Microsoft® Mobile Development Handbook

Andy Wigley
Daniel Moth
Peter Foot

PUBLISHED BY
Microsoft Press
A Division of Microsoft Corporation
One Microsoft Way
Redmond, Washington 98052-6399

Library of Congress Control Number: 2007924652

Printed and bound in the United States of America.

1 2 3 4 5 6 7 8 9 QWT 2 1 0 9 8 7

Distributed in Canada by H.B. Fenn and Company Ltd.

A CIP catalogue record for this book is available from the British Library.

Microsoft Press books are available through booksellers and distributors worldwide. For further information about international editions, contact your local Microsoft Corporation office or contact Microsoft Press International directly at fax (425) 936-7329. Visit our Web site at www.microsoft.com/mspress. Send comments to mspinput@microsoft.com.

Acquisitions Editor: Ben Ryan
Developmental Editor: Lynn Finnel
Editorial and Production Services: Waypoint Press
Copy editor: Christina Palaia
Technical Reviewer: Danial Hughes

Body Part No. X13-68393

For Stephanie, thanks for your support and tolerance while I was writing this book (and for putting up with the awful jokes).

–Peter Foot

To the two people in my life who have shaped and are still shaping who I am: my mother, Rita, and my wife, Jenny.

–Daniel Moth

For my mother, Margaret. Thank you, Mags, for being such a caring, loving person.

–Andy Wigley

Contents at a Glance

Table of Contents

Part III New Developments

Foreword

Is the era of the desktop computer drawing to a close? PCs may remain the focus of computing in the office and the home for a long time to come, but increasingly we find ourselves away from our homes and offices, yet still demanding information at our fingertips. The computing world is in the midst of a transition in which mobile devices are emerging as the world's dominant computing platform. In 2006, approximately 1 billion cell phones were sold worldwide-more than the total installed base of desktop computers. The fastest-growing segment of this exploding cell phone market is high-end Smartphones.

And smartphones are only part of the picture. We use computers of all kinds when we listen to our portable music players, drive our cars, work out on our treadmills, or play games on our handheld game players. All these computers start out simple, but little by little they evolve into full-blown computing platforms, connected to the Internet, and ready to run more complex and sophisticated software.

The Microsoft .NET Compact Framework was designed exactly for this mobile device revolution. Developers may want to run their software on ever physically smaller and more mobile devices, but they deserve the same first-class runtime platform and development environment that they know and use for their nonmobile software projects. They shouldn't have to relearn a different set of skills, languages, tools, and methodologies to run on these new devices-they should be able to capitalize on the skills, knowledge, and experiences they already have.

This book is a practical guide to developing applications for the .NET Compact Framework running on Microsoft Windows CE- and Windows Mobile-powered mobile devices. The authors, Andy Wigley, Daniel Moth, and Peter Foot, are veteran Microsoft Most Valuable Professionals (MVPs) who have worked with the .NET Compact Framework since its earliest prerelease versions. (Daniel is an ex-MVP who is currently employed by Microsoft.) In their roles as MVPs, they have translated their first-hand experiences developing software for .NET Compact Framework-based projects into requirements and feedback that have been incorporated directly into newer versions of the platform. In essence, they are part of a select community of experts who extend the eyes and ears of the product team in Redmond directly to the front lines with developers like you.

This is one of the first books on the market that directly addresses version 2.0 of the .NET Compact Framework, including the differences between version 1.0 and version 2. This is especially timely because at the time of this writing retail Windows Mobile devices containing version 2.0 in ROM are just beginning to show up on shelves in large volumes. The authors not only explain what the new features in version 2 are, but they provide straightforward explanations of why the new features are useful, and how they can be effectively used to improve your own mobile applications. The book also takes a first look at the forthcoming version 3.5 of the .NET Compact Framework as well, providing an interesting preview of additional features and improvements that will arrive in Microsoft Visual Studio Code Name "Orcas"-features such as compression, unit testing support, and compact versions of Language Integrated Query(LINQ) and Windows Communication Foundation (WCF).

Although this book would be useful to anyone interested in writing applications for smart devices, it will be most useful for the experienced desktop .NET developer who is interested in branching out to devices for the first time. The advice contained in this volume doesn't get bogged down in theory or esoterica. Instead, it provides practical guidelines and knowledge for writing efficient and functional mobile software. It is full of useful code samples and examples that you can use to turbocharge your own device development. It doesn't assume that devices exist in a vacuum, understanding instead that your application may be part of an overall architecture involving desktop computers, servers, and so forth. And it addresses not just writing your application and getting it to function correctly, but also performance and deployment of your applications-difficult areas that may surprise developers new to the mobile environment.

The guys who wrote this book know what they're talking about. They are part of the vanguard leading the next computing revolution: the mobile revolution. Take up the challenge of this revolution. Make your next software project a mobile project based on the .NET Compact Framework!

Richard Greenberg
Group Program Manager
.NET Compact Framework Team
Microsoft Corporation

Acknowledgments

Writing a book such as this is fun and immensely rewarding, but authors are a bit like long-distance runners–they are perhaps a little unimaginative about how painful the experience is going to be and just how long it takes. Nonetheless, having traveled along this long and occasional painful road, we, the authors, at least have the pleasure of seeing the product of our labors published as a book. Our families and friends, though, have suffered our absence through long hours of working and, although undoubtedly relieved that the project is over, don't get quite as much satisfaction from the finished product as we do. So, the first people to thank are our friends and families, for their love and support.

Second, a big thank you to Rob Miles. Although his name does not appear on the cover, he is one of the authors of this book as well because he contributed Chapter 13 about programming advanced graphics with Microsoft Direct3D Mobile.

Thanks to the excellent team at Microsoft Press–editor Lynn Finnel and copy editor Christina Palaia–and to the editorial and production team at Waypoint Press. Thanks to our technical editor, Danial Hughes, who spent a lot of time checking the accuracy of our words and our code. Thanks also to commissioning editor Ben Ryan, and also to Tim Cooke of Content Master, both of whom kept the flame alive for this book during the many months that this book was under consideration and we were waiting for the approval to get started.

We also enjoyed fantastic support from the other Device Application Development Most Valuable Professionals (MVPs), who volunteered to review our chapters as we produced them. Thanks, then, to Nick Randolph, Maarten Struys, Nino Benvenuti, Pete Vickers, Chris Muench, Jan Yeh, Alejandro Mezcua, Mark Arteaga, Ginny Caughey, Rolf Hoepli, César Fong, and Alex Feinman. People from the product group and the MVP program at Microsoft were also very supportive and went out of their way to answer technical queries, supply us with samples and advice, and review our chapters. Thanks to Mike Fosmire, Steven Pratschner, Mark Prentice, Ilya Tumanov, Sergiy Kuryata, Sriram Krishnan, Brian Cross, and Richard Greenberg.

Finally, thank you for reading this book. We hope you find plenty in it to help you create many great mobile applications.

Introduction

Microsoft released .NET Compact Framework version 1.0 as part of the Microsoft Visual Studio .NET 2003 product in April 2003. The .NET Compact Framework brings the benefits of managed code development to mobile devices with a slimmed-down class library and an execution engine optimized for use on Microsoft Windows CE–based operating systems. The .NET Compact Framework doesn't support the full feature set of the desktop framework, but that is what you expect on a small, battery-powered device, and most mobile application developers agree that version 1.0 was a great product. There were a few stand-out omissions though; in the .NET Compact Framework team today, the term *DateTimePicker* has become a generic description for "any dumb decision to leave out an essential feature," as in, "Is that a *DateTimePicker* feature?"

In November 2005, Visual Studio 2005 was released, and with it .NET Compact Framework version 2.0. This major release adds many new features and implements features missing from version 1.0 that caused pain to developers, including the aforementioned *DateTimePicker* control. Large enterprises built sophisticated applications using .NET Compact Framework 1.0, but the improved feature set of this new release, coupled with the increasing performance and widespread availability of devices from many different hardware vendors, make the .NET Compact Framework more and more attractive as a platform for enterprise application development.

This book focuses on managed code development using .NET Compact Framework 2.0, which is supported on Pocket PC devices running Windows Mobile 2003 and later, Smartphone devices running Windows Mobile 5.0 and later, and custom hardware running Windows CE 4.2 and later. It also covers programming with managed application programming interfaces (APIs) specific to different platforms, such as the *Microsoft.WindowsMobile* APIs available under Windows Mobile 5.0. We also cover programming of Microsoft SQL Server 2005 Compact Edition, which is the lightweight relational database that runs on devices and also on desktop computers.

If you are just starting out as a mobile application developer, welcome to a vibrant and exciting developer community! A couple of years back, the microsoft.public.dotnet.compactframework newsgroup was the second busiest of all .NET Framework newsgroups—busier even than microsoft.public.dotnet.framework! There are two ways of interpreting that statistic of course: Either the level of activity showed how many people were building .NET Compact Framework applications, or people were asking questions because they found it hard to use! The truth is probably a bit of both, but hopefully this book will go some way to addressing the second reason.

Who This Book Is For

This book is for new and existing mobile application developers who already have some experience developing applications using the .NET Framework (either desktop or compact version). If you are completely new to .NET, we suggest you start with one of these books: *Microsoft Visual C# 2005 Step By Step* by John Sharp or *Microsoft Visual Basic 2005 Step By Step* by Michael Halvorson, both published by Microsoft Press. Those books can teach you the programming basics, and you will then be well prepared to use this book to unlock the secrets of mobile application development.

If you are a developer with experience developing mobile applications using .NET Compact Framework 1.0 or desktop applications using .NET Framework 1.*x* or 2.0, this book can help you develop mobile applications using .NET Compact Framework 2.0 and will introduce you to some of the new features that are in .NET Compact Framework version 3.5, which will be released with the next release of Visual Studio, currently code-named "Orcas."

The predecessor to this book was *Microsoft .NET Compact Framework Core Reference*, which covered .NET Compact Framework 1.0 development using Visual Studio .NET 2003. That book was a Core Reference that explained pretty much every control and most basic programming techniques. At the time it was written, .NET programming was still relatively little understood, particularly in the device application development community, so the book did not assume much knowledge and included quite a lot of basic programming advice. However, much of the programming advice it contains, and descriptions of programming specific Windows Forms controls, are readily available online, at sites such as the Microsoft MSDN Web site (*msdn.microsoft.com*) or community sites such as the CodeProject Web site (*www.codeproject.com*), not to mention numerous blogs and newsgroups.

This book is different from its predecessor in that it does not attempt to cover every control or language feature. Along the way, the book does highlight features that are new to .NET Compact Framework 2.0 so that the developer who has experience building applications using the version 1.0 product can identify new features that can help build new applications. However, the main purpose of this book is to give you the essential information you need to design and build great applications that work on a constrained device such as a Pocket PC or Smartphone, or on embedded hardware. It tells you how to build and debug applications, how to design graphical user interfaces (GUIs) that work on small devices, and how to deploy applications. It also delves into problems that are unique to mobile device applications, such as how to design and build applications that work well with unreliable, slow network connections, which is the usual state of affairs with phone-enabled mobile devices. This book is a handbook for the mobile developer that explains how to tackle the common problems that mobile application developers encounter.

How This Book Is Organized

The book is divided into three parts:

- Part 1, Mobile Application Development Essentials, contains six chapters that everyone should read because they take you through topics that all mobile application developers must understand.

  Chapter 1, ".NET Compact Framework–a Platform on the Move," is an introduction to the .NET Compact Framework and explains the tools you need to build applications for smart devices. Chapter 2, "Building a Microsoft Windows Forms GUI," explains how to build effective Windows Forms applications on personal digital assistants (PDAs) and Smartphones, and Chapter 3, "Using SQL Server 2005 Compact Edition and Other Data Stores," extends this theme by looking at data persistence on devices in SQL Server 2005 Compact Edition databases and how you can build a graphical user interface that binds to data. In Chapter 4, "Catching Errors, Testing, and Debugging," you'll learn how to test and debug your applications on real devices and emulators, and how to trap and handle errors at run time. In Chapter 5, "Understanding and Optimizing .NET Compact Framework Performance," you'll learn how to create applications that perform well, something that requires a little more care to achieve on a smart device with limited RAM and storage than it does in a desktop application. The final chapter in this section, Chapter 6, "Completing the Application: Packaging and Deployment," looks at packaging and deployment and how Visual Studio 2005 makes it easy to build installation packages so that you can install your application on your target devices.

- Part 2, Solutions for Challenges in Mobile Application Development, contains 10 chapters that examine areas that present particular challenges to applications running on a smart device.

  These include how to exchange data with a backend server and how to keep local copies of data you store on a device synchronized with the master copy held on a server. Networking presents challenges because mobile devices often are equipped with many different kinds of networking hardware, including universal serial bus (USB) cable, WiFi, Bluetooth, and mobile phone network, but at times may have to operate in an environment where none of these are usable. Two chapters examine the kinds of network programming you can do and how you can get a usable network connection.

  Chapter 10, "Security Programming for Mobile Applications," is about security programming, an essential topic for any software developer, but of particular interest to mobile application developers who are responsible for keeping valuable data secure on a mobile device that can be lost or stolen, and one that must send data over public communications networks such as the Internet. Chapter 11, "Threading," looks at how to do multithreaded programming in the .NET Compact Framework, and this is followed by two chapters on graphics programming. Chapter 14, "Interoperating with the Platform," explains how to call native APIs that are available in the underlying Windows CE operating system to perform tasks that are not possible using the .NET Compact Framework APIs alone. The following chapter looks at developing custom Windows Forms controls that you can use in .NET Compact Framework applications, and the chapter after that explains how to create applications that are easily localizable to different cultures and languages. This section rounds up with a look at the Windows Mobile 5.0 managed APIs, a set of APIs that are unique to mobile devices and that expose system information and allow programmatic access to data stores such as Microsoft Office Outlook Mobile contacts, calendars, and tasks lists.

- Part 3, New Developments, contains a single chapter that provides an early look at the next version of Visual Studio and at the next version of the .NET Compact Framework, version 3.5. This new version, which is in beta at the time of this writing, builds on top of the solid foundation laid by version 2.0 and adds exciting new features for querying data collections, messaging, testing, and many other innovations and enhancements.

System Requirements

You'll need the following hardware and software to build and run the code samples for this book:

- The Windows Vista operating system, Microsoft Windows XP with Service Pack 2 (SP2), Microsoft Windows Server 2003 with Service Pack 1 (SP1), or Microsoft Windows 2000 with Service Pack 4 (SP4).
- Microsoft Visual Studio 2005 Standard Edition or higher.
- Microsoft .NET Compact Framework Service Pack 1 or Service Pack 2. If you install Service Pack 1, make sure you download and install the .NET Compact Framework 2.0 Service Pack 1 Patch to ensure that the Compact Framework binaries that Visual Studio uses are updated. If you try to run the sample code with Visual Studio 2005 without applying this update, you will get compilation errors.
- If you are developing under Microsoft Windows XP, you also need:
    - Microsoft ActiveSync 4.0 or later.
- If you are developing under Windows Vista, you also need:
    - Microsoft Windows Mobile Device Center Driver for Windows Vista.
    - Visual Studio 2005 SP1.
    - Visual Studio 2005 SP1 Update for Windows Vista.
    - Microsoft Device Emulator 2.0 or later. (Visual Studio 2005 ships with Device Emulator 1.0, which does not work correctly on Windows Vista.) Note that you do not need to install Device Emulator 2.0 separately if you install one of the Windows Mobile 6 software development kits (SDKs) because they install Device Emulator 2.0.

- Microsoft Windows Mobile 5.0 SDK for Pocket PC and/or Microsoft Windows Mobile 6 Professional SDK.
- Microsoft Windows Mobile 5.0 SDK for Smartphone and/or Microsoft Windows Mobile 6 Classic SDK.
- Microsoft SQL Server 2005 Express (included with Visual Studio 2005) or Microsoft SQL Server 2005.
- 600-megahertz (MHz) Pentium or compatible processor (1-gigahertz [GHz] Pentium recommended).
- For Microsoft Windows XP, 256 megabytes (MB) of RAM (512 MB or more recommended). For Windows Vista, 512 MB of RAM (1 gigabyte [GB] or more recommended.
- Video monitor (800 × 600 or higher resolution) with at least 256 colors (1024 × 768 High Color 16-bit recommended).
- Microsoft Mouse or compatible pointing device.

Configuring SQL Server 2005 Express Edition

Some chapters of this book require that you have access to SQL Server 2005 Express Edition (or SQL Server 2005). If you are using SQL Server 2005 Express Edition, follow these steps to grant access to the user account that you will be using to perform the exercises in this book:

1. Log on to Windows on your computer by using an account with administrator credentials.
2. On the Start menu, click All Programs, click Accessories, and then click Command Prompt to open a command prompt window.
3. In the command prompt window, type the following case-sensitive command:

   ```
   sqlcmd -S YourServer\SQLExpress -E
   ```

   Replace *YourServer* with the name of your computer.

   You can find the name of your computer by running the *hostname* command in the command prompt window before running the *sqlcmd* command.
4. At the 1> prompt, type the following command, including the brackets, and then press Enter:

   ```
   sp_grantlogin [YourServer\UserName]
   ```

   Replace *YourServer* with the name of your computer, and replace *UserName* with the name of the user account you will be using.

5. At the 2> prompt, type the following command, and then press Enter:

```
go
```

If you see an error message, make sure that you have typed the `sp_grantlogin` command correctly, including the brackets.

6. At the 1> prompt, type the following command, including the brackets, and then press Enter:

```
sp_addsrvrolemember [YourServer\UserName], dbcreator
```

7. At the 2> prompt, type the following command, and then press Enter:

```
go
```

If you see an error message, make sure that you have typed the `sp_addsrvrolemember` command correctly, including the brackets.

8. At the 1> prompt, type the following command, and then press Enter:

```
exit
```

9. Close the command prompt window.
10. Log out of the administrator account.

Code Samples

The downloadable code includes projects for most chapters that cover the code samples and examples referenced in the chapters. All the code samples discussed in this book can be downloaded from the book's companion content page at the following address:

http://www.microsoft.com/mspress/companion/9780735623583/

Support for This Book

Every effort has been made to ensure the accuracy of this book and the companion content. As corrections or changes are collected, they will be added to a Microsoft Knowledge Base article.

Microsoft Press provides support for books and companion content at the following Web site:

http://www.microsoft.com/learning/support/books/

Questions and Comments

If you have comments, questions, or ideas regarding the book or the companion content, or questions that are not answered by visiting the site just mentioned, please send them to Microsoft Press by e-mail to

mspinput@microsoft.com

Or by postal mail to

Microsoft Press
Attn: Microsoft Mobile Development Handbook *Editor*
One Microsoft Way
Redmond, WA
98052-6399

Please note that Microsoft software product support is not offered through the above addresses.

Part I

The Essentials of Mobile Application Development

In this part:

Chapter 1

.NET Compact Framework—a Platform on the Move

In this chapter:

Mobile device application developers work in a world where devices come in a wide variety of shapes and sizes, and with different capabilities, and so the first chapter of this book sets the scene by describing the different Microsoft Windows–powered mobile device platforms. It also explains the major programming differences between the full Microsoft .NET Framework used on desktop and laptop computers and the .NET Compact Framework used on devices. This chapter also summarizes the differences between version 1.0 and version 2.0 of the .NET Compact Framework.

The first section is primarily for developers who are new to developing applications for mobile devices. You'll learn about the mobile device platform choices, the different versions of the .NET Compact Framework, and the development tools you may require. This chapter summarizes the new features in .NET Compact Framework versions 2.0 and 3.5. The chapter ends by looking at some of the community resources that are available to augment the Microsoft-supplied tools, many of which have proved essential for .NET Compact Framework developers.

Getting Started with Mobile Application Development in Visual Studio

If you are creating your very first mobile device application, straightaway you must know the answers to some questions that may be confusing to developers new to the field:

- Which version of the Microsoft Visual Studio development system do you need?
- Which platform should you target: Pocket PC, Smartphone, or Microsoft Windows CE?

- What are the differences between these platforms?
- Which version of .NET Compact Framework should you use?

Choosing the Version of Visual Studio

The majority of mobile application developers use Visual Studio as their preferred integrated development environment (IDE). Different versions of Visual Studio are available, and you can install multiple versions side by side on your development computer. Each version of Visual Studio supports development of .NET Compact Framework applications, though the set of supported target devices differs, as explained in Table 1-1.

Table 1-1 Visual Studio Versions

Visual Studio Version	Supported Platforms
Visual Studio .NET 2003	.NET Compact Framework 1.0 development on Pocket PC 2002 and Windows Mobile 2003–based devices, and embedded devices running Windows CE 4.1 or 4.2. .NET Compact Framework 1.0 Service Pack 1 (SP1) adds support for phone devices running Windows Mobile 2003 for smartphones.
Microsoft Visual Studio 2005 Standard Edition or later	.NET Compact Framework 1.0 and 2.0 applications running on: ■ Windows Mobile 2003–powered Pocket PCs and Smartphones (but note that only .NET Compact Framework 1.0 is supported on the Windows Mobile 2003–powered Smartphone) ■ Windows Mobile 5.0–powered Pocket PCs and Smartphones ■ Windows Mobile 6.0–powered Pocket PCs and Smartphones ■ Embedded devices running Windows CE 5.0 ■ Embedded devices running Windows CE 6.0
Visual Studio v.Next (code-named Orcas)	The next version of Visual Studio will support development of .NET Compact Framework 2.0 applications for devices running Windows Mobile 5.0 and later and for embedded hardware running Windows CE 5.0 or later. It also will support development of .NET Compact Framework 3.5 applications.

> **Note** .NET Compact Framework 2.0 SP1 is supported on Windows CE 4.2, but Visual Studio 2005 does not support building applications targeting Windows CE 4.2. You must build your application for Windows CE 5.0 and then deploy to your Windows CE 4.2–powered device.

This book is primarily about development of .NET Compact Framework 2.0 applications. However, we mention version 3.5 of the framework in Table 1-1, and some of you may be wondering what happened to .NET Compact Framework 3.0. In fact, it never existed. The .NET Compact Framework product team maintains version numbering in sync with the desktop framework. Version 3.0 of the desktop .NET Framework was actually .NET Framework 2.0 with the addition of the first release of Windows Communication Foundation, Windows Presentation Foundation, Windows Workflow Foundation, and Windows Cardspace. There was no comparable release of the .NET Compact Framework. The version of the desktop .NET Framework that ships with Microsoft Visual Studio 2007 is 3.5, and the version of the .NET Compact Framework that ships with Visual Studio 2007 is also 3.5.

In this book, we use Visual Studio 2005 because with it you can create applications for devices that run the Windows Mobile 5.0, the Windows Mobile 6.0, or the older Windows Mobile 2003 operating system, and also for devices that run Windows CE 5.0 and Windows Embedded CE 6.0–which covers the majority of devices that are available today. You can create applications to run on either .NET Compact Framework 1.0 or 2.0 runtime, and so Visual Studio 2005 supports the broadest choice of platforms and runtimes.

Other Development Software You Need

Out of the box, Visual Studio 2005 does not support development of applications for Pocket PCs or Smartphones running Windows Mobile 5.0 or later. For that, you must download and install the following additional software:

- Windows Mobile 5.0 SDK for Pocket PC
- Windows Mobile 5.0 SDK for Smartphone

The Windows Mobile 5.0 SDKs contain documentation, samples, and software libraries for these platforms. They also install device emulators on your development computer that runs the Windows Mobile 5.0 operating system, and you can use these during development in Visual Studio 2005.

Developing .NET Compact Framework applications without using Visual Studio

It is not mandatory to use Visual Studio as your IDE because .NET Compact Framework 2.0 has its own software development kit (SDK) that supplies all the command-line tools and libraries you need to build and compile applications–something that was not available in version 1.0. The .NET Compact Framework SDK is not available separate from the framework, but instead it is included in the .NET Framework 2.0 SDK. The .NET Framework SDK includes documentation, sample code, tools, and reference assemblies that you can use to develop code that targets the .NET Compact Framework. To install the tools and assemblies you need for .NET Compact Framework development, install NETCFSetUpV2.msi, located in the CompactFramework subdirectory in the .NET Framework 2.0 SDK.

In addition to the .NET Framework 2.0 SDK, you must download the following products from the Microsoft MSDN Web site at *msdn.microsoft.com/netframework/downloads*:

- .NET Compact Framework 2.0 Redistributable
- Optionally, the standalone Device Emulator
- Microsoft SQL Server 2005 Compact Edition SDK if you plan to develop applications using this database

After you have these components installed, you have all the basic tools you require. You can then install an alternate IDE to help with application development (or indeed, you can write your applications in Notepad and compile them from the command line if you are that peculiar breed of developer who loves to do things the hard way). One IDE you can use is SharpDevelop, which you can download for free from the SharpDevelop Web site at *http://www.sharpdevelop.net*. You can find instructions on how to develop .NET Compact Framework 2.0 applications using SharpDevelop on the company's Wiki site at *http://wiki.sharpdevelop.net/default.aspx/SharpDevelop.CompactFramework2Development*.

If your development computer is running versions of Windows other than the Windows Vista operating system, you must also download Microsoft ActiveSync version 4.0 or later, which is required to manage connectivity and data synchronization between a mobile device and your development computer. Windows Vista has the basic connectivity capabilities built in that you require for software development on mobile devices..

If you are developing on Windows Vista, you should download and install Microsoft Windows Mobile Device Center Driver for Windows Vista from *www.microsoft.com/downloads*, along with the following updates:

- Visual Studio 2005 SP1
- Visual Studio 2005 SP1 Update for Windows Vista

- Microsoft Device Emulator 2.0 or later (Visual Studio 2005 ships with Device Emulator 1.0, which does not work correctly on Windows Vista). Note that you do not need to install Device Emulator 2.0 if you inst5all one of the Windows Mobile 6 SDKs.

If you want to develop applications for Windows Mobile 6.0–powered devices, download a Windows Mobile 6.0 SDK that contains documentation, tools, and new emulators that run Windows Mobile 6.0 that you can use during development. Note that Microsoft has changed the way different editions of the SDK are named, as follows:

- **Windows Mobile 6 Standard** This SDK is for devices that do not have a touch screen, those devices that were referred to in Windows Mobile 5.0 as Smartphones. You must download the Windows Mobile 6 Standard SDK to develop for these devices.
- **Windows Mobile 6 Classic** This SDK is for devices that have a touch-sensitive screen but no phone capabilities; these devices were formerly known as Pocket PCs. Use the Windows Mobile 6 Professional SDK to develop for these devices.
- **Windows Mobile 6 Professional** These are high-end devices with a touch screen and phone capabilities formerly known as Pocket PC Phone Edition. As with Windows Mobile 6 Classic, you use the Windows Mobile 6 Professional SDK to develop for these devices.

Visual Studio 2005 includes support for developing applications for targets running Windows CE 5.0. If you want to develop applications for devices running Windows Embedded CE 6.0, you must download the Windows Embedded CE 6.0 SDK.

You can download these components from the Microsoft Download Center Web site at *http://www.microsoft.com/downloads/Browse.aspx?displaylang=en&categoryid=8*.

Choosing Your Platform: Pocket PC, Smartphone, or Windows CE?

There are three broad categories of mobile platform: Pocket PCs (which run Windows Mobile), Smartphones (which also run Windows Mobile, although a version specific to smartphones), and embedded or custom hardware (which runs Windows CE). The key differences between these platforms are illustrated in Table 1-2.

Table 1-2 Key Physical Differences Between Mobile Platforms

Platform	Pocket PC/Windows Mobile 6 Classic and Professional	Smartphone/Windows Mobile 6 Standard	Windows CE
Touch-sensitive screen	Yes	No	Custom: Decision of device original equipment manufacturer (OEM)
Keypad	No keyboard, or QWERTY keyboard	Phone triple-tap keys, or QWERTY keyboard	Custom: Decision of OEM

Table 1-2 **Key Physical Differences Between Mobile Platforms**

Platform	Pocket PC/Windows Mobile 6 Classic and Professional	Smartphone/Windows Mobile 6 Standard	Windows CE
Telephone capability	Yes if Pocket PC Phone Edition or Windows Mobile 6 Professional; otherwise, no	Yes	Custom
Operating system	Windows Mobile 2003 for Pocket PC Premium Edition Windows Mobile 2003 for Pocket PC Professional Edition Windows Mobile 2003 for Pocket PC Phone Edition Windows Mobile 5 for Pocket PC Windows Mobile 6 Classic Windows Mobile 6 Professional	Windows Mobile 2003 for Smartphone Windows Mobile 5 for Smartphone Windows Mobile 6 Standard	Windows CE 4.2 Windows CE 5.0 Windows Embedded CE 6.0

As Table 1-2 shows, Pocket PCs always have touch-sensitive screens and may or may not have a keyboard. Smartphones have non-touch-sensitive screens and usually include a phone keypad, although occasionally a full QWERTY keyboard is included. Windows CE–based devices can have any kind of screen (or no screen at all in the case of headless devices) and keyboard because they are custom embedded hardware.

As shown in Figure 1-1, in the New Project dialog box, Visual Studio 2005 offers different project types that correspond to these categories. You may see different platform versions for Pocket PCs, smartphones, or Windows CE (for example, Figure 1-1 shows the version for Windows Mobile 2003 and Windows Mobile 5.0 options for Pocket PCs and Smartphones), but they still fall under the three categories mentioned.

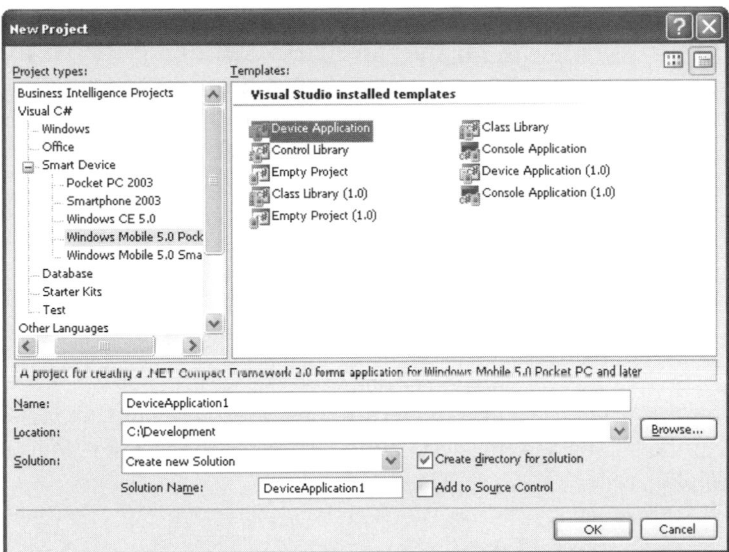

Figure 1-1 Visual Studio 2005 New Project dialog box, which divides mobile platforms into three categories

Important When you first install Visual Studio 2005, you will not see Windows Mobile 5.0 or Windows Mobile 6.0 platforms in the list of project types. To target these platforms, you must install additional software, as described earlier in this chapter in the section titled "Other Development Software You Need."

Choose the project type that matches the hardware on which your application will run, and then choose which kind of project you want to build.

The Difference Between Windows CE and Windows Mobile

Not understanding the difference between Windows CE and Windows Mobile often causes great confusion among new mobile developers. Are Windows Mobile and Windows CE simply different mobile device operating systems? Actually, that is quite a good way of thinking of it, although many people do not understand how closely they are related.

The Windows CE Operating System

Windows CE is an operating system. However, it is a *modular* operating system that is intended to be completely adaptable to its intended use–a kind of tool kit that device makers use for building customized operating system images for a variety of nondesktop devices. Embedded developers can use an application called Platform Builder to pick exactly which modules of Windows CE they want to build into their operating system. They then generate their custom operating system image and install it on custom hardware.

Some Windows CE modules include essential functionality that is required in all Windows CE–based operating systems, but many modules are optional, including the .NET Compact Framework runtime. Therefore, there is no one definitive version of Windows CE; every Windows CE operating system is simply a collection of whichever modules the designer decided to include. Microsoft has renamed the most recent version of Windows CE as Windows *Embedded* CE 6.0, to emphasize its intended use.

Note With the release of Windows Embedded CE 6.0, the Platform Builder functionality no longer operates as a separate product but instead integrates with Visual Studio 2005 as a plug-in.

We don't discuss how to use Platform Builder in this book. For more information about Platform Builder, visit the Microsoft Windows Embedded Developer Center Web site at *http://msdn.microsoft.com/embedded/default.aspx*.

Windows Mobile Operating Software

Windows Mobile is the operating environment for Pocket PCs and smartphones. Consumers and enterprise customers who require a stable platform on which to run their software use these devices. The platform customizability that is possible with Windows CE implementations—such as one that has networking and another that doesn't—is of no use to these customers. They need consistency between devices and clear upgrade paths from one version release to the next.

Consequently, device manufacturers who design and build Windows Mobile–powered devices do so within the terms of a license agreement with Microsoft that dictates the basic hardware functionality of the device and the software that is included in the basic package (although the manufacturer may add software). This is so that software that runs on one manufacturer's device also runs on a different manufacturer's device. The user finds the same kinds of buttons available, similar screen dimensions, and a consistent way of using the device.

Some years ago, the license terms were very restrictive so that all Pocket PC devices had a 240 × 320 pixel screen, portrait orientation, and no keyboard. This standardization was great for developers because they knew the exact characteristics of the target devices, regardless of manufacturer. Today the license restrictions are much less restrictive. Square, landscape, and high-resolution screens are common, as are keyboards on Pocket PCs, all of which offer great selections for users but add challenges for software developers who must build a graphical user interface (GUI) to run on multiple devices.

The Windows Mobile product group at Microsoft is a customer of the Windows CE group. Windows Mobile is built on Windows CE. The Windows Mobile group uses Platform Builder to build a particular implementation of Windows CE using the modules they require, and then they add their own software, such as the Pocket PC or Smartphone shell (a *shell* is a set of user interface components and underlying support routines that translate user input into useful operating system actions), plus standard add-on software such as Microsoft Internet Explorer Mobile, Word Mobile, Excel Mobile, and so on. Windows Mobile 2003 was built on Windows CE version 4.2; Windows Mobile 5.0 and Windows Mobile 6.0 both are built on Windows CE 5.0.

Choosing Between Windows Mobile and Windows CE

If it is your job to select the platform to use on devices for a new project, you may be confused about which one you want. The choice is relatively simple. If you are writing applications for a device with telephone capability that does not have a stylus and that can be operated one-handed from the keypad, Smartphone (or, to use the modern terminology, Windows Mobile 6 Standard) is the correct choice. If you are writing for custom hardware, obviously you must use Windows CE.

The choice between using Pocket PC (now called Windows Mobile 6 Classic or Professional) and Windows CE can be a little more complicated. Most of the large enterprise mobile device manufacturers, such as Intermec and Symbol, offer Pocket PC–style devices that come with a choice of Windows Mobile or Windows CE running on identical hardware. The implementation of Windows CE used on these devices usually uses the standard graphical Windows-style shell (one of the components included in Platform Builder) so that devices from different manufacturers tend to give a similar user experience.

When you compare the way the standard Windows CE shell works to the way the Windows Mobile for Pocket PC shell works, you see the obvious difference is in the screen layout and the way you start programs. On Pocket PC, the Start button is at the top, and menus are displayed from the upper-left corner downward, as shown in Figure 1-2. To select a menu item, you tap once with the stylus. All applications running on a Pocket PC display objects in full-screen mode (except for a very few types of pop-up dialog boxes).

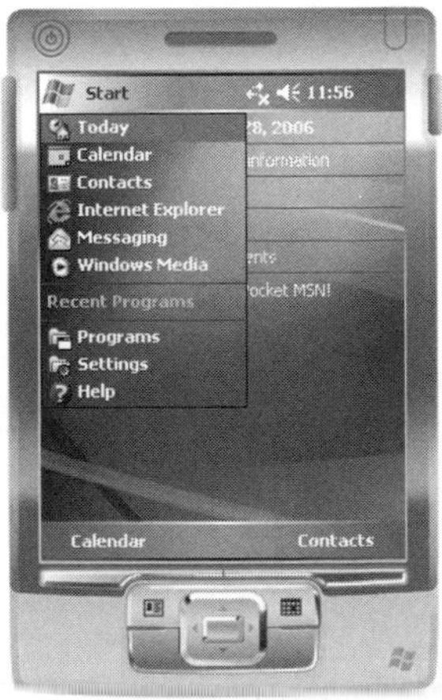

Figure 1-2 On Pocket PC, the Start button at the upper-left

On Windows CE using the standard graphical shell, the screen layout is similar to a desktop computer that runs the Windows operating system, as shown in Figure 1-3. The taskbar is along the bottom of the screen, and each time you start an application its icon appears in the taskbar. The Start button is lower left, and the menus open upward from the lower left. As on desktop computers, a single click or tap with the stylus selects a menu item. To start a program from an icon displayed on the desktop, you must tap twice with the stylus (the equivalent of a double click with a mouse). When an application runs, it does not necessarily run in full-screen mode. Also, in Windows CE, application windows typically include the Close button (cross) and the Minimize button. On Pocket PCs, you never see a Minimize button, and if there is a Close button, it actually works as a "Smart Minimize" button and not a Close button. For more information about Smart Minimize, see the section titled "Closing a Form" in Chapter 2, "Building a Microsoft Windows Forms GUI."

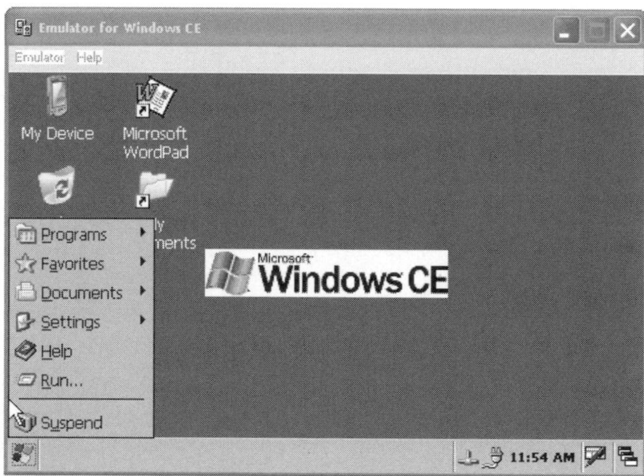

Figure 1-3 The Windows CE standard shell

> **Note** Remember that the Windows CE shell described here is only one of potentially many options you may encounter if you develop applications for hardware that runs Windows CE. A Windows CE–based platform can have its own unique shell that is developed and customized for a device and its target audience, which supplies a different user interaction experience from the one described here.

Smartphones supply yet another user experience. These devices do not have touch-sensitive screens, and they are designed to be used one-handed. The primary navigation method is to use the five-way joystick, and you can select items by using the two buttons under the screen. The convention is that the left button offers a single option, such as OK, View, or Start, or whatever is the most likely user choice, whereas the right button offers a menu of options. Figure 1-4 shows the smartphone interface in which the Home screen assigns Start to the left button. When you activate the Start menu, it is displayed as a full screen of icons, as shown in the smartphone interface on the right side of Figure 1-4. Applications are always displayed in full-screen mode on smartphones.

Figure 1-4 The five-way joystick and command buttons on a smartphone

You do not see buttons in the user interface (UI) of a smartphone application. In fact, there is no *Button* control in the Visual Studio Toolbox for smartphone projects because a button is better suited to a touch-sensitive screen where the user can tap the button to select that option, whereas on a smartphone screen the user would be required to highlight an on-screen button by using the five-way controller and then press the center controller button to select the on-screen button. This gives a poor user experience, and so buttons are not used. Instead, you can use the left and right action buttons under the screen to give users buttonlike functionality.

Differences in device behavior affect programmers as well. Not only do you have a more limited selection of controls to work with if you are developing applications for devices without a touch screen, but you will also find that Windows Forms exhibit different basic behavior. For example, on devices running Windows Mobile, all forms display full screen by default, whereas on devices running Windows CE, they do not. You learn more about these differences and how to program Windows Forms on each of the platforms in Chapter 2.

The differences in shell behavior are not significant enough to influence your choice of platform greatly. In fact, the usual reason developers choose Windows CE (apart from the obvious reason when a solution requires custom hardware) is that it is easier to configure a Windows CE–powered device so that it runs only your application and nothing else than it is to configure a device running Windows Mobile in such a way. For example, enterprise managers like to lock down devices to prevent users from playing games, downloading additional software, or pressing the hardware buttons to access built-in functions such as contacts and e-mail.

You can take steps to lock down a Windows Mobile–powered device, as described in Chapter 6, "Completing the Application: Packaging and Deployment," but it is more difficult to achieve complete lockdown on a Windows Mobile–powered device than it is on a Windows CE–based device. On a Windows Mobile–powered device, you must always use (and try to control) the standard Windows Mobile shell, which is designed to be a user-friendly interface to allow users to access all the capabilities of the device, whereas on a device running Windows CE, if you don't like the behavior of the shell you have, you can fairly easily create a custom shell dedicated to running your application.

Programming API Differences

If you have to choose between a device running Windows Mobile and a similar device running Windows CE, the other factor you must consider is the availability of application programming interfaces (APIs) on each platform. The most obvious difference is that on Windows Mobile 5.0 and later you have access to additional managed code libraries that are not available on Windows CE; these libraries make it easier to interact with the platform. For example, the *Microsoft.WindowsMobile.Status* namespace contains classes you use to query system status for many different items, such as the current active network connection and Internet Protocol (IP) address, battery power, screen orientation, phone status, media player information, or whether the device is cradled. You can also register to receive notifications when a system status changes. Also, you can use classes in the *Microsoft.WindowsMobile.PocketOutlook* namespace to query and set Microsoft Office Outlook Mobile data on tasks, appointments, and e-mail. You can use other libraries to access hardware on the device such as the phone, a Global Positioning System (GPS) receiver, or a camera. See Chapter 16, "The Windows Mobile 5 Managed APIs," for more detail on these libraries.

Of course, whenever possible managed code developers call APIs only in managed libraries, but sooner or later, every managed code application developer has to resort to Platform Invocation Services (PInvoke) calls to native APIs to access functions that are available on the platform but not through managed APIs. Having a broad understanding of features available in native APIs on Windows Mobile that are missing from Windows CE can help you choose between platforms. To access a native API, you must use PInvoke to call functions in native APIs (for more information, see Chapter 14, "Interoperating with the Platform") or use a third-party managed API, such as the OpenNETCF managed wrappers (see the section titled "Using Community Resources" later in this chapter for more information about the OpenNETCF) that effectively do all the hard PInvoke work for you.

There are too many differences in native APIs to describe them all here. To get an understanding of which native APIs are available on Windows Mobile that are not in the underlying Windows CE platform, study the documentation that comes with the Windows Mobile SDKs.

Choosing the .NET Compact Framework Version

We have established what the different device platforms are, and so the next question is which version of the .NET Compact Framework should you choose to target? "The latest version" would seem to be the obvious answer, but, as with many things concerning devices, it's not quite that simple! As the developer, you choose a version of the .NET Compact Framework on which to build your application. If you choose version 1.0, you can be reasonably confident that your application will run on all devices because versions 2.0 and later of the .NET Compact Framework runtime run applications that were built to run on an earlier version. However, if you write code that uses features only available in .NET Compact Framework 2.0, that version of the .NET Compact Framework runtime must be installed on your target device for your application to operate.

The versions of the .NET Compact Framework runtime that are supported by the different mobile platforms are illustrated in Figure 1-5. Note that the figure does not represent an accurate timeline for the release of the different mobile platforms (for example, Windows CE 5.0 was released earlier than the Windows Mobile 5 operating systems) but is purely intended to illustrate run-time support.

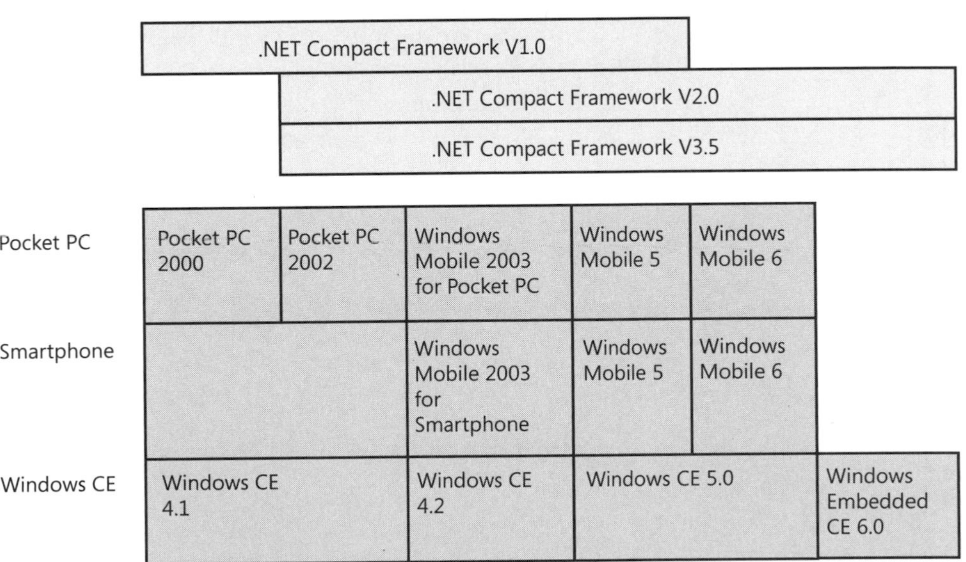

Figure 1-5 Supported platforms for different .NET Compact Framework versions

Microsoft does not manufacture mobile devices, but it does supply the software for such devices. As part of the license agreement, device manufacturers that manufacture devices that use Windows Mobile software must agree to preinstall the .NET Compact Framework runtime on all Windows Mobile–based smartphones and Pocket PCs. However, because it takes quite a long time to design and release a new device, the availability of the newest version of the runtime on devices in the marketplace lags behind the release of the software by Microsoft.

At the end of 2006, the majority of devices in use by consumers, including those running Windows Mobile 5.0, had the .NET Compact Framework 1.0 SP3 runtime preinstalled, although it is becoming more common to see version 2.0 on new devices coming to market. If a device has version 1.0 installed, you can install version 2.0 alongside it. However, if your application requires .NET Compact Framework 2.0 but the target user's device has only version 1.0 installed, either the user must download and install the version 2.0 runtime prior to installing your application or you must distribute the .NET Compact Framework 2.0 redistributable with your application. See Chapter 6 for more information about this issue and how to resolve it.

Figures 1-6, 1-7, and 1-8 illustrate some typical configurations you will encounter with commercially available devices. Figure 1-6 shows a typical Pocket PC device that has Windows Mobile 2003 Second Edition installed. Typically, these devices either did not have .NET Compact Framework installed into read-only memory (ROM) or had version 1.0 SP2 or SP3 factory installed into ROM (from where it is copied into random access memory [RAM] by the operating system). You can install later versions of the .NET Compact Framework or the Microsoft SQL Server runtime in RAM to run alongside any earlier version already on the device.

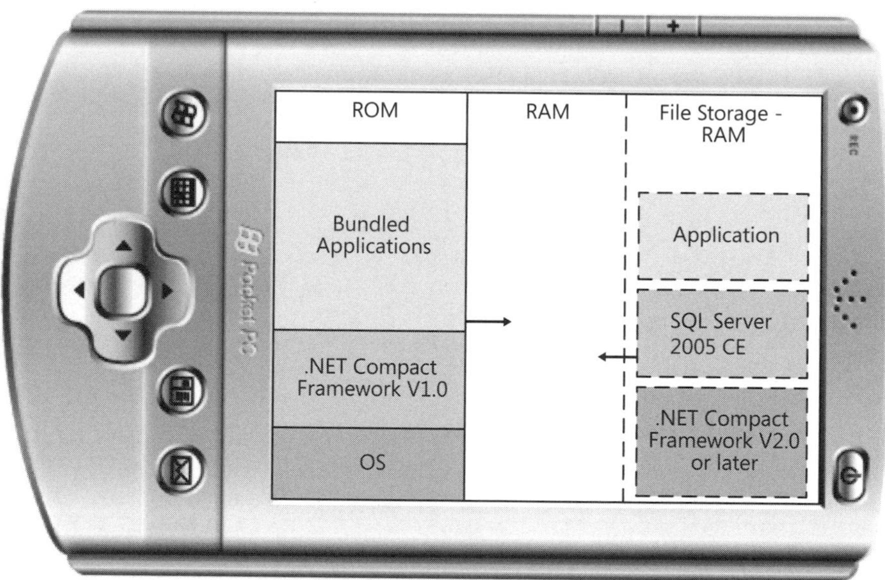

Figure 1-6 Typical configuration of a device running Windows Mobile 2003 Second Edition

Figure 1-7 shows the typical configuration of a device running Windows Mobile 5.0. On such devices, generally you will find that .NET Compact Framework 1.0 SP3 is preinstalled in ROM. Again, you can install version 2.0 of the framework on the device alongside the preinstalled version.

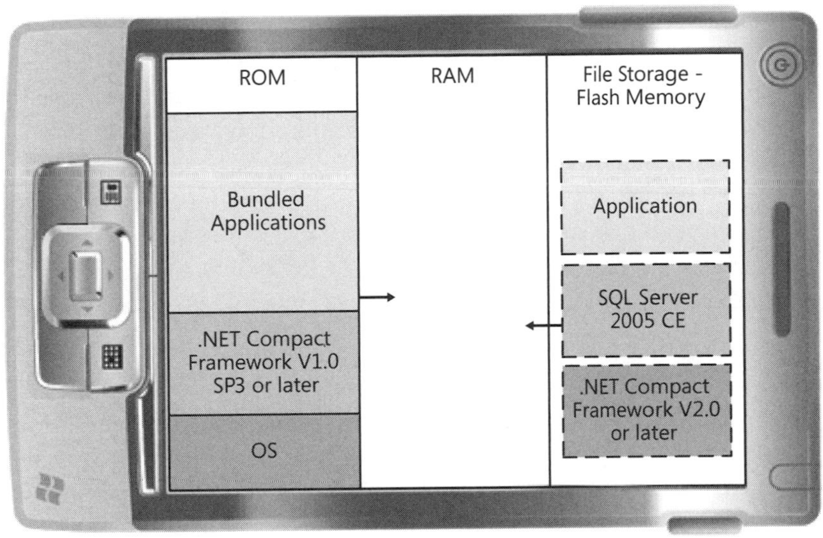

Figure 1-7 Typical configuration of a device running Windows Mobile 5.0

Another change that sometimes trips up developers is in the handling of registry changes. The registry, too, is persisted in flash memory, but because fast access to the registry is crucial to good system performance, Windows Mobile maintains a RAM-based cache that is used for all registry operations. Whenever you make a change to a setting in the registry, that change is applied to the RAM-based cache and is only flushed to the persistent store periodically by the operating system. The Windows Mobile team put great effort into flushing registry changes whenever necessary to avoid losing updates, but there are still some situations when you may change the registry and then reset the device, losing the change. Developers can force a flush by calling the *RegFlushKey* native API function.

On devices running Windows Mobile 6, you will find .NET Compact Framework 2.0 SP1 or later preinstalled into ROM, as shown in Figure 1-8. You will also find the SQL Server 2005 Compact Edition runtime preinstalled so that all the run-time components you need for the majority of your applications are already on the device. If you want to use some future version of the .NET Compact Framework, such as version 3.5, you can install that alongside the preinstalled versions in the same way as you can on devices that run earlier versions.

File store changes between Windows Mobile 2003 and Windows Mobile 5.0

The hardware of Pocket PC devices underwent substantial change with the move from Windows Mobile 2003 to Windows Mobile 5.0, as illustrated in Figures 1-6 and 1-7. All devices have ROM to store the factory-installed operating system and other preinstalled software, and to operate this software is copied into RAM—the program memory—by the operating system. On devices that run Windows Mobile 2003 and earlier versions, the file system, including the space where you store application executables and files, is also stored in RAM so that the available RAM is divided between the program memory and the file system. The dividing line between them is managed by the operating system on Pocket PCs, although there is a Control Panel item you can use to move the slider one way or the other to influence the space allocation. In Windows CE, the operating system does not try to manage the division for you; you set it manually by using the Control Panel item or programmatically.

In Windows Mobile 5.0 for Pocket PCs, the picture changes substantially. These devices have the same ROM region for preinstalled software, and they have RAM for program memory to run the operating system and applications. However, they also contain a region of flash memory where the file system sits. No longer is there a Control Panel item or memory slider bar to use to allocate memory use. (Note that Smartphone 2003 has used this model from the beginning.)

The major effect of adding flash memory is that at last you could run down the battery on a Pocket PC device and not lose all your installed applications or data: flash memory does not require any electrical current to retain the data written to it. The RAM-based file store on devices running Windows Mobile 2003 requires a tiny trickle of current to maintain state, even when the device is turned off. So when the battery runs out completely, the RAM-based file store is wiped and the user must restore data and applications from backup or reinstall them. Enterprises have expended much time reinstalling custom software and resetting registry settings on devices running Windows Mobile 2003 to get them operational again after the battery has gone flat, but thanks to flash file storage, this cost and effort are no longer required.

It is also worth mentioning that the flash-based file system has presented an unexpected challenge to application developers. It takes more time to write to flash memory than it takes to write to RAM, although it is still much faster than typical hard disk drives in desktop computers. If you have code that writes to the file system a lot and it has worked acceptably on devices running Windows Mobile 2003, you may experience performance problems using the same code on devices running Windows Mobile 5.0. You may have to rewrite your code to do more caching before committing data to a file. Built-in applications such as Word Mobile and the SQL Server 2005 Compact Edition database have been optimized to work well with a flash-based file store, and you must take special care to optimize your own applications as well.

Another unexpected effect of using a flash-based file store occurs when the store becomes full. Flash memory wears out quickly if you keep writing to the same physical location in memory. To prevent this from happening, the file system drivers continuously write to different locations in memory and keep a logical map to track used blocks. As the flash memory fills, the drivers have to work much harder to locate free memory, and so write performance degrades substantially—sometimes as much as 70 times. To optimize flash memory performance, keep plenty of free space in your file store.

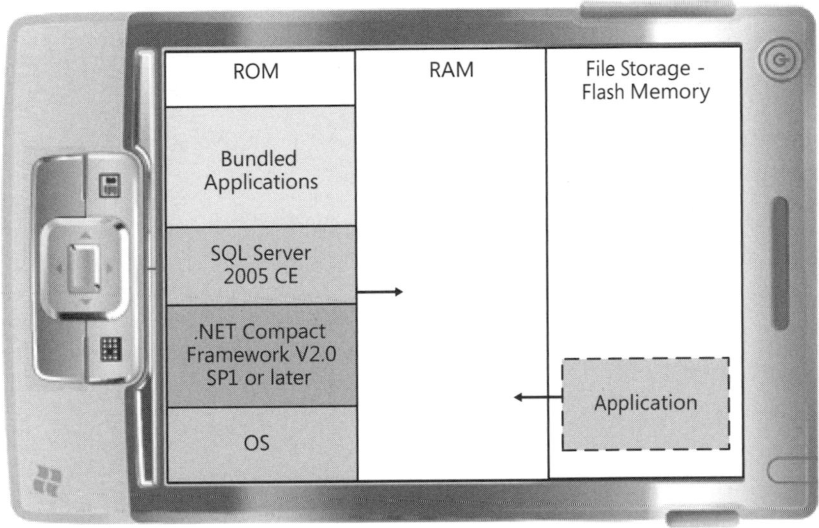

Figure 1-8 Typical configuration of a device running Windows Mobile 6.0

Caution Figures 1-6 through 1-8 show typical device configurations. The specific version of .NET Compact Framework and/or SQL Server 2005 Compact Edition installed is up to the device manufacturer, and so you may find variations.

If you are an enterprise developer, you are best advised to build your applications on .NET Compact Framework 2.0. More likely than not, you will have complete control over the configuration of your target devices so that you would be foolish not to take advantage of the superior performance and functionality of version 2.0.

See the section titled "Understanding the Differences Between .NET Compact Framework Version 1.0 and Version 2.0" later in this chapter for more information about the new features introduced in .NET Compact Framework 2.0.

.NET Compact Framework Service Packs

Microsoft has released three service packs for .NET Compact Framework 1.0 and, at the time of this writing, two service packs for version 2.0. You can install a service pack release alongside any earlier versions. For example, if your device has .NET Compact Framework 2.0 installed in ROM, you can install version 2.0 SP2 alongside it. By default, your applications will run using the version of the runtime they were compiled against or, if that version is not installed on the device, a more recent version, although you can override this behavior at run time by using configuration files. See Chapter 6 for more information.

On the whole, service packs fix bugs that have been discovered in the runtime or BCL, but Microsoft often uses service packs as a vehicle for introducing (limited) new functionality. For example, version 2.0 SP1 fixes some bugs but also widens support for more platforms and introduces some useful tools for developers, including the following:

- It introduces official support for running version 2.0 applications on Windows CE .NET 4.2.
- It adds support for running .NET Compact Framework 2.0 applications on headless devices; that is, custom Windows CE hardware that does not have a display monitor.
- It introduces the Remote Performance Monitor tool that you can use to monitor application performance in real time. See Chapter 4, "Catching Errors, Testing, and Debugging" for more information.

Version 2.0 SP1 also introduces a minor new programming feature: the ability to override the drawing of cells in a *DataGrid* control to perform custom drawing. Obviously, if you take advantage of any new functionality such as this in your application, you must take steps to ensure that the correct service pack or a later one is installed on all your target devices.

Understanding the Differences Between the .NET Framework 2.0 and .NET Compact Framework 2.0

Quite often, we read forum posts from desktop developers who are trying development using the .NET Compact Framework for the first time and who have discovered that some favorite class that they use in their desktop .NET applications is not supported in the .NET Compact Framework Base Class Libraries (BCL). They express their outrage at the perceived inadequacies of the mobile environment and express their astonishment that the .NET Compact Framework is so "limited."

Actually, where it matters the .NET Compact Framework is not at all limited. Yes, many of the more specialist classes may be missing, or you might have to program some piece of application functionality by using multiple lines of code where the desktop framework provides a convenient method. But the essential classes, methods, and properties are all there so that desktop and mobile developers can enjoy a consistent programming experience and can transfer their skills fairly easily between the two frameworks.

The .NET Compact Framework is a compatible subset of the full .NET Framework. To suit the constrained nature of the devices on which it operates, the .NET Compact Framework implements approximately 30 percent of the classes and methods of the full framework. The full .NET Framework has a minimum footprint of around 40 megabytes (MB), which is clearly inappropriate for mobile devices that typically have storage capacity in the range 32 MB to 128 MB. A mobile device is usually battery powered and has limited RAM (typically 64 MB). Clearly, the .NET Compact Framework requires a special run-time engine to run well in this demanding computing environment. In mobile computing as in all areas of computing, each year CPU power and storage capacity increase, but in the mobile world the march of technological progress is always tempered by the requirement of running the device on a battery for long periods of time. The size and functionality of the .NET Compact Framework will also likely increase with each new release (the footprint increased from 1.5 MB to around 4 MB in moving from version 1.0 to version 2.0), but device constraints will ensure that it remains a subset of the full framework.

Classes are excluded from the .NET Compact Framework for two main reasons:

- They expose Windows system services available on desktop versions of Windows but not in Windows CE. For example, ASP.NET classes, which require Microsoft Internet Information Server (IIS) in the underlying operating system services, are excluded from the .NET Compact Framework.
- They are too large in footprint or too computationally expensive to implement, and alternatives exist. A major design goal for the .NET Compact Framework is to keep the footprint as small as possible and to limit demands on the CPU and hence battery power. Consequently, the .NET Compact Framework excludes functionality such as Remoting and Extensible Stylesheet Language Transformations (XSLT).

Figure 1-9 shows a high-level overview of the namespaces in the full .NET Framework. Those that are not included in the compact implementation are shaded.

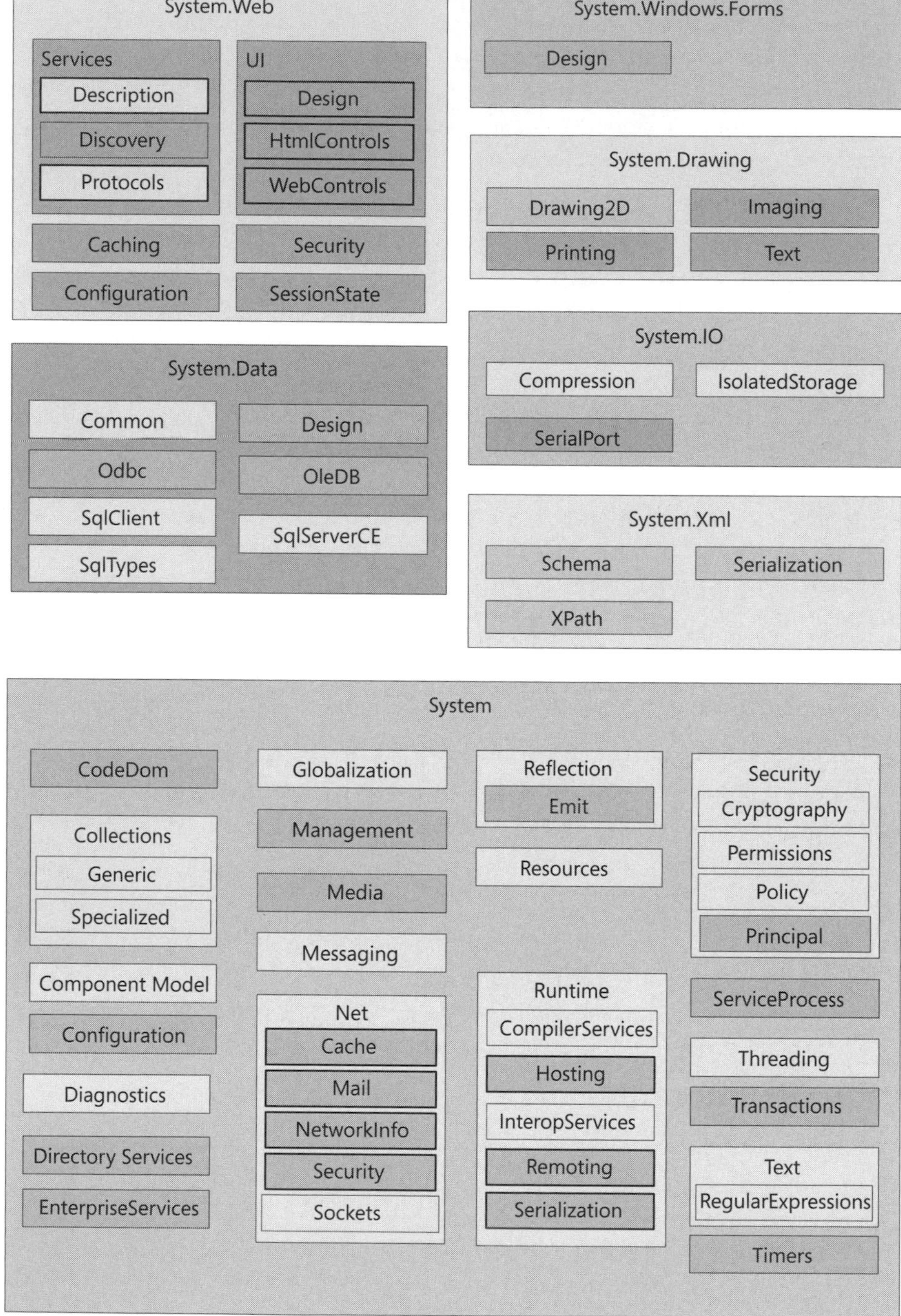

Figure 1-9 The full .NET Framework namespaces and those that are absent from the .NET Compact Framework

In Figure 1-9, the presence of a namespace in both implementations does not mean that all the classes, methods, enumerations, and interfaces are found in both. The .NET Compact Framework namespaces contain fewer classes, and the classes that exist might not include exactly the same methods as the corresponding classes in the full .NET Framework.

Tip The quickest way to find out if a class or method you want to use is supported in the .NET Compact Framework is to look up the class or method in the MSDN documentation included with Visual Studio and also available online. The documentation clearly states for which platforms the class or method is available; if there is no mention of .NET Compact Framework 1.0 or 2.0, that class or method is available only in the full .NET Framework.

The *System.Net* and *System.Net.Sockets* namespaces contain classes found only in the .NET Compact Framework that enable infrared communication. The *System.Data.SqlServerCE* namespace does not ship in the BCL of the .NET Compact Framework because it is implemented in supplementary libraries that come with the SQL Server 2005 Compact Edition database. Not shown in Figure 1-8 are the *Microsoft.WindowsMobile* namespaces that expose managed classes you can use to work with device-specific functionality on a Windows Mobile 5.0–powered device, such as system state counters and Outlook Mobile tasks, contacts, and e-mail. Although these are managed libraries for use by a .NET Compact Framework developer, they are additional capabilities provided by the platform, not a part of the .NET Compact Framework itself.

Classes in the .NET Compact Framework with the same name as a class in the full .NET Framework are designed to be semantically compatible with the corresponding full .NET Framework classes, ensuring that if a method or class is present in both frameworks, the techniques to use that method and class remain the same. In fact, .NET Compact Framework code is *retargetable*, meaning that you can take application code that has been built referencing the .NET Compact Framework BCL and run it without modification on a computer that uses the full .NET Framework–as long as you haven't called any methods that are specific to devices, such as those in the *Microsoft.WindowsMobile* namespace. However, the reverse is not true: you cannot run code compiled against the full .NET Framework on the .NET Compact Framework.

Application Configuration Files

In the full .NET Framework, the System.Configuration namespace contains classes that allow an application to read and update settings stored in an Extensible Markup Language (XML) configuration file. Storing constants in an external file rather than embedded in the code allows for easier reconfiguration later on. For example, a typical usage might be to define a connection string to a database in the application configuration file. If the assembly name is MyAssembly.exe, the configuration file name is MyAssembly.exe.config and is located in the same directory as the assembly.

The .NET Compact Framework does not include built-in support for reading settings in configuration files. However, the runtime will read a configuration file to look for directives to force applications that were compiled against an older version of the .NET Compact Framework runtime to use a newer version if both are available on the device. For example, if you have an application called AppA that was compiled against version 1.0 SP3 and another called AppB compiled against version 2.0 SP1, by default each application executes using the version of the runtime that they were compiled against, as long as both runtimes are installed on the device. If only the later version of the runtime is installed, both applications would run using the version 2.0 SP1 runtime, which should still work fine because each new release maintains backward compatibility with previous versions. However, if both versions of the runtime are installed on the device, but you want to promote AppA to run using the version 2.0 SP1 runtime (which you might do to take advantage of the superior performance compared with version 1.0), you can do this by placing a configuration file called AppA.exe.config in the folder where the application is deployed that contains the following, where each line represents the specific version number of each successive release of the runtime, from version 1.0 at the bottom through 1.0 SP1, 1.0 SP2, 1.0 SP3, version 2.0, 2.0 SP1, and 2.0 SP2:

```
<configuration>
  <startup>
    <supportedRuntime version="v2.0.7045"/>
    <supportedRuntime version="v2.0.6129"/>
    <supportedRuntime version="v2.0.5238"/>
    <supportedRuntime version="v1.0.4292"/>
    <supportedRuntime version="v1.0.3316"/>
    <supportedRuntime version="v1.0.3111"/>
    <supportedRuntime version="v1.0.2268"/>
  </startup>
</configuration>
```

If you want to use configuration files to store application settings in the same way as you do in desktop .NET Framework applications, libraries are available in both the Mobile Client Software Factory and the OpenNETCF Smart Device Framework; see the section titled "Using Community Resources" later in this chapter for more information.

ClickOnce

With the full .NET Framework, you can publish Windows Forms applications to a server or network share. Clients typically check for an update whenever they start, and you have the option of installing the application on the client to allow for offline working, or you can configure the application to be online to the publisher at all times. This brings the "deploy once, run on many clients" convenience of Web applications to Windows Forms.

ClickOnce is not supported on the .NET Compact Framework. See Chapter 6 to find out how to deploy applications onto handheld devices.

Ngen.exe

Ngen.exe is a tool used with the desktop common language runtime (CLR) to precompile assemblies to native code at installation time, also known as install-time just in time (JIT). This leads to faster startup time because the Microsoft intermediate language (MSIL) does not need to be compiled to native code before running. The option of precompiling to native code is not available in the .NET Compact Framework mainly because the size of assemblies compiled to native code far exceeds the size of the same assembly in MSIL. In general, handheld devices do not possess a large amount of storage for program files. Pocket PC devices do not have a physical hard disk drive and must store all program code that is not preinstalled into ROM in virtual storage in RAM, which is typically 32 MB or 64 MB, with some of that space required for program execution.

Remoting

The .NET Compact Framework does not support .NET Remoting. If you need to communicate with .NET components situated on a remote computer, you should implement an XML Web Services façade for the component and access it that way.

Serialization

Because of size and performance considerations, the .NET Compact Framework doesn't support the serialization of objects using the *BinaryFormatter* or *SoapFormatter* class in the *System.Runtime.Serialization* namespace. However, it does support the *System.Xml.XmlSerializer* class to serialize objects to and from XML.

Printing

Printing support is something that has been of interest only to a minority of handheld developers. Handheld applications tend to be used for information retrieval and information gathering and rarely involve requirements for printed output. However, a printed receipt to support a doorstep sale is one scenario in which printing can be of value. Windows CE does not support printing, and so far, providing support for this functionality has been left to third-party suppliers.

In the .NET Compact Framework, there is no support for printing from managed code. If you want to use an infrared, Bluetooth, or serially connected printer from a managed application, third-party products are available (for example, those from PrintBoy and Zebra) that include managed libraries to allow printing.

Web Forms

The *System.Web* namespace in the full .NET Framework contains all the ASP.NET classes (*System.Web.UI.**), as well as those classes that serve and consume XML Web Services. Serving

Web content is not a common function for handheld devices, and so this part of the .NET Framework is not implemented in the .NET Compact Framework. Windows CE–based devices might act as a client for ASP.NET applications (or any other Web server technology) by using the Pocket Internet Explorer browser bundled into the handheld package, but this does not require the presence on the device of any additional run-time components such as the .NET Compact Framework. On the Web server, you might use ASP.NET to develop Web applications targeted at Pocket Internet Explorer.

Understanding the Differences Between .NET Compact Framework Version 1.0 and Version 2.0

If you are a mobile application developer who already has experience developing using .NET Compact Framework 1.0, you want to know what has changed with version 2.0. One of the most agreeable differences is that the version 2.0 runtime is much faster than the version 1.0 runtime is. In 2005, at the Microsoft Mobile and Embedded Developer Conference (MEDC) in Las Vegas, Richard Greenberg, group program manager for the .NET Compact Framework at Microsoft, gave a presentation in which he described the performance gains achieved by .NET Compact Framework 2.0. Some of the statistics he gave for a Pocket PC device with a 400-megahertz (MHz) XScale processor running Windows Mobile 2003 are shown in Figures 1-10 and 1-11.

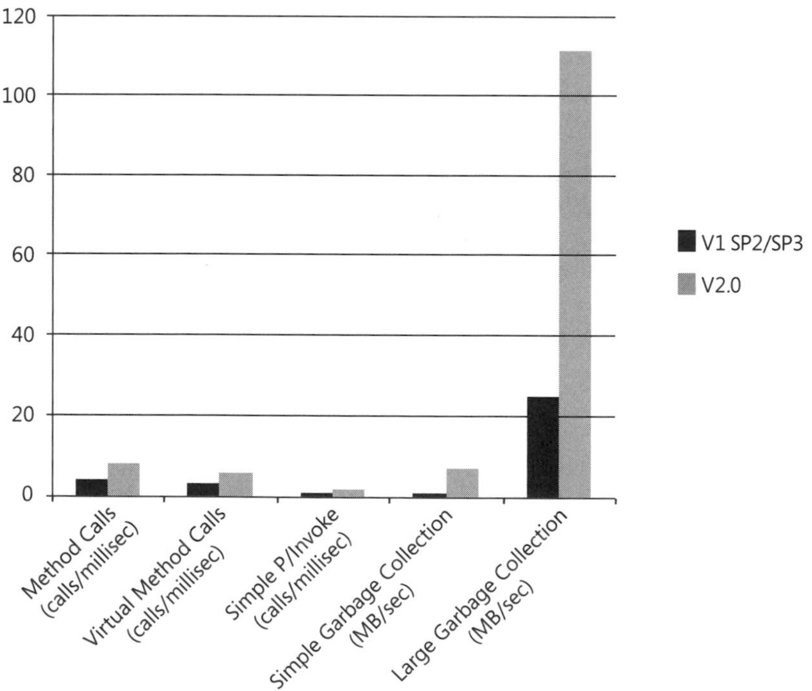

Figure 1-10 Performance improvements in method calls and garbage collection (larger is better)

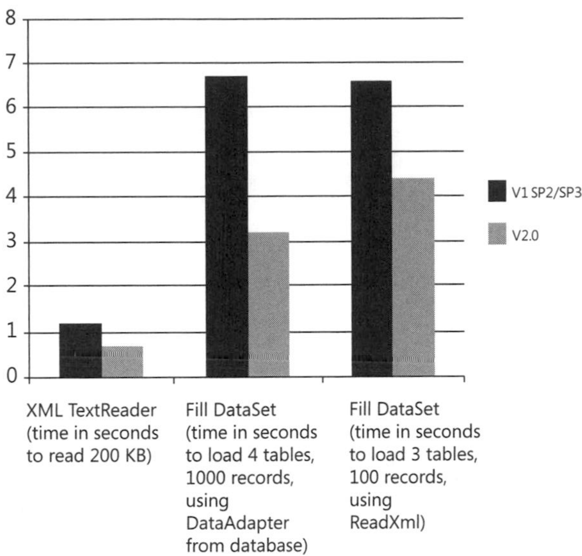

Figure 1-11 Performance improvements in data loading (smaller is better)

In addition to these raw performance gains, version 2.0 of the .NET Compact Framework contains many new capabilities in the BCL. These improvements are designed to improve developer productivity, improve compatibility with the full .NET Framework, and make it easier to use features specific to mobile devices.

The following sections provide a brief summary of all the new features of version 2.0. The chapters in the rest of the book discuss these features in much more detail. You can also find a detailed description of all version 2.0 new features in the online Visual Studio 2005 documentation on the MSDN Web site at *http://msdn2.microsoft.com/en-us/library/ws1c3xeh.aspx*. Also, a resource on the Internet at *http://compactframework2.net/compare* lists the method changes right down at the API level.

Windows Forms

Many new controls are included in version 2.0. One major change is support for user controls. A *user control* is a graphical component you can create in Visual Studio. After a user control is created, it is visible in the Toolbox and can be dragged onto Windows Forms. In addition to user controls, .NET Compact Framework 2.0 supports many new standard controls:

- *MonthCalendar* The *MonthCalendar* control is a useful way for users to select dates.
- *DataGrid* The *DataGrid* control is available in version 1.0, and the functionality has scarcely changed. However, it is now supported on the Smartphone platform as well as on the other platforms.
- *DateTimePicker* Another date selection control, but the *DateTimePicker* appears as a text box that the user can edit directly, or the user can click an icon to display a *MonthCalendar* control to select the date.

- *DocumentList* The *DocumentList* control is available only on Pocket PCs and provides a means for the user to navigate the file system on the device and to perform actions on files, such as Open, Close, Rename, Delete, and E-mail. It provides a user interface similar to the standard File dialog boxes included in standard applications such as Word Mobile and Excel Mobile.
- *LinkLabel* The *LinkLabel* control displays a link as a hyperlink. When clicked, it raises a *Click* event, similar to a *Button* control.
- *Notification* The *Notification* control is available only on the Pocket PC platform and provides a simple way for developers to use the platform's Notifications feature. A pop-up message box appears and can be used to convey information, but it can also include buttons and links to receive user input.
- *Splitter* The *Splitter* control is used to divide a screen into different resizable areas. You can dock controls in different areas, which can be a fixed size, or you can program the control to allow the user to resize an area.
- *WebBrowser* You can use the *WebBrowser* control to access the browser on the device from in your own application.

Display and Layout Management

One of the more recent challenges that mobile application developers face is how to handle the nonstandardization of device screen sizes and orientation. In the past, screen size and orientation were fixed so that the developer could build the UI of applications to work on the standard screen size for a Pocket PC or a smartphone (of course, Windows CE developers have never enjoyed that luxury).

Today devices come with square, portrait, or landscape screen orientation in different dimensions. Some devices, such as the HTC TyTn, use portrait orientation until you pull out the retractable keyboard (which is hidden in the side of the screen), whereupon the screen switches to landscape orientation. How does the developer create a UI that can operate well on such a device?

Docking and Anchoring

.NET Compact Framework 2.0 supports docking and anchoring of controls to help developers lay out an adaptable UI. You can dock a control against the edge of the parent control, such as a *Form* or *Panel*. The docked control will lock itself to that edge of its parent, filling that edge. When the parent control is resized, the docked control automatically resizes so that it always fills the specified edge of the parent control. Controls can also be docked to fill the entire parent.

Anchoring is a similar feature. An anchored control is not in direct contact with the edge of its parent but instead maintains a fixed distance from the edges of the parent to which it is anchored. When the parent control is resized, the anchored control automatically resizes so that the anchored sides of the control remain the appropriate distance from the corresponding edges of the parent control.

Automatic Scrollbars

If docking and anchoring are not sufficient to adapt your UI to work in different orientations, and you find some controls are positioned off the visible area, you can at least get the runtime to add scrollbars automatically to your display so that the user can move the visible area. To add scrollbars automatically, you can set the *AutoScroll* property of the *Form* or *Panel* control to *true*.

Screen Resolution Handling

These days, mobile devices also come with different screen resolutions. For example, Pocket PCs always used to have screens that were 320 × 240 pixels (QVGA), but today a number of devices are available that are 420 × 680 (VGA). If you have developed a UI for a Quarter VGA (QVGA) display, what will it look like on a Video Graphics Adapter (VGA) display? The only way you really know is to test it, and Visual Studio provides you with both QVGA and VGA emulators to help in that task.

From a programming point of view, you can set the *AutoScrollMode* property of container controls such as the *Form* or *Panel* to *AutoScrollMode.Dpi*, which causes all child controls of the container to be scaled to match the resolution of the display, even if a control was originally designed for a different resolution. You can also find out at run time what the horizontal and vertical dots per inch of the current display are by querying the *DpiX* and *DpiY* properties of the *Graphics* object.

Tab Support and Keyboard Management

Another main enhancement related to how a user interacts with your UI is support for keyboards, which are becoming more common on devices. Controls on a form now have tab order (a feature that was actually added in .NET Compact Framework 1.0 SP2) so that the user can use the Tab key to move between controls. Controls also now receive *KeyUp*, *KeyDown*, *KeyPress*, and *KeyPreview* events. You can use the *KeyPreview* event to intercept key presses, and if you like, set *KeyPressEventArgs.Handled* to *true* to prevent the key event from being sent to the control.

Data

Database handling has received major improvements. The *System.Data.SqlClient* classes for accessing back-end SQL Server databases have been enhanced to work with SQL Server 2005 databases, as have the remote data access and merge replication functionalities. The *System.Data.SqlServerCe* classes for accessing databases on the device work only with SQL Server 2005 Compact Edition (formerly called SQL Server 2005 Mobile Edition) and not with SQL Server CE 2.0. SQL Server 2005 Everywhere Edition is a much faster, more reliable database than SQL Server CE 2.0 is and includes many enhancements, such as support for more than one concurrent connection. However, the best innovation is the *SqlCeResultSet*, which is a bit like an updatable data reader, giving very fast query and update performance. You learn more about programming SQL Server 2005 Compact Edition in Chapter 3, "Using SQL Server 2005 Compact Edition and Other Data Stores."

If you work with datasets, you can now call the *GetChanges* method to return only rows that have changed, which is useful when you want to minimize network usage and send only data changes to a server. Complementary to this is the *Merge* method that you can use to merge one dataset with another, for example, to merge the changed rows back into a master dataset.

The *DataBinding* class is available to make binding easier between databound controls such as a *DataGrid* and a data source such as an *SqlCeResultSet*, a *DataSet*, or a collection. The *DataBinding* class exposes methods to set the current record position in the data source and exposes change events.

Communications

.NET Compact Framework 2.0 supports the *SerialPort* class that managed code developers can use to control communications with devices over a serial port. It also supports Microsoft Message Queuing (MSMQ), which is a great way of implementing reliable data message delivery to and from devices in a local area network (LAN) and from devices to a server over the Internet. See Chapter 8, "Networking," for more information.

COM Interop

You can use COM interop in .NET Compact Framework 2.0 to use native Component Object Model (COM) components from your managed code or create new COM components using managed code. See Chapter 14 for more information about COM interop and other techniques for interoperating with native code.

Graphics Programming

If you do custom drawing in your applications, you will find new methods to manipulate bitmaps and to save bitmaps to a file or stream. You can also draw text using the *LogFont* class, which supports drawing text at any angle. Version 2.0 also supports custom pens for which you specify the color and the size. See Chapter 12, "Graphics Programming," for more information.

For advanced graphics programming, .NET Compact Framework 2.0 includes support for the Microsoft Mobile DirectX and Direct3D Mobile APIs. The former is supported on all platforms, whereas the latter is supported on devices running Windows Mobile 5.0 or later. See Chapter 13, "Direct3D Mobile," for more information.

Security

.NET Compact Framework 1.0 does not support any managed classes to support encryption. Version 2.0, however, provides extensive support for cryptography, including MD5 and SHA1 hashing; RC2, RC4, Triple DES (3DES), Data Encryption Standard (DES), and Rijndael (as used in the U.S. Federal Government Advanced Encryption Standard) symmetric encryption; and RSA asymmetric encryption.

.NET Compact Framework 2.0 supports NTLM and Kerberos authentication, as well as the digest authentication also supported in version 1.0, for passing credentials to network resources that demand authentication. For more information about cryptography and authentication, see Chapter 10, "Security Programming for Mobile Applications."

Threading

Version 1.0 of the .NET Compact Framework provides limited support for multithreading programming but lacks some essential features such as the ability to abort threads. All threads are foreground threads, which means that you must be very careful to ensure that worker threads exit; otherwise, they prevent your application from closing.

Multithreaded programming is always a programming activity that demands care, but the task is made easier in version 2.0 with the capability to create threads as background threads. Background threads terminate when the main program thread terminates. You can also use the *Abort* method to terminate threads, and you can block waiting for a thread to exit by using the *Join* method.

Performance Monitoring

In version 1.0 of the .NET Compact Framework, it is difficult to diagnose performance problems because the only diagnostic tool you can implement is to set a registry key to cause the runtime to accumulate limited statistical data on internal counters and dump the data to a file when the application exits.

In version 2.0, the range of counters that are measured is greatly increased. Also, Service Pack 1 includes the Remote Performance Monitor tool that you can use to monitor the counters in real time and even display the results in Windows Performance Monitor on your development computer. To learn more about Remote Performance Monitor, see Chapter 4.

Introducing .NET Compact Framework Version 3.5

This book is primarily focused on developing applications using .NET Compact Framework 2.0. However, at the time of this writing, early versions of the next version, version 3.5, are available from the MSDN Downloads Center as Community Tech Preview releases. Version 3.5 will be included in the next release of Visual Studio, currently code-named Orcas.

Important The following list describes features in the Community Tech Previews. There is no guarantee that this feature list will be available in the final released product.

You can learn more about the new features and how to program them in Chapter 18, "A First Look at .NET Compact Framework Version 3.5," but a summary follows:

- **Compact Windows Communication Foundation (WCF)** This allows mobile devices to take part in distributed applications that use WCF for reliable communications. The implementation is planned to include a Hypertext Transfer Protocol (HTTP) transport for reliable networks, an implementation of WS-Security for secure message transfer, and the ability to use e-mail as a message transport over unreliable networks, using Microsoft Exchange Server 2007 for store and forward. This interesting development promises to provide a solution to the problem of sending unsolicited messages to a mobile device that is connected to a mobile operator's network, something that is very difficult to do today because of the network architectures that are employed, which make it problematic to open a Transmission Control Protocol/Internet Protocol (TCP/IP) connection to a device unless the device initiates the connection in the first place. WCF using an e-mail message channel takes advantage of the push e-mail capability that is a feature of Windows Mobile–powered devices connected to Exchange Server.
- **Compact Language Integrated Query (Linq)** Linq is the name given to new query capabilities added to the Microsoft Visual C# and Visual Basic languages to allow easier querying of collections. The implementation of Linq in .NET Compact Framework 3.5 is a subset of the desktop .NET Framework implementation and supports querying of datasets and XML, but not to a SQL Server or SQL Server Compact Edition database.
- **Compatibility with Desktop .NET Framework Features** A number of new features are implementations of features available in the desktop .NET Framework, including the following:
    - *SoundPlayer* (plus added device mixing)
    - *CreateGraphics* support for custom drawing on *TabPage*, *Panel*, *Splitter*, and *PictureBox* controls
    - The ability to change the *BackColor* on read-only controls
    - Addition of *SelectionStart* and *SelectionLength* properties to the *ComboBox*
    - *System.IO.Compression* support in file input/output (I/O) and communication
    - Extending the *PlatformID* class to include enums for Smartphone and Pocket PC
- **New Tools** The Remote Performance Monitor, which was first released as a standalone tool in .NET Compact Framework 2.0 SP1, is now fully integrated into Visual Studio. There is also a new CLR Profiler tool that will provide graphical displays of object

allocations, histograms of live objects categorized by age, and similar information about the memory management of the CLR.

- **Logging enhancements** Enhancements are made to interop logging and to finalizer logging, including logging of the order in which finalizers are run and the timing. Log files may be read at run time; they are currently locked while the application is running.
- **Debugging enhancements** The debugger will break in the correct location on unhandled exceptions instead of always at *Application.Run*.

Apart from the new capabilities in the .NET Compact Framework runtime, Visual Studio Orcas also contains version 3.0 of the Device Emulator, which brings many performance and functionality improvements over earlier incarnations. Support for unit testing using Visual Studio Team System is also included.

Using Community Resources

Application development with the .NET Compact Framework presents two particular challenges:

- The BCL contains only a subset of the functionality of the full .NET Framework. The product group at Microsoft decided what to implement and what to leave out, and those choices have been, on the whole, good ones. However, inevitably some functionality is missing that some developers may find useful.
- Mobile development is challenging because of the demanding computing environment in which mobile applications operate: network connections may be intermittent or unreliable, security is a prime concern because of the risk of a device being lost or stolen, and, for the GUI developer, there are problems writing a GUI that will work well on square, portrait, landscape, and/or high-resolution screens.

Members of the mobile developer community have been very supportive of each other in providing advice and workarounds to meet these challenges, and online forums are well populated by Microsoft support personnel, Microsoft Most Valuable Professionals (MVPs), and other experts. In particular, MSDN Forums where you can post questions and search for answers exist to support application development for devices. You can find MSDN Forums on the MSDN Web site at *http://forums.microsoft.com/MSDN/default.aspx?ForumGroupID=11&SiteID=1*. Also, many newsgroups are listed on the Mobile Development Center Web site at *http://msdn.microsoft.com/mobility/community/newsgroups/default.aspx*.

In addition to these community resources, two software libraries are available that have helped to address mobile application development challenges and that have become valuable tools for the .NET Compact Framework developer: The Microsoft patterns & practices Mobile Application Blocks and the OpenNETCF Smart Device Framework.

Microsoft patterns & practices Mobile Application Blocks

The Mobile Application Blocks are part of a free software product from the Microsoft patterns & practices group called the Mobile Client Software Factory. This encourages development of mobile applications using an asset called the mobile Composite UI Application Block, or mobile CAB for short. The mobile CAB is quite difficult to adopt and is intended for use by large enterprise software development departments, but the other application blocks can be used in any .NET Compact Framework 2.0 application running on Windows Mobile 5.0 or later.

These application blocks include the disconnected service agent, which makes it easy to call Web services on a device connected to an unreliable network; the Mobile Configuration Application Block, which implements support for application configuration files; and the mobile Password Authentication Application Block, which makes it easy to build solid password verification into your application and to encrypt and decrypt sensitive data such as database connection strings or user names and passwords. You can use the Orientation-Aware control to develop UIs that adapt automatically to changes in screen orientation. The Mobile Client Software Factory ships with full source code so that you can modify and extend the blocks to suit your own needs.

We explain how to use some of the Mobile Application Blocks in later chapters. To download the Mobile Client Software Factory, go to the patterns & practices Mobile Client Software Factory home page at *http://www.codeplex.com/smartclient*.

OpenNETCF Smart Device Framework

The Smart Device Framework (SDF) was started as an open source project by a group of MVPs with the goal of filling in the missing bits in .NET Compact Framework 1.0. Their libraries have evolved over time and now implement many classes that are in the full framework that were missing from the .NET Compact Framework and also include many useful additional libraries.

Best of all, version 1.*x* of the OpenNETCF SDF is free and shipped with full source code. There is no better resource on how to build good class libraries, in particular how to use PInvoke to call Microsoft Win32 APIs! You can still download the version 1.4 SDF source for free; see *http://www.opennetcf.org* for details. With the release of version 2.0 of the SDF, the source code is no longer available for free. You can download the binaries of the Smart Device Framework 2.0 Community Edition at *http://www.opennetcf.org* and browse the documentation, but if you want the source code, unfortunately you must now pay for it.

Summary

This chapter describes the mobile device platforms you may encounter as a mobile application developer, the tools you will require to develop .NET Compact Framework applications, and an overview of the differences between the full .NET Framework and the .NET Compact Framework.

We discussed the differences between .NET Compact Framework 1.0 and 2.0 and introduced version 3.5, and finally we described some additional resources that are available to make the job of the mobile application developer a little bit easier.

In the next chapter, we look at the process of mobile application development and explain how to build Windows Forms applications on mobile devices.

Chapter 2

Building a Microsoft Windows Forms GUI

In this chapter:

This and the next chapter explain how to build a Microsoft Windows Forms graphical user interface (GUI) for your mobile application. In this chapter, you learn about handling and navigating forms, handling user input, working with different screen orientations and resolutions, and the differences between the user interface (UI) on Pocket PCs and Smartphones. In Chapter 3, "Using SQL Server 2005 Compact Edition and Other Data Stores," the focus moves to how to bind controls to data sources.

Mobile devices come with the obvious constraint of a relatively small screen that can make it challenging to design an effective UI. In addition, Pocket PCs and Smartphones differ in their user input capabilities: Typically, Pocket PC applications must accommodate the on-screen keyboard (the software-based input panel, or SIP), whereas input in Smartphones is usually through a phone keypad. However, you must be aware that devices today are released in many different configurations; you may have to design your GUI to present a well-laid-out GUI in both portrait and landscape orientations, or on screens using Video Graphics Adapter (VGA) or quarter VGA (QVGA) resolutions. All these factors can make it more challenging to design a GUI for a mobile device than it is to design one for a desktop computer.

In addition to studying the information in this book, we strongly encourage you to read the UI guidelines for the Pocket PC and Smartphone platforms (links from here: *msdn.microsoft.com/mobility/windowsmobile/partners/mobile2market/participatevendors.aspx*) and to study the behavior of built-in applications on your chosen target platform.

One obvious UI design guideline for Pocket PC is to place near the bottom of the screen items that require the user to tap so that when the user taps to make a selection, the user's hand does not obscure the screen. This is why the tabs of the *TabControl* and the menus of the menu bar appear at the bottom of the screen.

Using the software-based input panel (SIP) is tedious for a user, and so you should always try to minimize the amount of data a user must enter wherever possible. Besides text boxes, you can use alternative controls such as combo boxes, check boxes, and radio buttons as applicable. If you must use text boxes, place them near the top of the display so that when the SIP becomes visible, it does not obscure the text boxes.

Also, do not populate lists with hundreds of items. Not only will the user not scroll through that many items on a device, but loading them all in a *Listview* or *Listbox* will negatively affect performance. Instead, consider on-demand loading of items, alphabetical categorization, and other techniques you can use to limit the number of items.

Again, a developer new to the platform should read the Microsoft Windows Mobile UI guidelines first.

Understanding Windows Forms Version 2.0 Enhancements

Most device applications include a GUI to present information to the user and accept input. In almost all modern environments, including Microsoft Visual Studio 2005, GUIs are built by adding objects to a design surface. In the Microsoft .NET Framework, the design surface is the form and the objects are Windows Forms controls.

The .NET Compact Framework version 2.0 Windows Forms controls include numerous enhancements. Some of the changes are part of the overall version 2.0 full .NET Framework such as *generics*, and others were intended to catch up with the functionality in the version 1.1 full .NET Framework, such as additional members in the *Control* class.

Other changes mean that existing code with workarounds for version 1.0 functionality can now be removed. For example, with .NET Compact Framework 1.0, adding a non-full screen *TabControl* to a form is not obvious; you have to place it in a panel first and then position the panel according to your desired design layout. With .NET Compact Framework 2.0, you can use the *TabControl* for absolute positioning as you see fit.

Only a few of the new features have been covered in this chapter and Chapter 1, ".NET Compact Framework—a Platform on the Move." For a comprehensive list of new .NET Compact Framework 2.0 features, please visit the Microsoft MSDN Web site at *msdn2.microsoft.com/en-us/library/hyc18s6t.aspx*.

Partial classes

When you create new forms in Visual Studio 2005 you may observe a new feature of .NET Framework 2.0. Unlike in earlier versions of Visual Studio, in Visual Studio 2005 the code generated when you add controls to a form in the design phase and when you tweak the appearance and behavior of those controls in the Properties window resides in a separate code file named *<FormName>.Designer* (for example, Form1.Designer.cs or Form1.Designer.vb). If you are using C# to view the generated code file, you must expand the Form node in Solution Explorer. If you are using Microsoft Visual Basic, first select Show All Files in Solution Explorer.

This split of designer-generated code from developer-written code is made possible by a new feature named *partial classes*. You can use partial classes to define a class in multiple files by using the same class name in multiple files and prefixing the class name with the new language keyword *partial*. It is important to note that all of the related files of the same class must be included in the same project because they are combined during compilation to represent a single class. A simple example of this is to examine a form's code-behind in Visual Studio 2005 following the steps described earlier to view the generated code file. Partial classes have even more uses in device development combined with conditional compilation, as you'll see at the end of this chapter.

Using the Same Workflow as for Developing Desktop Applications

As you know, to create a Windows Forms application on the desktop, you start by selecting New Project on the File menu. You create a new Smart Device project in the same way. After you expand the node that represents your managed language of choice (C# or Visual Basic), you see the Smart Device node, which includes a wealth of project templates. To create a Windows Forms GUI, choose the Device Application option under Windows Mobile 5.0 Pocket PC, as shown in Figure 1-1 in Chapter 1. This dialog box will look familiar only if you've installed the Windows Mobile 5.0 software development kit (SDK) as explained in Chapter 1.

Tip In the next version of Visual Studio code-named Orcas, the Windows Mobile 5.0 SDKs will be part of the install. You may still need to install the SDK for Windows Mobile 6.

To create a UI for a device application, follow the same basic process you use to create a UI for any desktop application. The form design surface represents a screen, and you add controls from the Toolbox onto it. After you add controls, you set their properties to customize their behavior and appearance. The last step is to handle events from the controls to respond to user interaction. The event handlers are methods in code that you fill with your business logic.

The obvious difference between building a UI for a device application and building one for a desktop application is that for the former the form design surface actually looks like a device. You can turn this appearance on and off by right-clicking the form and toggling the Show Skin option, as shown in Figure 2-1. You can set the default behavior to show the skin or not when a form is opened by selecting Options on the Tools menu.

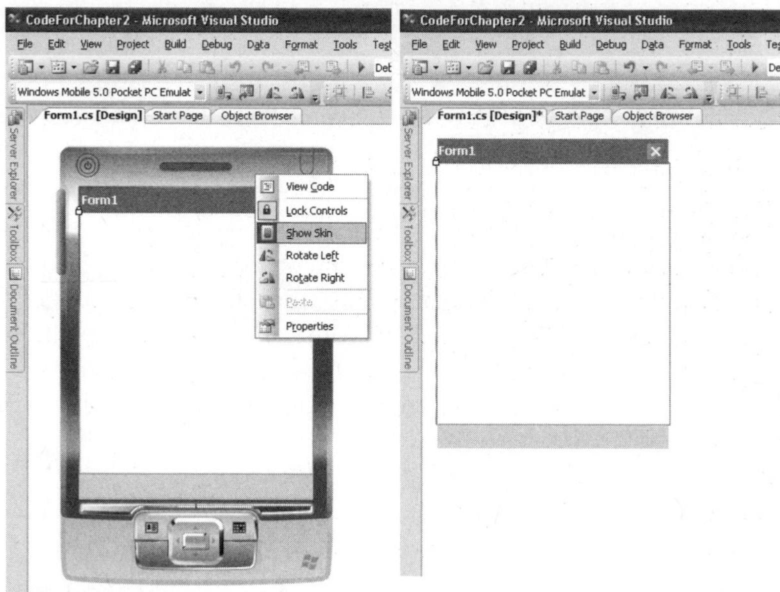

Figure 2-1 Show Skin option: with skin (and the context menu) on the left; without skin on the right

You can change the orientation and size of the skin by opening the form Properties dialog box and selecting an alternative form factor, as shown in Figure 2-2.

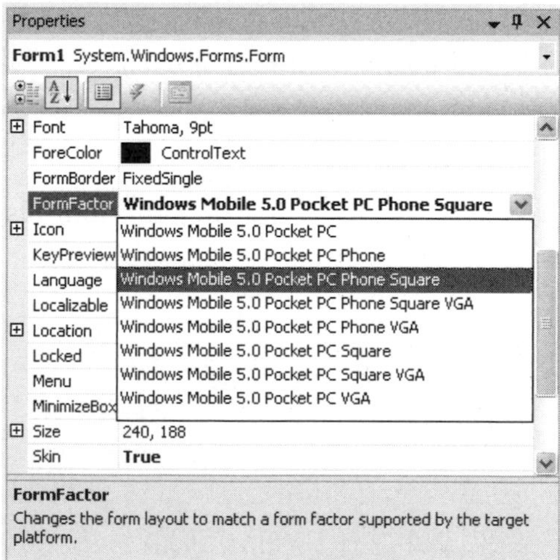

Figure 2-2 *FormFactor* option for Windows Mobile 5.0 Pocket PC project

Another significant difference between Windows Forms application development for devices and desktop computers is that the Toolbox of controls for Windows Forms is not as rich as is the one for desktop development. Figure 2-3 shows the Toolbox for both Pocket PC and Smartphone controls.

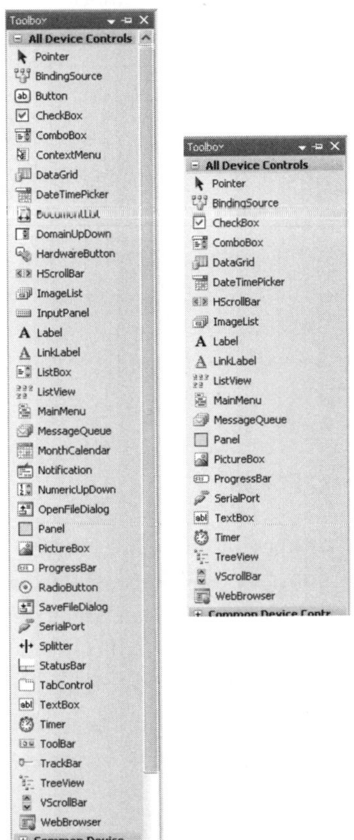

Figure 2-3 Toolbox for Pocket PC (left) and Smartphone (right) device projects

As you can see, the controls that do not make sense to use on a device (for example, *ToolTip*, *EventLog*, *DirectorySearcher*) or that may not offer enough value to justify their considerable footprint (for example, *Error Provider*, *TableLayoutPanel*, or any of the *Print* controls) are not included in the Toolbox. Only a subset of the desktop controls is available.

You can see a third difference between creating device projects compared with desktop projects when you press F5 to run the project. For desktop projects, the application runs on the desktop, but for device projects, the device application is deployed either to an emulator or to a real device, provided you have one available.

> **Tip** The Visual Studio 2005 emulators are great development tools. However, if you have a real device on which to test and debug your applications, you *may* find that you can deploy and debug your application more quickly than you can using an emulator (depending on the specification of your development computer). Remember that for Windows Mobile 5.0–powered devices, you need Microsoft ActiveSync version 4.0 or later (or Windows Mobile Device Center on the Windows Vista operating system).

For more deployment options, click the Tools menu and explore two of the options: the Connect To Device submenu and the Device Emulator Manager submenu. Chapter 4, "Catching Errors, Testing, and Debugging," covers these tools in more depth. It is important to note that with Visual Studio 2005, the emulators are Advanced RISC Machines (ARM) emulators that can provide a high-fidelity experience with machine code–level emulation. You must use a real device to measure performance accurately, diagnose networking issues, and of course perform final quality assurance (QA) testing (for example, using a stylus rather than a mouse), which is paramount before shipping your application. After you open the emulator, explore the rich options by selecting the File menu and then clicking Configure.

Mapping Device Screens to Device Forms

After you understand the mechanics and workflow of creating GUI projects, the next step is to understand the behaviors and configurability of all the controls. The Microsoft MSDN Web site at *msdn2.microsoft.com/en-us/library/hf2k718k(VS.80).aspx* provides copious amounts of information on controls, so we do not discuss them in depth in this book. Rather, we highlight the most important controls later in this chapter. Now it is essential to discuss some platform considerations and how they map to form properties.

Screen Layout

You can think of forms on devices as having three areas: a strip at the top, a strip at the bottom, and the main area in between the strips, as shown in Figure 2-4.

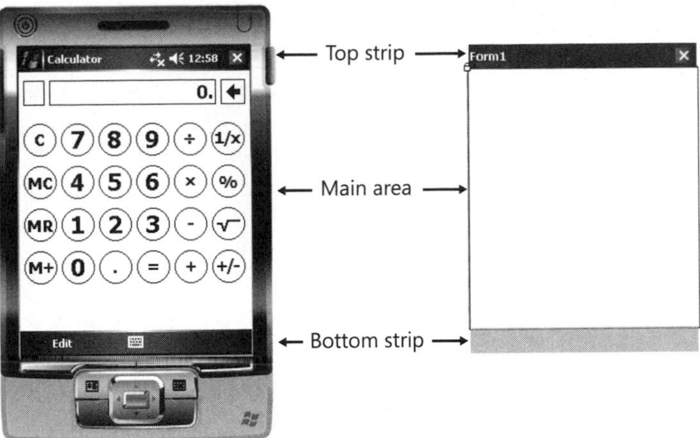

Figure 2-4 A Pocket PC application annotated to emphasize the screen layout

The top strip is for the application title/caption bar. The device also uses the top strip for such features as the device start menu, clock, and signal indicators. The bottom strip is for the soft keys (menu/toolbar in devices that use operating systems earlier than Windows Mobile 5.0) and also the SIP for Pocket PCs. The area in the middle is where you design your main UI.

It is generally advisable that you do not alter this layout, but if you do want to hide the top or bottom strip, you can. In Visual Studio, by default each form is given a *MainMenu* control. (In Windows Mobile 5.0 this is used for the soft keys, and for devices that use earlier versions of Windows Mobile, it is used for menu and toolbar.) You can delete the menu control from your form to hide the bottom strip. To hide the top strip, you must set the *WindowsState* property of the form to *Maximized* (instead of its only other value, *Normal*).

Closing a Form

Now that you understand the screen layout, the next thing to realize about forms is that you have a main form, and then there are all the other forms, that is, the nonmain forms. The main form is the one you passed to *Application.Run* in your static *Main* method, which resides in the Program.cs file that Visual Studio generates for you:

```
static class Program
{
  static void Main()
  {
    Application.Run(new Form1());
  }
}
```

Note By default, Visual Basic projects do not expose the *static Main* method. Instead, the developer can set the main form for the project through the project Properties dialog box. On the Application tab, select the form name in the Startup Object combo box or, even better, select Sub Main. You then must add a *Shared Sub Main* method to one of your classes (or to a new class). The benefit you gain is that you can then cleanly add code before the form is shown; you will see that this is useful later in this chapter when we talk about resolution awareness and in Chapter 4 when we talk about global exception handling. You can find an example of the preceding steps in the code samples for Chapters 2 and 4.

When the main form closes, the application also closes–other forms that you create during the lifetime of your application do not have that power. You can, of course, exit an application at any time by using *Application.Exit*, but that is not advisable because that technique does not run a *Closing* event method handler and instantly stops processing any Windows messages that are in the message loop queue. The clean way is to design your application so that it closes only when the user closes the main form.

Caution Any foreground threads that are running will keep your process up even when your application is not showing any UI elements. Always make sure you have terminated any threads that you have created. For more information about foreground threads and correct thread termination, see Chapter 11, "Threading."

Of course, you can decide, as is done for most device applications, not to offer a way to exit the application. Instead, you can configure your application to smart minimize (that is, it hides and reveals whatever application is running or showing beneath it); this is the default behavior.

When to close applications, when to minimize?

According to the design guidelines mentioned in the introduction to this chapter, Pocket PC and Smartphone applications should not include a way to close the application–no Exit menu option or button. It used to be the case that if you submitted an application for testing under the Designed for Windows Mobile logo program and it included an Exit option, your application failed verification. However, the requirements have been relaxed now so that you are allowed to provide a way for a user to close your application, although it is still preferred to leave it running.

If you do not provide an Exit option, after your application is started, it remains running on the device until either you reset the device, you close it using a task manager application, or the operating system orders the application to close because the device is running low on memory. On a Smartphone, the application smart minimizes (that is, disappears into the background) when the user presses the Back key to navigate away from your application or selects a new application from the Start menu. Similarly, on a Pocket PC, the application smart minimizes when the user selects a different application from the Start menu or presses a hardware button to select one of the built-in applications such as Contacts or E-Mail. Your application still runs, but in the background.

There is another way to smart minimize a Pocket PC application: by tapping the Close button on the application title bar (the icon with the *X* in it). An unfortunate inconsistency runs across the Windows platform here because on a desktop computer, the Close button means close, not minimize, and the Exit button is represented by a button with an *X* in it. However, the decision to use an *X* to represent the minimize function on a Pocket PC was made many years ago when the Pocket PC user interface was being refined into the current style.

If you are wondering whether to provide an Exit option in your application, consider the different ways a handheld device and a desktop computer are used. Desktop computer users are accustomed to running many applications simultaneously and minimizing or closing them as needed. A handheld device, however, is more of an always-on appliance. On a handheld device, the user expects to start Microsoft Windows Media Player Mobile and be listening to music almost instantaneously, or to run the Contacts application and gain instant access to contacts. On such a device, starting an application is slow, and it is much quicker to reactivate an application that is simply running in the background. The philosophy goes that a handheld device user doesn't care about closing or minimizing applications, just fast switching between them–and it doesn't matter how that happens. As a result, your users will perceive faster startup time for your application if, when they select it from the Programs menu, they simply reactivate a smart-minimized application that is already running rather than starting the application all over again.

For more information about the smart minimize feature, see the Windows Mobile Team Blog Web site at *blogs.msdn.com/windowsmobile/archive/2006/10/05/The-Emperor-Has-No-Close.aspx*.

On Pocket PCs, whether an application smart minimizes or actually closes is determined by the *ControlBox* appearance and, in particular, whether a close button or an OK is displayed, as shown in Figure 2-5.

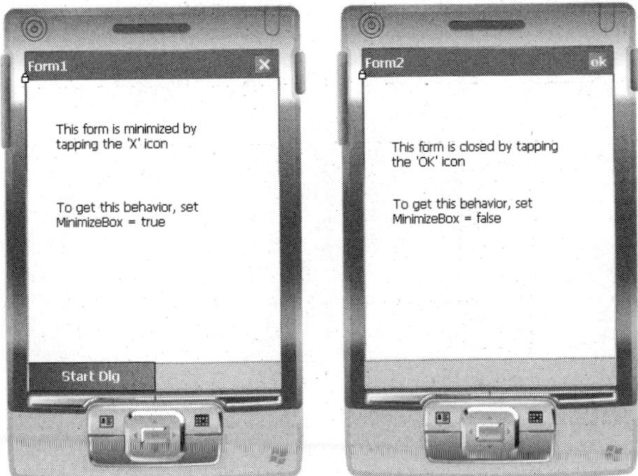

Figure 2-5 Using the Close button (on the left) or the OK button (on the right)

> **Note** On the Smartphone, the dedicated hardware Back button is the equivalent of the Close button. You must provide your own Done soft key to simulate the Pocket PC OK button. You can read more on soft keys later in this chapter in the section titled "Exploring Important Windows Forms Controls."

On a Pocket PC device, you can customize the minimize behavior in code by toggling the *Boolean* value of the form's *MinimizeBox* property (*false* displays an OK button; *true* displays a Close button). Setting the form's *ControlBox* property to *false* leaves the upper-right corner blank, and then it is up to you to provide an alternative means for the user to switch away from the form. At this point, it is worth mentioning that you can use the *Form.Show* and *ShowDialog* methods to open secondary forms just as on the desktop. If you use the *ShowDialog* method, the form will have an OK button in the upper-right corner (with the associated behavior described earlier) and the *MinimizeBox* property will be ignored. Note that using the *ShowDialog* method, as on the desktop, results in a modal dialog box.

A couple of relevant pieces of information follow. When any form switches to the background, its *Deactivate* event is raised. If the user closes a nonmain form by using the OK button in the upper-right corner, the *Closing* event is raised instead. Also, if a form displays the Close button but you actually really want to close the form by using code, you can use the form's *Close* method (note that this is the only route available on the Smartphone). The following code examples demonstrate:

```
private void frmShown_Closing(object sender, CancelEventArgs e)
{
  // When this form is closed
  // by using OK or Close method call
  Debug.WriteLine("Closing");
}

private void frmShown_Deactivate(object sender, EventArgs e)
{
  // When this form goes to the background
  // (closed, smart minimized, or otherwise)
  Debug.WriteLine("Deactivate");
}

private void menuItem1_Click(object sender, EventArgs e)
{
  // Same as clicking the OK button
  // If form has Close button, this still closes the form
  // as if it had an OK button.
  this.Close();
}
```

Form Navigation

This section discusses form navigation. Forms on a Windows Mobile device (with the exception of message boxes) are always full screen,[1] and the user can interact with only one form at a time. This makes navigating between forms fairly tricky—not to mention that if a specific task requires more than one screen, users are expected to remember what the previous screen displayed! You should try to minimize the number of screens/forms with which the user must interact and try especially to minimize the dependencies between forms.

To be notified when your form is navigated to (or navigated away from), use the *Activated* and *Deactivate* events. The forms that you do decide to open should generally be very task specific, with a shorter lifetime than the main screen of the application, and generally they should be shown by using the *ShowDialog* method (that is, modal forms). You can use *Show* (instead of *ShowDialog*) if you'd like the original form to continue with some processing instead of being blocked while waiting for the shown form to return. You'll see later, however, that this is rarely a good idea.

The only built-in mechanism that a user can use to navigate between different top-level windows on a Pocket PC is a long-winded path of taps: First, tap the Start menu, and then the Settings menu, and then the System tab, and then the Memory icon, and finally tap the Running Programs tab. Note that this is not a list of processes, but rather this sequence displays all top-level windows that have a nonzero-length caption. Typically, in the Running Programs screen the user of the device sees all current programs (with a UI) that are running.

Ensuring That an Application Shows Only Once in the Running Programs List

If you create and run a two-form project in Visual Studio, and then browse to the Running Programs list, you'll notice that both forms are showing and that you can browse to either:

```
private void button2_Click(object sender, EventArgs e)
{
  frmShown f = new frmShown();
  if (checkBox1.Checked) // show modal
  {
    f.ShowDialog();
  }
  else
  {
    f.Show();
  }
}
```

1 Technically, on a Pocket PC, you can change the size of the form by setting the *FormBorderStyle* to *None*. Not only will your form look funny, but other issues will arise, and so it is our opinion that you should stick with the platform guidelines.

This is generally not desirable. If you have shown a modal form (that is, by using *ShowDialog*), users can see the parent form in the Running Programs list, but when they try to activate it, the modal form appears instead (as you would expect). If you have shown a second form non-modally (that is, by using *Show*), users can activate the parent form when you probably intended for them to see only the second form. We present the solution next.

Conceptually, you can think of your application as having just one screen (a screen that may change its appearance but that is always one screen nonetheless). The first step to achieving the appearance of a one-screen application is to keep the same caption (use the form's *Text* property) constant across any forms that you open. The second step is to ensure that only one form appears in the Running Programs list. You can achieve both goals by setting the *Owner* property of the form you are about to show as follows:

```
// Show form, ensuring that:
// 1. only one entry appears in the Running Programs list
// 2. the single entry has the same caption regardless of form shown
private void button3_Click(object sender, EventArgs e)
{
  frmShown f = new frmShown();
  f.Owner = this;
  f.ShowDialog();
}
```

Note that using the *Owner* property approach works if the form is shown by using *ShowDialog*. If the form is shown by using *Show* (you should really be sure that modality was not desired), you must use code as follows:

```
// Show form, ensuring that:
// 1. only one entry appears in the Running Programs list
// 2. the single entry has the same caption regardless of form shown
private void button3_Click(object sender, EventArgs e)
{
  frmShown f = new frmShown();


  f.MinimizeBox = false;
  this.caption = this.Text;
  f.Text = this.caption;
  this.Text = ""; //hides the form from the list
  f.Closed += new EventHandler(f_Closed);
  f.Show();
  // Code in this form still runs (that is, it is not modal),
  // but users cannot navigate to it until they close the form shown.
}

private string caption;
void f_Closed(object sender, EventArgs e)
{
  this.Text = caption;
this.BringToFront();
}
```

Visual form inheritance

When you design forms in Visual Studio, you may be tempted to use visual form inheritance. *Visual inheritance* is inheritance (in the object-oriented sense) in which both the parent and the child classes are forms. The benefits are that you can visually design a form once and then reuse that visual design in other forms by inheriting from the base form. You can use visual inheritance in Visual Studio 2005 by selecting Add New Item from the Project menu and selecting Inherited Form from the list of templates (see Figure 2-11). However under certain circumstances it is possible for the designer to break when using visual form inheritance, as shown in Figure 2-6.

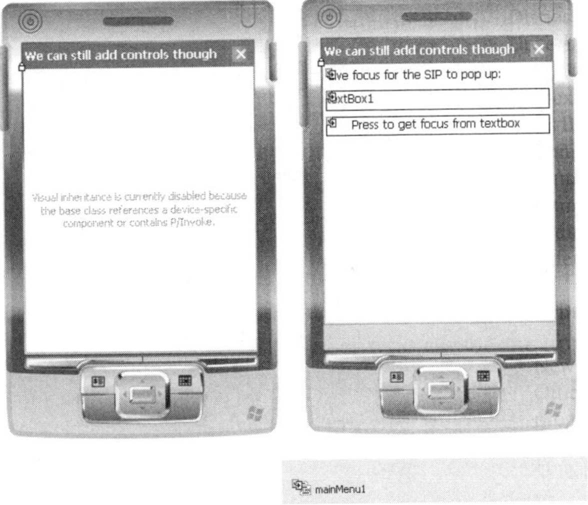

Figure 2-6 Broken forms designer when base form uses device-specific functionality; on the right, same form after the fix (note the inherited controls with arrows)

To rectify this, follow these steps:

1. Right-click frmBase, and then select View Class Diagram.
2. Select the class shape, and then go to the Properties dialog box.
3. Select Custom Attributes to open the Custom Attributes window for the form.
4. Add the following line of code to the window, and then click OK: *DesktopCompatible(true)*
5. Rebuild your solution, and the form should appear fine in the designer.

Exploring Important Windows Forms Controls

As mentioned earlier, the Windows Forms controls available to device projects are a subset of the controls available to desktop projects. Even when a control is supported on both platforms, the members of the class on the device platform are a subset of the members you find in the same class on the desktop platform. For example, the *Button* control in the .NET Compact Framework does not have an *Image* property. As on the full framework, all controls ultimately inherit from the *Control* class. Figure 2-7 shows what is available in the base *Control* class, but note that not all of those members are implemented in the controls you will instantiate (that is, not all controls provide implementations by overriding the members you see in the figure).

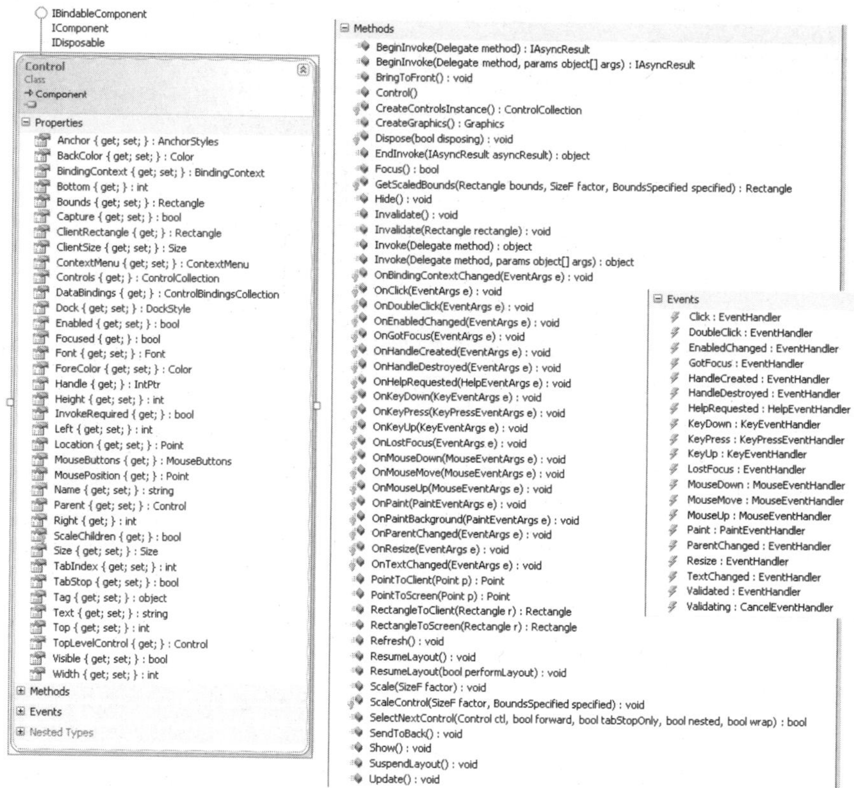

Figure 2-7 Base *Control* class properties, methods, and events (created with the new Class Designer in Visual Studio 2005)

It could take multiple pages to discuss each control in detail, but the goal is not to duplicate the free online MSDN documentation. Instead, the following sections highlight some key controls, in particular how they work on the device platform, and address some frequently asked questions.

Panel

Although the .NET Compact Framework does not include a *GroupBox* control, there is a *Panel* control. Fundamentally, the *Panel* control is a container for other controls (much as the *Form* control is) and can be used, for example, to group together multiple *RadioButton* controls. Its only interesting members are the *AutoScroll* property and the *Resize* event. Both of these are relevant for when the screen changes orientation (covered in the section titled "Orientation [and Size]" later in this chapter). For now, suffice it to say that when you set *AutoScroll* to *true*, a scroll bar will appear when any controls contained by the panel do not fit in its visible boundary. Also, every time the size of the panel changes, the *Resize* event can be handled to lay out the child controls again according to the new size.

So, that is one use of a panel: to group certain controls together to treat them all as one unified item. (If you want the user to treat these controls as one set, you can change the *BackColor* property of the panel as a visual aid.) For example, disabling the panel disables its children. Another use of the *Panel* control is for hiding and showing a group of controls. Simply place the controls in the panel, and then toggle the *Boolean Visible* property of the panel. You can use this technique to avoid creating multiple forms. Instead of switching between forms, you can switch between panels on the same form by toggling the visibility of the panels. Although this may reduce the overhead of multiple forms, it does increase the complexity of the form that hosts the multiple panels, so you must consider carefully whether to use this technique. In particular, if you cite performance as one reason to employ this technique, ensure that you have measured both approaches because the results sometimes can be surprising.

Another scenario in which to use a *Panel* control is for a login screen. Some applications require users to log in before they can interact with the remainder of the application. A mistake many developers make is to design the main form as the login form and then to show the rest of the UI in other forms. This is a mistake because the login form has no use for most of the lifetime of the application, but you have to keep it around because closing the main form closes the application. An alternative approach is to open a main form and then immediately open yet another modal form for the user to log in; this may be sufficient in many scenarios. Instead, the main form can start by using a panel (which contains login controls) that is visible, and after the user authenticates, you can simply hide the panel (optionally removing or disposing of the controls) and allow the user to interact with the main form. The following code assumes you have added over your main form design a *Panel* control containing login controls:

```
// Your login method
private void Login(...)
{
  if (LoginSuccess()) // your login success criteria
  {
    // Hide the login panel with all the login controls.
    panel1.Visible = false;
```

```
        // You will not use those controls again in this instance of the app.
        this.Controls.Remove(panel1);
        panel1.Dispose();

        // Required because the last control with focus will be on the panel.
        this.Focus();
    }
}
```

TabControl

One of the popular controls for Pocket PC development is the *TabControl*. You can use this control to load the form with many controls while allowing the user to switch quickly between different tabs. Notice how on the device the tabs appear at the bottom of the display, which is contrary to desktop applications in which tabs appear on the top (the sample code of this chapter shows this). This is a common design paradigm for touch screen devices. Try, when possible, to restrict the area users must tap to the bottom of the screen so that when they tap, their hand does not obscure the screen and hence the design of the *TabControl*.

A *TabControl* is generally used to occupy the entire form; however, you can resize it and change its location by using its *Dock* and *Location* properties, respectively. Another property that you are sure to use is the *TabPages* property, which represents a collection of *TabPage* objects that are the containers for controls you can place in each one. The most useful event is the *SelectedIndexChanged* event that notifies you when the user changes tabs.

Many developers want to know how to remove *TabPage* objects and prevent navigation from one *TabPage* to the next. The only way to hide a *TabPage* is actually to remove it from the *TabPages* collection (and then add it later when you need it again). Also, unfortunately, there is no easy way to prevent navigation from one *TabPage* to another; for example, if a user clicks the second *TabPage* but for some reason (that is, validation) you want to keep the user on the first *TabPage*, you must write code specifically to handle this. An example follows:

```
private int lastIndex = 0;
private void tabControl1_SelectedIndexChanged(object s, EventArgs e)
{
  int newIndex = tabControl1.SelectedIndex;
  if (newIndex == lastIndex)
  {
    // Validation failed.
    tabControl1.TabPages[lastIndex].BackColor = Color.Red;

    // Prevent infinite loop.
    return;
  }

  if (checkBox1.Checked) // Replace with your own validation logic.
```

```
    {
      tabControl1.SelectedIndex = lastIndex; // Raises this event again.
      return;
    }

    // Update your knowledge.
    tabControl1.TabPages[lastIndex].BackColor = Color.White;
    lastIndex = newIndex;
}
```

Menu (Soft Keys), *ToolBar*

Menus on Windows Mobile–powered devices appear near the bottom of the screen (for the same design reasons discussed earlier for the *TabControl*). In a Pocket PC project, if you add a *MainMenu* control and a *ToolBar* control and populate each with its items (menu items and toolbar buttons, respectively), they appear next to each other. In other words, only one bar on the Pocket PC shows the results of merging a menu bar and a toolbar, as shown in Figure 2-8.

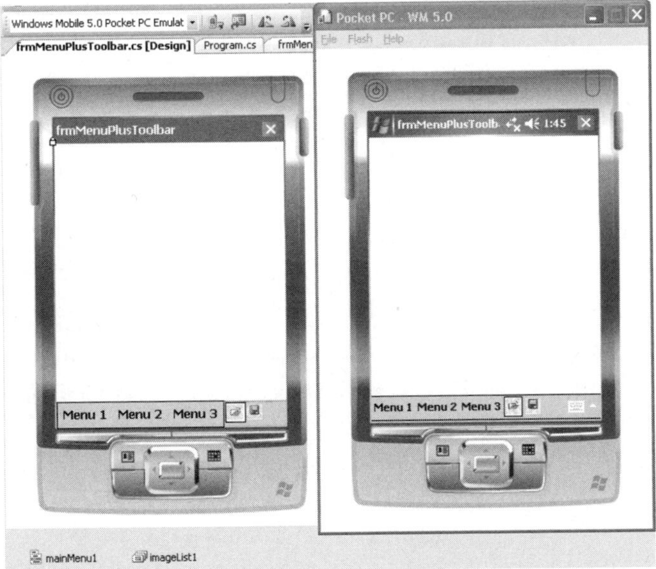

Figure 2-8 *MainMenu* and *ToolBar* controls, at design time (left) and at run time (right)

On devices that use Windows Mobile 5.0 and later, a unification on the menu concept occurred between the Pocket PC and the Smartphone platforms. As a result, the guidelines suggest that there should be no toolbar and that applications should have only two top-level menus known as soft keys. (See Figure 2-9.)

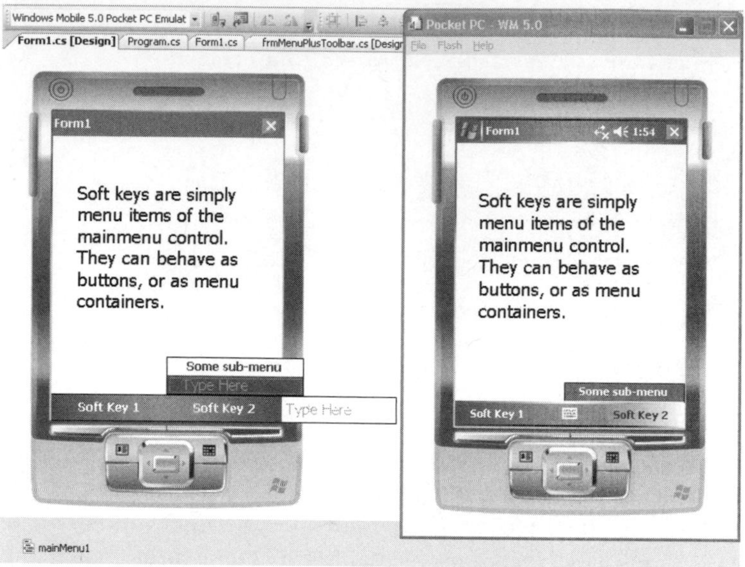

Figure 2-9 Soft keys at design time (left) and at run time (right)

Soft keys are clickable on touch screens but are usually paired with two hardware buttons that users can use to click the soft keys. As always, from a code perspective soft keys are simply menu items, and their *Click* event is handled in the usual way.

Soft keys are a powerful concept, and you should strive to make as much use of them as possible. Try to move all actions and commands to the soft keys, and try to contextualize the soft keys by changing their *Text* (and behavior) based on what is selected on the screen. The official guidelines go further by stating that the left button should represent the primary function and the right button should hold all other menu options.

Tip There is no *MenuItem.Visible* property, so the workaround is to remove the *MenuItem* instead (and readd or reinsert it as appropriate).

Microsoft.WindowsCE.Forms

Although we like to think of the .NET Compact Framework as a subset of the full desktop framework, in reality it is not a true subset because it includes some additional assemblies. Specifically, the *Microsoft.WindowsCE.Forms* assembly contains certain classes useful only in the context of device development (mostly Pocket PC only).

DocumentList (Pocket PC Only)

The *DocumentList* control is a full-screen control that provides the same interface as the built-in file explorer for working with folders and files in the My Documents folder. Simply create an empty form, double-click the control in the Toolbox to add it to the form, and then run the project to see what it looks like and how the user can work with it (see Figure 2-10).

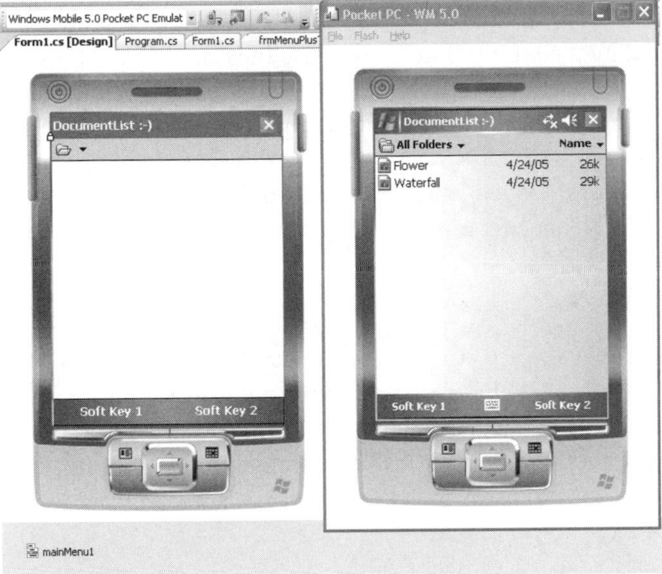

Figure 2-10 *DocumentList* control

The *DocumentList* control has three interesting properties, *Filter*, *FilterIndex*, and *SelectedDirectory*, and three events, *DocumentActivated*, *DeletingDocument*, and *SelectedDirectoryChanged*. It is extremely easy to use: simply place the control on your form, where it fully docks to take up the entire form. Then set its properties through the Properties window. An online example demonstrates the control in action on the MSDN Web site at *msdn2.microsoft.com/en-us/library/ms172535.aspx*.

Notification (Pocket PC Only)

The *Notification* component is used to show notifications to the user in the standard Pocket PC fashion (a "balloon popup" at the top or "toast popup" from the bottom). Simply drop it on a form, set its *Text* property and optionally its other properties (*Title*, *Icon*, *InitialDuration*, and *Critical*) while hooking into its two events (*BalloonChanged* and *ResponseSubmitted*). The component becomes more useful if you set *html* in its *Text* property to present a richer UI. Remember to dispose of the control when you are done with it and want to remove its icon from the title bar. You can find an online example on the MSDN Web site at *msdn2.microsoft.com/en-us/library/ms172539.aspx*.

Other Classes

Microsoft.WindowsCE.Forms contains other classes worth exploring because, after all, it is a device-specific assembly. We discuss *InputPanel*, *HardwareButton*, and *SystemSettings* in the following sections. With *LogFont*, you can draw text at an angle, and in addition to the excellent online sample on the MSDN Web site (*msdn2.microsoft.com/en-gb/library/microsoft.windowsce.forms.logfont.aspx*), we discuss this control further in Chapter 12, "Graphics Programming." *Message* and *MessageWindow* have been included since version 1.0, but their usefulness has diminished in version 2.0 because the *Control.Handle* property was added as was the capability to define native callbacks when doing platform invoke and thus to subclass forms–in the native sense of subclassing, as covered in Chapter 15, "Building Custom Controls." Finally, there is the *MobileDevice* class with a single static event (*Hibernate*) that, when raised, is an indication that you should clear resources; see Chapter 5, "Understanding and Optimizing .NET Compact Framework Performance," for more on this.

Creating Your Own Controls

Although .NET Compact Framework 2.0 contains many rich controls, there will be times when you require a slightly different behavior on a control, a means to reuse a collection or combination of controls in multiple places, or even a control that looks entirely different from the out-of-the-box controls and that exhibits some very domain-specific behavior. In such scenarios, you have four options: extend an existing control, create a *UserControl*, write a custom control, or obtain a third-party control that achieves the goal.

- Extending an existing control is as simple as writing a class that inherits from the control that includes most of the functionality you desire and then extending it by adding your own members. With the .NET Compact Framework, sometimes you cannot override fundamental methods (that is, *OnClick*, *OnPaint*), and hence this technique has limitations. For an example, see Chapter 15 on custom controls and also the article titled "How to Create a Numeric Text Box" on the MSDN Web site at *msdn2.microsoft.com/en-us/library/ms229644.aspx*.
- Grouping a few controls together and treating them as a unified control are achieved by using the *UserControl*. Simply add it to your project, and then add controls on its design surface as you do for a form. A fuller discussion and an example are given in Chapter 15.
- Writing a custom control gives you full flexibility (at the cost of complexity) and is the subject of Chapter 15.
- Obtaining a third-party control is almost always the cheapest option in the long run, but only if the control exactly fits the project's requirements. In this latter case, it is preferable to obtain controls that are extensible and easily customizable and, if possible, that include source code.

Your starting point to extending an existing control, writing a *UserControl*, or writing a custom control is in the Add New Item dialog box, which contains templates for all three options, as shown in Figure 2-11.

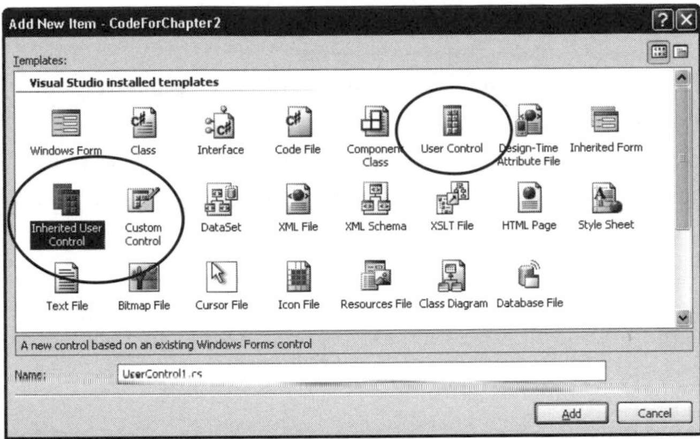

Figure 2-11 Add New Item dialog box

Handling Input

In general, when you think of input methods for a computer, you probably think of a keyboard and a two-button mouse (sure, you can get a mouse with more than two buttons, but fundamentally a mouse can do two unique actions). On a device, input is a bit more complex. Some devices have a touch screen (Pocket PCs), whereas others don't (Smartphones). On devices with a touch screen, the user can use a stylus or a finger to interact with the device (in the latter case, controls should be large enough to accommodate the size of a person's finger). Devices with touch screens also often include a SIP that effectively replicates the keyboard of a desktop computer. Some devices even include a full QWERTY hardware keyboard (and Smartphone devices always include a hardware numeric phone pad). In addition to any hardware keyboard, most devices have a handful of hardware buttons dedicated to specific tasks (for example, opening the calendar) as well hardware buttons for up, down, left, right, Enter navigation (also known as the directional pad, or d-pad for short).

Taps

When the user taps the screen of a touch-sensitive device, from a programmatic perspective it is basically the equivalent of a mouse click. All the control events with which you may be familiar from the full .NET Framework apply: *MouseDown*, *MouseUp*, *MouseMove*, *Click*, and *DoubleClick*. Be sure to check that the control you use actually supports the event you require. To do so, simply create a small project and write the event handler method for the event you are testing. Set a breakpoint in the event handler, and then run the project. Take the user action that should raise the event (for example, tap the control), and check whether your breakpoint is hit to determine whether the control actually supports the event. We can't stress enough that some members of the .NET Compact Framework are missing and hence not all events are exposed by all controls. The documentation indicates which members are supported by the .NET Compact Framework, and although it is much better now than it was in version 1.0, it still isn't perfect, which is why we suggest testing for the event before relying on it in your design.

Because there is no mouse, at first you may assume that there is no right-click functionality. However, right-clicking is achieved by pressing and holding down the stylus on the screen (known as tap-and-hold). For this reason, many controls expose a *ContextMenu* property that you can assign a *ContextMenu* control that will appear when the user taps and holds the control, for example, a *ListView* or a *TreeView*. Because tapping and holding with the stylus is not the most intuitive action for users, we recommend you do not rely on and design your application to use this feature unless you really must.

The absence of a mouse is coupled with the absence of a mouse pointer. On a device, the closest functionality to a mouse pointer is the busy cursor animation that appears at the center of the screen. You can use the following code to display the busy cursor:

```
Cursor.Current = Cursors.WaitCursor;
…
// Some logic…
…
Cursor.Current = Cursors.Default; // Turn it off again.
```

An often asked question is how to simulate a tap on the screen, for example, a tap on a button. In that particular example the best answer is: by calling the event handler method directly *or* inheriting your own control from *Button*, and then adding a *PerformClick* method that simply calls *base.Click()*. However, if you really want to simulate a user's click, you can use the Platform Invocation Services (PInvoke) to call *mouse_event*, as the following example shows for opening the main menu:

```
private void button1_Click(object sender, EventArgs e)
{
  PerformMouseClick(this.Left + 5, this.Height + 5, this);
}

// Wrapper for mouse_event, performing click action on coordinates given
public static void PerformMouseClick(Int32 x, Int32 y, Control f)
{
  Point p = f.PointToScreen(new Point(x, y));

  Int32 m1 = (65535 / Screen.PrimaryScreen.Bounds.Width);
  Int32 m2 = (65535 / Screen.PrimaryScreen.Bounds.Height);

  Int32 x2 = m1 * p.X;
  Int32 y2 = m2 * p.Y;

  mouse_event(2 | 0x8000, x2, y2, 0, 0);
  mouse_event(4 | 0x8000, x2, y2, 0, 0);
}

[System.Runtime.InteropServices.DllImport("coredll.dll")]
public static extern void mouse_event(Int32 dwFlags, Int32 dx, Int32 dy,
                                      Int32 dwData, Int32 dwExtraInfo);
```

The last thing we have to say about tapping is that you should strive to make your applications operable entirely without the use of the touch screen—in fact, you might even aim for one-handed navigation! This makes sense because users are often on the go when they use their devices and hence will need their other hand for some other activity. Operation without a touch screen is also a great goal if you plan to target both Pocket PCs and Smartphones because the main difference between the two is the touch screen. In fact, many of the advancements in Windows Mobile 5.0 and Windows Mobile 6 focus strongly on single-handed navigation of the operating system GUI components and nonreliance on the touch screen.

SIP and Hardware QWERTY Keyboard

Handling presses on the SIP and from a hardware keyboard is the same as handling key presses on a desktop computer keyboard. Simply handle the regular control events: *KeyDown*, *KeyUp*, and *KeyPress*. The same advice applies as mentioned in the previous section: check that the control you use actually supports the event you require.

In some situations, you may prefer to handle the key events in the form and not for each individual control. In that case, you can set the form's *KeyPreview Boolean* property to *true* and handle the form's events that are raised when one of its controls receives the input. It is in the form's *KeyDown* event handler that d-pad events are handled (and in the Smartphone case, the phone pad button presses as well). Relevant to key navigation is tabbing, and the good news is that .NET Compact Framework 2.0 controls support the *TabIndex* and *TabStop* properties.

You also should know how to deal programmatically with the SIP. In many cases, you can let the user decide whether to use the SIP, and users can show it manually (and then hide it manually). In those cases, you may need to know when the SIP is shown or hidden so that you can change the appearance of the form; for example, if a text box is placed near the bottom of the screen, you might want to move it upward when the SIP is shown (and then move the text box back in its original place when the SIP is hidden). Also, you may want to programmatically show the SIP when the user gives focus to a text box and hide the SIP when the text box loses focus. To achieve these goals, you must use a control from the *Microsoft.WindowsCE.Forms* assembly (introduced earlier), namely, the *InputPanel*. An example follows:

```
// Add a TextBox to the form and add the two event handlers.
// Add an InputPanel control to the form.
private void textBox1_GotFocus(object sender, EventArgs e)
{
    inputPanel1.Enabled = true;
}

private void textBox1_LostFocus(object sender, EventArgs e)
{
    inputPanel1.Enabled = false;
}
```

If you have placed input controls near the bottom of the screen, the SIP will hide them when it appears. If you can, place input controls at the top of the screen. If you must place an input control where it might be obscured by the SIP, you can handle the *InputPanel.EnabledChanged* event to be notified when the SIP is raised, and reposition the input control. An example of handling the event follows (this example assumes a *textBox2* control is placed near the bottom of the form/screen):

```
private void inputPanel1_EnabledChanged(object sender, EventArgs e)
{
  if (inputPanel1.Enabled)
  {
    textBox2.Top -= inputPanel1.Bounds.Height;
  }
  else
  {
    textBox2.Top += inputPanel1.Bounds.Height;
  }
}

private void frmBaseWithSIP_Closing(object sender, CancelEventArgs e)
{
  // Must do this to make sure the inputPanel releases
// its reference to this form
  inputPanel1.EnabledChanged -=
new EventHandler(this.inputPanel1_EnabledChanged);
}
```

In a real-world scenario, you would lay out all the controls again, not just *textBox2*. If there are too many controls to fit the screen, you can use an alternative design technique: Place all controls in a *Panel* control that has the *AutoScroll* property set to *true*; when the *InputPanel.EnabledChanged* event is raised, resize the *Panel.Height*.

With .NET Compact Framework 2.0, you can further choose the input method you desire (keyboard, transcriber, and so forth.) by using the *CurrentInputMethod* and *InputMethods* properties of the *InputPanel* (for more information, see "How to Set Pocket PC Input Methods" on the MSDN Web site at *msdn2.microsoft.com/en-us/library/ms172538.aspx*).

Hardware Keys

Pocket PCs can have up to six standard hardware buttons (think of them as ApplicationButton1 through ApplicationButton6). With the new *HardwareButton* component, you can capture events when these buttons are pressed (in the *KeyDown*, *KeyUp* events of the form, after you set *Form.KeyPreview* to *true*). Simply create the components, associate them with a *Form* or *UserControl* (no other control types can be used) by using the *AssociatedControl* property, and then indicate to which button the settings apply (in the *HardwareKey* property). You must supply a separate *HardwareButton* control for every hardware button that you want to handle. Be sure to handle the exception that may be thrown if the device does not include a particular button for which you have written code to capture events! An example is online at *msdn2.microsoft.com/en-us/library/microsoft.windowsce.forms.hardwarebutton.aspx.*

Considering the Physical Screen

An advantage of the Windows Mobile platform is that it supplies multiple device form factors all capable of running the same platform while catering to the needs of a variety of users. With this advantage comes a burden, however: The developer must write code that adjusts to all those requirements. One particular area of concern is screen size, orientation, and resolution.

Orientation (and Size)

Orientation on some devices is fixed, whereas on others it can change on the fly (and your application must react sensibly to that). Some devices use portrait orientation whereas others use landscape, and most current devices can toggle between the two. Further challenges arise with square screens that are available on some models. *Screen size* does not refer to the physical dimensions of the screen, although those do vary considerably, but rather to the resolution of the display measured in pixels, for example, 320 × 240, 240 × 320, and 240 × 240 (higher resolution is discussed later). Note that many Smartphones have a resolution of 176 × 220 and Windows Mobile 6 introduces the resolution 320 × 320. As a developer, you have tools to deal with some of these screen issues.

To detect the orientation of the device when your application starts (or indeed to change the orientation programmatically), you can use the static property *ScreenOrientation* of the *SystemSettings* class in the *Microsoft.WindowsCE.Forms* assembly, as the following example shows:

```
// Read the orientation.
label1.Text = "Orientation is " + SystemSettings.ScreenOrientation.ToString();
//  Set the orientation.
SystemSettings.ScreenOrientation = ScreenOrientation.Angle90;
```

To query the exact resolution of the device, you can use the *Screen* class (from the *System.Windows.Forms* namespace), as the following example demonstrates:

```
label2.Text = "Screen size is " + Screen.PrimaryScreen.Bounds.Width +
                    " x " + Screen.PrimaryScreen.Bounds.Height;
```

Finally, to be notified at run time when the orientation changes, you can handle the *Resize* event of the *Form* (or from other containers, for example, the panel as mentioned earlier in this chapter).

With the preceding three techniques, you can gather all the information you need. The next step, of course, is to actually do something with this information. One obvious but less than ideal choice is to design for square. If your entire UI can fit in a square, on both landscape-oriented and portrait-oriented devices you simply do not use the extra space on the right and the bottom, respectively. Figure 2-12 shows an example of a square design.

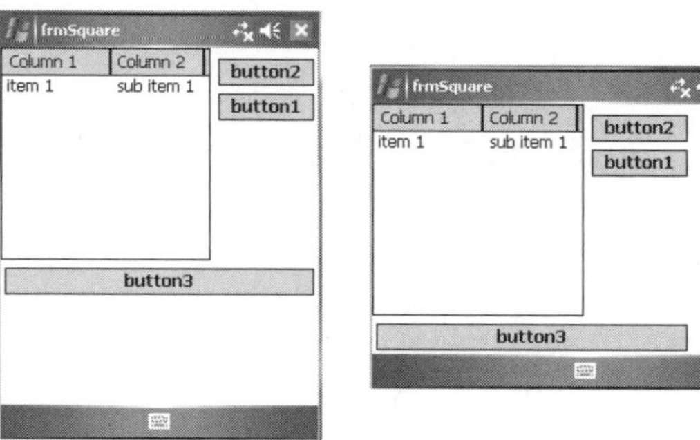

Figure 2-12 Design for square

Although this solution is not always possible, it is always worth considering because it can work for some of the less complex screens of an application. Another solution is to use scroll bars. In other words, design the application for one orientation (for example, portrait) and set to *true* the *AutoScroll* property of the form (or of a panel, as mentioned earlier). When the user runs the application on a different orientation (for example, landscape or square), a scroll bar appears so that the user can scroll to the portions that do not fit on the screen.

Again, the solution of using scroll bars is not the best but may be acceptable for some of your screens. The best solution is actually to design your screens for each orientation, portrait, landscape, and square, and lay out the UI at run time every time as appropriate. With version 2.0 of the .NET Compact Framework, you can do this more easily because controls have docking and anchoring properties. Docking[1] and anchoring[2] behave exactly as they always have for the full .NET Framework and are not discussed further here (see Chapter 1 for a brief overview). Figure 2-13 shows docking and anchoring effects.

1 Control aligns itself with the docked edges of its parent control.

2 Control's anchored edges remain in the same position relative to the edges of the parent control.

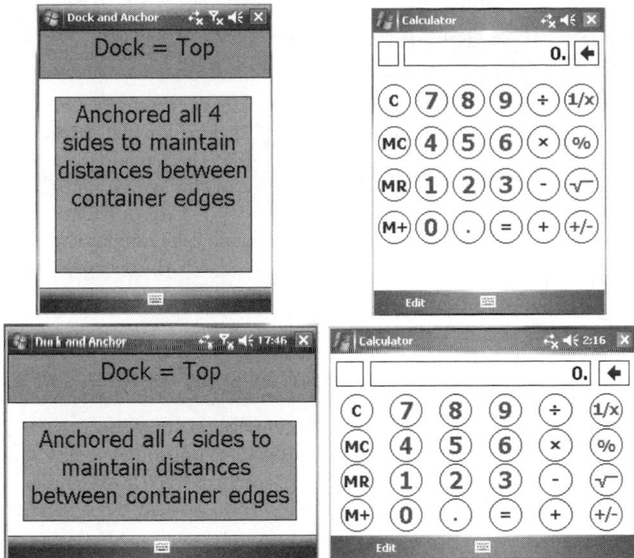

Figure 2-13 Docking and anchoring effects

If you use docking and anchoring (or if you have done nothing yet for orientation support), you can test what your application will look like under different orientations in Visual Studio without ever running the application. Simply right-click the form, and select Rotate Right and Rotate Left. If you do have run-time logic, of course you must run your application to test that (and the emulator supports that through the Calendar hardware button, which is mapped to rotate the screen).

Resolution

What if you must support resolutions of 480 × 640 (for Smartphone, 352 × 440), 640 × 480, and 480 × 480? Notice how these resolutions are simply the resolutions described earlier multiplied by two? This means that all the strategies described earlier for handling orientation changes apply exactly to these higher resolutions.

When you first encounter the latter three screen resolutions, you may think, "More space equals more controls." Actually, that is not true and implementing such a scheme is strongly recommended against. Higher resolution simply means better-looking UIs. It means more precision, higher-resolution icons, and an overall better user experience. It does not mean you should place more controls on the screen; this becomes obvious after you realize that these higher resolutions are not actually running on screens that are twice the physical size but simply have more dots per inch (dpi). What you must do is scale your UIs to the higher resolutions so that the look and feel are identical.

If you set the form's *AutoScaleMode* to *AutoScaleMode.Dpi* (located in the Properties dialog box when the form is selected in the forms designer), the .NET Compact Framework controls scale automatically. This is the default behavior for new version 2.0 projects, but you may need to configure this setting manually for upgraded projects. You can test what an application will look like under different resolutions in the designer without running the application. Go to the form's Properties dialog box and select a different value in the *FormFactor* combo box (for example, Pocket PC Square VGA). It is interesting to understand what the property does in code to achieve the results. To see what it does, simply look at the *FormName.Designer* file (as discussed in the sidebar titled "Partial Classes" earlier in this chapter) and find the one line of code responsible for the behavior:

```
this.AutoScaleDimensions = new System.Drawing.SizeF(192F, 192F);
this.AutoScaleMode = System.Windows.Forms.AutoScaleMode.Dpi;
```

Effectively, the dpi is changing from 96 to 192, which is what the higher resolutions use (recall that the higher resolutions are twice the dpi of the earlier resolutions). Note that after you assign the *AutoScaleDimensions* property, it is the call to the form's *ResumeLayout* method that actually does the scaling. If the *AutoScaleDimensions* property indicates the dpi under which you designed the form, how can you query to find the dpi of the device on which your application is running? This is discussed next.

In some situations, automatic scaling as described in the preceding paragraph is not enough. Such scenarios include custom drawing (for example, in custom controls in the *OnPaint* method), adding controls at run time, and images loaded in your UI (for example, in a *PictureBox*). First, you must determine the dpi of the device and store that information with global access:

```
static class Program
{
  /// <summary>
  /// The main entry point for the application
  /// </summary>
  [MTAThread]
  static void Main()
  {
    frmScaling f = new frmScaling();

    const float designResolution = 96.0f; //typical
    System.Drawing.Graphics g = f.CreateGraphics();
    float runningResolution = g.DpiX; //g.DpiY will return the same value
    ScaleFactor = runningResolution / designResolution;
    g.Dispose();

    Application.Run(f);
  }

  // Multiply all custom drawing with Program.ScaleFactor.
  // Most of the time this will have one of three values.
```

```
    // 1     , when we designed for exactly what we run on
    // 2     , when we designed for 96 dpi but we are running on 192
     // 1.365, when we designed for 96 dpi but we are running on
  //          131 (QVGA Smartphone)
    internal static float ScaleFactor;
  }
```

Then you must scale the size and position of any custom drawing, as the following code shows (see Figure 2-14 for an illustration of the effects).

```
// Run this project on both VGA and non-VGA devices.
private void frmScaling_Paint(object sender, PaintEventArgs e)
{
  int left = 5, right = 5, width = 200, height = 200;

  Rectangle r = new Rectangle((int)(left * Program.ScaleFactor),
                              (int)(right * Program.ScaleFactor),
                              (int)(width * Program.ScaleFactor),
                              (int)(height * Program.ScaleFactor));

  float thickness = 2;
  Pen p = new Pen(Color.Red, thickness * Program.ScaleFactor);

  e.Graphics.DrawEllipse(p, r);

  Brush b = new SolidBrush(Color.Blue);
  float x = 75, y = 100;
  e.Graphics.DrawString("scales well", this.Font, b,
                                      x * Program.ScaleFactor,
                                      y * Program.ScaleFactor);

  p.Dispose();
    b.Dispose();
}
```

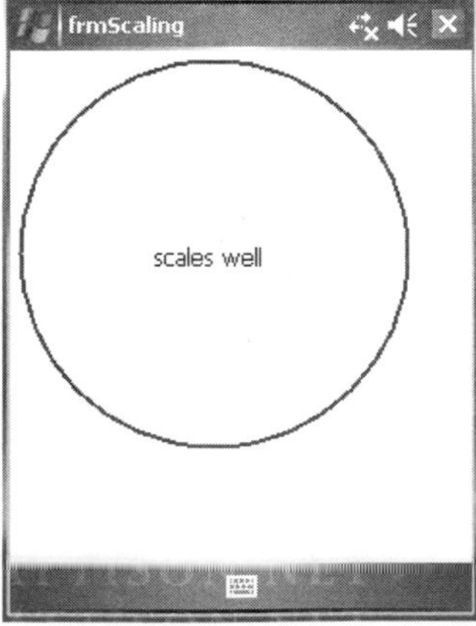

Figure 2-14 Custom scaling; result of code sample given in the text

By following this advice, you never have to call the *Control.Scale* method; we only mention it here so that you are aware that manual on-demand scaling is possible. This may become relevant when you build custom controls for which scaling may not be straightforward (in which case you may need to override *ScaleControl*, which is the method that *Control.Scale* calls).

Don't forget that for every image in your project, you must create another image at twice the size for the higher-resolution devices. Don't forget to do this also for the icons included with the application (that is, in addition to 16 × 16/32 × 32 also include 64 × 64).

Microsoft patterns & practices Orientation-Aware Control

One of the useful components in the Microsoft patterns & practices Mobile Client Software Factory is a control that you can use to design your form layouts at different screen orientations and screen resolutions and that applies the appropriate layout automatically at run time. Windows Mobile 5.0 and later versions support this control. See the section titled "Using Community Resources" in Chapter 1 for more information about the Mobile Client Software Factory, including how to download it.

After installing the Mobile Client Software Factory, you can easily use the *OrientationAware* control in your projects, as described here.

Using the Orientation-Aware Control

1. In your project, add a reference to *Microsoft.Practices.Mobile.UI.OrientationAware*. You must also add a reference to *Microsoft.WindowsMobile.Status* (and its dependency, *Microsoft.WindowsMobile*) because the *OrientationAware* control hooks events exposed by classes in that namespace to detect changes in the screen orientation of the device at run time.
2. Add a new *UserControl* to your project. After it is added, close the design view of the new control, open the control again in code view (right-click the control in Solution Explorer and click View Code), and then modify it so that the control inherits from the *ResolutionAwareControl* as follows:

```
...
namespace MyApplication
{
    public partial class MyUserControl :
        Microsoft.Practices.Mobile.UI.OrientationAwareControl
    {
```

3. Now build the project. After it has built successfully, open the user control in design view again. If you look beneath the Properties dialog box, you will see additional actions that are specific to the *OrientationAware* control, including Rotate and Switch To Default Layout.

4. The control shows the default layout initially. Resize the control to the required size; for example, to match a standard Pocket PC screen in QVGA resolution, set it to 240 pixels wide by 320 high. Then lay out the UI by dragging controls from the Toolbox in the usual way.

5. Click the Rotate command shown below the Properties dialog box. The designer repaints the control in landscape orientation, 320 × 240, but the controls that you positioned on it in portrait orientation are almost certainly not in the best position in landscape. Reposition the controls as you want them in the new orientation. This process is illustrated in Figure 2-15.

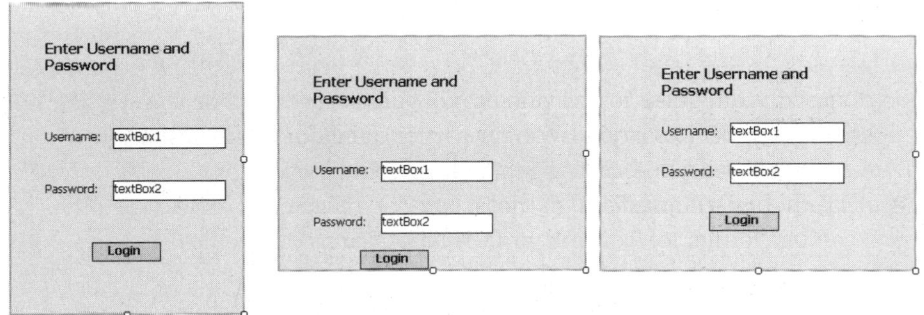

Figure 2-15 With the *OrientationAware* control, designing the default layout (left), rotating the control to an alternative orientation (center), and then modifying the layout to suit the new orientation (right)

6. The control stores the positions of controls you have placed inside it in resource files. You can create layouts for different screen dimensions and for different resolutions. When you use this user control on a form in your application, the control detects the current screen orientation and resolution, looks for stored layout settings that you created for that orientation and resolution, and applies them. If there are no settings that match, it uses the default settings.

The *OrientationAware* control makes it easy to design a UI that adapts to different run-time conditions, and it gives you more control over layout than if you use docking and anchoring alone.

Alternative Design

Making complex GUI applications orientation and resolution aware while maintaining a nice look and feel on various screen sizes is certainly possible but at the cost of code complexity and sometimes with undesirable tradeoffs. For this reason, some enterprises choose a specific device model to deploy to their workforce, and consequently the enterprise's developers must write code only for a certain device. Not only does deployment of standard devices to users result in code that is easier to maintain, but it also significantly reduces the test matrix.

Another alternative is to design different forms for different device form factors. This shifts the run-time decisions to design time at the expense of maintaining different codebases. This option becomes even more attractive when you have to support both Smartphones and Pocket PCs. Because not all controls are available for both platforms (this is discussed further in the next section), if you want to support both form factors with a single codebase that makes the decisions at run time, you must use only a subset of all the features available and also limit the user's experience to the lowest common denominator. Remember, the best GUIs are target-specific.

Maintaining different codebases and making UI layout and positioning decisions at design time are fairly straightforward activities almost identical to the technique you can use to share code between the device platform and the desktop. First, you must ensure that the application's business logic is not mingled with the UI code. In other words, the main functionality of the application should be contained in classes (or in classes that reside in a separate dynamic-link library) and not directly in the event handler methods on the form. When you look at the form code, you should see only logic that manipulates the UI (for example, through control properties) and that ultimately calls a method or two on external classes that carry out the real work.

More Info For more information about layering an application, look at the multiple resources on the Web and in books about the Model View Controller (MVC) and Model View Presenter (MVP) patterns.

The next step is to create separate Windows Forms projects for each target (for example, one for Smartphone and one for Pocket PC) and design target-specific forms. If the classes that contain the business logic are in a separate class library, you can simply reference the dynamic-link library (or libraries) and make the calls to the same classes from both UI projects, thus sharing the business logic. The alternative is to include the same code files in both UI projects, ensuring that a copy is not made and that indeed changing one class file updates both projects. You can do this from the second project you create by linking the code file to the project (on the Project menu, select Add Existing Item, browse to the existing file, and then select Add As Link).

Finally, if you do want to alter the business logic as well, you can use conditional compilation because the projects have been separated; for example:

```
    private void SomeMethod()
    {
#if PocketPC
        // Do something Pocket PC-specific.
#elif Smartphone
        // Do something Smartphone-specific.
#else
        // Do something desktop-specific.
#endif
    }
```

Remember the partial classes feature mentioned earlier in this chapter? As an alternative to conditional compilation, you can use partial classes. You can move methods that do not apply for a given platform to a separate file that is still a part of the class for the platform to which they do apply but is not included in the project that targets the platform for which they do not apply. By doing so, you reduce the amount of unusable code that is compiled in the binary while making maintenance of the code easier.

As a parting thought, remember not to hard-code various approaches based on today's technology. A better practice is to write generic code that will work on future new devices. For example, when the first landscape-oriented Smartphone device was launched, it caused issues because in the past all Smartphones used portrait orientation. Many applications were not usable on this new Smartphone because developers had made hard-coded assumptions in their code. Another example is Windows Mobile 6, which introduces the new 320 × 320 resolution at 129 dpi; will your application look correct on such a device?

Developing for Smartphones

Please do not view this section as the only one addressing the Smartphone. In all the previous sections of this chapter, although the advice applies to Smartphone development the focus has been on Windows Mobile Pocket PC development, highlighting where methods do not apply to Smartphone and noting relevant differences.

Developing UI applications for Smartphones requires you to understand the Smartphone platform. Reading the guidelines mentioned at the beginning of this chapter is essential, as is understanding the one-handed paradigm mentioned earlier as a good goal for Windows Mobile–powered devices.

Control Behaviors

Table 2-1 provides quick descriptions of the behavior of some of the controls available for Smartphones.

Table 2-1 Smartphone Control Commentary

Control	Function
Label, Panel, PictureBox, ProgressBar, Timer, ImageList, VScrollBar, HScrollBar, WebBrowser	No user interaction, just provide information.
CheckBox *ComboBox* *TextBox*	Should be the only interactive control on a single line/row on the screen. Use the Up and Down buttons to move to the previous and next control on the form.

Table 2-1 Smartphone Control Commentary

Control	Function
ComboBox	Use the Left or Right button to navigate through the items in the combo box list. Pressing Enter displays a full-screen list of the items from which the user can select by scrolling using the Up and Down buttons. Use the Up and Down buttons to move to the previous and next controls on the form.
TextBox	Left/Right button moves the caret in the text box. The Back button erases a character. If the text box is *Multiline=true*, pressing Enter displays a full-screen text box (with scroll bars if needed). Use the Up and Down buttons to move to the previous and next controls on the form.
CheckBox	Left/Right/Enter toggles the state. Use the Up and Down buttons to move to the previous and next controls on the form.
ListView, TreeView, DataGrid	Must be the only (interactive) control on the form because there is no automatic way for these controls to pass focus to another control.
TreeView	Up/Down moves through the visible tree node items. Left/Right scrolls horizontally if there is a scroll bar visible. Enter expands/collapses a tree node.
ListView	Up/Down moves through the *ListView* items. Left/Right scrolls horizontally if there is a scroll bar visible. Enter generates the *ItemActivate* event.
DateTimePicker	Left/Right moves between the different fields of the control (that is, day, month, year). You can edit the values by using the numeric keypad. If no other focusable control is on the form, the Up/Down buttons also change the selected field in the control; otherwise, they pass the focus.

Note from the list of controls the absence of a *Button* or any other control that requires direct tapping. You cannot tap on the screen, and hence such controls are absent. This makes it even more important for you to make good use of the two soft keys that map to the menu control, as mentioned earlier in this chapter.

Navigation Paradigm

Study Table 2-1, and use some of the built-in applications on the Smartphone; for example, populate and navigate the contacts list, and do the same for the appointments and tasks. A three-view navigation paradigm will become apparent: Items are listed in a vertical list (literally or virtually); selecting an item shows a new screen with more details about the item; and choosing to edit the item shows yet another screen with edit capabilities. You will find this list-based UI pattern useful for many Smartphone applications.

InputModeEditor

Microsoft.WindowsCE.Forms.InputModeEditor is a class with a single static method (*SetInputMethod*) that accepts two arguments: a control object (which can only be an instance of a *TextBox*) and an enumeration (*InputMode*) that specifies how the phone pad keys should behave (*Text*, *T9*, and *Numeric*). The behavior of this class is self-descriptive, but you can see an example online on the MSDN Web site at *msdn2.microsoft.com/en-us/library/ms172542.aspx*.

IntelliSense for Smartphone Projects

Some developers may paste Pocket PC (or even desktop) code into a Smartphone project and rely on no build errors to verify that the code works. If you do so, it is paramount that you also check the Warnings in the Error List window because for some types or members a line of code may compile but will at best have no effect at run time (for example, assigning the *Form.MinimizeBox* property) and at worst will throw a *NotSupportedException* at run time (for example, creating an *InputPanel* class in code). You can catch both cases by checking the Warnings list because they will appear there.

However, the preceding situation does not occur if you let Microsoft IntelliSense help you when you type in code. Only applicable types and members show up in the IntelliSense window.

Developing for Windows CE–Powered Devices

If you are developing for a custom Windows CE–powered device (that is, a device that runs Windows CE and not Windows Mobile), you may have felt left out reading this chapter because we have focused on the Windows Mobile story. The truth is that although the .NET Compact Framework behaviors are largely identical on Windows CE–based and Pocket PC devices, there are some differences, and most of them are at the UI level. What is also true is that no two custom Windows CE–powered devices are identical because, by definition, they are custom hardware that have different capabilities running on a customized version of Windows CE. This section highlights some of the UI differences and, along with the previous sections, gives the Windows CE developer enough information to start developing UI applications using .NET Compact Framework 2.0.

The shell on custom Windows CE–powered devices (whether aygshell or the standard shell) appears different from the Windows Mobile shell. Menus, toolbars, tab controls, combo boxes, and all the other controls appear the same on Windows CE–powered devices as they do on the desktop. (There are slight differences between Windows Mobile and Windows CE, as noted earlier.) You can choose to make windows any size (but they still are not resizable by the user at run time), and the user is not restricted to a form per screen. Windows have both Minimize and Maximize buttons that behave like their desktop counterparts, and the Close button will close the form (that is, no smart minimize behavior is included, and there is no OK button option for Windows Forms). The SIP on Windows CE–powered devices is not restricted to the bottom of the screen but is a window that can be moved around. Just as on the desktop, the taskbar contains the Start menu and any minimized windows. It is important to note that a custom Windows CE–powered device may have any screen size and any resolution that the original equipment manufacturer (OEM) chose. It may even have a mouse and a real mouse pointer on the screen.

By now, you might conclude that there is little point in starting development unless you have the actual device on which to debug (or at least a high-fidelity emulator provided by the OEM). We think it is actually easier to target a custom Windows CE–powered device compared to a Windows Mobile–powered device because you can simply work with a very particular locked-down platform. From a UI development perspective, this is actually closer to developing for desktop computers than it is to developing for the Windows Mobile platform.

Summary

The collection of tips and tricks in this chapter can be distilled into the following pieces of high-level advice:

- Understand the platform you are targeting from an end user perspective.
- Understand how the .NET Compact Framework controls behave on the chosen platform.
- Understand how the .NET Compact Framework controls differ from desktop controls.
- When designing your solution, always test any assumptions by building a prototype and running it on the target device.

Chapter 3

Using SQL Server 2005 Compact Edition and Other Data Stores

In this chapter:

Most business applications require data to be stored, organized, and viewed. A simple application can simply persist data in a file, whereas more complex applications can benefit by using a database because of its capability of organizing data in tables, providing fast searching using indexes, and representing master–child relationships between data in different tables through foreign keys. As well as storing the data, the application usually must display data to users so that they can read and update it.

This chapter looks at the different ways you can organize and persist data. First, it explains how to create Microsoft SQL Server 2005 Compact Edition databases to use in your application, and then it looks at how you can use the visual designer tools in Microsoft Visual Studio 2005 to define project data sources and bind them to controls in your graphical user interface (GUI). You will learn how to program the *SqlCeResultSet* object, which allows fast, updatable access to data in a SQL Server 2005 Compact Edition database and is a high-performance alternative to the typical ADO.NET *TableAdapter–DataTable* pattern. Finally, for those situations in which a database is too complex a solution, you will learn how to use lighter-weight data stores such as simple class objects that you can persist using Extensible Markup Language (XML) serialization.

This chapter restricts itself to describing solutions where data is stored on the device. If you want to know how to synchronize data with back-end servers, or fetch and store data in a SQL Server 2005 database on a network, see Chapter 7, "Exchanging Data with Back-end Servers."

Using SQL Server 2005 Compact Edition Databases

SQL Server 2005 Compact Edition (which we refer to from here on as SQL Server CE) is a lightweight relational database that supports data types that are compatible with full SQL Server 2005. It runs in-process in your application, meaning that it does not require a separate server process to operate. You can use it in Microsoft .NET Compact Framework applications running on Microsoft Windows CE or Windows Mobile, and also in .NET Framework applications running on Windows 2000, Windows XP, or Windows Vista. SQL Server CE also comes with application programming interfaces (APIs) that you can use in native applications.

Important When Visual Studio 2005 and .NET Compact Framework version 2.0 were first released, the database for devices was called SQL Server 2005 Mobile Edition. At that time, it was supported only on mobile devices and Tablet PCs. SQL Server 2005 Compact Edition is the same product, although it is now supported on all Windows desktop platforms as well as on devices. It has been renamed to emphasize the fact that it can be used on more than just mobile devices. To see the new name used for the product in the Visual Studio 2005 user interface, you must install Visual Studio 2005 Service Pack 1 (SP1) or later and install the new version of the run-time components. To see the new name in SQL Server Management Studio, you must install SQL Server 2005 SP2 or later. You can download service packs for Visual Studio and SQL Server from the Microsoft MSDN Download Center Web site at *www.msdn.microsoft.com/downloads*.

The previous version of this product, called SQL Server CE 2.0, was supported for managed applications built using .NET Compact Framework version 1.0. Existing applications built with .NET Compact Framework 1.0 and SQL Server CE 2.0 will run on devices that have the .NET Compact Framework 2.0 runtime installed, but you cannot create new .NET Compact Framework 2.0 applications using SQL Server CE 2.0; you must use SQL Server 2005 Compact Edition.

Note The other (incorrect) name that is often used in developer forums for SQL Server 2005 Compact Edition is SQL Server CE 3.0.

Creating a Database Using Visual Studio 2005

One way to create a new database is to use the Add New Item dialog box in Visual Studio, which adds a SQL Server Mobile database to your project and sets up a connection to the database in the Server Explorer window. Visual Studio creates the database and then displays the Data Source Configuration Wizard, which you can use to design a *DataSet* or *SqlCeResultSet* graphically to read and update data from tables in the database. At this stage, you have created an empty database that contains no tables, and so you should close the wizard.

Alternatively, and perhaps more easily, you can create a database by using the Add Connection dialog box. Click the Connect To Database icon at the top of the Server Explorer window, or click Connect To Database on the Tools menu. In the Add Connection dialog box, as shown in Figure 3-1, first ensure that the Data Source box at the top displays *.NET Framework Data Provider for SQL Server CE*. If it does not, click Change to open a dialog box where you can select it. Then click Create to open the Create New SQL Server 2005 Compact Edition Database dialog box. Note that creating a database in this way does not actually add it to your project, and so you can use the Add Existing Item dialog box to navigate to the newly created database file and include it in your project.

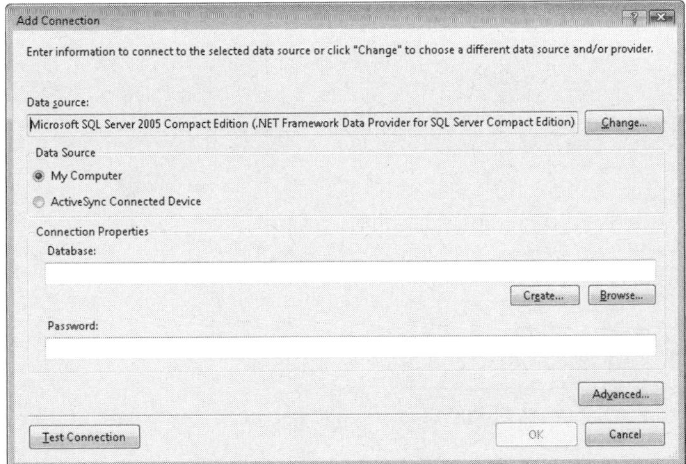

Figure 3-1 Using the Add Connection dialog box to create a new database

Tip After you have added a database to your project, you must ensure that the database will be deployed to your target device. In the Properties dialog box, verify that the Build Action property is set to Content and the Copy To Output Directory property is set to Copy If Newer.

Options for Database Security

In the Create New Database dialog box, you must specify the path to the database and optionally select the required sort order and/or specify a database password. If you set a password, you must include it in the connection string every time you open a database connection, and so this password forms your first line of defense against unauthorized access to the data in your database. In the examples in this chapter, we use the database password MobileP@ssw0rd.

If you specify a password, you can also specify that the data in the database be encrypted. The database password alone protects access to the database for usual methods of connection such as by using SQL Server Management Studio, Visual Studio, or through code, but a determined attacker could still dump out the raw data and so gain access to it; encryption provides a deterrent against such an attack.

Creating a Database Using SQL Server 2005 Management Studio

You can also create and modify Compact Edition databases in SQL Server 2005 Management Studio. To create or connect to a SQL Server CE database, open the Connect To Server dialog box, and select SQL Server Compact Edition in the Server Type drop-down list. Then, in the Database File text box, enter the path to an existing database, or select <*New Database...*> from the drop-down list, as shown in Figure 3-2. If you select to create a new database, the same Create New SQL Server 2005 Compact Edition Database dialog box that you see in Visual Studio 2005 opens, which includes identical security options as described previously.

Figure 3-2 Connecting to a SQL Server CE database in SQL Server Management Studio

From a developer's point of view, nearly everything you can do with SQL Server CE databases using SQL Server 2005 Management Studio you can do in the Server Explorer window in Visual Studio 2005, and so for the rest of this chapter, we concentrate mainly on using the tools built into Visual Studio.

Installing the SQL CE runtime on your target devices

To run an application that uses SQL Server CE, first you must install the runtime on the device. During application development, Visual Studio automatically installs the run-time components onto your development device or emulator the first time you debug an application that uses SQL Server CE.

Important All Windows Mobile 6–powered devices come with SQL Server CE already installed, so the following instructions apply only to devices running Windows CE or earlier versions of Windows Mobile.

The SQL Server CE runtime comes in three .cab files. If you need to get the run-time .cab files so that you can install the runtime on a number of devices, you can do so in two different ways:

1. If you have Visual Studio 2005 installed, navigate to *drive*:\Program Files\Microsoft Visual Studio 8\SmartDevices\SDK\SQL Server\Mobile\v3.0.
2. If you have SQL Server 2005 installed, navigate to *drive*:\Program Files\Microsoft SQL Server 2005 Mobile Edition\Device\Mobile\v3.0.

Whichever method you choose, the directory structure is the same:

- You will find the .cab files for devices that run Windows Mobile 2003 and Windows CE 4.0 in the \wce400\armv4 folder. (Only Pocket PC targets with Advanced RISC Machines [ARM] microprocessors are supported on Windows Mobile 2003.)
- The .cab files for devices that run Windows CE 5.0 and Windows Mobile 5.0 are in the \wce500*processor* folder, where *processor* is one of the supported microprocessors, such as armv4i, mipsii, or x86.

You need three .cab files:

- The main runtime, called sqlce30.*platform*.wce5.*processor*.cab, where *platform* is *phone* for smartphone, *ppc* for Pocket PC, and blank for Windows CE.
- Replication support, called sqlce30.repl.*platform*.wce5.*processor*.cab. This cab contains support for using Remote Data Access (RDA) or replication. (See Chapter 7 for more on these technologies.)
- Development support, including the Query Analyzer tool, which is in sqlce30.dev.ENU.*platform*.wce5.*processor*.cab.

You can install the .cab files on devices by copying the files and opening them in File Explorer.

Connecting to an Existing Database

As you have seen, you can use the Connect To Database dialog boxes in both Visual Studio 2005 and SQL Server Management Studio to connect to an existing database. That database can be in the file system on your computer or on a network share on your local area network (LAN). However, the database can also be on a mobile device that you currently have connected to your development computer using Microsoft ActiveSync technology. If you look back at Figure 3-1, you can see that the dialog box offers a choice between a location on My Computer or on an ActiveSync Connected Device. SQL Server Management Studio offers a similar ability to connect to a device if you select the *<Browse for more...>* option in the Database File text box in the Connect To Server dialog box.

This ability to connect to a database on a device is a welcome new feature in SQL Server 2005 Compact Edition. You cannot do this with SQL CE 2.0 databases using the tools shipped with that version of the product, although excellent third-party products exist that you can use to do this (and more!), including SQL CE Console from Primeworks and RemoteSQLCe from GUI Innovations.

Warning Be careful if you connect to a database that is on a device and modify tables and/or data in the database during application development. Remember that you are not modifying the version of the database that is included in your project, which is more likely than not sitting in your project folder along with your code. Unless you manually copy the modified database back to your computer and replace the copy in your project folder, you risk losing your changes if you deploy the project to a different device or deploy the project version over the modified version on your development device.

Creating Tables, Indexes, and Foreign Keys

After you have created a database, you must create some tables in it. It is not a goal of this book to teach database design, so for more information about basic database operations you can consult the Books Online for Microsoft SQL Server 2005 or other information sources. However, to set the scene for later parts of this chapter, we create two tables that happen to use many common features of a typical SQL Server CE database such as foreign key relationships: one called *ProductCategory* that stores details of different categories in the fictional Adventure-Works company product catalog and one called *Product* that contains details of individual products.

Creating a Table

In Visual Studio, open Server Explorer and expand the folders under the connection to your database. Right-click the Tables folder, and click Create Table so that the Create Table dialog box opens.

In the New Table dialog box, shown in Figure 3-3, you can define the columns in a new table, in this case the *ProductCategory* table, which has just two columns, *ProductCategoryID* and *Name*. The first thing to observe in Figure 3-3 is how both columns have been set to disallow *Null* values, which means that if you try to store a value in the database with a null value, the SQL CE runtime will throw an exception–an example of how you can set constraints on the data in your database to ensure that it is not possible to store incorrect or invalid data.

The second thing to observe is that the *ProductCategoryID* column is defined as a *Primary key*, meaning that the database will create an index in this table to assist lookups using the *ProductCategoryID* value. Also, *Unique* is set to *true* on both fields, meaning that a database constraint is applied to ensure that every record in this table has a unique value in both fields. *ProductCategoryID* is also defined as an *Identity* field, meaning that each time you add a new record to this table, the database will assign a unique value to this field. The *Identity Seed* is 1, which is the value that is used for the very first record you add to this table, and *Identity Increment* is also 1 so that for each subsequent record, the value assigned increments from the previous record by 1.

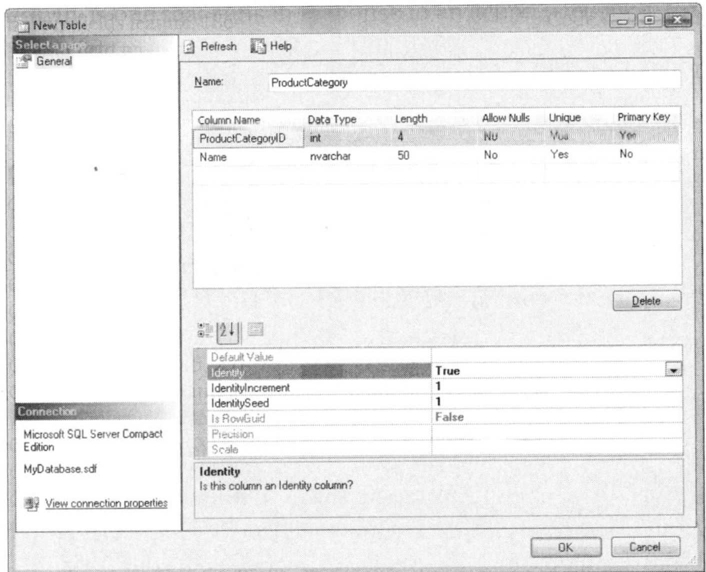

Figure 3-3 Using the Edit Table dialog box to define the columns and primary key of a new table

Create the *Product* table in a similar way. Set up the columns as follows:

- *ProductID*: int, not null, unique, primary key, identity
- *Name*: nvarchar(50), not null
- *Color*: nvarchar(15), null
- *ListPrice*: money, not null
- *Size*: nvarchar(5), null
- *ProductCategoryID*: int, not null

Creating a Foreign Key

The last column in the *Product* table is the *ProductCategoryID*, which cannot be null and clearly is intended to match a valid *ProductCategoryID* in the *ProductCategory* table. This is an example of a foreign key, meaning that for each *Product* record, the value stored in this column must match the *ProductCategoryID* of an existing record in the *ProductCategory* table. You could write code in your application to check that this relationship is working correctly, but it is much easier to let the database do the checking for you by setting up a foreign key.

The database design tools built into Visual Studio do not offer any direct way to create a foreign key, and so you will have to execute a Transact-SQL (T-SQL) query against the database. If you have access to SQL Server Management Studio, you can connect to the database and then create and execute a query such as the following:

```
ALTER TABLE Product
ADD CONSTRAINT Product_ProductCategory_FK
FOREIGN KEY (ProductCategoryID) REFERENCES ProductCategory(ProductCategoryID)
ON DELETE CASCADE
ON UPDATE CASCADE
```

This query creates a foreign key constraint so that the database will not allow a value to be entered in the *ProductCategoryID* column in the *Product* table that does not already exist in the *ProductCategory* table. The *ON DELETE CASCADE* clause means that if a record in the master table (*ProductCategory*) is deleted, records in the child table (*Product*) that referenced the *ProductCategoryID* of the deleted record are also deleted. *ON UPDATE CASCADE* means that if the *ProductCategoryID* of a master record is changed to a new value, the *ProductCategoryID* value in any child records is updated to match automatically. If you don't want this behavior, you can use *ON UPDATE NO ACTION* (the default) instead of *CASCADE*.

If you do not have access to SQL Server Management Studio, you can use Visual Studio 2005 to execute a query, although the technique for doing this is a little obtuse. Right-click your database in Server Explorer, and then click New Query, which opens the Query Graphical Designer that you would typically use to build *SELECT* statements to read data from the database. Close the Add Table dialog box, and then delete the *SELECT FROM* statements in the query pane. Write your query here, right-click the query pane, and then click Execute SQL.

Two other courses of action are to execute the query using the Query Analyzer tool on the device or to write some code to do it, such as that shown in Listing 3-1.

Listing 3-1 Creating Foreign Key Constraints in Code

```
using System;
using System.Data.SqlServerCe;
using System.IO;
using System.Reflection;

namespace MobileDevelopersHandbook
{
    class SetupForeignKey
    {
        public static void DefineKey()
        {
            // Set up the connection string.
            string databasePath = Path.GetDirectoryName(
                Assembly.GetExecutingAssembly().GetName().CodeBase);
            string connString = "Data Source=" + databasePath +
                "\\MyDatabase.sdf; Password=MobileP@ssw0rd";
```

```
                string commandText = "ALTER TABLE Product " +
                    "ADD CONSTRAINT Product_ProductCategory_FK " +
                    "FOREIGN KEY (ProductCategoryID) REFERENCES " +
                    "ProductCategory(ProductCategoryID) " +
                    "ON DELETE CASCADE " +
                    "ON UPDATE CASCADE";

                using (SqlCeConnection conn = new SqlCeConnection(connString))
                {
                    using (SqlCeCommand cmd = new SqlCeCommand(commandText, conn))
                    {
                        conn.Open();
                        cmd.ExecuteNonQuery();
                        conn.Close();
                    }
                }
            }
        }
    }
```

When you run this code the first time, it creates the foreign key constraint. If you run it a second time, you will get a *SqlCeException*. You can learn how to find out what the error is in the section titled "Deciphering *SqlCeExceptions*" later in this chapter.

> **Tip** You can use code such as that shown in Listing 3-1 to execute all sorts of queries, not just to create foreign keys. You could even execute a series of data definition language (DDL) queries using the *CREATE DATABASE* and *CREATE TABLE* statements to create a new database in code.

Creating an Index

Developers often overlook one step in improving the performance of SQL Server CE databases. Consider the foreign key that you just created. If your code has read a *Product* record and you want to find out the name of the *ProductCategory*, you read the *ProductCategoryID* value from the *Product* record and look up the corresponding record in the *ProductCategory* table. The *ProductCategoryID* field is the primary key of the *ProductCategory* table, and SQL Server CE has built an index for it so that the lookup is very fast.

Consider the reverse operation, though. If you have a *ProductCategory* record and you want to find all the *Products* that are in that product category, you need to find all records in the *Product* table that have a *ProductCategoryID* that matches the value in the *ProductCategory* record. Although you created a foreign key constraint linking these two tables, SQL Server CE did not create an index to help in the lookup you now want to do. The only way that SQL Server CE can find the required records is to do a full table scan, as shown in Figure 3-4, which could take a long time if the *Product* table contains many thousands of records.

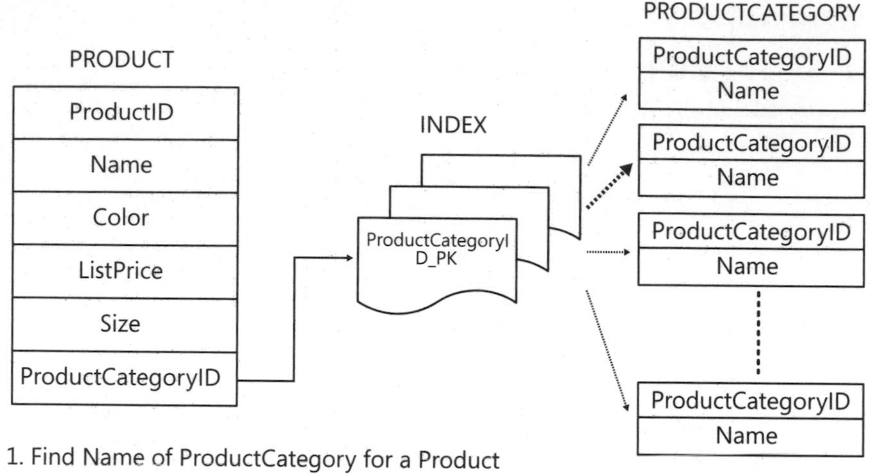

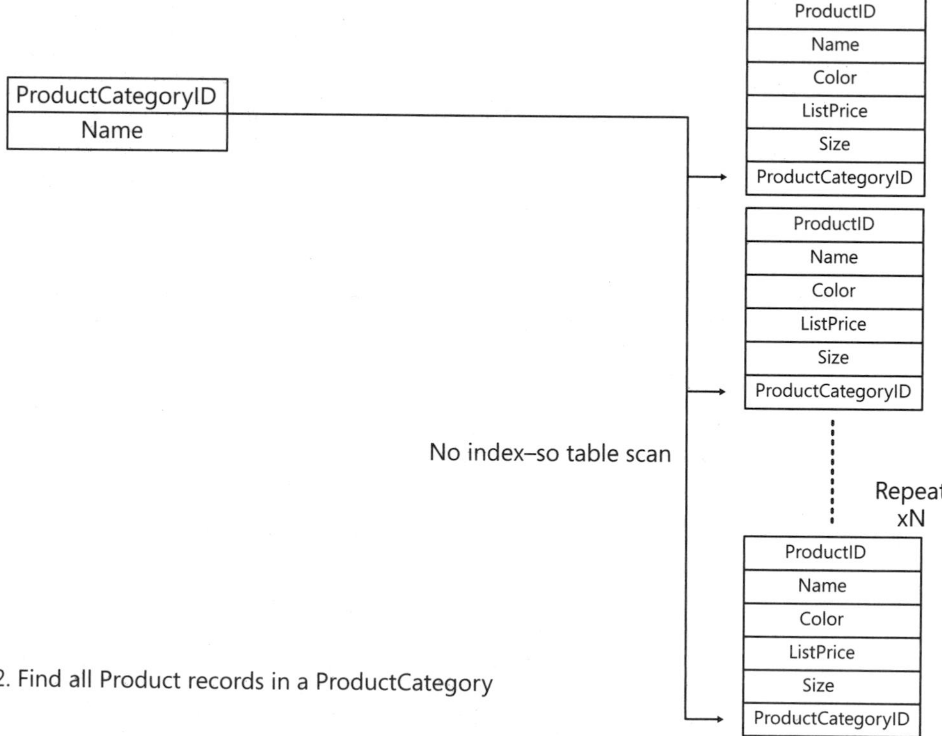

Figure 3-4 Lack of an index, which causes SQL Server CE to perform a full table scan

It is good practice to create an index on the foreign key field in a child table to help with these common searches. To do this in Visual Studio 2005, locate the *Product* table in Server Explorer, right-click Indexes, and then click Create Index. In the New Index dialog box, shown in Figure 3-5, give the index a suitable name, and click Add to select the column(s) that make up the index.

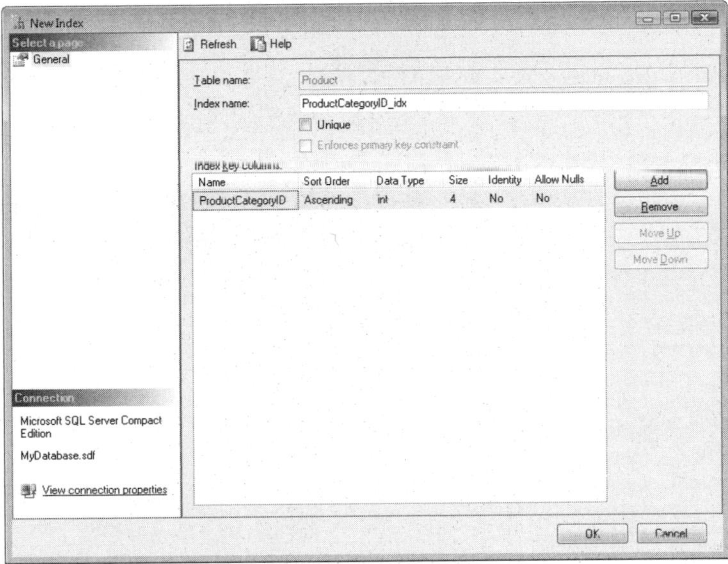

Figure 3-5 Creating a new index

You should create indexes where appropriate to help lookup performance. Beware of overusing them, though, because each index you create imposes extra work on the database: Every time you add a record, the database must maintain the indexes in addition to adding the new record.

Deciphering *SqlCeExceptions*

The SQL Server CE runtime raises a *SqlCeException* when an operation fails. *SqlCeException* has an *Errors* property of type *SqlCeErrorCollection* that always contains at least one *SqlCeError* instance describing the error condition that has occurred. A *SqlCeError* object exposes more details of the error in its *HResult, NativeError, NumericErrorParameters*, and *ErrorParameters* properties. For example, the following code (taken from SQL Server 2005 Compact Edition [SSCE] Books Online) displays the full contents of a *SqlCeException* in a message box:

```
private void DisplaySQLCEErrors(SqlCeException ex)
{
    SqlCeErrorCollection errorCollection = ex.Errors;

    StringBuilder bld = new StringBuilder();
    Exception inner = ex.InnerException;
```

```
        if (null != inner)
        {
            MessageBox.Show("Inner Exception: " + inner.ToString());
        }
        // Enumerate the errors to a message box.
        foreach (SqlCeError err in errorCollection)
        {
            bld.Append("\n Error Code: " + err.HResult.ToString("X"));
            bld.Append("\n Message   : " + err.Message);
            bld.Append("\n Minor Err.: " + err.NativeError);
            bld.Append("\n Source    : " + err.Source);

            // Enumerate each numeric parameter for the error.
            foreach (int numPar in err.NumericErrorParameters)
            {
                if (0 != numPar) bld.Append("\n Num. Par. : " + numPar);
            }

            // Enumerate each string parameter for the error.
            foreach (string errPar in err.ErrorParameters)
            {
                if (String.Empty != errPar)
                    bld.Append("\n Err. Par. : " + errPar);
            }

            MessageBox.Show(bld.ToString());
            bld.Remove(0, bld.Length);
        }
    }
```

The *SqlCeException* object also has *Message* and *NativeError* properties that are set to the same values as the properties of the same name in the first *SqlCeError* object in the *Errors* collection; this is a change from SQL CE 2.0, where you must interrogate the *Errors* collection to find the real cause of an error because the *SqlCeException* object does not set these properties.

The cause of an error is usually clear to the developer from the *Message* property, but if you want to identify specific errors programmatically, instead of searching for specific text in the *Message* property, it is better to read the *NativeError* and *HResult* properties. If you want to investigate the cause of an error further, the best resource for finding out more is the Troubleshooting book in the SQL Server Compact Edition (SSCE) Books Online, which lists the error numbers and their meanings. (You can find Books Online by clicking the Start menu, pointing to All Programs, and looking under Microsoft SQL Server 2005 Compact Edition.) For example, if you run the *CreateForeignKey* sample shown previously in Listing 3-1, and click the Create Key button twice, the second click raises a *SqlCeException* with a *NativeError* property of 25083 and the message "The referential relationship will result in a cyclical reference that is not allowed. [Constraint name = Product_ProductCategory_FK]." The message is fairly clear in this case, but if you look up 25083 in the Troubleshooting book in Books Online, you will find that the error is accompanied by a string parameter that gives the name of the constraint concerned. Knowing this, you might code an exception handler as follows to display a friendly message if the foreign key already exists:

```
private const int SSCE_M_CYCLEDETECTED = 25083;

private void button1_Click(object sender, EventArgs e)
{
    try
    {
        SetupForeignKey.DefineKey();
        MessageBox.Show("Foreign Key Created!");
    }
    catch (SqlCeException ex)
    {
        // Display friendly message if the foreign key already exists.
        if ((ex.NativeError == SSCE_M_CYCLEDETECTED) &&
            (ex.Errors[0].ErrorParameters[0] == "Product_ProductCategory_FK"))
        {
            MessageBox.Show("Key already exists. Continuing...");
        }
        else
        {
            // Display detailed error message.
            DisplaySQLCEErrors(ex);
        }
    }
}
```

Note The SQL Server CE managed libraries do not provide an enumeration for all the error codes that you can use to refer to them using their SSCE_M_* symbolic name. You must refer to the documentation to determine the correct values and then define your own constants, as shown in the preceding code example.

Creating Connections to Data in Your Project

Visual Studio 2005 introduces the concept of a project data source. In Visual Studio .NET 2003, you can drag a table from Server Explorer and drop it onto a form, and it automatically generates a data-bound user interface (UI), using a *Datagrid* control. In Visual Studio 2005, you must first create a project data source and then bind your controls to it. The data source can be created from tables in a database, from data returned from a Web service, or from any object that exposes one or more public properties. Compared with Visual Studio .NET 2003, the use of project data sources in Visual Studio 2005 gives you much more flexibility in the data to which you can bind and the way Microsoft Windows Forms controls in your GUI bind to data.

Creating a Project Data Source

The easiest way to work with data sources is through the Data Sources dialog box. You can open this dialog box by clicking Show Data Sources on the Data menu. A new project does not have any existing data sources, and so you can create a data source by clicking the Add Data Source link in the dialog box. You can have as many data sources as you want in a project; add data sources by clicking the icon at the top of the dialog box or click Add New Data Source on the Data menu.

With the Data Source Configuration Wizard, you can choose between database, Web service, or object as the source of your data, as shown in Figure 3-6. Choose Database to bind to the SQL Server CE database you created earlier in this chapter. You can learn more about working with Web services in Chapter 7.

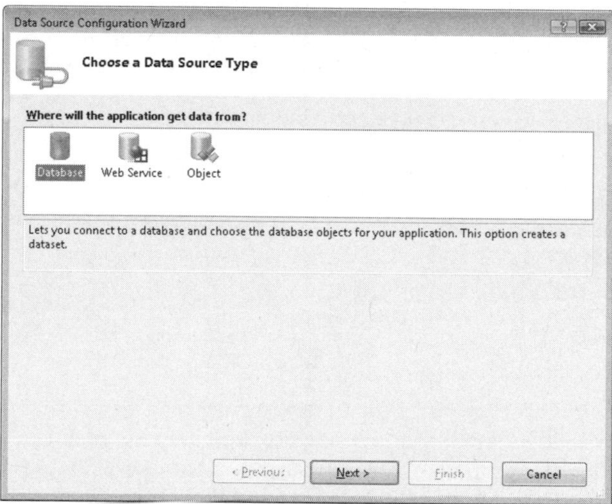

Figure 3-6 Data Source Configuration Wizard

The wizard then asks you for the database from which it should get the data. You can select an existing connection to a database that you created earlier or browse to a new database to create a new connection. If the database you select is not already in your project, Visual Studio detects this and helpfully asks if it should add the database. If you add a connection to a database that requires a password, Visual Studio detects that as well and displays the message: "This connection string appears to contain sensitive data (for example, a password) which is required to connect to the database. However storing sensitive data in the connection string can be a security risk. Do you want to include sensitive data in the connection string?" Visual Studio is warning you here that if you continue, it will generate code that includes the database password hard coded into the database connection string, which constitutes a security risk. We advise you to ignore the warning for now and reply Yes; otherwise, the visual designer tools will prompt you for the password every time you try to connect to your database.

> **Warning** Do not be tempted to leave database passwords in clear text in your code. Your code can be decompiled and the password can be uncovered by an attacker. See Chapter 10, "Security Programming for Mobile Applications," for advice on how to make the database password available to your application code in a secure way.

Next, the Data Source Configuration Wizard displays the Choose Your Database Objects page on which you select the tables and/or views to include in the data source. This is actually the first stage of building a strongly typed *DataSet* and *SqlCeResultSet*, which are objects you use to work with data in a SQL Server CE database. The *SqlCeResultSet* generally gives faster access to data than a *DataSet* can, although with some reduction in flexibility for the programmer, as explained in the section titled "Which Data Source: *DataSet* or *SqlCeResultSet?*" later in this chapter.

What is a strongly typed *DataSet*?

A *strongly typed DataSet* is an object that inherits from *System.Data.DataSet* but exposes additional properties that represent the table schema to which it is strongly typed. For example, if a *DataSet* instance called *myDataSet* contains two tables that store data from the *Orders* and *OrderDetails* tables in a database, in a *System.Data.DataSet* you can get a reference to the contained tables by indexing the *Tables* collection, for example, *myDataSet.Tables[0]* and *myDataSet.Tables[1]*. In a strongly typed *DataSet*, you can get a reference using intuitive names such as *myDataSet.Orders* and *myDataSet.OrderDetails*.

The visual designer tools in Visual Studio such as the DataSet Designer make it easy to generate strongly typed *DataSet* and *SqlCeResultSet* objects. The DataSet Designer also generates strongly typed *TableAdapter* objects that expose methods such as *Fill*, which fills a table in the *DataSet* with data read from the database, and *Update*, which updates the database using data in a *DataSet* table.

Designing and Programming Strongly Typed *DataSets* and *SqlCeResultSets*

The Data Source Configuration Wizard displays the Choose Your Database Objects page, where you select the tables and/or views to include in the data source (shown in Figure 3-7), and then builds a strongly typed *DataSet* or *SqlCeResultSet* object that it adds to your project in the form of an XML schema (.xsd file).

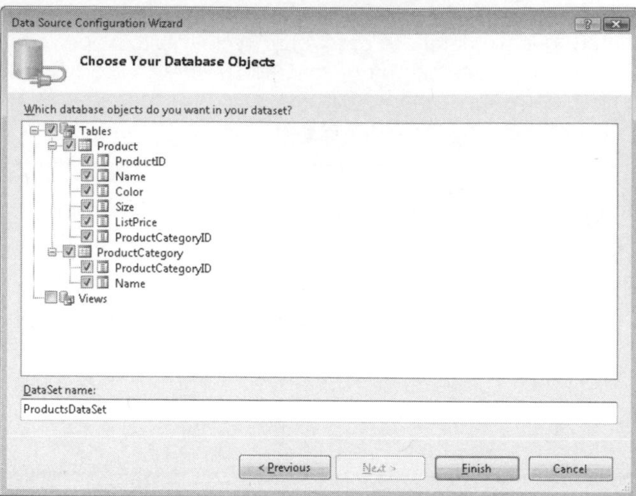

Figure 3-7 Selecting tables and/or views to include in a strongly typed *DataSet*

Tip You can select a subset of the columns in a database table on the Choose Your Database Objects page. This selection is honored in a typed *DataSet* object, but if you generate a *SqlCeResultSet* object, you will get all of the columns in the table. This is because the *SqlCeResultSet* by default uses a Table Direct mode, which bypasses the SQL Server CE Query Processor and is therefore highly performing but at the cost of a reduction in flexibility.

You can override this default behavior so that you can use complex queries with a *SqlCeResultSet* to select a subset of columns or columns from more than one table, but then you do not enjoy the raw speed of Table Direct mode. To find out how, see the section titled "Using Strongly Typed *DataSets* and *SqlCeResultSets* with Queries That Use Joins" later in this chapter.

The *DataSet* or *SqlCeResultSet* is the object that encapsulates your access to the data in the database. By default, Visual Studio creates a strongly typed *DataSet*, but if you want to create a *SqlCeResultSet* instead, you simply select the .xsd file in Solution Explorer and in the Properties dialog box change the custom tool to MSResultSetGenerator (shown in Figure 3-8). If you click the Show All Files icon at the top of Solution Explorer and then open the .Designer.cs (or .vb) file that is normally a hidden child of the .xsd, you can see the tool-generated code for both the *DataSet* and the *SqlCeResultSet*. If you want to generate both a strongly typed *DataSet* and a *SqlCeResultSet* at the same time, change the custom tool property to MSDataSetResultSetGenerator. Admittedly, the times that you would want to generate both a strongly typed *DataSet* and a strongly typed *SqlCeResultSet* for the same source data in the database will be few, but occasionally you might want to create a *SqlCeResultSet* for fast, direct access to the data (perhaps when binding to a *DataGrid*, as explained later in this chapter) and also create a *DataSet* instance that you would use when you need an object that takes a copy of the data in the database, for example, for sending over the network in a Web service call.

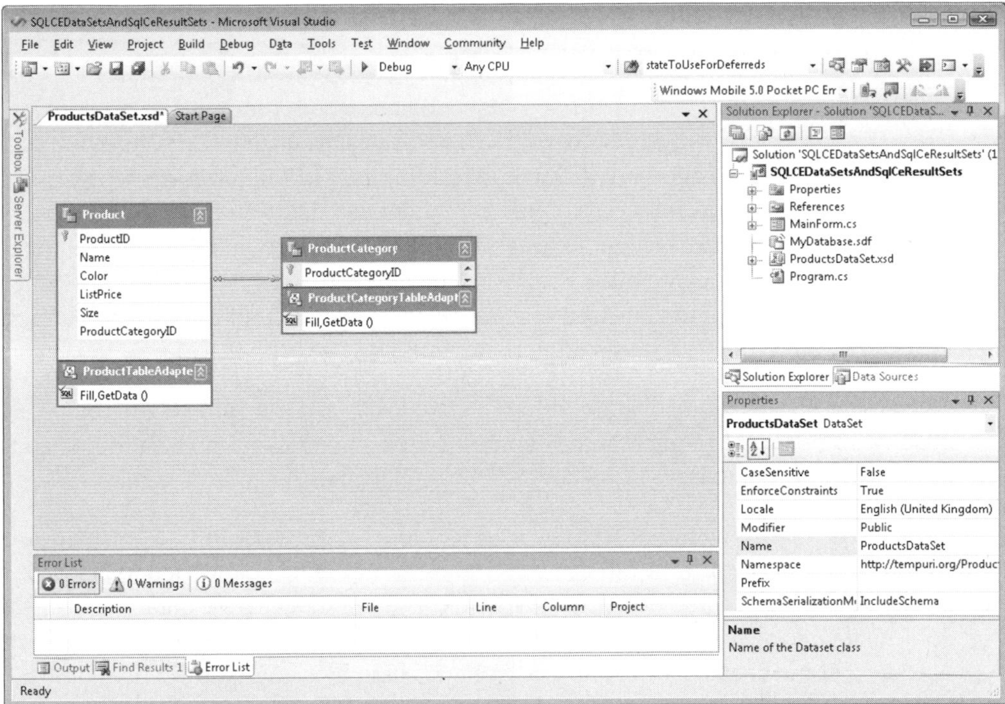

Figure 3-8 Changing the code generator tool

In Figure 3-8, you can also see the DataSet Designer displayed in the main workspace. You can open this window either by double-clicking the .xsd file in Solution Explorer or by clicking the Edit DataSet With Designer icon at the top of the Data Sources dialog box. With this graphical designer, you can drag in additional tables or views from the database shown in Server Explorer, edit existing queries, or you can right-click the design surface to open a menu of options, including designing a new query on data in the database.

In Figure 3-8, notice how the Data Source Configuration Wizard has detected the foreign key relationship between the *Products* and the *ProductCategory* tables and represents it graphically in the designer. This relationship, and the *TableAdapter* objects that are used to transfer data between the database and the *DataSet* (represented graphically in Figure 3-8 by the information at the foot of each table), are visual representations of programmable objects that are accessible through properties of the *DataSet* object but not the *SqlCeResultSet* object. You can see this for yourself if you expand the node for the .xsd file in Solution Explorer and then open the .Designer.cs/.vb file exposed beneath. This is the code that the visual tools generate and that defines the strongly typed *DataSet* or *SqlCeResultSet* that you program against. If you change the code generator tool to the MSResultSetGenerator, the visual appearance of the DataSet Designer does not change even though you will not find any foreign key or *TableAdapter* objects in the generated code.

Which Data Source: *DataSet* or *SqlCeResultSet*?

Both a *DataSet* and a *SqlCeResultSet* are suitable to be used as the data source for a data-bound GUI or as a means of manipulating data in a database, but that is where the similarities end. The *DataSet* object is functionally very rich and can store data in *DataTable* objects, each of which consists of a collection of *DataColumn* objects, with data records represented by *DataRow* objects. A *DataSet* can impose constraints on data you store in the tables, such as requiring all values in a column to be nonnull or unique, and can represent relationships such as foreign keys, in fact, very like a relational database. It also has the ability to remember the values in each row at the time the row was filled with data from the database and can separately store the new values after a row is updated.

A *SqlCeResultSet* is quite different. It does not store data, it is a lightweight object that you can use to read data that comes directly from the database, and you can also use it to update data directly in the database.

Figure 3-9 shows the difference. The *DataSet* model is the same as used by many distributed applications built with the full .NET Framework. A *DataSet* is designed to be used in situations where you use a *TableAdapter* object to copy some data from a database and store it in an object and then close the connection to the database. You can then ship that object (the *DataSet*) somewhere else, perhaps to a remote client by using Web Services or .NET Remoting, or you can even persist it to a file and transfer it manually to the other side of the world (well, not seriously—but the architecture does allow it), and then the remote client can make some changes to the data and ship it back again. Back in your data access logic code, you use the *TableAdapter* object to identify changed rows in the *DataTable* objects in the *DataSet* and write the changed values back into the database. This update is usually protected by a technique called *optimistic concurrency*, which means that the update logic uses the original data values stored in the *DataSet* to check that the target row has not been changed by someone else while you were off updating the *DataSet*. If it has been changed by someone else, the update fails, ensuring that updates from different clients cannot overwrite each other.

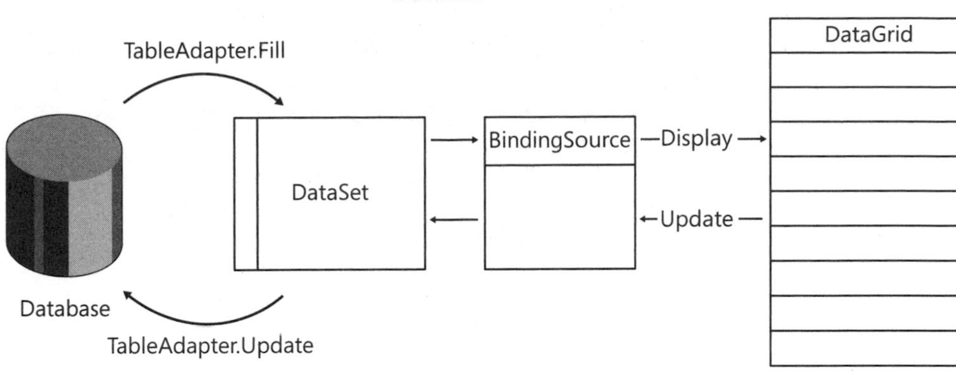

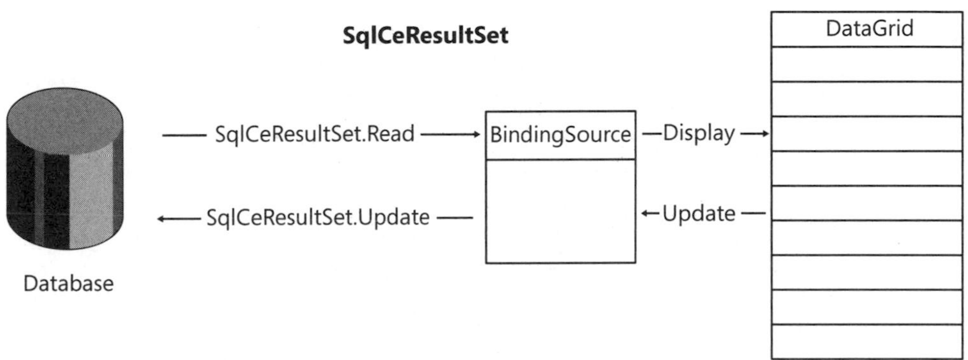

Figure 3-9 The difference—in a data-bound GUI—between reading and updating data using a *DataSet* and a *SqlCeResultSet*

That architecture is fine, and if you want to send data to a remote system over a Web Service call, it is still a good choice. However, on memory-constrained devices such as handheld devices, if all you want to do is show or update some data in a GUI, it is pretty wasteful to go to the trouble of using a heavyweight object such as a *DataSet*, which exhibits many of the characteristics of a relational database, when the database is sitting there begging to be used!

This is what a *SqlCeResultSet* is good for. A *SqlCeResultSet* is an object that you can use to query some data from a database, read it, and bind it to a GUI control such as a *DataGrid*, and also (as long as the source data is from a single table) update it. You are working directly with the database, using something called a server-side cursor (when you use a *DataTable* in a *DataSet*, you work with a client-side cursor). You should use a *SqlCeResultSet* whenever you can unless you specifically need the advanced features of a *DataSet*.

Working with Strongly Typed *DataSets* and *SqlCeResultSets*

So that you can compare the coding experience between the two objects, following are two examples that are functionally equivalent. The code reports the number of records in the *ProductCategory* and *Product* tables, adds two *ProductCategory* records, ensures that no duplicate records can be created, and then adds two *Product* records that are in the *ProductCategory* table with an ID of 1. You can find a full program that includes this code in the downloadable code samples on this book's companion Web site.

The first code listing, Listing 3-2, uses a *DataSet*.

Listing 3-2 Reading Records and Adding New Records Using a *DataSet*

```
using System.Data;
using System.Text;
…
private void DoStuffWithDataSet()
{
    // Create an instance of the strongly typed DataSet.
    ProductsDataSet productsDS = new ProductsDataSet();

    // Create a table adapter for product categories
    ProductsDataSetTableAdapters.ProductCategoryTableAdapter catTA =
        new ProductsDataSetTableAdapters.ProductCategoryTableAdapter();
    // ... and for products.
    ProductsDataSetTableAdapters.ProductTableAdapter prodTA =
        new ProductsDataSetTableAdapters.ProductTableAdapter();

    // FIRST: Get any existing data in these tables from the database.
    // Fill the ProductCategory table in the DataSet with data from the
    // database
    catTA.Fill(productsDS.ProductCategory);
    // ... and the products.
    prodTA.Fill(productsDS.Product);

    // Report count of records to the screen....
    ReportRecords(productsDS);

    // SECOND: Add some product categories.
    // To make sure you don't duplicate names, productCategory.Name has a
    // unique constraint.
    try
    {
        productsDS.ProductCategory.AddProductCategoryRow(
            "Rock Climbing Equipment");
        productsDS.ProductCategory.AddProductCategoryRow(
            "Scuba Diving Equipment");

        // Update to write changes back to the database.
        catTA.Update(productsDS.ProductCategory);
        textBox1.Text += "\r\nProduct Categories added.\r\n";
    }
    catch (ConstraintException)
```

```
    {
        // If the categories already exist, just continue.
        textBox1.Text += "\r\nProduct Category addition failed, "
            + "items already exist.\r\n";
    }

    // THIRD: Add some products in the category with categoryID of 1.
    ProductsDataSet.ProductCategoryRow prodCatRow =
        productsDS.ProductCategory.FindByProductCategoryID(1);
    productsDS.Product.AddProductRow(
        "Contoso Single Rope", "Red/Blue", 155.95M, "60m", prodCatRow);
    productsDS.Product.AddProductRow(
        "Contoso Rock Shoes", "Black", 89.95M, "8", prodCatRow);

    // Write to database.
    prodTA.Update(productsDS.Product);
    textBox1.Text += "\r\nProducts added.\r\n";

    // Report count of records to screen....
    ReportRecords(productsDS);
}

private void ReportRecords(ProductsDataSet productsDS)
{
    StringBuilder sb = new StringBuilder(textBox1.Text);
    sb.Append("There are currently ");
    sb.Append(productsDS.ProductCategory.Rows.Count);
    sb.Append(" product categories.\r\n");
    sb.Append("There are currently ");
    sb.Append(productsDS.Product.Rows.Count);
    sb.Append(" products.\r\n");
    textBox1.Text = sb.ToString();
}
```

The code is well commented and so should be fairly self-explanatory. However, note the following points:

- You do not have to do any management of the database connection. The *TableAdapter Fill* and *Update* methods both open the connection to the database before they execute and then close it again at the end.
- In the code that follows the comment that starts "SECOND," notice that there is some code that catches a *System.Data.ConstraintException*. If you execute this code more than once, the *ProductCategory* records will already exist, and when you try to add them to the *DataTable* (the two calls to the *AddProductCategory* method at the start of this section), the *ConstraintException* is thrown. The important thing to understand here is that when you create the strongly typed *DataSet* by dragging in the tables from the database, the tools detect the unique constraints and foreign key constraints and configure the *DataSet* with these constraints also. The *DataSet* mimics the behavior of the database.

Now examine Listing 3-3, which implements the same functionality but by using a strongly typed *SqlCeResultSet*.

Listing 3-3 Reading Records and Adding New Records Using a Strongly Typed *SqlCeResultSet*

```
using System.Data;
using System.Data.SqlServerCe;
using System.Text;
...
private const int SSCE_M_KEYDUPLICATE = 25016;

private void DoStuffWithResultSet()
{
    using (ProductsResultSetResultSets.ProductCategoryResultSet prodCatRS =
        new ProductsResultSetResultSets.ProductCategoryResultSet())
    {
        using (ProductsResultSetResultSets.ProductResultSet productRS =
            new ProductsResultSetResultSets.ProductResultSet())
        {
            try
            {
                // Report count of records to the screen....
                ReportRecords(prodCatRS.Connection, productRS);

                // SECOND: Add some product categories.
                // To make sure you don't duplicate names,
                // productCategory.Name has a unique constraint.
                try
                {
                    prodCatRS.AddProductCategoryRecord(
                        "Rock Climbing Equipment");
                    prodCatRS.AddProductCategoryRecord(
                        "Scuba Diving Equipment");
                    textBox1.Text += "\r\nProduct Categories added.\r\n";
                }
                catch (System.Data.SqlServerCe.SqlCeException sqlEx)
                {
                    if (sqlEx.NativeError == SSCE_M_KEYDUPLICATE)
                    {
                        // If the categories already exist, just continue.
                        textBox1.Text += "\r\nProduct Category addition "
                            + "failed, items already exist.\r\n";
                    }
                    else
                    {
                        throw;
                    }
                }

                // THIRD: Add some products in the category with categoryID 1.
                productRS.AddProductRecord(
                    "Contoso Single Rope", "Red/Blue", 155.95M, "60m", 1);
                productRS.AddProductRecord(
                    "Contoso Rock Shoes", "Black", 89.95M, "8", 1);
                textBox1.Text += "\r\nProducts added.\r\n";
```

```
                // Report count of records to the screen....
                ReportRecords(prodCatRS.Connection, productRS);
            }
            finally
            {
                // Close the DataReaders.
                productRS.Close();
                prodCatRS.Close();
                // Close and dispose of the database connections.
                productRS.Connection.Close();
                prodCatRS.Connection.Close();
                // Explicitly dispose of the connection objects
                // because the tool-generated code fails to do so.
                productRS.Connection.Dispose();
                prodCatRS.Connection.Dispose();
            }
        }
    }
}

private void ReportRecords(SqlCeConnection conn,
    ProductsResultSetResultSets.ProductResultSet productRS)
{
    int categoryCount;
    // One way of counting the records is to ask the database.
    using(SqlCeCommand cmd = new SqlCeCommand(
        "SELECT COUNT(*) FROM ProductCategory", conn))
    {
        categoryCount = (int)cmd.ExecuteScalar();
    }

    // Alternatively, get count by casting the ResultSet to IListSource.
    int productCount = ((IListSource)productRS).GetList().Count;

    StringBuilder sb = new StringBuilder(textBox1.Text);
    sb.Append("There are currently ");
    sb.Append(categoryCount);
    sb.Append(" product categories.\r\n");
    sb.Append("There are currently ");
    sb.Append(productCount);
    sb.Append(" products.\r\n");
    textBox1.Text = sb.ToString();
}
```

In comparing the two examples, you should see that the code to work with the *SqlCeResultSet* is simpler because you do not have to work through an intermediate data container such as the *DataSet*. You should note the following points about Listing 3-3:

- Unlike a *TableAdapter*, with a *SqlCeResultSet* you are responsible for writing code to open and close the connection to the database. In fact, there is no code in Listing 3-3 to open the connection because that is done for you automatically by the constructor of the tool-generated strongly typed *SqlCeResultSet* (look at the constructor and the *Open* method in

ProductsResultSet.Designer.cs). However, you must provide code to close and dispose of the connection.

- A *SqlCeResultSet* subclasses a *SqlCeDataReader*, and as with a *DataReader*, you must close it and dispose of it when you are finished with it. The *finally{...}* block in the code closes the *SqlCeResultSet* objects (and closes the database connections), while the *using* clauses around all the code in the *DoStuffWithResultSet* method ensure their disposal.
- As with a *SqlCeDataReader*, the *SqlCeResultSet* does not directly expose a *Count* property for you to find the number of records that will be read. One way of finding out how many rows there will be is to issue a *SELECT COUNT(*)* query to the database separately, as shown in the *ReportRecords* method. Alternatively, because *SqlCeResultSet* implements *IListSource*, you can use the following code to find the count of records:

```
((IListSource)productRS).GetList().Count
```

  Note that when you use a *TableAdapter* object to fill a *DataTable* in a *DataSet*, it reads all the records from the database and copies them into the *DataTable*, after which getting the record count is simple. The real performance advantage of a *SqlCeResultSet* is the fact that you do not have to read all the records into it before starting to read records. However, the internal implementation of the *SqlCeResultSet.GetList()* method must traverse the entire result set to determine the record count, so you lose some of that performance advantage. If the *SqlCeResultSet* returns a large number of records, it may be more efficient to execute a *SELECT COUNT(*)* query to establish the record count before you start reading the records.

Of course, this simple example only scratches the surface of how to work with a *SqlCeResultSet* and doesn't describe how to use a simple *SqlCeResultSet*, one that has not been subclassed and extended by the Data Designer tools.

Fixing the *SqlCeResultSet*

Unfortunately, the code for the typed *SqlCeResultSet* that the tools generate has a bug in it, so here's a warning to make this point as clearly as possible:

> **Caution** Do not use a typed *SqlCeResultSet* that has been generated by the tools unless you extend it to add your own constructor and override the tool-generated *Open* method. In Visual Studio 2005, the tool-generated code has a default constructor that calls the *Open* method, which creates a *SqlCeCommand* object but does not dispose of it after the call to *ExecuteResultSet*. This is a bug, and if you create many instances of one of these classes in your application, eventually you will get a Memory Exceeded exception from the SQL Server CE engine. This bug was not fixed in Visual Studio 2005 SP1.

If you locate the constructor for the typed *SqlCeResultSet* in <*yourResultSetName*>.Designer.cs, you find code similar to Listing 3-4.

Listing 3-4 Tool-Generated Code for a Strongly Typed *SqlCeResultSet*

```
public ProductsCategoryResultSet() {
    // Create default options.
    //
    resultSetOptions = System.Data.SqlServerCe.ResultSetOptions.Scrollable;
    resultSetOptions =
      (resultSetOptions | System.Data.SqlServerCe.ResultSetOptions.Sensitive);
    resultSetOptions =
      (resultSetOptions | System.Data.SqlServerCe.ResultSetOptions.Updatable);
...
    // Call Open() to initialize the ResultSet.
    //
    this.Open();
}

public void Open() {
    System.Data.SqlServerCe.SqlCeCommand sqlCeSelectCommand;
    // Open a connection to the database.
    //
    sqlCeConnection = new
      System.Data.SqlServerCe.SqlCeConnection(this.resultSetConnectionString);
    sqlCeConnection.Open();
    // Create the command.
    //
    sqlCeSelectCommand = sqlCeConnection.CreateCommand();
    sqlCeSelectCommand.CommandText = "ProductsCategory";
    sqlCeSelectCommand.CommandType = System.Data.CommandType.TableDirect;
    // Generate the ResultSet.
    //
    sqlCeSelectCommand.ExecuteResultSet(this.resultSetOptions, this);
}
```

Notice how the constructor calls the *Open* method, and how the *Open* method creates a *SqlCeCommand* object and then calls *ExecuteResultSet* to generate the result set? Unfortunately, that *SqlCeCommand* object is never disposed of, which causes a memory leak.

To overcome this limitation, you must extend the typed *SqlCeResultSet* that the tools generated. Fortunately, the tools generated it as a partial class, so you can simply view the *SqlCeResultSet* in the DataSet Designer window, right-click the background, and then click View Code to open a class file where you can add your own customizations.

To extend the *SqlCeResultSet*, add your own override of the constructor and a new implementation of *Open* (called *OpenEx*), such as that shown in Listing 3-4. The new version of the constructor takes two parameters:

- *bool openTable* If set to *true*, the constructor calls the default implementation of *Open* to read the table in *TableDirect* mode. If *false*, it does not call *Open*.
- *string connString* The database connection string.

The new version of *Open* is called *OpenEx* and is functionally identical, apart from the fact that it correctly disposes of the *SqlCeCommand* object (by virtue of the *using* statement). This new version also implements *IDisposable* so that when you dispose of the typed *SqlCeResultSet*, it also disposes of the *SqlCeConnection* object, and you don't have to explicitly do this yourself, as you did in Listing 3-3. Listing 3-5 shows the code to extend the *ProductsCategoryResultSet* from the sample application. You should create a similar class to extend each of the strongly typed *SqlCeResultSets* in your applications.

Listing 3-5 Extending the Strongly Typed *SqlCeResultSet* to Correctly Dispose of Dependent Objects

```
namespace MobileDevelopersHandbook.JoinQueryResultSetResultSets
{
    using System;
    using System.Data;
    using System.Data.SqlServerCe;

    partial class ProductsCategoryResultSet : IDisposable
    {
        /// <summary>
        /// Calling this method with an openTable value of true provides
        /// the same behavior as using the default constructor.
        /// </summary>
        /// <param name="openTable">Open the result set</param>
        /// <param name="connString">Connection string to the database</param>
        public ProductsCategoryResultSet(bool openTable, string connString)
        {
            resultSetOptions = ResultSetOptions.Scrollable |
                ResultSetOptions.Sensitive | ResultSetOptions.Updatable;
            resultSetConnectionString = connString;
            if (openTable)
                this.Open();
        }

        /// <summary>
        /// Use only with TableDirect mode. ResultSet will contain those
        /// records.
        /// </summary>
        public void OpenEx()
        {
            using (SqlCeCommand sqlCeSelectCommand =
                CreateConnectionAndCommand())
            {
                sqlCeSelectCommand.CommandText = "ProductCategory";
```

```
                sqlCeSelectCommand.CommandType =
                    System.Data.CommandType.TableDirect;

                sqlCeSelectCommand.ExecuteResultSet(ResultSetOptions, this);
            }
        }

        /// <summary>
        /// Creates a connection, opens it, and factories a command instance
        /// from the connection
        /// </summary>
        /// <returns></returns>
        protected SqlCeCommand CreateConnectionAndCommand()
        {
            sqlCeConnection = new
           System.Data.SqlServerCe.SqlCeConnection(resultSetConnectionString);
            sqlCeConnection.Open();

            return sqlCeConnection.CreateCommand();
        }
    }

    public new void Dispose()
    {
        if (this.Connection != null)
        {
            this.Connection.Dispose();
        }
        base.Dispose();
    }
}
```

To call this, update the original code in Listing 3-3 as follows:

```
private void DoStuffWithResultSet()
{
    string conn = "Data Source ="
        + (System.IO.Path.GetDirectoryName(System.Reflection.
        Assembly.GetExecutingAssembly().GetName().CodeBase)
        + "\\MyDatabase.sdf\\; Password =\"MobileP@ssw0rd\";");

    // Create the ResultSets using our own constructor to override the
    // default behavior.
    using (ProductsResultSetResultSets.ProductCategoryResultSet prodCatRS =
        new ProductsResultSetResultSets.ProductCategoryResultSet(false, conn))
    {
        using (ProductsResultSetResultSets.ProductResultSet productRS =
            new ProductsResultSetResultSets.ProductResultSet(false, conn))
        {
            try
            {
```

```
                // Open the two ResultSets.
                prodCatRS.OpenEx();
                productRS.OpenEx();

                // Report count of records to the screen....
                ReportRecords(prodCatRS.Connection);
            ...
            }
            finally
            {
                // Close the DataReaders.
                productRS.Close();
                prodCatRS.Close();
                // Close the database connections.
                productRS.Connection.Close();
                prodCatRS.Connection.Close();
            }
        }
    }
}
```

Warning The preceding code uses a hard-coded database password and is shown that way for brevity only. Do not hard-code passwords into your own applications! See Chapter 10 for advice on how to protect passwords and other sensitive data in your applications.

Enabling Insert, Update, and Delete in Strongly Typed *DataSets* and *SqlCeResultSets*

In Listing 3-2, you use a strongly typed *DataSet* to both read records from the database and insert new records. In Listing 3-3, you do the same operations with a *SqlCeResultSet*. You can use strongly typed *DataSet* and *SqlCeResultSet* objects to read, create, insert, and delete database records only if that object describes columns from a single database table.

Updating the Database with a *DataSet* Look at Figure 3-8 again: You can see that there are two separate tables represented in the *DataSet/SqlCeResultSet*, one for *Products* and one for *ProductCategory*. The *Products* table contains columns only from the products table in the database, and the *ProductCategory* table contains columns that are found only in the corresponding table in the database. When you drag a table directly from Server Explorer onto the Data Designer, as you did to build these objects, what you are really doing is defining a database query that performs a T-SQL *SELECT* statement on the columns in only that table. With such a simple query, the tools can generate corresponding *INSERT*, *UPDATE*, and *DELETE* statements. You can see the generated statements if you go to the Data Designer window, select one of the *TableAdapter* objects, and then go to the Properties dialog box (as shown in Figure 3-10); you can see the *SelectCommand*, *InsertCommand*, *DeleteCommand*, and

UpdateCommand properties that contain the T-SQL commands that the *TableAdapter* object uses to interact with the database.

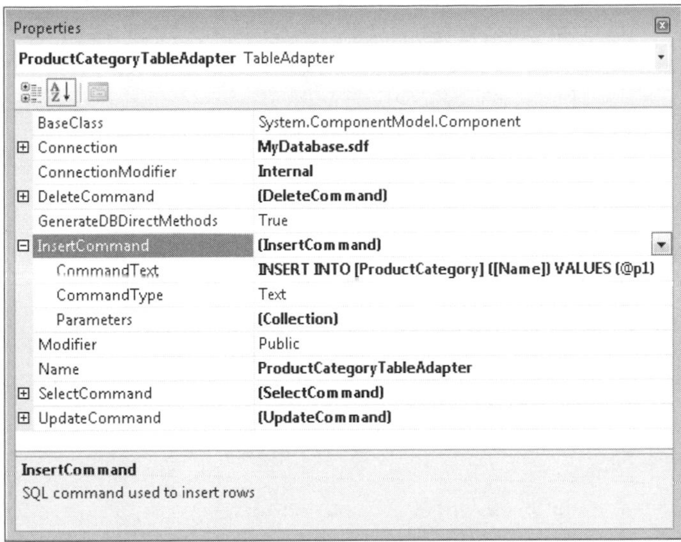

Figure 3-10 Viewing the *TableAdapter* properties that contain the T-SQL commands

When you call the *TableAdapter.Fill* method, it executes a T-SQL *SELECT* statement to read the data from the database using the data in the *SelectCommand* property and loads it into the *DataTable* in the *DataSet*. It closes the connection to the database, and now your application code works with the data in the *DataTable*, displaying the data and possibly updating or deleting records, or inserting new records.

Whenever you update, insert, or delete records in a *DataTable*, the *DataTable* records this activity by setting the *RowState* of the affected row to *DataRowStatus.Modified*, *DataRowState.Added*, or *DataRowState.Deleted*, respectively. Unchanged rows have a *RowState* of *DataRowStatus.Unchanged*. When you call the *TableAdapter.Update* method, the *TableAdapter* object first finds all rows in the source *DataTable* in the *DataSet* that have the *RowState DataRowStatus.Deleted*, and then uses the *DeleteCommand* to delete the corresponding record in the database. It then finds all rows in the *DataTable* with the *RowState DataRowStatus.Inserted* and uses the command in the *InsertCommand* property to insert the record into the database. Finally, it finds rows with the status *DataRowStatus.Updated* and uses the *UpdateCommand* to update the database rows.

All this happens for you "under the covers" so that the code to read records from the database and then later to update the database is not much more complex than a call to the *Fill* and *Update* methods of the relevant *TableAdapter* is, as you can see in Listing 3-1.

> **Tip** Many developers who are starting out with *DataSets* make the mistake of making changes to data in a *DataTable* and then calling the *AcceptChanges* method of the *DataSet* before calling the *TableAdapter.Update* method. What *AcceptChanges* actually does is set the *RowState* of every row to *DataRowState.Unchanged*. If you call *TableAdapter.Update* after you have accepted changes, the *TableAdapter* will not be able to discover which rows have changed and so is unable to make any changes to the database.
>
> However, the *AcceptChanges* method can be useful in certain circumstances, for example, when you want to send a *DataTable* you have built in code to another component and then discover the changes yourself when it is returned.

Updating the Database with a *SqlCeResultSet* As with the strongly typed *DataSet*, you can use a strongly typed *SqlCeResultSet* to insert, delete, and update records in the database—but only if the *SqlCeResultSet* performs a query on a single database table. If the query involves a *JOIN* across multiple tables, you can use a *SqlCeResultSet* (or a *DataSet*) only to read records, not update them; how you do this is explained in the next section.

You have already seen in Listing 3-2 how to insert a record. The tool-generated strongly typed *SqlCeResultSet* provides a convenient *Add<table>Record* method with arguments appropriate to that record. For example, the code to add a record to the *Product* table from Listing 3-2 is

```
productRS.AddProductRecord(
    "Contoso Single Rope", "Red/Blue", 155.95M, "60m", 1);
```

If you go to the definition of this method (in Visual Studio, right-click the code that calls this method, and then click Go To Definition), you can see what the tool-generated code does:

```
public void AddProductRecord(string Name, string Color,
    decimal ListPrice, string Size, int ProductCategoryID) {
    System.Data.SqlServerCe.SqlCeUpdatableRecord newRecord =
        base.CreateRecord();
    newRecord["Name"] = Name;
    newRecord["Color"] = Color;
    newRecord["ListPrice"] = ListPrice;
    newRecord["Size"] = Size;
    newRecord["ProductCategoryID"] = ProductCategoryID;
    base.Insert(newRecord);
}
```

As you can see, it creates a *SqlCeUpdateableRecord* by calling *base.CreateRecord()*, where *base* in this case is the parent class, which is a *SqlCeResultSet*. Then it sets the values in the correct columns and calls the *Insert* method of the *SqlCeResultSet* to insert it into the database.

Deleting records is very simple. Again, the tools have generated a method for this action in the strongly typed *SqlCeResultSet*:

```
public void DeleteRecord() {
    base.Delete();
}
```

To update a record, you simply position the cursor at the required record using a call to *Read* (which reads the next record in sequence) or *ReadAbsolute* (which reads a specific record by index number), make your changes, and then call the *SqlCeResultSet.Update* method. For example:

```
// Create a typed SqlCeResultSet.
using (ProductsResultSetResultSets.ProductResultSet productRS =
    new ProductsResultSetResultSets.ProductResultSet())
{
    try
    {
        // Update the third record.
        productRS.ReadAbsolute(3);
        productRS.Name = "Contoso Half Rope";
        productRS.ListPrice = 129.95M;
        productRS.Size = "70m";

        // Write changes to the database.
        productRS.Update();
    }
    finally
    {
        // Close the DataReader.
        productRS.Close();
        // Close and dispose of the database connection.
        productRS.Connection.Close();
        productRS.Connection.Dispose();
    }
}
```

Using Strongly Typed *DataSets* and *SqlCeResultSets* with Queries That Use Joins

You can use the Data Designer tools to create *DataSet* or *SqlCeResultSet* objects that encapsulate queries to the database that read data from more than one table by using a *JOIN* to retrieve a value from one table using a key value supplied in a different table. The resulting record set combines data from two or more tables.

For example, say you want to display a list of products, but instead of showing the *Product.CategoryID*, you want to display the actual name of the product category. You can build a project data source that encapsulates the correct database query in the following way:

Creating a Project Data Source That Makes a Complex Query

1. You can create a new query in a new *DataSet* or *SqlCeResultSet* or inside an existing data source.

    a. To create a new *DataSet* or *SqlCeResultSet*, click Add New Item on the Project menu, and then select a *DataSet* in the Add New Item dialog box. When the Data Designer window opens, right-click the background and click Add Table Adapter. (Don't choose Add Query because that does not give you the option of designing a query that returns rows, only a single value.)

       Change the Custom Tool to MSDataSetGenerator or MSResultSetGenerator to determine what kind of data source you want, as you did earlier in this chapter.

    b. b.To create a new query inside an existing data source, select an existing data source in the Data Sources dialog box, and click the Edit DataSet With Designer icon at the top of the dialog box. Then right-click the background of the Data Designer window and click Add Table Adapter. Note that if this is a *DataSet*, the tool will generate a new *DataTable* inside the *DataSet* to store the results of this query in addition to the existing *DataTables*.

> **Caution** If your existing data source is a *SqlCeResultSet*, the tool will generate a new typed *SqlCeResultSet* that is supposed to allow you to access the record set resulting from the query. However, the tools do not do a great job here, and you must do some additional coding to get this to work. See the section titled "Complex Queries and *SqlCeResultSets*" later in this chapter for more information.

2. The TableAdapter Configuration Wizard opens. On the first page, select the database connection. The second page is titled Choose A Command Type and offers two options: Use SQL Statements and Use Existing Stored Procedure. SQL Server CE does not support stored procedures, so select Use SQL Statements.

3. On the third page of the TableAdapter Configuration Wizard, you can enter your query. For example, to enter a query to return rows from the *Product* table but include the *Category Name* instead of the *CategoryID*, you would enter the following:

```
SELECT    Product.ProductID, Product.Name, Product.Color, Product.ListPrice,
          Product.Size, ProductCategory.Name AS CategoryName
FROM      Product, ProductCategory
WHERE     Product.ProductCategoryID = ProductCategory.ProductCategoryID
```

   (See Figure 3-11.)

> **More Info** If you find T-SQL syntax confusing, don't worry; you are not alone. Unfortunately, we don't have space to explain much about T-SQL. You can learn more by reading the SQL Server 2005 Compact Edition Books Online.

As an alternative to entering the query yourself, you can click the Query Builder button to use the graphical query designer to help you build complex queries and test them while you are developing them. See "Query and View Designer Tools" in the Visual Studio 2005 documentation for more information about using the graphical query designer tool.

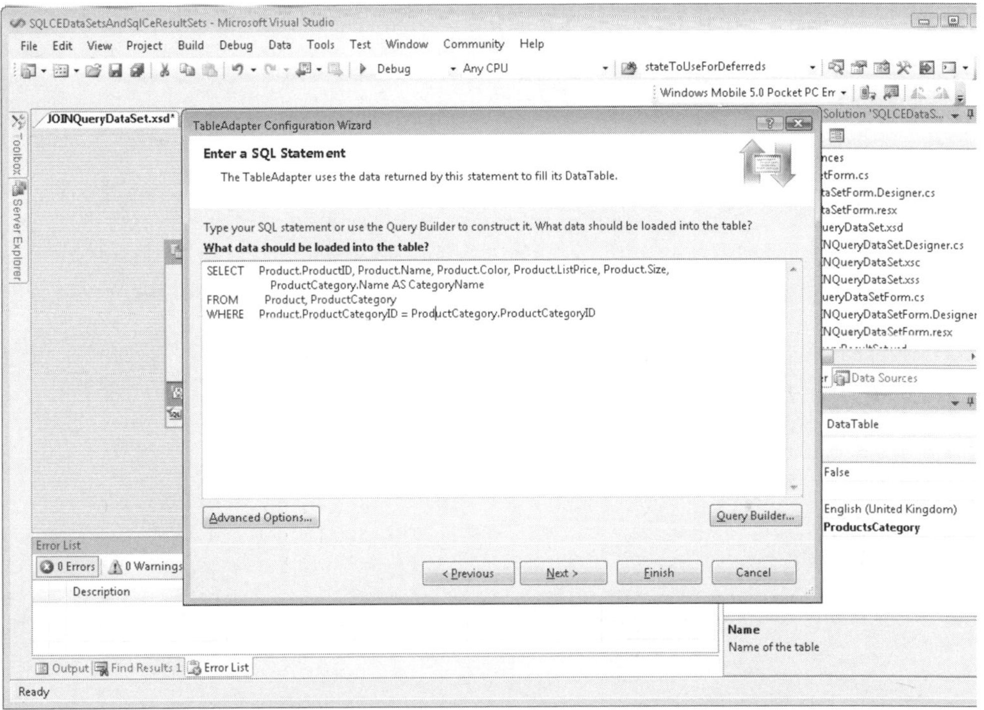

Figure 3-11 Entering a T-SQL query in the TableAdapter Configuration Wizard

4. Click Finish, and then rename the new table from *DataTable1* to an appropriate name–*ProductsCategory*, for example, in this scenario. Notice that if you select the *ProductsCategoryTableAdapter* on the Data Designer and then look at the Properties dialog box, you can see that the tools have detected that this is a complex query and so have not set the *InsertCommand*, *UpdateCommand*, or *DeleteCommand* property.

If your data source is a *DataSet*, you call *Fill* on the *TableAdapter* object to execute the query and load the results into the *DataTable*, just as you did before. For example:

```
// Get a DataTable filled with the results of a query with a JOIN.
JOINQueryDataSet ds = new JOINQueryDataSet();
JOINQueryDataSetTableAdapters.ProductsCategoryTableAdapter ta =
    new JOINQueryDataSetTableAdapters.ProductsCategoryTableAdapter();
ta.Fill(ds.ProductsCategory);

// Fill a ListView control with the results.
foreach (JOINQueryDataSet.ProductsCategoryRow row in ds.ProductsCategory)
{
    // Simple list in the format: <product name> - <product category name>
    listView1.Items.Add(
        new ListViewItem(row.Name + " - " + row.CategoryName));
}
```

Complex Queries and *SqlCeResultSets* If you design a data source that uses a complex database query as explained in the previous section, you might expect that you can simply change the custom tool from the *MSDataSetGenerator* to the *MSResultSetGenerator*, and you will be able to use the strongly typed *SqlCeResultSet* to perform the query instead of a *DataSet*.

Unfortunately, the tool-generated code does not work for strongly typed *SqlCeResultSet* objects that use a *JOIN* in the *SELECT* statement. If you create an instance of the tool-generated *SqlCeResultSet* (which you have also extended in the way explained earlier in the section titled "Fixing the *SqlCeResultSet*"), you will get a *SqlCeException* thrown at run time when you try to create an instance using code such as the following:

```
// Create an instance of the typed SqlCeResultSet.
JoinQueryResultSetResultSets.ProductsCategoryResultSet set =
    new JoinQueryResultSetResultSets.ProductsCategoryResultSet(false);
set.OpenEx();
```

The *SqlCeException* error message reads: The specified table does not exist. [ProductsCategory]. *ProductsCategory* is the name you gave to your new table in the Data Designer, but from this message it is clear that the generated code is not performing the query you entered earlier:

```
SELECT    Product.ProductID, Product.Name, Product.Color, Product.ListPrice,
          Product.Size, ProductCategory.Name AS CategoryName
FROM      Product, ProductCategory
WHERE     Product.ProductCategoryID = ProductCategory.ProductCategoryID
```

Instead, the code is trying to find records from the (nonexistent) *ProductsCategory* table in the database.

To understand why, you must look at the implementation of the *OpenEx* method shown in Listing 3-5 (which is functionally equivalent to the *Open* method the tools generated) and understand a bit more about the different ways you can use a *SqlCeResultSet*. The *OpenEx* method contains code similar to the following:

```
/// <summary>
/// Use only with TableDirect mode. ResultSet will contain those
/// records.
/// </summary>
public void OpenEx()
{
    using (SqlCeCommand sqlCeSelectCommand =
        CreateConnectionAndCommand())
    {
        sqlCeSelectCommand.CommandText = "ProductCategory";
        sqlCeSelectCommand.CommandType =
            System.Data.CommandType.TableDirect;

        sqlCeSelectCommand.ExecuteResultSet(ResultSetOptions, this);
    }
}
```

Notice how the *SqlCeCommand* is configured: The *CommandType* property is set to *TableDirect*. This is a clue to one of the reasons a *SqlCeResultSet* is faster than a *DataSet* for accessing data. *TableDirect* means that the database access is done by completely bypassing the SQL Server CE Query Processor. (The Query Processor is the engine that analyzes your query and works out the quickest way to execute it, taking into account which indexes are available.) The Query Processor is there to make sure your queries execute as fast as possible, but of course it imposes its own overhead on execution time, so if you bypass it, you avoid that overhead. However, to use *TableDirect* mode, you must set the *CommandText* to the name of the table you want to access, and that is why you get the exception; there is no table called *ProductsCategory*.

So how do you use a *SqlCeResultSet* with a complex query involving joins across different tables? You must get it to use the Query Processor again and supply it with the full query string. To do that you must extend the typed *SqlCeResultSet* in a slightly different way from how you first extended it to override the memory leak in the *Open* method, first shown in Listing 3-5. Add a new version of the *Open* method that you can use to specify a query string and that creates the *SqlCeCommand* in *Text* mode so that it does not bypass the Query Processor, as shown in Listing 3-6. You don't need the *OpenEx* method because that works only in Table Direct mode.

Listing 3-6 Extending the Strongly Typed *SqlCeResultSet* to Support Complex Queries

```
namespace MobileDevelopersHandbook.JoinQueryResultSetResultSets
{
    using System.Data;
    using System.Data.SqlServerCe;

    partial class ProductsCategoryResultSet
    {
        /// <summary>
        /// Calling this method with an openTable value of true provides
        /// the same behavior as using the default constructor.
        /// </summary>
        /// <param name="openTable">Open the result set</param>
        /// <param name="connString">Connection string to the database</param>
        public ProductsCategoryResultSet(bool openTable, string connString)
        {
            resultSetOptions = ResultSetOptions.Scrollable |
                ResultSetOptions.Sensitive | ResultSetOptions.Updatable;
            resultSetConnectionString = connString;
            if (openTable)
                this.Open();
        }

        /// <summary>
        /// ResultSet will contain those records.
        /// </summary>
        /// <param name="commandText"></param>
        public void Open(string sqlCommandText)
        {
            using (SqlCeCommand sqlCeSelectCommand =
                CreateConnectionAndCommand())
            {
                sqlCeSelectCommand.CommandText = sqlCommandText;
                sqlCeSelectCommand.CommandType = System.Data.CommandType.Text;

                sqlCeSelectCommand.ExecuteResultSet(resultSetOptions, this);
            }
        }

        /// <summary>
        /// Creates a connection, opens it, and factories a command instance
        /// from the connection.
        /// </summary>
        /// <returns></returns>
        protected SqlCeCommand CreateConnectionAndCommand()
        {
            sqlCeConnection = new
           System.Data.SqlServerCe.SqlCeConnection(resultSetConnectionString);
            sqlCeConnection.Open();

            return sqlCeConnection.CreateCommand();
        }

        public new void Dispose()
```

```
        {
            if (this.Connection != null)
            {
                this.Connection.Dispose();
            }
            base.Dispose();
        }
    }
}
```

To call this, use code similar to the following:

```
string conn = "Data Source ="
    + (System.IO.Path.GetDirectoryName(System.Reflection.
    Assembly.GetExecutingAssembly().GetName().CodeBase)
    + "\\MyDatabase.sdf\\; Password =\"MobileP@ssw0rd\";");

// Create an instance using your own constructor–don't open it yet.
JoinQueryResultSetResultSets.ProductsCategoryResultSet rsltSet =
    new JoinQueryResultSetResultSets.ProductsCategoryResultSet(false, conn);

// Define the query.
string query = "SELECT Product.ProductID, Product.Name, Product.Color,"
    + "Product.ListPrice, Product.Size, ProductCategory.Name AS CategoryName "
    + "FROM Product, ProductCategory "
    + "WHERE Product.ProductCategoryID = ProductCategory.ProductCategoryID";

// Open it, and supply your query.
rsltSet.Open(query);

// List the results in a ListView.
while (rsltSet.Read())
{
    // Simple list in the format: <product name> - <product category mame>
    listView1.Items.Add(
        new ListViewItem(rsltSet.Name + " - " + rsltSet.CategoryName));
}
```

Warning The preceding code uses a hard-coded database password and is shown that way for brevity only. Do not hard-code passwords into your own applications! See Chapter 10 for advice on how to protect passwords and other sensitive data in your applications.

Taking Advantage of Indexes with the *SqlCeResultSet*

If you have experience coding with *SqlCeDataReader* objects, you may be wondering what the strongly typed *SqlCeResultSet* offers that a *SqlCeDataReader* doesn't. What you get with the technique just described is the ability to refer to individual fields in the rows you are reading by using a descriptive name, such as *rsltSet.Name* and *rsltSet.CategoryName* in the preceding sample. Apart from that, at least when you are performing a complex query such as in this example, the strongly typed *SqlCeResultSet* does not offer any additional functionality over a *SqlCeDataReader* (remember that the *SqlCeResultSet* class descends from *SqlCeDataReader* in any case).

However, when you use a *SqlCeResultSet* in Table Direct mode, not only can you avoid the overhead of the Query Processor, but you can take advantage of additional optimizations. If the table you are reading has an index, you can sort the result set on that index by setting the *Index* property of the *SqlCeCommand* to the name of the index. You can also filter on a range of values in that index by calling *SqlCeCommand.SetRange*. *SetRange* takes three parameters: a *DbRangeOptions* enumeration, a start value, and an end value. Use *DbRangeOptions* to specify how the start and end values you supply are used; for example, whether the selected values are inclusive or exclusive of the start and end values. See the Visual Studio documentation for a full description of the options. To make use of this, you can further extend the methods in the partial class shown in Listing 3-6 to include a utility method to sort and filter on an index, as shown in Listing 3-7. Although this may seem like more work than using a T-SQL query is, in low-memory situations avoiding the Query Processor can result in dramatic performance improvement.

Listing 3-7 Extending the Strongly Typed *SqlCeResultSet* to Allow Sorting and Filtering on an Index

```
/// <summary>
/// ResultSet will contain only those records where the value of the specified
/// index falls within rangeStart and rangeEnd inclusive. Records will be
/// returned in the order of the index.
/// If rangeStart is null, the ResultSet will contain the whole table with the
/// records returned in the order of the index.
/// </summary>
/// <param name="indexName"></param>
/// <param name="rangeStart"></param>
/// <param name="rangeEnd"></param>
public void Open(string indexName, object[] rangeStart, object[] rangeEnd)
{
    using (SqlCeCommand sqlCeSelectCommand = CreateConnectionAndCommand())
    {
        sqlCeSelectCommand.CommandText = tableName;
        sqlCeSelectCommand.CommandType = System.Data.CommandType.TableDirect;
        sqlCeSelectCommand.IndexName = indexName;

        // If a range value specified, call SetRange-start without end is
        // legal, but not vice versa.
        if (rangeStart != null)
            sqlCeSelectCommand.SetRange(DbRangeOptions.Default,
                rangeStart, rangeEnd);

        sqlCeSelectCommand.ExecuteResultSet(this.resultSetOptions, this);
    }
}
```

> **Tip** In the downloadable sample code for this chapter, you will find a code snippet you can use to generate these extensions for a *SqlCeResultSet*, with instructions on how to install it in Visual Studio. Both Microsoft Visual C# and Visual Basic versions can be found there. Credit must be given to Most Valuable Professional (MVP) Jim Wilson, who first developed this code snippet.

Building a Data-Bound GUI

So far in this chapter, you have learned how to design project data sources using the designer tools in Visual Studio 2005. Now it is time to use them in a data-bound GUI.

Building a Quick UI Using the Visual Tools

The Visual Studio 2005 Forms Designer includes a tool that you can easily use to generate a set of forms to manipulate the records from a *DataTable*, to display the records in a *DataGrid*, to add new records, and to view or edit existing records. This tool is useful for building quick test programs, and it also serves as an excellent way of learning how to program the *BindingSource* control, a new control in .NET Framework 2.0 that makes it easy to build data-bound UIs, which is the main topic of this part of this chapter. This tool is available only from the SmartTag menu on a *DataGrid* bound to a *DataSet* data source. A SmartTag is the arrow shown on the upper right of a control displayed in the Windows Forms Designer; you can click the arrow to display a menu of actions you can perform that relate to that control.

Unfortunately, if your data source is a *SqlCeResultSet*, Visual Studio does not support this functionality, so the SmartTag does not appear and you have no option but to build the forms to add, view, or edit records manually.

Generating Data Forms

1. First, create a data source that is a *DataSet* containing a table that includes all the columns from a single database table, as you did earlier in this chapter. For example, create a *DataSet* that includes the *Product* and *ProductCategory* tables from your test database.
2. Open a form in design view. Then go to the Data Sources dialog box and expand the ProductsDataSet. Under it you will see the table or tables in your *DataSet*. If you click a table, you will see that a drop-down menu is associated with it that you can use to select between *DataGrid*, *Details*, or *None*. These are options for how the designer builds a UI bound to this *DataTable*, and we explain them in more detail very soon; for now, select *DataGrid*, as shown in the following:

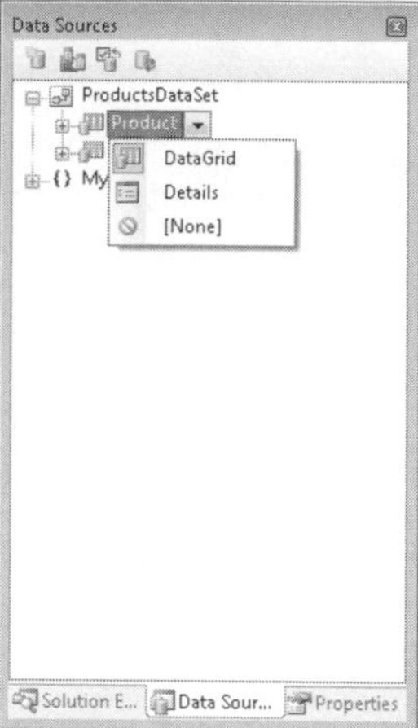

3. Drag the *Product* table onto the form. The tools create a *DataGrid* control that is data bound to the *Product DataTable*. In the Properties dialog box, change the *Dock* property so that the *DataGrid* fills the form.

4. Click the *DataGrid* in the Designer. On the SmartTag menu, you can see some design options, one of which is Generate Data Forms. Click this option as shown in the following:

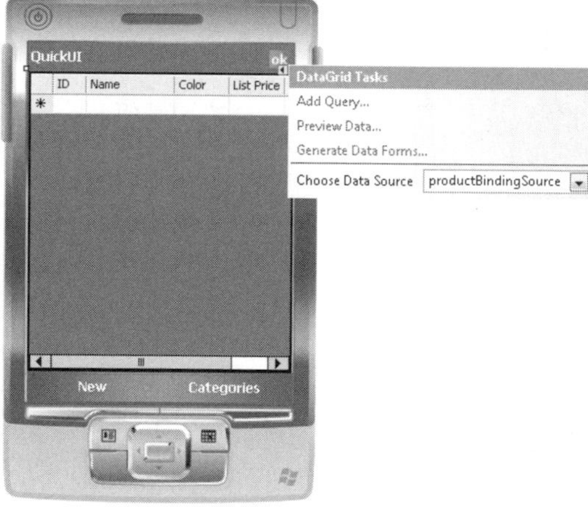

5. Visual Studio creates two new forms, ProductEditViewDialog and ProductSummary-ViewDialog, and adds them to your project. It also adds a menu item to the main form with the text Add and wires up a *Click* event handler for the *DataGrid*. If you run this application now, you'll find that you can add new records, click a row in the *DataGrid* to view existing records in the Summary View, and from there edit details of existing records.

Now, this sort of functionality in the integrated development environment (IDE) is quite fun, and a gift to demo gods who have to do presentations to show off the capabilities of Visual Studio, but for real development at best it serves as a starting point for a real application. If you study the code it has generated, you can see that it has added a call to *ProductTableAdapter.Fill* in the *Form1_Load* event handler, but there is no code to call *ProductTableAdapter.Update* to write the changes back to the database; you must add this code. The other problem you can fix in this particular example is to supply a list of product categories in a drop-down list, rather than ask the user to enter an integer *ProductCategoryID*, as is required by the tool-generated ProductEditViewDialog form.

Before you fix these issues, look at how the generated code uses the *BindingSource* control because it serves as a good, simple introduction. In .NET Compact Framework 2.0, you should always use *BindingSource* controls because it makes data binding a lot easier than it is in .NET Compact Framework 1.0.

Programming the *BindingSource* Control

In .NET Compact Framework 1.0, you accomplish data binding by setting the *DataSource* and *DataMember* properties directly to the data source (such as a *DataSet*), but in .NET Compact Framework 2.0, the best approach is to bind your controls to a *BindingSource*.

A *BindingSource* control simplifies binding controls on a form to data by providing a layer of indirection, currency management, change notification, and other services. This is accomplished by attaching the *BindingSource* component to your data source and then binding the controls on your form to the *BindingSource* component. All further interaction with the data, including navigating, sorting, filtering, and updating, is accomplished with calls to the *BindingSource* component.

An easy way to learn how to program a *BindingSource* control is by examining the code that was generated in the Quick UI. If you look at the Forms Designer for your main form where Visual Studio created the *DataGrid*, you can see that visible in the component tray is a *BindingSource* instance called *productBindingSource*, an instance of your strongly typed *DataSet* called *productsDataSet*, and an instance of the *productsTableAdapter* (see Figure 3-12). If you look at the Forms Designer–generated code for your form, you can see that the Forms Designer creates an instance of each of these objects in the *InitializeComponent* method, which is called from your form's constructor.

Why the *BindingSource* is a good thing

The *BindingSource* provides a solution to some problematic data-binding issues in .NET Compact Framework 1.0. By sitting between the data source and controls, the *BindingSource* can provide services on behalf of the data source. The most important services provided by the *BindingSource* are the following:

- **Provides *IBindingList* services for non-*IBindingLists,* including *IEnumerable* binding** Windows Forms complex data binding (that is, binding list-based controls such as *DataGrid* or *ListView* to a set of records) in Visual Studio 2005 works correctly against lists of type *IEnumerable* when bound through a *BindingSource* (version 1.0 requires *IList*). In the case of *IEnumerable*, the *BindingSource* copies all data source elements into an internal list and indirectly binds controls to the internal list.
- **Supports type-based binding** The Windows Forms 1.0 designer requires an instance of a type to exist at design time to set up design-time data binding. The *BindingSource* provides type binding services such that it can "project" a type to bound controls as an empty list of that type. For example, you can use the following code, which is illegal with the *DataSource* property of standard Windows Forms controls:

  ```
  myBindingSource.DataSource = typeof(Customer);
  ```
- **Provides centralized control for binding operations** A common binding request is the ability to suspend and resume binding for a data source. In version 1.0, the *CurrencyManager* provides *SuspendBinding*() and *ResumeBinding*() methods, but these work only for simple binding (simple binding of a property on a control to a property on an object). When binding through a *BindingSource*, you can suspend both simple and complex binding by having the *BindingSource* disable firing of *ListChanged* events (*ListChanged* events control binding). To do this, set the *BindingSource RaiseListChangedEvents* property to *false*.
- **Simplifies currency management** The *BindingSource* component exposes most of the *CurrencyManager* events and properties. This enables you to program against common currency-related events such as *CurrentChanged* and *PositionChanged* at design time.

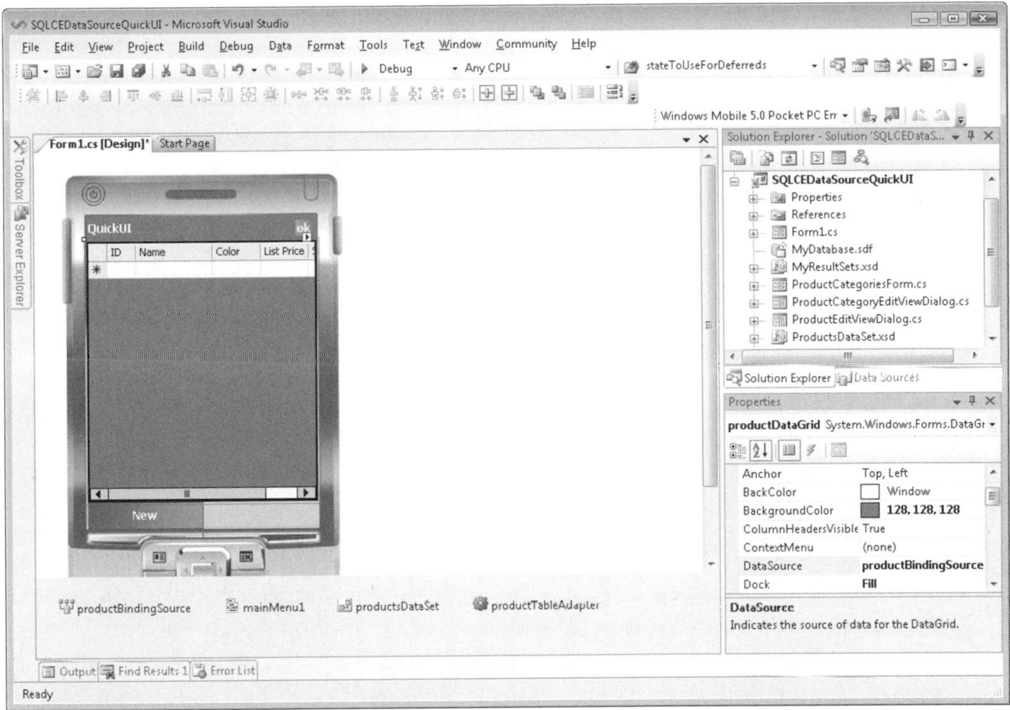

Figure 3-12 The Forms Designer–created *BindingSource*, *DataSet*, and *TableAdapter* instance that result from dragging a data source onto a form

If you look at the properties for the *DataGrid*, you can see that the *DataSource* property is set to *productBindingSource*. The *DataSource* property of the *productBindingSource* is set to *productsDataSet*, and the *DataMember* property is set to the *Product* table, so you can see how the *BindingSource* object sits between the control and the data source.

When you load this form, the *DataGrid* receives details of all records in the data source and displays them in the grid.

Adding Records to a Record Set Using *BindingSource*

Now look at the code in the *menuItem1 Click* event handler. This adds a new record to the record set simply by calling *AddNew* on the *BindingSource*:

```
productBindingSource.AddNew();
```

This adds a new record to the underlying record set in the data source (which is the *Product DataTable* in the *DataSet* in this example). Because the *DataGrid* is data bound to the *BindingSource*, it also displays a new row in the grid automatically. The *BindingSource* also operates as a currency manager that keeps track of the current position in the collection of records, and when you call *AddNew*, the *BindingSource.Position* property is automatically set to the index of the newly added record.

One disadvantage of simply calling *AddNew* is that you cannot initialize any columns in the new record. One workaround for this if your underlying data source is a *DataTable* is to set the default value on the columns, which you can do in the Data Designer at design time or in code at run time; for example:

```
// Set some default column values.
this.productsDataSet.Product.ProductCategoryIDColumn.DefaultValue = 1;
this.productsDataSet.Product.SizeColumn.DefaultValue = "M";
```

You can also trap the *DataTable.TableNewRow* event to set columns in a new row.

A different way of changing fields in the new record, and the technique you will have to use if your data source is not a *DataTable* is to trap the *BindingSource AddingNew* event. The *AddingNew* event occurs before a new object is added to the underlying list represented by the *BindingSource.List* property. This event is fired after the *AddNew* method is called but before the new item is created and added to the underlying list. By handling this event, the programmer can provide custom item creation and insertion behavior without being forced to derive from the *BindingSource* class. This is accomplished in the event handler by setting the *NewObject* property of the *System.ComponentModel.AddingNewEventArgs* parameter to the new item.

Beware if you try to use the *AddingNew* event when you are bound to a *DataTable* (as in this example) or a *DataView*. When you bind to a *DataTable*, the *BindingSource* actually binds to a *DataView* of that *DataTable*. A *DataView* contains a collection of *DataRowView* objects, but you cannot create a new instance of *DataRowView* in your *AddingNew* event handler and add it to the *DataView* exposed by *BindingView.List*; you will get a *System.ArgumentException*: Cannot add external objects to this list. There is a workaround for this: You can actually ask the *DataView* to create the new row for you, by calling *DataView.AddNew*. For example, if you add a new *Product* record and want to set the *ProductCategoryID* field to 1, use this code:

```
private void productBindingSource_AddingNew(
    object sender, AddingNewEventArgs e)
{
    MessageBox.Show("AddingNew event fired");
    // Create a DataRowView.
    DataRowView datarowview = ((DataView)productBindingSource.List).AddNew();

    // You can set fields in the new row like this:
    datarowview["ProductCategoryID"] = 1;
    // Or by getting the underlying DataRow in the data source
    ProductsDataSet.ProductRow productRow =
        (ProductsDataSet.ProductRow)datarowview.Row;
    productRow.ProductCategoryID = 1;
```

```
        productRow.ListPrice = 0.00M;

        // Tell it that this is the new row.
        e.NewObject = datarowview;

        // Set the position of the BindingSource.
        productBindingSource.Position = productBindingSource.Count - 1;
    }
```

Note that if you handle the *AddingNew* event, you must position the current record to the new row, as shown by the last line of this method. If you don't handle the *AddingNew* event, you do not have to set the position of the *BindingSource* manually when you add a new record because it is handled for you automatically by the internal implementation of *BindingSource.AddNew*.

Navigating Through a Record Set Using a *BindingSource*

As just mentioned, you use the *BindingSource.Position* property to set the current record in the rowset. *BindingSource* has a bunch of methods you can use for navigating through the records, including *MoveFirst*, *MoveLast*, *MoveNext*, and *MovePrevious*.

In fact, *BindingSource*-aware controls such as the *DataGrid* set the current row position when you click a row displayed in the grid. The code in the *Click* event for the *DataGrid* in the sample application takes advantage of this and implicitly passes the current row position by passing a reference to its *productBindingSource* object to the static *Instance* method of the Summary View form, as shown in the following:

```
private void productDataGrid_Click(object sender, EventArgs e)
{
    ProductSummaryViewDialog productSummaryViewDialog =
        ProductSummaryViewDialog.Instance(this.productBindingSource);
    productSummaryViewDialog.ShowDialog();
}
```

If you look now at the code of the *ProductSummaryViewDialog.Instance* method (shown just below), you can see that it does three important things:

1. It implements the singleton pattern. It creates a new instance if the object does not already exist; otherwise, it returns the previously created instance.
2. It sets the *productBindingSource.DataSource* property to the *BindingSource* that has been passed in. This particular *productBindingSource* is a new instance of *BindingSource* that is local to the ProductSummaryViewDialog form.
3. The code sets the *Position* property of this local *productBindingSource* to the same position of the *BindingSource* passed in, which is the current selected row in the *DataGrid* on the entry form.

```
public static ProductSummaryViewDialog Instance
    (System.Windows.Forms.BindingSource bindingSource)
{
    System.Windows.Forms.Cursor.Current =
        System.Windows.Forms.Cursors.WaitCursor;
    if ((defaultInstance == null))
    {
        defaultInstance = new ProductSummaryViewDialog();
        defaultInstance.productBindingSource.DataSource = bindingSource;
    }
    defaultInstance.AutoScrollPosition = new System.Drawing.Point(0, 0);

    defaultInstance.productBindingSource.Position = bindingSource.Position;
    System.Windows.Forms.Cursor.Current =
        System.Windows.Forms.Cursors.Default;
    return defaultInstance;
}
```

The result of this processing is that the *productBindingSource* object on this form is bound to the same position in the same data collection as the entry form. Controls on this form are, of course, bound to the *productBindingSource* object on this form, resulting in the display of the correct record on this form as the one that was clicked in the *DataGrid*.

If you look at the ProductSummaryViewDialog form, you can see that it does not contain a *DataGrid* but actually contains a lot of *Label* controls, some of which are data bound and some of which are not; this is an example of a details form.

Data Binding Details Forms

A details form is one designed to view or edit the fields in a single record. Both the ProductSummaryViewDialog and ProductEditViewDialog forms that Visual Studio generated are details forms.

If you look at the *Label* controls, some, such as *productIDLabel1*, are there to display the values from the current record. If you expand the *(DataBindings)* property in the Properties dialog box, you can see that the *Text* property of this *Label* is bound to the *ProductID* field in the *productBindingSource* (Figure 3-13); you can click the drop-down menu to select a different field to bind to.

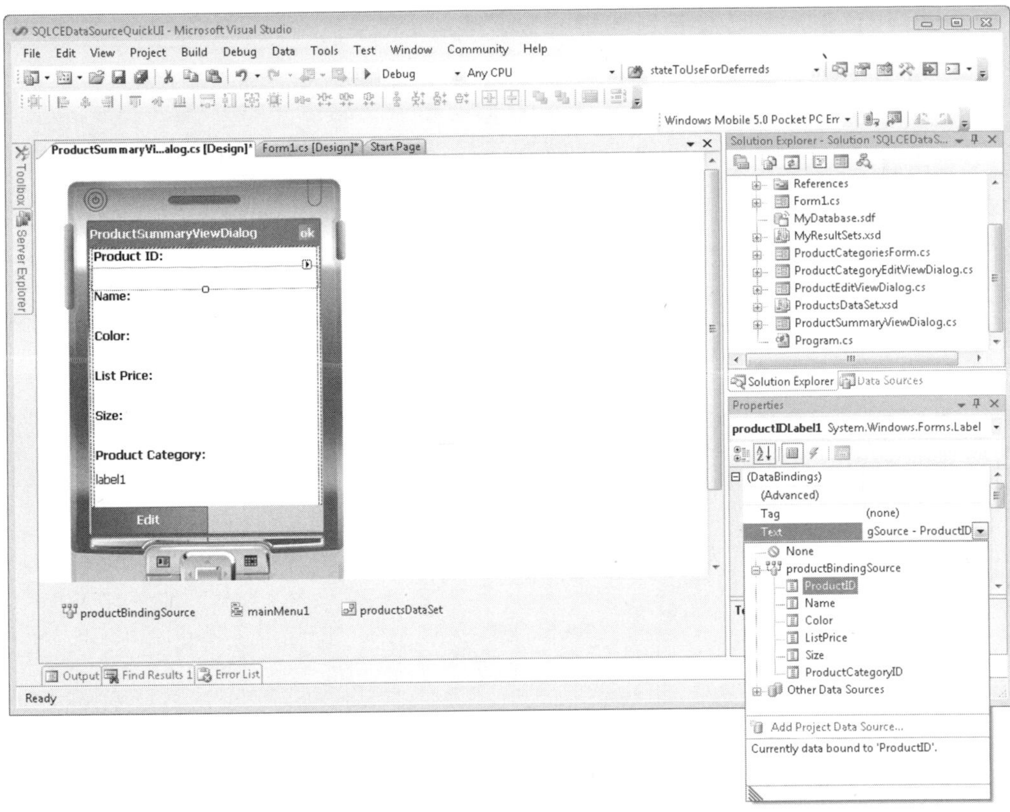

Figure 3-13 Data-binding properties for a field on a details form

You can change the way a field is displayed by clicking the ellipsis button by the *Advanced* property. For example, the *ListPrice* field should be formatted as currency, and you can set this in the Formatting And Advanced Binding dialog box, as shown in Figure 3-14.

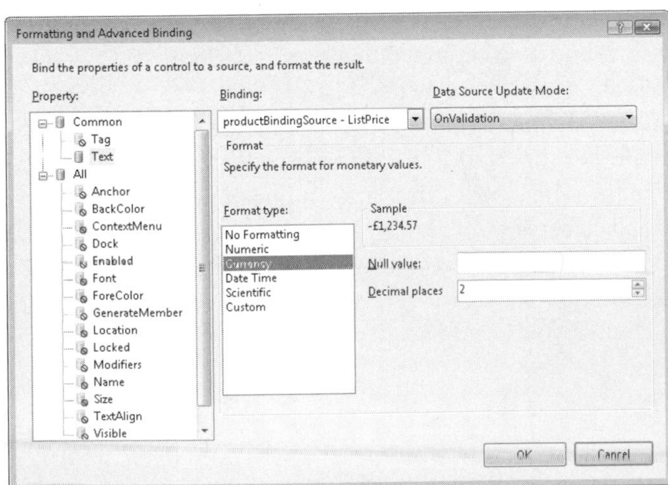

Figure 3-14 Setting formatting in the Formatting And Advanced Binding dialog box

Creating Your Own Details Forms

You can easily generate your own details forms. In the Data Sources dialog box, you can use the drop-down menu associated with each data source to choose between a *DataGrid* or a *Details* view. Previously, you chose *DataGrid* when you dragged the data source onto a form, but if you choose *Details*, the designer generates separate controls for each field, each with a *Label* control to identify it. When you select *Details* view, by default the designer generates *TextBox* controls for each field, but you can change these to other controls, such as *Label*, *ListBox*, *ComboBox*, *NumericUpDown*, or *None*, as shown in Figure 3-15.

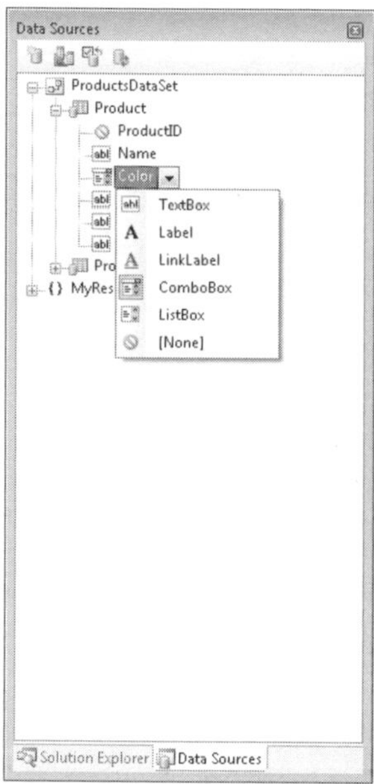

Figure 3-15 Setting field data-binding options for details forms

When you auto-generated the data forms, the tools created one form for viewing records (ProductSummaryViewDialog) and another for editing records (ProductEditViewDialog). On the ProductSummaryViewDialog, the tools generated *Label* controls to show the values in all the fields so that you could view them but not change them; on the ProductEditViewDialog, it used *TextBox* controls to allow editing. Notice that on the ProductEditViewDialog form, the *ProductID* field is not shown (in other words, the data-binding control for that field is *None*). This is as you should expect because it is an identity field, meaning that the value is assigned for you by the database to identify that record, and although it is reasonable to edit the other fields in the record, you should not change the record's identity field. If you are generating your own details form for editing, you should set the data binding for the identity field in a record to *None*.

Accepting and Canceling Updates with *EndEdit* and *CancelEdit*

If you run this sample application now and click the New menu option to create a new product, and then simply click OK on the ProductEditViewDialog form without supplying a name for the product, you will get a *System.Data.NoNullAllowed* exception. This exception is actually thrown at the following line in the *ProductEditViewDialog_Closing* event handler:

```
private void ProductEditViewDialog_Closing(object sender, CancelEventArgs e)
{
    this.productBindingSource.EndEdit();
}
```

The reason the exception is thrown is that the *BindingSource* control introduces another layer of update buffering to your applications. Any changes you make to values in controls that are bound to a *BindingSource* are buffered and not applied to the underlying record collection until you call *EndEdit* on the *BindingSource*. In this example, the underlying data source is the *Product DataTable* that disallows *Null* values in the *Name* and *ListPrice* fields. Because you did not enter a name, you get the *System.Data.NoNullAllowed* exception when the changes are applied to the *DataTable*.

Note If your *BindingSource* is bound to a *SqlCeResultSet* (more on this in the next section), the changes are applied directly to the database. In this case, if there are errors when you call *EndEdit*, you will get a *System.Data.SqlServerCe.SqlCeException*, not one of the ADO.NET exceptions from *System.Data*.

You should put a *try..catch* around calls to *EndEdit* to catch data validation errors. In this case, you can simply display an error message and cancel the close of the form so that the user can correct the error, as shown in the following code. Incidentally, this is also a good place to call an update on the *TableAdapter* to write changes from the *DataTable* back to the database, which is done in the code sample in the *ApplyUpdatesToDatabase* method–when your data source is a *DataTable*, you have to code this somewhere in your application yourself because the tools do not generate any code to do this.

```
private void ProductEditViewDialog_Closing(object sender, CancelEventArgs e)
{
    try
    {
        this.productBindingSource.EndEdit();

        // If the changes are applied correctly to the DataTable, apply them
        // also to the database.
        ApplyUpdatesToDatabase();
    }

    // If your data source is a DataTable, you will get an exception from
```

```
        // System.Data.
        // If your underlying data source is a SqlCeResultSet, EndEdit causes
        // changes to be applied to the database, hence you will get a
        // SqlCeException if a constraint is violated; or some other error.
        catch (System.Data.NoNullAllowedException)
        {
            MessageBox.Show("You have not entered one or more of the following " +
                "required values: Name, ListPrice");

            // Cancel the form closing.
            e.Cancel = true;
        }
    }

    private void ApplyUpdatesToDatabase()
    {
        // Write the changes back to the database.
        // Get the DataTable.
        DataTable sourceDataTable =
            ((DataRowView)this.productBindingSource.Current).DataView.Table;
        ProductsDataSet.ProductDataTable productTable =
            (ProductsDataSet.ProductDataTable)sourceDataTable;

        // Update
        ProductsDataSetTableAdapters.ProductTableAdapter ta =
            new ProductsDataSetTableAdapters.ProductTableAdapter();
        ta.Update(productTable);
    }
```

Tip A common cause of data validation errors occurs when the user has entered a text value that is longer than the maximum allowed length of the field in the table. When you drag a *TextBox* onto a form, its *MaxLength* property is always set to 32767. Be sure to change this to the correct length allowed for that field.

Canceling Updates You can also ask the *BindingSource* control to discard any updates by calling the *CancelEdit* method. For example, you can add a Cancel menu button to your form, and then in the *Click* event handler call *BindingSource.CancelEdit* and set the *DialogResult* property of the form to cause it to close:

```
private void cancelMenuItem_Click(object sender, EventArgs e)
{
    this.productBindingSource.CancelEdit();
    this.DialogResult = DialogResult.Cancel;
}
```

Getting at the Underlying *DataRow* from the *BindingSource*

The *ApplyUpdatesToDatabase* method in the preceding code sample illustrates how to get at the underlying data when your data source is a *DataTable*. The *BindingSource.Current* property returns an object that is the current row in the list of records maintained by the *BindingSource*, and you must cast this to the correct type of row for the data source you are using. When the underlying data source is a *DataTable*, the *BindingSource* list is actually a *DataView*, and each row is a *DataRowView*. If the underlying data source is a *SqlCeResultSet*, the *BindingSource* record list is actually a *ResultSetView* object, which contains *RowView* objects.

Knowing this you can see that to get at the underlying *DataRow* and/or *DataTable* when your data source is a *DataTable*, you can use code such as follows:

```
DataRowView currentRowView =(DataRowView)myBindingSource.Current;
DataRow currentDataRow = currentRowView.Row;
DataTable currentDataTable = currentRowView.DataView.Table;
```

Similarly, if you are using a *SqlCeResultSet*, use code such as the following to retrieve the underlying record in the *SqlCeResultSet*:

```
RowView currentRowView =(RowView)myBindingSource.Current;
SqlCeUpdatableRecord currentRecord = currentRowView.UpdatableRecord;
```

Data Binding with the *SqlCeResultSet*

The *BindingSource* control works fine with a *SqlCeResultSet* as well. You can find out how by extending the sample application to allow you to enter product categories. You can do this simply enough by adding a new form to your project and adding a menu option to your main form with the legend Categories, which creates an instance of that form and then calls *ShowDialog* on it. Create a strongly typed *SqlCeResultSet* in your project for the *ProductCategory* table, as explained earlier in this chapter, and then drag the *ProductCategory* table from the Data Sources dialog box onto the new form, having first selected *DataGrid* as the control to use for the UI. This form displays all *ProductCategory* records in the *DataGrid*.

Tip When you are using data binding to display a list of records, you get a substantial performance improvement using a *SqlCeResultSet* over a *DataSet* only if the control is a *DataGrid*. The *DataGrid* fetches only visible rows from the *SqlCeResultSet* (and hence from the database). All other controls must retrieve all the records to load the control, and so if there are a large number of rows, the *SqlCeResultSet* will not give you a performance advantage over the *DataSet*.

On the other hand, the performance improvement that comes from using a *DataGrid* can be so substantial that you may consider using an appropriately formatted *DataGrid* bound to a *SqlCeResultSet* instead of a list control.

In this example application, there's no point in creating a summary view form to view product categories such as the one you have for viewing product details because there are only two fields in the *ProductCategory* table, and you can easily see both in the *DataGrid*. However, you need to create a new form that allows the user to edit new or existing records. When the new empty form is displayed in the Forms Designer, go to the Data Sources dialog box and change the data-binding options for the *SqlCeResultSet* so that it generates a *Details* view, set the control to use for the *ProductCategoryID* field (the identity field) to *None*, and then drag the *ProductCategory* data source onto the new form as shown:

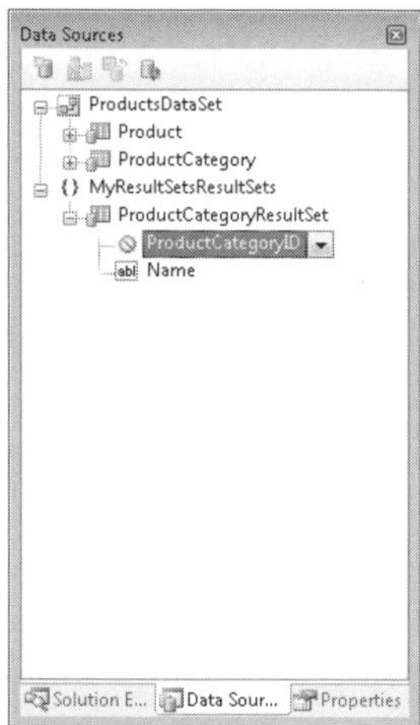

Because this new form was not generated by the Generate Data Forms tools, you are required to change some of the code. You must pass the *BindingSource* from the form displaying the *DataGrid* so that you can identify the correct record to edit. Add a static *Instance* method similar to the one generated for you by the tools earlier, which creates the form and sets up the *productCategoryBindingSource* instance in this form correctly. Also, improve the usability by adding Save and Cancel menu options, and set the *ControlBox* property of the form to *false*. Your form should look something like the one in Figure 3-16.

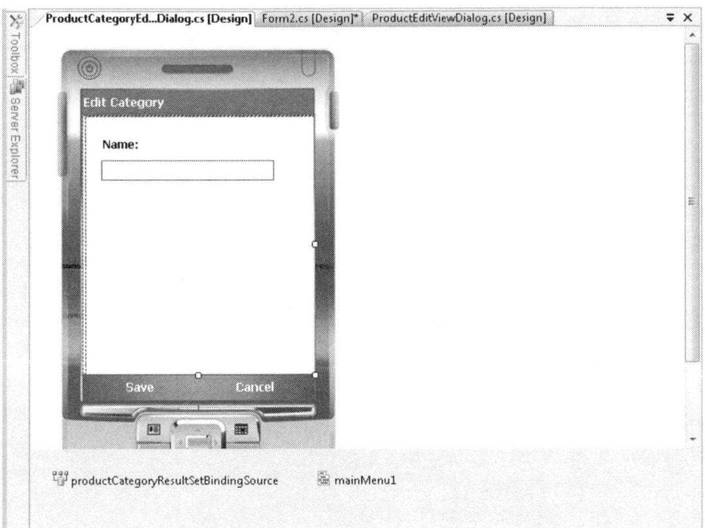

Figure 3-16 Screen layout for a details form to edit product categories

The code for this form is shown in Listing 3-8. Notice that the code that runs when the user clicks the Save button calls *EndEdit* on the *BindingSource*, just as you did by using a *DataTable* data source. However, this time the changes are applied directly to the database, so if there is an error, you will get a *System.Data.SqlServerCe.SqlCeException*, not an exception from *System.Data*.

Listing 3-8 Code for the Form to Edit Product Categories That Uses a *SqlCeResultSet* Data Source

```
using System;
using System.ComponentModel;
using System.Windows.Forms;

namespace MobileDevelopersHandbook
{
    public partial class ProductCategoryEditViewDialog : Form
    {
        private static ProductCategoryEditViewDialog defaultInstance;

        public static ProductCategoryEditViewDialog Instance
            (System.Windows.Forms.BindingSource bindingSource)
        {
            System.Windows.Forms.Cursor.Current =
                System.Windows.Forms.Cursors.WaitCursor;
            if ((defaultInstance == null))
            {
                defaultInstance = new
                    MobileDevelopersHandbook.ProductCategoryEditViewDialog();
                defaultInstance.productCategoryResultSetBindingSource
                    .DataSource = bindingSource;
            }
            defaultInstance.productCategoryResultSetBindingSource
                    .Position = bindingSource.Position;
```

```
            System.Windows.Forms.Cursor.Current =
                System.Windows.Forms.Cursors.Default;
            return defaultInstance;
        }

        public ProductCategoryEditViewDialog()
        {
            InitializeComponent();
        }

        private void cancelMenuItem_Click(object sender, EventArgs e)
        {
            this.productCategoryResultSetBindingSource.CancelEdit();
            this.DialogResult = DialogResult.Cancel;
        }

        private const int SSCE_M_NULLINVALID = 25005;

        private void saveMenuItem_Click(object sender, EventArgs e)
        {
            try
            {
                this.productCategoryResultSetBindingSource.EndEdit();
                // Close the form
                this.DialogResult = DialogResult.OK;
            }
            // If your underlying DataSource is a SqlCeResultSet, EndEdit
            // causes changes to be applied to the database, hence you will
            // get a SqlCeException if a constraint is violated, or some
            // other error.
            catch (System.Data.SqlServerCe.SqlCeException sqlEx)
            {
                if (sqlEx.NativeError == SSCE_M_NULLINVALID)
                {
                    MessageBox.Show("You must specify a name");
                }
                else
                    throw;
            }
        }
    }
}
```

All that remains is to program event handlers for the *Click* event on the *DataGrid* to display the new form to edit an existing record and for the *Click* event on the New menu option to edit the details of a new record:

```
private void newMenuItemMenuItem_Click(object sender, EventArgs e)
{
    productCategoryResultSetBindingSource.AddNew();
    ShowEditDialog();
}

private void productCategoryResultSetDataGrid_Click
    (object sender, EventArgs e)
        {
            ShowEditDialog();
        }

private void ShowEditDialog()
{
    ProductCategoryEditViewDialog productcategoryEditViewDialog =
        ProductCategoryEditViewDialog.Instance(
            this.productCategoryResultSetBindingSource);
    productcategoryEditViewDialog.ShowDialog();
}
```

Advanced Data Binding

Before leaving the subject of data binding, we discuss how you solve two common requirements:

- Bind a *ComboBox* or *ListBox* to a list of records so that they display details from a lookup table (perhaps a description or name), but store the index of the selected record when an item in the list is selected
- Create a master–detail UI, where selection of a record in one list causes a secondary grid or list to show only records from a different table that are related to the selected record

Data-Binding Combo Boxes to a Lookup Table

It is quite common to store in one table the ID of a record in another table. For example, a *SalesOrder* record might contain a *CustomerID* and a *ProductID*. In the fictional example you have been developing in this chapter, each *Product* record contains the *ProductCategoryID*.

On the details forms, you can view and edit *Product* records, and on both forms that it created for you, it displays the *ProductCategoryID* field. Wouldn't it be better to display the product category *name* in a drop-down list on the ProductEditViewDialog form but still to store the correct *ProductCategoryID* when the user makes a selection? Fortunately, this is quite easy to do.

The *ComboBox* and *ListBox* controls have five properties you can use in this scenario:

- *DataSource* Set the *DataSource* to the data source that provides the data that is displayed in the list's control.
- *DataMember* If the *DataSource* is a compound object such as a *DataSet*, set this property to the particular *DataTable* that provides the data.
- *DisplayMember* Set the *DisplayMember* to the name of the field that is displayed in the drop-down list.
- *ValueMember* Set the *ValueMember* to the name of the field that supplies the value for items in the control. Although the user cannot see this field in the list, when the user selects an item, the *Value* property of the control is set to the value of the selected item.
- *SelectedValue* The *SelectedValue* property exposes the value of the selected item. In the (Data Bindings) section of the Properties dialog box, you can data-bind this property to an item in a data source.

To display the list of items, use a data source that exposes the data items you require, set the *DataSource* and (if needed) *DataMember* properties to the source table, and set the *DisplayMember* and *ValueMember* properties to fields in that table. To do this in the sample application, do the following:

1. Drag a *BindingSource* from the Toolbox onto the component tray under the ProductEditViewDialog form (in Designer view). Rename it to productCategoryBindingSource. Set the *DataSource* property of this component to the *ProductCategoryResultSet* you created earlier.
2. Add the following code to the *Load* event handler for the form to create a new instance of the *ProductCategoryResultSet*, and bind the *BindingSource* to it:

```
productCategoryResultSet =
    new MyResultSetsResultSets.ProductCategoryResultSet();
productCategoryResultSet.Bind(this.productCategoryBindingSource);
```

3. Delete the *TextBox* that currently exists to allow the user to enter the *ProductCategoryID*. Drag a *ComboBox* there instead.
4. Set the *DataSource* property of the *ComboBox* to *productCatgoryBindingSource*, set *DisplayMember* to *Name*, and set *ValueMember* to *ProductCategoryID*.

Now you must take the *SelectedValue* of this *ComboBox* and write it away into the *Product* record that this form is editing. To do this, use the (Data Bindings) section of the Properties dialog box to bind the *SelectedValue* property to the *ProductCategoryID* field in the *productBindingSource*—the original *BindingSource* on this form that binds to the *Product* record being edited (see Figure 3-17).

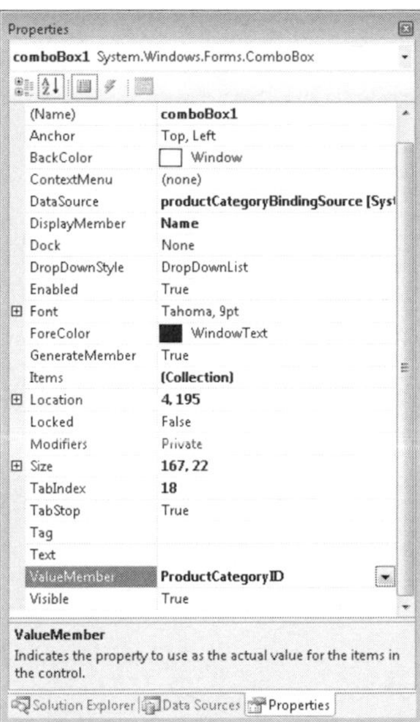

Figure 3-17 Setting properties to display records from one data source and store selected values in another

Creating a Master–Detail GUI

A master–detail display is one in which selecting a record from a master category list results in a different list of related records to be automatically filtered to show only relevant child records. The second list could be on the same form or on another one. For example, in the simple database you have been working with, if you show a list of product categories, when the user selects a category, you want to show only products in that product category.

Master–Details with *DataSets* This is one of those occasions when the relative complexity of a *DataSet* object compared to a *SqlCeResultSet* makes your job a little bit easier. To show why, create a new project, copy in the database you have been working with throughout this chapter, and then use Server Explorer to open each table and enter a few records. Create a typed *DataSet* with the *ProductCategory* and *Product* tables in it, just as you did before. Now drag the *ProductCategory* table from the Data Sources dialog box onto a form to create a *DataGrid*. You now have a *DataGrid* that displays all the product categories.

Creating the dependent child list is very simple. Remember that foreign key you created between the *ProductCategory* and *Product* tables that is shown in the Data Designer as a link between the two tables (as shown in Figure 3-8)? That foreign key is represented in the *DataSet* object, and you can make use of that now to generate the correct data binding, If you expand the *ProductCategory* table in the Data Sources dialog box, you can see that the *DataSet* already represents the parent–child relationship between the two tables because it shows the *Product* table as a child of *ProductCategory*:

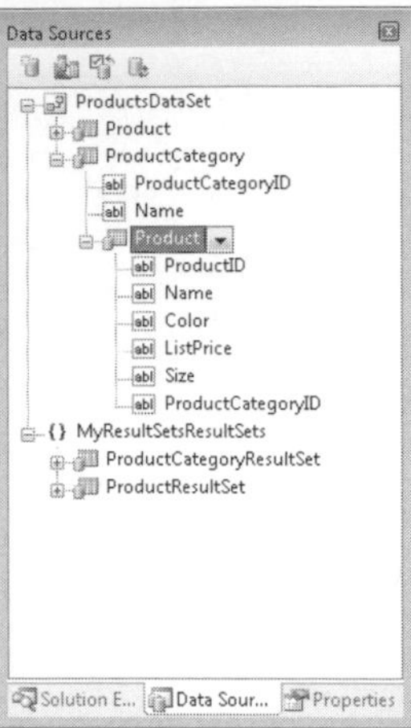

All you have to do is drag the child *Product* table (selecting *DataGrid* for the control to generate) from the Data Sources dialog box onto your form, and you have the functionality you require. The tools create a *DataGrid* on the form that is bound to a *BindingSource*. That *BindingSource*, called *product_productCategory_FKBindingSource*, is configured so that its *DataSource* property is the *productCategoryBindingSource* (which is bound to the *DataSet* instance, of course), but its *DataMember* property is set to *Product_ProductCategory_FK*—the foreign key between the *ProductCategory* and *Product* tables. This gives you the functionality you want, as shown in Figure 3-18.

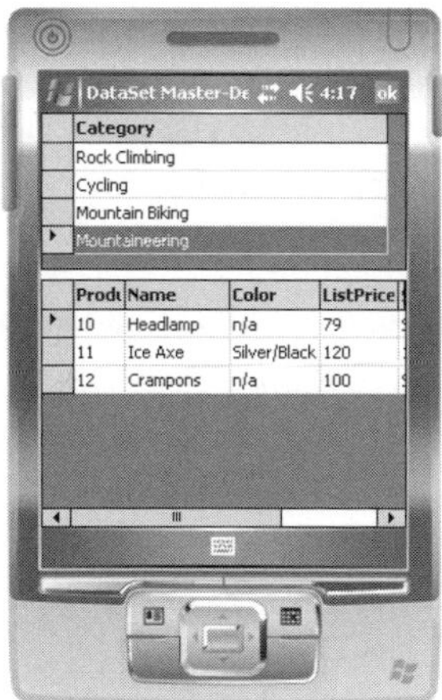

Figure 3-18 Master–detail: Selecting a category in the top grid, which automatically shows related records in the lower grid

Of course, you don't have to use the visual tools to create this kind of relationship. But if you want to learn the code required to achieve it, the easiest way is to create a tool-generated example such as this and then look at the code the tools have generated.

Master–Detail with *SqlCeResultSets* If you are using *SqlCeResultSet* objects, you have to write some code to handle this relationship. Create a typed *SqlCeResultSet* containing both the *ProductCategory* and *Product* tables, and extend each strongly typed *SqlCeResultSet* with a new constructor and custom *Open* methods as you did earlier in this chapter (as shown in Listing 3-7). Then drag the *ProductCategory* from the Data Sources dialog box onto the form to create the first *DataGrid*. You can also drag the *Product* table onto the form to create the second *DataGrid*, but initially it will contain all the *Product* records unfiltered.

You must create a new *SqlCeResultSet* instance containing only the required product records each time the user clicks a new category in the Product categories grid. To do this, write an event handler for the *CellChanged* event of the *productCategoryDataGrid* containing code to dispose of the old *SqlCeResultSet* instance and generate a new one containing only *Product* records in the required *ProductCategory*. You can take advantage of the index you created on the *ProductCategoryID* field at the beginning of this chapter. The complete code for this is shown in Listing 3-9.

Listing 3-9 Code to Manually Re-Create the *SqlCeResultSet* for the Required Child Records in a Master–Detail GUI

```
using System;
using System.Data.SqlServerCe;
using System.Windows.Forms;

namespace MobileDevelopersHandbook
{
    public partial class ResultSetForm : Form
    {
        private MyResultSetsResultSets.ProductResultSet productResultSet;
        private MyResultSetsResultSets.ProductCategoryResultSet
            productCategoryResultSet;

        public ResultSetForm()
        {
            InitializeComponent();
        }

        private void ResultSetForm_Load(object sender, EventArgs e)
        {
            // NOTE: Lines here were marked TODO: and have now been deleted
            // to remove the default AutoFill for ProductResultSet.

            // Default AutoFill for ProductCategoryResultSet
            productCategoryResultSet = new
                MyResultSetsResultSets.ProductCategoryResultSet();
            productCategoryResultSet.Bind(
                this.productCategoryResultSetBindingSource);

            // Set up the child records data source.
            SetProductResultSet();
        }
```

```
        private void productCategoryResultSetDataGrid_CurrentCellChanged(
            object sender, EventArgs e)
        {
            // Save reference to existing result set.
            SqlCeResultSet oldRS = this.productResultSet;

            // User has clicked the grid.
            SetProductResultSet();

            // Dispose of the redundant SqlCEResultSet.
            oldRS.Dispose();
        }

        private void SetProductResultSet()
        {
            // Find the ProductCategoryID of the selected record.
            int prodCatID =
            (int)((RowView)this.productCategoryResultSetBindingSource.Current)
                .UpdatableRecord["ProductCategoryID"];

            // Create new result set using the "custom" constructor.
            productResultSet = new
                MyResultSetsResultSets.ProductResultSet(false);

            // Filter on the index created earlier, and select only the
            // required ProductCategoryID.
            productResultSet.Open("ProductCategoryID_idx",
                prodCatID, prodCatID);

            // Bind the BindingSource.
            productResultSet.Bind(this.productResultSetBindingSource);
        }
    }
}
```

You should be careful to dispose of unused *SqlCeResultSet* objects (and also *SqlCeCommand* and *SqlCeConnection* objects). In Listing 3-9, the code in the *CurrentCellChanged* event handler saves a reference to the existing instance of the *productResultSet* before calling the *SetProductResultSet* method that generates a new instance that is filtered on the correct *ProductCategoryID* key value. When that call returns, the code in *CurrentCellChanged* disposes of the original instance that is no longer required.

For a working example demonstrating these techniques, see the MasterDetail sample in the downloadable code on this book's companion Web site.

Formatting Data in *DataGrid* Controls

All the instruction in this chapter has focused on how to bind controls to data, but nothing has been said about how to affect the appearance of data in the control.

The *DataGrid* control has many properties that affect the way users select cells, whether column and row headers are displayed, and what colors are used for the headers, background, and rows, including *BackColor*, *BackgroundColor*, *ColumnHeadersVisible*, *Font*, *ForeColor*, *GridLineColor*, *RowHeadersVisible*, and others. The most important property, however, is *TableStyles*, which exposes a collection of *DataGridTableStyle* objects.

By default, the collection returned by the *TableStyles* property does not contain any *DataGridTableStyle* objects. To create a set of customized views, complete the following steps:

1. Create a *DataGridTableStyle*.
2. Set the *MappingName* of the grid table object to the name of the *DataTable*.
3. Add *DataGridColumnStyle* objects, one for each grid column you want to show, to the *GridColumnStylesCollection* returned by the *GridColumnStyles* property.
4. Set the *MappingName* of each *DataGridColumnStyle* to the *ColumnName* of a *DataColumn*.
5. Add the *DataGridTableStyle* object to the collection returned by the *TableStyles* property.

Although you can do this programmatically, Visual Studio 2005 provides tools to do this graphically in the Forms Designer. To start, click the ellipsis button shown for the *TableStyles* property in the Properties dialog box. Next, click the Add button to add a *DataGridTableStyle*. If the underlying data source is a *DataSet*, you must set the *MappingName* to the name of the *DataTable* that you are displaying in the grid, but if it is a *SqlCeResultSet*, leave *MappingName* blank as shown here:

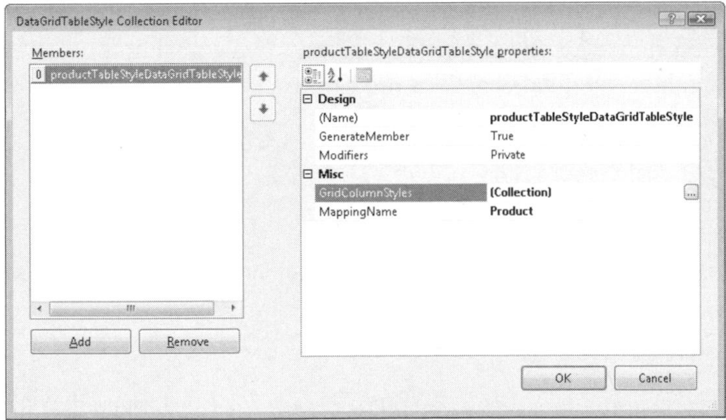

Next, you must define *DataGridColumnStyle* objects for each column you want to display. To start, select the *GridColumnStyle* property and click the ellipsis button to start the *DataGridColumnStyle* editor. Click Add to create a new object for each column you want to display. Set the *MappingName* to the name of the column in the *DataTable* or *SqlCeResultSet*, set the *HeaderText* and the *Width* as shown in the following example, and you are done.

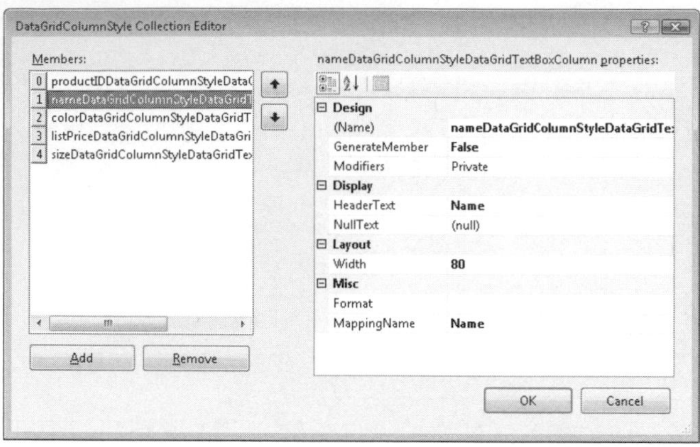

Note that you can create columns only of type *DataGridTextBoxColumn*, which is different from the *DataGrid* in the full .NET Framework, which supports additional column types, such as columns optimized for displaying numeric values and columns that include *CheckBox*, *Button*, or *LinkLabel* controls. The ability to customize data display in a *DataGrid* has been a much requested feature, and in .NET Compact Framework 2.0 SP1 the *DataGrid* supports custom *DataColumn* objects. You can download a sample that shows you how from *blogs.msdn.com/netcfteam/attachment/583542.ashx*. (Rename the download file to have an .msi extension, and install it on a computer that has .NET Compact Framework 2.0 SP1 installed.)

Persisting Data Without a Database

SQL Server CE is a good choice for storing and organizing your data, but it is not the only choice. There are two lighter-weight alternatives you can use:

- You can create your own *DataSet* and use its built-in capability to persist itself as an XML file.
- You can use a custom object and use XML serialization to save its state to a file.

Persisting to a file is often used for simple data records such as the settings for an application.

Serializing *DataSet* Objects

You can add a *DataSet* to your project and use the Data Designer to design tables in it, or you can create a *DataSet* programmatically. Then you store your data in it in the same way you do using a *DataSet* that you created by dragging tables from a SQL Server CE database. You can also simply use a *DataTable* object rather than a *DataSet* because that too supports the methods required to persist and restore data.

When you must save the data, use the *WriteXml* method. With the different overrides, you can save to a file, a stream, a *TextWriter*, or an *XmlWriter*; for example:

```
private void WriteXmlToFile(DataSet thisDataSet)
{
    // Create a file name to write to.
    string filename = "XmlDoc.xml";

    // Write to the file with the WriteXml method; write the schema also.
    thisDataSet.WriteXml(filename, XmlWriteMode.WriteSchema);
}
```

There are three options for the *XmlWriteMode* enumeration:

- **DiffGram** Writes the entire *DataSet* as a DiffGram, including original and current values. To generate a DiffGram containing only changed values, call *GetChanges*, and then call *WriteXml* as a DiffGram on the returned *DataSet*.
- **IgnoreSchema** Writes the current contents of the *DataSet* as XML data, without an Extensible Schema Definition (XSD) schema.
- **WriteSchema** Writes the current contents of the *DataSet* as XML data with the relational structure as inline XSD schema.

Many overrides of *WriteXml* take only the first parameter, which is equivalent to *XmlWriteMode.IgnoreSchema*. You should write the schema if you have to reload the data into an untyped *DataSet*, and then the reload will be much more efficient because the schema will not have to be inferred from the structure of the incoming data.

To reload the data, use *ReadXml*:

```
using System.Data;
…

private DataSet newDataSet;

private void ReadXmlFromFile()
{
    // Set the file name to read from.
    string filename = "XmlDoc.xml";

    // Create a new DataSet.
    newDataSet = new DataSet("New DataSet");

    // Read the XML document into the DataSet.
    newDataSet.ReadXml(xmlFilename);
}
```

Serializing Objects

One of the new features in .NET Compact Framework 2.0 is support for XML serialization. You can use XML serialization to persist the public properties of any class object, a useful technique not only for persisting an object to a file (as described in this section) but also for serializing objects prior to exchanging them with another program over a network. The sample described here called XMLSerialization, also available in the downloadable code on the book's companion Web site, shows how to use XML serialization.

The test application is for smartphones and simply draws some text on the screen using different colors and fonts (see Figure 3-19).

Figure 3-19 Screen of test application that stores graphics settings in a file stored using XML serialization

> **Tip** The sample application also uses a *DataSource* that is bound to an object—the *Settings* file. Although we do not say much in this chapter about creating data sources from an object (actually, there's not much to say), you can see an example in the XMLSerialization sample application, in the GUI for the *SettingsForm*.

The application code has a class called *Settings* in which you save the *Font Name* and *Size* and the background and foreground colors. At its simplest, this class just exposes the required public properties and is implemented as a singleton, as shown in Listing 3-10.

Listing 3-10 Basic Class to Store Settings

```
using System;
using System.Collections.Specialized;
using System.Text;
using System.Xml.Serialization;

namespace MobileDevelopersHandbook
{
    public class Settings
    {
        /// <summary>
        /// Static private member stores ref to single instance of this class.
        /// </summary>
        private static Settings thisClass = null;

        public static Settings Instance
        {
            get { return Settings.GetSettings(); }
        }

        /// <summary>
        /// Static method returns single instance of the settings class.
        /// </summary>
        /// <returns>single instance of the Settings class</returns>
        private static Settings GetSettings()
        {
            if (Settings.thisClass == null)
            {
                // Create instance of the class.
                Settings.thisClass = new Settings();
            }
            return Settings.thisClass;
        }

        #region Properties
        /// <summary>
        /// stores the individual settings
        /// </summary>
        private ListDictionary settingsHashTable = new ListDictionary();

        /// <summary>
        /// Font for text display
        /// </summary>
        public String Fontname
        {
            get
            {
                return (String)settingsHashTable["FontName"];
            }
            set
            {
                settingsHashTable["FontName"] = value;
            }
        }
```

```
        /// <summary>
        /// Size of font used for display on learn
        /// </summary>
        public int FontSize
        {
            get
            {
                return (int)settingsHashTable["FontSize"];
            }
            set
            {
                settingsHashTable["FontSize"] = value;
            }
        }

        /// <summary>
        /// color for background
        /// </summary>
        public System.Drawing.Color BackgroundColor
        {
            get
            {
                return (Color)settingsHashTable["BackgroundColor"];
            }
            set
            {
                settingsHashTable["BackgroundColor"] = value;
            }
        }

        /// <summary>
        /// color for text
        /// </summary>
        public System.Drawing.Color TextColor
        {
            get
            {
                return (Color)settingsHashTable["TextColor"];
            }
            set
            {
                settingsHashTable["TextColor"] = value;
            }
        }
        #endregion
    }
}
```

To serialize this to XML, add a static method that simply creates an instance of *XMLSerializer* and then calls the *Serialize* method; for example:

```
private static readonly String settingsFileName
        = "MobileDeveloperHandbookSettings.xml";

   /// <summary>
/// Save the settings to the persistence file.
/// </summary>
public static void SaveSettings()
{
XmlSerializer serializer =
                  new XmlSerializer(typeof(Settings), "http://tempuri.org/");
string _path = Path.GetDirectoryName
                  (System.Reflection.Assembly.GetExecutingAssembly().
                   GetName().CodeBase);
TextWriter writer = new StreamWriter(_path + "\\" +
                  settingsFileName, false);
serializer.Serialize(writer, Settings.Instance);
writer.Close();
}
```

Tip Creating an *XMLSerializer* like this is quite an expensive operation because it uses reflection to analyze the object to be serialized. It is better to create the serializer object only once in your application and then cache it to be reused next time you need it. See the XMLSerialization sample application in the downloadable code for this chapter on the book's companion Web site for an example of how to do this.

Note that the full .NET Framework software development kit (SDK) provides the Sgen.exe tool to generate serialization assemblies you can use in your full .NET Framework applications. Unfortunately, this tool does not create assemblies for the .NET Compact Framework.

The reverse operation to deserialize from the XML file is somewhat similar. In the sample application, this code is run when the *Settings* class is first instantiated, which is the obvious time you would want to deserialize settings that were stored away to file last time the application was run:

```
string _path = Path.GetDirectoryName
   (System.Reflection.Assembly.GetExecutingAssembly().GetName().CodeBase);

if (File.Exists(_path + "\\" + settingsFileName))
{
    XmlSerializer serializer =
        new XmlSerializer(typeof(Settings), "http://tempuri.org/");
    TextReader reader = new StreamReader(_path + "\\" + settingsFileName);
    try
    {
        Settings myClass = (Settings)serializer.Deserialize(reader);
```

```
        Settings.thisClass = myClass;
    }
    catch (InvalidOperationException ex)
    {
         System.Windows.Forms.MessageBox.Show(
             "Error reading Settings file: " + ex.Message);
    }
    finally
    {
        reader.Close();
    }
```

Serializing *System.Color*

If you try to run this code now, you will get an error. The problem is with the two public properties that expose colors. *System.Color* does not support XML serialization, and you must add some functionality to implement custom serialization for these colors.

First, create two methods to serialize a color to a string and to handle the reverse for deserialization:

```
public string SerializeColor(Color color)
{
        return string.Format("{0}:{1}:{2}",
                color.R, color.G, color.B);
}

public Color DeserializeColor(string color)
{
        int r, g, b;

        string[] pieces = color.Split(new char[] { ':' });

        r = int.Parse(pieces[0]);
        g = int.Parse(pieces[1]);
        b = int.Parse(pieces[2]);

        return Color.FromArgb(r, g, b);
}
```

Next, put an *XmlIgnore* attribute on the existing public properties that expose *Color* objects, and create a new property that exists solely to support serialization. You can also tell it which XML element name to use for the property using an *XmlElement* attribute. For example, you would implement the following properties to serialize and deserialize the *TextColor* property:

```
/// <summary>
/// color for text
/// </summary>
[XmlIgnore()]
public System.Drawing.Color TextColor
{
        get
        {
                return (Color)settingsHashTable["TextColor"];
        }
        set
        {
                settingsHashTable["TextColor"] = value;
        }
}
[XmlElement("TextColor")]
public string XmlTextColor
{
        get
        {
                return Settings.Instance.SerializeColor(TextColor);
        }
        set
        {
                TextColor = Settings.Instance.DeserializeColor(value);
        }
}
```

You can implement custom serialization for any complex object that does not itself support serialization. You simply must translate it to some object that does support serialization, such as the *string* used here for *System.Color*.

Summary

In this chapter, we have discussed some ways to store and organize data. You have learned how to use a SQL Server CE database in your application and how to use the tools in Visual Studio 2005 to create typed *DataSet* and *SqlCeResultSet* objects to read and manipulate data. We demonstrated how to create project data sources, which can be a *DataSet*, a *SqlCeResultSet*, or any object that exposes public properties, and also how to use the *BindingSource* control to link controls in your GUI to your data sources.

Finally, we looked at how to serialize *DataSets* by using their built-in serialization capability and how to serialize any class object using an XML serializer.

We return to SQL Server CE later in Chapter 7 and look at the powerful capabilities in this product for copying and synchronizing data from SQL Server. Before that, however, the next chapter explores how to test and debug your applications and how to implement effective exception handling.

Chapter 4

Catching Errors, Testing, and Debugging

In this chapter:

This chapter discusses how to connect to an emulator or real device so that you can debug your code during development. You learn what kind of errors can occur at run time and how you should code your applications to trap and respond to exceptions. You also learn about the different log files that the Microsoft .NET Compact Framework runtime can generate and how you can use them to diagnose specific problems, and you learn about instrumentation–how to write trace messages to the integrated development environment (IDE) or to a log file to help during development, or to log activity in a deployed application so as to provide a diagnostic tool to help support personnel.

Connecting to a Target

Before we discuss debugging techniques, best exception handling practices, and tips for troubleshooting common scenarios, you must understand how to connect Microsoft Visual Studio to the target. The target can be a real device or an emulator. We refer to *target*, *device*, and *emulator* interchangeably for the rest of this book.

Remote Tools

Visual Studio 2005 provides a single device development tool for both managed and native developers. Previously, native developers had to use the embedded Microsoft Visual C++ IDE for application development. One of the benefits of this unification is that the Remote Tools that were formerly in embedded Visual C++ but not in Visual Studio .NET 2003 are now included in Visual Studio 2005 and available to both classes of developer (see Figure 4-1).

Figure 4-1 Access Remote Tools from the Start menu, under the Visual Studio group

Remote Zoom In is very convenient for capturing bitmap screen shots from the device. An often-used tool is the *Remote Registry Editor*, which allows the developer to access and modify registry settings remotely on the target. *Remote File Viewer* is an alternative to Microsoft ActiveSync technology for remotely accessing the file system on the target, including importing and exporting. *Remote Spy* is similar to its desktop counterpart, and you can use it to browse the active windows and what messages are sent to each window handle; it is not a tool you use every day, but when you need it, it can be very handy. *Remote Process Viewer* is useful for viewing the list of processes currently running on the target, the threads they own, and the modules that each one has loaded; it can also be used to kill processes. Finally, the usefulness of *Remote Heap Walker* is limited for managed development because managed developers are not generally concerned with heap identifiers and flags for managed processes.

The Remote Tools help decrease the pain of developing on one computer (your PC) while running on another (your device). Another tool that was made available with .NET Compact Framework version 2.0 Service Pack 1 is the *Remote Performance Monitor* (RPM). The RPM is described in Chapter 5, "Understanding and Optimizing .NET Compact Framework Performance."

Device

Connection to a device is supported by ActiveSync (AS) version 4.*x* (or Microsoft Windows Mobile Device Center (WMDC) on the Windows Vista operating system as discussed in Chapter 1, ".NET Compact Framework–a Platform on the Move"). If you own a Windows Mobile–powered device, chances are you have already plugged it into your computer with the universal serial bus (USB) cable and you have used ActiveSync. Both the software and the cable ship in the box with every Windows Mobile–based device. ActiveSync allows connections by USB typically but also allows Bluetooth, infrared, and serial connections (see Figure 4-2). After the connection is established, the device can be targeted from Visual Studio.

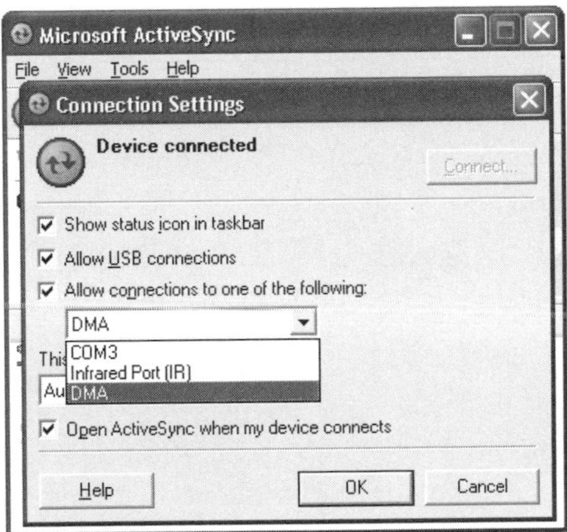

Figure 4-2 ActiveSync 4.2 Connection Settings, accessible from the File menu

In Visual Studio, you can configure the connection to a real device on the Tools menu by selecting the Options menu item. In the Options dialog box, scroll down to the Device Tools node, expand it, and select Devices. Select your chosen platform (for example, Microsoft Windows Mobile 5.0 Pocket PC), select the Device from the list (rather than the emulator), and finally click the Properties button. In the Properties dialog box, click Configure to open the Configure TCP/IP Transport dialog box, as shown in Figure 4-3.

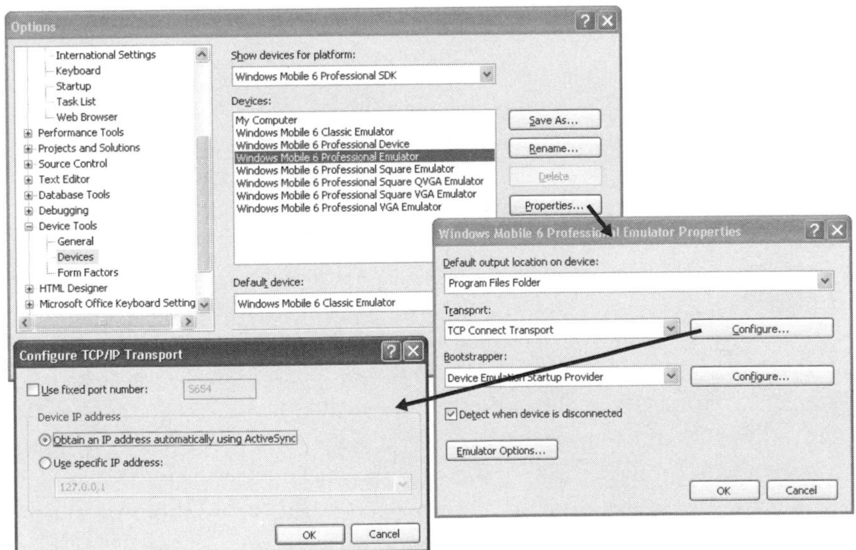

Figure 4-3 Visual Studio 2005 configuration of the device transport

By default, debugging simply works out of the box with devices connected by ActiveSync, as the dialog box in Figure 4-2 shows. When you deploy for the first time to a device that doesn't contain the .NET Compact Framework, the framework binaries are pushed to the target, and then your application follows. To install the .NET Compact Framework on your target manually, you must copy to the target the relevant .cab file (from SDK\CompactFramework under your Visual Studio installation) and run it there. Depending on the device that you use, you may see one or more security prompts. This is typical because your binaries are not signed, so make sure you watch the device to allow the binaries to run.

For devices that do not support ActiveSync, that is, some custom Microsoft Windows CE–based devices, the alternative is to connect directly over Transmission Control Protocol/Internet Protocol (TCP/IP) as follows:

1. First, prepare the device for the connection by copying the three .exe files and two .dll files from Program Files\Common Files\Microsoft Shared\CoreCon\1.0\Target\wce400\<*CPU*> on your development computer to the Windows folder of your device.
2. Run the Conmanclient2.exe file on the device (it is one of the three files copied in the preceding step).
3. Then, in the Configure TCP/IP Transport dialog box (shown in Figure 4-3), tell Visual Studio to connect to the IP address of the device.
4. If security is enabled on the device, you must also run cMaccept.exe on the device before attempting to connect from Visual Studio.

Emulator

Connecting to the emulator, like connecting to a device over ActiveSync or WMDC, simply works out of the box. Visual Studio 2005 includes emulators, for Windows Mobile 2003 Pocket PC and Smartphone. To use Windows Mobile 5.0 emulators you must download the free software development kit (SDK). You can download many other emulator images for specific device form factors. Emulators are released independently of the development environment. You can download them from the Microsoft Download Center or follow links from the Windows Mobile Developer Center Web site at *www.microsoft.com/windowsmobile/developers/default.mspx*. Emulators from other vendors (for example, from Palm) are available for specific devices, and you can visit the vendor's Web site to obtain those.

In Figure 4-3, observe how there are emulator options in the Options dialog box. If you select one and then click Properties, a dialog box similar to the one in the figure appears. You may notice some differences in the appearance of the dialog box, the main one being that an additional transport is available called DMA Transport. *DMA* stands for Direct Memory Access, and it is the new default transport in Visual Studio 2005—think of it as direct Component Object Model (COM) communication between processes without having to go through TCP/IP. Not having to go through TCP/IP means that connections are faster and no additional configuration is required when you are not connected to the Internet, for example, a loopback adapter that was required with Visual Studio .NET 2003.

You can select the emulator you want to deploy when you run the project (for example, by pressing F5), or in the Options dialog box (see Figure 4-3), or from the Tools menu (select Connect To Device), or in the project properties window, or by using the Device toolbar in Visual Studio. You can see the last two options in Figure 4-4.

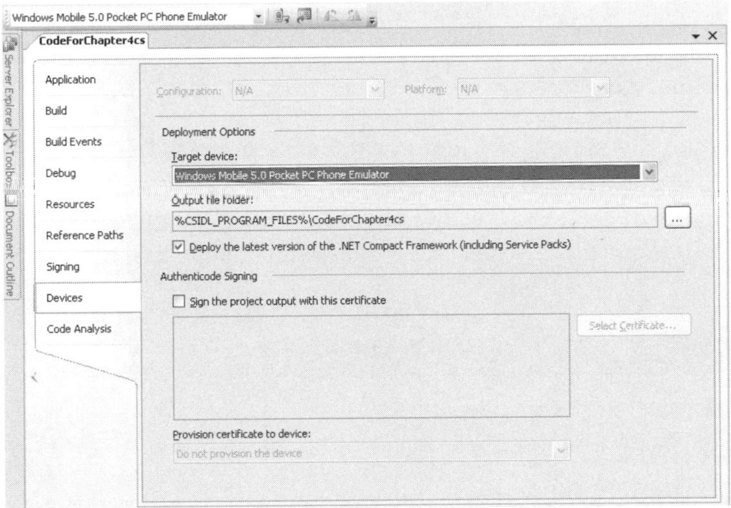

Figure 4-4 Selecting the emulator by using the project properties window or the Device toolbar

Yet another way to start an emulator is by using the Device Emulator Manager. You can start this tool from the Tools menu, as shown in Figure 4-5.

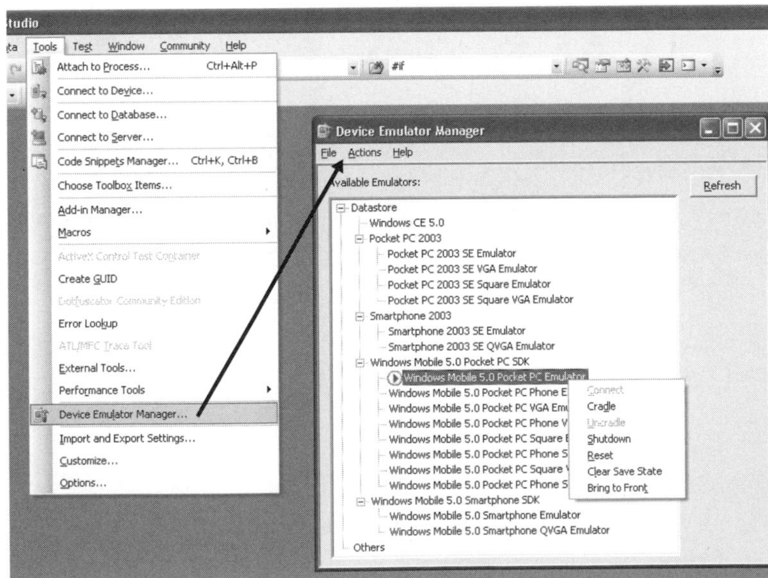

Figure 4-5 The Device Emulator Manager and the Tools menu (frequently referred to in this chapter).

One of the advantages of the Device Emulator Manager is that once an emulator is launched, you can cradle it by using the Actions menu. With the cradling feature, you can test your applications as if they were running on a real device with an ActiveSync connection. Also, when cradled, the emulator can connect to the Internet using the computer's Internet connection. You can also use the ActiveSync Explore option to open an explorer window and copy files to and from the emulator. Another benefit of the Device Emulator Manager is that you can install it standalone on a computer that does not have Visual Studio installed, and this can be useful for testing and demo purposes.

Finally, explore the emulator options. On the emulator's File menu, select Configure to open the Emulator Properties dialog box, as shown in Figure 4-6. One useful option is the Shared Folder setting, which allows you to treat a folder from a desktop computer as a Storage Card folder on the device, thus providing easy access to files sitting on the desktop computer from the device.

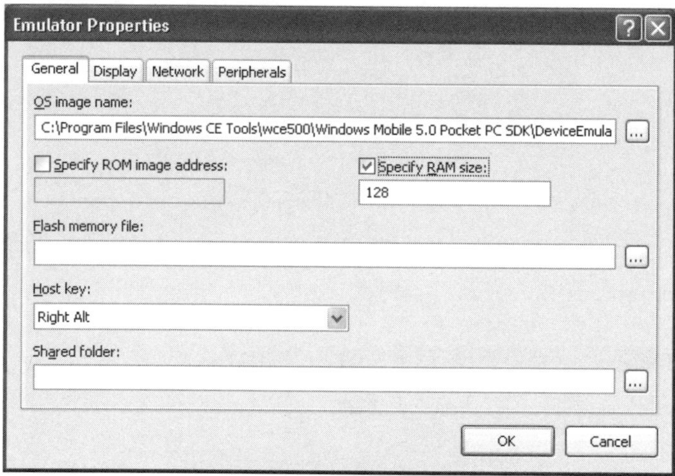

Figure 4-6 Emulator Properties dialog box

By downloading the Windows Mobile 6 SDK, you will also get Device Emulator V2 that among other useful features is much faster than version 1. Visual Studio Code Name "Orcas" will ship with version 3 of the Device Emulator.

Command-line debugging

One of the new .NET SDK tools in .NET 2.0 is a command-line debugger for managed applications, Mdbg.exe (*msdn2.microsoft.com/en-us/library/ms229861(vs.80).aspx*). This enables debugging applications without having Visual Studio installed on the desktop computer. Service Pack 1 of version 2.0 of the .NET Compact Framework includes an extension for Mdbg called MdbgNetcf.dll that you can use to debug devices from the command line. You can load the extension using the Mdbg Load command as per the documentation in the preceding link.

Command-line debugging is the only supported way to debug managed code on targets that run Windows CE 4.2 because Visual Studio 2005 does not support that platform any longer. It can also be useful in other scenarios when Visual Studio is not available. Note that command-line debugging with an emulator works only over the TCP/IP transport, not over DMA (you can select the transport in the Options dialog box, as discussed earlier in this chapter).

For more information about command-line debugging and many other debugging tips and tricks, see David Kline's blog at *blogs.msdn.com/davidklinems/*.

Best Choice

With deployment to either the emulator or the device being so easy, which method should a device developer choose for everyday development? There is no right or wrong answer. If you don't have a device, clearly the emulator is the only choice and it will serve its purpose well. For final quality assurance (QA) testing and user acceptance testing, a device must be used for testing the interaction model, which on the emulator, without a stylus, is not realistic enough. In debugging scenarios that involve close interaction with the hardware, a physical device is probably best and in some cases essential. When you are measuring performance, always use a device (for more on performance aspects, read Chapter 5).

An emulator serves the purpose of testing on form factors that you may not have available; for example, not everybody has a square Windows Mobile 5.0 Pocket PC, or a landscape Windows Mobile 5.0 Smartphone, or a Windows Mobile 2003 SE Pocket PC device. If your target devices include those, the emulators are good enough for your everyday developing. You can also download localized emulators in other natural languages (for example, Greek) and test on them your application if you do not have a device that supports the language you need to test against.

Finally, some developers claim that developing on the actual device is faster, that is, deployment is faster and hence development time is saved. This is true most of the time, but if you are running on a high-powered computer and have allocated large amounts of random access memory (RAM) to the emulator and, more important, you have downloaded the latest fast device emulator, that argument may not always be true.

Compile-Time Errors

In an ideal world, once the code is written, the developer would hit the Build button, and the computer would find all possible errors. Unfortunately, although compilers are getting better at identifying potential issues in the code beyond simple syntactical errors, they still cannot find all errors that may occur. The result is that after you build a project and see no errors, you will find errors when you run the application. We discuss run-time errors in the following sections, but because they are more expensive to identify and fix, you should strive to make the compiler do as much work for you as possible.

> **Troubleshooting** The compiler errors and warnings are displayed in the Error List dialog box, accessible from the View menu in Visual Studio 2005. Always start from the top down in the error and warning lists. You can double-click the description to navigate to the file and the exact line that causes the issue. Also, you can right-click the entry and select Show Error Help to show more information in the built-in Help. Finally, you can search for the exact error description (enclose it in double quotation marks) using your favorite search engine; this will bring back results that discuss the issue. In other words, you can find more information to understand the compiler error in a short period of time using different methods.

One way to take advantage of compile-time diagnostics is to ensure that warnings in addition to errors are also examined in the Error List (see Figure 4-7).

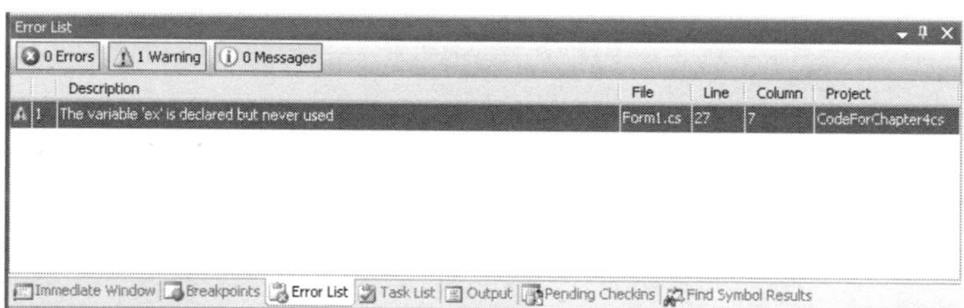

Figure 4-7 Error List dialog box

In the project properties window, accessible from the Project menu, on the Build tab, set the Warning Level to 4. Level 1 warnings are for situations in which the compiler is almost certain that there is an error but the code is syntactically and semantically correct. Level 4 warnings are for cases in which the beginner developer may have done something wrong and the compiler wants to make sure the developer acknowledges this. Level 2 and Level 3 warnings are for scenarios in between the other two extremes.

In Microsoft Visual Basic projects, the equivalent is the Compile tab, which contains a list of nine conditions for which you can change the notification for each one. We strongly advise you to configure the first three and the last five conditions to Error as per Figure 4-8.

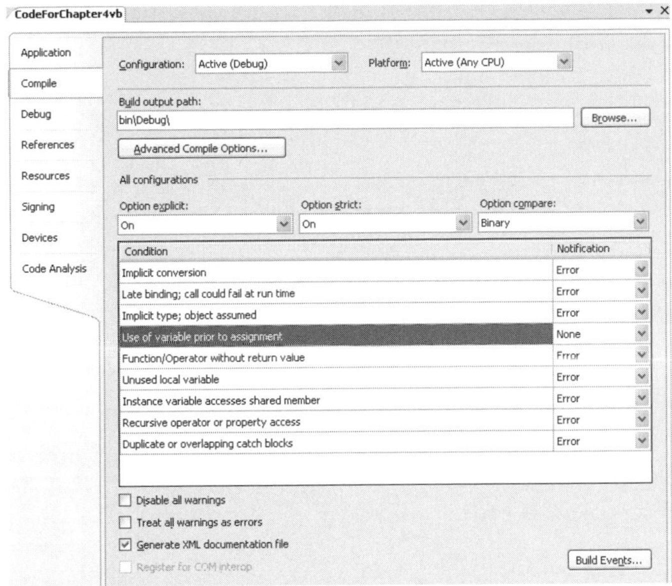

Figure 4-8 The Compile tab in the Visual Basic project properties window

If your Visual Basic project properties window does not look like the one in Figure 4-8, you are throwing away the opportunity to catch errors at compile time and potentially deferring the errors to run-time issues that are usually harder to diagnose.

You could set the fourth condition (Use Of Variable Prior To Assignment) to Warning, but it will yield so many false positives that it will probably cause you more irritation than be of help. The feature was not fully implemented to cover all possible conditions with no errors, and so, again, it can be helpful sometimes but not always. It is, however, a promise of things to come! If you decide to set the condition to Warning or Error, look at the following examples, which demonstrate the false positives to look out for:

```
Public Sub FalsePositive1()
  Dim s As String
  s = s & "why?" ' WARNING ?! - it is a valid statement
End Sub
Public Sub FalsePositive2()
  Dim o As Collection

  ' some other code here

  If o Is Nothing Then  ' WARNING ?! - just checking if it is null
    o = New Collection()
  End If
End Sub
```

```
Public Sub FalsePositive3()
  Dim s As Object
  Me.GetValueByRef(s) ' WARNING ?!
  ' I don't want to initialize s. The function will.
End Sub

' If only Visual Basic had "out" like C# has
Private Function GetValueByRef(ByRef methodAssignIt As Object) As Boolean
  methodAssignIt = "some value to return"
  Return True
End Function
```

If you have one of the Visual Studio 2005 Team Edition versions, you can take advantage of another compile-time aid called Code Analysis (formerly known as FxCop). In the project properties window, on the Code Analysis tab, select the Enable Code Analysis check box. This produces additional warning messages that generally help raise the quality of the code you write. For example, given this piece of code:

```
public class MyType
{
  public int NoOfWidgets; // CA1051

  public void DoSomething()
  {
    string s = "start";
    for (int i = 0; i < 30; i++)
    {
      s += "let's kill perf"; //CA1818
    }
  }
}
```

you get at least these two warnings:

1. CA1818 : Microsoft.Performance : Change MyType.DoSomething():Void to use StringBuilder instead of String.Concat or +=
2. CA1051 : Microsoft.Design : Make 'NoOfWidgets' private or internal (Friend in VB, public private in C++) and provide a public or protected property to access it.

Unfortunately, the warnings are not tailored to smart device projects specifically, so some warnings will be irrelevant and applicable only if you were writing code for the computer platform using the full .NET Framework. In fact, even in full .NET Framework projects, do not strive to eliminate all FxCop warning messages because they may not always be applicable to your specific goals. Having said that, there is still value to be gleaned from Code Analysis in smart device projects, so do turn on the feature, even if it is used only occasionally and just before you release code to your QA team.

Tip To suppress FxCop warning messages per method, class, and even assembly, you can use the *System.Diagnostics.CodeAnalysis.SuppressMessageAttribute*. Right-click the warning and select Suppress for the attribute to be automatically inserted. You can also turn off a specific warning completely or change it from a warning to an error by using the project properties window.

Exception Handling: Same as the Full .NET Framework

After following the advice of the preceding section, you will have done the best you can to let the compiler find errors for you before running the application. However, no application exists without issues and bugs manifesting in two ways:

- As logical errors where the application produces incorrect results and/or behavior (this is discussed in later sections of this chapter)
- As exceptions that get thrown at run time

We discuss the different kinds of run-time exceptions and how to deal with them in the following sections, but first, we talk a bit about .NET exception handling.

Essentially, exception handling with the .NET Compact Framework is identical to exception handling with the full .NET Framework. Exceptions are used for exceptional circumstances and not for normal flow of communication (where return values and events are much better and faster alternatives). Exceptions are thrown and caught in the same way using the familiar constructs of *throw*, *try*, *catch*, and *finally*. In Visual Basic, you can use the *when* keyword, and even the legacy *On Error GoTo* /*On Error Resume Next* is supported. Just because it is supported, though, doesn't mean you should use it! This advice is consistent with advice given for the desktop, and one reason is because of performance implications. When some feature has negative performance implications on the desktop, rest assured the issues will be more severe on mobile devices. For more information about performance implications, see Chapter 5.

When an exception is thrown, it passes up the call stack from method to method. Each method has an opportunity to handle the exception in a *catch* block and deal with it, or to let it bubble up, or to rethrow it, as the following piece of nonrealistic sample code shows:

```
private void SomeMethod()
{
  // 1. There is no try..catch around this call, so if an
  //    exception is thrown inside MethodThatMayThrow(),
  //    let it bubble up to be handled by some method higher
  //    up the call stack.
  this.MethodThatMayThrow();

  // 2. Rethrow.
  try
```

```
    {
      this.MethodThatMayThrow();
    }
    catch (Exception ex)
    {
      // Do something with the exception object, such as log it.
      LogException(ex);
      // or do something else such as cleanup in this code block,
      DoCleanup();
      // now rethrow to allow this exception to be handled elsewhere.
      throw;
    }

    // 3. Catch exception.
    try
    {
      this.MethodThatMayThrow();
    }
    catch (Exception ex)
    {
      // FULLY deal with this exception.
      RunSomeCodeSpecificToThisException();
    }

    // 4. Swallow.
    try
    {
      this.MethodThatMayThrow();
    }
    catch (Exception ex)
    {
      // Swallow, just so it doesn't go up to other methods.
      // DO NOT do this!
    }
  }
```

Good exception handling advice from the desktop also applies to device development. Never, ever "swallow" exceptions! When an exception occurs at run time, it has all the information you need to fix your bug: it has a message, a type, and a call stack. By swallowing an exception, you are throwing all that information away. Simply catching an exception and not doing anything about it leads to serious bugs that are hard to diagnose. Even if your application seems to run fine after swallowing an exception, it is probably hiding corrupt state that will lead to failures further down in the execution, and you will not be able to trace them back to the root cause.

> **Note** When catching an exception and then deciding to rethrow it, you should use the *throw;* statement rather than *throw ex;*. The former preserves the call stack, whereas the second resets it, thus losing important information. The code examples in this chapter follow this guideline and serve as a good example to follow in your code.

Another good practice is to catch specific exceptions. So, unlike the code example in the preceding section, the calling code should know what type of exceptions to expect and specify them precisely in the *catch* block. For example:

```
private void UpdateTimer(ref System.Threading.Timer tmr)
{
  try
  {
    tmr.Change(2000, 10000);
  }
  catch (ObjectDisposedException)
  {
    tmr = new System.Threading.Timer(...);
    tmr.Change(2000, 10000);
  }
}
```

The only reason to catch the generic *Exception* object is so that you can perform some action and then rethrow it, or because the code you are calling hasn't documented what types of exception it throws. Even in that latter case, if your calling code decides to handle exceptions typed as *Exception*, it should be able to genuinely deal with any kind of exception that is thrown! Of course, a *try* block can have more than one corresponding *catch* block, and in that case, it is common to make the last *catch* block handle the generic *Exception* type, perform some cleanup, and then rethrow (while the first *catch* block must handle the most specialized exception).

Warning In the .NET Compact Framework, some circumstances yield exception types different from the exception types for the same behavior on the full .NET Framework, contrary to the online documentation. For example, the following piece of code results in a *TargetInvocationException* exception (with the *InnerException* property set to *InvalidOperationException*) on the desktop, whereas it results in an *InvalidOperationException* exception under the .NET Compact Framework:

```
private void button2_Click(object sender, EventArgs e)
{
  Type t = this.GetType();
  MethodInfo m = t.GetMethod("DoIt");
  m.Invoke(this, null);
}

public void DoIt()
{
  throw new InvalidOperationException("my msg");
}
```

> **Warning** It is by design and as a result of footprint constraints. This becomes important when you write cross-platform code trying to keep the same codebase. You must catch both exception types so that the code can work as expected on both platforms.

In previous sections, we talked about performing cleanup. This shouldn't be confused with the *finally* code block. In earlier sections, *cleanup* refers to code that must run only when an exception is thrown, whereas in the *finally* block you place code that must run always, regardless of whether there was an exception. Once again, the advice for the desktop world holds true here: there should be more *try..finally* blocks in a program than there are *try..catch* blocks. In other words, catch an exception only if you are able to handle it, while at the same time always ensure your cleanup code will execute even if an unexpected exception or an exception that you are not catching occurs.

Now that we reviewed the exception handling construct in .NET and offered some advice, it is time to look at run-time exceptions in detail.

Runtime Exceptions

If an exception is not caught and dealt with, you have an unhandled run-time exception. Figure 4-9 shows what that may look like to the end user on a Pocket PC.

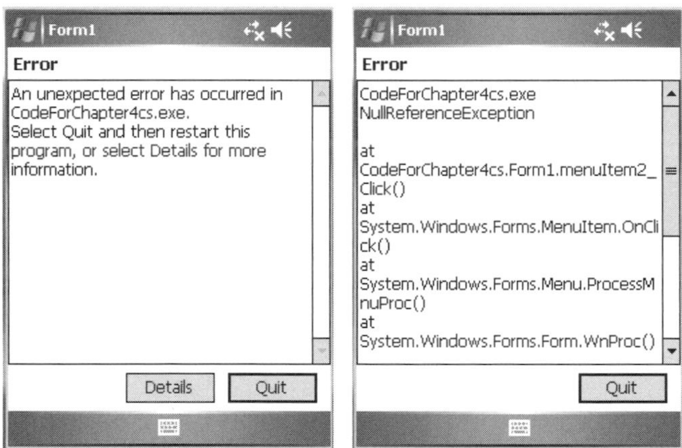

Figure 4-9 Built-in error dialog box shown for an unhandled run-time exception: the option to quit the application (left); the results after clicking Details (right)

In the section titled "Exception Handling: Same as the Full .NET Framework" earlier in this chapter, a rule was established: Never swallow exceptions. The second rule is: Run-time exceptions are something that the user should never see. In the following sections, we describe how to follow the rule by discussing the following:

- How to debug and find the cause of an exception
- Why any unhandled exception is the developer's fault
- How to avoid the exception being thrown in the first place
- How to deal with the exception if it is unavoidable that it will get thrown
- Global exception handling, the hard way

If you noted the advice earlier in the chapter never to swallow exceptions, it is easy to deduce that unhandled run-time exceptions should never occur.

Diagnosing the Cause of the Exception

Although the end user should never see unhandled run-time exceptions, as discussed in the next section, a regular developer will see quite a few exceptions while debugging and testing applications.

Typically, a developer writes code, makes sure it compiles, and then runs the project in Visual Studio with the debugger attached by pressing the F5 key (or selecting Start Debug on the Debug menu). If while the code is executing on the target, an exception gets thrown, the debugger breaks in Visual Studio in the code file and on the exact line that caused the exception to be thrown. For example, if you observe a *NullReferenceException* on the second line in the following piece of code, it is easy to deduce that you forgot to initialize *obj*, and it is easy to rectify; for example, *obj = new SomeClass();*:

```
...
SomeType obj = null;
obj.SomeMethod();  // NullReferenceException
...
```

Here is another example. The following code causes an *InvalidCastException*, and the debugger stopped on the problem line, as shown in Figure 4-10.

```
private void AnotherMethod(SomeClass obj)
{
  ((ISomeInterface)obj).DoIt();
}
```

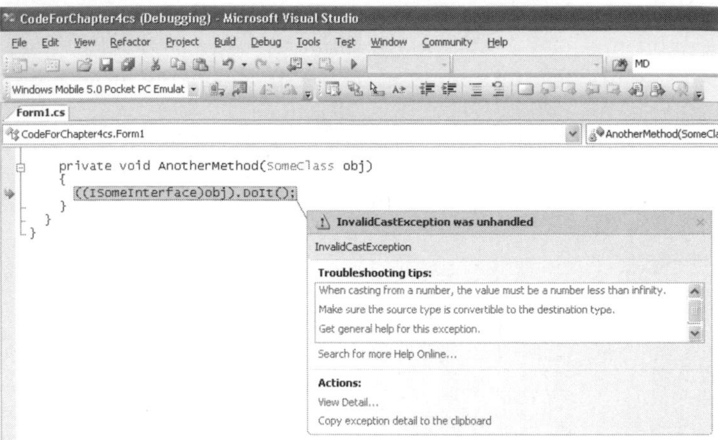

Figure 4-10 An unhandled exception while attached to the debugger that goes straight to the offending line of code

Just by looking at the name of the exception and the line of code, oftentimes you can make a "guesstimate" as to where the problem is. In some cases, though, further investigation is required. For example, in the preceding example code, you may guess that *SomeClass* does not implement the *ISomeInterface* interface. Based on that assumption, the code can change to the following, but it still throws an exception:

```
private void AnotherMethod(SomeClass obj)
{
  ISomeInterface i = obj as ISomeInterface;
  if (i != null)
  {
    i.DoIt(); // still throws here!
  }
  else
  {
    // Do something else!
  }
}
```

Because the same exception is still thrown at the same line, it should be clear that the exception is actually coming from somewhere deeper, and in this case the *DoIt* method itself.

> **Tip** This simplified example demonstrates how joining multiple lines of code into one line is not clever and instead may hinder debuggability. It is best to split such lines, which also aids readability.

The *DoIt* method and the *SomeClass* type reside in an external library, and hence the debugger breaks in the line of code that makes the call. However, you could have identified that the first time without any code changes simply by looking at the call stack. When the debugger stopped on the line of code farther up in the first example, you should have also looked at the Call Stack window, as shown in Figure 4-11.

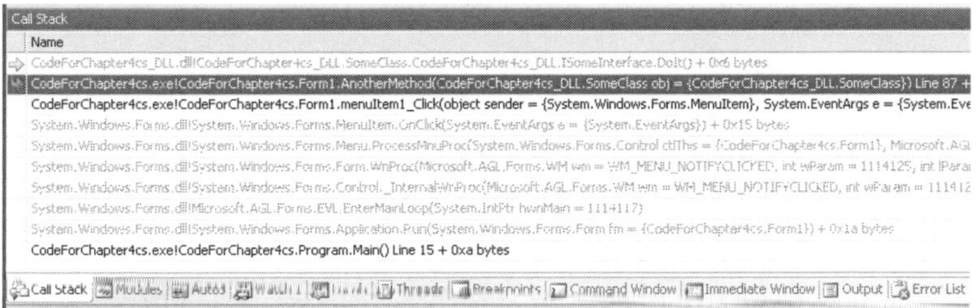

Figure 4-11 The Call Stack window, useful in debugging

Notice how the call stack shows both the lines of code in the program and also lines of code from other libraries that are unavailable. At the top of the stack, it would have been easy to spot that the *DoIt* method is the source of the exception.

> **Tip** In Figure 4-11, notice how there are other windows that can assist with debugging. You can access these on the View and Debug menus in Visual Studio. A discussion of what each does is beyond the scope of this book, but we encourage you to learn what they do by reading the Visual Studio documentation.

The call stack is also accessible on the device if you run the application without the debugger attached (for example, by executing the .exe file directly). If you run the application on the target, the built-in error dialog box that the user sees for unhandled exceptions has a Details button. Click the Details buttons to show the call stack, as shown in Figure 4-12.

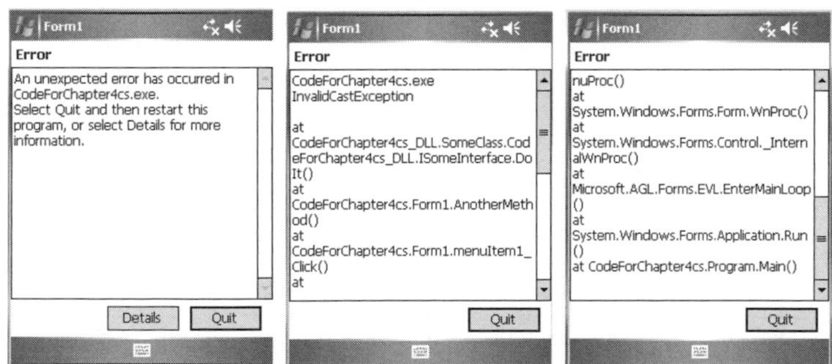

Figure 4-12 Built-in error dialog box for unhandled exceptions: the Details view showing the call stack—of no use to end users but useful for developers while debugging

In version 2.0 of the .NET Compact Framework, the call stack is also available programmatically through the *StackTrace* property of the *Exception* class. If the code is modified as follows, the output window will show the call stack (see Figure 4-13).

```
private void AnotherMethod(SomeClass obj)
{
  try
  {
    ((ISomeInterface)obj).DoIt();
  }
  catch (InvalidCastException ex)
  {
    // Log the exception to file.
    Debug.WriteLine("The stacktrace: \r\n" + ex.StackTrace);
    // Take some real recovery action!
  }
}
```

```
private void AnotherMethod(SomeClass obj)
{
  try
  {
    ((ISomeInterface)obj).DoIt();
  }
  catch (InvalidCastException ex)
  {
    // log the exception to file
    Debug.WriteLine("The stacktrace: \r\n" + ex.StackTrace);
    // take some real recovery action!
  }
}
```

```
Output
Show output from: Debug
A first chance exception of type 'System.InvalidCastException' occurred in CodeForChapter4cs_DLL.dll
The stacktrace:
at CodeForChapter4cs_DLL.SomeClass.CodeForChapter4cs_DLL.ISomeInterface.DoIt()
at CodeForChapter4cs.Form1.AnotherMethod()
at CodeForChapter4cs.Form1.menuItem1_Click()
at System.Windows.Forms.MenuItem.OnClick()
at System.Windows.Forms.Menu.ProcessMnuProc()
at System.Windows.Forms.Form.WnProc()
at System.Windows.Forms.Control._InternalWnProc()
at Microsoft.AGL.Forms.EVL.EnterMainLoop()
at System.Windows.Forms.Application.Run()
at CodeForChapter4cs.Program.Main()
```

Call Stack | Modules | Autos | Watch 1 | Locals | Threads | Breakpoints | Command Window | Immediate Window | Output | Error List

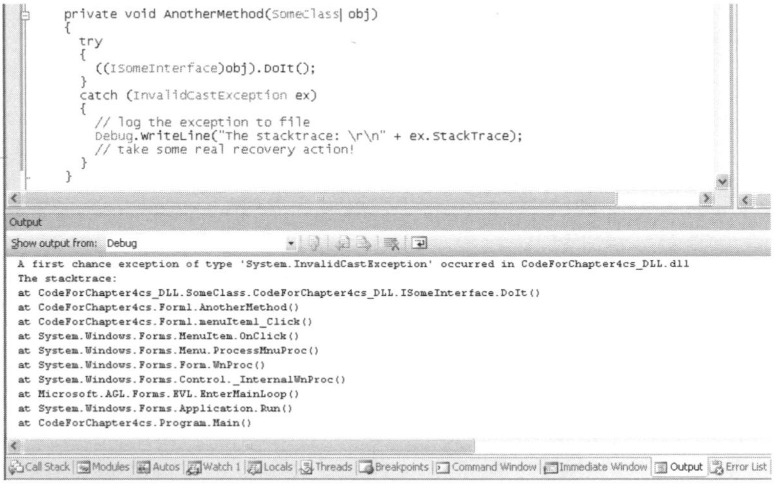

Figure 4-13 *Exception.StackTrace* that returns a string that in this case is printed to the Output window

It Is Your Fault

Now that you know how to find the cause of an exception, you must ask: Why do unhandled run-time exceptions occur? The fact is, and some find this controversial, unhandled run-time exceptions occur as a result of programmer error. With the exception of catastrophic common language runtime (CLR) exceptions such as *OutOfMemoryException*, *StackOverflowException*, or *ExecutionEngineException*, the developer should be able to write code that avoids any other exception from being thrown or at least to write code that gracefully handles the exception.

When do exceptions occur? The answer is obvious, but by emphasizing it, you can better understand the statement of the preceding paragraph. Exceptions occur as a result of a coding statement, typically a method call. Before you make a method call, you know all the different kinds of exceptions that the method can throw and you also know why they have been thrown. You know this because it is either documented (if it comes from Microsoft or a third party) or because you wrote the method in the first place (and have remembered to document what exceptions it might throw). Even for methods that are not fully documented, your testing should have stressed the method to discover what type of exceptions it may throw, and therefore allow you to write the calling code in a way that deals with them. If after deployment you discover an alternative type of exception, that simply means you didn't test thoroughly enough. Have a look at every *statement* you've written in your code and ask the question: "Could that line of code result in an exception?" If the answer is positive, rethink how you can avoid the exception.

Avoiding Exceptions Getting Thrown

Consider the following code sample:

```
private void DoSomethinginterestingWith(string path)
{
    FileStream fs = File.Open(path, FileMode.Open);
    // Do something interesting with fs.
}
```

That line of code makes assumptions—and assumptions may lead to exceptions. The code assumes that there is actually a file at the path that it is given. Indeed, if you couldn't guess this, you can get help by looking at the documentation that lists the possible exceptions that can be thrown, one of them being a *FileNotFoundException*. One naïve and wrong way to fix this is to change the code to look like this:

```
private void DoSomethinginterestingWith(string path)
{
  try
  {
    FileStream fs = File.Open(path, FileMode.Open);
    // Do something interesting with fs.
  }
  catch (FileNotFoundException ex)
  {
    // TODO deal with the invalid input
  }
}
```

This catches the exception and deals with it. However, the exception could have been avoided altogether by writing the statement the correct way, like this:

```
private void DoSomethinginterestingWith(string path)
{
  if (File.Exists(path))
  {
    FileStream fs = File.Open(path, FileMode.Open);
    // Do something interesting with fs.
  }
  else
  {
    // TODO deal with the invalid input
  }
}
```

The preceding pattern is very common. Most times, you can avoid a *try..catch* by replacing it with an *if* statement. Recall that this is also the first line of defense in the example in the preceding section with the *InvalidCastException*.

Handle the Exception and Recover Appropriately

Of course, in some scenarios it is impossible to code in a way that avoids exceptions getting thrown from method calls you make. In those cases, you have a choice to make. Either let the exception bubble up the stack if you cannot handle it or actually handle and deal with the exception. At the beginning of this section, there is an example dealing with an exception with a *Timer* that threw an *ObjectDisposedException*. Here you'll see a couple more.

You can deal with an exception by translating the exception to some change in state. The following piece of code shows how the method raises a custom event for a specific exception condition, propagates up an exception for another condition, and logs any other unexpected exception before letting it also bubble up:

```
    private void ConnectToThis(IPEndPoint ep)
    {
      Socket s = new Socket(AddressFamily.InterNetwork,
SocketType.Stream, ProtocolType.Tcp);
      try
      {
        s.Connect(ep);
      }
      catch (SocketException)
      {
        // Translate exception to own custom event.
        if (CantConnect != null)
          CantConnect(this, EventArgs.Empty);
      }
      catch (ArgumentNullException)
```

```
    {
      // IPEndPoint passed in is null. Pass it up, caller's fault.
      throw;
    }
    catch (Exception ex)
    {
      LogException(ex); //our own logging method
      throw;
    }
  }
```

Another way to handle the preceding is by using a return result:

```
  private bool ConnectToThis2(IPEndPoint ep)
  {
    Socket s = new Socket(AddressFamily.InterNetwork,
SocketType.Stream, ProtocolType.Tcp);
    try
    {
      s.Connect(ep);
      return true;
    }
    catch (SocketException)
    {
      // Translate exception to return result.
      return false;
    }
  ... ...
```

As in the first example, the exception was translated to some state change, this time notifying the calling code by returning a value. The principle is always the same: Never swallow an exception; either deal with it fully or let it bubble up so some other method has a chance to deal with it or continue to let it bubble up.

A variation of letting the exception bubble up to the other layers is wrapping it with another exception and throwing that one instead. Wrapping an existing exception with another one can be useful when you want the calling code to get a more meaningful exception than what it would do otherwise. In this case, you can either use a different framework exception that makes more sense or create your own custom one. In the previous socket example, if you did not want to translate the exception to some state, you could opt to throw your own *CantConnectException* rather than let the *SocketException* bubble up, as the following example shows:

```
private void ConnectToThis3(IPEndPoint ep)
{
  Socket s = new Socket(AddressFamily.InterNetwork,
SocketType.Stream, ProtocolType.Tcp);
  try
  {
```

```
    s.Connect(ep);
  }
  catch (SocketException ex)
  {
    // Wrap existing exception with more descriptive one.
    throw new CantConnectException(ex); //Nest the existing exception.
  }
... ...
```

Always remember that exceptions are not an alternative to events and return values for communicating between methods. Only throw an exception (your own or an existing one) if there is nothing sensible for the method to do instead. When you are certain that throwing an exception is the right action but cannot decide if you should throw an existing one or your own, throw the existing one.

Protecting the Boundaries (or Global Exception Handling, the Hard Way)

By examining your code statements and method calls, you can avoid exceptions altogether (that is, use a conditional instead), deal with them (that is, translate the .NET exception to some meaningful state in your business logic), or let them bubble up. If you let an exception pass up the call stack and no method handles it eventually, what is the result? The result is an unhandled exception that the user sees, which is what you want to eliminate. You can make sure users do not see unhandled exceptions by following the guidance in this section.

Some methods are special in that they are the ones that "protect the boundaries." Boundary methods are candidates for being the root method in a call stack:

- An event handler of a graphical user interface (GUI) control, for example, a button click. These protect the user interface (UI) boundary; in other words, they are the entry points of your main UI thread. An exception that escapes one of these methods (one that bubbles up right out of the top of the call stack) will appear in the UI in the built-in error dialog box.
- The first method on which a thread runs. An exception that escapes the first thread method will appear in the UI in the built-in error dialog box.
- Event handlers from external libraries that provide input to your application. If you are handling an event from a third-party library and you throw an exception, the exception will pass up the call stack into the library's root method. How it will then deal with that exception is out of your hands. You should not let the exception escape your boundary.

Boundary methods are special for two reasons. The first one is that they cannot let any exception bubble up any farther up the stack because the next level up is the end user. So identify every method that fits the preceding criteria and wrap its entire method body with a *try..catch* statement. In the *catch* block, log the exception because it was an entirely unexpected exception, inform the user, and gracefully exit the application. In some rare circumstances, particularly for methods that are event handlers of GUI controls, you may decide that it is safe to let the application run. In other words, you may decide that the application is not in an indeterminate state and hence there is no reason to exit. Note that just because boundary methods have a *try..catch* block around the entire method body does not mean that they should not have inner *try..catch* blocks around methods that may throw specific exceptions. That is to say, the exception handling added to boundary methods is a last resort, a safety net for catching your own mistakes.

The second reason these methods are special is that they must protect the rest of the application from invalid input. So validate every piece of input to these methods before executing any logic. If some input violates the preconditions of the method, do not proceed with calling other internal methods. If it was a user action, for example, invalid entry in a text box, let the user know.

Consider the previous example with the *Socket.Connect* again. This time, look at the method that calls the *ConnectToThis* method, and presume it is called from a menu click:

```
private void menuItem2_Click(object sender, EventArgs e)
{
  IPAddress ipAddress = this.GetIpAddressSomehow();
  int port;
  port = Convert.ToInt32(textBox1.Text);
  IPEndPoint ipe = new IPEndPoint(ipAddress, port);
  this.ConnectToThis(ipe);
}
```

Now, based on the preceding advice, this is a boundary method and hence it must not let any exception bubble up. After you have analyzed the method, you can make these changes to achieve that end:

```
private void menuItem2_Click(object sender, EventArgs e)
{
  IPAddress ipAddress = this.GetIpAddressSomehow();

  if (ipAddress == null)
  {
    MessageBox.Show("Sorry could not get ip address.");
    return;
  }

  int port;
  try
  {
    port = Convert.ToInt32(textBox1.Text);
  }
  catch (FormatException)
  {
    MessageBox.Show("Please provide a valid port number.");
```

```
    return;
  }
  IPEndPoint ipe = new IPEndPoint(ipAddress, port);


  try
  {
    this.ConnectToThis(ipe);
  }
  catch (CantConnectException ex)
  {
    MessageBox.Show("Sorry, could not connect");
  }
}
```

Notice how various pieces of advice given in this chapter so far have been applied and in addition, because it is a boundary method, you have not let any exception bubble up.

The final task, because this is a boundary method, is to protect against your own bugs or in this case against your own potential incomplete analysis of the boundary method and all the methods that it calls. Remember this point because we refer back to it in the section titled "Global Exception Handling" later in this chapter. This means wrapping the whole method for unexpected exceptions:

```
private void menuItem2_Click(object sender, EventArgs e)
{
  try
  {
    IPAddress ipAddress = this.GetIpAddressSomehow();

    if (ipAddress == null)
    {
      MessageBox.Show("Sorry could not get ip address.");
      return;
    }

    int port;
    try
    {
      port = Convert.ToInt32(textBox1.Text);
    }
    catch (FormatException)
    {
      MessageBox.Show("Please provide a valid port number.");
      return;
    }

    IPEndPoint ipe = new IPEndPoint(ipAddress, port);

    try
    {
      this.ConnectToThis(ipe);
```

```
    }
    catch (CantConnectException ex)
    {
      MessageBox.Show("Sorry, could not connect");
    }
  }
  catch (Exception ex)
  {
    LogException(ex);
    MessageBox.Show(
      "An unexpected error has occured. Please shut down this app.");
    ExitApplication();
  }
}
```

You can see that if you did this for all your boundary methods, no exception would ever escape the application.

Note For class libraries, the definition of boundary methods extends to all public methods of all public classes, that is, the entry points to the class library. The same guidelines apply, except instead of notifying the user and/or exiting the application, class libraries should throw an appropriate exception to their external caller. In this instance, *class libraries* also cover the notion of layers. As a class library developer, remember that all exceptions that leave your boundaries should be logged.

Global Exception Handling

One of the most requested features from the .NET Compact Framework team was the ability to catch unhandled run-time exceptions globally in a single place. This has always been possible in the full .NET Framework, but is not fully possible in .NET Compact Framework version 1.0. Before we look at those, though, and more important before we show how version 2.0 of the .NET Compact Framework delivers on the popular request, it is worth evaluating what the purpose of global exception handling (GEH) really is.

The purpose of GEH is to log all unhandled exceptions and not to allow any of them to escape to the user. You will recall this is the second rule of exception handling as established in the section titled "Runtime Exceptions" earlier in this chapter. If you are looking for global exception handling for recovering from unhandled exceptions, no framework can provide that. With the definition of this paragraph in place, the astute reader will not be surprised by the following paragraph.

Global exception handling is something that you can implement already on all versions of .NET simply by following the guidelines discussed earlier in this chapter, and particularly in the section about boundary methods. From boundary methods, and in particular from the *catch* blocks of those methods, you can log the exception to file before informing the user and exiting the application.

So our advice is for you to achieve global exception handling the hard way, protecting all your boundary methods, because this will force you to analyze all the entry points to your application and encourage you to take appropriate specific action on a case-by-case basis. Having said that, not everybody wishes to be as rigorous, and so an easier way of achieving global exception handling that is not as complete as the boundary methods approach is described next.

GEH on the Full .NET Framework

On the full .NET Framework, you must do three things to catch all exceptions:

- Wrap the call to *Application.Run* with a *try..catch* block.
- Handle the *Application.ThreadException* event.
- Handle the *AppDomain.UnhandledException* event.

Because this is a mobility book, there is no point in getting into the mechanics of these steps, but if you would like more information, see the article titled "Unexpected Errors in Managed Applications" on the Microsoft MSDN Magazine Web site at *msdn.microsoft.com/msdnmag/issues/04/06/NET/default.aspx*.

GEH in NET Compact Framework 1.0

As mentioned earlier, GEH in the .NET Compact Framework 1.0 is not fully possible. This is partly because the two events *Application.ThreadException* and *AppDomain.UnhandledException,* used in the full .NET Framework, are not available. Furthermore, wrapping the call to *Application.Run* with *try..catch* works for exceptions thrown on the main UI thread but not completely for exceptions thrown on worker threads. (For more on threading, please see Chapter 11, "Threading".) In addition, exceptions thrown in a method that was called by using *Control.Invoke* from a worker thread will hang the application. In our opinion, this issue alone renders the attempt for GEH with version 1.0 of the .NET Compact Framework not worth exploring. If you must achieve GEH with version 1.0 of the .NET Compact Framework, your only choice is to use the approach discussed earlier about protecting the boundary methods.

GEH in .NET Compact Framework 2.0

The good news is that version 2.0 of the .NET Compact Framework fixes the issue mentioned previously and in fact makes GEH even easier to achieve than on the desktop! Although the *Application.ThreadException* event is still not available, the *AppDomain.UnhandledException* is available and, unlike the desktop version, does catch every type of exception so that no complementary actions are needed. The following example demonstrates:

```
static class Program {
    [MTAThread]
    static void Main() {
        // Add global exception handler.
        AppDomain.CurrentDomain.UnhandledException +=
            new UnhandledExceptionEventHandler(OnUnhandledException);

        Application.Run(new Form1());
    }

    // In .NET Compact Framework case only,
    // ALL unhandled exceptions come here.
    private static void OnUnhandledException(Object sender,
        UnhandledExceptionEventArgs e) {
        Exception ex = e.ExceptionObject as Exception;
        if (ex != null) {
          // TODO write the ex.ToString() to file
          return; // exit
        }
    }
}
```

Tip Visual Basic developers should take the advice of Chapter 2, "Building a Microsoft Windows Forms GUI," and use a Program.vb file for specifying the startup form just as C# projects do by default. It is then a simple modification, as noted in the preceding code example, that offers global exception handling.

Note that after your method is called, your application has very limited time before it actually exits automatically, so there is no point trying to salvage the situation or even putting a UI up for the user. Simply log to file the unexpected exception. This should help you fix the bug in the next version of your software. To be clear, you should never design your application to solely rely on this method to be called–it should be called only for exceptions that you were simply not expecting, that is, bugs in your code.

GEH Choice: Single-Method vs. Multiple-Method Approach

To be clear, using the single method *AppDomain.UnhandledException* is a much simpler alternative to protecting the boundary methods but not as powerful. To reinforce the point, remember the last change made in the example in the section titled "Boundary Methods" earlier in this chapter. A catchall handler was added to the method, and from there you would exit the application after logging some details and informing the user. Consider the amount of information you have about the state of the application in that method should you want to be detailed in your report to the log file and/or in the message you present to the user. Then consider the results if you do not do that and instead use the single-method approach. All you get in your *AppDomain.UnhandledException* handler is the exception with the stack trace. Very useful indeed, but not as detailed as what you can get using the multiple-method approach. Another drawback of the single-method approach is that you incur a time limit before the application automatically exits, whereas by using the boundary methods approach, the choice is yours.

You may find it very tempting to follow this single-method approach rather than putting the effort into protecting multiple methods. It is debatable if the benefits outweigh the complexity, but you, dear reader, now understand both approaches and can formulate your opinion. Our opinion is that the boundary methods approach is the best approach, and the *AppDomain.UnhandledException* should be used as the ultimate backup–in addition to and not instead of.

Informing the User and Getting the Log Files Back

Two questions arise that have similar answers: "How do I inform the user of the error?" and "How do I get the log files to examine?" A simple, yet effective approach is to do so the next time your application is started. Every time your application is started, check to see whether a GEH log file was generated by the application last time. If so, move the log file to a different (archive) folder so that the next time the application is started your check for the file fails as expected. After that, apologize to the user for the application crashing last time, and ask the user to send you additional information so that you can diagnose and fix the issue encountered. In the UI, you could point users to the archive folder so that they can get the log file and send it to you (by whatever means you or they see fit).

An even more helpful UI simply offers a button that when clicked (by the user) automatically sends the log files back to you (the developer). The communication medium could be File Transfer Protocol (FTP; you would have to use a third-party solution because FTP libraries are not available in the .NET Compact Framework) or a Web Service call (on your server, you can host a Web service that accepts your log files). Another method is simply to send the log files attached to an e-mail message. Programmatically, sending e-mail messages with attachments is very easy on devices that run Windows Mobile 5.0 and later. See Chapter 17, "Developing with Windows Mobile," for the six lines of code required to accomplish that.

You can offer an even greater user experience that addresses two issues of the preceding approach:

1. When your application crashes, the user must start it again manually.
2. The user does not see what happened to your application until *after* he or she starts it again.

If you don't find these issues important enough to address, you'll be glad to learn that the better solution comes at the cost of extra complexity and, in particular, by introducing an additional process (.exe file) that you must distribute with your application as part of your package. This .exe file is what you start from your GEH method, and it is this process that immediately apologizes to the user and offers the option of sending the log file to you. After it sends the log files, it launches your application ready for users to continue where they left off before the application crashed.

Some Exceptions Worthy of Further Mention

Most exceptions are self-describing. For example, it is apparent in an *ObjectDisposedException* that your code attempted to use an object that has already been disposed of. Other exceptions that are self-explanatory include *InvalidArgumentException*, *InvalidCastException*, and *NullReferenceException*.

Whenever you catch an exception whose type and message are not enough to fully describe the problem, always check whether it exposes any custom properties that can help. A nonexhaustive list of examples of such exceptions includes *WebException*, *SocketException*, and *SqlCeException*. After these three, another set of four exceptions deserve special mention: *InvalidOperationException*, *MissingMethodException, System.Resources.ManifestResourceException*, and *TypeLoadException*.

WebException

The *System.Net.WebException* is a great example of an exception class where the exception type alone does not tell you what the precise error is. You must further explore its other two properties.

The *WebException.Status* property is typed as the *WebExceptionStatus* enumeration, and it has 16 possible values that usually are enough to inform you of precisely what the error is, for example, *Timeout*, *NameResolutionFailure*, *ConnectFailure*.

In some cases, it is necessary to query the *WebException.Response* property for more information. The *WebException.Response* property returns a *WebResponse* object. The *WebResponse* object has a *StatusCode* property typed as *HttpStatusCode* enumeration that has dozens of possible values that you can use to precisely determine the return code, for example, *NotFound* (404), *Unauthorized* (401), *Moved* (301). For a list of all the possible values, look up the enumeration in the MSDN Help or in the Object Browser in Visual Studio.

Following is a short code example:

```
      try
      {
        HttpWebRequest wr =
  (HttpWebRequest)WebRequest.Create(textBox1.Text);

        HttpWebResponse rsp = (HttpWebResponse)wr.GetResponse();
        label1.Text = rsp.StatusCode.ToString();
        rsp.Close();
      }
      catch (WebException ex)
      {
        if (ex.Status == WebExceptionStatus.ProtocolError)
        {
              if (ex.Response != null)
              {
                label1.Text =
    ((HttpWebResponse)ex.Response).StatusCode.ToString();
ex.Response.Close();
              }
        }else{
// TODO handle other status values
}
      catch (Exception ex2)
      {
        Debug.WriteLine(ex2.Message);
      }
    }
```

SocketException

Another exception that has an additional property that helps identify the cause of the exception is the *System.Net.SocketException* class. When you work with sockets, the crucial bit of information that points to the error is the native error. The *SocketException* class returns the native error through its integer *ErrorCode* property, for example, 10060 (ConnectionTimedOut) or 10061 (ConnectionRefused).

You can look up the descriptions for all the socket errors on the Microsoft Help and Support Web site at *support.microsoft.com/default.aspx?scid=kb;en-us;819124*.

SqlCeException

Like *SocketException*, *System.Data.SqlServerCe.SqlCeException* is a wrapper for native errors. Its *NativeError* integer property returns the first native error, but to obtain all of them you should iterate the *Errors* property, which returns a collection of *SqlError* objects. The *SqlError* class has a *NativeError* property to help you narrow down the precise reason the exception was thrown, and you can potentially get additional information by using its other two properties: *ErrorParameters* and *NumericErrorParameters*.

A short code example follows:

```
try
{
    // some SqlCe operation
}
catch (SqlCeException e)
{
    for (int i = 0; i < e.Errors.Count;i++)
    {
     SqlCeError error = e.Errors[i];
        if (error.NativeError == 29045)
        {
            // TODO handle specific error
        }else{
     // Check for other errors.
}
    }
}
```

For more information, see the section titled "Deciphering *SqlCeExceptions*" in Chapter 3, "Using SQL Server 2005 Compact Edition and Other Data Stores."

InvalidOperationException

The *System.InvalidOperationException* may seem to have a cryptic name at first, but the name is actually fairly accurate when you realize what it is conveying. Whenever you encounter this exception as a result of a method call, check the state of the object on which you are trying to perform the action. The documentation for the class of the object will detail under what circumstances it is invalid to perform the action that you are attempting. For example, it is illegal to attempt to modify a collection while it is being iterated. Another example is trying to open a serial port when it is already open. So remember to check the state of the object and its documentation whenever one of its methods throws this particular exception.

System.SR.dll

When working on the full framework, developers are accustomed to examining the error messages associated with each exception (by using the *Exception.Message* string property). Because exceptions are not intended to propagate up to the user, these messages are only an aid for developers while debugging. On the .NET Compact Framework, these exception strings have been moved to a resource assembly (System.SR.dll) to conserve space.

When deploying from Visual Studio, you should deploy this assembly as well, but do not rely on it for your production environment. Any attempt to access the exception strings when the System.SR.dll is not on the device results in a "Could not find resource assembly" message. If you observe this while debugging, do not confuse it with the actual exception that caused this message as a side effect!

Do not deploy System.SR with your application installation because you should never let an unhandled exception bubble up to the UI, as discussed earlier. If you still feel that you must deploy it, you must deploy the System_SR_<*locale*>.cab file (or System_SR_<*locale*>_wm.cab for Windows Mobile 5.0–powered devices) instead of the .dll file directly, to avoid violating the End User License Agreement (EULA).

MissingMethodException

The *System.MissingMethodException* is usually observed when you use Platform Invocation Services (PInvoke; see Chapter 14, "Interoperating with the Platform," for more information about PInvoke). This is a good example of the importance of checking the *Message* property of the exception to identify the issue exactly. Consider the following two declarations:

```
[DllImport("ws22.dll", SetLastError = true)]
public static extern Int32 sethostname(byte[] pName, Int32 cName);

[DllImport("ws2.dll", SetLastError = true)]
public static extern Int32 sethostnamee(byte[] pName, Int32 cName);
```

Calling either of those results in a *MissingMethodException*, which means that the method could not be found. If you examine the *Message* for the exception for each case, you find the exact reason for each case:

"Can't find PInvoke DLL 'ws22.dll'"

"Can't find an Entry Point 'sethostnamee' in a PInvoke DLL 'ws2.dll'"

> **Tip** Rather than exercise all the code paths in your application to test your PInvoke declarations, on startup of your application during testing you can call the *Marshal.PreLinkAll* static method once for each class that contains *DllImport* declarations. It will throw an exception if any of your declarations are wrong.

After identifying the misnaming, in most cases it is obvious what the correction should be. If it isn't, you can use the Dumpbin or Depends.exe tools to assist you further with the exact naming of the exported function. For more on interop, including the aforementioned tools, see Chapter 14.

MissingManifestResourceException

In online forums, developers have made many requests for help regarding the *System.Resources.ManifestResourceException*. Fundamentally, most developers seem to get the fully qualified name of the resource (for example., image in a *PictureBox*) incorrect, especially in Visual Basic projects. So if you do encounter this error, the first thing to do is inspect the assembly to check what the correct resource names are. To do this, search your computer for a tool named Ildasm.exe, which comes with the .NET Framework SDK, and start it. Then, from the tool, locate and open your assembly. Double-click the Manifest label with the red triangle in front of it, and scroll to the bottom of the window that opens to read the embedded resource names.

TypeLoadException

A *TypeLoadException* is self-describing in that it indicates a failure to load a type, for example, a class. This typically means that the assembly is not present on the target where the runtime expects it to be, for example, in the applications folder or in the global assembly cache (GAC). It is worth mentioning, though, another common cause of this exception: trying to use a desktop assembly on the device. Unfortunately, under certain circumstances, it is possible in Visual Studio to reference an assembly built against the desktop framework or indeed a desktop framework assembly. Although you may get away with it in Visual Studio, it will not work at run time and is categorically an unsupported scenario. An example of such an exception in a Visual Basic project is: Could not load type Microsoft.VisualBasic.CompilerServices.ProjectData from assembly Microsoft.VisualBasic, Version=7.0.5000.0, Culture=neutral, PublicKeyToken=B03F5F7F11D50A3A. Regardless of whether you are using Visual Basic or C#, you can tell from the exception string that the application has tried to directly or indirectly load a desktop assembly on the device. You can tell because the PublicKeyToken is a desktop PKT. Desktop framework assemblies start with a *B*, whereas device assemblies start with a 9.

For more help with diagnosing *TypeLoadException* exceptions, always refer to the loader log, discussed in the following section.

The Log Files

The .NET Compact Framework runtime version 2.0 can create diagnostic text files on the target while your application is running. These log files contain information that can help debug four areas: loading, interop, networking, and error.

Before looking at each area, you must enable logging globally through the registry on the device. Use Remote Registry Editor or some other device registry editing tool of your choice.

1. Navigate to HKLM\Software\Microsoft\.NETCompactFramework\. If it doesn't exist, create a key named Diagnostics. Under that key, create a key named Logging.
2. Under the Logging key, create a new *DWORD* value: *Enabled*. Set it to 1. Logging is now enabled.
3. Optionally, create three additional *DWORD* values (described later) as shown in Figure 4-14.

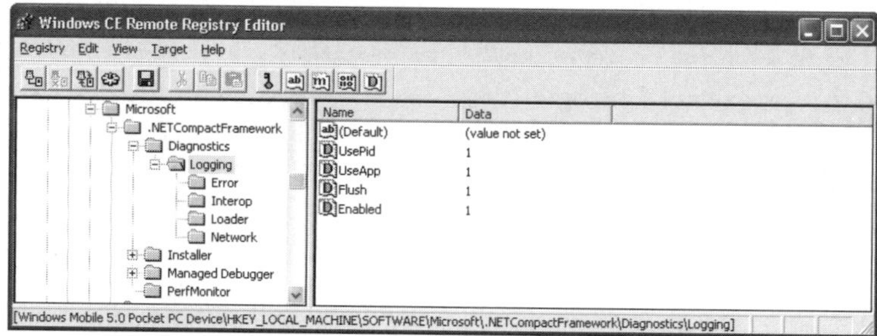

Figure 4-14 Remote registry with logging keys and values configured

The *UsePid* and *UseApp* values ensure that the log file names generated are distinguishable from other log files of other managed applications and from other runs of the same application. The *Flush* value ensures that writes to the log file are not delayed and hence, if your application ends abruptly, no log entries are missed.

To activate a log file with loader information, in addition to the steps outlined earlier, you must perform the following:

1. Under the Logging key, create a new key called Loader.
2. Under the Loader key, create a new *DWORD* value called *Enabled*, and set it to 1.

After this, every time your application exits, a new log will be created: netcf_ APPNAME_ Loader_PID.log.

To enable additional log files for network, interop, and error, you must also create three additional corresponding keys under the Logging key: Network, Interop, and Error. Under each one of these newly created keys, create a new *DWORD* value called *Enabled* and set it to 1.

Every time your application encounters an exception or other unexpected behavior, you can open the log files and examine the contents for clues. The easiest way to open the files is to transfer them from the device to your development computer (for example, by using Remote File Explorer or the ActiveSync explorer) and open them there in your preferred text editor, such as Notepad.

Logging hinders the run-time performance of your application, and so it is advisable that you turn logging on only in debugging scenarios and not in production environments. After you have created the registry keys and values described here, you can set an individual *Enabled* value to 0 to turn off logging of that area; for example, set HKLM\Software\Microsoft\.NETCompactFramework\Diagnostics\Logging\Network\Enabled value to 0 to disable network logging. To turn off logging of all areas for your device, simply set the HKLM\Software\Microsoft\.NETCompactFramework\Diagnostics\Logging\Enabled value to 0.

Loader Log

In simplistic terms, every time your managed application creates an object or uses a value type or calls a static method and so forth, the runtime has to locate the assembly that contains the type and load it. Every time this fails, an exception is thrown. Should that exception be missed (swallowed or masked by another exception), the log file can help. If the runtime fails to find a member of a type (*MissingMethodException* or *MissingFieldException*) or the type itself (*TypeLoadException*), you can see the history of the assemblies that were loaded along with the one that failed that ultimately led to one of the run-time exceptions mentioned previously. The assembly loading information includes public key tokens, versions, and path locations that the runtime probed to find the assembly. In other words, you can get rich information that otherwise is not available anywhere else. If you are familiar with the fusion log on the desktop, this is the closest equivalent.

Seeing what a loader log file looks like is left to you as an exercise. Simply run any managed application on the device and copy the log file to the desktop for examination. To observe erroneous entries, perform the following steps:

1. From a smart device application project, reference a smart device class library project. In a button *Click* event handler, create a class from the class library.
2. Deploy and debug the project from Visual Studio onto the target. Collect the log file.
3. On the device, browse to the application folder and delete the .dll file. Run the .exe file directly, click the button, and observe the crash. Collect the log file and note the differences from the log file collected earlier.

Interop Log

Even though version 2.0 of the .NET Compact Framework plugs many of the gaps in version 1.0, developers occasionally still need to call into native methods in Windows .dll files by using Platform Invocation Services (PInvoke). This is covered in detail in Chapter 14.

When things go wrong with PInvoke (or COM interop), various exceptions may be thrown (for example, *DllNotFoundException*, *EntryPointNotFoundException*), and in other scenarios, marshaling errors may just lead to incorrect results. The interop log is an aid to diagnosing marshaling errors by listing every interop method in both its managed signature and the unmanaged equivalent. Sometimes the unmanaged equivalent can help developers identify an incorrect declaration.

Again, seeing what an interop log file looks like is left for you as an exercise. Simply run any managed application that performs PInvoke calls on the device and copy the log file to the desktop for examination. For examples of such managed applications, see the ones provided in Chapter 14.

Network Log

Network logs gather rich information about networking activities. Unlike all the other log files, they do not contain just American Standard Code for Information Interchange (ASCII) data and they do require a parser to decrypt some of the binary data found therein. In Service Pack 1 of .NET Compact Framework 2.0, such a tool exists. Search your computer for the Logviewer.exe application and run it. You can use this tool to open a network log file and examine its contents, namely, the packets that are sent and received.

Attaching to a debugger

In some scenarios, you must debug an application that is already running on a device but that has not been started with Visual Studio. What you must do is attach to the running process on the device from Visual Studio. This is possible, but only if the capability has been explicitly activated. You can configure this setting through the registry. Use Remote Registry Editor with the device connected to create a key called Managed Debugger under HKEY_LOCAL_MACHINE\SOFTWARE\Microsoft\.NETCompactFramework\ (Figure 4-14 shows this). Under that key, create a *DWORD* value called *AttachEnabled*, and set it to 1.

Then, on the Visual Studio Debug menu, select Attach To Process to open the relevant dialog box. In the dialog box, change the Transport to Smart Device, and from the Qualifier combo box, select your device. In the list, select your managed process, and then click the Attach button.

Like the logging options, this setting negatively affects the performance of all managed applications on the device, and so turn it on only when you expect to have to attach to debug the application.

Error Log

The error log is available only with version 2.0 SP1 and later of the .NET Compact Framework. It was added to help with debugging headless devices, but of course you can use it for devices with displays as well. Recall the built-in error dialog box that the .NET Compact Framework opens for unhandled exceptions in your application? It is described in earlier sections of this chapter, and you can see what it looks like in Figure 4-9 and Figure 4-12. The error log is simply a textual version of this dialog box.

Finalizer Log (Version 3.5)

In the version 3.5 of the .NET Compact Framework that will ship with Visual Studio Code Name "Orcas," there will be an additional log type: the finalizer log. The usefulness of the finalizer log is that it shows which objects are being finalized, which means you omitted calling their *Dispose* method. This helps with performance tuning because letting an object be finalized rather than explicitly disposed hinders performance. We discuss finalizers and performance in Chapter 5.

The .NET Compact Framework team has briefly described this new finalizer log on its blog Web site at *blogs.msdn.com/netcfteam/archive/2006/12/18/NetCF-3.5_2700_s-Finalizer-Log.aspx*.

Remote Performance Monitor

Service Pack 1 of .NET Compact Framework 2.0 includes a new tool to use primarily for measuring the performance of managed device applications. We discuss Remote Performance Monitor (RPM) thoroughly in the next chapter, so please visit that for more information.

But it is worth noting here that from RPM and specifically from the Device menu, you can open the Logging Options dialog box, which you can use to make *some* of the registry configurations described earlier. Figure 4-15 will whet your appetite.

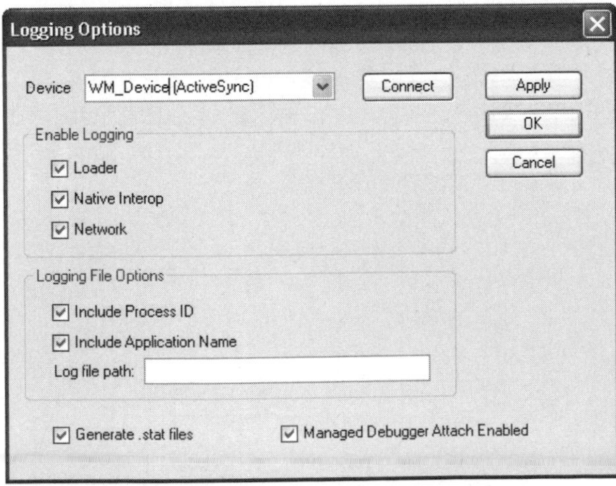

Figure 4-15 Remote Performance Monitor Logging Options dialog box accessed from the Device menu

Instrumentation

Errors that do not result in an exception but rather make the application exhibit incorrect behavior are called silent logical errors. To investigate such errors, you must add to your real code extra debugging code that informs you of the code's internal state. This is also known as *instrumenting* your code.

Before we look at instrumentation, it is important to review a fundamental debugging concept: breakpoints.

Breakpoints

When you observe unexpected results while testing your application, you will have an idea approximately where in your code the error occurs. Maybe you can guess the method or the class that causes the error. In a worse-case scenario, you'll be able to guess which boundary method is called when the undesired behavior is exhibited. Knowing where to start debugging means that you can review the code and run it mentally in your head to see where the issue with your logic lies. If that exercise does not prove fruitful, the next step is to set a breakpoint on a line of code and to run the project under the debugger. Execution of the program halts when the debugger reaches the line with the breakpoint, and you are now able to examine the state of your variables and identify where the logic as coded is flawed after single-stepping each line of code.

Tip In Visual Studio 2005 and .NET Compact Framework 2.0, you can change the statement that is executed next because the *Set Next Statement* command is available. However, the desktop feature *Edit and Continue* is not yet available.

Consider the following code, which is simple; you can imagine a more complex realistic scenario if you want:

```
private void menuItem1_Click(object sender, EventArgs e)
{
  ArrayList ar = new ArrayList(4);
  ar.Add(new MyType(1));
  ar.Add(new MyType(1));
  ar.Add(new MyType(2));
  ar.Add(new MyType(0));
  ar.Add(new MyType(1));
  this.DoSomething(ar);
}

private void DoSomething(object o)
{
  ArrayList col = (ArrayList)o;
  int lastObject = col.Count - 1;
  int total = 0;
```

```
    for (int i = 0; i < lastObject; i++)
    {
      total += ((MyType)col[i]).NoOfWidgets;
    }

    MessageBox.Show("Total = " + total);
  }
```

that uses this class:

```
public class MyType
{
  public int NoOfWidgets;

  public MyType(int widgets)
  {
    NoOfWidgets = widgets;
  }
}
```

When you run the code, you observe that the total is short by 1. You can set a breakpoint in the line that calculates the *total* and assigns it to the variable, and then single-step on each iteration to find out where the issue is. Figure 4-16 shows the breakpoint and the Locals window after the fourth iteration.

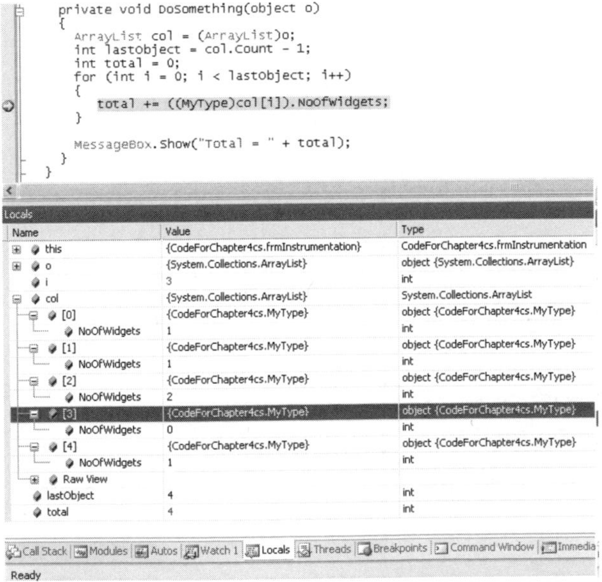

Figure 4-16 Breakpoints in Visual Studio

On each iteration, you can mentally note the value of *total* and what it should be after you *step into* it based on the value of the *NoOfWidgets*. On the fourth iteration, everything is as predicted so that the values of your objects are as they were when you passed them in; the *total* variable was incremented each time as expected. However, when you *step in* to evaluate the variables on the next iteration, you notice that the execution does not go through the loop and instead moves on to the statement with the message box. Looking at the *i* variable confirms the suspicion that the loop exits prematurely because of an incorrect condition on the line with the *for* statement. Changing it to the following fixes the problem:

```
for (int i = 0; i <= lastObject; i++)
```

Tracepoints

Even in the simplistic example described in the preceding section, it is tedious to hit the breakpoint and step into the code to examine the variables. In more complex scenarios, the approach described would take longer than it is worth. An alternative is not to break execution of the running program and instead to output to the Visual Studio output window the variables of interest. This is also useful for multithreading scenarios in which breakpoints make it less than ideal to debug a piece of code that is traversed by multiple threads simultaneously. You can output variables to the Visual Studio output window by using a feature called tracepoints. A *tracepoint* is a breakpoint with a *print message* and the option to *continue execution* automatically. It is a new feature in Visual Studio 2005.

To create a tracepoint, right-click a breakpoint in the code editor or in the Breakpoints window, and select When Hit to open the When Breakpoint Is Hit dialog box, as shown in Figure 4-17.

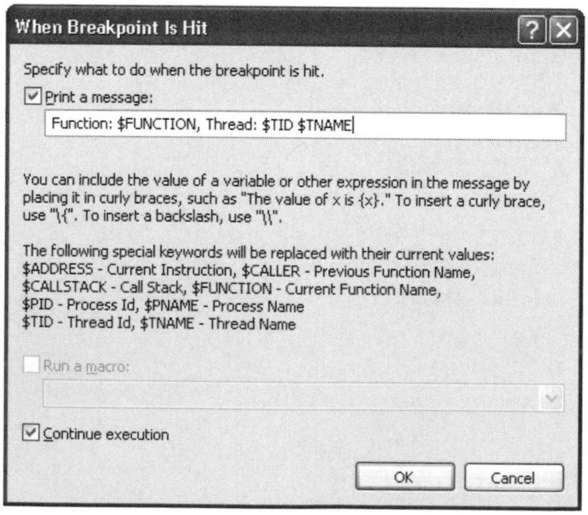

Figure 4-17 Tracepoints in Visual Studio

You can configure the behavior of the breakpoint by selecting or clearing the check boxes in the dialog box. The appearance of the breakpoint will become diamond-shaped rather than circular when both options are selected. When the line of code that contains the tracepoint is hit, the message you enter in the Print A Message text box is printed to the Visual Studio output window and execution continues. Like with breakpoints, tracepoints take effect before the line of code executes. So if you enter the following in the Print A Message text box, when you run the project, the output window displays the message shown in Figure 4-18:

```
Iteration {i}:The 'total' is {total} and I will now add {((MyType)col[i]).NoOfWidgets}
```

Notice how you can extract the same conclusions as you can by using the breakpoint approach but much more quickly and without stopping execution of the program.

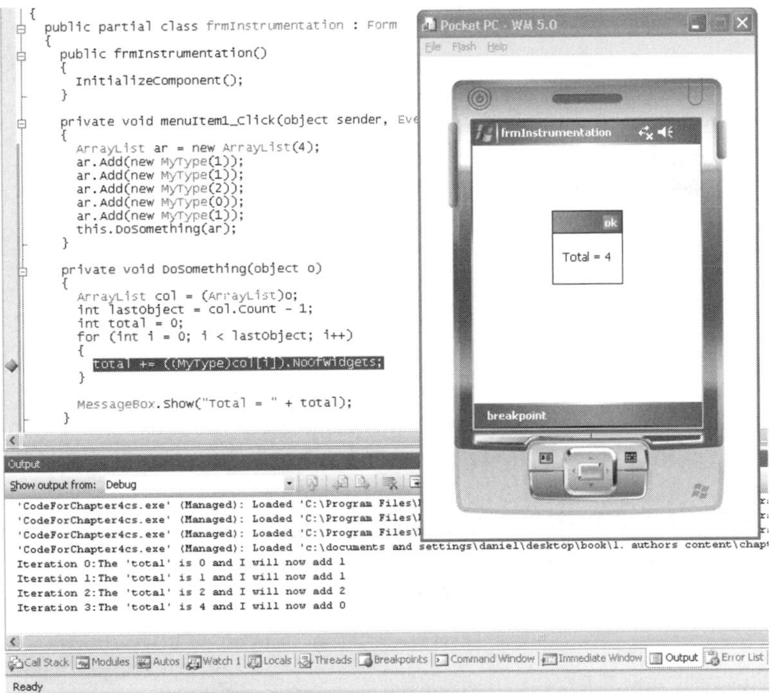

Figure 4-18 Output window in Visual Studio following run with tracepoint

Debug.WriteLine

The traditional mechanism for outputting helpful debug messages that externalize the internal variable state of your running application is by using the *System.Diagnostics.Debug* class and its *WriteLine* method. With Visual Studio 2005, this method now works as expected for device projects as well. The following code example shows how you can change the code method to use this approach:

```
Debug.WriteLine(
  String.Format(
    "Iteration {0}:The 'total' is {1} and I will now add {2}",
    i,
    total,
    ((MyType)col[i]).NoOfWidgets
  )
);
total += ((MyType)col[i]).NoOfWidgets;
```

Although the *Debug.WriteLine* statement is spread over eight lines of code, you can see how it achieves the *exact* same effect as the tracepoint. The difference is that it is now clear what the code does, and the debugging information has the same lifetime as the code file it is associated with. Tracepoints do not add verbosity to the code but are best suited for short-lived debugging tasks that are not expected to be used beyond the particular debugging session in which they are introduced.

Note that the *Debug* statements have effect only in builds where the DEBUG conditional compilation constant is defined. When the DEBUG constant is not defined, the statements have no effect and hence do not affect performance either because they are not compiled into the binary. You can inspect the constants defined in the project properties window on the Build tab (in Visual Basic, the Compile tab). For an example that uses the DEBUG constant directly in code, see the code in the *MyTrace* class mentioned in the following section.

Tracing to File

The techniques discussed in the three previous sections are all great when you can establish a connection from Visual Studio to the target. If you need to gather such information about the internal state of your application while it is running somewhere other than your development computer, for example, on a beta tester's device, you should log all the debug information to file. In fact, you will certainly want to add some kind of logging support to your application so that you can get diagnostic information from your customers' devices from around the world.

On the desktop, many logging frameworks exist but very few work with device projects. One product that does work with the .NET Compact Framework is log4net, but we do not explore it in this book. Most of the .NET Framework classes that facilitate building such infrastructures are absent from the .NET Compact Framework, for example, the *Trace* class has only 3 members compared with its desktop counterpart, which has around 40! This changes with version 3.5, which ships with "Orcas," where not only the *Trace* class is significantly enhanced but also the *TextWriterTraceListener* class is added. Having said that, you still need a solution today when targeting version 2.0 or even version 1.0 of the .NET Compact Framework.

Consider what the specification for a class that logs to file is. It should write the debug information to a file as well as output it to the Visual Studio console if connected; thus, it can be used instead of *Debug.WriteLine* and it also offers value when not connected by Visual Studio. It should behave accordingly when the DEBUG and TRACE constants are not defined and be further configurable so that performance is not affected if you do not need the diagnostic information. Ideally, it should be small so that it can be easily included in projects, for example, a single class with a collection of static methods. Its use would be something like the following examples in pseudo code:

```
MyTrace.Info("ClassName: MethodName", "Diagnostic msg");
MyTrace.InfoIf(SomeCondition, "ClassName: MethodName", "Diagnostic msg");
MyTrace.Warning("ClassName: MethodName", "Diagnostic msg");
MyTrace.WarningIf(SomeCondition, "ClassName: MethodName", "Diagnostic msg");
MyTrace.Assert(SomeCondition, "ClassName: MethodName", "Diagnostic msg");
MyTrace.LogError("SomeMessage");
MyTrace.LogError(SomeException);
```

You can find an example of such a class that satisfies the preceding specification online at *www.danielmoth.com/Blog/2004/11/debugwriteline.html.*

As you can see, there are three levels of diagnostic information—at one extreme, it can be very verbose, outputting INFO, WARNING, and ERROR, whereas at the other extreme, it can output just ERROR information. Typically, the ERROR level logs unrecoverable exceptions such as from your global exception handler. The WARNING level is used for code paths that were unexpected and for exceptions that your code thinks it has recovered. Finally, you can use the INFO level for tracing into and out of methods, thus creating a call stack in the file. Typically, you deploy the application with ERROR and WARNING on and instruct the user to turn on INFO only when trying to diagnose a situation.

Once the log file is created on the device, you could automate its retrieval by following the same suggestion discussed in the section titled "Global Exception Handling" earlier in this chapter.

Unit Testing

Unit testing is only one of the many good practices that became popular with agile and test-driven methodologies such as XP and SCRUM. At its most basic, a unit test is a code test method that tests an actual code method of your application.

For every method you write in your application, you have one or more corresponding unit test methods. Your goal is to run all the unit tests at set intervals or events, for example, daily or every time you check in code to source control or every time you build. If all unit tests run and *pass*, you know that all your code works as expected. Of course, for this to happen you must always include unit tests for every new method that you add to ensure 100 percent code coverage.

Unit tests are invaluable for detecting code changes that break existing functionality. That is, if a unit test passed before but then fails after you make some code changes, it means you have introduced a bug somewhere. By examining which unit test fails, you can pinpoint the buggy method.

Unit testing is interesting from a nontechnical perspective as well; some very vocal advocates of the technique go so far as to claim that they never debug applications, they just run unit tests! This means that your code quality is only as good as the quality of your unit tests. Regardless of what approach to development you take, having unit tests for your code is a good thing. Without going to extremes, unit testing is certainly something that must be part of a good developer's arsenal. It is beyond the scope of this book to go into detail about unit testing, but it is our goal simply to make you aware of the options of using unit testing in smart device development.

Unit testing requires tool support. It requires a framework on which to base the actual tests and test results, and it requires some way of automatically deploying the unit tests to the device and running them on there while recording the results on the desktop. Of course, nice IDE integration is also important.

Community Project

Version 1.0 of the .NET Compact Framework and Visual Studio .NET 2003 provide no support for unit testing. An open source project called CFNunitBridge (use an Internet search engine to find more details) attempted to fill this gap, but support for it ended fairly abruptly before it evolved into an easily used tool. Nevertheless, the code is accessible to anyone who would like to put effort into developing it further.

Deploy to My Computer

In 2005, with the release of Visual Studio 2005, unit test support was included in the more recent versions of Visual Studio, but the support is only for the full .NET Framework and not for device projects. However, you can unit-test your device code by running it on the desktop.

Follow the instructions for unit testing given in the documentation, and when you run the tests your device code will be executed on the desktop against the full .NET Framework.

When you unit-test your device applications against the full .NET Framework, you cannot test any libraries that use device-specific functions, and any attempt do so results in exceptions. Even if you have used only the compatible namespaces, types, and type members, any differences in the runtimes and implementations of the framework methods skew the unit test results. In addition, you are not able to test anything that relies on the device environment because the code is running on the desktop.

Patterns and Practices

In 2006, the patterns & practices team from Microsoft released the Mobile Client Software Factory package, as mentioned in Chapter 1. The code for all the application blocks is available, as are unit tests for all of them. This is achieved mainly by a GuiTestRunner utility that the team wrote in conjunction with a unit testing framework you can also use for your own code. With the unit testing framework, you can run unit tests on the target by driving a GUI on the target. The roundtrip communication from device to desktop isn't that great, but at the time of writing it is the best solution for your unit test needs.

Visual Studio Code Name "Orcas"

The subsequent version of Visual Studio after 2005 is code-named "Orcas" and will include full support for unit testing for devices. The experience will be identical to unit tests for the desktop except that the tests will run on the device (but still be controlled, reported on the desktop). When "Orcas" becomes available, its documentation will cover the details. If it has not shipped by the time you read this, feel free to download the Community Technology Preview (CTP) of "Orcas" to preview this feature. There is a brief description on the Visual Studio for Devices blog at *blogs.msdn.com/vsdteam/archive/2006/11/12/unit-testing-for-net-compact-framework.aspx*.

Summary

This chapter explains how to test and debug your applications and offers strategies for catching errors and fixing bugs. It describes the tools and features available to you in Visual Studio 2005 and .NET Compact Framework 2.0, and it discusses best practices you can use to design solutions with managed languages such as C# and Visual Basic. The main points of advice to take away are the following:

- Use the compiler to its fullest so that you can catch potential errors very early.
- Never swallow exceptions.

- Never let an unhandled exception be presented to the user in the in-built error dialog box.
  - Analyze your boundary methods so that no exception goes uncaught.
  - On .NET Compact Framework 2.0, handle the *AppDomain.UnhandledException* event for exceptional scenarios that you missed on the previous point.

The next chapter explains how to identify performance bottlenecks and how to write efficient code for mobile devices, which by their nature are constrained in both memory and power.

Chapter 5

Understanding and Optimizing .NET Compact Framework Performance

In this chapter:

Despite massive improvements at the hardware and operating system levels, mobile devices are still constrained in their raw power, and that makes performance considerations all the more important during device development. Also, given that these devices run on battery, the old adage "do as little as possible" is essential not only for performance reasons but for power preservation reasons as well.

This chapter discusses the principles of writing well-performing code. The key to achieving good performance is to set performance goals early in the development process, understand how the common language runtime (CLR) manages memory, and avoid coding practices that create unnecessary garbage in memory. It is also important to understand what the runtime is doing when your application is running and how to get the runtime to do as little as possible.

What Every Developer Should Know

In some circles, developers are obsessed with making processes as fast as possible, applying every optimization thinkable, and making high performance the driving factor in design decisions without consideration for anything else. That is wrong. Your code should run "fast enough." The goal is to identify what fast enough is for your application.

For example, if your application takes 3 seconds to run a certain action (for example, connecting to a server to verify login credentials) and the users are happy with that, investing time to make that action faster is not a good use of resources. In this situation, the required performance level of the use case implementation has been identified in the user acceptance criteria. Meeting required performance levels for user acceptance should be the only driver in determining how fast your code must run. If you need more factors to help in that determination, consider the following questions: How fast did the previous version run? How fast do similar competing products run? Again, the only criterion you must consider in deciding whether to optimize a code path should be if users are happy with the speed. If your product is faster than whatever method users were using before (including manual processes) and is equally as fast as other similar applications, there really is no point in optimizing further.

When you write feature specifications, you should include specific minimal and ideal performance requirements and avoid using just descriptive text such as "this function must be fast" to describe how a feature must perform. Unfortunately, many developers write vast amounts of code only to find out at the last minute that their code is not fast enough, and only then do they try to optimize the code, hoping for performance improvements. You must specify performance requirements and enumerate expectations of stakeholders early in the development process to avoid nasty surprises later. Part of your test cycle should be to continuously measure the performance of those features to establish if they are in line with the specifications and if any code modifications have negatively affected the results.

Well-performing code does not happen as an afterthought—performance is designed into an application. For example, consider a feature that populates a *ListView* with entries. You implement the feature, and then find that it takes an unacceptably long time to load 10,000 items. Should you then profile individual methods to try to optimize the code or should you reconsider the design? The process of loading 10,000 items on a constrained device will perform badly regardless of how you write the code. Even if you were prepared to pay the performance penalty for such a decision, does it make sense to require users to scroll through thousands of items on a device where only a dozen items can be visible on the screen at any one time? The solution, of course, is to design the feature for performance by default: load only 100 to 200 items at a time, and load more as the user scrolls down, or offer buttons to navigate to the previous and next pages, splitting the data alphabetically or by category or by some other characteristic.

It is better to focus first on perceived performance (for example, time it takes for the wait cursor to appear after the user clicks a button) than it is to focus initially on actual performance (for example, time to load a form). Design your application so that users are continuously given feedback about their actions. It is amazing how users will insist that one application is faster than another when both applications take the same time to complete an action but the one that is perceived as faster offers visual feedback. For example, you can place a *ProgressBar* on the screen, show the busy cursor, or update the status bar with intermediate messages to keep the user informed of progress rather than expecting the user to stare at a blank screen waiting for an action to complete. Intermediate feedback is important and may not be available for all actions unless you design for it early. For example, it may not be acceptable for search results to appear on-screen 10 seconds after a user taps a search button. However, if every 2 seconds the list is populated with intermediate search results, the complete search may even take 15 seconds and still be perceived as fast by the user.

So far, we have given generic advice that applies to any software development project. The other piece of advice we offer is that you must always understand the characteristics of the platform on which you are working. This is especially true with the Microsoft .NET Compact Framework. Almost every optimization trick you come across makes sense when you understand the common language runtime (CLR) of the .NET Compact Framework.

Understanding the Compact CLR Engine

In software, developers usually must make a trade-off between fast code and code that uses little memory. That is, certain design decisions can err on the side of faster performance that consumes a lot of memory (for example, by caching results in memory) or processes can be slower and use very little memory (for example, by spending central processing unit cycles calculating certain results every time they are asked for). Under the compact CLR, trading random access memory (RAM) usage for speed doesn't always work. You must write code that is both memory-efficient and fast at the same time. To understand why, you must understand the inner workings of the garbage collector (GC) and the just-in-time (JIT) compiler, also known as the JIT compiler or JITter.

The descriptions that follow are high level, with a focus on what affects performance rather than full coverage of the CLR. We aim to simplify as much as possible the mechanics at the cost of details.

JIT Compiler

When you compile Microsoft Visual Basic or C# code, the binaries that are produced (that is, the .exe or .dll file) do not contain native central processing unit (CPU) instructions and instead contain intermediate language (IL) code. At run time, the JIT compiler further compiles each IL method into native code, which then is executed. It is important to note that JIT compiling occurs per method and only when the method is requested to execute. When the method is called, a check is made to see if there is native code for the method. If there is, the native code is executed; if there isn't any native code, the JIT compiler compiles the IL code to native code, which is then associated with that method entry (stored in an in-memory cache), and of course then the native code is executed.

Every time a method is JIT compiled, there is a performance cost. To minimize the cost, try to reduce deep method call hierarchies or really long methods or recursion because the JIT compiler works best with short code paths. On the desktop CLR, the cost is paid only once because the generated native code for the method is associated with the method for the lifetime of the application run. This is different from the compact JIT compiler surfaces: The native code that is generated by the compact JIT compiler can be thrown away at run time in certain circumstances, such as when the system comes under severe memory pressure. This is known as code *pitching*. Should pitching occur, the obvious effect is that the JIT compiling performance penalty is paid more than once per method. See the section titled "Garbage Collector" later in this chapter for more information about pitching.

Another difference from the desktop CLR is that there is no support for native images. In other words, you cannot use the Ngen tool from the software development kit (SDK) to generate native images at install time, which in turn would mean the JIT performance penalty would not be paid at run time. This is because a native image is three to four times larger than a managed assembly is, so the footprint implications are severe when you consider that the .NET Compact Framework version 2.0 libraries alone are almost 5 megabytes (MB).

Inlining

The JIT compiler includes an optimization feature called *method inlining*. This means that some methods can be inlined to the calling method. The calling method's body grows to include the body of the inlined method, thus avoiding making the method call altogether. All this happens at the machine code level after the IL has been JIT compiled. If you were to picture the effects of inlining at the managed code level, it would look something like the following two methods:

```
public int CallingMethod()
{
  // code that performs some task A

  this.SomeOtherMethod();

  // code that performs some task C
}

private void SomeOtherMethod()
{
  // code that performs some task B
}
```

At run time, they become a single method, that is, *SomeOtherMethod* is inlined and doesn't exist separately:

```
public int CallingMethod()
{
  // code that performs some task A

  // code that performs some task B

  // code that performs some task C
}
```

The compact JIT compiler inlines only the most basic of methods; realistically it happens only for simple accessor methods, that is, properties. Rules determine whether a method can be inlined.[1] Note that method inlining is an internal implementation detail subject to change, and you should not design your application specifically with inlining in mind; however, it might be useful to keep performance-critical methods as simple as possible to give them a better chance of being inlined. Certain types of methods are never inlined, however; these are virtual methods.

Virtual Methods

Tip Virtual methods are methods that are marked as *virtual* in C# and *Overridable* in Visual Basic. They are one of the building blocks that facilitate the elegant design of object hierarchies that can result in polymorphism, that is, the ability of a method in an inherited class to redefine the behavior of a method in a base class. The ability for a method to be redefined does come at a cost, which is why it is not enabled by default.

With the compact JIT compiler, virtual method calls are approximately 40 percent more expensive[2] than are nonvirtual method calls! Although we do not advise designing your solution based on this fact, an important aspect here is that virtual methods are not subject to inlining. Be particularly careful about defining *virtual properties* because properties are in fact methods despite any superficial differences. For example, consider the following two methods, which are identical except one calls a virtual property and the other calls an identical nonvirtual property:

```
private int myVar = 1;
public int MyProperty
{
  get { return myVar; }
  set { myVar = value; }
}

private int myVVar = 1;
public virtual int MyVirtualProperty
{
  get { return myVVar; }
  set { myVVar = value; }
}

public void Test1()
{
  int total=0;
```

1 To be inlined, a method must have 16 bytes of IL or less, no branching (typically an *if*), no local variables, no exception handlers, no 32-bit floating-point arguments, and no return value. Also, if the method has more than one argument, the arguments must be accessed in order from lowest to highest (as seen in the IL).

2 The compact JIT compiler does not use a v-table, which means that virtual methods must be interpreted the first time they are called, rather than just looked up.

```
    for (int i = 0; i < 1000000; i++)
    {
      total += this.MyProperty;
    }

    MessageBox.Show(total.ToString());
  }

  public void Test2()
  {
    int total =0;
    for (int i = 0; i < 1000000; i++)
    {
      total += this.MyVirtualProperty;
    }

    MessageBox.Show(total.ToString());
  }
```

If you run the preceding code, notice that *Test2* performs worse than *Test1* does. On a Pocket PC device that runs Microsoft Windows Mobile 2003 Standard Edition, *Test1* takes 240 milliseconds in debug and 45 milliseconds in release mode; *Test2* takes 320 milliseconds in debug and 190 milliseconds in release mode. If the code is built in debug mode, the performance difference will be smaller than the performance difference when the code is built in release mode (release mode is faster than debug mode is overall, of course). In debug mode, the difference in performance is because the virtual call is inherently slower, and in release mode the effect worsens because only the nonvirtual property benefits from inlining.

Garbage Collector

The garbage collector is responsible for allocating objects and freeing objects when they are no longer referenced. One of the biggest claims of programming in a managed environment is that you do not have to think about memory management. However, that claim is not exactly true: although memory management is taken care of for you, if you design an application with no consideration for memory usage, the application will probably perform badly. So you do have to think about memory management, but in a way different from how you do in native code. Before we analyze memory usage of an application, it will help to explain the garbage collector's role with respect to performance.

Windows CE and Windows Mobile memory management

As a managed developer, if the CLR performs its duties, you should not worry about memory management. Having said that, we call out a few useful points that some managed developers come across occasionally. Under Microsoft Windows CE, only 32 processes can be running, and after you realize how many processes run on a Windows Mobile–powered device by default, you can see how easy it is to reach that limit. Also, each process has only 32 MB of virtual address space, so, for example, if you load large bitmaps into memory in your application, don't be surprised if you run out of memory even though the device in total has free memory to use. The restrictions on number of processes and virtual address space are issues that native and managed developers must be aware of and design for. Note that in Windows Embedded CE 6.0, both limitations have been removed, but there isn't a Windows Mobile version running on Windows Embedded CE 6.0 yet.

Also note that when a Windows Mobile–powered device is running low on memory, it will send a WM_HIBERNATE windows message to applications, starting with the longest inactive one and stopping after it has sufficient resources. When the applications receive that message, they should dispose of any resources that are not absolutely necessary. If the system still needs to free memory resources after sending WM_HIBERNATE messages, it starts shutting down applications first by sending a WM_CLOSE message and then by calling *TerminateProcess* if necessary, again stopping after it has sufficient resources. When a managed application receives a WM_HIBERNATE message, a full garbage collection will take place. If your application can additionally free references that are active, it should do so by handling the *Microsoft.WindowsCE.MobileDevice.Hibernate* event (new in version 2), after which a full garbage collection will run.

If you are interested in understanding Windows CE memory management, see the article titled "Windows CE .NET Advanced Memory Management" on the Microsoft MSDN Web site at *msdn2.microsoft.com/en-us/library/ms836325.aspx*. If you are interested in further understanding the internals of the CLR and what its cost model is against Windows CE, see the blog titled ".Net Compact Framework Advanced Memory Management" on Mike Zintel's Weblog Web site at *blogs.msdn.com/mikezintel/archive/2004/12/08/278153.aspx*.

When a new object is created, a memory block in RAM is required to store the contents of the object. That place is called the heap, and each process has its own. From your code you have a reference to where your object storage starts in the heap. This reference, also known as a handle or a pointer, is stored on the stack and is 4 bytes long on 32-bit systems, such as Windows CE. In nonmanaged environments, when the program needs a new place in memory to store an object, work has to be done to find an appropriate address in the heap with a large enough contiguous memory block to hold the object. When the object is no longer needed, it is the developer's responsibility to write code that explicitly deletes the memory held by the reference. How does that compare with managed code?

Allocating objects under the garbage collector is an extremely fast operation, generally faster than in unmanaged environments, because the garbage collector preallocates a portion of the heap and continues to increment the heap in 64-KB segments[1] as more objects are created. In other words, the space has already been allocated, and every time a new object creation is requested, an internal pointer is moved to the next available address, ready for the next object.

How about freeing objects in managed code? Freeing objects is known as a *garbage collection* (more details on this later). A collection is not an inexpensive operation, even on the full framework, where garbage collection details differ from the compact version. A garbage collection takes place on the thread that happens to be running when the collection is needed, and all other thread activity is paused. In simplistic terms, think of your application freezing while a collection takes place. Typically, this freeze is for a few milliseconds but, depending on how often collections take place, can have a negative impact on your application.

Six conditions can trigger a garbage collection:

1. A cumulative 1 MB of heap data has been allocated since the last collection (in version 1.0, this value is 750 kilobytes).
2. Your code calls *GC.Collect*.
3. Your application is moved to the background.
4. A failure to allocate memory for a managed object occurs.
5. The *System.Drawing* subsystem receives an out of memory error when trying to allocate an unmanaged resource.
6. Your application receives a WM_HIBERNATE message.

Warning It is important to understand and unequivocally accept that calling *GC.Collect* in production code is never a good idea. It is very expensive and it will probably not have the effects you hope for. This is as true on the Compact Framework as it is on the full .NET Framework. Generally, the system knows when it needs to do a collection, and because every collection involves freezing your application threads and walking the heap—even if there are no unreachable objects to collect—you may just be introducing more freezes in your app and not actually freeing any memory.

1 Should a single object require more than 64 kilobytes (KB) on its own, a segment for that entire object is created the exact appropriate size.

When a collection occurs, the garbage collector identifies the dead objects and marks their heap space as available. If the objects have a finalizer, they are moved to another queue, where their finalizer method is executed by the finalizer thread; their memory is reclaimed the next time the garbage collector runs.[1] The process described in this paragraph is known as a *simple collection*.

In addition to the preceding actions, as part of the collection a compaction may occur depending on heap fragmentation. A *compaction* is the movement of all live objects to a contiguous block at the beginning of the heap, while the unused memory blocks from the end are freed to the operating system. This is known as a *compact collection*.

Finally, in addition to the preceding actions, code pitching may occur (as defined in the section titled "JIT Compiler" earlier in this chapter) as part of the garbage collection. The result is that, apart from the methods of the current call stack, all others must be JIT compiled again when they are next called. This is known as a *full collection* and is triggered by any of the last four conditions in the preceding list. A full collection also shrinks the heap, which in all other cases would remain at 1 MB (if it had reached that size).

What does all this mean? Most of the conditions that precipitate garbage collection are beyond your control, but at least you can understand when a collection will occur and exactly what it will do. You can do nothing about your application switching to the background or if other applications on the device stress the overall available memory. However, in those cases you still pay the penalty of re-JIT-compiling methods in your application. Apart from those two conditions, you can avoid the rest by not allocating objects. The more objects you allocate, the more garbage is created and the more collections have to run, thus increasing the chances of paying the re-JIT-compiling cost and contributing to overall garbage collector latency. The garbage collector latency is directly proportional to the number of objects in your application because identifying which objects are live and which aren't involves traversing the heap. A generic principle holds true on this platform more than on any other: less code is faster code. You will see in a later section how to use performance counters to help identify whether any performance bottlenecks are caused by garbage collections.

Version 1.0 to Version 2.0 Improvements

Figures 1-10 and 1-11 in Chapter 1, ".NET Compact Framework–a Platform on the Move," summarize some of the performance improvements in different versions of the framework.

The bottom line is that every aspect of the .NET Compact Framework is faster in version 2.0 compared with version 1.0. The product team invested significant effort in reviewing both the engine and the libraries and optimizing them for our benefit. The JIT compiler was completely rewritten with performance in mind, the garbage collector algorithm was fine-tuned, the

1 A finalizer is a method that, when implemented for an object, runs before the object is collected by the garbage collector. Its purpose is to free any resources that the object may have, excluding managed references. A finalizer is almost always implemented in conjunction with the *Disposable* pattern, described later in this chapter.

speed of making method calls was improved, and core scenarios such as calling Web services and accessing data were optimized. Not only will the same application run faster under version 2.0 than it did under version 1.0, but application startup is also vastly improved. In short, one of the major reasons for moving from version 1.0 to version 2.0 isn't just the additional functionality, but so that your applications can run faster (see Chapter 1, ".NET Compact Framework–a Platform on the Move").

.NET Compact Framework Performance Statistics

After you have identified a performance issue with some aspect of your application, the next step is to diagnose which bit of code is responsible. In a managed environment, this isn't always straightforward because an engine is doing some work for you (as described in the preceding section) and there is a lot of code in the framework libraries not under your control; for example, you may create a single framework object, but that object may create another 10 objects on your behalf. It is for this reason that the .NET Compact Framework can generate performance statistics (or counters) that you can then examine for clues.

Performance statistics are available in .NET Compact Framework 1.0, but they are significantly enhanced in version 2.0: There are many more counters, they can be generated for more than one running application at a time, and they can be updated while the application is running, whereas in version 1.0 you must wait for your application to exit cleanly. Finally, version 2.0 includes a tool for viewing the data called Remote Performance Monitor (RPM), as described later in this chapter.

Activating Performance Counters

Performance counters are activated in the registry, much like the logging files discussed in Chapter 4, "Catching Errors, Testing, and Debugging," and particularly in the section titled "The Log Files." On the device, use Remote Registry Editor as explained in Chapter 4 to navigate to the HKEY_LOCAL_MACHINE\SOFTWARE\Microsoft\.NETCompactFramework key, and create a key under it named PerfMonitor. Under this newly created key, create a *DWORD* value named *Counters* and set it to 1. Note that this will affect the performance of your application and should be turned off by setting the *Counters* value to 0 when you do other performance tests or in a production environment.

Note that if you connect Remote Performance Monitor to your device as described in a later section, you can activate and disable the counters simply by selecting or clearing a check box. See Figure 4-15 in Chapter 4, and notice the Generate .stat Files option.

Viewing the Data

After you activate the counters, every time you run your application on the device, a file named <*application_name*>.stat is generated at the root of the device. When your application exits, you can copy the .stat file from the device to your development computer and open it in

Notepad or another text editor. You will see seven columns. The first column is a list of counter names, 63 in total. The other six columns show the data for each counter. Not every column is applicable for every counter and, when that is the case, rather than a number, a hyphen is shown. The six columns (with a friendlier name in parentheses) are as follows: total (Total), last datum (Last Value), n (Sample Count), mean (Average), min (Minimum), and max (Maximum). Figure 5-1 shows a heavily edited .stat file in which many counters have been deleted.

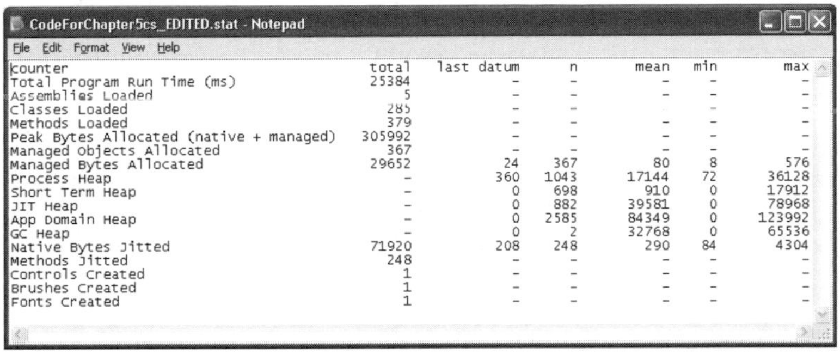

CodeForChapter5cs_EDITED.stat - Notepad

File Edit Format View Help

counter	total	last datum	n	mean	min	max
Total Program Run Time (ms)	25384	-	-	-	-	-
Assemblies Loaded	5	-	-	-	-	-
Classes Loaded	285	-	-		-	-
Methods Loaded	379	-	-	-	-	-
Peak Bytes Allocated (native + managed)	305992	-	-	-	-	-
Managed Objects Allocated	367	-	-	-	-	-
Managed Bytes Allocated	29652	24	367	80	8	576
Process Heap	-	360	1043	17144	72	36128
Short Term Heap	-	0	698	910	0	17912
JIT Heap	-	0	882	39581	0	78968
App Domain Heap	-	0	2585	84349	0	123992
GC Heap	-	0	2	32768	0	65536
Native Bytes Jitted	71920	208	248	290	84	4304
Methods Jitted	248	-	-	-	-	-
Controls Created	1	-	-	-	-	-
Brushes Created	1	-	-	-	-	-
Fonts Created	1	-	-	-	-	-

Figure 5-1 .stat file in Notepad showing some random counters

The .stat files can also be opened using the Remote Performance Monitor tool. On the File menu, select the Open .stat menu item (as explained in a later section). The next step is for you to understand all the counters.

Performance Counter Descriptions

The 63 counters of the .stat file can be grouped in 10 categories. In fact, when viewed in the RPM tool, they are grouped in 10 categories and helpful descriptions are shown for each counter. The following sections discuss the categories and counters, and the figures show the counter descriptions, so descriptions of each counter are not repeated in the text. One method of understanding these counters is to collect a .stat file from your own application and look at real data while reading the following subsections.

Loader

Figure 5-2 supplies the description of the counters for the CLR loader. Typically, you will have one AppDomain loaded, and you can calculate how many assemblies are loaded if you analyze your project. The number of classes and methods loaded would be a mystery if it were not for these two counters. They are a good indication of an application's size. The larger the numbers, the more metadata that must be kept in memory by the runtime. Use this information together with the loader log file discussed in Chapter 4.

Loader

Total Program Run Time (ms)	The elapsed time from CLR invocation.
App Domains Created	The count of App Domains created in the process.
App Domains Unloaded	The count of App Domains that have been unloaded from the process.
Assemblies Loaded	The count of assemblies that have been loaded - across all App Domains.
Classes Loaded	The count of classes that have been loaded - across all App Domains.
Methods Loaded	The total count of methods loaded - across all App Domains.

Figure 5-2 Loader: six counters with descriptions

Generics

Figure 5-3 shows the descriptions of counters for generics in your application. Don't be surprised if you are not using generics (a new version 2.0 feature) and you still observe positive numbers on these counters–internally, the runtime may use generics as a side effect of nongeneric method calls that your application makes. Also, it is worth recalling that generic methods do not have to belong to generic types! For more information about the generics implementation in the .NET Compact Framework, see Roman Batoukov's Weblog at *blogs.msdn.com/romanbat/archive/2005/01/06/348114.aspx.*

Generics

Closed Types Loaded per Definition	The maximum number of unique generic types created for a given definition across all AppDomains.
Closed Methods Loaded per Definition	The maximum number of unique generic methods created for a given definition across all AppDomains.
Closed Types Loaded	The count of unique generic types that have been loaded across all AppDomains.
Open Types Loaded	The count of open generic types created across all AppDomains. Open types are typically created only in Reflection scenarios.
Closed Methods Loaded	The count of unique generic methods that have been loaded across all AppDomains.
Open Methods Loaded	The count of open generic methods created across all AppDomains. Open methods are typically created only in Reflection scenarios.

Figure 5-3 Generics: six counters with descriptions

Locks and Threads

Figure 5-4 shows descriptions of the threading counters. You learn more about threading in Chapter 11, "Threading."

Locks and Threads

Threads in Thread Pool	The number of threads currently in the thread pool.
Pending Timers	The number of timers currently waiting to fire.
Scheduled Timers	The number of timers that are currently running or scheduled to run.
Timers Delayed by Thread Pool Limit	The count of timers that have been delayed by the thread pool limit.
Work Items Queued	The count of work items queued to the Thread Pool.
Uncontested Monitor.Enter Calls	Count of calls made to Monitor.Enter that are not contested.
Contested Monitor.Enter Calls	Count of calls made to Monitor.Enter with lock contention.

Figure 5-4 Locks and Threads: seven counters with descriptions

There are two important numbers in this category. The first one is the number associated with the Threads In Thread Pool counter. If that number is equal to or greater than the maximum number of threads the thread pool can hold (by default 25), it could explain a delay in your application to carry out work items. Look at this number in combination with the Work Items Queued counter to understand the ratio of jobs you are queuing compared with the number of threads available to handle them. The counters relating to timers refer to the *System.Threading.Timer* (not the *System.Windows.Forms.Timer*) and are relevant here because they also use threads from the thread pool.

The other important number is the number associated with the Contested Monitor.Enter Calls counter. Every time you explicitly use *System.Threading.Monitor.Enter* or implicitly use the C# *lock* keyword (or the Visual Basic *SyncLock*), you are protecting a region from being entered concurrently by more than one thread (more on this in Chapter 11). This has a small performance penalty of its own but can really delay processing if a thread encounters the region when another thread is already executing there, and hence the one thread must wait. Such cases are caught by this counter. Again, this is by design for most applications, but if the figure is not close to what you were expecting, you may have to revisit your design. See Chapter 11 for a more in-depth explanation.

GC

Figure 5-5 shows descriptions for the large number of garbage collector counters. If you read the section titled "Garbage Collector" earlier in this chapter, the counters in the figure are self-explanatory. Note that the numbers associated with the GC Latency Time, Garbage Collections (GC), GC Compactions, and Code Pitchings counters collectively expose the GC statistics.

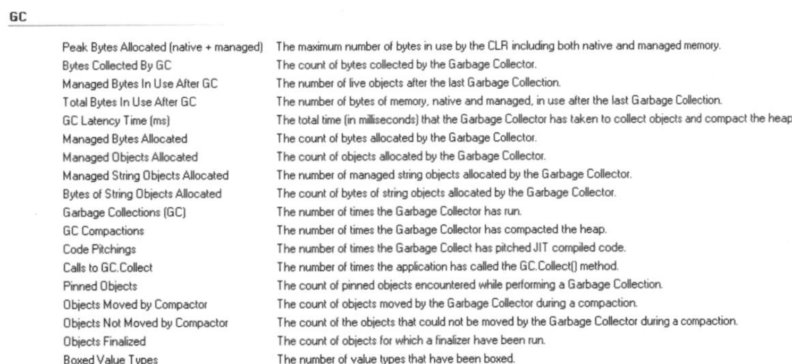

GC

Counter	Description
Peak Bytes Allocated (native + managed)	The maximum number of bytes in use by the CLR including both native and managed memory.
Bytes Collected By GC	The count of bytes collected by the Garbage Collector.
Managed Bytes In Use After GC	The number of live objects after the last Garbage Collection.
Total Bytes In Use After GC	The number of bytes of memory, native and managed, in use after the last Garbage Collection.
GC Latency Time (ms)	The total time (in milliseconds) that the Garbage Collector has taken to collect objects and compact the heap.
Managed Bytes Allocated	The count of bytes allocated by the Garbage Collector.
Managed Objects Allocated	The count of objects allocated by the Garbage Collector.
Managed String Objects Allocated	The number of managed string objects allocated by the Garbage Collector.
Bytes of String Objects Allocated	The count of bytes of string objects allocated by the Garbage Collector.
Garbage Collections (GC)	The number of times the Garbage Collector has run.
GC Compactions	The number of times the Garbage Collector has compacted the heap.
Code Pitchings	The number of times the Garbage Collect has pitched JIT compiled code.
Calls to GC.Collect	The number of times the application has called the GC.Collect() method.
Pinned Objects	The count of pinned objects encountered while performing a Garbage Collection.
Objects Moved by Compactor	The count of objects moved by the Garbage Collector during a compaction.
Objects Not Moved by Compactor	The count of the objects that could not be moved by the Garbage Collector during a compaction.
Objects Finalized	The count of objects for which a finalizer have been run.
Boxed Value Types	The number of value types that have been boxed.

Figure 5-5 Garbage Collector: 18 counters with descriptions

Note that a high number associated with the Boxed Value Types counter may indicate a performance issue because boxing and unboxing are expensive operations. A common situation in which boxing occurs is when you use types from the *System.Collections* namespace, and that is discussed in the section titled "Tips and Tricks" later in this chapter.

Boxing

Value types such as *int*, *bool*, enumerations, and structures are allocated on the stack. Stack allocation makes value types an attractive proposition from a performance perspective because they don't have to be allocated or freed on the heap and consequently the GC is not involved. Value types can be more expensive to pass by value in methods, but this is easily mitigated by declaring the method signatures to accept them by reference.

Value types can also be used wherever a reference type is expected. This seamless dual usage makes a *struct* a good choice from a performance perspective and does not break a basic object-oriented principle: everything is an object. However, there is a cost: When you use a value type as a reference type, an operation known as *boxing* occurs in which an actual reference type is created (on the heap, of course, and thus it is a candidate for garbage collection) that is equivalent to the value type. Casting back to the value type is known as *unboxing*. Boxing and unboxing are expensive.

In your application, if a value type is boxed often in its lifetime, any benefits of using value types are lost and it would be best if the type were a reference type instead. Finding the situations in which a value type is boxed requires analysis of your code. Look for clues such as implementing an interface from a value type, and so forth.

As a historical aside, boxing takes its name from the IL statement used to actually "convert" the value type to a reference type: *box*. An extreme technique would be to dump the IL from your assemblies and search for the *box* keyword to find where types are boxed.

You should also aim for a small number for the Objects Finalized counter because an object with a finalizer remains in memory longer and also results in a performance hit because a separate thread must traverse the finalization queue (this is explained earlier in the section titled "Garbage Collector"). Implement a finalizer only when the object directly holds on to native resources, and even then you should implement it in combination with a *Dispose* method, as detailed next.

Tip In version 3.5 of the .NET Compact Framework, an additional Finalizer log will be added to complement the other logs discussed in Chapter 4.

The following sample code demonstrates the disposable idiom that you should use, and it is applicable on both the .NET Compact Framework and the full framework. Pay attention to the inline comments and the key point following the code sample:

```
class NativeResourceHolder : IDisposable
{
  private bool alreadyDisposed = false;

  // This method does the cleanup.
  // Gets called only from finalizer(true) OR from Dispose(false).
  // Protected virtual so subclasses can override it.
  protected virtual void Dispose(bool calledFromFinalizer)
  {
    if (this.alreadyDisposed)
    {
      return;
    }
    this.alreadyDisposed = true;

    if (!calledFromFinalizer)
    {
      //If you hold other IDisposable references, call their Dispose method.
      //Cannot do this from finalizer; they may have already been disposed.
    }

    // Always free native resources, such as handles.
  }

  public void Dispose()
  {
    this.Dispose(false);
    // Get rid of finalizer
    // to avoid the object staying around for an extra GC cycle!
    GC.SuppressFinalize(this);
  }

  ~NativeResourceHolder()
  {
    this.Dispose(true);
  }
}
```

From your calling code, you should always ensure that you call the *Dispose()* method of the class when the object is no longer of use. Not doing so and relying on the finalizer negatively affect performance. Implementing a finalizer on a class is literally only for backup if the developer using the object has written bad code that forgets to call *Dispose*. For more information about this, read the article titled "Implementing a Dispose Method" on the Microsoft MSDN Web site at *msdn2.microsoft.com/en-us/library/fs2xkftw.aspx*.

Finally, look at the GC counters, and if the number associated with the Managed String Objects Allocated counter is larger than what you were expecting, examine the code for potential optimization opportunities of substituting strings with *System.Text.StringBuilder*—an example of how to do this and why is given in the section titled "Tips and Tricks" later in this chapter.

Memory

Figure 5-6 shows the Memory counter names and descriptions. The two counters that your application can affect are the JIT Heap counter, which holds the native representations of all the managed methods that were JIT compiled, and the GC Heap counter, which holds the memory for all the managed objects allocated. The other three heap counters can indicate the size of your application, so the principle of less code is faster code always applies.

Memory

GC Heap	The number of bytes in use by the Garbage Collector heap.
Short Term Heap	The number of bytes currently in use by the CLR's short term heap.
JIT Heap	The number of bytes in use by the JIT compiler's heap.
Process Heap	The number of bytes currently in use by the CLR's default heap.
App Domain Heap	The number of bytes in use by the CLR's App Domain heap.

Figure 5-6 Memory: five counters with descriptions

JIT

Figure 5-7 lists the JIT counters and descriptions. The larger the number associated with the Pitched counters, the more penalties your application pays for the runtime to re-JIT-compile those methods the next time they are called. If your application was not moved to the background while it was running, the numbers of pitched methods should be zero (0). Also, note that the JIT and Memory counters must be read in combination to help you form the complete picture of the run-time characteristics of your application.

JIT

Method Pitch Latency Time (ms)	The total time (in milliseconds) spent pitching methods generated by the JIT compiler.
Bytes Pitched	The count of bytes of native code generated by the JIT compiler which is pitched.
Native Bytes Jitted	The count of bytes of native code generated by the JIT compiler.
Methods Jitted	The count of methods generated by the JIT compiler.
Methods Pitched	The count of methods generated by the JIT compiler which is pitched.

Figure 5-7 JIT: five counters with descriptions

Exceptions

Figure 5-8 shows the single counter for exceptions. As mentioned in Chapter 4, throwing exceptions is expensive. Exceptions should be thrown only in exceptional circumstances. If this counter is high, your application has issues not only from a performance point of view but from an overall design perspective.

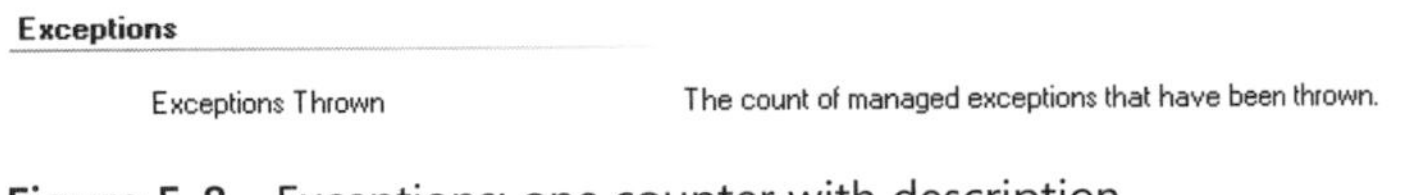

Exceptions

Exceptions Thrown	The count of managed exceptions that have been thrown.

Figure 5-8 Exceptions: one counter with description

Interop

Figure 5-9 describes the interop counters. The numbers you see for these counters should not surprise you if you are familiar with Platform Invocation Services (PInvoke) and using it in your code. If they do surprise you, you should investigate. Crossing the boundary from managed code to native does have a performance implication that is amplified when complex marshaling must take place. If you are in control of the native side or can introduce a native intermediary, try to design chunky calls rather than chatty ones. Of course, only do this after you identify interop as the source of a specific performance issue. Finally, combine the information you get from the interop counters with the information in the interop log, as described in Chapter 4 and Chapter 14, "Interoperating with the Platform."

Interop

Platform Invoke Calls	The count of Platform Invoke calls from managed code to native call, excluding internal CLR Platform Invoke calls.
COM Calls Using a vtable	The count of calls from managed code to native code using the COM Interop vtable method.
COM Calls Using IDispatch	The count of calls from managed code to native code using the COM Interop IDispatch method.
Complex Marshaling	The number of objects marshaled from managed code to native code that involved copying or transforming the data.
Runtime Callable Wrappers	The total count of COM Runtime Callable Wrappers that have been created.

Figure 5-9 Interop: five counters with descriptions

Networking

The pair of networking counters depicted in Figure 5-10 are self-explanatory. Combine the information given by these counters with the network log, as described in Chapter 4 and Chapter 8, "Networking."

Networking

Socket Bytes Sent	The total count of bytes sent via sockets.
Socket Bytes Received	The total count of bytes received via sockets.

Figure 5-10 Networking: two counters with descriptions

Windows.Forms

Figure 5-11 shows the counters and descriptions for Windows Forms objects. When you create an application with a single form and no controls–in other words, a default project with no code–one control is created (the form) with one brush, one font, and no other values. In your applications, if you observe high numbers for the various Windows.Forms counters, try to reuse the objects in your forms, such as the *Font* and *Brush* objects.

Windows.Forms

Controls Created	The total number of controls created by the application.
Brushes Created	The total number of brushes created by the application.
Pens Created	The total number of pens created by the application.
Bitmaps Created	The total number of bitmaps created by the application.
Regions Created	The total number of regions created by the application.
Fonts Created	The total number of fonts created by the application.
Graphics Created (FromImage)	The total number of graphics objects created by 'FromImage'.
Graphics Created (CreateGraphics)	The total number of graphics objects created by 'CreateGraphics'.

Figure 5-11 Windows Forms: eight counters with descriptions

Remote Performance Monitor

The file name of Remote Performance Monitor (RPM) is NetCFRPM.exe, and you can find it on your local hard drive if you have installed Service Pack 1 (SP1) of the .NET Compact Framework.

Tip Even if your target does not have SP1 installed, you can still use the RPM tool to connect to it.

All the screen shots in the figures in the preceding sections of this chapter were captured by using RPM when the .stat file was opened in it. For opening .stat files, RPM does not have to be connected to the device. You simply copy the file from the device across to the development computer, and then browse to it locally using RPM. We modified the previous screen shots by removing the columns with the actual numbers so that the images would fit properly on the page.

Earlier in this chapter, we mentioned the Logging Options dialog box that is shown in Figure 4-15 in Chapter 4. As you may recall, you can use the Logging Options dialog box to change the relevant registry entries that control logging and the performance counters remotely. To be able to do this, RPM must be connected to the device (described later).

Another feature of RPM is the capability of collecting performance statistics while the application is running, and optionally to publish the counters to the Performance Monitor (PerfMon) tool on the desktop. To be able to do this, again, RPM must connect to the device.

Connecting to the Device

To connect to the device, you must copy two files from your development computer to the Windows folder on your device: Netcfrtl.dll and Netcflaunch.exe. Both can be found by default in the C:\Program Files\Microsoft Visual Studio 8\SmartDevices\SDK\CompactFramework\2.0\v2.0\WindowsCE\wce400\armv4 folder. (For devices that run Windows CE 5.0 and Windows Mobile 5.0 or later, change *wce400* to *wce500*.) The first time you run RPM, you may see a security prompt on the device relating to Netcfrtl.dll, and you should of course accept it. On devices running Windows Mobile 5.0, you may further need to provision the device over Microsoft ActiveSync by using Rapiconfig, a desktop configuration tool that you can use to run provisioning Extensible Markup Language (XML) snippets. Either way, the XML with which to provision the device is as follows:

```
<wap-provisioningdoc>
   - <characteristic type="Metabase">
      - <characteristic type="RAPI\Windows\netcfrtl.dll\*">
         <parm name="rw-access" value="3" />
         <parm name="access-role" value="152" />
         <!-- 152 maps to "CARRIER_TPS | USER_AUTH | MANAGER"-->
      </characteristic>
   </characteristic>
</wap-provisioningdoc>
```

For more information about provisioning devices, including how to do it on the device with managed code by using the *Microsoft.WindowsMobile.Configuration* assembly, see Chapter 17, "Developing with Windows Mobile."

Assuming the preceding XML resides in a file named Rpmprovision.xml, you can run it on the device by using the following command:

```
rapiconfig rpmprovision.xml
```

When RPM is connected, you configure the registry using the Logging Options dialog box, which you open from the Device menu, and more important, you can collect live counters, as described next.

> **Note** The RPM tool that ships with version 2.0 SP1 of the .NET Compact Framework can connect only to a real device and not to the emulator. The next version of RPM will rectify this issue as well as include additional enhancements.

Collecting Live Counters

On the File menu, select Live Counters to open the Live Counters dialog box. In the Device combo box, you should see your device listed, assuming you followed the steps of the preceding section successfully. This is depicted in Figure 5-12.

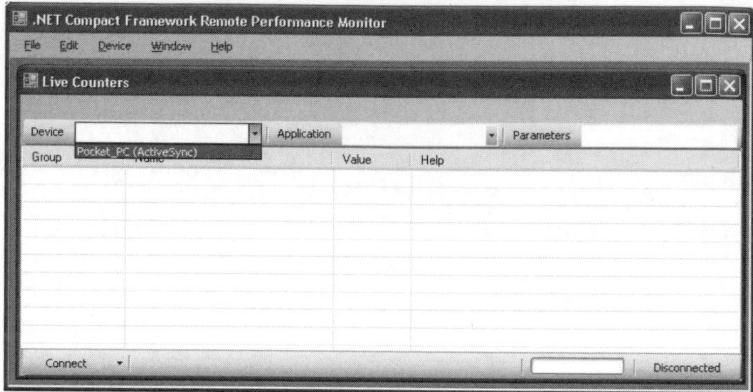

Figure 5-12 RPM Live Counters dialog box showing that the device is prepared but that RPM is not connected to an application yet

After choosing your device in the Device combo box, enter the full path to your application on the device in the Application combo box. If your application accepts command-line arguments, enter those in the Parameters text box. When you are done, click Connect. You should see something like the results shown in Figure 5-13.

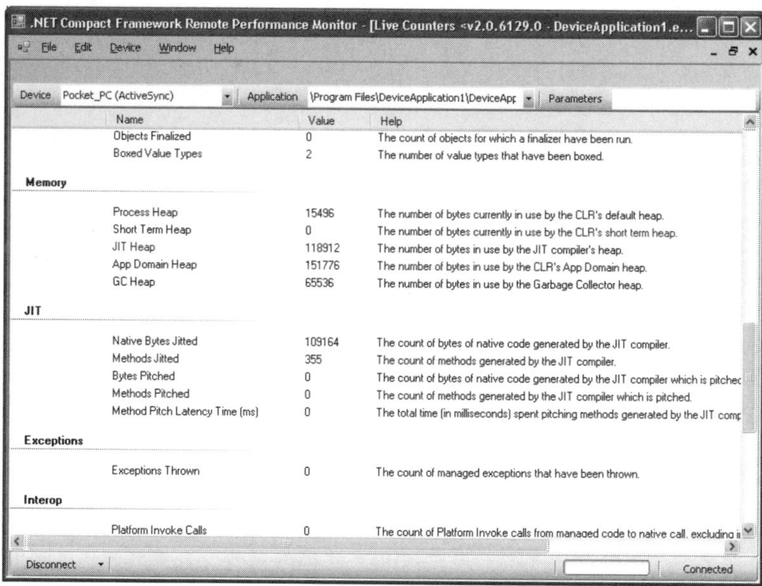

Figure 5-13 RPM Live Counters when the application is started

Unlike when you open the static .stat file, the counters are updated as the application runs. For example, if you scroll to the top and look at the Total Program Run Time counter, you will see that it is continuously incrementing. Live counters are great for observing differences as they occur while your application is running; for example, click a button and observe which numbers change and by how much. If you prefer to focus on certain counters and, for example, see them in a graph, you can use PerfMon, as described in the next section.

Using PerfMon

Run PerfMon (press Windows logo key + R) to open the management console with the performance snap-in. Right-click in the graph area and select Add Counters. You should see the .NET Compact Framework performance counters in the Performance Object list, as shown in Figure 5-14.

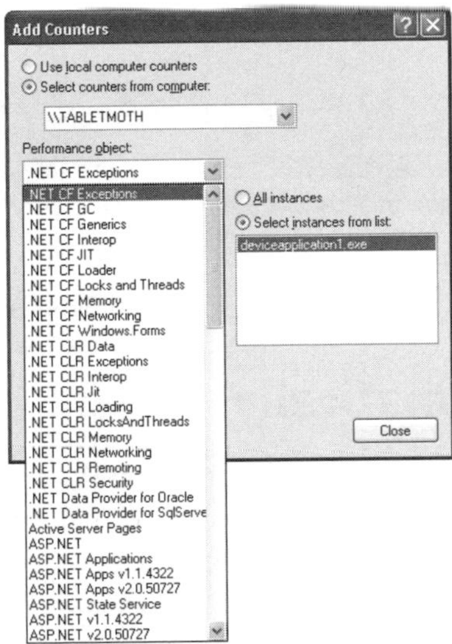

Figure 5-14 Performance Monitor: adding the .NET CF counters

We added two counters: Total Program Run Time and Managed Bytes Allocated. Clearly, you'd expect the first counter to increment linearly and the second to start at some value and then increment depending on the mechanics of your application. In the sample application, we have a button that allocates some strings, so whenever that button is clicked, we expect to see a small increase in the second counter. Figure 5-15 shows the complete graph: Both counters start at 0 before the application runs, they go up, and finally when the application exits they both go to 0 again.

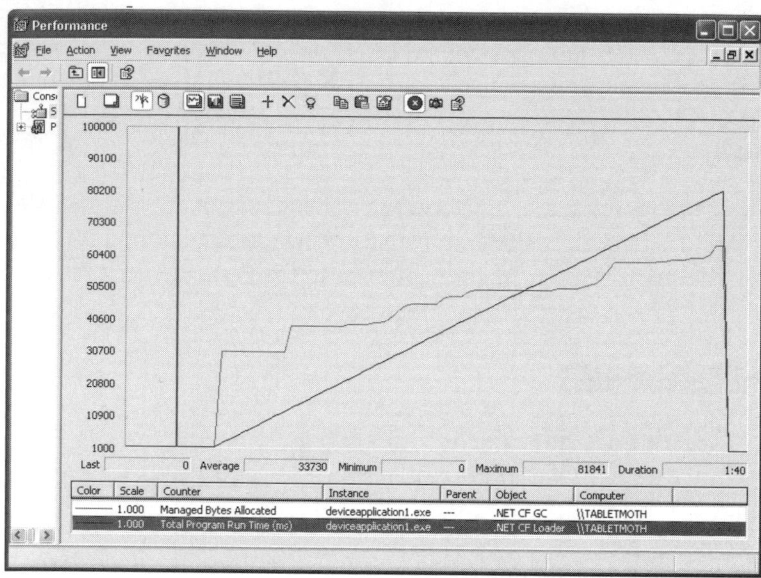

Figure 5-15 Performance Monitor: graph of Total Program Run Time, Managed Bytes Allocated

Measuring Performance Programmatically

This chapter starts by discussing the characteristics of the .NET Compact Framework runtime engine and notes how that may affect your application performance. In particular, you know that high memory usage negatively affects your application and that more code usually means slower code. Sometimes you may simply need to measure how long a particular method takes and, for example, optimize performance at the micro level of a particular algorithm.

Unfortunately, unlike the full .NET Framework, the .NET Compact Framework includes no profiling tools. This means that you cannot get a tool to report how long each method took to execute, how many times it was called, how long each code statement took, and so forth—all of this information is available by using tools on the desktop only. As mentioned in Chapter 4 for unit testing, you could run your code on the desktop, assuming it is not dependent on any device-only features and environment. Most of the time, this is not possible, but it is always worth considering.

The only option is to measure manually how long a method takes by inserting code to that effect and remembering to remove it when you release. Traditionally, measuring time is done by using the tick count, which is accessible through *Environment.TickCount* and returns the number of milliseconds since the system started. You can access this number before and after an operation runs, and the difference indicates how much time elapsed. The following code sample demonstrates:

```
private void SomeMethodB()
{
  int start = Environment.TickCount;

  // some long-running task
  Thread.Sleep(2000);

  int end = Environment.TickCount;

  int millis = end - start;

  MessageBox.Show(millis.ToString());
}
```

The full .NET Framework 2.0 introduces the *Stopwatch* class in the *System.Diagnostics* namespace. You can use it to accurately measure elapsed time. *Stopwatch* wraps the high-resolution native timer application programming interfaces (APIs) *QueryPerformanceCounter* and *QueryPerformanceFrequency*. If they are not available on your platform, *Stopwatch* falls back to using the *Environment.TickCount*. *Stopwatch* is not implemented in .NET Compact Framework 2.0, but you can get a *Stopwatch* implementation from Daniel Moth's Weblog at *www.danielmoth.com/Blog/2004/12/stopwatch.html*. Note that this community implementation does not include the fallback mechanism to calling *TickCount*, and version 3.5 of the .NET Compact Framework includes a full implementation of the *Stopwatch* class.

An example of using *Stopwatch* follows in the code sample:

```
private void SomeMethodA()
{
  Stopwatch sw = new Stopwatch();
  sw.Start();

  // some long-running task
  Thread.Sleep(2000);

  sw.Stop();

  long millis = sw.ElapsedMilliseconds;

  MessageBox.Show(millis.ToString());
}
```

While we're on the subject of programmatically measuring time, in some circumstances you may wish to measure memory consumption programmatically. The following line of code retrieves the number of bytes currently thought to be allocated by your application:

```
long bytesInUseByManagedObjects = GC.GetTotalMemory(false);
```

You can also use PInvoke on the native *GlobalMemoryStatus* method, which retrieves information about the system's current usage of both physical and virtual memory, as the following code sample shows:

```
private void ShowMemory()
{
  MemoryStatus ms = new MemoryStatus();
  GlobalMemoryStatus(ms);

  string result =
    "Memory Load % = " + ms.MemoryLoad +
    "\r\nTotal Physical (KB) = " + ms.TotalPhysical / 1024 +
    "\r\nAvailable Physical (KB) = " + ms.AvailPhysical / 1024 +
    "\r\nTotal Virtual = (KB) " + ms.TotalVirtual / 1024+
    "\r\nAvailable Virtual = (KB) " + ms.AvailVirtual / 1024;

  MessageBox.Show(result);
}


[DllImport("coredll.dll")]
public static extern void GlobalMemoryStatus(MemoryStatus lpBuffer);

public class MemoryStatus
{
  public int Length;
  public int MemoryLoad;
  public int TotalPhysical;
  public int AvailPhysical;
  public int TotalPageFile;
  public int AvailPageFile;
  public int TotalVirtual;
  public int AvailVirtual;

  public MemoryStatus()
  {
    Length = Marshal.SizeOf(this);
  }
}
```

You must consider several factors when you measure code. We attempt to summarize some of them here.

Always build your project in *release* mode using any optimizations that your chosen language allows to be set in the project properties window. Run the code directly on the device, not in the emulator and not through Microsoft Visual Studio. Ensure that no other user applications are running on the device. Close any Internet and other network connections unless they are needed by what you are measuring. The idea is to create an environment that is repeatable between tests and one that is not adversely affected by unexpected changes from other external factors. Never measure just once; measure the same operation multiple times and take an average. Discard the first measurement to compensate for JIT compilation time of the code involved. Ensure that you are logging the results either on-screen or to file, and don't make the common mistake of including the logging mechanism in your measurements!

Finally, focus on seconds and not milliseconds. Although performing operations in less than a second is definitely possible, generally speaking you should not rely on this. Given the by-design nondeterministic garbage collection behavior, expecting certain tasks to take less than 1 second can lead to disappointment–so do not expect it and do not promise it either. If your requirements do dictate deterministic subsecond measurements, consider using native code in a solution instead.

Performance Guidance

Most developers try to find the magic bullet for writing faster code. We must reiterate: No such thing exists. Performance is designed into an application, and micro-optimizations almost never have significant impact. Always measure before you attempt to optimize, and always measure the optimization to see if it has had an effect in your particular scenario. Performance guidance and several tips and tricks are included throughout this chapter in sections discussing other important topics, so please do read the whole chapter to find them all.

For more information about generic–not device-specific–performance advice given by the patterns and practices team, see the MSDN Web site at *msdn2.microsoft.com/en-us/library/ms998530.aspx*.

With that said, the section titled "Tips and Tricks" that follows summarizes the guidance offered directly by the .NET Compact Framework team. Please do not apply this advice blindly. Many times, implementing performance optimizations conflicts with writing extensible, maintainable code; use optimizations only when you must.

Tips and Tricks

One of the performance counters described earlier counts the number of exceptions that are thrown. Throwing new exceptions is expensive, and you should avoid throwing exceptions unless one must be thrown. In addition, if you are a Visual Basic developer, do not use the legacy *On Error GoTo/Resume Next*, which is very expensive even when an exception is not actually thrown; instead, replace that construct with *try..catch..finally* constructs to be more efficient.

Improve Start-Up Time

Loading applications with version 2.0 of the .NET Compact Framework is faster than loading them with version 1.0, and the Visual Studio 2005 designer generates more optimal form layout code. You can also write optimal layout code whenever you are manually populating, creating, and laying out controls. Use the following two pairs of methods wherever they are available: *SuspendLayout/ResumeLayout* and *BeginUpdate/EndUpdate*.

This tip helps you keep the user interface (UI) responsive. Another technique for creating a responsive UI is to load any data and perform other expensive tasks in a background thread. You learn more about this in Chapter 11. You can keep the UI flicker-free when performing custom drawing by using double buffering, which is a technique described in Chapter 12, "Graphics Programming."

Give your assemblies strong names only if they are placed in the global assembly cache (GAC), and place your assemblies in the GAC only if you really must. (For more information about how to place an assembly in the GAC, see Chapter 6, "Completing the Application: Packaging and Deployment".) Loading a strongly named assembly requires the runtime to verify the assembly, which is not a cheap operation. Also, Windows Mobile does some checks of its own on the hash of an executable when the executable is started. This means that the larger your assembly becomes, the longer it will take to load. One trick for keeping the overall assembly size small is to remove embedded resources and load them from the file system instead. Chapter 11 includes an example.

Strings, XML, and Data

There is no application that does not use strings. Strings are immutable objects, so if you have methods that perform multiple concatenation and other altering operations, what your code is really doing is creating and copying multiple string objects. Use a *System.Text.StringBuilder* instead. This same advice applies to the desktop world as well, but it has dramatic effects when used with the .NET Compact Framework, as shown in the following code examples on a device running Windows Mobile 2003 Standard Edition:

```
   // Takes ~ 5 minutes  (i.e., 300,000 seconds)
public static void UseString()
   {
     string result = string.Empty;
     for (int i = 0; i < 10000; i++)
     {
       result += "strings are immutable " +
         "but I still use them as if they are not";
     }
```

```
}

// Takes ~ 0.2 seconds (i.e., ~230 milliseconds!)
public static void UseStringBuilder()
{
  string result = string.Empty;
  StringBuilder sb = new StringBuilder();
  for (int i = 0; i < 10000; i++)
  {
    sb.Append("strings are immutable ").Append(
      "but I still use them as if they are not");
  }

  result = sb.ToString();
}
```

Like string manipulation, XML is commonly used in modern applications. XML is great because of its "toolability" and wide applicability, but it is a verbose format. If you are loading XML documents larger than 64 KB, it is best to use a *System.Xml.XmlReader* instead of the popular *System.Xml.XmlDocument*. Also, when you load XML documents, use performance-tuning properties such as *IgnoreWhitespace*, which can produce great savings in time. Other commonsense advice includes using short element and attribute names; try to keep the XML as concise as possible.

For data access advice, see Chapter 3, "Using SQL Server 2005 Compact Edition and Other Data Stores." In particular, if you are new to Microsoft SQL Server 2005 Compact Edition, learn to use *System.Data.SqlServerCe.SqlCeResultset*, which was designed with efficiency in mind for applications using a local, not remote, database. For that reason, it is a class unique to the Compact Edition of SQL Server 2005.

Math

When your application must perform complex math calculations, try to stick with 32-bit numbers because 64-bit numbers are not eligible for enregistration, which basically means the JIT compiler must use the CPU registers to store your variables. Floating-point math is slow on Advanced RISC Machines (ARM) devices because they do not have a floating-point unit (FPU), so regardless of whether you use managed or native code, it will not be fast. Having said that, with the .NET Compact Framework being used in Microsoft XNA[1] on other processors, a lot of work must have been done to optimize the floating-point implementation of the framework, and so future versions should improve.

Finally, the decimal type is very slow even on the desktop framework because it does not have a direct mapping to an IL type. You cannot expect it to be fast on the .NET Compact Framework; use the decimal type only when absolutely necessary.

1 XNA Framework is a set of managed code libraries for game development on the PC and Microsoft Xbox 360. Its implementation started with the .NET Compact Framework as the base, and any positive changes made on the way should be back-ported as applicable to devices that run the .NET Compact Framework for Windows CE.

Reflection

Reflection is a complex and advanced topic to which a whole book can be dedicated. We resist the temptation to go into too much detail and instead summarize the key points that you should revisit when you are required to use reflection in your application.

Reflection is expensive even on the desktop. On devices, you can expect to pay a penalty of 10 to 100 times slower code execution compared with making the calls early bound; plus, there is an increase in the overall memory usage of the application. Reflection-avoidance techniques are the same on devices as they are on the desktop or server.

Reflection usually refers to creating types dynamically and can sometimes be avoided by employing class factories instead. After you create a type, you invoke members on them next, and this can sometimes be avoided by using interfaces (for an example, see the code for this chapter on the companion Web site). Also, remember attributes and particularly custom attributes. Attributes are not expensive until they are called, which is always by reflection, and again, they can sometimes be avoided by using interfaces instead (for an example, see code for this chapter on the companion Web site).

It is interesting to note that when your code makes Web service calls reflection is used. If you identify Web service calls as a bottleneck, you may decide to invest in a custom serialization (binary) solution, although when Web service calls create a bottleneck it is usually because of the network rather than the device-side components. Another tip for when you use Web Services is to create a single instance of the Web service proxy object and use it throughout the application instead of re-creating it each time.

Collections

Collections in one form or another are used very commonly in applications. A common boxing scenario occurs when you use collections such as *ArrayList* to store value types such as *int.* Such is the perfect scenario for using generics and particularly the collections from the *System.Collections.Generic* namespace such as *List<T>*. Generic collections have the added advantage of strong typing and hence can reduce run-time exceptions by employing compile-time checking.

```
public static void UseArrayList()
{
  ArrayList a1 = new ArrayList(100000);
  ArrayList a2 = new ArrayList(100000);

  for (int i = 0; i < 100000; i++)
  {
    a2.Add(i * i); // boxing
  }

  for (int i = 0; i < 100000; i++)
  {
    int j = (int)a2[i]; //unboxing
    a1.Add(j); //boxing
```

```
  }
  // takes ~ 600 milliseconds
}

public static void UseGenerics()
{
  List<int> a1 = new List<int>(100000);
  List<int> a2 = new List<int>(100000);

  for (int i = 0; i < 100000; i++)
  {
    a2.Add(i * i);
  }

  for (int i = 0; i < 100000; i++)
  {
    int j = a2[i];
    a1.Add(j);
  }
  // takes ~ 75 milliseconds
}
```

In the preceding code, the method using generics is faster. However, comparing the generics case to a scenario in which an array is used directly shows that the array is still faster. This is no surprise because the array is what all other collection types wrap. It is left as an exercise for you to run the two preceding methods and the method that follows and to compare them to identify exactly how much they vary. Use *Stopwatch*, and also be sure to look at the performance counters for each case.

```
public static void UseArray()
{
  int[] a1 = new int[100000];
  int[] a2 = new int[100000];

  for (int i = 0; i < 100000; i++)
  {
    a2[i] = i * i;
  }

  for (int i = 0; i < 100000; i++)
  {
    int j = a2[i];
    a1[i] = j;
  }
  // takes ~ 30 milliseconds
}
```

Of course, different access characteristics vary, so always test your particular scenario. Once again, trading performance for elegant code should take place only when it must.

Other advice for using collections includes using a standard *for* loop instead of *foreach* because the latter uses reflection. Always presize your collections by using the constructor that accepts a *capacity*; otherwise, when you reach the capacity internally, a new, larger buffer must be allocated and all the existing items copied to it. You should get the size of the buffer right the first time.

Overriding *System.Object* Methods

Reflection is costly. Sometimes reflection can occur under the covers and not directly in your code. Consider the *Object.ToString()* method: Every object supports it, yet if you do not override this method in your code, when it is called, the base implementation will run. This is a case of a virtual call, but the performance cost of the virtual call is small compared with the performance cost of the default *ToString* implementation that uses reflection. Make a point of overriding the *ToString* method in your own classes if it is going to be called.

Similarly, for value types, make sure you override the *Equals* and *GetHashCode* methods. These methods create serious performance bottlenecks; improvements are there to be gained for your value types. These methods are virtual, use reflection, and also result in boxing because your value type must be boxed for the methods to be called. Overriding these two methods in your value type (that is, your *struct*) will eliminate boxing, the virtual call, and also the reflection if you can implement the methods in a way that does not use reflection.

Parting Thoughts

Please do not take all of the advice given in this chapter and start applying it blindly to your code. First, measure to see whether a performance issue exists. If so, evaluate the best way to optimize the code causing the issue, and only then see whether you can use one of the tips and tricks we give here. After you apply the change, measure performance again to see whether the optimization had an effect, which is the criterion for keeping the change. Some of the advice given here is in direct opposition to good design principles, that should be sacrificed for performance only when it is absolutely necessary to do so.

Summary

Performance optimization principles are generally the same across platforms. .NET performance advice on the desktop also applies in the device world. This chapter highlights some of the generic performance-optimizing advice and focuses on summarizing the techniques you can apply to resource-constrained devices. Understanding the compact CLR is paramount for writing efficient code. This chapter describes how to use the performance counters and Remote Performance Monitor. Also, the code samples in this chapter can help you measure memory consumption or the speed of an operation programmatically.

Good performance should be a requirement in your projects, one with the same importance as functional requirements. This chapter gives you the tools and information you need to optimize your code and write applications that are good citizens of the mobile platform: They are always responsive, they get the job done fast, and they do not consume resources that other applications could be using.

Chapter 6
Completing the Application: Packaging and Deployment

In this chapter:

In this chapter, we discuss the often overlooked tasks involved in packaging and deploying your completed code to your target devices. First, we talk about how to add online help content to your application, and then we describe some techniques you can use to lock down devices to your specific applications. Finally, we discuss the steps involved in producing a simple installer package that you can use to deploy your application and content files to smart devices.

Implementing Help

Implementing help content for an application is an important step in application development that is often left till late in the development process. Although it is beyond the scope of this book to describe the techniques involved in writing good help content, we must mention that it is important to keep the help content concise and arranged into short topics to minimize the need for scrolling. You have only limited screen space (see Figure 6-1), which is not ideal for reading large amounts of text, and the search and navigation functionalities on devices are limited in comparison with desktop versions of the Microsoft Windows operating system.

Figure 6-1 The Pocket PC Help application

Creating HTML-Based Help

Since the first version of Windows CE, the platform has supported a Hypertext Markup Language (HTML)–based help engine. Pocket PC continues to use the same technology. Smartphone does not have a help engine, so we discuss smartphones separately later in the chapter. Unlike on the desktop, help is accessed on the Start menu only. Users can open a specific help topic by tapping Help on the Start menu when your form is visible; if you don't provide an implementation for this feature, the full help contents on the system are displayed. The device help engine is far simpler than HTML Help on the desktop, and Microsoft does not ship any tools to build this content. However, because the help format is an extension of standard HTML, with a few additional tags you can create help content using any regular Web authoring software. The engine supports all the same tags as Microsoft Internet Explorer Mobile (known as Pocket Internet Explorer in earlier versions of the platform).

Each help file is a single .htm file that can contain multiple help topics. Standard HTML anchors are used to provide links between topics in the file. One anchor must be included in the file to indicate the location of the table of contents—the help engine uses this anchor to provide a permanent link to the contents as follows:

```
<A NAME="Main_Contents"></A>
```

The table of contents itself is simply created as a list of hyperlinks to the different topics contained in the document. A special tag is placed in the page header to tell the help application which topic represents the table of contents. This tag must match the anchor name of your table of contents page exactly; otherwise, the help application will display an error indicating that the help file cannot be found.

```
<meta http-equiv="Htm-Help" content="kiosk.htm#Main_Contents"/>
```

In the HTML file, each individual page is separated by a special comment tag. The name of the comment tag harkens back to the code name for Windows CE 1.0, which was Pegasus; hence, *PegHelp*:

```
<!-- PegHelp --><hr/>
```

This comment tag is used so that the document is still valid HTML and will display in any browser; it indicates to the Help application in Windows CE where each topic begins and ends to preserve the illusion that each topic is on a separate page. The horizontal rule tag is optional but makes working with the file from the desktop much easier.

The help file can contain keyword definitions that the built-in search application can use to find topics in your help file. These keyword definitions are specified in the <HEAD> section of your help file and take the following form:

```
<keyword value="kiosk;screen"
title="Kiosk Settings"
href="Kiosk.htm#kiosk" />
```

The *value* attribute is a semicolon-separated list of keywords. In the preceding example, we associate the keywords *kiosk* and *screen* with the topic. The *title* attribute stores a description of the specific topic that can be displayed to the user. Finally, the *href* contains the link to the help topic. Notice the number sign (#) is used to denote a named anchor in the document. The help engine cannot cope with relative paths, so it is customary to place your .htm file in the Windows folder on the device. Figure 6-2 shows the results of a search for the keyword we detailed in the sample help file.

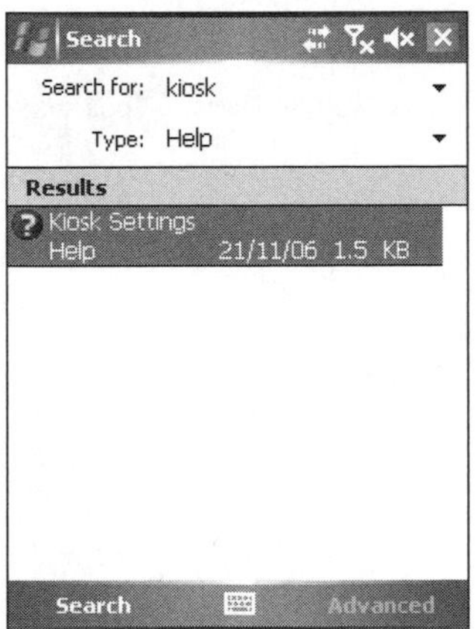

Figure 6-2 Searching the help system for the keyword *kiosk,* which is defined in the help file

There is little else to know about writing help content for Windows CE. A wide range of HTML tags is supported, as you would expect from Internet Explorer Mobile. One surprising limitation is that you can use only bitmap images, and these must be specified with absolute paths in the <IMG> tag. Realistically, this means the help file and associated images are usually deployed to the Windows folder on the target device. The following listing shows a completed help file.

```
<html>
<head>
    <title>Kiosk Sample</title>
    <LINK rel="stylesheet" type="text/css" href="file://\Windows\DeviceHelp.css" />
    <meta http-equiv="Htm-Help" content="kiosk.htm#Main_Contents"/>
    <keyword title="Kiosk Mode" value="Kiosk;Fullscreen" href="kiosk.htm#kiosk"/>
    <keyword title="Hardware Buttons" value="Hardware;Button"
href="kiosk.htm#buttons"/>
    <keyword title="Help Links" value="Help;Context" href="kiosk.htm#help"/>
</head>
<body><!-- PegHelp -->

<a name="Main_Contents"></a><h1>Table of Contents</h1>

<p><a href="kiosk.htm#kiosk">Kiosk Mode</a></p>
<p><a href="kiosk.htm#buttons">Hardware Buttons</a></p>
<p><a href="kiosk.htm#help">Help Links</a></p>

<!-- PegHelp --><hr/>

<a name="kiosk"></a><h1 class="dtH1">Kiosk Mode</h1>
<p>SHFullScreen is used to enable/disable various user interface features such as the
start menu.</p>

<ol>
<li>Hide StartMenu will disallow the user from tapping Start or any of the
notification tray icons.</li>

<li>Hide Taskbar will remove the entire taskbar. This only works if the Form has
WindowState = Maximized</li>
<li>Hide SIP will hide the Soft Input Panel button. On Windows Mobile 5.0, this will
reappear if you tap on the menu bar.</li>
<li>Hide Control Box changes the property to hide the OK button used to close the
form.</li>
</ol>

<h4 class="dtH4">See also</h4>
<p><a href="kiosk.htm#buttons">Hardware Buttons</a></p>
<p><a href="kiosk.htm#help">Help</a></p>

<!-- PegHelp --><hr/>

<a name="buttons"></a><h1 class="dtH1">Hardware Buttons</h1>
<p>Six Hardware Button controls are used to override their default behavior so that
the user cannot easily "escape" from our application.</p>
```

```
<h4 class="dtH4">See also</h4>

<p><a href="kiosk.htm#kiosk">Kiosk Mode</a></p>
<p><a href="kiosk.htm#help">Help Links</a></p>

<!-- PegHelp --><hr/>

<a name="help"></a><h1 class="dtH1">Help</h1>
<p>The sample implements help links from both the Start menu and through a main
application menu (so that it is accessible even in Kiosk mode).</p>
<p>The System.Windows.Forms.Help class is used to start the help system (Not supported
on Smartphone).</p>

<h4 class="dtH4">See also</h4>

<p><a href="kiosk.htm#kiosk">Kiosk Mode</a></p>
<p><a href="kiosk.htm#buttons">Hardware Buttons</a></p>
<!-- PegHelp --><hr/>
</body>
</html>
```

After you create a working multiple-topic help file, you can hook up the Help menu item to display the Help topics to the user.

Starting Help Topics from Code

The Microsoft .NET Compact Framework version 2.0 introduces a subset of the desktop *System.Windows.Forms.Help* class used to interact with the help engine. With the *ShowHelp* method, you can specify the file name and optionally the topic name to display. The topic name is appended as a standard HTML anchor, for example:

```
Help.ShowHelp(this, "MyApp.htm#MyTopic");
```

Typically, you would call this from your *HelpRequested* event handler for your form, but you could provide additional help links in your application:

```
private void Form1_HelpRequested(object sender, HelpEventArgs hlpevent)
{
Help.ShowHelp(this, "Kiosk.htm#Main_Contents");
}
```

If you want to add more flexibility, you can store the topic name in a string variable that you can set based on activity in the application to provide context sensitivity.

Master Table of Contents

There is one final step available that you can use to hook the help content into the master table of contents on the device—this master table of contents is the list displayed when a user taps Start and then taps Help when no application is in use. You hook the Help content to the master table of contents by placing a shortcut to the help file in the Windows\Help folder on the device. In Windows Mobile 5.0 and later, the help engine reads the title from your file and appends it to the "Help for Added Programs" topic that appears at the bottom of the main table of contents (see Figure 6-3). In earlier versions, custom Help files are added alphabetically to the table of contents.

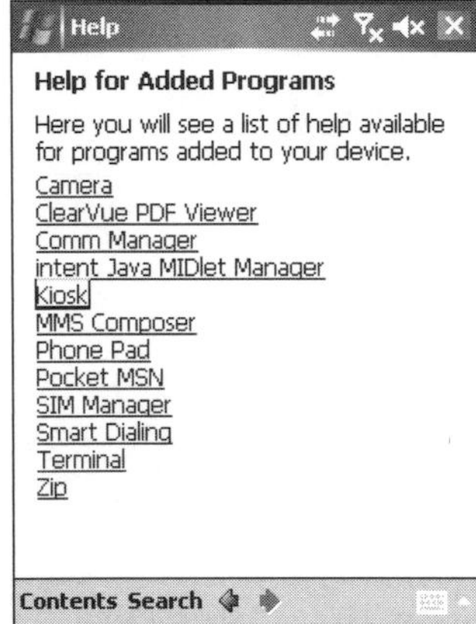

Figure 6-3 Custom Help link in the master table of contents

You can create these shortcuts in the device installer, as described in the section titled "Adding Shortcuts" later in this chapter. You can also create the shortcuts manually if necessary. In Windows CE, a shortcut is a file with an .lnk extension with contents such as follows:

```
18#\Windows\Kiosk.htm
```

The numeral represents the number of characters after the number sign (#), which is followed by the full path to the file. If you create this file manually, you must calculate the length yourself. If a path contains spaces, it must be enclosed in double quotation marks, and these are included in the character count. You can call an application programming interface (API) to create shortcuts programmatically: SHCreateShortcut. The techniques involved in calling API methods are discussed in Chapter 14, "Interoperating with the Platform."

Help on Smartphone Devices

If you need to distribute help content on smartphone devices, the easiest method is to write Help as simple HTML content. The content is probably best divided into separate .htm files for each topic along with a table of contents page. Although you can potentially use the same .htm file as the one you created for Pocket PC, it will be shown in its entirety and is not conveniently split into topics.

To start a help topic in your application, you can use the *Process* class in the *System.Diagnostics* namespace to start the .htm file. The following *ShowTopic* method is designed to behave much like the *System.Windows.Forms.Help.ShowTopic* method, which is not available on smartphones. You should pass in the full path of an HTML file containing your help content.

```
public static void ShowTopic(string url)
{
Process.Start(url, "");
}
```

The preceding code opens the topic in an Internet Explorer Mobile window. The user can navigate back to your application by pressing the Back hardware key. If you need to provide online help for a smartphone application, you should keep the help content as concise as possible and perhaps consider directing users to a manual that they can read on their desktop computer or on the Web.

Locking Down Your Application

When you deploy an enterprise application, often you want to restrict user access to only your application and not any other applications or settings. You can achieve this by using a combination of device configuration and changes to your application to avoid control passing away from your forms. Because the way devices are configured varies between manufacturers, the options available to you for device configuration vary depending on the device you deploy to.

Kiosk Mode

Essentially, Windows Mobile is designed as a consumer platform rather than as an industrial platform, and therefore the user interface is designed to provide easy access to built-in applications. Users can use many routes to access system features, many of which are outside your control, such as notification bubbles that can open above your application.

You have two options for writing a kiosk mode application. The first is new in .NET Compact Framework 2.0 and involves setting the *Form.WindowState* property to *Maximized*. This hides the entire taskbar and makes your form fill the entire screen space (if you remove the default *MenuBar* from your form, you'll have full screen real estate). Use this option with care because you will lose the ability to switch to other applications if necessary or view the notification area, including the clock.

The second option retains the basic shell components but disables the Start menu and restricts the user from tapping notification area icons, although these can still be used to display status. You can use the SHFullScreen API function, to which you can pass flags, to disable the Start menu and software-based input panel (SIP) buttons. Figure 6-4 shows a side-by-side comparison of an application with the *SHFullScreen* options and a maximized form. The .NET Compact Framework does not include a managed API for calling SHFullScreen, so you have to write the Platform Invocation Services (PInvoke) declaration yourself.

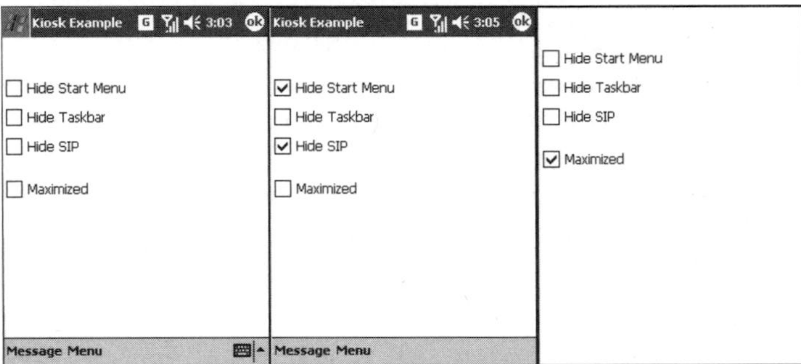

Figure 6-4 Comparison of a regular Windows Mobile application (left), when using *SHFullScreen* (middle) and when displaying with the form maximized (right)

```
[DllImport("aygshell.dll", SetLastError=true)]
[return: MarshalAs(UnmanagedType.Bool)]
private static extern bool SHFullScreen(IntPtr hwndRequester,
SHFS dwState);

[Flags()]
internal enum SHFS
{
SHOWTASKBAR = 0x0001,
HIDETASKBAR = 0x0002,
SHOWSIPBUTTON = 0x0004,
HIDESIPBUTTON = 0x0008,
SHOWSTARTICON = 0x0010,
HIDESTARTICON = 0x0020,
}
```

Hardware Buttons

.NET Compact Framework 2.0 includes support for reacting to application buttons on devices. If you register the hardware buttons to your application, you can ensure that the user can't use the buttons to switch to another application. There is no standard for which devices support which application buttons, and the order the buttons appear on the device may not match the numerical value of the button.

To use the HardwareButton component, you can drag it onto your form in the designer. Each *HardwareButton* component can capture only a single hardware button, and so you will probably need to add several *HardwareButton* controls to your form. Then you must set the AssociatedControl property (use your form) and the HardwareKey, and the control will pass through key presses to your form as KeyDown events. If you want to capture only the hardware buttons to restrict them from performing other functions, you don't need to write the event handler for *KeyDown*. Unlike a regular key press, the *HardwareButton* component doesn't raise an equivalent KeyUp event.

```
private void Form1_KeyDown(object sender, KeyEventArgs e)
{
            switch ((HardwareKeys)e.KeyCode)
            {
                case HardwareKeys.ApplicationKey1:
                    MessageBox.Show("Hardware Key 1");
                    break;
                case HardwareKeys.ApplicationKey2:
                    MessageBox.Show("Hardware Key 2");
                    break;
                case HardwareKeys.ApplicationKey3:
                    MessageBox.Show("Hardware Key 3");
                    break;
                case HardwareKeys.ApplicationKey4:
                    MessageBox.Show("Hardware Key 4");
                    break;
                case HardwareKeys.ApplicationKey5:
                    MessageBox.Show("Hardware Key 5");
                    break;
                case HardwareKeys.ApplicationKey6:
                    MessageBox.Show("Hardware Key 6");
                    break;
            }

}
```

Locking Down the User Interface

A simple, but not entirely bulletproof, method of disabling access to other applications is to remove the application shortcuts from the *Programs* folder on the device. You can, therefore, remove the shortcut to File Explorer to prevent the user from browsing to the application file. You can't delete or rename files already on the device from a setup project. The only workaround is to overwrite them with a zero-byte file, which effectively hides them. Files can be removed from a custom setup .dll file, or even from in your application code; we demonstrate these techniques in the section titled "Native CESetup.dll" later in this chapter.

Third-Party Solutions

For more detailed control in locking down your devices, you can use a number of third-party tools designed to enforce kiosk mode on Windows Mobile–powered devices. Symbol, for example, provides the AppCenter tool you can use to lock down devices to a single application. SPB Software House has a product that works on any Pocket PC that can provide access to multiple trusted applications and can be administered by password entry. More details are available at *www.spbsoftwarehouse.com/products/kioskengine/?en*.

Deploying the Runtime

All devices that run Windows Mobile 2003 or Windows Mobile 5.0 have at least .NET Compact Framework 1.0 in read-only memory (ROM). Devices running Windows Mobil 6 have version 2.0 of the Compact Framework in ROM. Microsoft ships releases of the platform to device manufacturers, who then customize and release to their devices on their own schedule. This can mean that different devices are running different versions of the framework as service pack updates are introduced with the Adaption Kit Update (AKU) releases that Microsoft ships to device manufacturers.

Because framework releases introduce performance improvements and bug fixes, it is preferable to ensure you are running on the latest available version. On current devices, .NET Compact Framework 2.0 is not built in as standard, but device manufacturers may choose to include it. Ensure that version 2.0 is installed so that your application runs properly; otherwise, if the version 2.0 runtime is not present, running a .NET Compact Framework 2.0 application will result in the error shown in Figure 6-5.

At the time of this writing, .NET Compact Framework 2.0 Service Pack 2 is the latest release; for optimal performance and reliability, ensure that the latest version of the runtime is installed. Microsoft has released a package containing all the redistributable components for Service Pack 2 version. To download, go to the Microsoft Download Center Web site at *www.microsoft.com/downloads/details.aspx?familyid=aea55f2f-07b5-4a8c-8a44-b4e1b196d5c0&DisplayLang=en*.

Figure 6-5 Error message displayed when attempting to run a .NET Compact Framework 2.0 application on a device without the version 2.0 runtime

The Compact Framework runtime is shipped by Microsoft as a collection of .cab file installers, each for a different version of Windows CE and Windows Mobile and different central processing unit (CPU) architectures (see Table 6-1). Microsoft bundles each of the separate .cab file installers together into the .NET Compact Framework Redistributable package. The Redistributable package starts the relevant .cab file installer through Microsoft ActiveSync and deploys the correct version of the runtime onto whichever device is currently connected. By directing your users to use this approach, you remove the need to ship the runtimes with your desktop installer and ensure that your users can always install the latest version without you having to repackage your application.

You may, however, wish to automate this step and push the correct .cab file to the device prior to installing your application. In the next section, we work through an example of this.

Table 6-1 .NET Compact Framework 2.0 .cab Files

File Name	Platform
NETCFv2.ppc.armv4.cab	Pocket PC 2003
NETCFv2.wce4.[CPU].cab	Windows CE .NET 4.2
NETCFv2.wm.armv4i.cab	Windows Mobile 5.0
NETCFv2.wce5.[CPU].cab	Windows CE 5.0

If you quickly want to determine the available runtime version from the device, you can open the Cgacutil.exe application, which is in the Windows folder. This application displays a window that lists the installed framework versions shown in Figure 6-6.

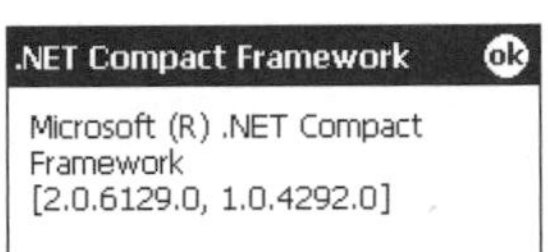

Figure 6-6 Cgacutil tool showing installed framework versions

Building a Device Installer

Windows CE supports a common installer type based on the Microsoft Cabinet format; packages have the .cab extension. These .cab files contain the application files and an installation script that specifies where to install the files and which shortcuts and registry settings to apply.

Visual Studio Installer Tools

Visual Studio 2005 introduces a project template specifically for building a .cab file installer directly from the integrated development environment (IDE). Previously, you could generate the .cab file installer only once, and then you had to manually alter an .inf file to regenerate the .cab file with any changed settings. The new approach, although not perfect, brings the experience closer to that of building an installer for a desktop project.

Device Installer Project Type

To create a new device installer, on the File menu, select New Project. Navigate to Other Project Types, Setup And Deployment, Smart Device CAB Project. With the project selected in the Solution Explorer tree, you can set a number of project-wide options. For example, Manufacturer and ProductName are used in combination as the display name for the component in the Remove Programs list in Settings. For this reason, it is recommended that the total length of the combined string be not longer than approximately 36 characters because the string will be truncated on most devices that use a portrait screen orientation. In the unlikely event that you don't want to allow the user to remove your product, you can exclude your application from the Remove Programs list by setting the NoUninstall property to *True*.

Adding Files and Setting Targets

Files are installed by pasting them into the File System Editor (Figure 6-7) in your setup project. You can use a variety of standard folder constants that deploy their contents to the correct localized folder on the target device. You can also create new folders and subfolders.

As the result of an issue with devices that run Windows Mobile 2003 and earlier, you may find that deploying files to a subfolder of Windows results in the files being placed directly in the Windows folder. The only workaround here is to manually create a directory called Windows and place your subfolder in there–do not use the Windows Folder system folder in the File System Editor.

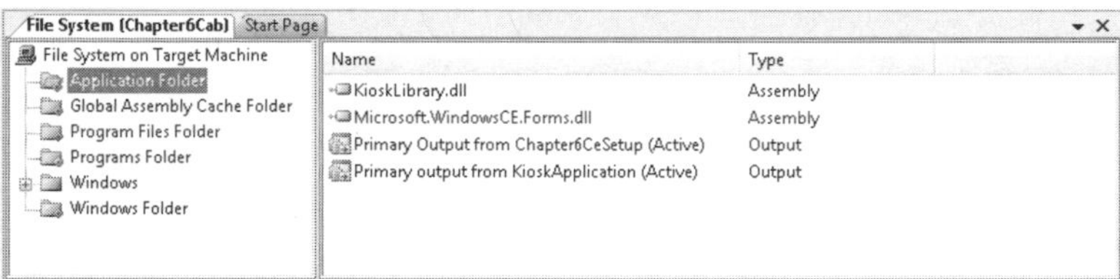

Figure 6-7 File System Editor, which you can use to drag program files to where they will be deployed to the file system on the target device

Adding Shortcuts

Shortcuts are just files, and as such are also added by using the File System Editor. To create a shortcut to a file in a project, right-click the file, and select Create Shortcut. You can then rename the shortcut to assign it the required display name, and you can place it in a folder, for example, the Programs Folder, if you want it to show on the Start menu Programs list.

Writing Registry Settings

As with setup projects for desktop Windows, built-in support is provided for provisioning registry settings in a device deployment project. Select the Registry Editor to see a tree prepopulated with root keys, as shown in Figure 6-8. You can add your own keys beneath the prepopulated values as required. They will be created if they are not already present on the target device.

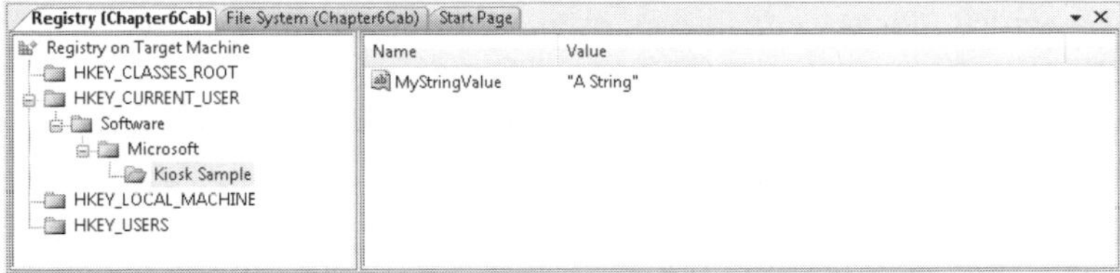

Figure 6-8 Registry Editor, which you can use to deploy specific keys and values for your application

Compression

Certain devices that run Windows Mobile, such as all smartphone devices and all devices running Windows Mobile 5.0 and later, support compressed .cab files. Although devices running Windows Mobile 5.0 Pocket PC still support uncompressed .cab files, using uncompressed files is not recommended. You can activate compression in the project properties window with your .cab file project selected. You may want to build the project twice—one version with compression enabled and one version with compression disabled—so that it supports all device types. Unfortunately, Visual Studio does not include a method to do this automatically for you.

Security Policies and Code Signing

Code signing was originally introduced in the Smartphone platform to address mobile operator concerns about malicious software affecting the security of their mobile networks. With Windows Mobile 5.0, the security model is extended to Pocket PC also. Smartphones support a one- or two-tier security model; Pocket PCs support only the one-tier model. Table 6-2 shows the differences between security tiers.

Table 6-2 Windows Mobile 5.0 Security Configurations

Authentication Level	Two-Tier Security (Most Smartphones)	One-Tier Security (Pocket PCs)
Signed with a Privileged Certificate	Application may access privileged and normal APIs and registry keys	Application may access privileged and normal APIs and registry keys
Signed with an Unprivileged Certificate	Application may not access privileged APIs and certain registry locations	Application may access privileged and normal APIs and registry keys
Unsigned	Application may be prevented from running	Application may be prevented from running

The default behavior on most devices is to prompt the user the first time an unsigned application is run. The user can then choose to trust the application, and if so, the user will not be prompted when running the application again. When you develop for smartphones, you need to know which APIs are considered privileged; these APIs are documented on the Microsoft MSDN Web site at *http://msdn2.microsoft.com/en-us/library/aa455835.aspx*. On some devices, privileged certificates are available only from the network operator for which the device is built. In many cases, privileged certificates can be obtained through the Mobile2Market signing program. See the upcoming section titled "Design Guidelines and Mobile2Market" for more information.

Microsoft has released a Security Configuration Manager Powertoy (Figure 6-9) that you can use to query and provision security policies on a connected device. In a future release of Visual Studio, this functionality will be built in.

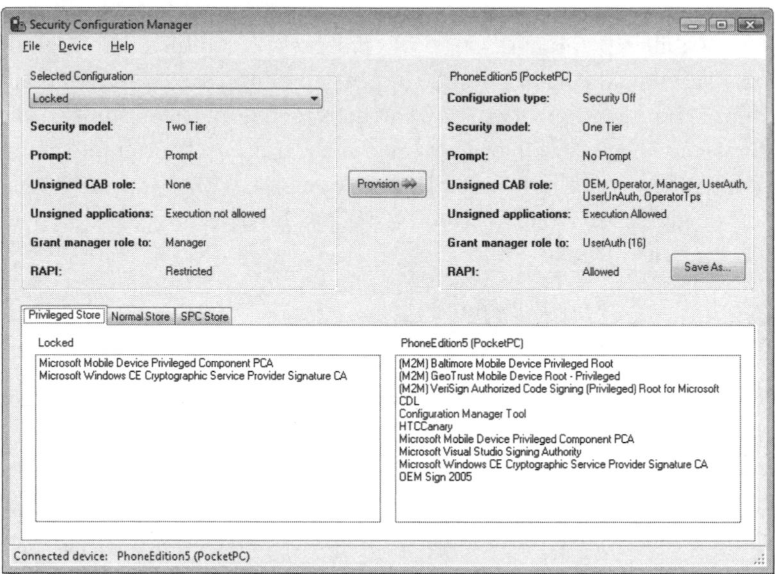

Figure 6-9 Security Configuration Manager Powertoy, which provides easy access to change the security policy on the device

You can quickly switch the device between various security modes, including turning security off, which allows any application to run without prompts. You can download Security Configuration Manager from the Microsoft Download Center at *www.microsoft.com/downloads/details.aspx?familyid=7E92628C-D587-47E0-908B-09FEE6EA517A&displaylang=en*. The next version of Visual Studio, currently code-named "Orcas," will include this functionality as standard.

Signing Your Code

Signing your application requires you to have an account with one of the code-signing bodies, such as VeriSign. The costs involved depend on the volume of signing events for which you apply. A signing event represents a single application file (.dll, .exe, or .cab) that is to be signed. If your application uses a large number of separate files, the cost of code signing can be significant.

When you have established an account with a signing authority, you are issued a personal key with which you must sign all of your application files. After you've built and signed your files, you upload them to the provider. The provider checks all of the files and replaces the signatures with your official signatures, which are derived from the Mobile2Market base key. Only when they contain these final signatures will your files be correctly recognized by the security system on the device and the application will be allowed to run without prompting.

Design Guidelines and Mobile2Market

Similar to the logo program for desktop versions of the Microsoft Windows operating system, Microsoft has a scheme to achieve a "Designed for Windows Mobile" logo. The guidelines for this were last updated in May 2004, and although they were written for a previous generation of the platform, they still apply to applications you write today.

Because of limitations in version 1.0 of the .NET Compact Framework, certain requirements were relaxed for managed code developers, such as the ability to provide an exit option and support for the platform's Help menu. You can decide whether to include an exit option in your application. The decision will depend on the usage patterns of the device and your target audience. In version 2.0 of the Compact Framework, you can support Help by handling the HelpRequested event of your form, as discussed earlier in this chapter. The advantages of using this built-in mechanism are consistency with other applications and less need to clutter your menus or toolbars with Help buttons.

Mobile2Market is a program that provides a stamp of approval on applications written to conform to a set of Designed for Windows Mobile guidelines, as mentioned at the beginning of Chapter 2, "Building a Microsoft Windows Forms GUI." These guidelines ensure that the application respects user interface standards, behaves well when run alongside other applications, and correctly allows for localization.

There is a cost involved in submitting your application for Mobile2Market testing. The program is designed to be used for consumer-focused applications; enterprise applications are not usually expected to go through the approval process because they are generally distributed internally only. You can find more information about Mobile2Market at *www.mobile2market.com*.

The Global Assembly Cache

The global assembly cache (GAC) provides a central repository for .NET .dll files that are shared across multiple applications. To support installation in the GAC, an assembly must be signed with a key pair to give it a strong name. Signing assemblies with a key pair ensures that if two assemblies with the same name are installed in the GAC, because they are different versions or were signed with different keys they will be treated as different assemblies.

Strong Naming Your Assemblies

Strong naming an assembly not only provides this unique versioning, it also provides authentication because to produce an assembly with a matching signature you must sign the assembly with the same key pair. To assign a strong name to your assembly, you need a key pair file. Generally, you create only one key pair file, and then you can use it with any managed assemblies you want to strong name. The same mechanism for strong naming is used for desktop and device .NET assemblies. Open the project properties window for the assembly project, and on the Signing tab select the Sign The Assembly option, as shown in Figure 6-10. If you don't have a key file (a file that uses the .snk extension), you can generate one by selecting New from the list of keys in the Choose A Strong Name Key File list.

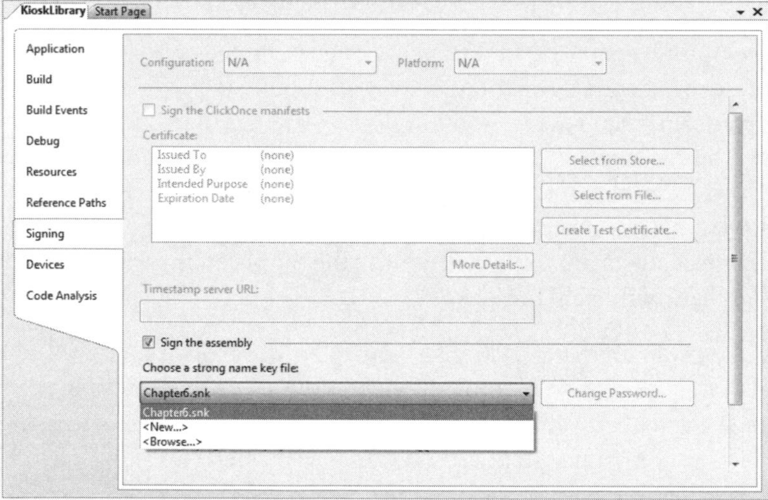

Figure 6-10 Project signing options showing selection of a key pair file

When and How to Use the Global Assembly Cache

Installing in the GAC is not always the right option for a .dll file. By installing your .dll files locally with your application, you ensure that your application will not be broken if a patched .dll file is installed on the system as part of another application. However, you can install common .dll files in the GAC to reduce the installation footprint. All of the framework base class libraries and Microsoft SQL Server assemblies are installed in the GAC.

Assemblies are added to the GAC by a text file placed in the Windows directory. This file simply contains a list of paths to .NET Compact Framework assemblies to be added to the GAC. When a .NET Compact Framework application is started, the system scans for new .gac files, and if any are present, it imports the .dll files specified. If a .gac file is removed, the .dll files that were registered in it are removed from the GAC.

Adding your assembly to the GAC through a device .cab file project is very easy. In the File System Editor, right-click File System On Target Machine, and select Add Special Folder. Then choose Global Assembly Cache Folder, which is at the bottom of the menu. Drag the managed .dll files into this folder to generate automatically the .gac files necessary to register them. If your assemblies do not have a strong name, you will receive a build error. The only caveat to using this method of installing in the GAC is that the file is not moved until the next time the .NET Compact Framework runtime is started. However, you can make this happen immediately by calling Cgacutil.exe with the */refresh* flag, as we demonstrate in the example CESetup.dll in the upcoming section titled "Native CESetup.dll."

On devices that run versions earlier than Windows Mobile 5.0, this technique doesn't work because the generated .gac file is Unicode encoded and older devices fail to recognize this correctly. In such scenarios, the solution is to hand-code the .gac file in Notepad, which saves the file in American Standard Code for Information Interchange (ASCII) by default. Place this file in the Windows Folder special folder in your .cab file project, along with the project output from the .dll file you want to add to the GAC. The .gac text file simply contains the path to the .dll files to add, one per line. In our example (shown later), it contains the following:

```
%CE2%\KioskLibrary.dll
```

Native CESetup.dll

The cab installer engine in Windows CE supports a mechanism for adding custom actions during the install process. For example, you may want to add a custom action to perform additional checks to see whether prerequisite components are present on the device or to make changes that cannot be made directly from a .cab file package, such as deleting files to lock down the device as described earlier in this chapter. You can create custom actions by creating a single native code (C++) .dll file for your .cab file project. This .dll file must expose four specific methods that are called at the beginning and end of the install and uninstall processes. You can create the required .dll file as a Smart Device Microsoft Win32 project.

Next, you must perform a couple of additional steps. In the main .cpp file for the project, add the following:

```
#include "ce_setup.h"
```

You can then define the four setup methods that are called by the installer engine:

```
codeINSTALL_INIT
Install_Init(
    HWND        hwndParent,
    BOOL        fFirstCall,
    BOOL        fPreviouslyInstalled,
    LPCTSTR     pszInstallDir
)
{
return codeINSTALL_INIT_CONTINUE;
}

codeINSTALL_EXIT
Install_Exit(
    HWND    hwndParent,
    LPCTSTR pszInstallDir,
    WORD    cFailedDirs,
    WORD    cFailedFiles,
    WORD    cFailedRegKeys,
    WORD    cFailedRegVals,
    WORD    cFailedShortcuts
)
{
//Hide games and File Explorer.
CreateDirectory(_T("\\Windows\\Start Menu Backup"), NULL);
CreateDirectory(_T("\\Windows\\Start Menu Backup\\Programs"), NULL);
MoveFile(_T("\\Windows\\Start Menu\\Programs\\File Explorer.lnk"),
_T("\\Windows\\Start Menu Backup\\Programs\\File Explorer.lnk"));
MoveFile(_T("\\Windows\\Start Menu\\Programs\\Games"), _T("\\Windows\\Start Menu
Backup\\Programs\\Games"));

//Force a refresh of the GAC.
CreateProcess(_T("cgacutil.exe"),_T("/
refresh"),NULL,NULL,FALSE,0,NULL,NULL,NULL,NULL);
return codeINSTALL_EXIT_DONE;
}

codeUNINSTALL_INIT
Uninstall_Init(
    HWND        hwndParent,
    LPCTSTR     pszInstallDir)
{
return codeUNINSTALL_INIT_CONTINUE;
}

codeUNINSTALL_EXIT
Uninstall_Exit(
    HWND    hwndParent)
{
//Restore games and File Explorer.
MoveFile(_T("\\Windows\\Start Menu Backup\\Programs\\File Explorer.lnk"),
_T("\\Windows\\Start Menu\\Programs\\File Explorer.lnk"));
MoveFile(_T("\\Windows\\Start Menu Backup\\Programs\\Games"), _T("\\Windows\\Start
```

```
Menu\\Programs\\Games"));

//Refresh GAC.
CreateProcess(_T("cgacutil.exe"),_T("/
refresh"),NULL,NULL,FALSE,0,NULL,NULL,NULL,NULL);
return codeUNINSTALL_EXIT_DONE;
}
```

Finally, so that these entry points are exported, add a new module-definition file to the project, and name it native.def. Place the following contents in it:

```
EXPORTS

Install_Init
Install_Exit
Uninstall_Init
Uninstall_Exit
```

If you want to test the .dll file and see when it is called, add a message box to each of the methods.

To have this .dll file called as part of the setup process, add the primary output to your Application Folder in your device .cab file project (see Figure 6-11). In the main properties of the .cab file project, you can designate this .dll file as the Windows CE Setup .dll file.

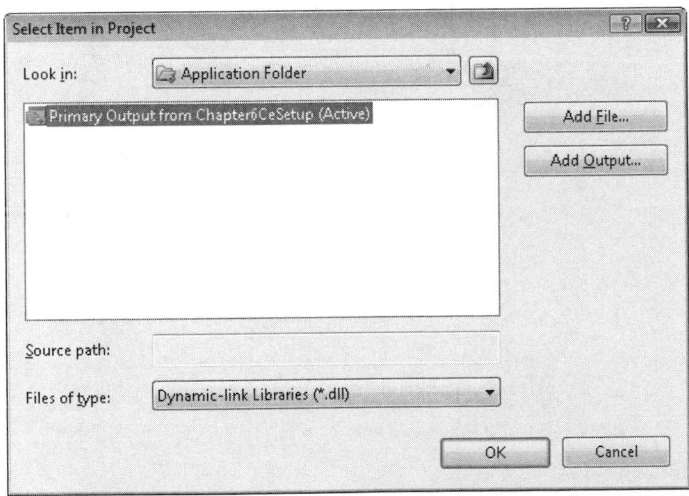

Figure 6-11 The project output of the CESetupDLL project that was previously added to the installer project

What you have done in this setup .dll file is to move a couple of key application shortcuts to make it difficult for the user to try to start the games or File Explorer applications on the device. You also force a refresh of the GAC so that the .dll file is registered immediately (rather than waiting until the next .NET Compact Framework application is started).

Testing Your .cab File

Your .cab file now contains everything necessary to install your application on the device. You can use ActiveSync (or Windows Mobile Device Center in the Windows Vista operating system) to explore the file system on the device and copy the .cab file to it. Then, from the device, you can locate and start the .cab file from the File Explorer to install your application. After you have successfully installed and run your application, the next step is to build a desktop installer.

Building a Desktop Installer

The preceding section describes how to create a device .cab installer that you can use to deploy the file to devices manually and install the product. Many device users have ActiveSync set up on their desktop computer, and this can be used to automate the installation process. In this section, we create a sample installation project to provide a package that can be run on a desktop computer and that will deploy and install the .cab file using ActiveSync. On the File menu, select New Project, and then select Other Project Types, Setup And Deployment, and Setup Project.

Adding Your .cab Project

You can add the output from another project in your solution to your Application Folder. We do this in this example to add in the .cab file created in the preceding section. Select Add, select Project Output, and then ensure your device .cab file project is selected, as shown in Figure 6-12.

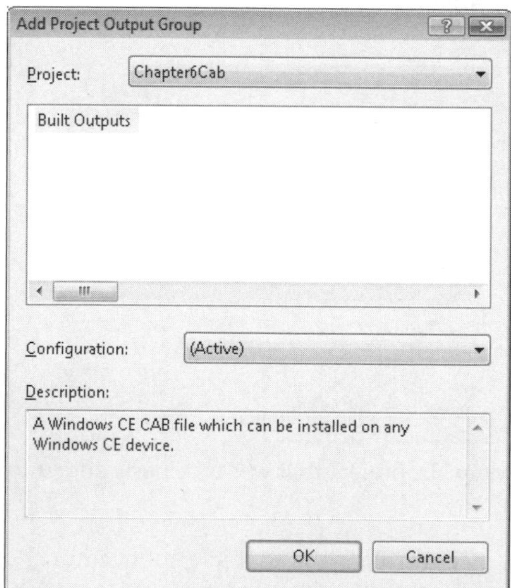

Figure 6-12 Adding project output from the device installer project

Adding Other Application Files

In the same way that you added the .cab file, you can add other files associated with your application that will be installed on the desktop computer, such as help files or a companion application.

Automating the Device-Side Installation

You can install an application to the Add/Remove Programs in ActiveSync or the Windows Mobile Device Center in Windows Vista by passing it a correctly formed .ini file that describes your application and the .cab file or files to install. Although Add/Remove Programs allows multiple .cab files to be listed, this capability is to be used for supporting the same component with versions for different CPUs or platforms; you can't use this method to deploy multiple distinct .cab files. If your .cab file project is created for Windows Mobile, only the Advanced RISC Machines (ARM) architecture is supported, so you won't have to deal with multiple .cab files.

The .ini file consists of a CeAppManager section that specifies attributes to describe the AppManager version (only 1.0 is valid) and the name of your component. This is followed by a section named exactly the same as the Component attribute in the first section that describes that component. This section contains a longer textual description of the package, optionally the name of the device-side package to use when uninstalling, and finally the comma-separated list of .cab files that make up the package.

```
[CEAppManager]
Version      = 1.0
Component    = Chapter6

[Chapter6]
Description  = Chapter Six Example
Uninstall    = Chapter6

;Because there are multiple .cab files specific to a CPU type,
;these files are relative to the installation directory.
CabFiles    = Chapter6Cab.cab
The Setup project types in VS2005 do not include the capability to automatically
install the device side component; therefore, we need to add a custom action to pass
this INI file to CeAppMgr.
```

Adding a Custom Installer Action

When you build a desktop installer project by using Visual Studio 2005, you can start only executables that you install through your package. However, in our example, we want to launch the CeAppMgr application with the .ini file we wrote to deploy our device installer to the connected device automatically. You can provide custom actions in the form of a managed installer .dll file, an executable, or a script. In our case, a Visual Basic Scripting Edition (VBScript) file is preferable because of the simple nature of the task to be performed, and it will not introduce .NET Framework dependencies for the desktop computer. Following is a very simple VBScript file that can be called from a custom action. It consists of only two lines:

```
Set objShell = CreateObject("Wscript.Shell")
objShell.Run(Session.Property("CustomActionData"))
```

Wscript.Shell is a component of the VBScript runtime that provides a number of shell methods. In this case, we use *Run*, which is passed a string containing the application name and optionally arguments separated with spaces. *It is similar to the System.Diagnostics. Process.Start method in managed code. CustomActionData* is a named property that you can set for each custom action in the installer project.

With the Custom Actions editor, you can set tasks to run at various stages in the installation process. To run the Add/Remove Programs tool, you must determine the path to the CeAppMgr component of ActiveSync. To determine the ActiveSync path, add a registry check to the start actions for the installer project. With the registry check, you can cancel installation of the package if a version of ActiveSync is not installed on the computer. The *ActiveSyncRegistrySearch* search looks in the *HKEY_LOCALMACHINE\SOFTWARE\Microsoft\Windows CE Services* key for the *InstalledDir* value, which is stored in a named value called *ACTIVESYNCDIR*. The custom installer action is run in the Commit phase of installation so that it runs only if the rest of the package is successfully installed. It passes the following string to the VBScript:

```
"[ACTIVESYNCDIR]\CeAppMgr.exe" "[TARGETDIR]\Terminal.ini"
```

Running the Installer

After you have built the project and created an .msi file, you can start the Windows Installer package to install your application. The installer package installs all the files onto the desktop computer and then starts the ActiveSync installer. If a device is connected, installation will take place automatically; otherwise, the user receives a message that the installation will take place when a device is next connected.

If you run the installer on Windows Vista, which includes the new User Account Control feature, the installation pauses until the user permits the installation to proceed by supplying Administrator credentials.

Summary

This chapter describes the process of adding Help content to your project, investigates methods you can use to lock down the target device user interface, and describes the process of building an installer. The .cab file generated by the installer can be deployed onto a device by using a storage card, from a Web link or an e-mail message, or manually by copying the file to the device. Finally, in this chapter we built a sample desktop installer package that can be run from the user's desktop computer to fully install the software on the device.

Part II

Solutions for Challenges in Mobile Applications

In this part:

Chapter 7

Exchanging Data with Backend Servers

In this chapter:

Chapter 3, "Using SQL Server 2005 Compact Edition and Other Data Stores," starts by stating, "Most business applications need to store, organize, and view data." You can easily extend that statement by adding *and transfer data to and from backend servers*. Very few enterprise applications run entirely self-contained on a mobile device with no need to communicate with the outside world. Instead, most applications are mobile components of a bigger enterprise solution. These solutions provide users the ability to gather data in the field, for example, in stock management or when support personnel who operate in customer-facing roles outside the office must take sales orders, service equipment, or track goods distribution. In all these cases, the devices need to hold data to allow the application to operate, and the devices must transmit data gathered in the field to enterprise servers. This chapter discusses how to synchronize data between applications running on the device and backend servers.

Architecting a Data Synchronization Application

When you connect mobile devices to an enterprise network, you must connect them directly to the local area network (LAN) using WiFi, Ethernet cradles, or Microsoft ActiveSync over a direct cable connection or Bluetooth to a LAN-connected computer, or you must provide some kind of gateway to which you can connect from the Internet–a mobile gateway. You can synchronize to a mobile gateway using Web Services or Microsoft SQL Server replication–both operate through a Web server running Microsoft Internet Information Server (IIS). The Web services or SQL Server on your mobile gateway can communicate with backend systems and servers, tying your mobile application into the wider enterprise operations. This basic architecture is shown in Figure 7-1.

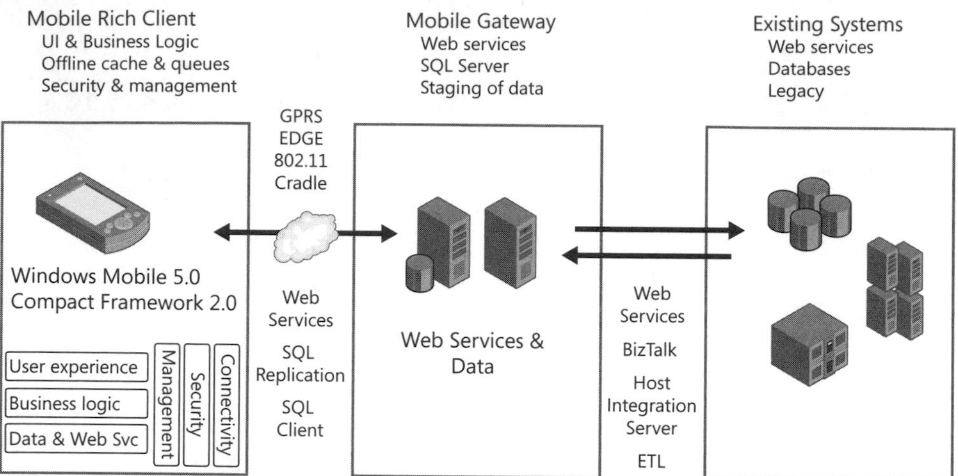

Figure 7-1 Mobile rich clients connecting to the enterprise by using Web Services or SQL Server, and then to backend systems

Designing for the Mostly Disconnected Client

One tenet of mobile application architecture is that you must design for a mostly disconnected network. A device that runs Microsoft Windows Mobile comes with many different communications capabilities: Depending on the particular device, you have a choice of universal serial bus (USB) cable, WiFi, Bluetooth, and—on a phone device—General Packet Radio Service (GPRS), Code-Division Multiple Access (CDMA), Universal Mobile Telecommunications System (UMTS), or High-Speed Downlink Packet Access (HSDPA). Despite all these connectivity choices, you cannot guarantee that at all times at least one of these will be available because you may be in an area without cellular coverage or WiFi, and Bluetooth and cable connections are really only practical for synchronizing with a computer (although there are exceptions).

As a result, usually you must design your applications to be able to operate without a live network connection. There are exceptions of course; for example, if your application is a stock control application operating in a warehouse or store that has reliable WiFi coverage, you can design the application under the assumption that the network will be available at all times. Or your application could be a Web application—the ultimate thin client for which the only software required on the device is a Web browser.

However, most mobile applications are *rich clients*, which means they are custom applications that must be installed on the device and that use a custom user interface (UI) and some local data storage such as a SQL Server Compact Edition (CE) database. A rich client application can operate without a live network but must occasionally connect to a backend server to transfer data. It relies on the occasional availability of cellular phone networks or WiFi, or it must be placed in a cradle connected to an Ethernet network or a desktop computer.

A typical design is when a device is left overnight in a cradle both to charge the device battery and to bulk upload lookup (reference) data from backend servers by direct connection to a

SQL Server or over the Internet using Web Services or SQL Server replication. For example, for a mobile sales assistant application, the uploaded data could be the current product catalog and price information. In the morning, the user removes the device from the cradle and takes it out on the road. Often, the user will send the data gathered on the road by using Web services; in the sales assistant application, this data could be relatively small messages required to enter new orders and/or check product availability. This architecture is shown in Figure 7-1.

Usually, you design a mainly disconnected application to provide the same functionality to the user regardless of the availability of an active network connection. Updates that must be sent to a server simply are queued until a network is available because this is the simplest implementation of a rich client. Other designs are possible, such as offering enhanced capabilities when a network is available and reduced capabilities when no network is available. These are design details that you must consider when analyzing the operational requirements of your application. Cost is another important consideration: updates sent over a phone network usually cost much more than those sent over a WiFi network or a direct cable connection, so this too may influence your decisions on what kind of data transfers you will allow over particular kinds of networks.

Designing for Stale Data

One thing is always true: Any data that you copy from a backend server and then store on the device to use when the device is disconnected from the network is inherently *stale* from the moment it is stored. The data may have been updated on the server, but the stored copy of the data that your application uses will not be up-to-date until you next synchronize. You must analyze the consequences of this and design appropriate safeguards to ensure that your mobile application cannot do any harm by using stale data.

You must also consider the potential consequences of data sent from the device that is based on stale data. The data on the server may have changed since the last device sync, so you may need to implement logic on the server to validate the update sent from the device before applying changes to your backend database.

The best advice is to try to cache lookup (that is, reference) data on the device that is not very volatile and make sure you perform appropriate business logic processes to validate data sent from a device.

Choosing the Synchronization Technique

This chapter discusses four synchronization techniques:

- **Web Services** This standards-based technique works over Web protocols and is perfect for small transactions. Web Services works with a wide variety of servers from different vendors and is simple to program. It is not solely a data synchronization technique, but it is designed as a request–response message transfer, and therein lies its attraction: It is very flexible.

- **SQL Server client** If your mobile client can connect directly to the enterprise LAN, the simplest approach is to connect directly to your backend SQL Server. You cannot use this technique over the Internet (unless you connect first over a virtual private network [VPN]).
- **SQL Server 2005 Compact Edition Remote Data Access (RDA)** This synchronization technique is quite simple to use, and with it you can copy a data table to the device, track any changes your application makes, and then simply upload the changes back to the server to update the master table. This is an excellent technique for a small number of clients, but the conflict resolution capabilities are not sophisticated–if you have two or more clients all working on copies of the same source table and they all update changes to the same rows, the last updater wins and overwrites changes made by the other clients.
- **SQL Server 2005 replication** This is a sophisticated synchronization technique designed for use by multiple updaters. Each time a client synchronizes, it uploads changes it has made and then downloads all changes made by all clients so that the local copy of the data remains up-to-date. SQL Server replication allows you to partition data to avoid update conflicts and has capabilities for conflict resolution.

Note Microsoft is working on new synchronization tools. At the time of this writing, it provides no tools support for Microsoft .NET Compact Framework clients but will provide support after the release of Microsoft Visual Studio Code Name "Orcas." For more information about Synchronization Services for ADO.NET, see the team's Weblog at *blogs.msdn.com/synchronizer/default.aspx.*

Using Web Services for Data Synchronization

When you add a Web reference to your client-side application project, the Visual Studio Add Web Reference tool generates a proxy class that includes methods that make it easy to make calls to the Web service, receive the response, and make the received data available to your application. When Visual Studio detects that the Web service returns a strongly typed *DataSet* object, it generates code in the proxy class that creates an instance of that strongly typed *DataSet* as the return value for the proxy class method that calls the Web method.

In .NET Compact Framework 1.0, the tool-generated code for a Web service that uses strongly typed *DataSet* objects requires classes that are not supported by the runtime and Base Class Libraries, and so you must be careful to use only vanilla *DataSet* objects (or, of course, your own custom data objects) as parameters or return types in Web methods that are for use by .NET Compact Framework 1.0 clients.

Fortunately, in version 2.0, such usability considerations are a thing of the past because the Visual Studio Add Web Reference tool generates code for strongly typed *DataSet* objects that is fully compatible with .NET Compact Framework 2.0. As a result, considerations with Web Services shift to more interesting problems, such as follows:

- How to authenticate Web Services clients
- How to use Web Services on a device that may be only occasionally connected to a network
- How to compress Web services payload to reduce communication costs

Authenticating Web Services Clients

Applications you write with the .NET Compact Framework that access Web Services do so over Hypertext Transfer Protocol (HTTP) protocols. If your Web service is a Microsoft ASP.NET Web service running on an IIS Web server, you can configure the Web service to require Basic, Digest, or Integrated Windows authentication, just as you can for a regular Web site (see Figure 7-2).

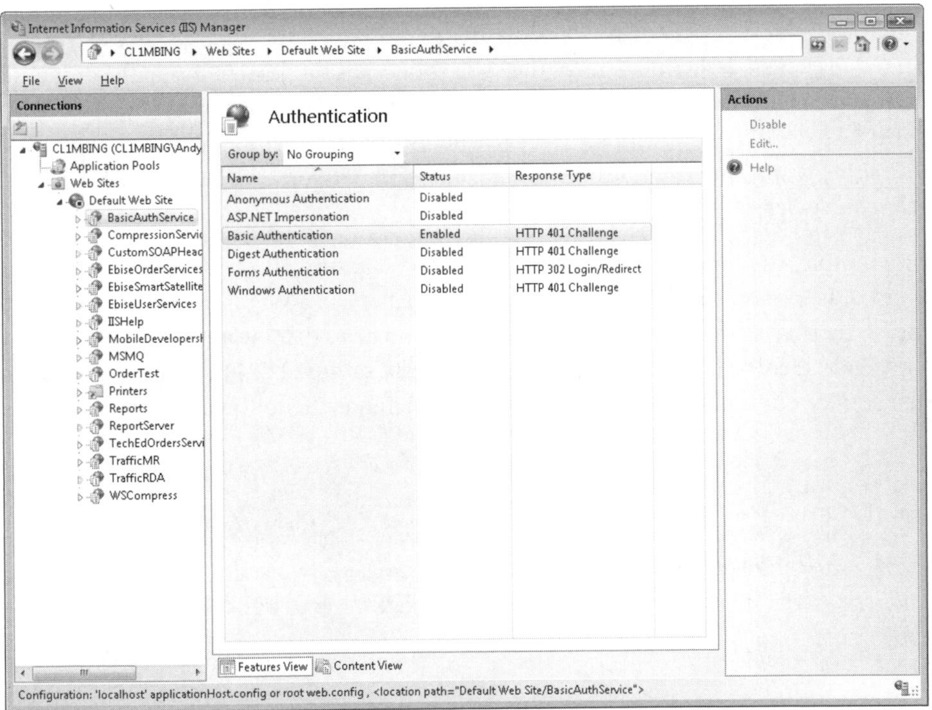

Figure 7-2 Setting authentication options in IIS Manager for an ASP.NET Web service

The mechanisms used for Basic authentication are actually a part of HTTP and are not vendor-specific, so you can authenticate Web Services clients using Basic authentication whether the server is a Windows server running IIS or a server running other Web server software, such as Apache. Remember that when you send credentials to a remote server using Basic authentication, the data transmits in clear text and is vulnerable to discovery by an attacker. Always use

Secure Sockets Layer (SSL) to encrypt data in transit to ensure that it cannot be intercepted. If your application operates over an intranet and accesses a Web service on a Windows server running IIS, you also can use Integrated Windows authentication to identify the client device.

When you add a Web reference to your Visual Studio .NET 2003 project for a Web service that requires authentication, the system prompts you for your credentials, as follows:

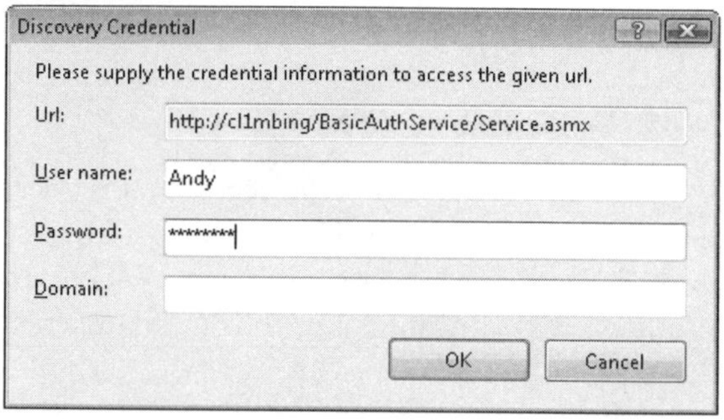

Discovery Credential

Please supply the credential information to access the given url.

Url: http://cl1mbing/BasicAuthService/Service.asmx

User name: Andy

Password: *********

Domain:

OK Cancel

Visual Studio uses the credentials you enter to download the Web Services Description Language (WSDL) file that defines the Web service, but it does not save the credentials in the client code it adds to your project to access the Web service. You must create a *System.Net.NetworkCredential* object and set the *Credentials* property of your Web Service proxy object. (The same technique is required when you make a network call using the *System.Net.WebRequest* class.)

For example, the following Windows Forms application contains two text box controls that accept a user name and a password, a button that starts a Web service when clicked, and a label to display the string sent by the Web method or to display an error message. The project has a Web reference to a Web service that has been set up to require Basic authentication. The Web service contains a single Web method, which has the following code:

```
[WebMethod]
public string HelloWorld()
{
    return "Hello authenticated user! Your username: "
        + System.Threading.Thread.CurrentPrincipal.Identity.Name;
}
```

The code for the *button1_Click* event in the client program is as follows:

```
private void button1_Click(object sender, System.EventArgs e)
{
    BasicAuthWebService ws = new BasicAuthWebService();
    // Create a NetworkCredential object with the user name
    // and password as entered in the TextBox controls.
```

```
        NetworkCredential creds = new NetworkCredential(
            UsernameTextBox.Text, PasswordTextBox.Text);
        // Use this NetworkCredential object with the Web service proxy.
        ws.Credentials = creds;

        try
        {
            ResponseLabel.Text = ws.HelloWorld();
        }
        catch (Exception exp)
        {
            ResponseLabel.Text = exp.Message;
        }
    }
```

This method creates a new instance of the Web Services proxy class *BasicAuthWebService*. It then creates a *NetworkCredential* object and sets the *Credentials* property of the Web Services proxy class instance to that. When the user enters an incorrect user name and/or password, the call to the Web method throws an exception with the message "The remote server returned an error: (401) Unauthorized." If valid credentials are entered, the Web method returns its response, a string that identifies the Windows user account with which the user has logged on.

Custom Authentication with SOAP Headers

Another option is to pass data in the Simple Object Access Protocol (SOAP) headers along with your Extensible Markup Language (XML) Web Services request. If you use this process, you do not implement authentication and authorization using the facilities of the IIS server, but instead you pass this information in code in your Web method. Consequently, this approach works with servers from any vendor. If you are using an IIS server, you should set the IIS authentication to Anonymous authentication.

To write a Web service using ASP.NET that requires a SOAP header to be present, you first define a class that derives from *System.Web.Services.Protocols.SoapHeader*, which defines the object to be passed in the SOAP header. Then you declare a public field of that type inside your Web Services class:

```
using System.Web;
using System.Web.Services;
using System.Web.Services.Protocols;

namespace MobileDevelopersHandbook
{

    // AuthHeader class extends from SoapHeader.
    public class AuthHeader : SoapHeader
```

```
    {
        public string Username;
        public string Password;
    }

    /// <summary>
    /// SOAPheaderService will contain a Web method that requires that a
    /// AuthHeader object be passed in the SOAP headers.
    /// </summary>
    public class SOAPheaderService : System.Web.Services.WebService
    {
        // Declare a public field of type AuthHeader, which becomes
        // part of the Web service contract.
        public AuthHeader AuthToken;
        . . .
    }
}
```

Then, for any Web method for which you require the client to pass an *AuthHeader* object in the SOAP headers, decorate the method with a *SoapHeader* attribute. The first parameter is the name of the public field in the class that defines the type of the header.

```
[WebMethod(Description=
    "This method requires a custom soap header set by the caller")]
[SoapHeader("AuthToken", Direction=SoapHeaderDirection.In)]
public bool Authenticate()
{
    // Check for header
    if (AuthToken == null)
    {
        throw new Exception("AuthHeader not passed in SOAP headers");
    }

    // Code to authenticate a user using the AuthToken object.
    // In this simple example, we just look for hard-coded values,
    // but a real application might look up users in a database or
    // use some other form of authentication.
    if (AuthToken.Username == "andy" & AuthToken.Password == "P455w0rd")
        return true;
    else
        return false;
}
```

In this example, the second parameter sets the *Direction* property of the *SoapHeaderAttribute* object, which takes a *SoapHeaderDirection* enumeration, which has the values shown in Table 7-1.

Table 7-1 ***SoapHeaderDirection*** **Enumeration**

SoapHeaderDirection Member	Description
In	The header is sent from client to server.
InOut	The header is sent to both the server and the client.
Out	The header is sent from server to client only.
Fault	The header is sent to the client only when the XML Web Services method throws an exception.

SoapHeaderAttribute can be used to decorate methods in a Web service, as shown in this example, and it can also be used to decorate methods in the proxy class used on the client side. When you use it on the client side, *SoapHeaderDirection.Fault* is not supported—if the client-side method throws an exception, it is not propagated back to the server as a SOAP exception.

On the client side, the public field *AuthHeader* is exposed in the WSDL for the Web service. When you add a Web reference to the Web service to your project, the code that is generated includes the definition of the *AuthHeader* class, and the proxy class that is generated for the Web service contains the *AuthHeaderValue* property, which the client-side code uses to set the value in the SOAP headers. The client creates an instance of *AuthHeader*, and then sets the *AuthHeaderValue* property to that instance. For example, the following method creates an instance of the Web Services proxy and calls the *Authenticate* method of the Web service, passing an instance of *AuthHeader* in the SOAP headers:

```
private void invokeIt()
{
    // Create a proxy for the Web service.
    SOAPheaderService ws = new SOAPheaderService();
    // Create the AuthHeader object for the SOAP header.
    AuthHeader hdr = new AuthHeader();
    hdr.Username = "andy";
    hdr.Password = "P455w0rd";
    // Set the AuthHeader SOAP header to the AuthHeader object instance.
    ws.AuthHeadervalue = hdr;

    // Call the Web method.
    bool response = ws.Authenticate();
}
```

This sample code uses string literals for the user name and password to keep the example simple. In practice, you should read this data from an external source and should not store this kind of data inside your program code. See Chapter 10, "Security Programming for Mobile Applications" for recommendations on good practice.

You can find a full working sample of this application in the CustomSoapHeaders project in the code samples on this book's companion Web site.

Using Web Services on Occasionally Connected Clients

Although Web Services provides a flexible solution that can be used for many applications and with servers from many different vendors, one thing it does not do is offer very much in the way of resilience or any built-in retry mechanisms. If you are developing client applications that are connected to a reliable broadband Internet connection, resilience and retry capabilities are not factors you need to worry about very much. However, if your client application runs on a mobile device that may be only intermittently connected to a USB cable, a WiFi network, or a cellular network, you must spend a great deal of time and effort considering what happens if you want to make a Web service call and there is no network available, or if a call fails halfway through.

Fortunately, the patterns and practices group at Microsoft has addressed this problem in the Mobile Client Software Factory, which works with devices that run Windows Mobile 5.0 and later. One of the application blocks included in this suite of tools is the Disconnected Service Agent. With the Disconnected Service Agent, you can queue Web service requests and have them automatically dispatched when a network becomes available, and, in the event of failure, you can configure the number of times the requests will be retried.

The downloadable code for this chapter on this book's companion Web site includes a sample application called DisconnectedServiceAgentExample. This application simulates a mobile sales assistant application and shows a *DataGrid* of some fictional products. If you click a product name, you see the details for that item and a menu link that you can use to post an order back to the server. This application requires a Web service to be running on your development computer. (For instructions on configuring the Web service and updating the Web reference in your project, see the readme file that accompanies the sample code.)

To run this test application, you need not download and install the Mobile Client Software Factory, but if you want to develop your own applications using the Disconnected Service Agent or run through the steps described in the next section that use add-ons the Mobile Client Software Factory installs in Visual Studio, you will need to do so. See Chapter 1, ".NET Compact Framework–a Platform on the Move," for details about how to obtain the Mobile Client Software Factory.

Getting Started with the Disconnected Service Agent

First, you must add a reference to the *Mobile.DisconnectedAgent* Application Block and to the four other Mobile Application Blocks that the Disconnected Service Agent uses. The Mobile Client Software Factory ships these application blocks as full Visual Studio 2005 projects with all source code, so either you can add a reference to the projects where you installed them (by default this is at C:\Program Files\Mobile Client SoftwareFactory\Application Blocks) or you can copy the projects into your own application directory structure and add them to your solution. The application blocks you need are the following:

- *Mobile.DisconnectedAgent*
- *Mobile.Configuration*
- *Mobile.ConnectionMonitor*
- *Mobile.DataAccess*
- *Mobile.EndpointCatalog*

Setting the Configuration File

The operation of the Disconnected Service Agent is controlled by settings in an application configuration file. There is no built-in support in .NET Compact Framework 2.0 for reading application configuration files, but the *Mobile.Configuration* Application Block adds that support. The .config file for the sample application is shown in Listing 7-1.

Listing 7-1 App.config File for a Disconnected Service Agent Application

```
<?xml version="1.0" encoding="utf-8" ?>
<configuration>
  <configSections>
    <section name="Connections"
      type="Microsoft.Practices.Mobile.ConnectionMonitor.Configuration. …
…ConnectionSettingsSection, Microsoft.Practices.Mobile.ConnectionMonitor"
    />
    <section name="Endpoints"
      type="Microsoft.Practices.Mobile.EndpointCatalog.Configuration. …
…EndpointSection, Microsoft.Practices.Mobile.EndpointCatalog"
    />
  </configSections>

  <Connections>
    <ConnectionItems>
      <add  Type="CellConnection" Price="8"/>
      <add  Type="NicConnection" Price="2"/>
      <add  Type="DesktopConnection" Price="1"/>
    </ConnectionItems>
  </Connections>

<Endpoints>
  <EndpointItems>
      <add Name="Orders"
        Address="http://myWebServer/OrdersServices/OrdersService.asmx"
        UserName="PDAUser" Password="P@ssw0rd"/>
  </EndpointItems>
</Endpoints>
</configuration>
```

The key point to notice about Listing 7-1 is that it consists of three main sections inside the *<configuration>* element:

- **<configSections>** The <configSections> section describes the types that define the format of the other configuration sections, <connections> and <Endpoints>.
- **<connections>** The <connections> section describes the three types of network connections you will find on a mobile device. You should not change this section. Each connection type has an associated price attribute that compares the types for their relative cost–both in terms of the likely financial cost of using the connection (in most countries, data communications over a cellular network are much more expensive than is communication over a USB connection to a broadband-connected computer) and in terms of bandwidth costs. The three connection types are as follows:
    - **CellConnection** A data connection over a cellular telephone network, using GPRS, CDMA, HSDPA, or UMTS
    - **NicConnection** Connection over WiFi or a wired Ethernet connection
    - **DesktopConnection** A connection through a computer over a USB cable that uses ActiveSync as the communications medium
- **<Endpoints>** The <Endpoints> section describes one or more endpoints, which is a name you give to an addressable resource, specifying the Uniform Resource Locator (URL) and optionally credentials needed to access that resource.

> **Caution** The configuration file shown here includes valuable data such as URLs and user credentials. Although it is shown in clear text here, in most commercial applications, you will want to encrypt this data. Fortunately, the *Mobile.Configuration* Application Block supports encrypted .config files. See Chapter 10 for an example of how to encrypt configuration data.

Generating the Disconnected Service Agent Proxy

The first thing you need to do is add a Web reference to your Web service in just the same way as you always do. Then you must activate the Visual Studio add-ons included in the Mobile Client Software Factory (MCSF) (called "recipes") to generate the Disconnected Service Agent wrapper for your Web service proxy class.

> **Note** You must activate the MCSF package only if you want to create a Disconnected Service Agent in an existing application. The Mobile Client Software Factory adds its own solution template to the Visual Studio project templates, and if you create your project that way, the MCSF package is already active. Be aware that if you use the MCSF project template, Visual Studio creates a project that is built around use of the mobile Composite UI Application Block, which is not covered in this book.

Enabling the MCSF Package When you install the MCSF, two prerequisites are the Guidance Automation Extensions (GAX) and Guidance Automation Toolkit (GAT) (see the MCSF installation guide for more information). These Visual Studio 2005 add-ons allow groups such as the Microsoft patterns and practices group to extend Visual Studio 2005 and integrate their own dialog boxes, wizards, and documentation. After you install the GAX and GAT, you will find the Guidance Package Manager on the Visual Studio 2005 Tools menu.

In the Guidance Package Manager, click the Enable/Disable Packages button, and on the next screen, select Mobile Client Software Factory, as shown in Figure 7-3, and then click Next.

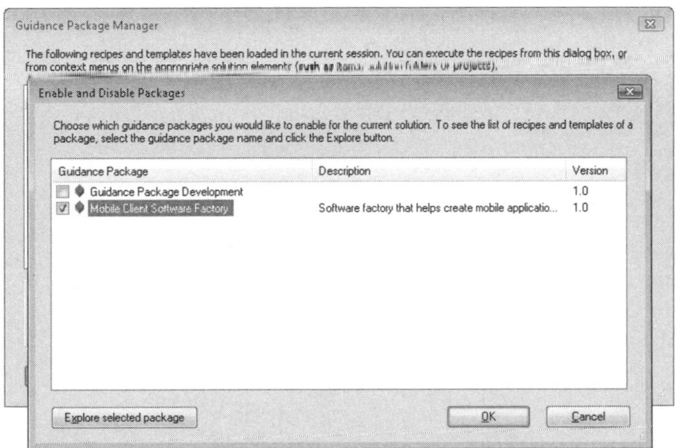

Figure 7-3 Activating the Mobile Client Software Factory guidance package

The Guidance Package Manager loads the package and, on the next screen, gives you the option of running the enclosed recipes immediately. Click Close because you need to run the Create Disconnected Service Agent recipe against a Web reference.

Configuring the Disconnected Service Agent Next, go to the Web References folder in Solution Explorer, right-click an existing Web reference, and click Mobile Factory – Create Disconnected Service Agent. This starts the Create Disconnected Service Agent Wizard that guides you through configuring your Disconnected Service Agent.

On the first page, enter the name of an endpoint you have defined in your App.config file, as shown in Figure 7-4. On the second page, you can define the default attributes for a request you queue with this Disconnected Service Agent. In the example shown in Figure 7-5, new requests are queued with three stamps, which means that the agent sends the request only if the currently active network connection has a price of three or less (in other words, a *DesktopConnection* or a *NicConnection*, according to the configuration shown in Listing 7-1). If the active network is a cellular connection, the request will be queued until a WiFi or desktop-passthrough connection becomes active. The example in Figure 7-5 also sets the maximum number of retries in the event of failure to 10 and sets an expiry time of 1 day. If a message cannot be delivered in the configured number of retries or expiry time, the agent moves it onto a dead letter queue, which is a table in a SQL Server 2005 Compact Edition database that you must provide for the use of the Disconnected Service Agent.

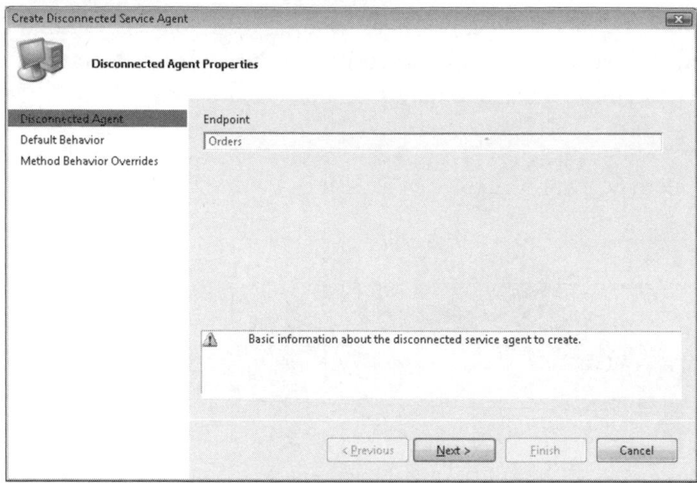

Figure 7-4 Setting the endpoint name for the Disconnected Service Agent

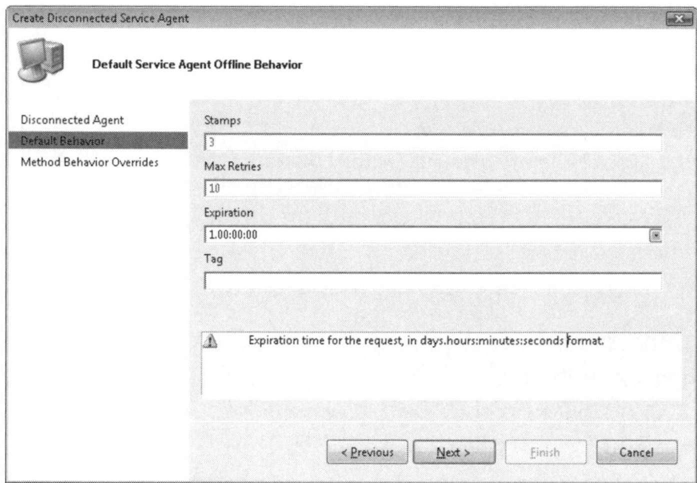

Figure 7-5 Configuring message expiry options

Any options you set in this wizard merely establish defaults for this Disconnected Service Agent; you can set different values at run time.

Initializing the Request Manager

The principal object that drives the Disconnected Service Agent functionality is the *Request Manager*, which you must configure in code at run time. Listing 7-2 shows the code that is required in the *InitializeRequestManager* method, which first creates an instance of a mobile connection monitor responsible for notifying the Request Manager of changes in the active network. The code then creates a *Microsoft.Practices.Mobile.DataAccess.Database* object for a SQL Server Compact Edition database that already exists in the project and an *IEndpointsCatalog* instance that the Request Manager uses to discover details of available endpoints from the configuration file. These different objects are all passed as arguments to the *RequestManager.Initialize* method, which sets up the required database tables in the SQL Server CE database and starts the Request Manager. The final line of this method calls *RequestManager.StartAutomaticDispatch*, which means that the Request Manager will start trying to process a queued Web service request as soon as it is queued. The alternative is to manage dispatch of messages yourself in your application code.

Listing 7-2 Abbreviated Code from the Sample Application That Initializes the Request Manager

```
using System;
using System.ComponentModel;
using System.Windows.Forms;
using Microsoft.Practices.Mobile.Configuration;
using Microsoft.Practices.Mobile.ConnectionMonitor;
using Microsoft.Practices.Mobile.DisconnectedAgent;
using Microsoft.Practices.Mobile.DataAccess;
using Microsoft.Practices.Mobile.EndpointCatalog;

namespace MobileDevelopersHandbook.DSAExample
{
    public partial class MainForm : Form
    {
        private ConnectionMonitor connectionMonitor;
        private RequestManager requestManager;
        private Database database;
        private IEndpointCatalog endpoints;

        public MainForm()
        {
            InitializeComponent();
        }

        private void Form1_Load(object sender, EventArgs e)
        {
            ...

            InitializeRequestManager();
        }

        /// <summary>
        ///  Initialize Disconnected Service Agent.
        /// </summary>
        private void InitializeRequestManager()
        {
            connectionMonitor =
```

```
                ConnectionMonitorFactory.CreateFromConfiguration();

            // Init database object
            string filename = System.IO.Path.Combine(
                DirectoryUtils.BaseDirectory, "AppDatabase.sdf");
            string connectionString =
                String.Format("Data Source=\"{0}\"", filename);
            database = new SqlDatabase(connectionString);

            // ...and an IEndpointsCatalog.
            IEndpointCatalogFactory factory =
                new EndpointCatalogFactory("Endpoints");
            endpoints = factory.CreateCatalog();

            // Finally, init the agent, using the database, endpoint
            // catalog, and connection monitor.
            IConnectionMonitor connections =
                new ConnectionMonitorAdapter(connectionMonitor);
            requestManager = RequestManager.Instance;
            requestManager.Initialize(endpoints, connections, database);
            requestManager.StartAutomaticDispatch();

            requestManager.RequestDispatched += new
EventHandler<RequestDispatchedEventArgs>(requestManager_RequestDispatched);
        }

        void requestManager_RequestDispatched(
            object sender, RequestDispatchedEventArgs e)
        {
            if (e.Result == DispatchResult.Failed)
            {
                MessageBox.Show("Request failed to endpoint: "
                    + e.Request.Endpoint);
            }
        }
        …
    }
}
```

Queuing a Request

After the Request Manager is initialized, you can post Web service calls to the queue. You post Web service calls by creating an instance of the Disconnected Service Agent you created earlier and then calling the method in that class of the same name as the Web method in the original Web service. For example, if your Web method is called *PostOrder*, you will find a method of the same name in the Disconnected Service Agent. For example, the following code is taken from the sample application:

```
using System;
using Microsoft.Practices.Mobile.DisconnectedAgent;
using
   MobileDevelopersHandbook.DSAExample.DisconnectedAgents.OrdersWebService;

namespace MobileDevelopersHandbook.DSAExample
{
    public partial class OrderProductDialog : Form
    {
        ...

        private void QueueWebServiceRequest()
        {
            // Queue the order to the Disconnected Service Agent;
            ServiceDisconnectedAgent agent = new ServiceDisconnectedAgent(
                RequestManager.Instance.RequestQueue);
            agent.PostOrder(this.customerNameTextBox.Text,
                Int32.Parse(this.productIdTextBox.Text),
                Int32.Parse(this.quantityTextBox.Text));
        }
    }
}
```

Note that when you queue a Web service request, the Disconnected Service Agent stores the request details in a table in the SQL Server CE database. This means that requests are stored and remain queued even if your application exits, to be handled next time your application runs. The Disconnected Service Agent Application Block provides an API you can use to interrogate the local request queue to find information about queued requests.

Handling the Callback

Processing is now under the control of the Request Manager. When a network of the appropriate cost is active, the Request Manager is responsible for calling the Web service using the user credentials (if any) specified in the endpoint definition in the configuration file.

When you created the Disconnected Service Agent, the wizard generated a *Callback* class containing two callbacks, one called *On<webmethod>Return* for a successful Web service call, and one called *On<webmethod>Exception* that is called when the Web service returns a *WebException*. The exception callback is also called if your own code running in *On<webmethod>Return* throws an exception.

In the example application, as shown in Listing 7-3, when a Web service call completes successfully, a *MessageBox* is displayed and some code runs to update a record in the local

SQL Server CE database; the exception handler method throws a *NotImplementedException*. Of course, you should implement more meaningful logic in a commercial application!

Listing 7-3 Callbacks for Handling a Successful and Unsuccessful Web Service Call

```
//------------------------------------------------------------------------------
// <auto-generated>
//     This code was generated by the Mobile Client Software Factory.
//     Runtime Version:2.0.50727.42
//
//     Changes to this file will be preserved if code is regenerated.
//     However, you must keep the method overrides in sync with the
//     generated ServiceDisconnectedAgentCallbackBase class.
// </auto-generated>
//------------------------------------------------------------------------------
using Microsoft.Practices.Mobile.DisconnectedAgent;
using System;
using System.Windows.Forms;

namespace
    MobileDevelopersHandbook.DSAExample.DisconnectedAgents.OrdersWebService
{
    // Generated code for the Web service
    // Use this proxy to make requests to the service when working in an
    // application that is occasionally connected.
    public class ServiceDisconnectedAgentCallback :
                     ServiceDisconnectedAgentCallbackBase
    {
        #region PostOrder

        public override void OnPostOrderReturn(
            Request request, object[] parameters, Int32 returnValue)
        {
            MessageBox.Show("Callback from Disconnected Service Agent");

            // Update the Orders table.
            OrdersResultSetResultSets.OrdersResultSet orders =
                new OrdersResultSetResultSets.OrdersResultSet();

            while (orders.Read())
            {
                …
            }
            orders.Dispose();
        }

        public override OnExceptionAction OnPostOrderException(
            Request request, Exception ex)
        {
            throw new NotImplementedException("Not implemented", ex);
        }

        #endregion PostOrder

    }
}
```

Compressing Web Service Payload

One criticism that is often leveled against Web Services is that the SOAP message format it uses, being XML, is verbose–you transfer a lot of bytes of data to convey a comparatively small amount of information. This is of particular concern over slow communications networks, such as the GPRS or CDMA over cellular networks we often have to use with mobile devices, because of the time taken to transfer data. Data communications over cellular networks are also expensive, so if you can compress the SOAP messages, your costs will be reduced and the communications will also be more reliable because the transfer time will be shorter.

One technique for compressing SOAP messages is to use SOAP extensions to intercept the SOAP message stream on dispatch, compress the message, and then on receipt decompress the message (you can also use SOAP extensions to apply other transformations on your messages, such as encryption). The following compression technique was described by Mobile Devices MVPs Chris Forsberg and Andy Sjöström in an article on their Web site at *www.businessanyplace.net/?p=wscompress2*; visit their site for additional technical information, including a description of how to use standard HTTP 1.1 compression as an alternative to the SOAP extensions technique described in the following subsections.

Coding a SOAP Extension for Compression

With SOAP extensions, you can access the actual network stream before it is deserialized into objects in the framework, and vice versa. You can learn more about how this works by reading the topic "SOAP Message Modification Using SOAP Extensions" in the .NET Developers Guide in the Visual Studio 2005 documentation.

At a technical level, you need a class that derives from *System.Web.Services.Protocols.SoapExtensionAttribute*, which defines an attribute you can place on any Web method, and another class derived from *System.Web.Services.Protocols.SoapExtension*, which implements the functionality associated with the attribute. Listing 7-4 shows the implementation of these classes for message compression. The code shown is compatible with both .NET Compact Framework 2.0 and the full .NET Framework 2.0.

Listing 7-4 Code to Define a *SoapExtension* and *SoapExtensionAttribute* for SOAP Message Compression and Decompression

```
using System;
using System.Collections.Generic;
using System.Text;
using System.IO;
using System.Web.Services.Protocols;
using ICSharpCode.SharpZipLib.GZip;

namespace CompressionSOAPExtensionLibrary
{
    /// <summary>
    /// Define a class for the CompressionSoapExtension attribute.
```

```
/// </summary>
[AttributeUsage(AttributeTargets.Method)]
public class CompressionSoapExtensionAttribute : SoapExtensionAttribute
{
    private int priority;

    /// <summary>
    /// Returns the type of the object that actually performs the logic
    /// associated with this SOAP extension
    /// </summary>
    public override Type ExtensionType
    {
        get { return typeof(CompressionSoapExtension); }
    }

    /// <summary>
    /// The Priority property indicates the order of processing when
    /// several SOAP extensions are applied simultaneously.
    /// </summary>
    public override int Priority
    {
        get
        {
            return priority;
        }
        set
        {
            priority = value;
        }
    }
}

public class CompressionSoapExtension : SoapExtension
{
    Stream oldStream;
    Stream newStream;

    public override Stream ChainStream(Stream stream)
    {
        oldStream = stream;
        newStream = new MemoryStream();
        return newStream;
    }

    public override object GetInitializer(
        LogicalMethodInfo methodInfo, SoapExtensionAttribute attribute)
    {
        return attribute;
    }

    public override object GetInitializer(Type serviceType)
    {
        return typeof(CompressionSoapExtension);
    }

    public override void Initialize(object initializer)
```

```
        {
            CompressionSoapExtensionAttribute attribute =
                (CompressionSoapExtensionAttribute)initializer;
        }

        public override void ProcessMessage(SoapMessage message)
        {
            Byte[] buffer = new Byte[2048];
            int size;

            switch (message.Stage)
            {
                case SoapMessageStage.AfterSerialize:
                    // This is called after a SOAP message is serialized
                    // but before it goes over the wire.
                    newStream.Seek(0, SeekOrigin.Begin);
                    GZipOutputStream zipOutputStream =
                        new GZipOutputStream(oldStream);
                    size = 2048;
                    while (true)
                    {
                        size = newStream.Read(buffer, 0, buffer.Length);
                        if (size > 0)
                            zipOutputStream.Write(buffer, 0, size);
                        else
                            break;
                    }
                    zipOutputStream.Flush();
                    zipOutputStream.Close();
                    break;

                case SoapMessageStage.BeforeDeserialize:
                    // This is called when the incoming message has been
                    // received.
                    GZipInputStream zipInputStream =
                        new GZipInputStream(oldStream);
                    size = 2048;
                    while (true)
                    {
                        size = zipInputStream.Read(
                            buffer, 0, buffer.Length);
                        if (size > 0)
                            newStream.Write(buffer, 0, size);
                        else
                            break;
                    }
                    newStream.Flush();
                    newStream.Seek(0, SeekOrigin.Begin);
                    break;
            }
        }
    }
}
```

> **Tip** You can create a simple class library containing the code shown in Listing 7-4. Create it as a Windows CE 5.0 class library, and then you can use it with all mobile platforms and also with the full .NET Framework.

The *CompressionSoapExtensionAttribute* class defines the *[CompressionSoapExtension]* attribute; the *ExtensionType* property in this class returns the type that actually performs the work, which is the *CompressionSoapExtension* defined in the other class in Listing 7-4.

In *CompressionSoapExtension*, the *ChainStream* method is the one that actually hooks the message stream. The real work occurs in *ProcessMessage*, which is called at four different stages of message processing so that you perform different processing depending on the value of the *Stage* property of the *SoapMessage*. The different stages are as follows:

- *BeforeSerialize* Called before the object to be sent out is serialized to SOAP
- *AfterSerialize* Called after the object has been serialized and before it gets sent out over the wire
- *BeforeDeserialize* Called when an incoming message has been received, but before it has been deserialized
- *AfterDeserialize* Called after the incoming message has been deserialized

You must compress outgoing messages after they have been serialized but before they are sent out over the wire, and decompress incoming messages when they have been received but before deserialization takes place. As you can see in Listing 7-4, the processing associated with *SoapMessageStage.AfterSerialize* takes the *oldStream* (the stream containing the SOAP message), zips it using a *GZipOutputStream*, and writes it to *newStream*, which then becomes the data that is sent out over the wire.

The processing for *SoapMessageStage.BeforeDeserialize* reverses this for incoming messages: the *oldStream* is processed by a *GZipInputStream* object to unzip it and the result is written to *newStream*. The *GZipOutputStream* and *GZipInputStream* objects that perform the compression and decompression operations are in the open source SharpZipLib library, available on the IC#Code Web site at *www.icsharpcode.net/OpenSource/SharpZipLib/*.

Using the *CompressionSoapExtension*

All that remains is to decorate the methods to which you want to apply compression. One advantage of using SOAP extensions is that you can apply the processing on a method-by-method basis so that if you have a Web service that sends only a small payload, you might not want to use compression because to do so would almost certainly increase the processing time with little benefit for the size of the message. The following code sample shows how the

CompressionSoapExtension is applied to a Web method called *GetCustomers*, which returns a *DataSet*:

```
[WebMethod]
[CompressionSoapExtension]
public CustomersDataSet GetCustomers()
{
    CustomersDataSet ds = new CustomersDataSet();
    ta.Fill(ds.Customers);
    return ds;
}
```

You must also apply the attribute to the matching method in the Web service proxy in the .NET Compact Framework client. The easiest way to do this is to add your Web reference to your project in the normal way and then click the Show All Files button at the top of Solution Explorer so that you can see the Reference.cs/.vb file:

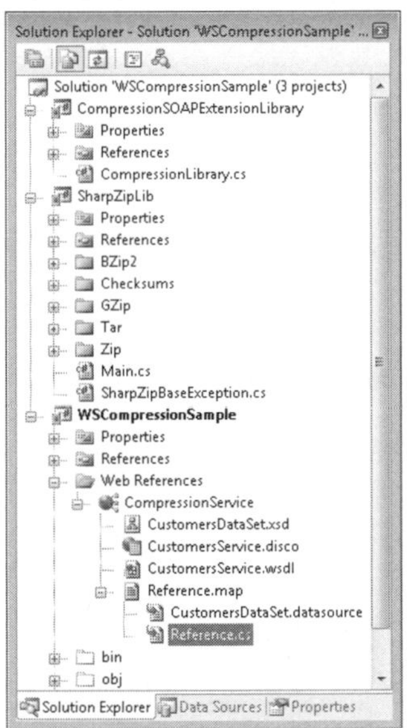

Edit this file, and apply the *[CompressionSoapExtension]* attribute to the appropriate methods, for example:

```
[System.Web.Services.Protocols.SoapDocumentMethodAttribute(
    "http://MobileDevelopersHandbook.org/GetCustomers", …)]
[CompressionSoapExtension]
public CustomersDataSet GetCustomers() {
    object[] results = this.Invoke("GetCustomers", new object[0]);
    return ((CustomersDataSet)(results[0]));
}
```

> **Warning** Remember that every time you refresh the Web reference, the contents of this file will be regenerated by the Visual Studio Add Web Reference tool, so you will have to reapply these updates. An alternative is to extend the tool-generated class by using partial classes and put your own methods in the partial class file, which will not be overwritten when you update the Web reference.

The results of this are quite impressive. In the code for this chapter on the companion Web site, you can find the WSCompression sample that calls a Web service that returns a *DataSet* containing the Customers table from the standard Northwind sample database. The Web service contains two Web methods: *GetCustomers()*, which returns the *DataSet* uncompressed, and *GetCompressedCustomers()*, which returns the same data, but using the *CompressionSoapExtension*.

If you use some kind of SOAP trace tool, such as the free TcpTrace from *www.pocketsoap.com/tcptrace/*, you can see the size of the HTTP messages that are sent. The size of the uncompressed message is 39,132 bytes, but once compressed, the size falls to 8,348 (as shown in Figure 7-6), a reduction of nearly 80 percent.

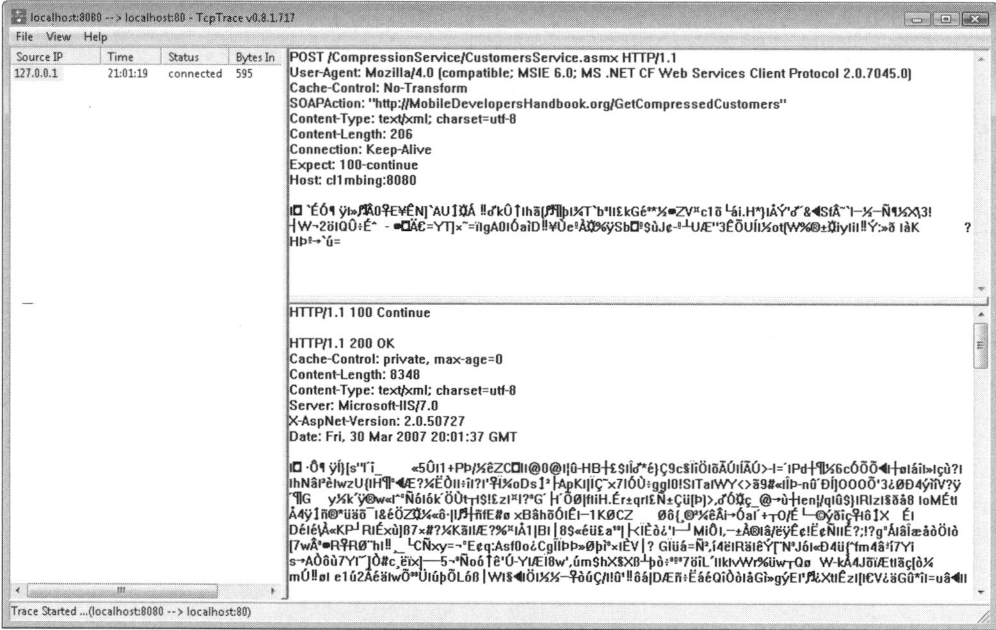

Figure 7-6 TcpTrace of the HTTP messages sent with the SOAP message compressed

You might suppose that the computational effort required to perform the compression and decompression on the mobile device client would make the call to the Web method take longer. In fact, even using the emulator, using virtually a direct network connection, the reduction in time to transfer the data easily compensates for the additional computation time. In a rough series of tests using the emulator (five calls, discarding the time taken to make the first call), transfer of the uncompressed data took an average of 5,128 milliseconds, while that of the compressed data took 4,936 milliseconds. Over a slower network, the time advantage for the transfer of compressed data should be even more pronounced, which leads to the conclusion that using compression with Web services that return medium to heavy payloads should be the norm, rather than the exception.

Accessing SQL Server Directly by Using *SqlClient*

If you can connect your device to your LAN, using WiFi or desktop passthrough (meaning your device uses ActiveSync to connect to a computer that is connected to the LAN), you can interact directly with a SQL Server 2000, SQL Server 2005, or SQL Server 2005 Express database server. Before you can connect to SQL Server from an application, you must add a reference in the Visual Studio .NET project to the SQL Server managed provider, which is listed in the Add Reference dialog box as *System.Data.SqlClient*. Alternatively, you can create a project data source that connects to your SQL Server and then drag it onto a form, in which case the designer adds the appropriate references to your project for you.

The ability to create a data source for a SQL Server database is a significant new feature in Visual Studio 2005. In Visual Studio .NET 2003, building applications running on the .NET Compact Framework 1.0 runtime, you cannot drag SQL Server database tables or views from the Server Explorer into Forms Designer to automatically generate managed provider and dataset objects. You must create any such objects that you need in code.

In Visual Studio 2005, if you are building a .NET Compact Framework 2.0 project, you can create a project data source and drag it from the Data Sources window into the Forms Designer in exactly the same way as we described for a SQL Server 2005 Compact Edition database in Chapter 3. You must remember three things when you are using a SQL Server 2000 or SQL Server 2005 database for your data source:

- When you create your database connection, at the beginning of the data source creation process, you must select the Microsoft SQL Server (*SqlClient*) data source, which uses the .NET Framework Data Provider for SQL Server, as shown in the following graphic:

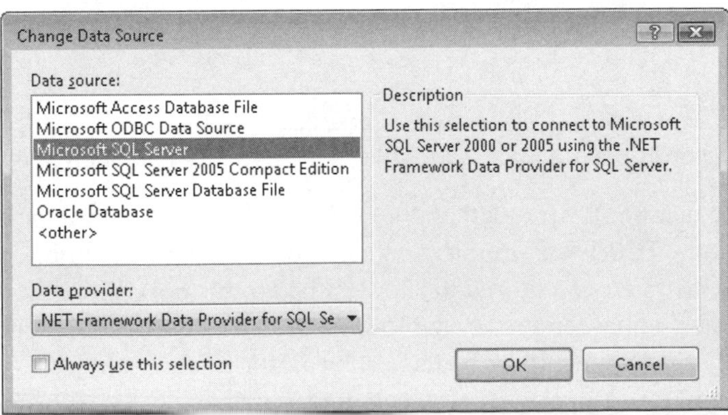

- You cannot use a *SqlCEResultSet* with a SQL Server data source.
- The connection string is different, in particular in presenting user credentials for logging on to the server. (More on this in the next section.)

In all other respects, you can follow the instructions on how to create a project data source and bind Windows Forms controls to your data using a *BindingSource* component given in Chapter 3.

Understanding Differences from the Desktop .NET Framework

Before we examine how you program the *System.Data.SqlClient* namespace in more detail, this section mentions some of the differences between the .NET Compact Framework and the desktop .NET Framework.

Only TCP/IP Connections Are Supported

Only TCP/IP connections to SQL Server are supported. You'll get an error if you use the Network Library keyword with any network library name (other than the default) in the connection string. Note that by default the TCP/IP transport is disabled in SQL Server 2005 Developer Edition, Evaluation Edition, and Express Edition. You must run the SQL Server Configuration Manager to turn it on, as shown in Figure 7-7, and then stop and restart the database service.

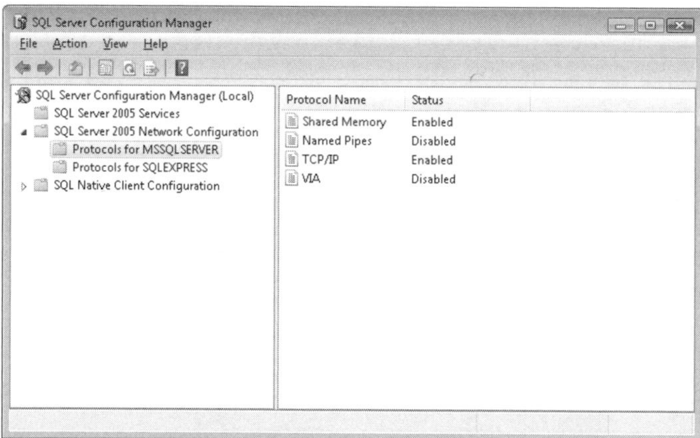

Figure 7-7 Turning on TCP/IP transport support in SQL Server Configuration Manager

Note that if you are using SQL Server 2000 or SQL Server 2005 configured to run only a single instance (the default), TCP/IP communication uses port 1433, so you should ensure that any firewalls you must cross are configured to allow traffic on this port. If you have configured a named instance, the database engine dynamically allocates an unused TCP port the first time it is started, so you must configure firewalls to allow traffic on that port. (Use the SQL Server 2005 Configuration Manager to discover which port is assigned.)

Implementing Transactions

The .NET Compact Framework doesn't support distributed transactions (such as those that can be achieved using SQL Server Distributed Transaction Coordinator [DTC], Microsoft Transaction Services [MTS], or COM+ components) across databases or servers. You can use transactions on a single database on one server.

Establishing Connections

The .NET Compact Framework doesn't support connection pooling. You can't use any of the connection-pooling keywords or values in the connection string. (You'll get an error if you try it!) Specifically, the connection string values that are not in use are *Connection Lifetime*, *Connection Reset*, *Enlist*, *Max Pool Size*, *Min Pool Size*, and *Pooling*. Using *Encrypt=true* to request an encrypted connection is not supported either.

Programming *System.Data.SqlClient*

A detailed look at accessing data in a SQL Server database, with a sample application, follows. The sample application, SqlClientExample, is available on this book's companion Web site. The sample retrieves some data from SQL Server that is to be read-only in the application and that can be collected all in one go. The sample application creates from scratch the ADO.NET objects it needs instead of creating a project data source (the technique described in Chapter 3, and a feature not supported by .NET Compact Framework 1.0) so that the code used is compatible with .NET Compact Framework 1.0 as well as version 2.0.

To run the sample, you must set up a database on your database server. There is an SQL script file and a readme file that contains instructions on how to set up the database. You must also configure an SQL login for a valid Windows account–again, see the readme for instructions.

Before you run the sample application, edit the code to set the name of your database server in the *Hostname* variable (see Listing 7-5). Then run it, supplying the user name and password of the Windows user account for which you created the database login.

> **Tip** Do not make the common mistake of using *localhost* or *(local)* for the server name in your connection strings. That works only when the client code runs on the same computer as the database server. Code running on a mobile device—even on a Visual Studio 2005 emulator—runs on a different computer, so you must use the correct name for the computer where SQL Server is running.

Figure 7-8 shows the application's form. The sample application retrieves the data into a *ListBox* control when the user clicks a button. (In practice, however, this sort of code might be found in the form's *Load* event handler, or it may run from some business logic rather than in a button's *Click* event handler.)

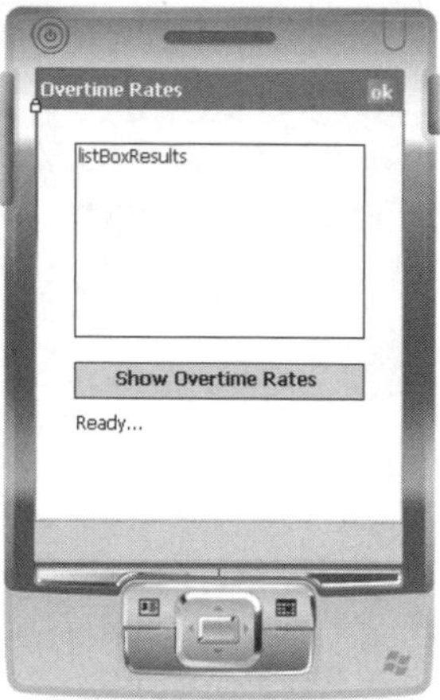

Figure 7-8 SqlClientExample sample application

The most important section of code in this sample application is shown in Listing 7-5. The application uses a custom class called *NetworkCredentials* and a form, *NetworkCredentialsForm* (both not shown), which are responsible for storing and setting a user name and password. Then it builds up the connection string, incorporating the user name and password, opens the connection, and reads the data using a *SqlDataReader*. Notice how the code is careful to dispose of the *SqlCommand* and *SqlConnection* objects; it is very important to dispose of database objects to avoid memory leaks.

Listing 7-5 Code to Open a Connection to a SQL Server Database and Use a *SqlDataReader* to Read Data

```
using System;
using System.Data;
using System.Data.SqlClient;
using System.Windows.Forms;
...

// TODO: Change this to your own server name.
private readonly string Hostname = "MYSERVER";

private void buttonGetData_Click(object sender, EventArgs e)
{
    // Get the user credentials, if not already set.
    if (NetworkCredentials.Instance.Username == null)
    {
        // Create an instance of custom form for gathering credentials.
        using (NetworkCredentialsForm dlg = new NetworkCredentialsForm())
        {
            dlg.ShowDialog();
        }
    }

    SqlConnection conSql;
    SqlDataReader rdrOvertimeRates = null;
```

```
    listBoxResults.Items.Clear();
    labelStatus.Text = "Connecting...";
    this.Refresh();

    string connString = "Server=" + Hostname + ";Database=DotNetCF;"
            + "Integrated Security=true;UID="
            + NetworkCredentials.Instance.Username + ";Password="
            + NetworkCredentials.Instance.UserPassword;

    using (conSql = new SqlConnection(connString))
    {
        using (SqlCommand sqlGetOvertimeRates = new SqlCommand(
            "SELECT OvertimeRateID,Description " +
            "FROM OvertimeRates " +
            "ORDER BY Description ",
            conSql))
        {
            try
            {
                //Open the connection.
                conSql.Open();
                //Get the records using a reader.
                rdrOvertimeRates = sqlGetOvertimeRates.ExecuteReader();
                //Put them in the list box.
                while (rdrOvertimeRates.Read())
                {
                    listBoxResults.Items.Add(rdrOvertimeRates.GetString(1));
                }
            }
            catch (SqlException errSql)
            {
                DisplaySQLErrors(errSql);
            }
            finally
            {
                //Always close the connection.
                if (rdrOvertimeRates != null)
                    rdrOvertimeRates.Close();
                conSql.Close();
            }
        }
    }

    labelStatus.Text = "Done";
}
```

Tip Notice that the SqlClientExample application can take some time to establish a connection to SQL Server. Connection pooling is not an option in the .NET Compact Framework, so the SqlClientExample application experiences this delay every time it connects to the database. To prevent this delay, one option is for the application to create a form-level reference to a connection, open it in the form's *Load* event, keep it open, and then close it when the application closes. However, this has the downside of keeping the connection alive as long as the application runs, which imposes additional burden on your database server.

Configuring your system for running the samples

To configure your system to run the code samples, the first thing you must do is create the databases in your SQL Server. Transact-SQL (T-SQL) scripts are included in the downloadable code. Refer to the accompanying readme for instructions.

Quite often, the hardest part of programming applications that access a backend server from a mobile device is configuring networking correctly. We suffered ourselves while getting these samples working for this book, and so here are the top tips:

- **TCP/IP** If you use *SqlClient* to access SQL Server directly, remember that only TCP/IP transport is supported. Remember also that TCP/IP transport is disabled by default in SQL Server 2005; you must activate it in the SQL Server Configuration Manager.
- **Cradle the emulator** If you are developing using the emulator, remember to cradle it (as described in Chapter 2, "Building a Microsoft Windows Forms GUI"), and also set the This Computer Connects To setting in ActiveSync Connection Settings to Work Network. You can now use desktop passthrough successfully to access resources on the LAN (or, indeed, on the Internet if you set the This Computer Connects To option to Internet and your computer has an Internet connection). This applies to direct access using *SqlClient* and also to HTTP access using RDA or merge replication.

  If your development computer is disconnected from a network, your client software running on the device will not be able to resolve host names and connections will fail. You can get around this by installing and activating the Microsoft Loopback Adapter. For more information, see the Microsoft Knowledge Base article titled "How to Install the Microsoft Loopback Adapter in Windows XP" on the Microsoft Help and Support Web site at *support.microsoft.com/kb/839013*. At the time of this writing, the best instructions for installing the Loopback Adapter in the Windows Vista operating system are on the following blog: *blogs.msdn.com/briankel/archive/2006/12/03/how-to-install-the-microsoft-loopback-adapter-on-windows-vista.aspx*.

  Remember that you can always use Microsoft Pocket Internet Explorer to check connectivity with the SQL Server CE agent. Just enter the URL that you configured in the Configure Web Synchronization Wizard (described later in this chapter), such as *http://myserver/mySyncVirtualDirectory/sqlcesa30.dll*, and it will return an identification string.

Apart from that, failures in using RDA or merge replication usually come down to incorrect user credentials that do not match those of either a Windows user account (where you are using Windows Integrated authentication in IIS) or a SQL Server database login, or you have not granted appropriate access permissions to the requested data in the database. For help in diagnosing problems in logging in to the database, or in accessing data in the database, you can start the SQL Server Profiler tool and request a trace that includes the *Audit: Login Failed* event. Then, you can easily see what user name requested access to the database. See SQL Server Books Online for more information about the SQL Server Profiler.

Setting the Connection String

Here is a sample of a connection string being passed to the constructor of a new *SqlConnection* object:

```
SqlConnection conSql2000 = new SqlConnection(
    + @"Data Source=MYSERVER\SQL2005; Database=DotNetCF"
    + "Integrated Security=true; UID=Andy; Password=p@ssw0rd "
    );
```

There are two points of interest in the preceding sample:

- Connecting to an instance of SQL Server
- Security options

Connecting to an Instance of SQL Server SQL Server 2000 and later allow the presence of more than one instance of SQL Server on a single physical server. You must specify both the server name and the instance name when connecting to a SQL Server that has been set up with a second instance. In the preceding sample, if you are connecting to a SQL Server 2005 instance called SQL2005 that is on the network server called MYSERVER, you would use the following:

```
Data Source=MYSERVER\SQL2005;
```

If you are connecting to just the default instance, you can specify only the server name.

Specifying Security Options An important role of the *SqlConnection* object is to specify the security access to the SQL Server database from your client application. Although the data stream between your application and the database server cannot be encrypted, access to the database can be authenticated using Windows Integrated security or SQL Server authentication.

It is generally recommended in all SQL Server documentation that you configure your database server to authenticate logins using Windows Integrated authentication rather than SQL Server authentication. Client programs running on a Windows-based computer or server, all of which run under the identity of a Windows user account, do not have to specify a user name and password in the connection string when connecting to a database server that requires Windows Integrated authentication. The Windows user who is running the client program has already logged on to Windows, specifying a correct user name and password, and so on login to the database server, the server receives an authentication token from the client computer identifying that user, which it uses to grant the login. However, if the database server is configured to require SQL authentication, the user name and password must always be specified in the connection string.

The security benefits of using Windows Integrated authentication on the database server are clear for a Windows-based computer or server client. However, a client running on a Windows CE– or Windows Mobile–powered device must always include a user name and password in the connection string, whether the database server uses Windows or SQL authentication. You do not log on to a mobile device, so there is no way that a Windows user token can be passed to the server for authentication.

If the server uses Windows authentication, set *Integrated Security=true*, and if it uses SQL authentication, simply set *Integrated Security=false*. In both cases, specify the user name and password with the *UID* and *Password* attributes.

> **Important** From a security point of view, you should not hard-code a user name and password into a connection string, such as in the code example at the beginning of the section titled "Setting the Connection String" earlier in this chapter. Instead, get the credentials from the user as demonstrated in the SqlClientExample sample application, or use one of the other techniques for storing credentials securely on the device as described in Chapter 10.

Using Transactions in the .NET Compact Framework

Transactions are used to ensure that data remains in a consistent state. They can ensure that all updates (even across different servers and organizations) are successful and, if a failure is detected, that all operations are rolled back to their original state.

One of the limitations of the .NET Compact Framework is that no support is provided for managing a transaction spanning databases or servers. However, the *SqlConnection* object does have a *BeginTransaction* method, which returns a *SqlTransaction* object that you can use to implement a transaction that is not distributed but is based on one SQL Server database.

You could take advantage of the SQL Server capability of coordinating transactions that span servers by writing a stored procedure that uses a transaction with a database on a linked server. For more detail about using linked servers, see SQL Server Books Online.

Overall, it is not recommended you use transactions from the user interface tier of a smart device application. You can perform only transactions that are not distributed across databases anyway, and database performance can be severely affected if you allow a client application to leave transactions uncommitted for any length of time (for example, if you allowed the application to start a transaction or begin an edit and then permitted users to go for lunch and not commit the changes until their return). The SQL Server host is the place to begin and commit transactions, and if you use stored procedures, you can use Transact-SQL code to perform the transactions. The following is an example of Transact-SQL structure for using a transaction:

```
CREATE PROC qUserTransaction
AS
BEGIN TRANSACTION
-- rest of the SQL here
IF @@ERROR=0 BEGIN
    COMMIT TRANSACTION
    RETURN 0 - success
END
ELSE BEGIN
    ROLLBACK TRANSACTION
    RETURN @@ERROR
END
```

Synchronizing Data Using SQL Server 2005 Compact Edition Remote Data Access

Many applications require you to load data from a central database, make changes or additions locally, and then send your changes back to the central SQL Server database so that other users can see them. Remote Data Access (RDA) is one technique you can use for loading from a central SQL Server database and sending updates back to the server at a later time.

RDA makes use of the SQL Server CE Database Engine and the SQL Server CE Client Agent on the smart device client. (See Figure 7-9.)

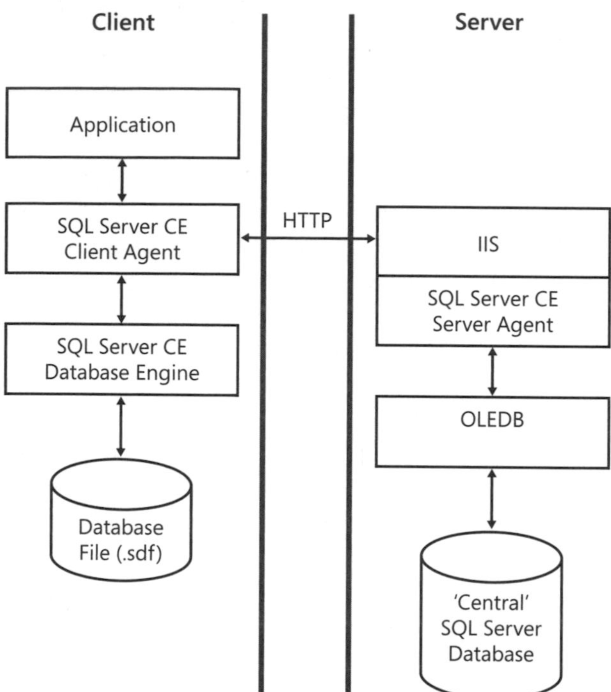

Figure 7-9 RDA and merge replication architecture

When data is required from the central SQL Server database, the SQL Server CE Client Agent makes a request to the SQL Server CE Server Agent over HTTP. The server agent runs as an Internet Server API (ISAPI) extension under IIS. It is implemented in the Sscesa30.dll file that is located on a Web site designated for the use of RDA.

There are three stages to setting up a server to support RDA and/or merge replication:

1. Install IIS on the server.
2. Install replication components for your SQL Server 2000 or SQL Server 2005 database.

   If your database is SQL Server 2005, install replication support from the product installation procedure.

   If your database is SQL Server 2000, you can find installers for the replication components in the *drive*:\Program Files\Microsoft Visual Studio 8\SmartDevices\SDK\SQL Server\Mobile\v3.0 folder. There are two choices in this folder:

   - **sql2kensp4.msi** Install this if the target database is SQL Server 2000 Service Pack 4 (SP4).
   - **sql2kensp3a.msi** Install this if the target database is SQL Server 2000 SP3.

3. Install the SQL Server CE Server Tools. You configure the Web site using tools you install from the SQL Server 2005 Compact Edition Server Tools package, which you can download from the Microsoft MSDN Download Center at *msdn.microsoft.com/downloads/details.aspx?FamilyID=4E45F676-E69A-4F7F-A016-C1585ACF4310*. Alternatively, if you have Visual Studio 2005 SP1, you can find the installer, called Sqlce30setupen.msi, in the *drive*:\Program Files\Microsoft Visual Studio 8\SmartDevices\SDK\SQL Server\Mobile\v3.0 folder.

You must install the SQL Server CE Server Tools on your Web server where IIS is located. You can configure your server-side components as follows:

- A single-server environment, with IIS and SQL Server running on the same computer
- A multiple-server environment, with IIS and SQL Server running on two separate computers

These options are illustrated in Figure 7-10. A multiple-server environment is the most common scenario for deployed applications. Multiple servers are typically used in production because they provide more flexibility and can better meet complex security needs. If you are setting up SQL Server CE for the first time, consider setting up a single-server environment. This lets you simplify the setup process by installing all the necessary server software on one computer.

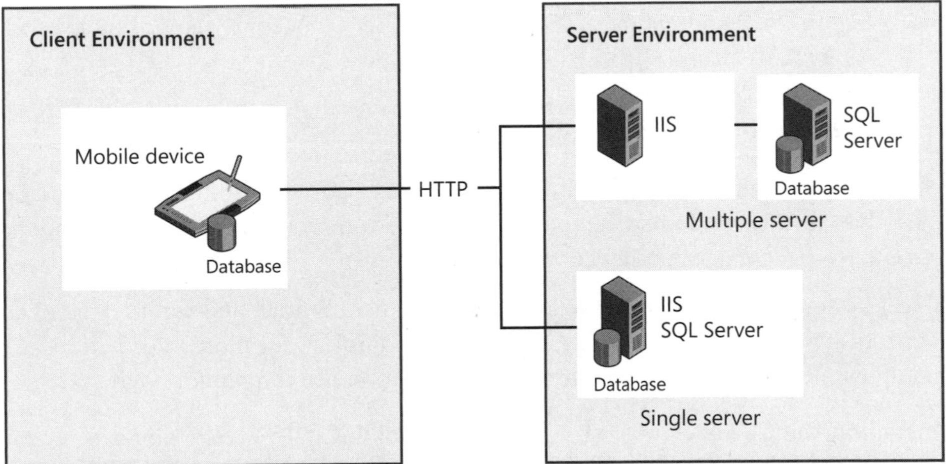

Figure 7-10 Server-side component configuration options to support RDA and merge replication

Understanding RDA Pull and Push

RDA *pull* retrieves data from the SQL Server database using OLEDB and then transmits it back to the client using HTTP. The SQL Server CE Server Agent manages communications on the server side, while on the client, the SQL Server CE Client Agent receives the data stream and stores it in a table in a local SQL Server CE database file. After data is in the local SQL Server CE database, it can be manipulated by the client smart device application.

You can return a pulled table from a local SQL Server CE database to update the central SQL Server database. RDA calls this the *push*. The SQL Server CE Client Agent sends the data across HTTP to the SQL Server CE Server Agent. The SQL Server CE Server Agent updates the SQL Server database using OLEDB and returns to the client any errors that occur.

In addition to the push and pull of data, RDA provides the *SubmitSQL* method for executing SQL statements directly on the server, as you will learn later.

You can use RDA with SQL Server 6.5 and later, and it is relatively simple to set up. The RDA communication protocol is suited to wireless transports; the data is compressed and may be encrypted during transmission. However, the process by which RDA merges data back into the central database is also simple and is not suitable for complex data structures or multiuser applications where many users are trying to update the same data. Note that you can't use RDA with a case-sensitive SQL Server database.

RDA Server Setup

The following shows you how to set up RDA for the sample application. Here is an outline of the tasks:

- Install the SQL Server CE Server Agent on your Web server.
- Use the SQL Server Connectivity Management tool to create a virtual directory (see Figure 7-12) containing the SQL Server CE Server Agent dynamic-link library (DLL) (Sqlcesa30.dll).
- Choose an authentication method for the new site (see the section titled "RDA Security Setup" that follows and Figure 7-14).
- Check that the identity authorized by IIS has a corresponding login to SQL Server and has permission to use the relevant database and permissions to access and make any required changes to the database objects.

Create a new database using SQL Server Management Studio, and run the MakeTrafficDatabase.sql script to create the tables used in these samples– for more information, see the readme in the downloadable code for this chapter on the companion Web site.

Installing the CE Server Agent Locate and run the SQL Server Compact Edition Server Tools setup program on the server that you will use as the Web server for RDA. This extracts files before presenting the Microsoft SQL Server CE Server Tools Setup Wizard. Follow the wizard through the system configuration check, SQL Server selection page, and location of program files to the Confirm Installation page. Click Install, and the wizard copies the server tools and the data access components onto the server.

When installation is complete, click Start, point to All Programs, click SQL Server 2005 Compact Edition, and then click Configure Web Synchronization Wizard to configure the SQL Server CE virtual directory in IIS (see Figure 7-11).

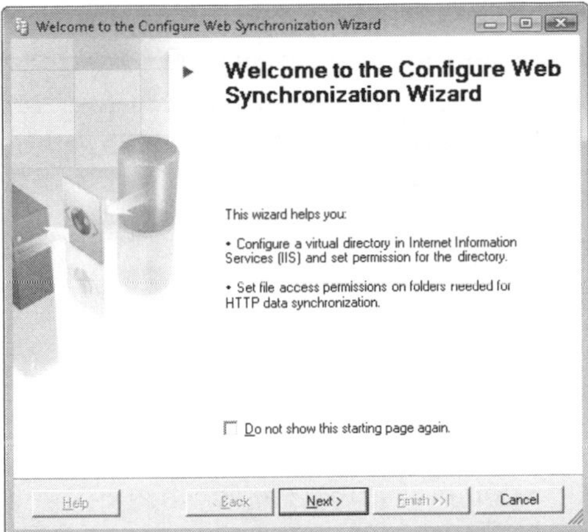

Figure 7-11 Configure Web Synchronization Wizard

Click Next to start the wizard. On the next page, you can select the subscriber type; you must select SQL Server 2005 Compact Edition. On the following page, you can select the computer running IIS and choose to set up a new virtual directory or use an existing one (see Figure 7-12).

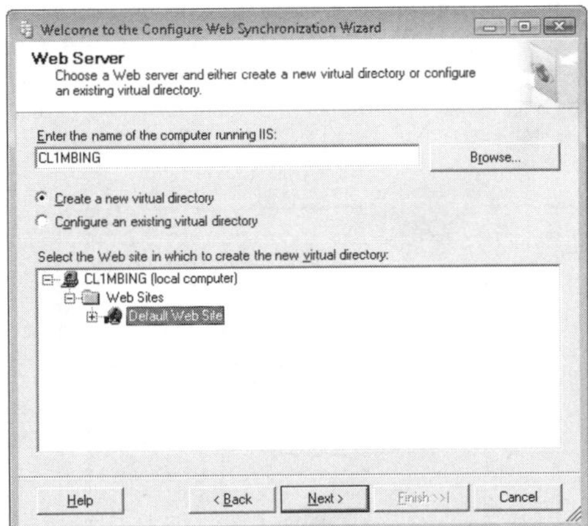

Figure 7-12 Select server, virtual directory, and Web site

On the Virtual Directory Information page, enter **TrafficRDA** in the Alias box, and click Next. The wizard creates the physical folder and asks if it should copy in the SQL Server CE Agent and register it; you must reply Yes.

On the Secure Communications page, you can specify whether a secure communications channel should be used. You must obtain and install a server certificate if you want to use secure communications, and you can also specify that client certificates be required for all clients. You can learn more about setting up secure communications in Chapter 10.

The wizard then displays the authentication choices for RDA.

RDA Security Setup Many of the problems you might encounter in practice when you use RDA will be caused by the security mechanisms in the chain of applications that participate in RDA operations. There are four checkpoints that you have to pass through between your smart device application and the data that you want out of the central SQL Server database. These are as follows:

- IIS authentication
- SQL Server authentication
- SQL Server database access
- SQL Server object permissions

Refer to Figure 7-13, which shows these checkpoints as gates (they open only if you are successfully authenticated and are authorized to have access). As well as the gates, you can see three stick people, who represent the three identities you might be assuming as you pass each control.

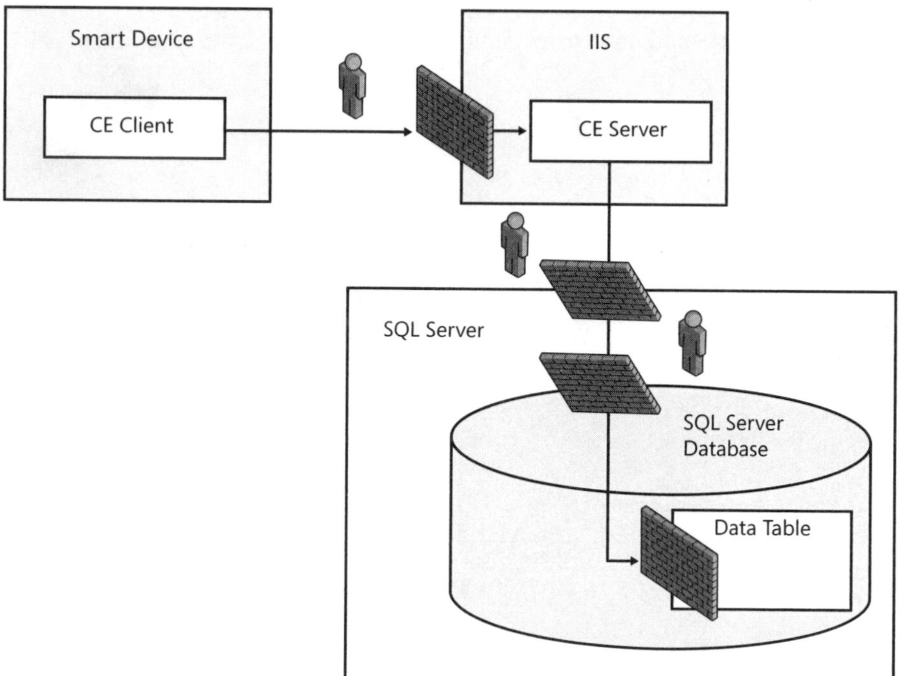

Figure 7-13 RDA security checks

Next, you are asked whether IIS should authenticate users (at the first gate). Figure 7-14 shows the Client Authentication page in the SQL Server CE Configure Web Synchronization Wizard. Select Clients Will Be Authenticated, and then click Next.

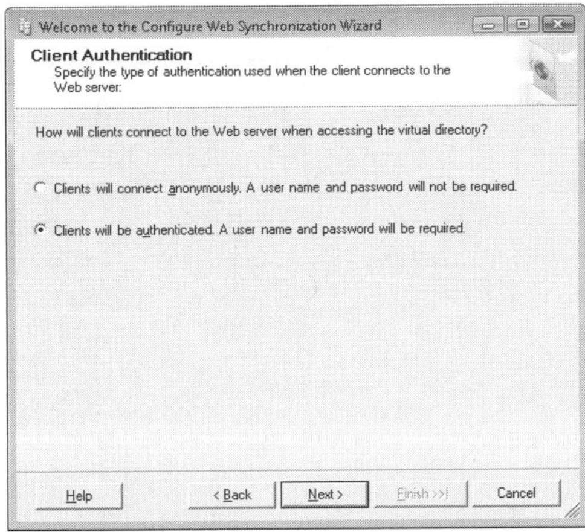

Figure 7-14 IIS authentication options

Then you are asked to choose the authentication control mode that IIS is to use (at the first gate). The sample application uses the Integrated Windows authentication mechanism, so you should check the top option and then click Next to proceed to the next stage of the security setup.

This set of authentication choices for IIS along with the option to specify a SQL Server login in the OLEDB connection string used by the RDA methods (more detail later in the sections titled "Using RDA Pull" and "Pushing Changes Back to the Remote Database") gives you four possible scenarios for the RDA security setup. Table 7-2 details the identities and authentication checks that will be made for each of these scenarios. It should help you check your security setup if you have problems connecting using one of the RDA methods.

Table 7-2 Identities and Authentication Checks in RDA

Authentication Scheme	IIS Authentication	SQL Server Authentication	SQL Server Permissions
IIS Anonymous, with logon to SQL Server authenticated by Integrated Windows authentication	You do not provide a user name or password but are instead logged on to the Windows server using the credentials specified for anonymous Internet access (by default, the IUSR_*ComputerName* local account is used, although you can configure a custom Windows user account to be used).	You are logged in to SQL Server as the Windows user account configured for anonymous Internet access (by default, *ComputerName* \IUSR_*ComputerName*).	You need to grant database access and relevant object permissions to the account configured for anonymous Internet access.

Table 7-2 **Identities and Authentication Checks in RDA**

Authentication Scheme	IIS Authentication	SQL Server Authentication	SQL Server Permissions
IIS Basic, with logon to SQL Server authenticated by Integrated Windows authentication	You must provide a Windows user name and password in the *InternetLogin* and *Internet-Password* properties of the *SqlCeRemoteDataAccess* instance. The credentials are passed to IIS in plain text. You should use Secure Sockets Layer to create a Secure HTTP (HTTPS) connection when using Basic authentication so that the credentials are transferred over an encrypted channel.	You are logged in to SQL Server as the Windows user identity used to authenticate to IIS.	You need to grant database access and relevant object permissions to the Windows user identity used to authenticate to IIS, or to the Windows group to which the user account belongs.
IIS Integrated Windows, with logon to SQL Server authenticated by Integrated Windows authentication	You must provide a Windows user name and password in the *InternetLogin* and *Internet-Password* properties of the *SqlCeRemoteDataAccess* instance, and these credentials are passed in an encrypted form to IIS. Note that you cannot use this form of authentication through a proxy server.	As above.	As above.
IIS Anonymous, Basic, or Integrated Windows, but with logon to the database server authenticated using SQL Server authentication	You must provide credentials for IIS Basic and IIS Integrated Windows as described above.	You are logged in to SQL Server using the user ID/password you specify in the connection string you supply to the *SqlCeRemote-DataAccess.Pull* and *.Push* methods.	You need to grant database access and relevant object permissions to the SQL Server user specified in the connection string.

The next step in the security setup for the sample application is to identify the Windows user accounts (or groups) that you will use for authenticating to IIS so that the wizard can grant appropriate NTFS file system access permissions to the virtual directory. Because the sample application uses Integrated authentication, you should enter the domain and user name of a test user, or the domain and group name of a test user, as shown in Figure 7-15.

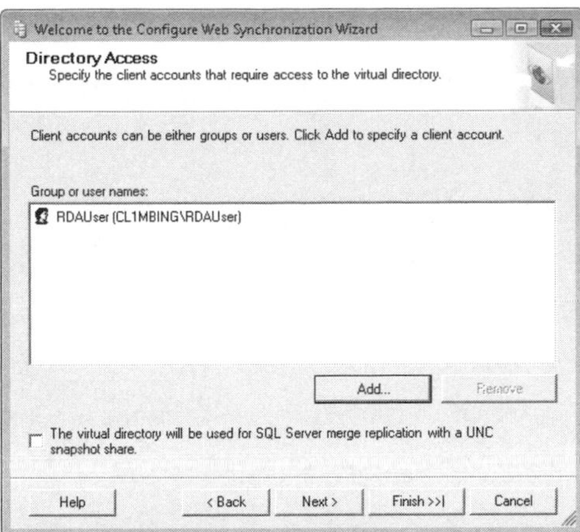

Figure 7-15 Identifying Windows user accounts that are used for IIS authentication so as to grant them NTFS access permissions

Leave the option The Virtual Directory Will Be Used For SQL Server Merge Replication clear, and click Next again. On the last page, click Finish to complete this part of the security setup.

To complete the security setup in the database, run the SQL Server Enterprise Manager and locate the sample database called Traffic. Make sure that the domain user account you have configured for use for RDA or its Windows group is added as logins to the server and has permission to access the Traffic sample database. Check that the account also has permission to read and update the Cars and Obs tables in the Traffic database. (For more information about setting permissions in SQL Server, see SQL Server Books Online.)

> **Tip** To check that you have configured the virtual directory correctly, and that your device has network connectivity to the SQL Server CE Agent, start Pocket Internet Explorer on the device, and enter the URL to the virtual directory. If you have connectivity, you will see a string returned from the server agent:

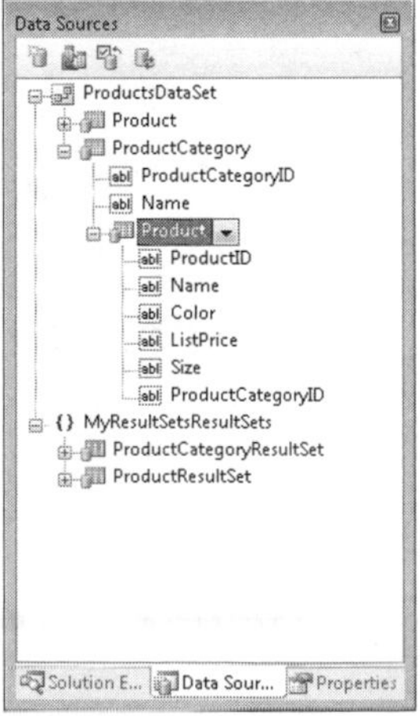

Pulling Data into a Local Database

This section extends the sample application of a parking management system. You will see how to load the initial data from a central SQL Server database using RDA.

Using RDA Pull You follow several steps to use RDA to pull data from a SQL Server database onto a smart device; they are as follows:

- Use the SQL Server CE Configure Web Synchronization Wizard to create a virtual directory on your Web server that is configured correctly for RDA.
- Check the security path from the Web server to the SQL Server database login.
- Create the target SQL Server CE database on the device using the *SqlCeEngine* object.
- If the target database already exists, connect using a *SqlCeConnection* object, and use a *SqlCeCommand* object to delete any tables that are part of the pull.
- Transfer the data using the *Pull* method of a *SqlCeRemoteDataAccess* object.

You have already done the first two steps in the preceding section. Now you need to do the housekeeping tasks of creating a local database and deleting any existing tables. For each table that you use to store the results of an RDA Pull, you also need a separate table to store details of any errors that are encountered (you specify the name of the errors table in the call to the *Pull* method, as explained later), so you must delete both these tables. The sample shows you how to do this in more detail, but in outline, you must use T-SQL Data Definition Language (DDL) to remove any existing tables, for example:

```
//Clear out old table.
using (SqlCeConnection cn =
    new SqlCeConnection(@"Data Source=\My Documents\TrafficRDA.sdf"))
{
    cn.Open();
    try
    {
        try
        {
            using (SqlCeCommand cmd =
                new SqlCeCommand("DROP TABLE Cars", cn))
            {
                cmd.ExecuteNonQuery();
            }
        }
        catch (SqlCeException sqlCeEx)
        {
            if (sqlCeEx.HResult != -2147217865) // Table does not exist
                DisplaySQLCEErrors(sqlCeEx);
        }
    }
    finally
    {
        cn.Close();
    }
}
```

Warning There is a bug in SQL Server 2005 Compact Edition that makes it difficult to delete an errors table using code similar to that shown in the preceding code example or even if you try to drop the table using Query Analyzer on the device. You may get an exception with the error "DDL Operations are restricted on this Table," and the DROP operation fails. Subsequent calls to *Pull* will also fail if the table name you specify for the errors table already exists.

There are two workarounds. You can delete the whole database rather than try to delete individual tables, and then create a new database before calling *Pull*. Alternatively, make sure your program executable runs from the same folder as where the SQL CE DLLs are installed, by default the Windows folder. The sample application that you can download for this chapter uses the latter approach.

You achieve the last step of pulling the data from SQL Server by creating a *SqlCeRemoteDataAccess* object and setting some properties, before calling its *Pull* method. Table 7-3 examines the properties needed.

Table 7-3 Properties of the *SqlCeRemoteDataAccess* Object

Property	Description	Comment
CompressionLevel	Specifies the amount of compression that will be used by the compression routines during *Push* and *Pull* operations.	A value of 0 turns off all compression. The maximum is 6. The default value is 1, which uses the lowest amount of processor time while still providing some compression.
ConnectionManager	On Windows Mobile–powered devices, *true* enables use of the Connection Manager application programming interface (API) to establish the connection to the server (recommended).	If the *ConnectionManager* property is set to *true*, the Connection Manager will always be used to establish a connection. If proxy settings are required, the Connection Manager proxy settings will be used unless the *InternetProxyServer*, *InternetProxyLogin*, or *InternetProxyPassword* property is set.
ConnectionRetryTimeout	Allows you to specify an amount of time that the SQL CE client will attempt to recover from a failed connection.	This property applies only to situations when the initial connection has succeeded and then the connection has been destroyed. If recovery occurs during the specified duration, the operation (*Push*, *Pull*, or *SubmitSql*) continues.
InternetURL	The URL string to the SQL CE Server Agent DLL.	You must include the name of the DLL (Sqlcesa30.dll).
InternetLogin	The IIS login name.	The default is no login string. You do not need to give a value if you are using Anonymous authentication.
InternetPassword	The IIS password string.	There is no need to give a password for Anonymous authentication.

Table 7-3 **Properties of the *SqlCeRemoteDataAccess* Object**

Property	Description	Comment
InternetProxyServer	Proxy server name and port.	Both the server name (or IP address) and port must be given using the format *ProxyServerName:Port*. You do not set this property if you are not using a proxy server.
InternetProxyLogin	Login for the proxy server.	You need to set this property if you are using Basic or Integrated authentication on the proxy server. You do not set this property if you are not using a proxy server.
InternetProxyPassword	Password for the proxy server.	You need to set this property if you are using Basic or Integrated authentication on the proxy server. You do not set this property if you are not using a proxy server.
LocalConnectionString	The OLEDB connection string for SQL Server CE.	The OLEDB connection string for logging onto SQL Server CE on the smart device.

The remaining details of the route from the central SQL Server database to the SQL Server CE database are provided by the arguments of the *Pull* method. Table 7-4 gives guidance on their use.

Table 7-4 **Arguments of the *Pull* Method**

Argument	Description	Comment
LocalTableName	The name of a SQL Server CE table that will receive the extracted SQL Server records.	You need to drop the table if it already exists.
SqlSelectString	SQL that specifies what columns and rows of SQL Server data to transfer.	This can contain any valid Transact-SQL statement or function. This SQL is executed against the SQL Server database; you must check that you have all the permissions needed.
OLEDBConnection String	The OLDB connection string for the SQL Server database.	This is the OLEDB connection string for the SQL Server CE Server Agent to use when it connects to the central SQL Server database.
RDATrackingOption	Indicates whether SQL Server CE should track changes made to the pulled table (to allow you to send them back to the SQL Server).	Options are *TrackingOn*, *TrackingOff*, *TrackingWithIndexesOn*, and *TrackingWithIndexesOff*. See Tracking Options below.

Table 7-4 Arguments of the *Pull* Method

Argument	Description	Comment
ErrorTableName	Name of a table in the local SQL Server CE database to be used for errors.	Each local table you create must use a separate local error table. If you try to reuse an error table name, the pull will fail.

Here is a sample function to achieve an RDA pull:

```
private void RDAPull()
{
    // First, ensure you have an empty local SQL CE database.
    if (System.IO.File.Exists(@"\My Documents\TrafficRDA.sdf"))
    {
        System.IO.File.Delete(@"\My Documents\TrafficRDA.sdf");
    }

    // Create new database.
    SqlCeEngine eng =
        new SqlCeEngine(@"Data Source=\My Documents\TrafficRDA.sdf");
    eng.CreateDatabase();

    // Perform the pull.
    using (SqlCeRemoteDataAccess rda = new SqlCeRemoteDataAccess())
    {
        string sCon = @"Provider=SQLOLEDB;Data Source=MYSQLSERVER;"
            + @"Initial Catalog=Traffic;"
            + @"integrated security=SSPI;Persist Security Info=False";

        rda.InternetUrl = @"http://MYSERVER/TrafficRDA/sqlcesa30.dll";
        rda.LocalConnectionString =
            @"Data Source=\My Documents\TrafficRDA.sdf";
        rda.InternetLogin = @"MyDomain\RDAUser";
        rda.InternetPassword = "P@ssw0rd";
        rda.CompressionLevel = 10;
        try
        {
            rda.Pull("Cars", "SELECT CarID,Reg,Location FROM Cars",
                sCon, RdaTrackOption.TrackingOn, "rdaCarErrors");
        }
        catch (SqlCeException sqlCeEx)
        {
            DisplaySQLCEErrors(sqlCeEx);
        }
        try
        {
            rda.Pull("Obs",
                "SELECT ObsID,CarID,ObsDateTime,ObsNote FROM Obs",
                sCon, RdaTrackOption.TrackingOn, "rdaObsErrors");
        }
        catch (SqlCeException sqlCeEx)
        {
```

```
                DisplaySQLCEErrors(sqlCeEx);
            }
        }

        MessageBox.Show("RDA Pull Done!");
    }
```

> **Caution** For simplicity, the preceding code example shows the *InternetLogin* and *InternetPassword* values hard-coded. Do not do this in your own applications because an attacker can decompile application code and discover these values, compromising your security. Instead, store these values securely as described in Chapter 10, or use a Windows Form to ask the user to enter credentials at run time, which is the technique used in the first sample in this chapter.

You can verify the operation of your code by using the Query Analyzer tool on the smart device. By connecting to the new database after executing the RDA pull and examining the Objects tab, you can see both the pulled tables and their error tables (see Figure 7-16).

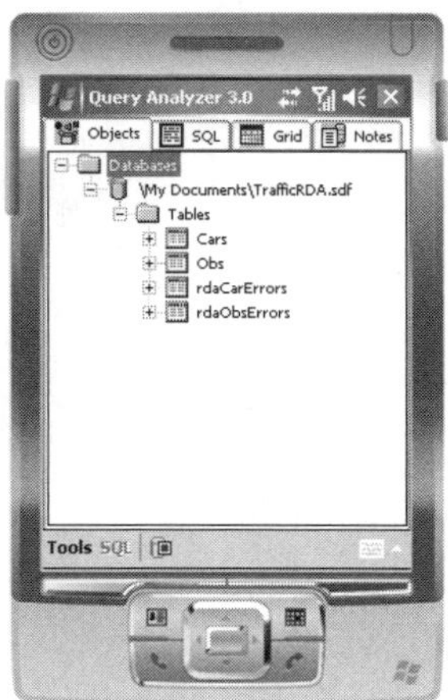

Figure 7-16 RDA pulled tables and error tables

Tracking Options There are four *TrackingOption* values to choose from when calling the *Pull* method of the *SqlCeRemoteDataAccess* object. Your choice is important because it affects whether you can subsequently call the *Push* method and the behavior of the pulled table. Table 7-5 lists the effects of each value.

Table 7-5 *RdaTrackOption* Values

Value	Description
TrackingOn	SQL Server CE will keep track of every record that is inserted, updated, or deleted. You will be able to push these changes back to the central SQL Server. You must select an updatable record set containing the primary key of the source table. In practice, this restricts the selection to a single table or a SQL Server updatable view. If you specify the name of an errors table, push errors will be logged in that table in the database on the device.
TrackingOff	No tracking of changes is done, and you will not be able to call the *Push* method.
TrackingWithIndexesOn	Same as *TrackingOn*, but additionally copies the indexes during the pull. For example, this may be useful if you have unique constraints on the table that are implemented by an index.
TrackingOffWithIndexes	Same as *TrackingOff*, but the indexes are copied during the pull.

Making Changes to a Pulled Table

Although a *SqlCeCommand* object generally gives you a wide range of DDL SQL commands, if you are trying to change a local table that has been pulled using RDA, there are some restrictions. You can drop a table that has been created in an RDA pull and add or drop indexes, default values, and foreign key constraints. You are not allowed to rename a table that has been created in an RDA pull; drop the primary key; add, drop, or rename columns; or alter the data type of a column.

Pushing Changes Back to the Remote Database

You can write code to update pulled tables in the local database in the same way as in any other table (subject to the restrictions described in the preceding section). When you are ready to update the central SQL Server database with additions, changes, and deletions you have made, you call the *Push* method of the *SqlCeRemoteDataAccess* object.

Optimistic Concurrency RDA uses optimistic concurrency control on the central SQL Server database. That is, when records are pulled, they are not locked on the central SQL Server database, and when you push changes back, the SQL Server CE Server Agent overwrites any changes that might have been made by another user. There are no built-in features to allow you to detect that two or more clients have updated the same records in a table. This means that the RDA *Push* method is suited to applications for which this kind of lost update is acceptable or for which you can implement some kind of mechanism to ensure that different clients work on a unique selection of records (for example, modifying the *SELECT* statement that you pass to the RDA *Pull* method so that each client pulls a unique range of records).

Using the *Push* Method You set the same set of properties on the *SqlCeRemoteDataAccess* object as mentioned in Table 7-3 for the *Pull*, so they are not repeated here. The *Push* method takes two or optionally three arguments, as described in Table 7-6.

Table 7-6 Arguments of the *Push* Method

Argument	Description	Comment
LocalTableName	The SQL Server CE table that will be the source of the changes	The name of the local table that contains the tracked changes.
OLEDBConnection String	The OLDB connection string for the SQL Server database	This is the OLEDB connection string for the SQL Server CE Server Agent to use when it connects to the SQL Server database.
BatchOption	Optional argument: *RdaBatchingOn* or *RdaBatchingOff*	This argument specifies whether SQL Server CE should apply each update in a separate transaction (*RdaBatchingOff*) or all together in a single transaction (*RdaBatchingOn*).

As with the *Pull* method, you must check that the authentication method you are using has access through to the table on the SQL Server database and that it also has authorization to change the data. Here is a sample function to perform an RDA *Push*:

```
private void RDAPush()
{
    using (SqlCeRemoteDataAccess rda = new SqlCeRemoteDataAccess())
    {
        string sCon = @"Provider=SQLOLEDB;Data Source=MYSQLSERVER;"
            + @"Initial Catalog=Traffic;"
            + @"integrated security=SSPI;Persist Security Info=False";

        rda.InternetUrl = @"http://MYSERVER/TrafficRDA/sqlcesa30.dll";
        rda.LocalConnectionString =
            @"Data Source=\My Documents\TrafficRDA.sdf";
        rda.InternetLogin = @"MyDomain\RDAUser";
        rda.InternetPassword = "P@ssw0rd";
        try
        {
            rda.Push("Cars", sCon);
        }
        catch (SqlCeException sqlCeEx)
        {
            DisplaySQLCEErrors(sqlCeEx);
        }
    }

    MessageBox.Show("RDA Push Done!");
}
```

Caution For simplicity, the preceding code example shows the *InternetLogin* and *InternetPassword* values hard-coded. Do not do this in your own applications because an attacker can decompile application code and discover these values, compromising your security. Instead, store these values securely as described in Chapter 10, or use a Windows Form to ask the user to enter credentials at run time, which is the technique used in the first sample in this chapter.

Examining the RDA Errors Table If an *ErrorTableName* argument was given during the *Pull* of the *LocalTableName* that is being pushed, if any errors are detected during the *Push*, they will be logged in the *ErrorTableName* table in the SQL Server CE database. You can examine this table by retrieving its records using standard database access techniques. See the upcoming section titled "Troubleshooting RDA" for more information about some of the errors you can encounter.

Running Commands on the Remote Database

In addition to pulling *Push* and *Pull*, the *SqlCeRemoteDataAccess* object has a *SubmitSQL* method that you can use to run SQL statements on the central SQL Server database. The *SubmitSQL* method requires you to set up the same properties to specify the URL of the SQL Server CE agent and user credentials as for the *Pull* method, and you must have the correct authorization to run the SQL on the central SQL Server database. The *SubmitSQL* method takes just two arguments, the SQL string to execute and the OLEDB connection string the SQL Server CE agent will use to connect to the SQL Server database.

The sample code here sets an archive flag on all the cars in the central database, used in the sample application at the end of the day to close off all observations:

```
private void SubmitSQLRDA()
{
    using (SqlCeRemoteDataAccess rda = new SqlCeRemoteDataAccess())
    {
        rda.InternetUrl = @"http://MYSERVER/TrafficRDA/sqlcesa30.dll";
        rda.LocalConnectionString =
            @"Data Source=\My Documents\TrafficRDA.sdf";
        rda.InternetLogin = @"MyDomain\RDAUser";
        rda.InternetPassword = "P@ssw0rd";
        try
        {
            string sCon = @"Provider=SQLOLEDB;Data Source=MYSQLSERVER;"
                + @"Initial Catalog=Traffic;"
                + @"integrated security=SSPI;Persist Security Info=False";
            rda.SubmitSql("UPDATE Cars SET Archive = 1", sCon);
        }
        catch (SqlCeException ex)
        {
            DisplaySQLCEErrors(ex);
        }
    }
}
```

Caution The same advice applies to this sample about not using hard-coded credentials as was given for the RDA *Pull* and *Push* samples.

However, there is another security point to make about the *SubmitSql* method. You must take care with how you use this if you use user input to help build up the command. For example, think about what could happen if you build up an SQL statement to send to the *SubmitSql* method using code such as *"UPDATE Cars SET Color ='" + TextBox1.Text + "'"*, and you are expecting the user to enter values such as Red, Blue, or Yellow.

What if the user enters: *"Red'; DROP TABLE Cars --"*? Because SQL Server is quite happy to execute multiple statements you pass to it in a single string, it will update the Cars table and then delete it!

This is an example of an SQL injection attack. You must always validate user input carefully and use regular expressions or some other technique to ensure that the input is in the format you intended. Remember the security maxim: Never trust user input.

Troubleshooting RDA

As described in the introduction to this section on programming RDA and in Figure 7-9, there are a number of layers making up the RDA architecture. When you are developing a system using RDA, a problem might occur in any one of the layers. Table 7-7 lists some of the problems you might encounter if you are developing applications using RDA, and it helps you track down their sources and reach resolutions.

Table 7-7 Potential Problems and Resolutions for Using RDA

Problem	Reason	Resolution
Cannot Pull Table (Native Error reports 0 or 4060)	You will get a pull error if you have not set up the security access correctly.	Check your security setup. See the section titled "RDA Security Setup" earlier in this chapter for guidance.
Cannot Push Table with no Primary Key (Native Error reports 29010)	You cannot update a central SQL Server table that has no primary key (although you will be able to pull it successfully).	Alter the table on the central SQL Server database to have a primary key.
Cannot Push Table with Identity Column (Native Error reports 28537)	The SQL Server CE Client Agent receives the error that it is unable to establish an identity range for any new records you add to a table that contains an identity column.	You will need to consider using merge replication if your application has to push identity columns back to the central SQL Server database. Consider a workaround if you want to stick to RDA. (See the SQLCE_RDA sample in the downloadable code on the companion Web site for one solution, where the application assigns unique record ID values when you create a new record, instead of relying on an identity column to assign these values.)

Table 7-7 Potential Problems and Resolutions for Using RDA

Problem	Reason	Resolution
Cannot drop Errors tables, either programmatically or in Query Analyzer	There is a restriction in SQL Server CE that means you cannot delete errors tables unless the application that created them is in the same folder as the SQL Server CE DLLs.	Either delete the whole database and create a new empty one before calling *Pull*, or deploy your application to the same folder as the SQL Server CE DLLs (by default, Windows).

For a full list of SQL Server CE error messages and numbers, search the SQL Server CE Books Online for "SQL Server CE Errors."

Replicating Data Using SQL Server Merge Replication

This section looks in detail at the alternative to RDA: SQL Server CE Merge Replication (referred to as *merge replication* from here). Merge replication is supported in SQL Server 2000 and later. Although merge replication is more powerful and simpler to program than RDA is, you will find that it is more complex to set up, especially the security configuration. We start by taking you through the main points.

SQL Server CE Merge Replication Architecture

Although SQL Server CE Merge Replication is similar to SQL Server 2000 and SQL Server 2005 Merge Replication, it is not identical. As with all forms of SQL Server replication, three databases are involved:

- Publisher
- Distributor
- Subscriber

The *publisher* is a database that makes data available for replication, the *distributor* is a database that contains the data and metadata required to manage the replication, and the *subscriber* is a database that receives the replicated data. In the simplest replication configuration, the publisher and the distributor reside on the same server. It is beyond the scope of this chapter to consider multiple-server configurations for SQL Server replication. Refer to SQL Server Books Online. The main difference between full SQL Server replication and SQL Server CE Merge Replication is that IIS sits between the client (and the subscriber database) and the other databases. This allows the replication data and communications to be sent over HTTP, as shown in Figure 7-17.

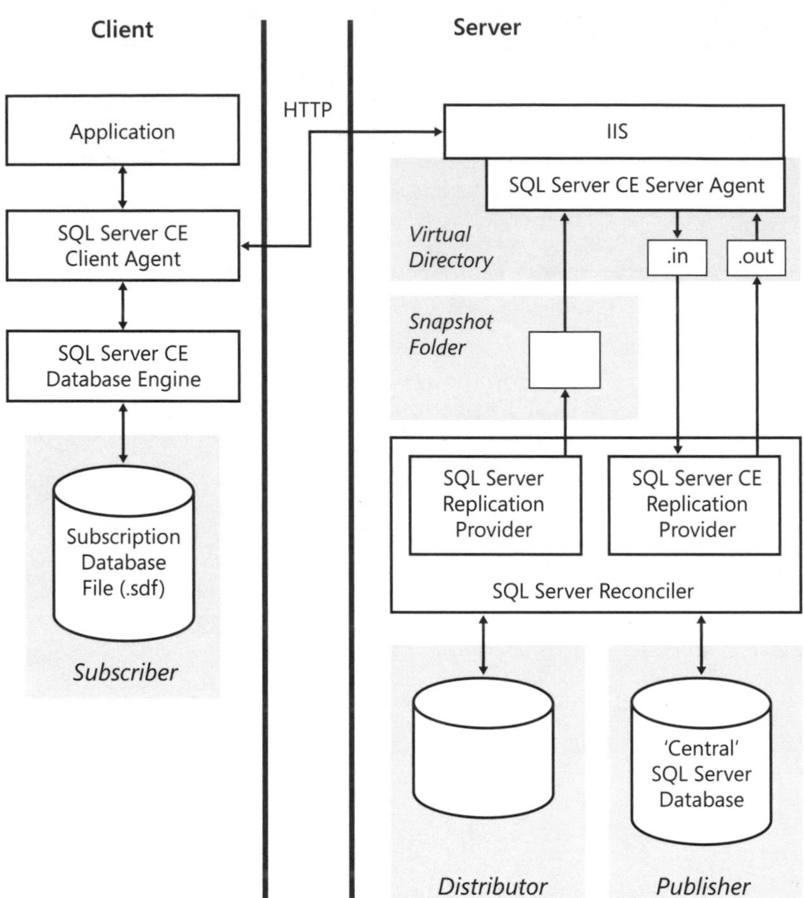

Figure 7-17 SQL Server CE Merge Replication architecture

Like RDA, SQL Server CE Merge Replication makes use of the SQL Server CE Database Engine and the SQL Server CE Client Agent on the smart device client. When data is first required (called *initialization*), the application calls a method that invokes the SQL Server CE Client Agent, which in turn calls the SQL Server CE Server Agent over HTTP. (This is the same server agent that is used for RDA.) The server agent invokes the SQL Server CE replication provider, and an initial record set (called a *snapshot*) is selected from the central SQL Server database and returned by HTTP to the client agent. The client agent is then able to build the local SQL Server CE database (called the *subscription database*) on the smart device.

After the subscription database has been built, you can use the *SQLServerCe* objects to manipulate its structure and data locally. The SQL Server CE Database Engine tracks all the changes you make using a small amount of tracking information for each record.

Periodically, your application is required to send its changes to the central SQL Server database and to receive any changes made centrally or by other remote users. This is the process of *synchronization*, and you will see later that it can be initiated from the client application using the *SQLCeReplication* merge replication object. The client agent calls the server agent over HTTP, sending details of the changes tracked since the last synchronization (or since initialization, if this is the first synchronization). The server agent then writes an input message (.in) file that is passed to the SQL Server CE replication provider for loading into the central SQL Server database. The SQL Server reconciler merges the new input data into the central database and then informs the SQL Server CE replication provider about changes made at the publisher that must be applied to the subscription database. The SQL Server CE replication provider writes an output message (.out) file that is passed back to the server agent and then on to the client agent. The client agent is finally able to apply the changes to the subscription database on the smart device. It is interesting to note that the output message file is written to the client and processed in blocks so as to avoid overloading the smart device with large quantities of changes all at once.

Setting Up Merge Replication

To set up merge replication, start by installing the server-side software to support replication, both in your SQL Server database and on the IIS server where the SQL Server CE agent will run. Refer to the opening paragraphs of the section titled "Synchronizing Data Using SQL Server 2005 Compact Edition Remote Data Access" for information about setting up the server-side software.

Some of the steps of the merge replication setup follow those for the RDA setup. However, there are extra steps both in SQL Server and in the creation and securing of the replication snapshot folder. The main steps are as follows:

- Set up a default replication snapshot folder for SQL Server.
- Create a publication of a SQL Server 2000 or SQL Server 2005 database.
- Install the SQL Server CE Server Agent on your Web server.
- Use the SQL Server 2005 Compact Edition Configure Web Synchronization Wizard to create a virtual directory containing the SQL Server CE Server Agent DLL (Sqlcesa30.dll).
- Choose an authentication method for the new site.
- Secure the virtual directory using NTFS.
- Share and secure the Snapshot folder using NTFS.
- Check that the identity that IIS authorizes has a corresponding login to SQL Server and has permission to subscribe to the publication.

Setting Up the Publication

You need administrator credentials to SQL Server for this setup. If you have not already used the SQL Server for replication, you first must start SQL Server 2005 Management Studio and run the Configure Distribution Wizard. (Skip this section and go straight to the section titled "Creating a New Publication" if you have already configured distribution on this SQL Server.)

Configuring SQL Server for Distribution Start the Configure Distribution Wizard by right-clicking the Replication folder and then clicking Configure Distribution. The Welcome page for this wizard explains that you have three options:

- Configure your server to be a Distributor that can be used by other Publishers
- Configure your server to be a Publisher that acts as its own Distributor
- Configure your server to be a Publisher that uses another server as its Distributor

You make your choice on the next page. If you are configuring a SQL Server for testing purposes, you should configure your SQL Server to perform both Publisher and Distributor roles by selecting the option <*server*> Will Act As Its Own Distributor, and then click Next. The next page shows the location of the Snapshot folder (this a folder where the SQL Server Snapshot Agent stores all relevant information about a publication's data). By default, the wizard creates the Snapshot folder in a folder in the <*drive*>:\Program Files\Microsoft SQL Server directory tree, but do not accept this. You are advised to create a network share and enter the path here (as shown in Figure 7-18). Remember its location–you will need it later when you set up the merge replication Web server.

Note The Snapshot folder is simply a directory that you have designated as a share; agents that read from and write to this folder must have sufficient permissions to access it. See the section titled "Merge Replication Security" later in this chapter for details on setting appropriate NTFS permissions on the snapshot share.

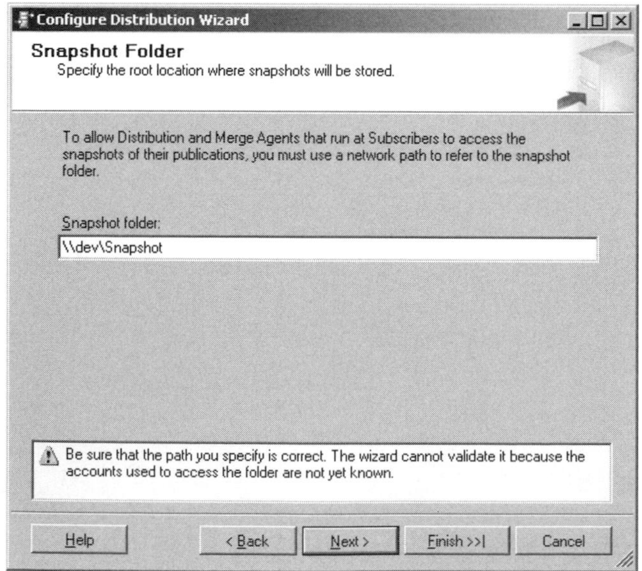

Figure 7-18 Setting the Snapshot share in the SQL Server Configure Distribution Wizard

Click Next, and on the Distribution Database page, accept the defaults. Click Next to move to the Publishers page, where you can configure which SQL Servers that are configured as publishers may use this server as a distributor. The server you are configuring is already shown in the list (because it is acting as both publisher and distributor), and so click Next, and then click Finish.

Creating a New Publication Run SQL Server 2005 Management Studio, and right-click the Replication – Local Publications folder. Click New Publication to run the New Publication Wizard. Click Next, select traffic Database For Replication, and then click Next. On the Select Publication Type page, click the bottom option for Merge Replication, and then click Next. On the Specify Subscriber Types page, select SQL Server 2005 Compact Edition and optionally select any other of the subscriber types you want to support with this publication, and then click Next.

On the Articles page, shown in Figure 7-19, select both the Cars and the Obs tables, and then click Next. The next page may display Article Issues, which is advice on changes the wizard will make to the selected tables to support merge replication. In the case of the tables you have selected, it warns that it will add a *Uniqueidentifier* column to each table. Read the advice, and then click Next.

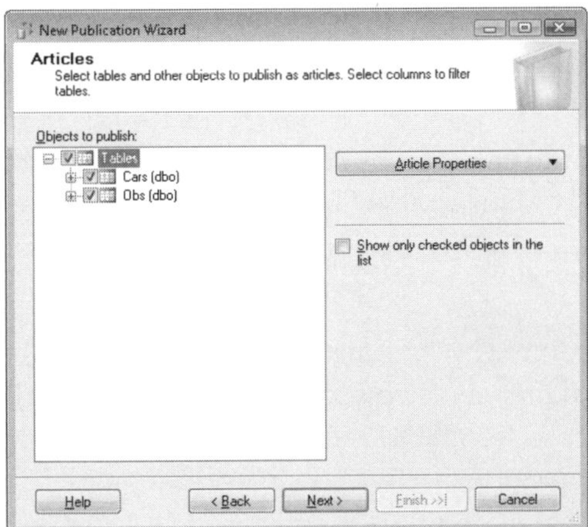

Figure 7-19 SQL Server Create Publication Wizard

On the next page, you can define filters, which is a useful way of limiting the number of rows of data that you send to each subscriber. Effectively, you use this page to define the *WHERE* clause in a *SELECT <publishedColumns> FROM <table> WHERE...* statement. For example, you can create a filter such that all subscribers receive the same subset of data: *WHERE Manufacturer='Contoso'*, or a filter that is parameterized so that each subscriber passes a parameter that is used to filter the rows it receives: *WHERE Salesman = SUSER_SNAME()*. You can also declare linked filters, where you filter table B based on a foreign key relationship to table A, which is better than using a single filter on a table based on joins and subqueries.

In the current example, do not define any filters, and click Next. On the next page, specify when to run the Snapshot Agent. Select Create A Snapshot Immediately, and also accept the default schedule for running the Snapshot Agent in the future.

Next, you must configure security for the Snapshot Agent. Click the Security Settings button, and then enter the user name and password of a Windows account under which the Snapshot Agent will run. This account must at least have the db_owner role in the distribution database and must also have Write NTFS permissions on the snapshot share. In the lower pane of the Security Settings page, select By Impersonating The Process Account (Recommended), or enter the name and password for a SQL Server login (that is, a login you have set up in SQL Server for SQL authentication). The account must at least have the db_owner role in the publication database.

Give the publication a name (this sample uses TrafficMR), and click Finish to complete the setup. The wizard then creates the subscription and, if you requested it to do so, runs the Snapshot Agent immediately.

> **Tip** If the Snapshot Agent fails to run successfully, it may be because the SQL Server Agent is not running. Open the SQL Server 2005 Configuration Manager to view the Server Agent status, and start it if necessary. Then right-click your publication in SQL Server 2005 Management Studio, and click View Snapshot Agent Status to open a window where you can start or monitor the agent.

You can modify any of these configuration details later by selecting your publication under the Local Publications folder in SQL Server Management Studio and clicking Properties.

Setting Up the Web Server

Start the setup for the merge replication sample by running the SQL Server CE Web Synchronization Wizard that was installed on your Web server when you set up RDA for the preceding sample. You can also start this tool from SQL Server 2005 Management Studio by right-clicking your publication and clicking Configure Web Synchronization.

Run through the Web Configuration Wizard exactly as you did for RDA when you created the TrafficRDA virtual directory, as described earlier in the section titled "RDA Server Setup." Create a new virtual directory called TrafficMR, and as before, select Integrated Authentication on the Authenticated Access page. As before, enter the domain\user name or domain\group to configure NTFS access to the virtual directory. One important difference from RDA, though, is you must select the box for SQL Server merge replication, as shown in Figure 7-20.

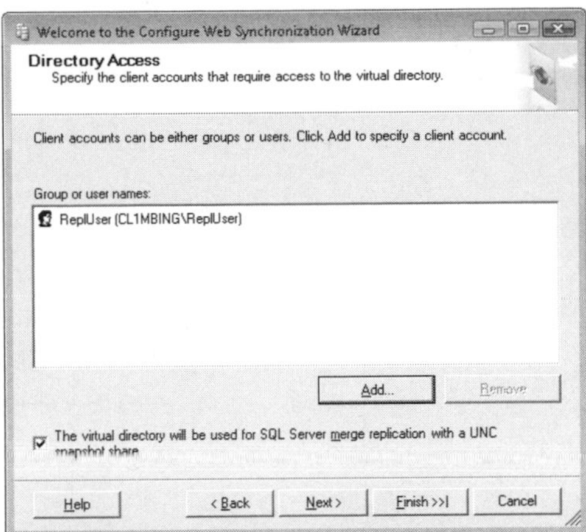

Figure 7-20 Merge replication option selected when configuring NTFS security

The final step is to secure the merge replication user for access to the Snapshot folder. Enter the network location of the Snapshot folder you created earlier in the section titled "Configuring SQL Server for Distribution," click Next, and then click Finish to complete the setup. The Web server part of the setup for merge replication is now complete.

Merge Replication Security

NTFS file security is used to control access to the two folders that merge replication uses: the Web site *virtual directory* and the *Snapshot folder*. This is in addition to the user authentication provided by IIS and SQL Server. SQL Server also controls access at a database level and, through the Publication Access List (PAL), it controls access to the publication. There is an additional optional level of security in SQL Server called the Check Permissions. The Check Permissions provide an enhanced level of control by ensuring that the SQL login that the SQL Server CE Server Agent uses has permissions to perform insert, update, and delete operations on the data.

Figure 7-21 shows the general security scheme using the gates to represent security checks and the stick figures to represent the identities that you might assume at the various stages.

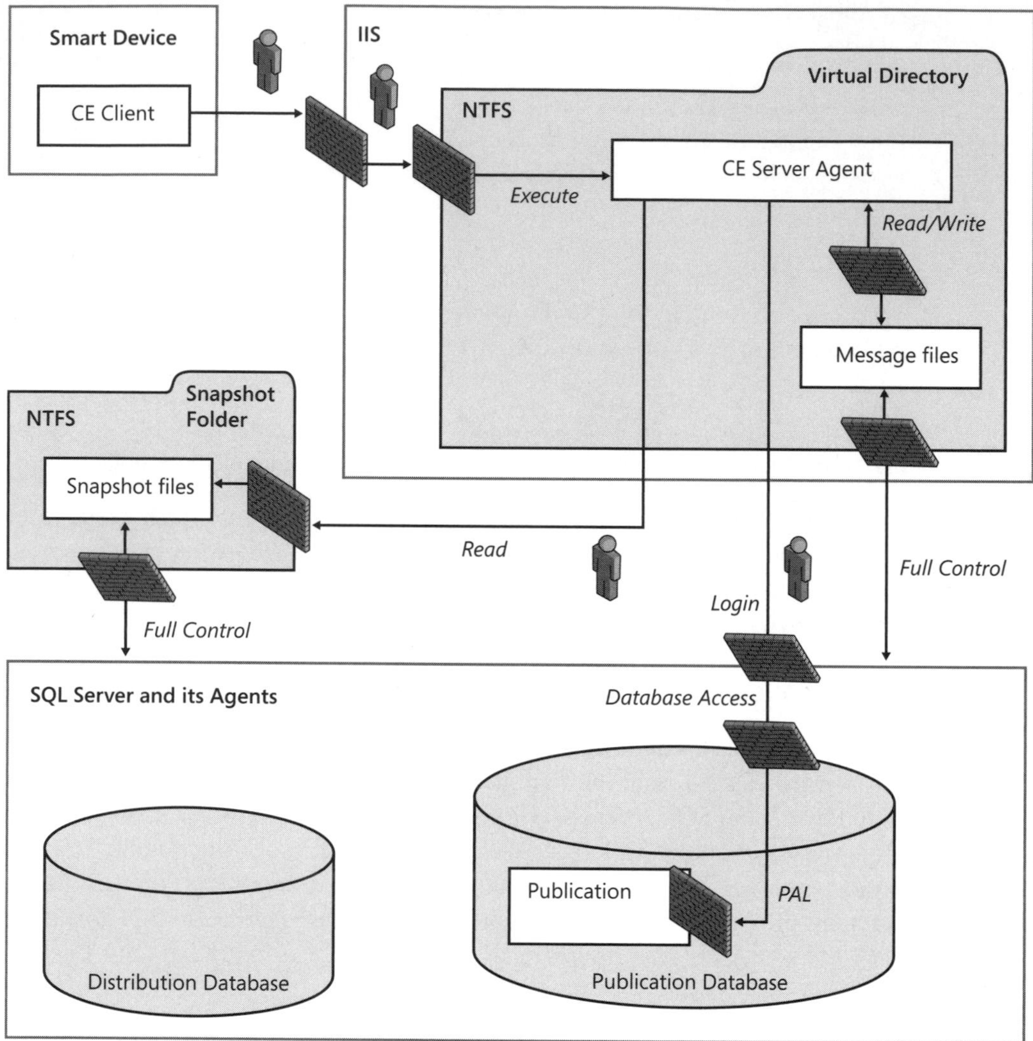

Figure 7-21 Merge replication security

With RDA, you only had to worry about how to authenticate to IIS, and then whether you logged in to SQL Server using the Windows account credentials or using SQL Server authentication; these options were described in Table 7-2. With merge replication, there are many more gates to pass through. As with RDA, you have three choices for IIS authentication: Anonymous, Basic, or Integrated Windows, which you select when you use the SQL Server CE Web Synchronization Wizard to configure the virtual directory (as described in the preceding section). If you are using Basic or Integrated Windows authentication, you specify the user name and password to supply to IIS by setting the *InternetLogin* and *InternetPassword* properties of the *SqlCeReplication* instance.

If you successfully pass IIS authentication, the SQL Server CE Server Agent must connect to the Distributor and Publisher databases, and for that you use some additional properties of *SqlCeReplication*. The *DistributorSecurityMode* determines how the login to the SQL Server Distributor database is authenticated and may be set to either *SecurityType.DBAuthentication* (meaning that SQL Server authentication is used to connect to the Distributor database) or *SecurityType.NTAuthentication* (Windows Authentication is used, and the default). If *SecurityType.NTAuthentication* is selected, the agent logs on to the Distributor database using the Windows account that you used to log on to IIS. If *SecurityType.DBAuthentication* is selected, you must supply the *DistributorLogin* and *DistributorPassword* properties to supply the SQL Server authentication user name and password. The *PublisherSecurityMode* property sets the authentication mode for the Publisher database, and if it is set to *SecurityType.DBAuthentication*, you must supply the *PublisherLogin* and *PublisherPassword*.

Table 7-8 shows scenarios in which SQL Server is configured as both publisher and distributor and identifies the identities and authentication checks involved.

Table 7-8 Authentication in Merge Replication

IIS Authentication	SQL Server Authentication	SQL Server Permissions
IIS Anonymous, with *PublisherMode* and *DistributorMode* set to *SecurityType.NTAuthentication* (Integrated Windows authentication)	You do not provide a user name or password but are instead logged on to the Windows server using the credentials specified for anonymous Internet access. (By default, the IUSR_*ComputerName* local account is used, although you can configure a custom Windows user account to be used.)	You need to grant database access and add to the PAL the computer \IUSR_*machinename* login.
Basic authentication, with *PublisherMode* and *DistributorMode* set to *SecurityType.NTAuthentication* (Integrated Windows authentication)	You must provide a Windows user name and password in the *InternetLogin* and *InternetPassword* properties of the *SqlCeReplication* instance. The credentials are passed to the IIS server in plain text. You should use Secure Sockets Layer to create an HTTPS connection when using Basic authentication so that the credentials are transferred over an encrypted channel.	You need to grant database access and add to the PAL the login specified by the Internet login, or to a Windows NT group to which the Internet login belongs.

Table 7-8 Authentication in Merge Replication

IIS Authentication	SQL Server Authentication	SQL Server Permissions
Integrated Windows, with *PublisherMode* and *DistributorMode* set to *SecurityType.NTAuthentication* (Integrated Windows authentication)	You must provide a Windows user name and password in the *InternetLogin* and *InternetPassword* properties of the *SqlCeReplication* instance, and these credentials are passed in an encrypted form to IIS. Note that you cannot use this form of authentication through a proxy server.	As above.
Anonymous, Basic, or Integrated Windows, with *PublisherMode* and *DistributorMode* set to *SecurityType.DBAuthentication* and SQL Server user ID/password specified in the *PublisherLogin/ PublisherPassword* and *DistributerLogin/ DistributorPassword* properties.	You must provide credentials for IIS Basic and IIS Integrated Windows as described above. You are logged in to SQL Server using the user ID/password specified in the *PublisherLogin/ PublisherPassword* and *DistributerLogin/ DistributorPassword* properties.	You need to grant database access and add to the PAL the SQL Server user specified in the *PublisherLogin* or *DistributerLogin* property.

For merge replication, in addition to the IIS and SQL Server setup, you will need to set up NTFS permissions. Note that when you run the SQL Server CE Web Synchronization Wizard and the SQL Server 2005 Management Studio New Subscription Wizard, the required NTFS permissions are correctly set for you. However, note the following:

- Allow SQL Server and its agents Full Control to create the initial snapshot files and folder structure in the Snapshot folder.
- Allow the SQL Server CE Agent to Read the snapshot files in the Snapshot folder.
- Allow the SQL Server CE Agent to Read and Write the message files in the virtual directory.
- Allow SQL Server and its agents Full Control over the message files in the virtual directory.
- Allow the user to Execute the SQL Server CE Agent (Sscesa.dll).

Table 7-9 expands the information in the preceding list for each of the four authentication scenarios and includes additional file security requirements to give a full list of the NTFS permissions you need to set up.

Table 7-9 NTFS Permissions for Merge Replication

IIS Authentication Mode	NTFS Permissions
SQL Server CE Server Agent	
Anonymous; you do not give a user name/password.	For the computer \IUSR_*machinename* login, you need to grant Read and Write access to the virtual directory, and Read access to the Snapshot folder.
Basic; you must give a user name/password.	For the login specified by the Internet login or to a Windows NT Group to which the Internet login belongs, you need to grant Read and Write access to the virtual directory, and Read access to the Snapshot folder.
Integrated Windows; you must give a user name/password.	As above.
Anonymous, Basic, or Integrated Windows, with SQL Server user ID/password specified in the *PublisherLogin*/*PublisherPassword* or *DistributorLogin*/*DistributorPassword* properties.	Apply NTFS permissions as per the previous scenario that matches the IIS authentication mode chosen.
SQL Server Replication Agent	
SQL Server agents	The user account under which SQL Server and its agents run must be given Full Control to the virtual directory and to the Snapshot folder.

The Snapshot folder is simply a directory that you have designated as a share; agents that read from and write to this folder must have sufficient permissions to access it, as described in Table 7-9. You can test that the replication agent will be able to connect to the Snapshot folder by logging on under the account that the agent will run under and then attempting to access the Snapshot folder.

Programming Merge Replication

With the server setup completed, you are ready to program SQL Server CE Merge Replication. You can find the UsingSqlCeMRSample application in the sample code for this chapter on the companion Web site. This sample application contains the code shown in the rest of this section and uses the TrafficMR publication and virtual directory you just configured in the section titled "Setting Up Merge Replication."

If you have downloaded and opened the sample application, locate the *Merge* function in the code for the FormMR form. You can see that the first step for programming merge replication is to create an instance of the *SqlCeReplication* object, which is part of *SqlServerCe*. Table 7-10 lists the methods available on the *SqlCeReplication* object and outlines their use.

Table 7-10 Methods of the *SqlCeReplication* Object

Method	Description
SqlCeReplication constructor	We used the second overload of this in the example: This takes arguments for all the properties that are required for synchronization.
AddSubscription	Used to create a new subscription to the published database; optionally can also create the local SQL Server CE database. You must call the *Synchronize* method to actually retrieve the data.
DropSubscription	Used to drop the subscription to the published database, and optionally to delete the local SQL Server CE database file.
ReinitializeSubscription	Used to mark a subscription for reinitialization (SQL Server re-creates the snapshot of data). You must call the *Synchronize* method (which reloads the snapshot) to see data based on the reinitialization.
Synchronize	Call this to invoke the merge replication.

Note SQL Server CE Merge Replication supports the same set of data types as RDA and uses the same mappings from SQL Server data types.

Adding a Subscription

For the first stage of merge replication, you must create the subscription database on the smart device and create the subscription to the published database on the server. You do this by creating a *SqlCeReplication* object and setting the required properties listed in Table 7-11. You can either set them directly or specify them as arguments to the *SqlCeReplication* constructor, and then call its *AddSubscription* method.

Table 7-11 Required Properties of the *SqlCeReplication* Object

Property	Description
InternetURL	The URL to the Sqlcesa30.dll.
InternetLogin	Required only if you are not using Anonymous Authentication mode.
InternetPassword	Required only if you are not using Anonymous Authentication mode.
Publisher	Name of the publishing server. If this is a named instance of SQL Server, it will be in the format *ServerName/InstanceName*.
PublisherDatabase	The name of the published database.
Publication	The name of the publication on the published database.
Subscriber	The name of your subscription; this is just an identification string.
SubscriberConnection-String	The local connection string for the SQL Server CE database file (*.sdf).

After calling the *AddSubscription* method, your local SQL Server CE database file will have been created, but the tables and their initial snapshot of data will not yet be present. (You could confirm this by using the Query Analyzer to look at the local database objects.) You must call the *Synchronize* method to transfer the initial snapshot of data to the new SQL Server CE database.

Synchronization

The *Synchronize* method of the *SqlCeReplication* object gets the initial snapshot of data for your local SQL Server CE database if this is the first time you call it (or the first time after the publication has been marked for resynchronization). After the initialization of data has taken place, subsequent calls you make to the *Synchronize* method invoke the merge replication, and only changes to the data will be sent and received.

The following sample code (from the UsingSqlCEMRSample application) shows a subscription being set up only if the local database file does not already exist. Notice how the code disposes of the *SqlCeReplication* object at the end but doesn't drop the subscription. The next time it executes this method, there is no reinitialization of the data in the local database.

```
using System.Data.SqlServerCe;
...

private void Merge()
{
    using (SqlCeReplication rep = new SqlCeReplication(
        @"http://MyServer/TrafficMR/sqlcesa30.dll", //URL to Agent
        @"MyDomain\ReplUser",   // InternetUser
        "P@ssw0rd",             // InternetPassword
        "MYSQLSERVER",          // Publisher server
        "Traffic",              // Publisher Database
        "TrafficMR",            // Publication name
        "Testing",              // Subscriber name
        @"Data Source=\My Documents\TrafficMR.sdf") //Connection string to
                                                    //local database
        )
    {
        try
        {
            // If the local database does not exist, subscribe to the
            // publication, creating the local database at the same time.
            if (!System.IO.File.Exists(@"\My Documents\TrafficMR.sdf"))
            {
                rep.AddSubscription(AddOption.CreateDatabase);
            }

            // Synchronize with the publication.
            rep.Synchronize();
        }
```

```
            catch (SqlCeException ex)
            {
                DisplaySQLCEErrors(ex);
            }
        }
    }
```

After you have created a subscription, and the initial transfer of snapshot data has been used to create the local database, your application code can update the copy of the data in the local SQL Server CE database. Any changes that you make are merged into the published database on the backend SQL Server the next time you call the *Synchronize* method.

Troubleshooting Merge Replication

As with RDA, most of the problems you will encounter with merge replication can be traced back to the security setup. The following gives a sequence of checks you can use to locate and resolve problems with merge replication:

- Check the users and permissions at each stage of the sequence from the *InternetLogin* to the published database.
- Check that you are using the correct version of the SQL Server replication objects for the version of SQL Server and service pack you are using. (See the opening paragraph of the section titled "Synchronizing Data Using SQL Server 2005 Remote Data Access" earlier in this chapter.)
- If you are using an *Identity* column, you must find the next available number and reseed before an insert can be successful. You will also have to set up ranged identity columns on the published database to prevent errors when the new data is merged.

Summary

This chapter explains how to use *SqlClient* and SQL Server CE RDA and merge replication, and it looks at some useful techniques for using Web Services.

Web Services provides a flexible solution that is not tied to the use of SQL Server as the backend resource. It requires more programming effort to implement a sophisticated data synchronization solution than RDA or merge replication requires. You can use the Disconnected Service Agent to allow your applications to use Web Services over an intermittently connected network, and you can use compression to reduce the volume of data sent over the network.

You can use *SqlClient* only where you have a direct network connection to SQL Server over a LAN. SQL Server RDA and merge replication work over a LAN or over the Internet, and both are excellent ways of copying data from a backend SQL Server, using the copied data in your application on the mobile device, and then later synchronizing the changes with the master copy of the table in SQL Server. Of these two, RDA is simpler to set up and is secure and works well on a simple table, though it has no built-in conflict resolution; the last updater wins, overwriting any updates that may have been applied by other clients. Merge replication is harder to configure but once set up is ideal for situations where you have multiple updaters for a table, all of which need to keep a synchronized copy of the table.

You might think (correctly) that the fastest way to get up and running with sharing central SQL Server data with smart device applications is by using RDA. However, it is recommended that you invest the extra initial (and setup) effort and use merge replication. With the considerable extra server-side functionality provided by SQL Server replication, you can deal with any future increase in the complexity of your application and ultimately can support larger numbers of users through your ability to improve the SQL Server replication configuration by partitioning data and using more physical servers.

Chapter 8
Networking

In this chapter:

This chapter looks at a number of networking technologies that are available to a developer of mobile applications. We begin with a recap of Web Services, which is covered in Chapter 7, "Exchanging Data with Backend Servers," and then look at a couple of methods of sending data over the Internet and TCP/IP networks. We then look at personal area networking technologies of the Infrared Data Association (IrDA), Bluetooth, and RS-232 serial transfer. The chapter ends with a look at the *System.Messaging* namespace, which is a set of technologies for supporting loosely coupled messaging over TCP/IP networks. Chapter 9, "Getting Connected," looks at topics surrounding making a connection and responding to changes in connection states.

Understanding Complications of Networking and Mobile Devices

Writing networking code for mobile devices can be much more difficult than it is for a static computer. You have to work around the fact that network availability will be intermittent, and often there are costs involved based on the volume of network traffic. For example, many mobile networks calculate their bills for data services by the number of kilobytes transferred. You can mitigate these issues by implementing your own scheme for encoding your data to be as efficient as possible. The Microsoft .NET Compact Framework doesn't include binary serialization, so you must implement something specific to your needs or use a third-party solution. One such solution is the CompactFormatter, which is designed to work similarly to the desktop *BinaryFormatter* class (*www.freewebs.com/compactFormatter/index.html*).

You may not necessarily choose a binary solution. If your data can be represented purely as alphanumeric characters, you can encode it as American Standard Code for Information Interchange (ASCII) text rather than the default Unicode, and this will halve the size of your data. To combat the cost issue, you can build your application to send data only if the user initiates the operation, or only at certain times or when a specific network connection is active. The next chapter investigates connection types and status in further detail. You also must gracefully handle the scenario when the network connection drops during an operation.

Initiating a connection from the server to a device can be made difficult by constantly changing IP addresses, which in most cases are not assigned from a public range. There are two ways to overcome this: You can invest in a third-party middleware product such as Broadbeam or IBM WECM, or you can write your own mechanism. You might do this by having your client devices establish a connection to the server and wait for a response. This is similar to the Direct Push technology used between Microsoft Windows Mobile 5.0 and Exchange Server 2003. You can read more about Direct Push on the Windows Mobile Home Web site at *www.microsoft.com/windowsmobile/business/directpushemail.mspx.*

Microsoft is aware of the challenge, and in the forthcoming version 3.5 of the Compact Framework it will add an e-mail-based provider for Windows Communication Framework (WCF), a fully managed extensible mechanism for messaging. You can read about the current desktop version of WCF on the Microsoft MSDN Web site at *msdn2.microsoft.com/en-us/netframework/aa663324.aspx.*

Using Web Services

Web services are self-describing, platform-independent remote method calls. Microsoft Visual Studio and the .NET Framework are designed so that you can call a Web service from your code very easily. You can browse to your chosen Web service through the Visual Studio integrated development environment (IDE) and have the necessary device-side code generated for you. This generated code then makes calling a Web service just the same as calling a local method in your own code.

Because of the nature of mobile devices, you have to design your application so that it can gracefully fail if no network connection is currently available. You must also understand that many devices will be connected to low-bandwidth connections, and so operations may take considerably longer than they would for a desktop computer application connected to broadband. As well as the apparent speed of the operation, you should also be aware that most mobile networks are charged by the volume of data transferred, so it is probably in your interest to look carefully at reducing the volume of data sent and received in a Web service call. Chapter 7 describes this in the section titled “Compressing Web Service Payload.” Chapter 7 also includes a sample based on the Microsoft patterns & practices Disconnected Services Agent, which supports queuing Web Services operations.

Understanding *System.Net*

Networking functionality is housed in the *System.Net* namespace, which in turn is in System.dll. This is a subset of the functionality available in the full .NET Framework. The two main areas of networking functionality are the *WebRequest* classes, which perform Hypertext Transfer Protocol (HTTP) request/response communication, and the *Socket* class, which allows a lower level of two-way communication.

WebRequest

The *WebRequest* and associated *WebResponse* classes provide a base implementation for performing operations over a number of network technologies. You can use specific derived classes for working with different protocols such as http://, ftp://, and file://. The Compact Framework has only a limited implementation and doesn't have any built-in File Transfer Protocol (FTP) support. You can extend the support to additional protocols by writing your own class derived from *WebRequest*, and this can be registered to a particular Uniform Resource Identifier (URI) scheme so that your class is created from a call to *WebRequest.Create*. Discussing this is out of the scope of this book, but you can find details of a shared-source example later in this chapter in the section titled "Using IrDA and Bluetooth."

Out of the box, the Compact Framework supports the HTTP and Secure HTTP (HTTPS) protocols through the *HttpWebRequest* class. With this support, you can perform *GET*, *PUT*, and *POST* operations to the Web. In the following example, we demonstrate how easy it is to download a file from a specific *URI* and save it locally on the device.

System.Uri is a class you can use to encapsulate a unique address, and a new instance can be created by passing in the URI as a string. With the class, you can then query individual parts of the URI string, as shown in Table 8-1.

Table 8-1 *System.Uri* Properties

Property	Value
OriginalString	http://www.microsoft.com/windowsmobile/devicecenter.mspx
Scheme	http
Host	www.microsoft.com
AbsolutePath	/windowsmobile/devicecenter.mspx

A new *HttpWebRequest* is created either by calling *WebRequest.Create* with the URI or by using the *HttpWebRequest* constructor. The advantage of the latter is that you don't need to cast from the base *WebRequest* class to use HTTP-specific properties of the class. By default, you don't need to set any other properties on the request object. The default operation is a *GET*, which you can use to retrieve content. After it is created, you call *GetResponse* on the *WebRequest* and it returns a *WebResponse* object. This includes a stream to allow you to read from the response.

To help you put all these concepts together, the following code sample shows a method to perform a download and save the received data to the device file system.

```
private void Download(Uri address, string localPath)
{
string filename = address.Segments[u.Segments.Length - 1];
WebRequest request = WebRequest.Create(u);

//Perform the GET request.
   WebResponse response = request.GetResponse();

   //Get stream containing received data.
   Stream s = response.GetResponseStream();

   //Open filestream for the output file.
   FileStream fs = new FileStream(Path.Combine(localPath, filename),
FileMode.Create, FileAccess.Write);

//Copy until all data is read.
   byte[] buffer = new byte[1024];
   int bytesRead = s.Read(buffer, 0, buffer.Length);
   while (bytesRead > 0)
   {
   fs.Write(buffer, 0, bytesRead);
   bytesRead = s.Read(buffer, 0, buffer.Length);
   }

   //Close both streams.
   fs.Close();
s.Close();
   response.Close();
}
```

You can use the *WebRequest* approach to download or upload content for your application, or even to download application packages that you can then install. (Building .cab files is described in Chapter 6, "Completing the Application: Packaging and Deployment".)

Sockets

Sockets represent a lower-level method of sending and receiving data over a network connection. The *System.Net.Sockets* namespace contains the *Socket* class and associated classes and enumerations. Under the hood, this uses the Windows Sockets (winsock) implementation on the host operating system, which in turn is modeled on the Berkeley Sockets architecture for UNIX. Out of the box, the Compact Framework supports User Datagram Protocol (UDP) and TCP/IP socket communications similar to the full .NET Framework. Additionally, IrDA is supported by a library specific to the Compact Framework–System.Net.IrDA.dll.

Tip Because this solution involves using a TCP port other than port 80, which is used for HTTP and Web Services, you must ensure that any firewalls on your network are configured to allow traffic on the port you choose.

Differences Between the Desktop Framework and the Compact Framework

The Compact Framework implementation of *Socket* includes a subset of the features contained in the desktop version because of differences in the underlying native Windows Sockets functionality. For example, it is not possible to set the send and receive buffer sizes and timeouts. Also, a number of Internet Protocol version 6 (IPv6) properties are not implemented. The Compact Framework socket doesn't support the Disconnect method and subsequent reuse of the same *Socket* object. This isn't really a problem because you can call Close on a *Socket* and create a new one easily. Finally, the desktop version has a method to send an entire file over the *Socket*. This method is not included in the Compact Framework, but it is easy to work around that fact: The file can be read into a buffer and this buffer written to the socket in a loop until the entire file has been read. The following sample includes a helper method to do this synchronously.

```
//Send file contents to a socket.
private static void SendFile(Socket s, string filename)
{
FileStream fs = new FileStream(filename, FileMode.Open);

byte[] buffer = new byte[256];
int bytesRead = fs.Read(buffer, 0, buffer.Length);
while (bytesRead > 0)
{
   s.Send(buffer, bytesRead, SocketFlags.None);

   //Read next block.
   bytesRead = fs.Read(buffer, 0, buffer.Length);
}

fs.Close();
}
```

SocketException

As described in Chapter 4, "Catching Errors, Testing, and Debugging," errors encountered are raised in the form of exceptions. In the case of the *Socket* class, the majority of possible exceptions will be caused by Windows Sockets errors returned from the native functions. A specialized exception type, the *SocketException*, is provided to encapsulate these errors. The *ErrorCode* property returns the socket error message. A transfer can fail for numerous reasons, such as inability to contact the remote computer or a connection breaking partway through the transfer. This is especially an issue on a mobile device where a continuous network connection cannot be relied upon.

You can handle these issues by wrapping your network code in *try..catch* blocks to catch *SocketExceptions*. You can then make informed decisions about the reason for the exception. For example, a Connect attempt may fail if the specific port you are using is blocked, the remote computer is unavailable, or the network connection has been lost. If an exception occurs during data transfer, it is often because of a network problem, or possibly the remote computer disconnected because it did not receive the expected data. Probably the most common socket exception has the code 10054 and message "An existing connection was forcibly closed by the remote host." This can commonly occur after you open a connection to a remote device and then first try sending data to it or reading from it. This is because a TCP socket doesn't throw an exception at the time you connect, even if the remote computer is unreachable or not listening on the specified port.

Using Sockets

To demonstrate sending and receiving information over sockets, we use the example of a simple tool that records sales prospects for a sales professional. By using sockets, we send data to a colleague or the central server. We revisit the same scenario later in the chapter when we look at another networking technology–*System.Messaging*. The custom data type is the *Prospect* class, which simply has three fields–*Name*, *Company*, and *Number*. Related to the *Socket* class, there are a number of helper classes to do some of the common tasks. For TCP networking, these are the TcpClient and TcpListener classes. These are also found in the *System.Net.Sockets* namespace and wrap a *Socket* instance. TcpClient is used to establish an outgoing connection over TCP/IP, and TcpListener contains the functionality to listen for incoming connections from remote devices.

A Simple Server

In our sample, we create a TcpListener and run a background thread to listen for incoming connections. In a production system, the server would create a new thread to handle each incoming connection. To make the example code easier to follow, the server uses a single thread and so handles only a single connection attempt. When a connection is made, we read raw text from the socket and send a response to indicate success or failure. The equivalent code using just sockets and not the *TcpListener/TcpClient* helper classes is shown in inline comments in the code sample.

```
private void ListenerThread()
{
//Create a new listener to listen on the custom port.
TcpListener listener = new TcpListener(
new IPEndPoint(IPAddress.Any, port));
listener.Start();

//Socket listenerSocket =
//new Socket(AddressFamily.InterNetwork,
//SocketType.Stream, ProtocolType.Tcp);
//listenerSocket.Bind(new IPEndPoint(IPAddress.Any, port));
//listenerSocket.Listen();

try
{
while (true)
{
//Get incoming connection (blocking).
TcpClient incomingClient = listener.AcceptTcpClient();
//Socket incomingSocket = listenerSocket.Accept();

//Get address of remove device.
IPEndPoint ep = (IPEndPoint)incomingClient.Client.RemoteEndPoint;
//IPEndPoint ep = (IPEndPoint)incomingSocket.RemoteEndPoint;
IPAddress senderAddress = ep.Address;

//Get a stream to read from the socket.
NetworkStream ns = incomingClient.GetStream();
//NetworkStream ns =
//new NetworkStream(incomingSocket, true);

StreamReader sr =
new StreamReader(ns, System.Text.Encoding.Unicode);
StreamWriter sw =
new StreamWriter(ns, System.Text.Encoding.Unicode);

string operation = sr.ReadLine();

if (operation == "PROSPECT")
{
//sending the data as a plain string
string rawProspect = sr.ReadLine();
string[] fields = rawProspect.Split(',');

//Perform simple validation of received data
//and send a response.
if (fields.Length == 3)
{
//Send acknowledgment.
sw.WriteLine("OK");
}
else
{
sw.WriteLine("ERROR");
```

```
}

Prospect receivedProspect = new Prospect();
receivedProspect.Name = fields[0];
receivedProspect.Company = fields[1];
receivedProspect.Number = fields[2];

this.Invoke(
new AppendToListBoxDelegate(AppendToListBox),
new object[] { senderAddress.ToString()
+ " " + receivedProspect.ToString() });
}
else if (operation == "FILE")
{
string filename = sr.ReadLine();
byte[] len = new byte[8];
ns.Read(len, 0, 8);
Int64 fileSize = BitConverter.ToInt64(len, 0);

string filepath =
Path.Combine(System.Environment.GetFolderPath(Environment.SpecialFolder.Personal),
filename);
FileStream fs = new FileStream(filepath,
FileMode.CreateNew);
byte[] buffer = new byte[256];
int bytesread = ns.Read(buffer, 0, buffer.Length);
int totalbytesread = bytesread;
try
{
while (totalbytesread < fileSize)
{
fs.Write(buffer, 0, bytesread);

bytesread = ns.Read(buffer, 0, buffer.Length);
totalbytesread += bytesread;
}
fs.Close();

sw.WriteLine("OK");

this.Invoke(
new AppendToListBoxDelegate(AppendToListBox),
new object[] { senderAddress.ToString()
+ " " + filename });
}
catch
{
sw.WriteLine("ERROR");
}

}
ns.Close();
}
}
```

```
finally
{
//Stop the listener.
listenerClient.Stop();
//listenerSocket.Close();
}
}
```

To show the user what happened, we insert the received record into a list box. Because we are sending this from a background thread to a user interface (UI) control, we must use Control.Invoke.

Client Connections

To allow the user to send an outgoing prospect record, we use a text box to accept the IP address (for example, of the server). The IPAddress class has a static Parse method to read the IP address from a string. In a real scenario, you wouldn't expect the user to know this information, but here it clearly illustrates what is happening. We can test the application by using the localhost IP address 127.0.0.1, and our own application will receive the incoming connection. When the Share button is tapped, a Socket is created to connect to the remote device, and then the Prospect details are sent over the Socket as a string. We wait for a response from the remote device and record whether the transfer was successful or not. Because any network communication is potentially a slow operation, you would typically perform such tasks in a background thread so that your application remains responsive.

```
private void btnShare_Click(object sender, EventArgs e)
{
IPAddress target;

try
{
target = IPAddress.Parse(txtRecipient.Text);
}
catch
{
MessageBox.Show("Invalid IP address");
return;
}

//Create prospect object.
Prospect p = new Prospect();
p.Name = txtName.Text;
p.Company = txtCompany.Text;
p.Number = txtNumber.Text;
```

```
//Create new outbound socket.
Socket clientSocket = new Socket(AddressFamily.InterNetwork,
SocketType.Stream, ProtocolType.Tcp);

clientSocket.Connect(new IPEndPoint(target, port));

NetworkStream ns = new NetworkStream(clientSocket, true);
StreamWriter sw = new StreamWriter(ns);
StreamReader sr = new StreamReader(ns);

try
{
//Write a header to say that following data is a prospect record.
sw.WriteLine("PROSPECT");

sw.WriteLine(p.ToString());
string response = sr.ReadLine();
switch (response)
{
case "OK":
this.Invoke(
new AppendToListBoxDelegate(AppendToListBox),
new object[] { target.ToString() +
" Sent successfully" });
break;
case "ERROR":
this.Invoke(
new AppendToListBoxDelegate(AppendToListBox),
new object[] { target.ToString() +
" Failed to send" });
break;
}
}
catch(SocketException se)
{
MessageBox.Show("Exception trying to send: " + se.ToString());
}
finally
{
//Close the stream and underlying socket.
ns.Close();
}
}
```

Using IrDA and Bluetooth

The Compact Framework provides an IrDA library; however, there is no matching library in the full framework. Fundamentally, this was designed to work in the same way as sockets programming over TCP. The main difference is that IrDA has the ability to search for nearby devices using the *IrDAClient.DiscoverDevices* method. The following code sample shows how to perform a discovery:

```
private void btnDiscover_Click(object sender, EventArgs e)
{
IrDAClient ic = new IrDAClient();
IrDADeviceInfo[] devices = ic.DiscoverDevices(6);
dataGrid1.DataSource = devices;
}
```

The *IrDADeviceInfo* class groups together information on a specific device such as its address, display name, and hint bits, which are used to describe the type of device. The address is not a fixed identifier and is valid only for the current session because it is created during negotiation between devices. Because IrDA requires a clear line-of-sight connection to a nearby device, you can use it only for exchanging data with one device at a time. Typical client and server applications are created using the *IrDAClient* and *IrDAListener* classes, respectively; these are analogous to the *TcpClient* and *TcpListener* classes described in the section titled "Using Sockets" earlier in this chapter. As with TCP connections on a mobile device, it's very important to handle connection errors gracefully in your applications because an IrDA connection can easily be broken.

There is no inbuilt support for Bluetooth in the .NET Framework, desktop version or Compact Framework. An added complication is that the device manufacturer can choose to use a Bluetooth networking stack, which may either be the Microsoft version, which is part of the Windows CE modular operating system, or be from a third-party provider. A Bluetooth stack follows a layered architecture to support the connectivity and protocols used for a whole range of connection types over Bluetooth. Microsoft provides a native application programming interface (API) around its Bluetooth networking stack that is based on sockets; however, you need to add some additional classes before you can use System.Net.Sockets functionality. The easiest way to take advantage of this is to use a free shared-source library called 32feet.NET (*32feet.net*), which supports both IrDA and Bluetooth, has both Windows CE and Windows XP versions, and is useful if you want to reuse code on Tablet PCs or laptop computers.

Using Serial Ports

Serial ports are a communications technology that you can use to talk to peripheral devices attached to your device. The technology is tried and tested, and lots of specialist hardware sensors and accessories such as Global Positioning System (GPS) receivers communicate by using serial ports. .NET Compact Framework version 2.0 supports the *SerialPort* component, which was also introduced in version 2.0 of the full framework.The key port properties exposed are listed in Table 8-2.

Table 8-2 *SerialPort* Properties

Property	Description
PortName	This is the full name for the port without the trailing colon.
BaudRate	Physical baud rate in bits per second; this must match that used on the remote device.
StopBits	Number of stop-bits transmitted, usually 1.
NewLine	Determines the character used to represent a new line. Used by the *ReadLine()* method. Examples are *\r* and *\r\n*.

We demonstrate using the SerialPort component by stepping through the process of building a simple terminal application designed to connect to a serial port and send and receive data. This is a very simple application with a single form. The SerialPort component exposes events when data is received, and these are marshaled through to the UI thread. The SerialPort component has defined buffers that are used for both incoming and outgoing data. The class exposes a simple set of properties, methods, and events and works directly with the Windows CE file APIs under the hood. A simple way of testing the application is to open a port connected to a GPS receiver. When a connection is established, the device will send back National Marine Electronics Association (NMEA) text data. We don't go into detail about parsing this data to determine the GPS location because it is out of the scope of this book, and some free utility libraries will do this for you–see *www.hardandsoftware.net* for the DecodeGPS library.

Before you can open a *SerialPort*, you need to know the port name. The *SerialPort* class exposes a static method GetPortNames() to return a list of available serial ports. We call this on the *Load* event of our main form and assign the resulting string array to a *ComboBox*:

```
private void Form1_Load(object sender, EventArgs e)
{
//Populate the combo box with available port names
//(not all may actually be valid)
//such as Bluetooth etc emulated ports.
cbPort.DataSource = System.IO.Ports.SerialPort.GetPortNames();
}
```

The user can choose the port from the *ComboBox* and set other properties such as *BaudRate*, and then tap Connect. In the method handling this menu item, we provide the code to establish a connection if the current state is disconnected or to disconnect the current connection. After the port is opened, a handler is set up for the *DataReceived* event, and this event is raised whenever the port has data ready for processing.

```
private void mnuConnect_Click(object sender, EventArgs e)
{
//Button functionality toggles depending on port status.
if (spPort.IsOpen)
{
//Unhook the event handler.
spPort.DataReceived -= new
System.IO.Ports.SerialDataReceivedEventHandler(
spPort_DataReceived);
//Close the port.
spPort.Close();
mnuConnect.Text = "Connect";
btnSend.Enabled = false;
}
else
{
//Reset the data text box.
txtData.Text = "";
//Set the port settings.
spPort.PortName = cbPort.SelectedValue.ToString();
spPort.BaudRate = int.Parse(txtBaud.Text);

try
{
//Try opening the port and hook up the events.
                spPort.Open();
                spPort.DataReceived += new
System.IO.Ports.SerialDataReceivedEventHandler(
spPort_DataReceived);
                mnuConnect.Text = "Disconnect";
                btnSend.Enabled = true;
         }
         catch
         {
//An exception may be thrown
//if the port isn't actually valid.
MessageBox.Show("Port not recognized", "Error",
MessageBoxButtons.OK, MessageBoxIcon.Exclamation,
MessageBoxDefaultButton.Button1);
}

}
}
```

The spPort_DataReceived method receives data and appends it to a *TextBox*. Because this event is not raised on the user interface thread, we must use *Control.Invoke* to another method ShowNewData, which updates the *TextBox*.

```
//method invoked on ui thread to append text to text box
void ShowNewData(string data)
{
txtData.Text += data;
}
//custom delegate to receive a single string for marshaling
//to the user interface thread
private delegate void InvokerDelegate(string data);

//event handler for serial port data received
void spPort_DataReceived(object sender,
System.IO.Ports.SerialDataReceivedEventArgs e)
{
this.Invoke(new InvokerDelegate(ShowNewData),
new object[] { spPort.ReadExisting() });
}
```

We can send data to the port using the *SerialPort Write* and *WriteLine* methods. *WriteLine* writes a string and follows it with the newline character that is defined on the specific serial port. Tapping the Send button in our sample sends the contents of the outgoing text box to the serial port:

```
//Send an outgoing message to the remote device (appends a line break).
private void btnSend_Click(object sender, EventArgs e)
{
if (spPort.IsOpen)
{
    if (txtOutgoing.Text.Length > 0)
       {
           spPort.WriteLine(txtOutgoing.Text);
       }
}
}
```

As with any other networking or communication technology we have described, you can encode your data in any way you see fit. The example application works only with devices that return data as plain text and will display garbage characters if binary data is used.

Virtual Serial Ports

Most devices support serial port emulation to expose Bluetooth devices to legacy applications that support only serial ports. For example, navigation software expects a GPS receiver to be connected to a serial port; in the case of a Bluetooth receiver, you must assign a virtual serial port that can be selected from in the navigation software. Because the way these are configured can vary between devices and the Bluetooth networking stack used on the device, it is not possible to provide definitive instructions. On Windows Mobile 5.0, when the Microsoft Bluetooth stack is used, there is a section of the Bluetooth control panel used to configure virtual serial ports, and these are configured in the device registry. After a virtual port is set up on your device, you use it programmatically just as you would a device connected by a serial cable.

Understanding *System.Messaging*

Although *System.Messaging* is a new set of functionality in .NET Compact Framework 2.0, it wraps a technology called Microsoft Message Queuing (MSMQ), which has been available to native code developers for some time and is present in the desktop .NET Framework. MSMQ provides loosely coupled store-and-forward messaging between applications and different computers. Each message contains a packet of raw data that can be up to 4 megabytes (MB) in size, though it is uncommon to create such large messages. As with many APIs, this is a subset of a standard Windows API that is exposed as a set of Component Object Model (COM) interfaces and C functions. The *System.Messaging* namespace removes all complexities of calling into this native code and provides a subset of the *System.Messaging* namespace that is present in the full .NET Framework.

Installing MSMQ

MSMQ is an optional component of Windows CE: It can be built into a custom platform by the operating system developer, or in the case of Windows Mobile, it is shipped separately to be installed in device memory. The standalone Windows Mobile 2003 software development kit (SDK) includes the required files to be installed manually on the target device. The Windows Mobile 5.0 SDK does not include the MSMQ components, but instead they are deployed separately as part of the Redistributable Server Components Package for Windows Mobile 5.0 on the Microsoft Download Center Web site at *www.microsoft.com/downloads/details.aspx?FamilyID=cdfd2bb2-fa13-4062-b8d1-4406ccddb5fd&DisplayLang=en*. Because this updated version is packaged as a compressed .cab file, it cannot be installed on device versions prior to Windows Mobile 5.0. Another difference in the Windows Mobile 5.0 version is that it supports using HTTP as a transport, rather than just the default binary transport. This can simplify your network configuration because data is sent over TCP port 80. The Windows Mobile 2003 SDK, which is included with Visual Studio 2005, does not include the MSMQ components, so if you are targeting devices that run Pocket PC 2003, you must install the standalone Pocket PC 2003 SDK, which you can download from the Microsoft Download Center Web site at *www.microsoft.com/downloads/details.aspx?FamilyID=9996b314-0364-4623-9ede-0b5fbb133652&DisplayLang=en*.

To install these Pocket PC 2003 files on the device, you must copy them all to the Windows directory. For Windows Mobile 5.0, simply copy the .cab file onto the device and install. Some further steps that apply to both versions are required to set up the MSMQ service on the device.

You can use the Msmqadm.exe application to control the service, and you must issue it with a number of commands to register the service correctly on the device. These can be called from your managed application using the *System.Diagnostics.Process.Start* method and checking the process *ExitCode* for status. The following code example shows these called from a method in the sample application.

```
//helper function to launch a process and wait for the result code
private static int ShellWait(string app, string args)
{
if (!File.Exists(app))
   {
   return -1;
}
Process p = Process.Start(app, args);
p.WaitForExit();
return p.ExitCode;
}

[DllImport("coredll.dll", SetLastError=true)]
private extern static int CloseHandle(IntPtr handle);

[DllImport("coredll.dll", SetLastError = true)]
private extern static IntPtr ActivateDevice(string lpszDevKey,
int dwClientInfo);

private static void InitMsmq()
{
string msmqadmPath = "\\Windows\\msmqadm.exe";

if (ShellWait(msmqadmPath, "status") < 0)
{
   //failed, msmq isn't present
string apppath = Path.GetDirectoryName(
System.Reflection.Assembly.GetExecutingAssembly().GetName().CodeBase);


if (System.Environment.OSVersion.Version.Major < 5)
{
//copy files (PPC2003)
File.Copy(Path.Combine(apppath, "msmqadm.exe"), "\\Windows\\msmqadm.exe");
File.Copy(Path.Combine(apppath, "msmqadmext.dll"),
"\\Windows\\msmqadmext.dll");
File.Copy(Path.Combine(apppath, "msmqd.dll"),
"\\Windows\\msmqd.dll");
File.Copy(Path.Combine(apppath, "msmqrt.dll"),
"\\Windows\\msmqrt.dll");
}
```

```
else
{
//Install CAB (WM5.0)
string cabname = Path.Combine(apppath, "msmq.arm.cab");
ShellWait("\\Windows\\wceload.exe", "\"" + cabname + "\"");
}
//initialize
ShellWait(msmqadmPath, "register cleanup");
ShellWait(msmqadmPath, "register install");
ShellWait(msmqadmPath, "register");
ShellWait(msmqadmPath, "enable binary");

//Register the service.
IntPtr handle = ActivateDevice("Drivers\\BuiltIn\\MSMQD", 0);
CloseHandle(handle);

//final check on the status
if (ShellWait(msmqadmPath, "status") < 0)
{
throw new ApplicationException("Failed to register MSMQ");
}

}

}
```

The Windows CE version of MSMQ doesn't support reading from remote queues, and neither does it support some of the more advanced security features such as encryption and access control lists (ACLs) for queues. It is not possible to search for public queues published in the Microsoft Active Directory directory service. Queues must be created as private queues on the server to be used by Message Queuing on Windows CE.

Set Up a Private Queue

The Windows operating system doesn't have MSMQ installed by default, so you must add it by using Add/Remove Programs in Control Panel and selecting Add/Remove Windows Features. After it is installed, you can manage message queuing from Computer Management in Administration Tools in Control Panel, as shown in Figure 8-1.

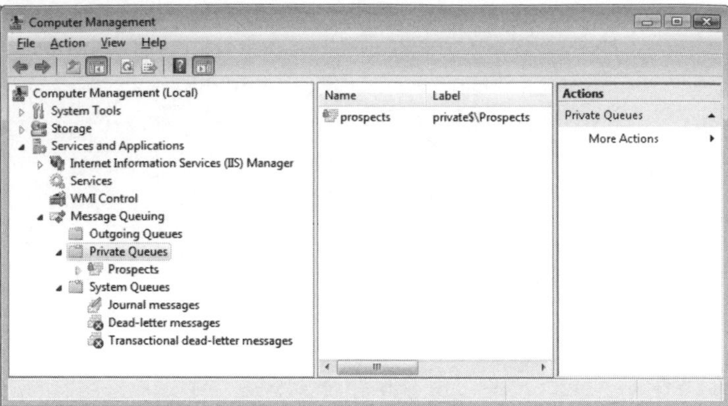

Figure 8-1 Microsoft *MessageQueue* Management Console

Transaction Support

Message queuing on Windows CE supports only basic transaction support to ensure once-only delivery in the order the messages were originally sent. It doesn't support multimessage transactions using Microsoft Transaction Coordinator (MTC). You can set transaction support on a server queue simply by selecting the option when creating the queue. You can't change this setting once the queue has been created. Figure 8-2 shows the New Private Queue dialog box you can use to create a new private queue.

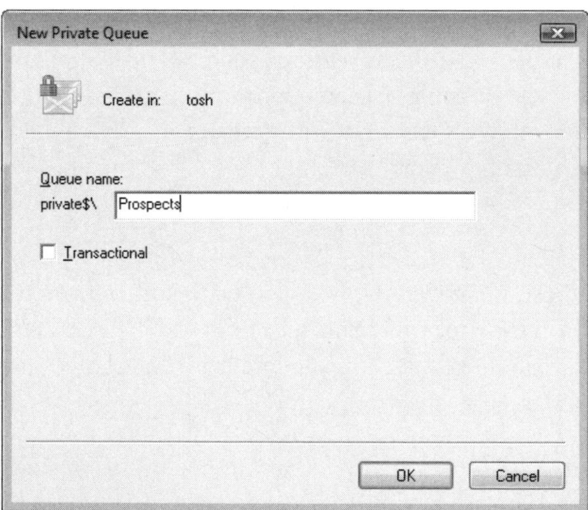

Figure 8-2 New Private Queue dialog box

Formatters

Formatters are used to convert your data into a form that can be sent in an MSMQ message. The desktop .NET Framework has three built-in formatters: *ActiveXMessageFormatter*, *BinaryMessageFormatter*, and *XmlMessageFormatter*. Because the Compact Framework includes no support for Microsoft ActiveX or binary serialization, it's no surprise that it supports only *XmlMessageFormatter*. This uses the Extensible Markup Language (XML) serialization built into the framework to produce an XML fragment that on the receiving computer can be deserialized into the same object type. This does, however, mean that individual messages are quite large in comparison with a binary representation of an object, which can be a concern when run over slow and expensive networks.

You must make sure you use the same formatter on both ends of the same queue. You are not, however, limited to the single *MessageFormatter* provided by the Compact Framework because it is possible to implement your own custom *MessageFormatter*. Nothing is stopping you from implementing your own version of the missing *BinaryMessageFormatter* or other missing features such as encryption. Writing a custom *MessageFormatter* is discussed in the article titled "How to create a custom message formatter by using Visual C#" on the Microsoft Help and Support Web site at *support.microsoft.com/default.aspx?scid=kb%3bEN-US%3b310683*.

Queuing Messages from the Device

After MSMQ is installed on the device and the server queue is created, you can start to queue some messages. You can use the *MessageQueue* class to do this. You must supply the queue name. Queue names are similar in concept to Uniform Resource Locators (URLs), but the format is different; the target computer can be addressed either by IP address or by machine name. MSMQ uses the Domain Name System (DNS) and Windows Internet Name Service (WINS) as available to determine the target computer. A queue name, therefore, looks like either of the following:

```
FormatName:DIRECT=OS:CUBE\Private$\Prospects
FormatName:DIRECT=TCP:192.168.2.2\Private$\Prospects
```

You can also use a local queue. For this, the machine name or IP address is replaced with a single period:

```
.\Private$\Prospects
```

This can be set in code by using the *Path* property, or you can drop a *MessageQueue* onto your form in the designer and set the path in the properties window.

```
this.mqRemote.Path = "FormatName:Direct=OS:CUBE\\Private$\\Prospects";
```

The *MessageQueue* can then be used to send messages. For example, this is our sample *Prospect* class:

```
Prospect p = new Prospect();
p.Name = txtName.Text;
p.Company = txtCompany.Text;
p.Number = txtNumber.Text;

mqRemote.Send(p);
```

To send messages to a transactional queue requires two changes to your code. First, you must add the *XACTONLY* identifier to the queue path, so our previous two examples become the following:

```
FormatName:DIRECT=OS:CUBE\Private$\Prospects:XACTONLY
FormatName:DIRECT=TCP:192.168.2.2\Private$\Prospects:XACTONLY
```

Second, you must call the overload of the *Send* method, which accepts a *MessageQueue-TransactionType*, for example:

```
mqRemote.Send(p, MessageQueueTransactionType.Single);
```

If you do not make these changes, your message will not be delivered to the transactional queue.

The formatter on the receiving queue must have the *TargetTypes* or *TargetTypeNames* properties set to tell it into what types to convert the XML. You must do this only once when setting up the queue. The receiving thread to read from a local queue is very simple. No processing of the received object is done in this example; it's simply added to the on-screen list.

```
private void ReceiveThread()
{
XmlMessageFormatter formatter = new XmlMessageFormatter(
new Type[] { typeof(Prospect) });
mqLocal.Formatter = formatter;

while (listening)
{
Message m = mqLocal.Receive();
Prospect p = (Prospect)m.Body;
this.Invoke(new AppendToListBoxDelegate(AppendToListBox),
new object[] { p.ToString() });
}
}
```

One potential use for a local queue is as an interprocess communication (IPC) method. Because another application could listen on the queue and you could pass messages back and forth. The other application need not be a managed application because MSMQ also has a native API.

Summary

This chapter looks at the range of networking and communication methods available in the Compact Framework. When you use any of these techniques, you must understand the cost and performance issues you may encounter on wireless networks, and you must design your code so as not to assume the connection will always be available. You can control this to an extent by how you encode your data to send over a connection, a factor completely in your control when you use low-level sockets or *SerialPort*. The next chapter looks at techniques to establish network connections and monitor connection state.

Chapter 9

Getting Connected

In this chapter:

Mobile application developers often spend more time and effort than their desktop colleagues do on interacting with the mobile device platform on tasks that are not directly related to the business functionality of the application but that are still essential to a successful solution. Mobile devices usually support a number of different networking technologies, including direct cable connections or wireless connections over a mobile phone network, such as WiFi or Bluetooth. This chapter looks at the tasks necessary to establish a network connection and how to manage the network adapters on your device.

Understanding Connections on Windows Mobile

Microsoft Windows Mobile includes settings that are responsible for all the configured connections on the device. Because the settings screens manage a variety of connection types, they can sometimes look confusing, but they are central to how the Connection Manager on the device works. Later in this chapter, we use the Connection Manager application programming interfaces (APIs) to establish connections, so it is important to understand the architecture.

You can access the settings by tapping Start, Settings, and on the Connections tab, tapping the Connections item. This opens the Settings dialog box, as shown in Figure 9-1, which contains two tabs labeled Tasks and Advanced. The first thing to notice is that the tasks are split into two clearly defined groups: My ISP, which contains tasks related to connections to the Internet, and My Work Network, which contains tasks relevant to connecting to a corporate network either directly or by using a virtual private network (VPN) connection. *Work* refers to a corporate network; you would typically use it to access servers within your firewall, including, for example, a Microsoft Exchange Server. The Internet destination network supports all other traffic destined for the wider Internet. The concept of two main destination networks—Internet and Work—is central to the way Connection Manager works.

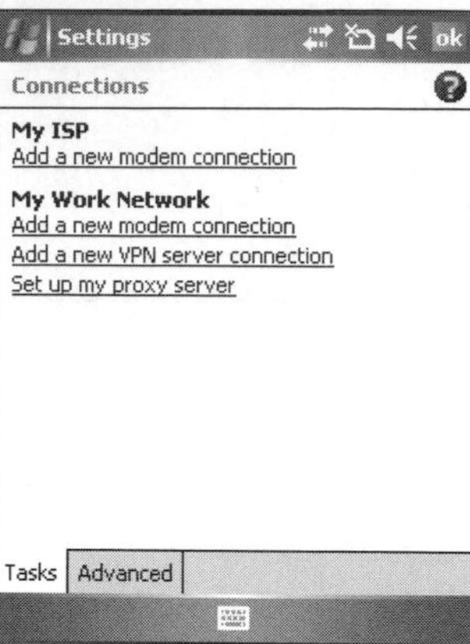

Figure 9-1 Connection settings in Windows Mobile

If your device was supplied by a mobile operator, it should have available Internet connections set up for you. We quickly step through the process of setting up a General Packet Radio Service (GPRS) network connection manually. Tap Add A New Modem Connection under My ISP to open the Make New Connection Wizard, as shown in Figure 9-2, which can help you configure your new connection.

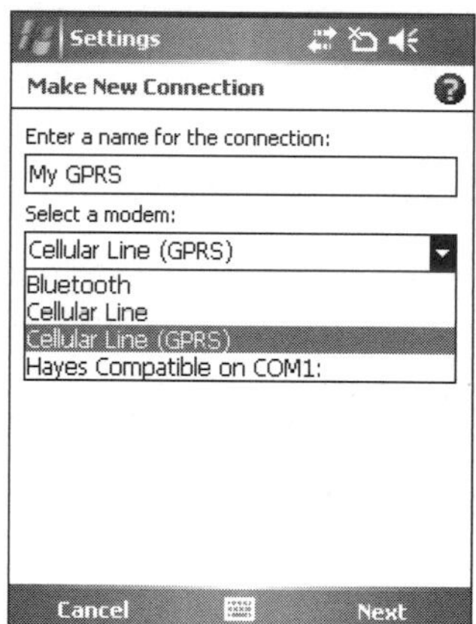

Figure 9-2 The Make New Connection Wizard

In the wizard, first, you enter a display name for the connection, and then you select a device from the Select A Modem drop-down list. In our example, we call the new connection My GPRS and configure it to use the Cellular Line (GPRS) device. This device name is a special case because it uses the same cellular line device as a circuit-switched call, but the settings required for a GPRS connection are different from the ones for a circuit-switched call. Next, you enter an access point name (APN). The name will vary depending on your mobile operator; in this example, we use .myapn. The final page of the wizard is for entering user name and password settings; these are not used on most public GPRS services, but as with all the settings, you should check with your mobile operator.

When there is at least one network connection configured, the Manage Existing Connections option appears on the Tasks tab of the Settings dialog box. It displays a list of connections, as illustrated in Figure 9-3, and with it you can edit and delete connections and set which connection to use as the default. You can select the Auto Pick option to allow the system to choose a connection for you.

Figure 9-3 Managing existing connections

On the Tasks tab on the Connections page of the Settings dialog box, the My Work Network section contains a similar option for defining dial-up connections. In this section, you can create a VPN connection that provides a private channel over an existing public network connection.

The Advanced tab, shown in Figure 9-4, includes additional options. You can tap the Select Networks button to select which connection group connects to which network. By default, these are set so that the My ISP connections are the default for applications connecting to the Internet, and My Work Network connections are used to connect to a private (intranet) network. You can tap the Dialing Rules button to define the way telephone numbers are dialed. If your connections use a circuit-switched connection, you may need to set these up when roaming on foreign networks. Telephone numbers stored with the connections must have a valid number, including a dialing code, because generally network short codes do not work when roaming. The Exceptions button is important when using Connection Manager because it helps you define whether a particular Uniform Resource Locator (URL) resides on a private network or the Internet and therefore whether Connection Manager can establish the correct connection.

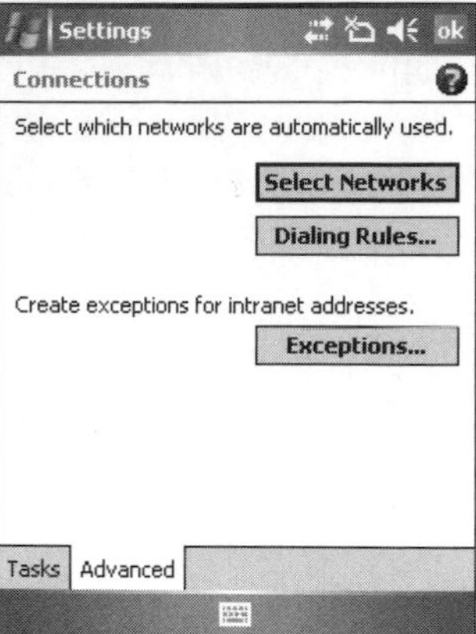

Figure 9-4 Options on the Advanced tab of the Connections page in the Settings dialog box

By default, any host name that includes a period is considered to be a public address, but you can override that behavior. The Work URL Exceptions page, shown in Figure 9-5, shows a list of currently stored exceptions. Tap Add New URL to add a new entry to the list. The form to add a new exception, shown in Figure 9-6, shows examples of the expected format. For example, you can add ***.mydomain** to ensure that exchange.mydomain is interpreted as an intranet server and that the correct dial-up or VPN connection is established.

Figure 9-5 Work URL Exceptions page

Figure 9-6 Adding a new Work URL exception

All of the settings exposed on the Connections page can be deployed to the device through the Extensible Markup Language (XML) configuration API. This configuration API is described in Chapter 17, "Developing with Windows Mobile." These can be deployed either through a compiled deployment package, programmatically through an API call, or by an operator over the air.

Using Desktop Passthrough

Microsoft ActiveSync is an application shipped for the desktop Windows operating system to support connecting and synchronizing devices that run Windows Mobile. In the Windows Vista operating system, ActiveSync received a face-lift and is now called the Windows Mobile Device Center–but it is still the same ActiveSync technology under the hood. In this book, we use the term *ActiveSync* to mean both Windows Mobile Device Center in Windows Vista and ActiveSync in earlier operating systems.

ActiveSync works over universal serial bus (USB), serial, or Bluetooth connections and provides a passthrough network connection so that you can access the wider Internet using your desktop computer rather than establish a GPRS or similar wireless connection.

ActiveSync uses the same concept of destination networks as Connection Manager when routing requests from the device. From ActiveSync on your desktop, you can specify to which of these network types your computer is connected in the Connection Settings dialog box, as shown in Figure 9-7. The default setting in the This Computer Is Connected To box is Automatic, so any attempt to access either a Work or an Internet resource should be passed through the ActiveSync connection. You are unlikely to need to change this setting. In the preceding section, we discussed the standard rules for how Windows Mobile determines whether a URL is on a Work network and how you can override this rule to fit your particular network topology.

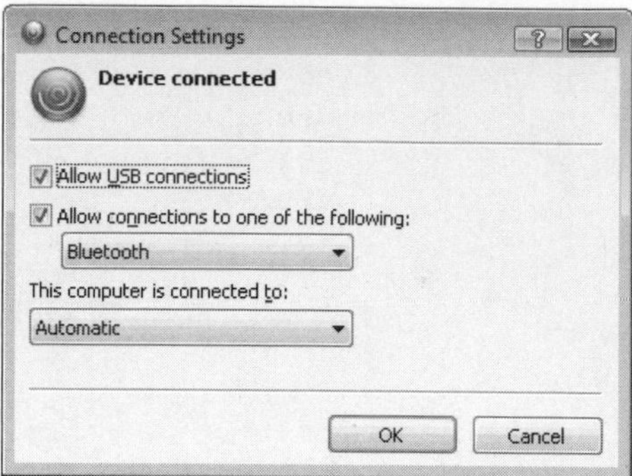

Figure 9-7 The Connection Settings dialog box

There are no APIs to allow you to change these settings programmatically. On the device side, the connection is invisible and appears just as if the device has an active Internet connection. Sometimes, for example, when you want to upload certain information only when you're on a high-bandwidth connection with no costs to send data, you may need to know if the device is connected through ActiveSync or another connection such as a mobile phone network. In Windows Mobile 5.0, the *Microsoft.WindowsMobile.Status.SystemState* class contains the *ConnectionsDesktopCount* property you can query to determine whether the connection is active. It might seem odd to expose it in this way because the device can have only one desktop connection active at a time, but it follows the pattern used for all other connection types.

On older devices, you can indirectly determine the type of connection by checking whether you can resolve the host name used by ActiveSync. If you are connected by ActiveSync, the host name PPP_PEER will resolve to the Internet Protocol (IP) address of the desktop, and the device will be assigned its own address in the same range. When an ActiveSync connection is established, devices that run Windows Mobile and Windows CE close connections to other networks, such as WiFi, GPRS, or Code-Division Multiple Access (CDMA).

```
public static bool DesktopPassthrough
{
    get
    {
        try
        {
            System.Net.IPHostEntry ihe =
System.Net.Dns.GetHostByName("PPP_PEER");
            return true;
        }
        catch
        {
            return false;
        }
    }
}
```

The technique of using the *System.Net.Dns* class is equally useful to look up the IP address of remote computers over any IP-based network. As long as you can connect to a Domain Name System (DNS) server on the network and you pass a valid host name, you can determine the IP address. If you are programming using sockets as described in Chapter 8, "Networking," you must specify the IP address of the remote host to connect to, so you must perform a DNS lookup on the remote host name to obtain the IP address.

Making Voice and Data Calls

Data connections such as ActiveSync and WiFi are essentially always on as long as their hardware is activated. If you want to use a telephone network to send data using GPRS, CDMA, or Universal Mobile Telecommunications System (UMTS), you must programmatically establish a connection when required. If you use an *HttpWebRequest* or use Web Services code, the Microsoft .NET Framework runtime will attempt to establish an Internet connection for you automatically; when using lower-level networking technologies, you must create the connection yourself. Similarly, if as part of your application you want to initiate a voice call for the user, you must know the appropriate native APIs to call because the Microsoft .NET Compact Framework doesn't have any functionality for establishing voice connections.

Voice Calls

Windows Mobile provides a single high-level API call for starting a voice call on the user's behalf. Lower-level control of the phone functionality is possible through further Microsoft Telephony Application Programming Interface (TAPI) methods, a complete investigation of which is beyond the scope of this book.

Making a Voice Call on Windows Mobile 2003

The following code samples show the *MakeCall* method that wraps the *PhoneMakeCall* native API call and that requires just the destination number and a flag to indicate whether to display a prompt to the user before commencing dialing. First, you must define the native API and the structure used to pass it parameters.

```
using System.Runtime.InteropServices;

[DllImport("phone.dll", SetLastError = true)]
internal static extern int PhoneMakeCall(ref PHONEMAKECALLINFO ppmci);

internal struct PHONEMAKECALLINFO
{
public int cbSize;
public PMCF dwFlags;
[MarshalAs(UnmanagedType.LPWStr)]
public string pszDestAddress;
[MarshalAs(UnmanagedType.LPWStr)]
string pszAppName;
```

```
[MarshalAs(UnmanagedType.LPWStr)]
string pszCalledParty;
[MarshalAs(UnmanagedType.LPWStr)]
string pszComment;
}

internal enum PMCF
{
DEFAULT = 0x00000001,
PROMPTBEFORECALLING = 0x00000002,
}
```

Then you define a static wrapper method called *MakeCall*. Because many of the *PHONEMAKECALLINFO* members are unused, you need to pass only the phone number and a *Boolean* flag to determine whether to prompt the user to confirm before dialing.

```
public static void MakeCall(string number, bool prompt)
{
PHONEMAKECALLINFO pmci = new PHONEMAKECALLINFO();
pmci.cbSize = Marshal.SizeOf(pmci);
pmci.dwFlags = prompt ? PMCF.PROMPTBEFORECALLING : PMCF.DEFAULT;
   pmci.pszDestAddress = number;

   int result = PhoneMakeCall(ref pmci);

if (result != 0)
{
throw new System.ComponentModel.Win32Exception(result,
"Error calling PhoneMakeCall");
}
}
```

Making a Voice Call on Windows Mobile 5.0 and Later

Windows Mobile 5.0 introduces a managed API for making voice calls. By using the *Phone* class in the *Microsoft.WindowsMobile.Telephony* namespace, you can call the *Talk* method, passing it the number to dial. Therefore, you simply require two lines of code to make a voice call:

```
Microsoft.WindowsMobile.Telephony.Phone p = new
Microsoft.WindowsMobile.Telephony.Phone(); p.Talk(txtPhoneNumber.Text);
```

In Chapter 17, we investigate the Windows Mobile managed class libraries in detail.

Establishing Data Calls

Many applications require some kind of network connection while a device is away from a computer dock, and there are a number of ways to establish a data connection programmatically. On devices that run Windows Mobile (Pocket PC 2002 and later), the Connection Manager API is responsible for managing outgoing connections. On devices that run Windows CE, you can use Remote Access Service (RAS) APIs to establish dial-up and GPRS connections.

Connection Manager

Data connections can be established over connections such as GPRS. On devices that run Windows Mobile, a dedicated API handles setting up connections and monitoring their state: Connection Manager. Although this is a native code API, you can call it easily by using Platform Invocation Services (PInvoke) or a third-party wrapper library.

Connection Manager handles the low-level connection over different network media: WiFi, GPRS, circuit-switched data, and desktop passthrough, for example. Because the API manages connections across all applications in the system, it can make better decisions about which connections to use based on what other applications have requested. Connection Manager is built around the concept of destination networks and routes to those destinations, which can be made up of one or more connections. For example, a device may connect to a private Work network by first connecting to a public cellular packet-based network such as GPRS and then by establishing a VPN connection to the Work network. After these connections are set up in Connection Manager, you need to know only the destination network, and Connection Manager will manage the connection process to get you connected to the chosen network.

There are a number of standard destination networks for Internet, Work, and Wireless Application Protocol (WAP) networks. In most cases, your application will need to connect to either Internet or Work destinations. The parameters for the connections are configured through the XML configuration API (discussed with examples in Chapter 17).

The Connection Manager API supports notifications, which can be passed back to an application by window messages to a supplied window handle (HWND). Alternatively, the application can query the status at any time by using the *ConnMgrConnectionStatus* function. In the following code sample, we demonstrate how to establish an Internet connection by using Connection Manager to create the most appropriate connection type. The sample provides a very basic wrapper around Connection Manager. Third-party libraries (such as Mobile In The Hand at *www.inthehand.com/WindowsMobile.aspx* and the OpenNETCF Smart Device Framework at *www.opennetcf.org/sdf/*) are available and can provide more full-featured implementations.

Connection Manager uses several standard rules to determine whether a host name is in Internet format (contains a period) or is a single host name. You can customize the exceptions to this rule through XML configuration or the user interface. The *ConnMgrMapUrl* method is used to check your URL against these rules and return the destination network identifier. We use the following wrapper function, which returns the list of destination network identifiers.

```
public static Guid[] MapUrl(Uri url)
{
ArrayList al = new ArrayList();
Guid g;
int index = 0;
int hresult = 0;
while (hresult == 0)
{
hresult = ConnMgrMapURL(url.ToString(), out g, ref index);
if (hresult == 0)
{
al.Add(g);
}
}

return (Guid[])al.ToArray(typeof(Guid));
}

[DllImport("cellcore", SetLastError = true)]
private static extern int ConnMgrMapURL(string pwszURL, out Guid pguid,
ref int pdwIndex);
```

The *Guid* values returned are in priority order. You can create an instance of the ConnectionManager class and with the first returned value call the *EstablishConnection* or *EstablishConnectionSync* methods. These methods call the native *ConnMgrEstablishConnection* and *ConnMgrEstablishConnectionSync* methods, respectively. The *EstablishConnectionSync* method waits until either the connection is established or the attempt fails after a specified timeout. *EstablishConnection* starts the connection process and then returns control to your code. A handle is maintained for the lifetime of the connection request. We store this in the *ConnectionManager* instance.

```
public void EstablishConnection(Guid destination)
{
ReleaseConnection();

connectionInfo.guidDestNet = destination;

int hresult = ConnMgrEstablishConnection(ref connectionInfo,
out handle);
}
```

The connection settings are inserted in the *CONNMGR_CONNECTIONINFO* structure, which is defined in managed code as follows:

```
[StructLayout(LayoutKind.Sequential)]
internal struct CONNMGR_CONNECTIONINFO
{
public int cbSize;
public CONNMGR_PARAM dwParams;
public CONNMGR_FLAG dwFlags;
public ConnectionPriority dwPriority;
public int bExclusive;
public int bDisabled;
public Guid guidDestNet;
public IntPtr hWnd;
public uint uMsg;
public uint lParam;
public uint ulMaxCost;
public uint ulMinRcvBw;
public uint ulMaxConnLatency;
}
```

In the example, we prefill the structure with default values so that only the network globally unique identifier (GUID) need be set for the connection request. You can request the current connection state at any time by using the native *ConnMgrConnectionStatus* method, which in our sample is wrapped by the *ConnectionStatus* property.

```
public ConnectionStatus ConnectionStatus
{
get
{
ConnectionStatus status = ConnectionStatus.Unknown;
if (handle != IntPtr.Zero)
{
int hresult = ConnMgrConnectionStatus(handle, out status);
}
         return status;
}
}

 [DllImport("cellcore", SetLastError = true)]
private static extern int ConnMgrConnectionStatus(IntPtr hConnection,
out ConnectionStatus pdwStatus);
```

Windows Mobile 5.0 exposes a number of properties in the *Microsoft.WindowsMobile.Status.SystemState* class that describe the active network connections, both wired and wireless. We look at this class in more detail in Chapter 17.

Remote Access Service

For dial-up, GPRS, and VPN connections, you can use the Remote Access Service (RAS) API. Once again, this is a subset of a desktop Windows API. If your device supports Connection Manager, it is recommended that you do not use RAS directly–use Connection Manager instead, which will start the appropriate connection for you, handle connection sharing with other applications, share the connection state, and report it in the device user interface.

The RAS API exposes methods to read the devices, phonebook entries, and active connections available on the device. You must specify the name of a phonebook entry when calling the *RasDial* method to establish the connection. In the sample code for this chapter on this book's companion Web site, we created a class called *Ras* that exposes a property that returns all the names of available phonebook entries as an array of strings.

```
public static string[] Entries
{
get
{
int cEntries;
int len = Marshal.SizeOf(typeof(RASENTRYNAME));
IntPtr ptr = Marshal.AllocHGlobal(len);
Marshal.WriteInt32(ptr, Marshal.SizeOf(typeof(RASENTRYNAME)));
// The first call gives required buffer length.
int result = RasEnumEntries(null, null, ptr, ref len,
out cEntries);
ptr = Marshal.ReAllocHGlobal(ptr, (IntPtr)len);
// Call again with resized buffer.
Marshal.WriteInt32(ptr, Marshal.SizeOf(typeof(RASENTRYNAME)));
result = RasEnumEntries(null, null, ptr, ref len, out cEntries);
string[] names = new string[cEntries];
for (int iEntry = 0; iEntry < cEntries; iEntry++)
{
IntPtr p = (IntPtr)(ptr.ToInt32() +
(Marshal.SizeOf(typeof(RASENTRYNAME)) * iEntry));
RASENTRYNAME ren =
(RASENTRYNAME)Marshal.PtrToStructure(p,
typeof(RASENTRYNAME));
names[iEntry] = ren.szEntryName;
}

Marshal.FreeHGlobal(ptr);

return names;
}
}
```

The *RASENTRYNAME* structure is defined as follows:

```
internal struct RASENTRYNAME
{
public int dwSize;
[MarshalAs(UnmanagedType.ByValTStr, SizeConst=21)]
public string szEntryName;
}
```

After you know the name of the connection to use, you can use the *RasDial* method. In the sample code, the *Dial* method wraps the *RasDial* code, and instead of just returning the handle, it returns an instance of the *RasConnection* class, which stores the handle and exposes the *HangUp* method.

```
[StructLayout(LayoutKind.Sequential, CharSet=CharSet.Unicode)]
internal struct RASDIALPARAMS
{
public int dwSize;
   [MarshalAs(UnmanagedType.ByValTStr, SizeConst=21)]
   public string szEntryName;
   [MarshalAs(UnmanagedType.ByValTStr, SizeConst=129)]
   public string szPhoneNumber;
   [MarshalAs(UnmanagedType.ByValTStr, SizeConst=49)]
   public string szCallbackNumber;
   [MarshalAs(UnmanagedType.ByValTStr, SizeConst=257)]
   public string szUserName;
   [MarshalAs(UnmanagedType.ByValTStr, SizeConst=257)]
   public string szPassword;
   [MarshalAs(UnmanagedType.ByValTStr, SizeConst=16)]
   public string szDomain;
}

[DllImport("coredll", SetLastError = true)]
private static extern int RasDial(IntPtr dialExtensions,
string phoneBookPath, ref RASDIALPARAMS rasDialParam, int NotifierType,
IntPtr notifier, out IntPtr pRasConn);
```

The strings in the native *RASDIALPARAMS* struct are defined as inline character arrays rather than as string pointers. The size constants are taken from the structures definition in the ras.h header. Therefore, the *MarshalAsAttribute* must be applied to enforce this behavior. We look at marshalling structures in detail in Chapter 14, "Interoperating with the Platform."

Dial extensions are not supported in Windows CE and the phonebook is not stored in the file system, so the first two parameters to *RasDial* are ignored. The *RASDIALPARAMS* structure is used to pass all the settings. In this example, we do not use notifications, so the only other argument used is the handle, which is populated on success. On failure, the method returns one of the RAS error codes defined in the raserror.h header file in the software development kit (SDK) for your platform.

```
public static RasConnection Dial(string name, string username,
string password, string domain)
{
IntPtr handle;
RASDIALPARAMS rdp = new RASDIALPARAMS();
rdp.dwSize = Marshal.SizeOf(rdp);
rdp.szEntryName = name;
rdp.szDomain = "*";
rdp.szUserName = username;
rdp.szPassword = password;
rdp.szDomain = domain;
int result = RasDial(IntPtr.Zero, null, ref rdp, 0, IntPtr.Zero,
out handle);

if (result != 0)
{
throw new System.ComponentModel.Win32Exception(result,
"Error establishing connection");
}

return new RasConnection(handle);
}
```

Microsoft patterns & practices Network Monitor Application Block

The Microsoft patterns & practices Mobile Application Blocks introduced in Chapter 1, ".NET Compact Framework–a Platform on the Move," contain a Network Monitor Application Block that works on devices running Windows Mobile 5.0 and later. The Network Monitor Application Block makes it easy to get information about the physical network connections. Internally, it uses the Connection Manager API and the *SystemState* managed class, but it exposes a simple object model to request information about the state of network connectivity on the device and exposes events you can hook to be notified about changes in the active network.

It is important to note that the block doesn't actually contain functionality to establish a connection; it merely monitors the status. You need to add references to your project to both the Configuration and Connection Monitor blocks. The Network Monitor block uses the Configuration Application Block to read settings from the config file, where you define the relative price of each type of network connection. An example config file may look like this:

```
<?xml version="1.0" encoding="utf-8" ?>
<configuration>
  <configSections>
    <section name="Connections"
```

```
type="Microsoft.Practices.Mobile.ConnectionMonitor.Configuration.ConnectionSettingsSec
tion, Microsoft.Practices.Mobile.ConnectionMonitor" />
  </configSections>

  <Connections>
    <ConnectionItems>
      <add  Type="CellConnection" Price="8"/>
      <add  Type="NicConnection" Price="2"/>
      <add  Type="DesktopConnection" Price="1"/>
    </ConnectionItems>
  </Connections>

</configuration>
```

In your application code, you create an instance of *ConnectionMonitor* based on the configuration settings you have provided. The classes are contained in the *Microsoft.Practices.Mobile.ConnectionMonitor* namespace.

```
private ConnectionMonitor _cnMonitor =
ConnectionMonitorFactory.CreateFromConfiguration();
```

The *ConnectionMonitor* class exposes a single event called *ActiveNetworkChanged*, which occurs when a connection is opened or closed. Therefore, when you handle the event, you must determine whether the device is connected and use the *ActiveNetwork* and *ActiveConnection* properties to find out about the currently active connection method.

The *ConnectionMonitor* also exposes two collections–*Connections* and *Networks*–that contain all the available connections and network types supported on the device. All the *Connections* items returned contain the *Price* property so that you can decide whether to send data over the currently active network connection. See the documentation supplied with the Mobile Client Software Factory for more information. As with the rest of the application blocks, the full source code is available.

Tip If your application uses Web Services, you can use the Disconnected Service Agent Application Block to handle the dispatch of Web service calls, taking into account the state of network connectivity and queuing messages if no network is available. The Disconnected Service Agent uses the Network Monitor Application Block to get information about network availability, and it calls Connection Manager to establish a connection when a network becomes available.

Enabling and Disabling Adapters

Radios use power, and the battery power on a mobile device is a valuable resource. On consumer devices, which radios are active is a decision that rests with the user, but for enterprise line-of-business applications running on custom or ruggedized hardware, frequently the application developer is responsible for turning network adapters on or off. For example, your application may be used by users who visit public buildings. If the application runs in kiosk mode so that standard features to control radios built into the operating system are not available, you may have to build into the application some way for users to turn off the radios, perhaps when they enter a building such as a hospital where you must turn off cell phones and WiFi. This section explains how to turn wide area network (WAN), WiFi, and Bluetooth radios on and off.

Cellular Phones

Low-level phone functionality on a device is controlled through the native Telephony API (TAPI), which is a subset of TAPI as present in desktop versions of Windows for controlling modems and phone devices. A detailed look at TAPI is outside the scope of this book, and because it is a native API, it requires either numerous PInvoke definitions or a commercial wrapper library.

TAPI works on the basis of having a handle to an individual line device. Additionally, a number of Extended TAPI methods perform cellular-specific operations such as registering with a network provider and changing the status of the device. It is these operations that can be used to disable the phone hardware, putting it into the so-called flight mode. First, you must open a TAPI session and then obtain details of available line devices until you find the one that represents the cellular radio; it is named Cellular Line. Open this line, and then call the Extended TAPI methods on that line. Finally, you must remember to release these handles to free resources after you are finished working with TAPI. To use these TAPI methods, you must also define a number of structures and enumerations in managed code. The following code shows the necessary definitions:

```
[DllImport("coredll", SetLastError = true)]
internal static extern IntPtr GetModuleHandle(string lpModuleName);

//TAPI
[DllImport("coredll", SetLastError = true)]
internal static extern int lineInitializeEx(out IntPtr lphLineApp,
IntPtr hInstance, int lpfnCallback, string lpszFriendlyAppName,
out int lpdwNumDevs, ref int lpdwAPIVersion,
ref LINEINITIALIZEEXPARAMS lpLineInitializeExParams);
```

```
public struct LINEINITIALIZEEXPARAMS
{
public int dwTotalSize;
public int dwNeededSize;
public int dwUsedSize;
public LINEINITIALIZEEXOPTION dwOptions;
public IntPtr handle;
public int dwCompletionKey;
}

public enum LINEINITIALIZEEXOPTION
{
USECOMPLETIONPORT = 0x00000003,
USEEVENT = 0x00000002,
USEHIDDENWINDOW = 0x00000001,
}

[DllImport("coredll", SetLastError = true)]
internal static extern int lineShutdown(IntPtr hLineApp);

[DllImport("coredll", SetLastError = true)]
internal static extern int lineGetDevCaps(IntPtr hLineApp, int dwDeviceID,
int dwAPIVersion, int dwExtVersion, byte[] lpLineDevCaps);

[DllImport("coredll", SetLastError = true)]
internal static extern int lineOpen(IntPtr hLineApp, int dwDeviceID,
out IntPtr lphLine, int dwAPIVersion, int dwExtVersion,
int dwCallbackInstance, LINECALLPRIVILEGE dwPrivileges,
LINEMEDIAMODE dwMediaModes, IntPtr lpCallParams);

internal enum LINECALLPRIVILEGE
{
NONE = 0x00000001,
MONITOR = 0x00000002,
   //OWNER = 0x00000004,
}

[Flags()]
internal enum LINEMEDIAMODE
{
INTERACTIVEVOICE = 0x00000004,
}

[DllImport("coredll", SetLastError = true)]
internal static extern int lineClose(IntPtr hLine);
```

The Extended TAPI functions control cellular-specific features, and these methods are exposed from the Cellcore.dll file. They define functions that are not relevant to an ordinary wired phone device, such as the ability to turn the radio equipment on and off and to register or unregister with an available mobile operator. All of these methods require a standard TAPI line handle that is obtained from the *lineOpen* method. These four functions and their associated enumerations are defined in the following sample.

```
[DllImport("cellcore", SetLastError = true)]
internal static extern int lineSetEquipmentState(IntPtr hLine,
LINEEQUIPSTATE dwState);

internal enum LINEEQUIPSTATE : int
{
MINIMUM = 0x00000001,
//RXONLY = 0x00000002,
//TXONLY = 0x00000003,
//NOTXRX = 0x00000004,
FULL = 0x00000005,
}

internal enum LINERADIOSUPPORT : int
{
OFF = 0x00000001,
ON = 0x00000002,
UNKNOWN = 0x00000003,
}

[DllImport("cellcore", SetLastError = true)]
internal static extern int lineGetEquipmentState(IntPtr hLine,
out LINEEQUIPSTATE lpdwState, out LINERADIOSUPPORT lpdwRadioSupport);

[DllImport("cellcore", SetLastError = true)]
internal static extern int lineRegister(IntPtr hLine,
LINEREGMODE dwRegisterMode, string lpszOperator, int dwOperatorFormat);

internal enum LINEREGMODE
{
AUTOMATIC = 0x00000001,
}

[DllImport("cellcore", SetLastError = true)]
internal static extern int lineUnregister(IntPtr hLine);
```

You have created a *Telephony* class that includes all these definitions and a public property to activate and disable the phone. The constructor opens a TAPI session and reads the details of available line devices. When a line device named Cellular Line is found, the index is stored and the line is opened, obtaining a line handle.

```
public Telephony()
{
int numDevices;
int version = 0x20000;
LINEINITIALIZEEXPARAMS initParams = new LINEINITIALIZEEXPARAMS();
initParams.dwTotalSize = Marshal.SizeOf(initParams);
initParams.dwOptions = LINEINITIALIZEEXOPTION.USEEVENT;

//initialize tapi-negotiates API version and returns number of devices
int result = lineInitializeEx(out hLineApp, GetModuleHandle(null), 0,
"Chapter9", out numDevices, ref version, ref initParams);
int cellularLineIndex = 0;

//Loop through the devices looking for the cellular line.
for(int thisDevice = 0; thisDevice < numDevices; thisDevice++)
{
byte[] caps = new byte[Marshal.SizeOf(typeof(LINEDEVCAPS))+256];
BitConverter.GetBytes(caps.Length).CopyTo(caps,0);

result = lineGetDevCaps(hLineApp, thisDevice, 0x020000, 0, caps);
//length of the null-terminated line name
int namelen = BitConverter.ToInt32(caps, 32);
//offset in the buffer of the line name
int nameoffset = BitConverter.ToInt32(caps,36);
//Get the line name.
string lineName = System.Text.Encoding.Unicode.GetString(caps,
nameoffset, namelen);

//Strip the trailing null if present.
int nullIndex = lineName.IndexOf('\0');
if (nullIndex > -1)
{
lineName = lineName.Substring(0, nullIndex);
}

//If cellular line, store the index and leave the loop.
if (lineName == "Cellular Line")
{
cellularLineIndex = thisDevice;
break;
}
}

//Open a handle to the cellular line.
result = lineOpen(hLineApp, cellularLineIndex, out hLine, version, 0, 0,
LINECALLPRIVILEGE.NONE , LINEMEDIAMODE.INTERACTIVEVOICE,
IntPtr.Zero);
}
```

With this handle to the cellular line, you can then call the Extended TAPI functions to activate flight mode. This is wrapped up in the *PhoneEnabled* property.

```
public bool PhoneEnabled
{
   get
   {
        LINEEQUIPSTATE state;
        LINERADIOSUPPORT radio;
        lineGetEquipmentState(hLine, out state, out radio);

        if (state == LINEEQUIPSTATE.FULL)
        {
                return true;
        }
        return false;
   }
   set
   {
        if (value)
        {
                lineSetEquipmentState(hLine, LINEEQUIPSTATE.FULL);
                lineRegister(hLine, LINEREGMODE.AUTOMATIC, null, 0);
        }
        else
        {
                lineUnregister(hLine);
                lineSetEquipmentState(hLine, LINEEQUIPSTATE.MINIMUM);
        }
   }
}
```

Two steps are required to activate the phone. First, you set the hardware status to full functionality, and then you call *lineRegister*, which automatically registers with a cellular provider. This function returns instantly, although the registration may take up to 30 seconds. The status icon in the notification area shows the state of the mobile network because signal strength is shown only when the device is registered to a network. You have used a lot of complex PInvoke code to use these TAPI methods; the techniques of platform interop are described in more detail in Chapter 14, "Interoperating with the Platform."

WiFi

The situation with WiFi adapters is not quite as simple. Depending on the specific platform, the device may or may not support a high-level API such as the Microsoft Wireless Zero Configuration (WZC); otherwise, you must configure adapters at the driver level. Some device manufacturers provide their own API for controlling their wireless local area network (LAN) hardware. Although there isn't a documented way of activating and disabling the WiFi device, the very worst case scenario is to provide a link to the Wireless Manager tool from your own application. Wireless Manager is supported on devices that run Windows Mobile 5.0 and can be started by using the *Process* class:

```
Process.Start("\\Windows\\wrlsmgr.exe",null);
```

Wireless Manager is a simple tool you can use to toggle the state of all the wireless features of the device, as shown in Figure 9-8.

Figure 9-8 The Wireless Manager tool

Bluetooth

Working with Bluetooth on devices that run Windows CE is complicated by the fact that the device manufacturer can use a Bluetooth software stack of its choice. Different stacks have different programming models and not all have a freely available software development kit. Microsoft ships a Bluetooth stack implementation in Windows CE that is used in many devices that run Windows Mobile. The Bluetooth software stack provided with Windows CE exposes two API calls for changing the Bluetooth radio state. The shared source 32feet library (*32feet.net*) mentioned in Chapter 8 includes radio functionality for the Microsoft Bluetooth stack.

Because you must use only two API functions to get or set the status of the radio, we use a sample to show how you can wrap the APIs in your own code. The radio can be in one of three states, *Off*, *Connectable*, and *Discoverable*. These are defined in the code sample in the *RadioMode* enumeration. The difference between *Connectable* and *Discoverable* is that *Connectable* powers up the hardware but the device is not visible to new devices, so it can be used only with remote devices that have already paired and know the unique device address.

Discoverable responds to remote devices doing a device lookup. The following sample shows a property to wrap these two native methods to control the radio mode.

```
Using System.Runtime.InteropServices;

public static RadioMode Mode
{
     get
     {
          RadioMode val;
          int result = BthGetMode(out val);
          if(result!=0)
          {
               throw new System.ComponentModel.Win32Exception(result,
                      "Error getting Bluetooth radio mode");
          }
          return val;
     }
     set
     {
          int result = NativeMethods.BthSetMode(value);
          if(result!=0)
          {
               throw new System.ComponentModel.Win32Exception(result,
                      "Error setting BluetoothRadio mode");
          }
     }
}

[DllImport("BthUtil.dll", SetLastError=true)]
public static extern int BthSetMode(RadioMode dwMode);

[DllImport("BthUtil.dll", SetLastError=true)]
public static extern int BthGetMode(out RadioMode dwMode);

public enum RadioMode
{
     PowerOff,
     Connectable,
     Discoverable,
}
```

It is then very easy to change the state at any time by setting this property, for example:

```
BluetoothRadio.RadioMode = RadioMode.Connectable;
```

SMS Interception

Windows Mobile 5.0 introduces a set of managed APIs, one of which is a class capable of intercepting incoming Short Message Service (SMS) messages that match a rule of your choosing. This functionality is contained in the *Microsoft.WindowsMobile.PocketOutlook.MessageInterception* namespace. A rule consists of a property, a comparison type, and a string keyword or phrase. You can use either the message body or sender property for your rule, and the comparison is a member of the *MessagePropertyComparisonType* enumeration. You can set up a comparison rule to match messages beginning or ending with a specific phrase or messages containing the phrase in any location. When a matching message is received, you can then access the message properties, such as sender and body text, from your code.

The MessageInterceptor allows you to use SMS as a messaging transport in your application with no input from the user. You can register your rule so that even if your application is not currently running on the device, the system will launch it, allowing you to process the message. The rule must be registered with an identifier unique to your application. The identifier is stored in the registry, so must not contain any path characters. In this example, we use Chapter9, and it just so happens that this is also the keyword we use in the rule, but the two do not have to be the same. Because there are separate constructors for the *MessageInterceptor* class, depending on whether you are first setting up your rule or loading an existing saved rule, you should call the *IsApplicationLauncherEnabled* method to determine which constructor to use, as demonstrated by the following code in the *Load* event of the main application form.

```
private void Form1_Load(object sender, EventArgs e)
{
if(MessageInterceptor.IsApplicationLauncherEnabled("Chapter9"))
{
//Load existing settings.
mi = new MessageInterceptor("Chapter9");
}
else
{
//Set up rule and register with application id "Chapter9".
mi = new MessageInterceptor(InterceptionAction.NotifyAndDelete);
mi.MessageCondition = new MessageCondition(MessageProperty.Body,
MessagePropertyComparisonType.StartsWith, "Chapter9");

string appPath =
Assembly.GetExecutingAssembly().GetName().CodeBase;
mi.EnableApplicationLauncher("Chapter9", appPath);
}
mi.MessageReceived +=
new MessageInterceptorEventHandler(mi_MessageReceived);
}
```

An important item to note is the call to *EnableApplicationLauncher*. Besides persisting the rule in the registry for future use, it also stores the application path so that when a matching SMS message is received the system can automatically start your application and process the message. The last statement of this code sets up an event handler that is called each time a matching message is received. The method receives a *MessageInterceptorEventArgs* object that contains details of the message. Because the message is of the type *Message*, from which the *SmsMessage* is derived, you must cast it to the *SmsMessage* type to access all of the message properties. In this example code, we simply display the message body to the user.

```
void mi_MessageReceived(object sender, MessageInterceptorEventArgs e)
{
MessageBox.Show(((SmsMessage)e.Message).Body, "SMS Received");
}
```

Your application could do all manner of processing on this message using either string methods or regular expressions to parse the contents. You are limited only by your own imagination and the 160-character limit on an SMS message. You can use concatenated messages to send larger messages that are broken down into multiple SMS messages and reassembled before the event is raised containing the entire message contents. This, of course, incurs additional costs because each section is billed as a single message. You may also find that not all SMS sending mechanisms support concatenated messages. Windows Mobile and most other modern consumer handsets will support this, but some Internet SMS gateways do not.

Tip When you test your application using the device emulators, you can send a loopback SMS by using the fake phone number 14250010001. This allows you to test your interception code without incurring real network charges.

In Chapter 17, we look at the task of sending outgoing SMS messages.

Summary

In this chapter, we looked at the task of establishing a network connection to send and receive information. We discussed how ActiveSync, or Windows Mobile Device Center in Windows Vista, establishes a passthrough Internet connection that you can use when docked. For devices that run Windows Mobile, we discussed how Connection Manager provides a unified API for managing and prioritizing connection requests. We also looked at the lower-level RAS API used to establish connections on devices running Windows CE. Finally, we discussed using SMS as a means of sending and receiving application data. In Chapter 17, we revisit this topic with a more detailed look at the Windows Mobile managed libraries.

Chapter 10

Security Programming for Mobile Applications

In this chapter:

Mobile devices are easily lost or stolen. If a device contains data that is valuable to your business, loss of a mobile device can be a disaster. No one wants a device containing customer information or details of user names and passwords required for authentication to the company's systems to fall into the hands of a competitor or an attacker.

In some code samples in other chapters of this book, database passwords or user credentials are shown hard-coded—a necessary evil so that the real purpose of the sample is not obscured by code required to protect this sensitive information. Needless to say, hard-coding of secrets is very bad practice, so this chapter starts by discussing some methods you can use to store sensitive information securely.

Security programming is a field that many perceive to be difficult. If you start from a blank page, it undoubtedly is, but fortunately you can use a number of packaged solutions to make implementation of a secure system easier. This chapter walks you through using the Mobile Configuration and Mobile Password Authentication Application Blocks from the Microsoft patterns & practices Mobile Client Software Factory. These application blocks make user authentication and encryption of secrets quite simple. Of course, a solution built using the Mobile Configuration and Mobile Password Authentication Application Blocks will not be appropriate in all cases, so the chapter goes on to describe how to use symmetric and asymmetric encryption algorithms and how to generate hash tokens.

Finally, you should remember that one technique that contributes to good security is to implement *defense in depth*. Put as many obstacles as you can between your attackers and their goal, which means using a combination of secure design, application development, and device management and configuration. This book is aimed at application developers, so most of this chapter discusses topics of interest to that audience. However, the last section talks about perimeter security–configuration and management practices you can employ to prevent attackers from gaining access to the device in the first place–and about how to configure Microsoft Windows Mobile security policy to harden the device against certain forms of attack.

Implementing Good Security

Security is not something you bolt onto a solution after you have finished coding the interesting bits. Of course, most developers know this, and yet security is still too often considered only as an afterthought. You must consider security in the early stages of your design process to ensure that security requirements are gathered along with the functional requirements of your application and that you perform reviews of your design and your code from a security perspective.

Performing Security Reviews

You should always perform a security review of your code as a mandatory component of your code review process. Some things that you should look for include unvalidated user input; weak user authentication and authorization for accessing resources on Web servers; unsecured network connections; hard-coded user names, passwords, and other secrets; unencrypted sensitive data that is accessible to outsiders; and storing sensitive information on the device (either in memory or in persistent storage) longer than is absolutely necessary. On a more general level, ensure that your code checks return values from every function call and takes appropriate action. Attackers can take advantage of situations where code they are attacking does not check status returns–think of it as slipping something through while you are not looking. If the code is robust in this way, it is much harder to attack.

Much work has been done over the last few years in defining a repeatable process you can use to perform effective security reviews and in integrating security into the development life cycle. One process is called threat modeling, which breaks the security review process into six steps:

1. Identify the valuable assets in your solution that you must protect.
2. Create an architecture overview.
3. Decompose the application architecture that you created in step 2, identifying trust boundaries (that is, areas where security requirements differ) and identifying how data flows between them.

4. Identify the threats that could affect the application, keeping the goals of an attacker in mind.
5. Document the threats.
6. Rate the threats and prioritize them, considering the potential consequences if an attacker were able to exploit each threat to compromise your application.

The objective of this process is to uncover weaknesses in design and implementation and to direct your efforts toward addressing the most serious weaknesses. You must repeat this security review process at various times throughout the lifetime of your project to keep security concerns at the top of your agenda. One book that will help you adopt this technique and other good security practices is *The Security Development Lifecycle* by Michael Howard and Steve Lipner (Microsoft Press, 2006).

Why You Should Not Hard-Code Secrets

In Chapter 7, "Exchanging Data with Backend Servers," one example explains how to use Simple Object Access Protocol (SOAP) headers to pass user credentials across to a Web service. It includes the following sample code that creates an instance of a Web service proxy and calls the *Authenticate* Web method of the Web service, passing an *AuthHeader* object containing a user name and password in the SOAP headers:

```
private void invokeIt()
{
    // Create a proxy for the Web service.
    SOAPheaderService ws = new SOAPheaderService();
    // Create the AuthHeader object for the SOAP header.
    AuthHeader hdr = new AuthHeader();
    hdr.Username = "andy";
    hdr.Password = "P455w0rd";
    // Set the AuthHeader SOAP header to our AuthHeader object instance.
    ws.AuthHeadervalue = hdr;

    // Call the Web method.
    bool response = ws.Authenticate();
}
```

In Chapter 7 and elsewhere in this book, we warn against hard-coding credentials in this way and refer you to this chapter to find out how to store credentials properly.

Why is it wrong to hard-code credentials? Because Microsoft .NET Framework compilers compile your code not to architecture-dependent machine code but to Microsoft intermediate language (MSIL), which is a CPU-independent set of instructions that can easily be translated to native code at run time by a just-in-time (JIT) compiler. MSIL is optimized for efficient compilation by the JIT compiler but makes no effort toward securing your code or obscuring its purpose. You can take any .NET dynamic-link library (DLL) or executable and decompile it with a tool such as Lutz Roeder's Reflector (*www.aisto.com/roeder/dotnet/*) to reveal the original source code–not formatted exactly as it was first written but in a format that is functionally equivalent (note that you can use a tool such as Reflector to discover the code that exists in the Microsoft Base Class Libraries, which is useful for learning how to write class libraries). You may think that you could institute secure distribution procedures to prevent your compiled code from falling into the wrong hands, but this is impossible to police and does not constitute an effective security policy.

This issue is not limited to managed code. Passwords and other secrets you put in native modules can be just as easily located in the string table. Even if binary data such as a globally unique identifier (GUID) or something similar is used and obfuscated in the data section, simple entropy search tools can find such secrets very quickly.

Understanding Good—and Bad—Techniques for Hiding Secrets

So, if hard-coding secrets is no good, how should you hide secrets from attackers? Here is a list of the techniques that are commonly used, some of which are just plain wrong:

- **Hard-code the secret, but obfuscate the code.** Microsoft Visual Studio 2005 comes with the community edition of Dotfuscator (find it at <*drive*>:\Program Files\Microsoft Visual Studio 8\Application\PreEmptive Solutions\Dotfuscator Community Edition), which you can use to protect your intellectual property. It modifies the MSIL so that it functions the same way but substitutes symbolic names for variable names and performs other modifications. As a result, if you then decompile the MSIL with a tool such as Reflector, the resulting code is very difficult to understand (and hence to steal). However, this is *not* a security tool. Obfuscation cannot change the values of constants, so your hard-coded secrets are still there, still stored in variables, and they can still be discovered by a determined attacker.
- **Conceal the secret hidden inside some other block of code.** So you think that defining a byte array containing lots of seemingly random bytes, reading it in code into a stream, converting it to a string, and then reading characters 5 to 20 (or some similarly silly attempt at concealment) constitutes security? Your attacker would end up helpless on the floor with laughter.
- **Store it in the registry.** Unencrypted? You might as well paint your secrets in big letters on a billboard. The registry is not a secure store for secrets. An attacker who gets hold of your device can connect it to a computer where Visual Studio 2005 is installed and use the Remote Registry Editor tool to look at what is stored there, or the attacker could download and install a registry editor program on the device. If you can prevent attackers from accessing the device by using a strong power-on password, you can make it difficult for attackers to get access to data stored on the device, including that stored in the registry, although it is still not impossible. (See the section titled "Perimeter Security: Securing Access to the Device" later in this chapter for more information.)
- **Store it encrypted in the registry or in a config file.** Now you are getting there. However, you must have the code in your application to decrypt the stored data.

Encryption algorithms do not have to be kept secret because these algorithms are well understood, and their strength comes from rigorous examination by the cryptography community to validate their efficacy and confirm their unbreakability. However, encryption algorithms require as input an encryption key, along with the data to be encrypted or decrypted, which most definitely must remain a secret. We have seen supposedly secure applications in which the secret data is stored encrypted in a config file, but the key used to decrypt it is hard-coded into the application. This type of coding constitutes only a deterrent that might stop the casual observer of the config file from learning your secret but does not deter the determined attacker.

If you can introduce another secret, such as by requiring the user to enter a password from which you can derive the decryption key, this constitutes a secure solution.

- **Ask the user to enter it every time.** In some circumstances, this might be a solution. In fact, this is what you do every time you log on to your desktop computer that runs the Microsoft Windows operating system–you enter your user name and password to authenticate yourself to the system and gain access to your account. The SqlClient example program described at the beginning of Chapter 7 requires the user to enter the user name and password to pass to Microsoft SQL Server.

  Later in this chapter, we discuss how you can use a user-entered password to create an encryption key that is used to decrypt stored secrets. Often, this is the basis of a security solution if combined with the encryption techniques described later in this chapter. If you use this technique, you must consider the following issues: how often you ask the user for the password so that it does not become an irritation, how you handle the situation when users forget the password, and whether you should force the user to reauthenticate periodically–after all, a mobile device application can often run for days or weeks, so it is no good getting users to enter the secret just once at the beginning and never to ask them again. What if the device is lost or stolen?

  Bear in mind that keeping the original password in memory introduces a weakness where a malicious application could search your process memory at run time and extract the data. Instead, as explained later in this chapter, use the password to generate your encryption key or a hash (a *hash* is a cryptographically derived token for clear text data that cannot be decoded to reveal the original text) right away, and then lose the password–clear screen fields and overwrite the memory that contains the original password.

Good Security Requires User Input

If you read the preceding list carefully, you will come to the inescapable conclusion that the best thing you can do is ask the user directly for the secret or store the secret encrypted and ask the user for a password from which you can derive a decryption key to decrypt the secret. This raises other questions, such as follows:

- If you deploy the application to multiple users, are all users required to use the same password? This would be no good because, if the security is compromised and the password revealed, you would have to recall all your devices, reencrypt the secured data using a new password, and securely distribute the new password to all your users.

- How do you distribute encrypted data, such as a config file containing encrypted data or an encrypted SQL Server Compact Edition (CE) database, to perhaps thousands of devices but provide a way for users to enter their own unique password to decrypt the data?
- What if a user forgets his or her password? How do you reset the password? How do you validate the user's password?

The answer to these questions is to use a combination of encryption techniques, as explained throughout the rest of this chapter. The complete solution is surprisingly easy to implement, particularly if you use the application blocks in the Mobile Client Software Factory, as explained in the next section.

Storing Credentials and Other Secrets Securely

Consider the following requirements for a fictional application: it stores data in a SQL Server CE database, and it communicates with a Web service that authenticates users using Hypertext Transfer Protocol (HTTP) Basic authentication. Your threat analysis has identified the following vulnerabilities:

- The data in the database includes details of your company's customers, so must not fall into the hands of your competitors.
- The Uniform Resource Locator (URL) of the Web service and the credentials required to authenticate must also be kept secret, so as to reduce the likelihood of an attacker trying to break into your backend systems.
- Data transmitted must be unintelligible to anyone who manages to intercept it while it travels across public networks such as the Internet.

To mitigate these risks, you identify the following security requirements for your solution:

- Data in the database will be encrypted.
- The database password, the URL of the Web service, and the user name and password required for authentication to the Web service will be stored encrypted in a config file.
- Your application has many users. For ease of deployment, each device must have the same config file, so your application must have a secure way of storing the decryption key.
- Users of the application each will have their own user name and password that they must enter to start using the application. Only when the user authenticates successfully will the data in the config file be decrypted, the database opened, and the application become functional.

This list of security requirements looks as though it may be difficult to implement. Fortunately, the Microsoft patterns & practices team addressed this scenario in the Mobile Application Blocks in the Mobile Client Software Factory (MCSF). (See Chapter 1, ".NET Compact Framework—a Platform on the Move," for more information about the MCSF and how to download it.) The Mobile Application Blocks expose an application programming interface (API) that is easy to program and that hides the complicated cryptography code that underlies the solution. The description of how to program these application blocks that follows is not a detailed explanation of the underlying cryptography but more a discussion of the practical application of it. For readers who want to understand more about cryptography programming, the section titled "Encrypting Data" later in this chapter gives an introduction to symmetric and asymmetric cryptography. Interested readers are also advised to study the source code of the Mobile Authentication Application Block, which ships with the MCSF.

Protecting Data in SQL Server CE Databases

You can easily accomplish the first requirement in the list, to encrypt the data in the database, without calling on the services of the Mobile Application Blocks. You can apply a password to a SQL Server CE database and optionally encrypt the database using SQL Server 2005 Management Studio or by right-clicking the database in Server Explorer in Visual Studio 2005 and then clicking Database Properties. Select the Set password page, enter the password in the New Password and Confirm Password boxes, and then, if you want encryption, select Encrypt, as shown in Figure 10-1.

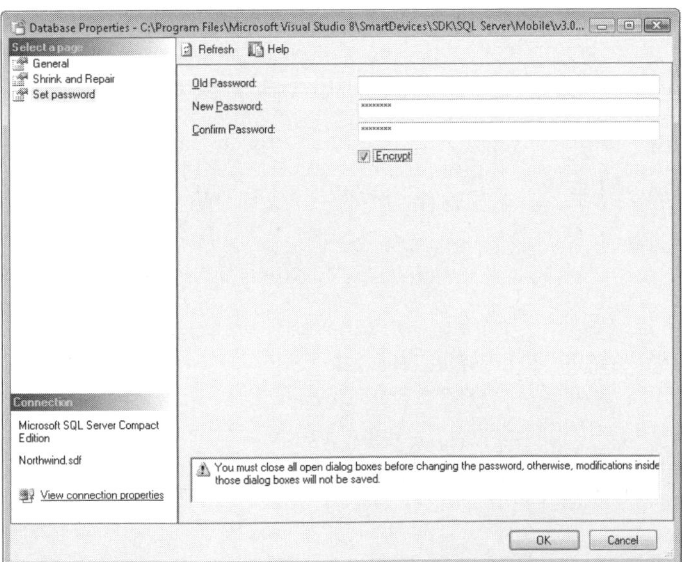

Figure 10-1 Setting a database password and database encryption

SQL Server CE uses the MD5 algorithm for hashing and the RC4 algorithm for encryption.

To access a password-protected database, whether you have turned on encryption or not, simply specify the database password in the connection string–but remember not to hard-code it!

```
private void OpenDatabase(string dbName, string password)
{
    // Connection string is:
    // Data Source="\My Documents\xyz.sdf"; password=pwd
    String connString = @"Data Source=""\My Documents\" + dbName +
        """; Password=" + password;
    SqlCeConnection connection = new SqlCEConnection(connString);
    ...
}
```

Tip There is a downside to encryption: the computational effort it requires means that application performance will suffer and battery life will be reduced. You can avoid these consequences by moving critical data to a separate database and encrypting only that database.

Encrypting a 500-megabyte (MB) database where critical data occupies only 1 MB is overkill and wasteful of resources.

Programming a Secure Solution by Using the Microsoft patterns & practices Application Blocks

The MCSF includes 10 different application blocks, three of which work together to offer the security framework you need to implement the security requirements of the application.

- **Mobile Configuration Block** Reads application configuration files
- **Mobile Authentication Block** Includes methods for validating user name and password
- **Endpoint Catalog** API to expose URLs and credentials stored in a config file

To use these application blocks in a solution, you must add a reference to the *Mobile.Configuration*, *Mobile.Authentication*, and *Mobile.EndpointCatalog* assemblies provided in the MCSF folders, or copy the projects for each of these application blocks into your own solution (the MCSF ships all the source code for the blocks), as has been done for the ApplicationBlocksSecure sample application you can find in the downloadable code for this chapter on this book's companion Web site.

Defining the Configuration File

The .NET Compact Framework version 2.0 does not include classes for reading application config files. The MCSF includes the mobile Configuration Application Block to provide this capability, and when used with the mobile Authentication Block, it also supports reading of encrypted sections in a config file.

The unencrypted configuration file looks something like this:

```
<?xml version="1.0" encoding="utf-8" ?>
<configuration>
  <configSections>
    <section name="Endpoints" type=
    "Microsoft.Practices.Mobile.EndpointCatalog.Configuration.EndpointSection
 ,Microsoft.Practices.Mobile.EndpointCatalog" />
    <section name="SystemSettings"
      type="MobileDevelopersHandbook.SystemSettingsSection,
 MobileDevelopersHandbook.ApplicationBlocksSecure"/>
  </configSections>

  <Endpoints>
 <EndpointItems>
      <add Name="ServerHost"
           Address="https://MyServer/SecureAppServices/Service.asmx"
           UserName="PDAUser" Password="PDAP@ssw0rd"/>
    </EndpointItems>
  </Endpoints>

  <SystemSettings>
    <SystemSettingsItems>
      <add Name="DatabasePassword" Value="M0bileP@ssw0rd" />
    </SystemSettingsItems>
  </SystemSettings>
</configuration>
```

The *<configSections>* element describes the classes that implement the configuration section handlers the runtime uses to decode the other sections in the config file. The first child element inside the *<configSections>* element specifies that the configuration section handler for the *<Endpoints>* section is defined in the *Microsoft.Practices.Mobile.EndpointCatalog* assembly from the MCSF, but the *<SystemSettings>* section is a custom section implemented just for this solution. In this application, you will use this custom section for storing a named item and an associated value and you can see that the example listing just shown uses it to store the value of the database password. Hence, the second child element in the *<configSections>* element that reads *<section name="SystemSettings" type="MobileDevelopersHandbook.SystemSettingsSection, MobileDevelopersHandbook.ApplicationBlocksSecure"/>* tells the runtime that the configuration section handler for the *<SystemSettings>* section is in the *MobileDevelopersHandbook.SystemSettingsSection* type in the *MobileDevelopersHandbook.ApplicationBlocksSecure* assembly (the name of the assembly file for this sample program, which you can find in the downloadable code for this chapter on the book's companion Web site). The code for the *SystemSettingsSection* configuration section handler is shown in Listing 10-1. For more information about using the *Mobile.Configuration* Application Block and defining custom sections, see the MCSF documentation.

Listing 10-1 Configuration Section Handler Definition

```
using System;
using Microsoft.Practices.Mobile.Configuration;

namespace MobileDevelopersHandbook
{
    public class SystemSettingsItemElement : ConfigurationElement
    {
        [ConfigurationProperty("Name", IsRequired = true)]
        public String Name
        {
            get { return (String)this["Name"]; }
        }

        [ConfigurationProperty("Value", IsRequired = true)]
        public String Value
        {
            get { return (String)this["Value"]; }
        }
    }

    public class SystemSettingsItemElementCollection :
        ConfigurationElementCollection
    {
        protected override ConfigurationElement CreateNewElement()
        {
            return new SystemSettingsItemElement();
        }

        protected override Object GetElementKey(ConfigurationElement element)
        {
            SystemSettingsItemElement e = (SystemSettingsItemElement)element;
            return e.Name;
        }
    }

    public class SystemSettingsSection : ConfigurationSection
    {
        [ConfigurationProperty("SystemSettingsItems")]
        public SystemSettingsItemElementCollection SystemSettingsItems
        {
            get
            {
                return
           (SystemSettingsItemElementCollection)(this["SystemSettingsItems"]);
            }
        }
    }
}
```

Encrypting the Configuration File

The next step is to create the encrypted sections in the config file. To help with that, the MCSF comes with a tool called ConfigSectionEncrypt, which you can find (as a Visual Studio 2005 solution) by clicking Start, pointing to All Programs, Microsoft patterns and practices, Mobile Client Software Factory, and then clicking Tools.

When you run the program, copy the text of a config file section that you want to encrypt onto the Section Xml tab, as shown in Figure 10-2 for the *<Endpoints>* section, and then click Encrypt Section. The program encrypts the clear text and displays the Encrypted Section tab, in which it displays the encrypted text. Copy the encrypted text into your app.config, and then delete the clear text version. Repeat the exercise for any other sections you want to encrypt, and after this is complete, your app.config should look something like the following code sample:

```
<?xml version="1.0" encoding="utf-8" ?>
<configuration>
  <configSections>
    <section name="Endpoints" type=… />
    <section name="SystemSettings" type=…/>
  </configSections>

  <EncryptedSection name="Endpoints">AQAQNu3F… …J2M+EN</EncryptedSection>
  <EncryptedSection name="SystemSettings">AQAQymI… …8r7aR</EncryptedSection>
</configuration>
```

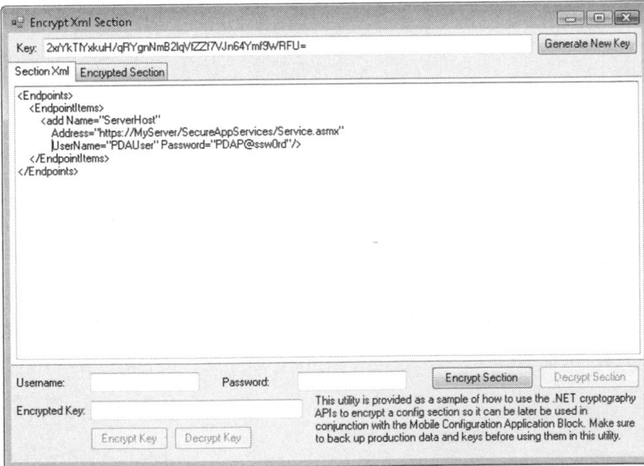

Figure 10-2 ConfigSectionEncrypt tool from the Mobile Client Software Factory

The *Key* text box at the top of ConfigSectionEncrypt shows an encryption key, Base64 encoded, which is very important to the whole system. It is an encryption key for use with the Rijndael symmetric encryption algorithm—symmetric because exactly the same key is used for encryption as is used for decryption. (You can learn more about encryption using symmetric algorithms later in this chapter in the section titled "Encrypting Using the AES Symmetric Algorithm".) If you study the code for the tool, you'll find that the code that generates this key is as follows:

```
using System.Security.Cryptography;
...
public static byte[] GenerateKey()
{
SymmetricAlgorithm algorithm = Rijndael.Create();
return algorithm.Key;
}
```

Advanced Encryption Standard

The Advanced Encryption Standard (AES) is the U.S. government–approved method for encrypting sensitive but unclassified information by U.S. government agencies and is the de facto standard for encryption in the private sector.

Encryption algorithms wear out in the sense that advances in computing power and encryption technology mean that, over time, algorithms become easier to crack and hence less secure. Previously, the U.S. government specification for encryption was the Data Encryption Standard (DES), which was approved in 1976. However, in February 2000, a team of researchers using very powerful computers cracked a DES key in 22 hours; by 2005, using modern computers, the time it took to crack a 56-bit DES key had dropped to less than 5 minutes.

A stronger algorithm, Triple DES (or 3-DES) uses three DES keys, which means that it should be secure enough to see us through the next security generation, which most experts agree will be the next 15 to 20 years, although that could change if computing technology advances faster than anticipated. Strong though 3-DES is, in 1999 the federal government started a process to identify and approve a stronger replacement, one that offers sufficient security to protect data for the next 20 or 30 years.

The result was the selection of the Rijndael algorithm for AES, which became the required method of encryption for the U.S. government in December 2001. AES is computationally more efficient than 3-DES is, and it supports longer key lengths.

It's important to remember that there is no such thing as 100 percent encryption: a 64-bit key in both 3-DES and AES can be cracked in around 70 days using modern computers. If you use a 256-bit key (which is not supported by 3-DES), the time required to crack it increases to 200 days, which effectively makes it computationally infeasible to crack. (Figures were taken from *intelligrid.info/IntelliGrid_Architecture/New_Technologies/Tech_Confidentiality.htm*.)

Creating User-Specific Encrypted Keys

Now you have a config file that contains sensitive data that has been encrypted using a key (which we call the *master* key from now on) and that you can distribute with your application to all target devices. On the device, you need to decrypt the encrypted data, for which you need exactly the same key that was used for encryption. How do you put the encryption key on the device without revealing it to an attacker?

The answer is to assign a user name and password to each user, derive another encryption key from that user name and password, and then use that user-specific encryption key to encrypt the master key. You must transfer the encrypted version of the master key onto the device by some method; this can be as simple as using an unsecured Web service—the data is encrypted, so it can be transferred over unsecure channels. On the device, the user enters his or her user name and password, and those inputs are used to derive the user-specific encryption key, which in turn is used to decrypt the encrypted master key.

This still sounds a little complicated, but fortunately the Mobile Application Blocks in the MCSF provide easy-to-use APIs that make creating user-specific encryption keys quite simple. The first part of the process happens on the server. The software you need is implemented in the ConfigSectionEncrypt tool that you used to encrypt the config file sections. This tool offers options where you can enter the user name and password, and then click the Encrypt Key button to display the encrypted version (in Base64 encoding) of the master Rijndael key, as shown in Figure 10-3.

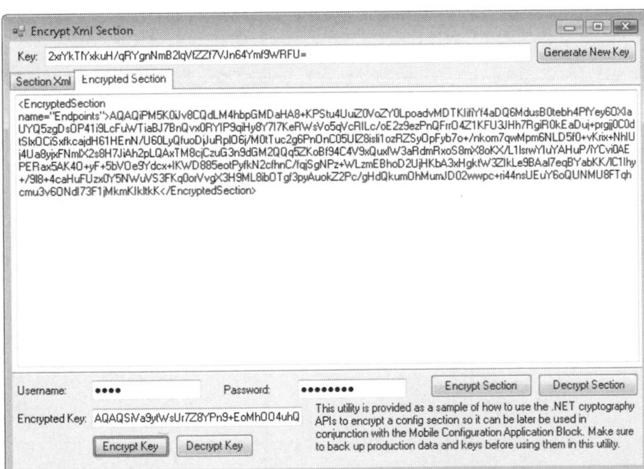

Figure 10-3 Encrypting the master key using an encryption key derived from the user name and password

When you click the button, the code that runs to create the encrypted key is as follows:

```
using System.Security.Cryptography;
using Microsoft.Practices.Mobile.PasswordAuthentication;
...
    public static byte[] EncryptKey(
        string username, string password, byte[] key)
    {
        using (RsaAesCryptographyProvider provider =
            new RsaAesCryptographyProvider(containerName))
        {
            PasswordIdentity identity =
                new PasswordIdentity(username, password, provider);
            Rijndael algorithm = Rijndael.Create();
            CryptographyBlock block =
                new CryptographyBlock(algorithm, identity.CryptoKey);
            return block.Encrypt(key, algorithm.IV);
        }
    }
```

This code creates an *RsaAesCryptographyProvider* instance, which is a class in the *Microsoft.Practices.Mobile.PasswordAuthentication* namespace that handles much of the work required for encryption and decryption. Its constructor takes a string parameter, which is the name of a key store where the Cryptographic Service Provider (CSP; the underlying cryptography provider exposed by the operating system) stores its keys; you should use an application-specific name for this. The *RsaAesCryptographyProvider* instance, along with the user name and password, is passed to the constructor of a *PasswordIdentity* instance. To get a cryptographic key derived from the user name and password, you get the *CryptoKey* property of the *PasswordIdentity* class, and this key is passed to the constructor of a *CryptographyBlock* object, along with a *System.Security.Cryptography.Rijndael* instance. The last line of this code uses the *CryptographyBlock.Encrypt* method to encrypt the master key. In this way, you have encrypted the master key using a key derived from the user name and password.

If you click the Encrypt Key button many times, you may notice something interesting. The encrypted key that is displayed changes each time you click the button. That is because the Rijndael algorithm actually uses two ingredients to encrypt data: an encryption key and an initialization vector (IV); an IV is otherwise known as a seed. Notice that the call to *CryptographyBlock.Encrypt* takes two parameters: the data to be encrypted and an IV. Each time you create an instance of the Rijndael class, which happens each time you run this method in the code *Rijndael algorithm = Rijndael.Create();*, it generates a new IV. Introducing a different IV each time means that the cipher text changes each time, which means that if you send a series of encrypted messages out over the network that were created from the same clear text data, the cipher text will be different each time, which makes it harder for an attacker who intercepts it to crack the encryption by looking for repeating patterns. It also means that when you are ready to decrypt the cipher text, you need to know not only the encryption key but also the IV that was used when the text was encrypted. If you study the code for the *Cryptography.Encrypt* and *Decrypt* methods (included in the source code for the mobile Authentication Application Block), you can see that the solution is to include the IV (unencrypted) at the beginning of the block of encrypted bytes, from where it can be retrieved by the *Decrypt* method.

At first glance, storing the IV at the beginning of the block of encrypted bytes seems to offer little in the way of security. After all, the attacker can find the IV there too. That is true, but what you are doing by using an IV (or seed) is introducing another random ingredient into the encryption process. Rijndael is more usually used to encrypt data to transfer between two entities, each of which possesses the same shared key. If these entities exchange a series of messages but no seed is used, and some of the messages are identical, the cipher text will also be identical; the attacker can gain information about the data by observing duplicates. If the same clear text messages are encrypted and sent but a seed *is* used, the cipher text will be different, so this route of analysis is blocked to the attacker. Revealing the seed to the attacker does not compromise the encryption because the attacker still needs the shared key—as well as the seed—to decrypt the data.

In this sample application, you store the user names and the encrypted keys in an Extensible Markup Language (XML) file, which looks something like the following (the XML file also includes an attribute called *Token*, which is explained in the next section):

```
<?xml version="1.0" encoding="utf-8" ?>
<Users>
  <User Name="Bill"
        Token="AQAKK90fWdPpq+Umc4tTmwy9u61JD+nPEPu6Hlke"
        EncKey="AQAQbQR3QmZ1wUNfJI73gllp5tCt9gGjAn… …04nl4thG+FvwL/Ng=="/>
  <User Name="Mary"
        Token="AQAYAVjIVA94wzLv2rXRRYSES14zJ3vjR2OFHrd4"
        EncKey="AQAQbqT2rGTFiwW/iZTBh85myiPHuu26eA0xuG99As… …VgMPeaFoQ=="/>
  <User Name="Joe"
        Token="AQAsocb1MW6WiOV/bzj1yqehrYAKP05dWq808gF5"
        EncKey="AQAQXG+00D408eajDnmoJ/… …LAMGZOKSOYquZQ7RdI9N/MjA=="/>
</Users>
```

Notice that although the user name is included in clear text, the password is not, for obvious reasons. Only a user who knows the correct password for the user name is able to decrypt the encoded key and hence decrypt the configuration file. For simplicity, this file is included in the sample application as content, but in a real application you could distribute it to clients using any of the techniques described in Chapter 7.

Creating Tokens for User Authentication

The code in the ConfigSectionEncrypt tool encrypts the master key, but that in itself is not sufficient for authenticating users. You could derive a key from the user name and password that the user enters and then try to decrypt the encrypted master key and the configuration file and see if the results made sense—but that is not an efficient way of testing whether the correct user name and password were entered.

Instead, the mobile Password Authentication Application Block provides the *AuthenticationToken* class to help with the process of authenticating users, which you use in two ways:

- To create a hash token from the user name and password, which you transfer to the point of authentication on the device (just as you do with the encrypted master key)
- To perform authentication of a user name and password using an existing hash token

Even if you know the user name and the hash token, you cannot derive the password, so hash tokens are a good way of passing a representation of users' credentials around a network without risk of exposing those credentials.

The code for creating the hash token is very simple. In the sample code for this chapter, in the ApplicationBlocksSecure sample, you can find the desktop program UserTokens. This simple program includes text boxes that accept the user name and password, and a button. When you click the button, the program displays the user token. The code behind the button is very simple:

```
using Microsoft.Practices.Mobile.PasswordAuthentication;
...
        private void buttonShowToken_Click(object sender, EventArgs e)
        {
            using (RsaAesCryptographyProvider provider =
                new RsaAesCryptographyProvider("MobileDevelopersHandbook"))
            {
                PasswordIdentity identity = new PasswordIdentity(
                    textBoxUsername.Text, textBoxPassword.Text, provider);
                AuthenticationToken token = new AuthenticationToken(identity);
                textBoxToken.Text = token.TokenData;
            }
        }
```

All you need to do is to include the user tokens in the XML user file (as shown previously), and the server-side processing is complete.

Authenticating the User and Decrypting the Config File on the Device

On the device side, you must implement a login screen where the user can enter the user name and password, such as the one shown on the left side of Figure 10-4.

Figure 10-4 Login screen and main form from the sample program

The code to authenticate the user and to decrypt the configuration file is quite simple, as shown in Listing 10-2. This *LoginForm* class takes a reference to a *Dictionary<string, string>* in its constructor, and it returns the decrypted information from the config file in this *Dictionary*. For simplicity (although not for efficiency!), this example reads the contents of the Users XML file into a *DataSet*.

The code to authenticate the user in the *AuthenticateUser* method is very simple and uses the alternative constructor to *AuthenticationToken* that takes an existing token, different from the one you used previously to create the token initially. The method then calls the *AuthenticationToken.Authenticate* method, which takes as parameters the user name and password the user entered on the login form, and also an instance of *RsaAesCryptographyProvider* to handle the encryption duties. Internally, it then generates a new token from the user name and password and checks that it matches the token you supplied. If this authentication succeeds, it returns a *PasswordIdentity* object; otherwise, *null*.

Listing 10-2 Login Form That Authenticates the User and Decrypts the Configuration File

```
using System;
using System.Collections.Generic;
using System.Data;
using System.Windows.Forms;
using Microsoft.Practices.Mobile.PasswordAuthentication;
using Microsoft.Practices.Mobile.Configuration;
using System.Security.Cryptography;

namespace MobileDevelopersHandbook
{
    public partial class LoginForm : Form
    {
        private DataSet users;
```

```
    private Dictionary<string, string> configSettings = null;

    public LoginForm(Dictionary<string, string> settings)
    {
        InitializeComponent();

        configSettings = settings;
    }

    private void LoginForm_Load(object sender, EventArgs e)
    {
        Cursor.Current = Cursors.WaitCursor;
        try
        {
            // Get the user details from the Users.xml file.
            users = new DataSet();
            users.ReadXml(GetApplicationDirectory() + @"\Users.xml");
        }
        finally
        {
            Cursor.Current = Cursors.Default;
        }
    }

    private void menuItemSubmit_Click(object sender, EventArgs e)
    {
        for(int rowidx = 0; rowidx < users.Tables[0].Rows.Count; rowidx++)
        {
            DataRow userRow = users.Tables[0].Rows[rowidx];
            if ((string)userRow["Name"] == textBoxUsername.Text)
            {
                Cursor.Current = Cursors.WaitCursor;

                try
                {
                    PasswordIdentity identity =
                        AuthenticateUser((string)userRow["Token"]);
                    if (identity != null && identity.IsAuthenticated)
                    {
                        // Success!! Decrypt the config file.
                        DecryptSettings(
                            identity, (string)userRow["encKey"]);

                        //Close this modal dialog box.
                        this.DialogResult = DialogResult.OK;
                    }
                }
                finally
                {
                    Cursor.Current = Cursors.Default;
                }
            }
        }
```

```
        // Show the login failed message.
        labelIncorrect.Visible = true;
    }

    private PasswordIdentity AuthenticateUser(string userToken)
    {
        using (RsaAesCryptographyProvider provider =
            new RsaAesCryptographyProvider("MobileDevelopersHandbook"))
        {
            // Create AuthenticationToken using existing token.
            AuthenticationToken token =
                new AuthenticationToken(userToken);
            PasswordIdentity identity = token.Authenticate(
                textBoxUsername.Text, textBoxPassword.Text, provider);
            // return result - caller checks Authenticated property to
            // see authentication result
            return identity;
        }
    }

    private void DecryptSettings(
        PasswordIdentity identity, string userEncryptedConfigurationKey)
    {
        // Obtain the user's key.
        byte[] userKeyBytes = identity.CryptoKey;

        // Create an instance of the CryptographyBlock class.
        SymmetricAlgorithm symmetric = Rijndael.Create();
        CryptographyBlock block =
            new CryptographyBlock(symmetric, userKeyBytes);

        // Get the user's encrypted configuration key.
        byte[] configKeyBytes =
            Convert.FromBase64String(userEncryptedConfigurationKey);

        // Decrypt the key
        byte[] configurationKey = block.Decrypt(configKeyBytes);

        // Create a configuration provider to decrypt the config file.
        RijndaelConfigurationProvider configProvider =
            new RijndaelConfigurationProvider(configurationKey);

        // Assign the new instance of the RijndaelConfigurationProvider
        // class to the ConfigurationManager.
        ConfigurationManager.ProtectedConfigurationProvider
            = configProvider;

        // Finally, use the GetSection method of the ConfigurationManager
        // to retrieve the section you want.
        String sectionName = "SystemSettings";
        SystemSettingsSection configSection =
            ConfigurationManager.GetSection(sectionName)
            as SystemSettingsSection;
```

```
            // Store the decrypted data in the settings collection.
            foreach (SystemSettingsItemElement item in
                configSection.SystemSettingsItems)
            {
                configSettings.Add(item.Name, item.Value);
            }
        }

        private string GetApplicationDirectory()
        {
            return System.IO.Path.GetDirectoryName(
                System.Reflection.Assembly.GetExecutingAssembly()
                .GetModules()[0].FullyQualifiedName);
        }
    }
}
```

After the user is authenticated, you can retrieve the key created from the user name and password by getting the *PasswordIdentity.CryptoKey* property. Use the *PasswordIdentity.CryptoKey* property to decrypt the master key, and use the decrypted master key to decrypt the configuration file. The code to do all this is in the *DecryptSettings* method in Listing 10-2 and is fairly self-explanatory.

Handling Changed or Forgotten Passwords

This system is easy to extend to handle a change password facility. On the device, you could run code similar to that already discussed in this chapter to decrypt the encrypted master key using the user name with the old password and then encrypt it again using the new password. You must use some method of sending the encrypted master key for that user to the server, such as a Web service call, so that the copies of user-specific keys held by your administration functionality are kept in sync.

If a user forgets his or her password, you must set a new one. The password is not stored anywhere in this system, and you cannot decode the user token to discover it. Instead, your administrator must set a new password for that user, generate a new user token and encrypted master key, and then get those onto the device either by simple file transfer (as in the sample used in this chapter) or by a Web service call or some other data synchronization method.

Encrypting Data

The Microsoft patterns & practices mobile Password Authentication and mobile Configuration Application Blocks provide encryption and authentication services that meet the needs of many line-of-business mobile applications. However, they do not provide solutions for every security and encryption need. In this section, we discuss how to use the *System.Security.Cryptography* namespace directly to perform common encryption tasks.

Encrypting Using the AES Symmetric Algorithm

A symmetric algorithm is one in which exactly the same key is used for encryption and decryption. The most commonly used symmetric algorithm is Rijndael, which is the algorithm selected for the U.S. government Advanced Encryption Standard (see the sidebar titled "Advanced Encryption Standard" earlier in this chapter).

The following example shows how to use Rijndael to save data in encrypted form in a file on the device or a storage card. The sample application, called Encryption, which is included in the downloadable samples for this chapter on the book's companion Web site, implements a personal encryption facility for a user. With this program, you can enter some text on-screen, and then the user can tap the Save menu button that prompts the user for a password, derives an encryption key from the password, encrypts the text, and saves it. The next time you run the program, the user can tap the Restore menu button, which prompts the user for the password again, derives the key from the password, and decrypts the cipher text for display on the screen (see Figure 10-5).

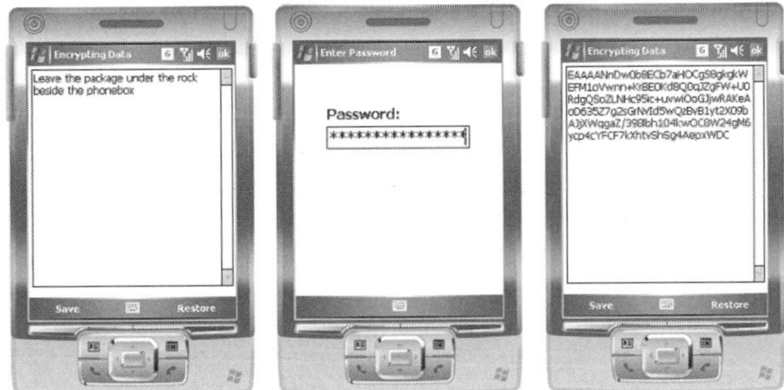

Figure 10-5 Screens from the Encryption sample that encrypts text using Rijndael

Deriving the Key from a Text String

The first piece of interesting code in this sample is used to derive an encryption key from the password text the user enters. The Rijndael algorithm requires a key that is 128, 160, 192, 224, or 256 bits in length (although only the 128-, 192-, and 256-bit key sizes are specified in the AES). No methods in any of the managed classes in *System.Security.Cryptography* can help you derive a key of a specified length from variable-length text, so you must make native function calls using Platform Invocation Services (PInvoke) into the native Crypto API. These calls are complex, and rather than explain them here, the sample takes the pragmatic approach of using the *CryptNativeHelper.GetPasswordDerivedKey* method in the mobile Password Authentication Block, which already wraps the necessary calls to create a 256-bit key. If you are interested in the exact logic, examine the source code for the mobile Password Authentication Block.

```
using Microsoft.Practices.Mobile.PasswordAuthentication;
...
       private byte[] DeriveKeyFromPassword(string password)
        {
            byte[] key;
            using (RsaAesCryptographyProvider provider =
                new RsaAesCryptographyProvider("DevelopersHandbook"))
            {
                CryptNativeHelper crypto = new CryptNativeHelper(provider);
                key = crypto.GetPasswordDerivedKey(password);
            }

            return key;
        }
```

Encrypting

Using the key, the sample calls the following method to do the encryption:

```
using System.IO;
using System.Security.Cryptography;
...
        /// <summary>
        /// Encrypts a string using Rijndael/AES symmetric key algorithm
        /// </summary>
        /// <param name="enckey">The encryption key</param>
        /// <param name="plainText">String to be encrypted</param>
        /// <returns>Encrypted data as a Base64 encoded string</returns>
        private string EncryptData(byte[] key, string plainText)
        {
            // Get the bytes to encrypt.
            byte[] plaintextByte =
                System.Text.Encoding.Unicode.GetBytes(plainText);

            // Create a Rijndael instance.
            RijndaelManaged rijndael = new RijndaelManaged();

            // Set encryption mode.
            rijndael.Mode = CipherMode.ECB;
            rijndael.Padding = PaddingMode.PKCS7;

            // Create a random initialization vector.
            rijndael.GenerateIV();
            byte[] iv = rijndael.IV;

            string encodedText = "";

            // Define memory stream that will be used to hold encrypted data.
            MemoryStream memStrm = new MemoryStream();

            // Write the IV length and the IV.
```

```
        memStrm.Write(BitConverter.GetBytes(iv.Length), 0, 4);
        memStrm.Write(iv, 0, iv.Length);

        // Create a symmetric encryptor.
        using (ICryptoTransform encryptor =
            rijndael.CreateEncryptor(key, iv))
        {
            // Create a CryptoStream to write to the output file.
            CryptoStream cryptStrm = new CryptoStream(
                memStrm, encryptor, CryptoStreamMode.Write);

            // Write the content to be encrypted.
            cryptStrm.Write(plaintextByte, 0, plaintextByte.Length);
            cryptStrm.FlushFinalBlock();

            // Convert encrypted data from memory stream into byte array.
            byte[] cipherTextBytes = memStrm.ToArray();

            // Close the streams.
            memStrm.Close();
            cryptStrm.Close();

            // Convert encrypted byte array into a base64-encoded string.
            encodedText = Convert.ToBase64String(cipherTextBytes);
        }
        return encodedText;
    }
```

The method generates an initialization vector (IV) and stores it unencrypted in the first few bytes of the block of encrypted data, preceded by 4 bytes that give the length of the IV. (We discussed IVs earlier in this chapter in the section titled "Creating User-Specific Encrypted Keys.") To actually perform the encryption, you create an encryptor (as an *ICryptoTransform* instance) by calling the *RijndaelManaged.CreateEncryptor(key, iv)* method:

```
using (ICryptoTransform encryptor = rijndael.CreateEncryptor(key, iv)) {…}
```

Pass the resulting *ICryptoTransform* object, along with the output stream where you want to write the result, to the constructor of a *CryptoStream* object:

```
CryptoStream cryptStrm =
    new CryptoStream(memStrm, encryptor, CryptoStreamMode.Write);
```

Then simply write the clear text (as a byte array) to the *CryptoStream*, which encrypts it using the encryptor and writes it to the output stream:

```
cryptStrm.Write(plaintextByte, 0, plaintextByte.Length);
```

Decrypting

Unsurprisingly, the method that does the decryption is very similar:

```
using System.IO;
using System.Security.Cryptography;
...
        private string DecryptData(byte[] key, string encryptedData)
        {
            string retStr = "";

            // Create a symmetric decryptor.
            RijndaelManaged rijndael = new RijndaelManaged();
            rijndael.Mode = CipherMode.ECB;
            rijndael.Padding = PaddingMode.PKCS7;

            // Convert the ciphertext into a byte array.
            byte[] cipherTextBytes = Convert.FromBase64String(encryptedData);
            // Define memory stream to use to read encrypted data.
            MemoryStream inStream = new MemoryStream(cipherTextBytes);

            // Read the IV length from the buffer.
            int ivLength = BitConverter.ToInt32(cipherTextBytes, 0);
            // Reposition to after 'length' bytes in stream.
            inStream.Position = 4;

            // Read the IV from the input stream.
            byte[] iv = new byte[ivLength];
            inStream.Read(iv, 0, ivLength);

            using (ICryptoTransform decryptor =
                rijndael.CreateDecryptor(key, iv))
            {
                // Create a CryptStream to read from the file.
                CryptoStream cryptStrm = new CryptoStream(
                    inStream, decryptor, CryptoStreamMode.Read);

                // Create another MemoryStream for the output.
                MemoryStream memStrm = new MemoryStream();
                byte[] buffer = new byte[2048];
                int totalbytes = 0;
                do
                {
                    int bytesRead = cryptStrm.Read(buffer, 0, buffer.Length);
                    if (bytesRead == 0)
                        break;
                    memStrm.Write(buffer, 0, bytesRead);
                    totalbytes += bytesRead;
                } while (true);

                // Write the content to be encrypted.
                memStrm.Flush();
                memStrm.Seek(0, SeekOrigin.Begin);
```

```
            // Get the string from the bytes you read.
            retStr = System.Text.Encoding.Unicode.GetString(
                memStrm.GetBuffer(), 0, totalbytes);
            cryptStrm.Close();
        }
        return retStr;
    }
```

The main difference from the encryption processing is that the length of the IV is retrieved from the first 4 bytes, and then the IV is retrieved. After that, you create a decryptor (as an *ICryptoTransform* instance) using *Rijndael.CreateDecryptor(key, iv)* and pass the input stream containing the encrypted bytes and the decryptor to the constructor of a *CryptoStream*, which this time you open using *CryptoStreamMode.Read*. You then read the encrypted bytes using the *CryptoStream*, which decrypts the stream and writes the clear text to an output buffer.

Encrypting Using the RSA Asymmetric Algorithm

The symmetric encryption algorithm just discussed is quite efficient, in encryption terms. Generally, if you want to encrypt large blocks of data, you should always use a symmetric algorithm such as Rijndael. However, symmetric algorithms have the disadvantage of using the same key for both encryption and decryption. If you want to send encrypted data over a network, how can you send the key to the recipient without it being revealed to an attacker? (Note that this is one of the problems that Secure Sockets Layer (SSL) solves; SSL is the underlying protocol that you use when you access *https://* URLs.)

The answer is to encrypt the symmetric key using an *asymmetric* algorithm and send it to the recipient first so that both sides have the same symmetric key, and then subsequent encryption can proceed using the symmetric key. An asymmetric algorithm, such as RSA (which stands for the initials of the algorithm's inventors, Rivest, Shamir, and Adleman), uses a pair of keys, one called the private key, the other the public key. With asymmetric algorithms, anything encrypted using the public key can be decrypted only by using the private key, and anything encrypted using the private key can be decrypted only by using the public key. When you generate a key pair, you keep the private key secure–it is for your personal use only–but the public key you distribute widely; publish it on the Internet if you want. If you know only the public key, you cannot derive the private key.

Now if someone–say his name is Bill–wants to send someone else–call her Alice–a secure message, all Bill has to do is encrypt the message using Alice's public key. The encrypted message can be decrypted only by the private key, which is held only by Alice. If Bill and Alice want to exchange a lot of encrypted data, Bill can generate a symmetric key (a Rijndael key), encrypt it using Alice's public RSA key, and then send the symmetric key to her. Alice decrypts the symmetric key using her private RSA key and waits for the next message from Bill, which will be a block of data encrypted using the symmetric key. Figure 10-6 shows how this process works.

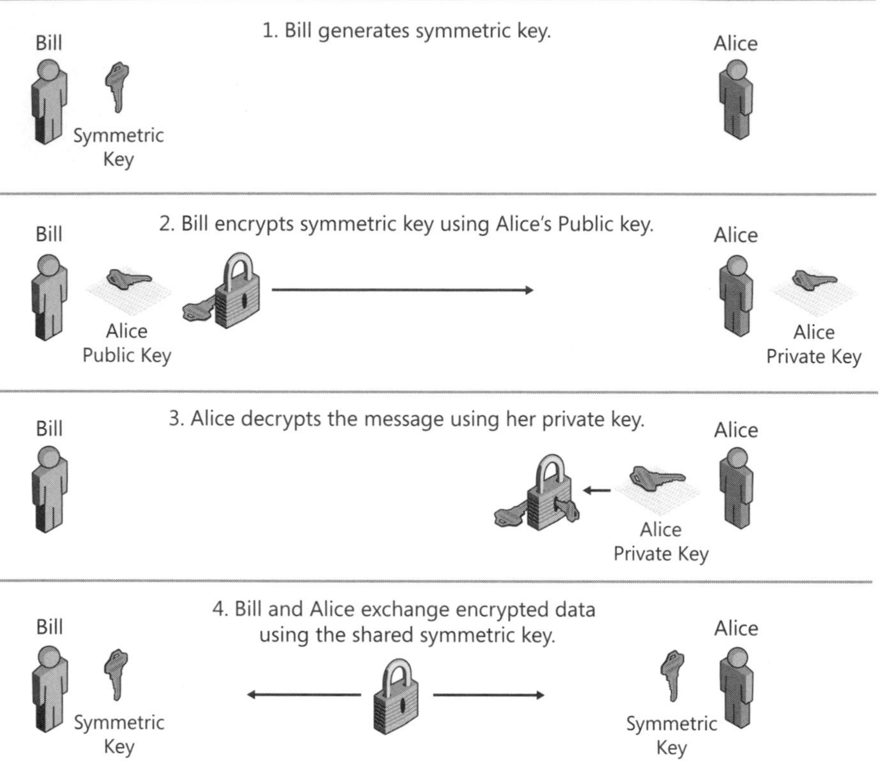
1. Bill generates symmetric key.
Bill
Alice
Symmetric Key
2. Bill encrypts symmetric key using Alice's Public key.
Bill
Alice
Alice Public Key
Alice Private Key
3. Alice decrypts the message using her private key.
Bill
Alice
Alice Private Key
4. Bill and Alice exchange encrypted data using the shared symmetric key.
Bill
Alice
Symmetric Key
Symmetric Key

Figure 10-6 Exchanging a shared key securely using a public–private key pair

Asymmetric encryption is slow compared to symmetric—1,000 times slower—and the computational effort required will drain a device battery quickly. These are the reasons why asymmetric key encryption is usually used for symmetric key exchange rather than for bulk encryption.

Using key pairs for authentication

Because of the properties of asymmetric keys, you can do digital signatures. Remember that Alice's public key is public property and can be used by many individuals. So how can Alice be sure that it is really Bill that is sending her the symmetric key encrypted using her RSA public key? Bill must generate his own pair of RSA keys and send his public key to Alice. Now, after he encrypts the symmetric key by using Alice's public key, he encrypts it again, but this time by using his private key. When Alice receives the data, she decrypts it using Bill's public key; if that succeeds, she knows the data must have come from Bill because only Bill can have encrypted it using his private key. She then decrypts the data again using her private key to obtain the symmetric key to use for subsequent message exchanges.

This description is somewhat of a simplification, but it explains at a high level how to use RSA to support encryption and authentication.

Generating RSA Keys

We can illustrate one use of RSA by extending the personal encryption example used earlier in this chapter. In that example, the user is asked for a password that is used to derive the key for encrypting and later decrypting the data. What if the user forgets his or her password? How could you access the encrypted data?

One solution is to use the public key of an RSA key pair to encrypt the user's password and save it to a file. If the user forgets the password, you can transfer the file to a desktop Windows computer, where you can run a program that uses the private key from the RSA key pair to decrypt the file. In the sample code for this chapter on the book's companion Web site, you can find the DesktopKeyUnlocker project, which implements the desktop component of this solution, and the EncryptionWithAdminUnlock project, which is the same as the Encryption sample used earlier and with the addition of the encryption of the user-entered password using the RSA public key.

The desktop component, DesktopKeyUnlocker, has two functions:

- To generate a key pair and print out the public key as an XML string
- To use the private key to decrypt some data that has been encrypted using the public key

The following code is used to fetch an existing key pair from a named key container (which is a name you specify for a user-specific logical container) or to generate a new key pair if the key container does not already exist. The key pair is persisted by a Windows component called the Cryptographic Service Provider (CSP); the exact location is implementation dependent but is usually the Windows registry:

```
using System.Security.Cryptography;
…
        private string GetRSAKeyPair(string containerName)
        {
            //Create a CryptoServiceProvider Parameter object.
            CspParameters cspParams = new CspParameters();
            // Set the key container name that has the RSA key pair.
            cspParams.KeyContainerName = containerName;
            //Set the CSP Provider Type PROV_RSA_FULL.
            cspParams.ProviderType = 1;
            //Set the CSP Provider Name
            cspParams.ProviderName =
                "Microsoft Enhanced Cryptographic Provider v1.0";

            //Create a new RSA provider, pass CspParameters to the constructor.
            //If specified key container doesn't exist, creates a new key pair
            rsaprovider = new RSACryptoServiceProvider(cspParams);
```

```
        //Indicate that you would like the new key pair to be persisted in
        // the key container specified.
        rsaprovider.PersistKeyInCsp = true;

        //Return the PUBLIC key info.
        return rsaprovider.ToXmlString(false);
    }
```

In the sample program, you call this method like this:

```
        string publicKey = GetRSAKeyPair("DesktopKeyUnlockerContainer");
```

When you run the program, it displays the public key, as shown in Figure 10-7. The first time you run it, it generates the key pair, but on subsequent runs, it retrieves the persisted key pair and so displays the same public key.

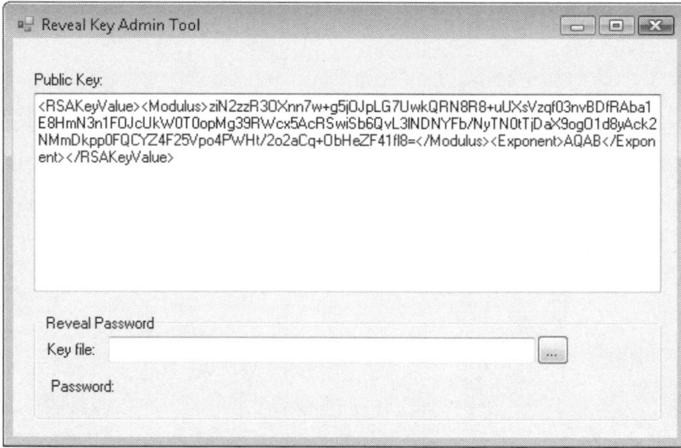

Figure 10-7 The DesktopKeyUnlocker program displaying the public key from the RSA key pair

Keeping Private Keys Secure

As you have probably realized already, keeping private keys secure is absolutely essential. On desktop Windows, that task is made easier by the *RSACryptoServiceProvider*, which persists key containers in a user-protected private key store; only the Windows user who created the keys can access the private key store because the master key used to unlock the store is derived from the Windows user credentials. You can also use the .NET Framework 2.0 *System.Security.Cryptography.ProtectedData* class, which wraps a native API called Data Protection API (DPAPI) and gives you an alternative way of securing private keys (and other secure data) in a user-specific (or machine-specific) secure store.

On Windows Mobile, the underlying platform does not provide the same level of support for this kind of functionality because users do not log onto a Windows CE–based device using Windows user credentials. You must use an encryption technique such as that described in the section titled "Encrypting Using the AES Symmetric Algorithm" earlier in this chapter. As an alternative, you can use the implementation of the *ProtectedData* class in the OpenNetCF Smart Device Framework (see Chapter 1 for details of how to get the OpenNetCF Framework). As mentioned earlier, *ProtectedData* wraps DPAPI, which on a device encrypts the data using a key it generates that is specific to the device on which you execute the code. This means that it can be decrypted only on the device where the data was encrypted, which removes the risk of off-device attacks.

Encrypting Using the RSA Public Key

In the sample application EncryptionWithAdminUnlock, the public key is stored in an XML file:

```
<?xml version="1.0" encoding="utf-8" ?>
<RSAKeyValue>
  <Modulus>ziN2zzR3OXnn7w+… …o2aCq+ObHeZF41f18=</Modulus>
  <Exponent>AQAB</Exponent>
</RSAKeyValue>
```

The complete code to read the key and modulus from the XML file, to encrypt the string, and to save it in a file is shown in Listing 10-3. The *SavePassword* method creates an instance of *RSACryptoServiceProvider*, imports an *RSAParameters* instance that has been set up with the key and modulus of the public key by the *ReadPublicKeyXML* method, and then calls the *RSACryptoServiceProvider.Encrypt* method to perform the encryption. The result is saved to a file.

Listing 10-3 *EncryptPasswordRSA* Class to Encrypt Using an RSA Public Key

```
using System;
using System.Text;
using System.Security.Cryptography;
using System.IO;
using System.Xml;

namespace Encryption
{
    class EncryptPasswordRSA
    {
        public void SavePassword(string cleartext)
        {
            RSACryptoServiceProvider rsaProvider =
                new RSACryptoServiceProvider();
            //Create a new instance of RSAParameters.
            RSAParameters RSAKeyInfo = new RSAParameters();
```

```
        RSAKeyInfo = ReadPublicKeyXML(RSAKeyInfo);

        //Import key parameters into RSA.
        rsaProvider.ImportParameters(RSAKeyInfo);

        //Encrypt the supplied data.
        byte[] cipherText = rsaProvider.Encrypt(
            new UnicodeEncoding().GetBytes(cleartext), false);

        //Save the ciphertext.
        using (System.IO.StreamWriter sw =
            new System.IO.StreamWriter(GetApplicationDirectory() +
                @"\UserKeyCipher.txt", false))
        {
            sw.Write(Convert.ToBase64String(cipherText));
            sw.Flush();
        }
    }

    private RSAParameters ReadPublicKeyXML(RSAParameters RSAKeyInfo)
    {
        // Read the public key from the XML file by using a reader.
        using (Stream stm = File.OpenRead(GetApplicationDirectory() +
            @"\PublicKey.xml"))
        {
            XmlTextReader reader = new XmlTextReader(stm);
            // Search the XML for the required element.
            string ev = reader.NameTable.Add("RSAKeyValue");
            while (reader.Read())
            {
                if (reader.LocalName == ev)
                {
                    // Process it!
                    int eventDepth = reader.Depth;
                    reader.Read();
                    while (reader.Depth > eventDepth)
                    {
                        if (reader.MoveToContent() == XmlNodeType.Element)
                        {
                            switch (reader.Name)
                            {
                                case "Modulus":
                                    RSAKeyInfo.Modulus =
                          Convert.FromBase64String(reader.ReadString());
                                    break;
                                case "Exponent":
                                    RSAKeyInfo.Exponent =
                          Convert.FromBase64String(reader.ReadString());
                                    break;
                            }
                        }
                        reader.Read();
                    }
                }
            }
```

```
            }
            return RSAKeyInfo;
        }


        private string GetApplicationDirectory()
        {
          return System.IO.Path.GetDirectoryName(
              System.Reflection.Assembly.GetExecutingAssembly().
              GetModules()[0].FullyQualifiedName);
        }
    }
}
```

Decrypting Using the RSA Private Key

The decryption function takes place in the DesktopKeyUnlocker program. In the sample scenario, you can help a mobile device user who has forgotten his or her password. Without knowing the password, the user can no longer view the data encrypted earlier, but the user can reveal the password he or she used by copying the file saved by the code in Listing 10-3 over to the administrator's computer. Remember, this file was encrypted using the public key of the administrator's key pair, and so can be decrypted only by the private key, which is known only to the administrator.

The administrator must run the DesktopKeyUnlocker program again. As it starts up, it retrieves the RSA key details from the key store using the *GetRSAKeyPair* method, as described in the section titled "Generating RSA Keys" earlier in this chapter. Then the administrator enters the path to the encrypted password file copied from the device, and the code in the *textBoxFilePath_TextChanged* method (shown just below) calls the *RSACryptoServiceProvider.Decrypt* method to decrypt the contents of the file using the private key and displays the result at the bottom of the screen (see Figure 10-8).

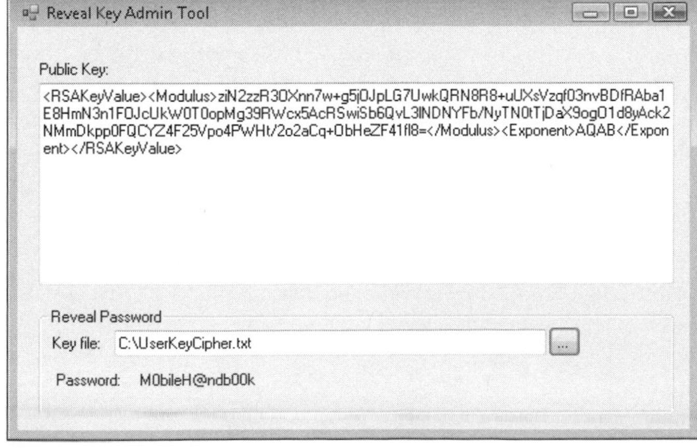

Figure 10-8 Decrypting using the RSA private key—the test program output

The code to do the decryption is in the *TextBox.TextChanged* event handler in the sample and is as follows (remember that the *RSAProvider* object has already been initialized by the *GetRSAKeyPair* method shown previously):

```
private void textBoxFilePath_TextChanged(object sender, EventArgs e)
{
    if (System.IO.File.Exists(textBoxFilePath.Text))
    {
        string cipherBase64 =
            System.IO.File.ReadAllText(textBoxFilePath.Text);
        byte[] cipherText = Convert.FromBase64String(cipherBase64);

        // Decrypt the file using the PRIVATE key.
        byte[] decipheredText =
            rsaprovider.Decrypt(cipherText, false);

        //Display the deciphered message.
        labelResult.Text =
            new UnicodeEncoding().GetString(decipheredText);
    }
}
```

This simple example demonstrates how to use RSA encryption. You can use this technique for encrypting data you send to recipients over an otherwise unsecure channel. You can also authenticate the sender, as described earlier in the sidebar titled "Using Key Pairs for Authentication."

Securing Network Connections

Your Windows Mobile–powered applications will frequently use HTTP to access network resources. If you use Web Services or the *WebRequest/WebResponse* classes described in Chapter 8, "Networking," data transfers take place over the network using HTTP. (HTTP is also used for SQL Server CE Remote Data Access [RDA] and merge replication.) You can encrypt data you transfer over the network using the RSA algorithm (for key exchange) and Rijndael algorithm as explained earlier, although in many cases you would be better advised to take advantage of Secure Sockets Layer (SSL).

SSL is a handshaking and encryption protocol that performs the key exchange and symmetric encryption for you without you having to code anything yourself—apart from changing URLs to start with *https://*. However, on your Web server you must have an X.509 server certificate, which is used to authenticate the Web server so that the client (your program on the mobile device) knows that it is talking to the correct server and has not been tricked by an attacker who has redirected requests to the target URL to its own server.

How you set up your Web server with a server certificate differs from server to server and is beyond the scope of this book. For instructions on setting up Microsoft Internet Information Server (IIS) 6.0 with a secure server certificate, search the IIS 6.0 Documentation page in Microsoft Windows Server 2003 documentation on the Microsoft TechNet at *www.microsoft.com/technet/prodtechnol/WindowsServer2003/Library/IIS*.

An X.509 server certificate contains a digital signature and a private–public key pair and can be used to authenticate the server, but only if it has been issued by a trusted public body called a Certificate Authority (CA). CAs are respected—and regulated—public companies such as VeriSign, GTE, and Thawte. They sell security solutions, including server certificates. You must prove your identity to the CA before the CA will issue a server certificate to you for a specific computer. All certificates they issue are "children" of that CA's root certificate and contain data that identifies their parentage.

As part of the handshake process in SSL, the server presents its digital certificate (which has been encrypted with the private key) and its public key to the client. SSL uses the data in the digital certificate to verify the authenticity of the certificate. It does this by comparing certain attributes with those of the issuing CA's root certificate, which must already be installed in the root certificate store on the device. Because the digital certificate was encrypted using the private key, which is held only by the sender (the Web server), and was issued by the CA, authenticity is established. If the certificate cannot be authenticated, a warning message is issued if you are accessing the site using a browser, or a *System.Net.WebException* will be thrown if you are accessing the server programmatically.

> **Tip** The Windows Mobile team at Microsoft has created a useful tool called SSLChainSaver that helps troubleshoot problems with SSL and also allows easy creation of an XML file you can use for provisioning certificates onto devices. See *blogs.msdn.com/windowsmobile/archive/2006/08/11/sslchainsaver.aspx* for more information.

Root Certificates Installed on a Windows Mobile–Powered Device

Verifiable third-party SSL certificates are issued by trusted root CAs that have a root store presence in Windows Mobile–powered devices. By default, the following root certificates are installed on a device that runs Windows Mobile 5.0:

- Class 2 Public Primary Certification Authority (VeriSign, Inc.)
- Class 3 Public Primary Certification Authority (VeriSign, Inc.)
- Entrust.net Certification Authority (2048)
- Entrust.net Secure Server Certification Authority
- Equifax Secure Certification Authority

- GlobalSign Root CA
- GTE CyberTrust Global Root
- GTE CyberTrust Root
- Secure Server Certification Authority (RSA)
- Thawte Premium Server CA
- Thawte Server CA

Note that devices running Windows Mobile 5.0 that have the Adaptation Kit Update 2 (AKU2) update (Messaging and Security Feature Pack) have the following additional root certificate installed:

http://www.valicert.com/

Note that original equipment manufacturers (OEMs) can choose to ship devices without all these root certificates, and if you are an enterprise user who has complete control over the configuration of the devices you deploy in your organization, you can remove them.

Certificate stores

Certificate stores contain the digital certificates of a mobile device. By default, Windows Mobile–powered devices have the following set of certificate stores:

- The ROOT store contains trusted root certificates that identify root Certificate Authorities. The ROOT store typically contains certificates from a trusted public Certificate Authority. You can view the contents of this store by using the Certificates function in Control Panel.
- The CA store contains trusted intermediate certificates that identify intermediate Certificate Authorities. You can view this store in Control Panel on Windows Mobile 6 but not on Windows Mobile 5 or earlier, and by default, no certificates are installed in this store in shipped devices.
- The MY store contains the user's personal client certificates that are used for client authentication to Web sites, the Microsoft Exchange Server, Secure/Multipurpose Internet Mail Extensions (S/MIME), and so forth. You can view the MY store by using the Certificates function in Control Panel.

- Privileged Execution Trust Authorities and Unprivileged Execution Trust Authorities certificate stores are used by the security loader (part of the Windows CE operating system that assigns security trust levels to code modules when you run them) to control code execution. If an executable can be chained to a certificate in either of these stores, it is considered signed by the security loader and is assigned a trust level depending on the device security policies. If a binary is signed using Microsoft Authenticode technology but cannot be chained to a certificate in either of these stores, it is considered unsigned by the security loader (and likely a message stating that will be displayed).
- The SPC store governs .cab file installation. The .cab installer tries to chain the signature on a .cab to a certificate in this store, following similar rules as described previously for other binaries. All code execution certificates in the previous two stores should also be in this store. For instance, if the device has the Mobile2Market (M2M) certificates, they will also be in this store for application installation. Certificates in the SPC store contain an additional property that indicates to the .cab installer what credential to use when installing the application.

Using a Self-Signed Certificate

For most applications, it is recommended that you install a certificate issued by a Certificate Authority that the device trusts. Alternatively, install a certificate issued by a company that is chained to an authority that the device trusts.

However, a server certificate costs money, and if your application is only for internal use in an organization or is in test phase, you can use a server certificate you issue yourself, called a *self-signed certificate*. On a computer running Microsoft Windows Server 2003, it is quite easy to install Certificate Services, which sets you up as your own CA. You can then create a server certificate.

For more information about self-signed certificates, see the topic "Issuing Your Own Server Certificates" on Microsoft TechNet at *www.microsoft.com/technet/prodtechnol/WindowsServer2003/Library/IIS/f72bde43-2f6a-4424-a890-f25b6c41425f.mspx?mfr=true*.

Validating a Server SSL Certificate in Code

If you are using a self-signed certificate on your Web server and you try to access a resource on the server using Microsoft Pocket Internet Explorer on a device, you receive a warning security alert indicating there is a problem with the site's security certificate, as shown in Figure 10-9.

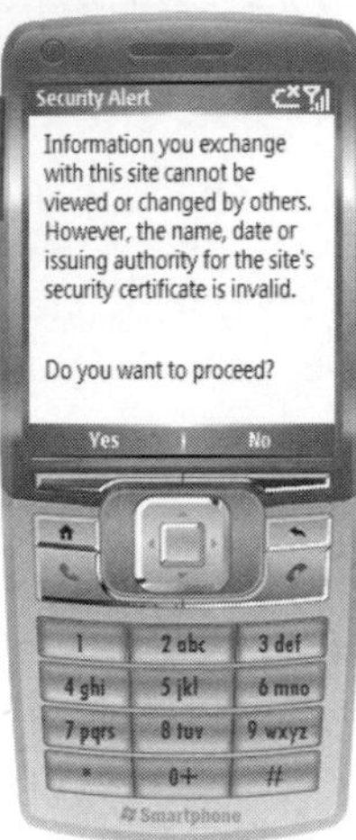

Figure 10-9 Security warning issued because the server certificate cannot be chained back to a root certificate on the device

This warning is issued because the certificate your server presents to the client to authenticate cannot be chained back to any of the root certificates installed on the device. The security alert asks, "Do you want to proceed?" You must click Yes to continue.

If you try to access a Web service on such a server, you get a *WebException* with the message "Could not establish trust relationship with remote server," as shown in Figure 10-10.

Figure 10-10 Message displayed when a Web service call to a server secured with a self-signed certificate fails with a *WebException*

One solution is to install the root certificate on your device, but this may be problematic if your device supplier has set security policy that prevents you from doing this. (See the sidebar titled "Installing Root Certificates on a Windows Mobile–Powered Device" later in this chapter.) The easier solution is to programmatically answer the question, "Do you want to proceed?" You must define a class that implements *System.Net.ICertificatePolicy*, which contains a single method, *CheckValidationResult*; return *true* from this to accept all server certificates. Then set the static *CertificatePolicy* property of *System.Net.ServicePointManager* to an instance of your class before calling the Web service, and the call will succeed. The code required is as follows:

```
using System.Windows.Forms;
using System.Net;
using System.Security.Cryptography.X509Certificates;

public class Form1: Form
{
    …

    private void SetPolicyAndCallWebService()
    {
        System.Net.ServicePointManager.CertificatePolicy =
            new TrustAllCertificatePolicy();
        // Call method to call the SSL-secured Web service.
        CallSecureWebService();
    }
}

public class TrustAllCertificatePolicy : System.Net.ICertificatePolicy
{
    public TrustAllCertificatePolicy()
    { }

    public bool CheckValidationResult(ServicePoint servicepoint,
        X509Certificate cert, WebRequest req, int problem)
    {
        return true;
    }
}
```

Note that in the full .NET Framework 2.0, the *System.Net.ServicePointManager.CertificatePolicy* property is obsolete, and instead you should define a callback on the *System.Net.ServicePointManager.ServerCertificateValidationCallback* property (not supported in .NET Compact Framework). On the full .NET Framework 2.0, use the following to achieve the same result:

```
System.Net.ServicePointManager.ServerCertificateValidationCallback =
    delegate { return true; };
```

Installing root certificates on a Windows Mobile–powered device

Often, installing a root certificate on a device running Windows Mobile 5 is quite problematic. Getting the certificate is usually easy enough; for example, if you have installed Certificate Services on a computer running Windows Server 2003, you can open *http://{server}/certsrv*, request the server certificate, and save it as an X.509 certificate in a .cer file. You can then copy this .cer file onto the device.

If your device is running Windows Mobile 6, the certificate installer is built into the platform so that you can copy the .cer file to your device; just tap on it in File Explorer, and Windows Mobile will install it. This approach usually works on Pocket PC devices running Windows Mobile 5 as well. However, if your device is a Windows Mobile 5 Pocket PC Phone Edition or a Smartphone, this probably will not work because the suppliers of such devices often ship them in a restricted configuration; the exact behavior varies depending on who is the network operator and/or device manufacturer. If you have a restricted device, you must use a utility program that itself has been signed with an appropriate certificate that grants it the rights to install certificates. Some network operators might provide such a utility to allow you to install a root certificate, so consult the support services of your operator to find out. Some device manufacturers who supply phone-enabled devices that are not locked to a particular phone network operator may also provide a utility; at the time of writing, iMate, for example, supplies a utility to install root certificates on its SP5 model Smartphone but not, curiously, for its JasJar Pocket PC Phone Edition device.

One technique–which I used successfully during the writing of this chapter–that may work with one-tier devices, such as Pocket PCs, is to install a root certificate through a .cab file. (See the section titled "One-Tier and Two-Tier Security" later in this chapter for more information about device security configurations). For more information about how to do this, see the article titled "Step-by-Step Guide to Deploying Windows Mobile-based Devices with Microsoft Exchange Server 2003 SP2" at *www.microsoft.com/technet/solutionaccelerators/mobile/deploy/msfp_d.mspx.*

Validating User Input

One of our favorite security maxims is "Never trust user input." Most other factors in your application are under your control, but anything a user supplies crosses a security boundary and should be mistrusted until proved benign.

We described a classic example of this in Chapter 7 when we discussed how a user could perform a SQL injection attack. For example, with the SQL Server CE RDA *SubmitSql* method or classes in *System.Data.SqlClient*, you can execute Transact-SQL (T-SQL) commands directly on a SQL Server database. You might construct the T-SQL statement using code such as "*UPDATE Cars SET Color* ='" + *TextBox1.Text* + "'", and then expect the user to enter values such as *Red*, *Blue*, or *Yellow*.

What if the user enters: "**Red'; DROP TABLE Cars --**" Because SQL Server is quite happy to execute multiple T-SQL statements delimited by a semicolon that you pass to it in a single string (something not supported by SQL Server Compact Edition, incidentally), it will update the Cars table and then delete it!

> **Warning** Although the type of SQL injection attack described here using multiple T-SQL statements affects only SQL Server, other forms of SQL injection attacks are possible with SQL Server CE.

There are two ways of handling this kind of problem:

- If you can limit user options to a known set of values, you can require the user to select from a list box or combo box. In any case, limiting user options to given choices rather than allowing the user to type in a value will probably result in a user interface (UI) that is cleaner and easier to use.
- If you must allow free-form text entry, validate the text users enter. If you are expecting only one word to be entered, you could use the following code to ensure that no punctuation is included:

```
private bool IsValidWord(string input)
{
    bool isValid = true;
    foreach (char c in input)
    {
        if (Char.IsLetterOrDigit(c))
        {
            isValid = false;
            break;
        }
    }
    return isValid;
}
```

You can also achieve this kind of validation—and much more complicated pattern matching—by using regular expressions. For example, the following code validates a name so that it includes only lowercase and uppercase characters, spaces, and an apostrophe for names such as O'Dell, plus the point character. It also limits the length of the field to 40 characters:

```
using System.Text.RegularExpressions;
...
        private bool IsValidName(string input)
        {
            Regex reg = new Regex(@"^[a-zA-Z'.\s]{1,40}$");
            return reg.IsMatch(input);
        }
```

For more information about crafting complex regular expressions, see the Regular-Expressions Web site at *www.regular-expressions.info/tutorial.html*.

The preceding example validates the input to ensure that it is no longer than 40 characters. Remember that in Windows Forms, you can also set the *MaxLength* property of the *TextBox* control to limit the number of characters the user can enter.

Perimeter Security: Securing Access to the Device

So far in this chapter, we've discussed applications of encryption, including how to authenticate a user name and password to protect access to your application and how to encrypt data in databases and files. We have also discussed input validation. If you, the developer, have done your job properly, it really doesn't matter if the device is lost or stolen, does it?

Because there's no such thing as perfect security, you must use defense in depth: Put many obstacles in front of your attackers. If your devices run Windows Mobile, the first thing you should do is use the built-in power-on password. This feature is disabled by default, and when activated you can choose between a simple four-digit personal identification number (PIN) and a strong alphanumeric password—needless to say, the latter is preferred.

Unfortunately, you cannot rely on users to keep the power-on password feature activated. In enterprise applications, you should consider a remote management solution. A number of vendors sell remote management solutions that you can use to enforce sign-on passwords and password complexity rules to deploy software onto devices and to remotely wipe all data from the device should the device be lost or stolen.

Remote Management Using Exchange Server 2003 SP2 and the MSFP

The Messaging and Security Feature Pack (MSFP) is the name of an update to Windows Mobile 5.0 that activated direct push e-mail to devices and certain remote management capabilities. It is also known as the AKU2 update (AKU stands for Adaptation Kit Update, which is the name for a Windows Mobile operating system build that is issued to device manufacturers). You need Exchange Server 2003 SP2 to use these capabilities.

You set security policies for all devices in your domain by using the Exchange System Manager. In Exchange System Manager, under Global Settings in the Mobile Services Properties dialog box, you can set device security settings, as shown in Figure 10-11. You can configure such settings as the minimum password length, the time of inactivity on the device before the password screen is redisplayed, and the number of failed password attempts allowed before the device is automatically wiped.

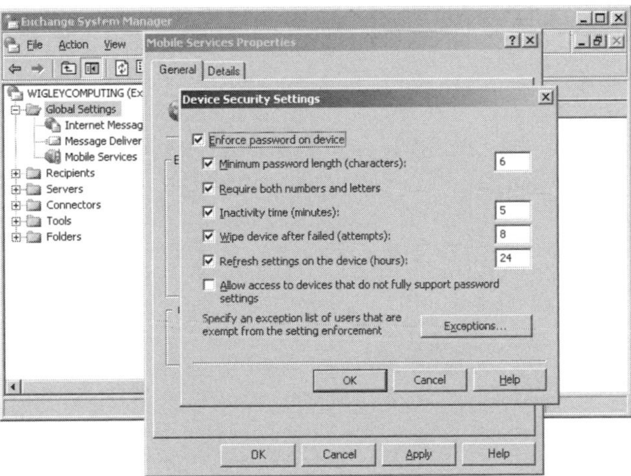

Figure 10-11 Device Security Settings dialog box in Microsoft Exchange System Manager

Once set, these settings are propagated to the devices by direct push over HTTP in under 10 minutes or when the device is next contactable. The next time the device owner performs e-mail synchronization, he or she is required to confirm that Exchange Server enforces the new security settings, as shown in Figure 10-12.

Figure 10-12 Accepting Security Settings Update on the device

If the user loses the device or the device is stolen, an administrator can remotely wipe the device. The administrator opens a Web management interface on the Exchange Server by browsing to *http://{servername}/mobileadmin*. The Remote Wipe option opens the Remote Device Wipe page, where the administrator can select the required device and then select to wipe it (see Figure 10-13). If the device is currently connected to the mobile phone network, or the next time it does connect, it resets itself and returns to its factory state with all applications and data removed. Remember, though, that the device will not be wiped until it connects to the phone network, so you should not rely on this security measure alone to secure sensitive data on your devices.

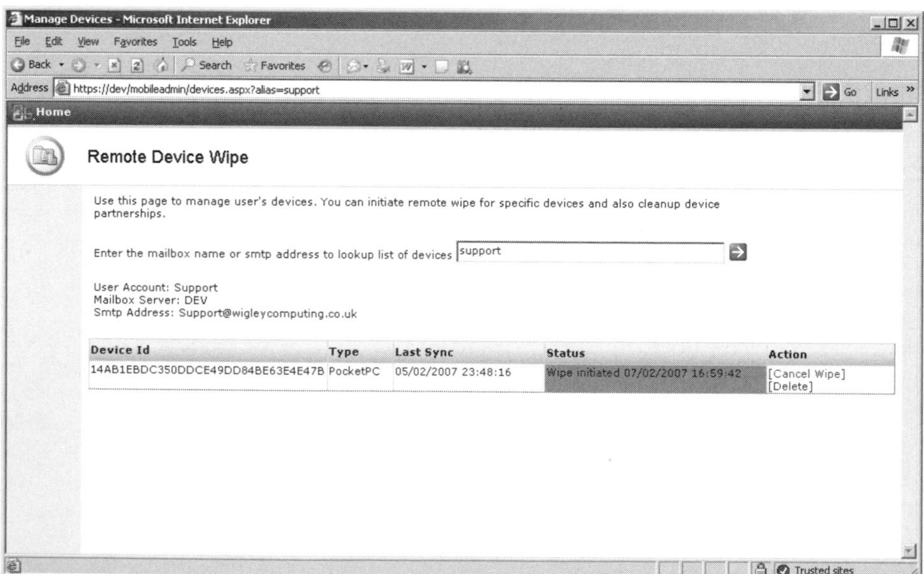

Figure 10-13 Initiating a remote wipe

In Exchange Server 2003, an administrator must initiate the wipe process, but in Exchange Server 2007, a user can connect to a public Web page on your enterprise Web site and initiate the wipe. With this capability, the user can respond more quickly to the event of a lost or stolen device rather than having to contact administrators to initiate the wipe.

Signing Applications

Windows Mobile checks each and every executable module such as dynamic-link libraries (.dll) and executable (.exe) files as they are loaded to validate that the code is signed, the signature is valid, and the signature matches a recognized certificate installed on the device. Software installation through .cab files is also protected by this process with a separate certificate store, and a revocation process is available on the device to block execution and installation of rogue applications.

Code signing provides two guarantees: that the code has not been modified since signing and that the owner of the code can be identified. How it does this is similar to how authenticity for X.509 server certificates is established, as described earlier. A CA issues the X.509 certificates used for code signing, which are derived from the root certificate (which provides a way for the authenticity of a certificate to be checked by verifying whether its parent certificate is one of the root certificates in the root store on the device). When you code-sign an application, the public certificate details, including the public key, are attached to the code module as a resource, and then a hash is generated from the whole code module, encrypted with the private key and attached to the code module as well. Chapter 6, "Completing the Application: Packaging and Deployment," discusses how to sign your code modules with digital signatures.

When the code begins to run, Windows Mobile extracts the public key from the resource section of the code module and uses it to decrypt the hash. Then it calculates a new hash for the module and compares it with the decrypted value–if they match, this guarantees that the code module has not been modified in any way since it was signed. Next, Windows Mobile extracts the public certificate from the code module, validates it to check that it is properly formatted and that the dates are valid, and then creates a hash from it and examines the Privileged Execution Trust Authorities and Unprivileged Execution Trust Authorities certificate stores on the device for a corresponding hash.

From a security point of view, you enhance the security of the device–where your own application must run–by signing your application and by setting appropriate security policy to prevent unsigned applications from executing. We discuss how to do this in a short while, but first, you must understand something about how Windows Mobile security policy works. What follows is a brief overview; for more information about application security, see the article titled "Windows Mobile 5 Application Security" in the Microsoft MSDN Smart Client Developer Center at *msdn.microsoft.com/smartclient/default.aspx*.

Understanding Windows Mobile Security Policy

Each Windows Mobile–powered device has a security policy that determines what is and what is not allowed to run, and what a running application is allowed to do. The security policy determines what level of trust the operating system will apply to applications according to the way the applications are signed.

Privileged, Unprivileged, and Unsigned Applications

The Windows Mobile security model recognizes three kinds of applications:

- **Privileged** An application that has been signed using a certificate that has a corresponding certificate in the Privileged Execution Trust Authorities certificate store
- **Unprivileged** An application that has a corresponding certificate in the Unprivileged Execution Trust Authorities certificate store
- **Unsigned** An application that is not signed

Trusted and Normal Execution Modes

The Windows Mobile security model also recognizes two different application execution modes:

- **Trusted** An application that is virtually unlimited in what it is allowed to do. It can write to any registry key and call any Windows API.
- **Normal** An application that is not allowed to call certain restricted APIs or modify restricted registry keys. Restricted items are typically APIs and registry entries used to control security functionality and other essential functions. For a list of restricted APIs and registry keys, see the topic titled "Trusted APIs" in the Windows Mobile software development kit (SDK) documentation.

One-Tier and Two-Tier Security

Before Windows Mobile 5.0, Pocket PCs had no security. With the advent of Windows Mobile 5.0, Pocket PCs have what is called a one-tier security policy. On a one-tier device, there is no difference between Trusted and Normal execution modes. If an application is allowed to run (and you can still set policy to prevent unsigned applications from running), it runs in Trusted mode. Pocket PCs running Windows Mobile 6.0 also come with a one-tier security policy.

Smartphones running Windows Mobile 5.0 and later, on the other hand, nearly always come with a two-tier security policy (although some suppliers configure them to be one tier). On a two-tier device, applications run as either Normal or Trusted.

Security Policies

A security policy is simply a key–value pair that determines some aspect of security behavior on a Windows Mobile–powered device. There are 24 key–value pairs; the important ones are as shown in Table 10-1.

Table 10-1 Windows Mobile Security Policies

Security Policy	Description
4102	Can unsigned apps run? 0—No, unsigned apps cannot run. 1—Yes, unsigned apps can run.
4122	Prompt user to run unsigned apps. 0—Yes, prompt user. 1—No, do not prompt user. Note that if policy 4102 = 0, the setting of 4122 is irrelevant because unsigned apps cannot run.
4123	Is the device two-tier or one-tier? 0—Two-tier 1—One-tier
4097	User rights when making Remote API (RAPI; an API used by desktop programs calling into a Microsoft ActiveSync–connected device) calls. 0—RAPI disabled. 1—RAPI allowed with full access rights. 2—Restricted so that the desktop application has the same rights as the device user. (Note: By default, many Windows Mobile 5.0–powered devices have RAPI disabled, so applications that used RAPI successfully with older versions of Pocket PC may not work unless you change this policy.)

Security Configurations

Windows Mobile combines the four security policies described in Table 10-1 into different combinations, each of which describes a security configuration. The five security configurations are described in Table 10-2.

Table 10-2 Windows Mobile Security Configurations

Configuration	4102 (Unsigned apps can run?)	4122 (Prompt user for unsigned apps?)	4123 (One-tier or two-tier?)	4097 (RAPI allowed?)
Locked	0—No	1—No	Either	0—Disabled
Third-Party-Signed	0—No	1—No	Either	0—Disabled
Two-Tier-Prompt	1—Yes	0—Yes	0—Two-Tier	2—Restricted
One-Tier-Prompt	1—Yes	0—Yes	1—One-Tier	2—Restricted
Security-Off	1—Yes	1—No	1—One-Tier	1—Allowed

Note that the Visual Studio 2005 Pocket PC emulator is configured with the One-Tier-Prompt security configuration, and the smartphone emulator is configured with the Two-Tier-Prompt configuration.

Viewing and Provisioning Security Configurations with the Security Manager PowerToy

You can download the highly useful Microsoft Device Security Manager PowerToy for Windows Mobile 5.0 from *http://www.microsoft.com/downloads*. It is a remote configuration tool that runs on a host workstation. You can use the Device Security Manager PowerToy to perform the following tasks:

- Examine the security configuration of a Windows Mobile–powered device.
- Provision one of the standard security configurations onto a mobile device.
- Save the security configuration of a mobile device.
- Add a development certificate to a mobile device.
- Sign a file with a signing certificate.
- Check a file's digital signature.

With this tool, you can modify the configuration of an unlocked device or an emulator so that you can test how your application operates on devices with different security configurations. To use the Device Security Manager PowerToy, connect your device with ActiveSync, and then run the tool. The main screen displays the security configuration of the connected device on the right, and on the left you can select a different security configuration and then provision it to the device by clicking the arrow in the center, as shown in Figure 10-14. The menus contain options you can use to sign a file (an .exe or .dll) with a privileged or nonprivileged certificate and provision root development certificates to the device.

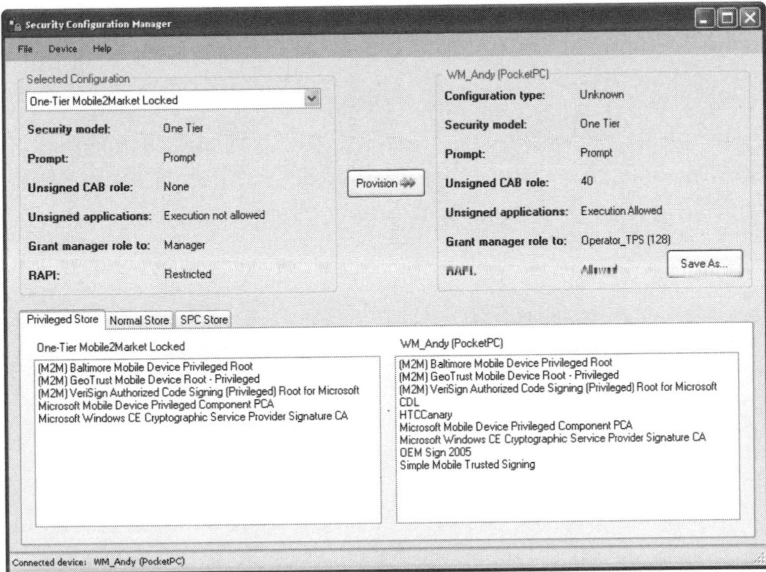

Figure 10-14 The Windows Mobile Device Security Manager PowerToy

Provisioning Windows Mobile–Powered Devices

Finally, the point of all the details of the Windows Mobile security policy: If you are an enterprise user who deploys a large number of unlocked devices into the field, the devices quite likely will come from your supplier with a Security-Off security configuration. Before you deploy devices to users in the field, you need to ensure that security policy is configured appropriately, and it is likely that part of that will be to configure them so as to prevent your users from running unsigned applications. Note that if your devices are commercially obtained from a phone network operator, they will almost certainly come with a Locked or Third-Party-Signed configuration, and unless the operator provides you with a tool to modify security configuration that is itself signed with a privileged certificate, you will not be able to change the security configuration of the device.

If you are working with a mobile operator or a mobile device manufacturer to deploy your Windows Mobile devices, you may be able to acquire mobile devices that have been preconfigured with the technologies and security settings that fit your needs.

If you cannot get suitably configured devices from your supplier, or you want to modify the configuration of one or more devices, you can create a .cab provisioning format (.cpf) file. You use this special form of .cab file to modify configuration settings on a device, such as to prevent unsigned applications from running.

Preventing Unsigned Applications from Running

To prevent unsigned applications from running, first create the provisioning XML. This is an XML fragment consisting of a *<wap-provisioning>* element that contains a *<characteristic>* element. There are many different characteristic types; see the Windows Mobile SDK documentation for a full list.

Inside the XML, you specify the *SecurityPolicy* characteristic type and then supply the new value for each security policy you want to change; to prevent unsigned applications from executing, set the 4102 security policy to 0. The XML looks like this:

```
<wap-provisioningdoc>
  <characteristic type="SecurityPolicy">
    <parm name="4102" value="0" />
  </characteristic>
</wap-provisioningdoc>
```

Save the file containing the XML with the name *_setup.xml*, and then run the MakeCab utility from a command prompt to create the .cab file. You can find the MakeCab utility in the <*drive*>:\Program Files\Microsoft Visual Studio 8\SmartDevices\SDK\SDKTools folder. Use the following syntax:

```
Makecab _setup.xml DisableUnsignedApps.cpf
```

Note that you do not have to use the .cpf extension for the output file, although this is the convention; a conventional .cab extension works just as well.

Tip As mentioned previously, current Windows Mobile–powered devices come with policy 4097 (RAPI Enabled) set to 0, meaning *Disabled*. RAPI is a valuable tool for developers; for example, you require RAPI to be activated to use the Remote Performance Monitor tool mentioned in Chapter 4, "Catching Errors, Testing, and Debugging," and Chapter 5, "Understanding and Optimizing .NET Compact Framework Performance." To enable RAPI on a device, create a provisioning .cab file as described here, but use *<parm name="4097" value="1" />*.

Install the resulting .cab file on your devices to apply the security configuration change. You can do this in many ways, such as by copying the .cpf file to the device through ActiveSync or using a storage card. Windows Mobile 5.0 also supports updates over the air by Open Mobile Alliance (OMA) Device Management (DM) push or by OMA Wireless Access Protocol (WAP) push, where a Microsoft Systems Management Server (SMS) message is sent to the device to trigger the update process. You can also send to the device an e-mail or SMS message that contains a link to a Web site where you deploy the .cpf file so that the device pulls the update from your server. For more information about these methods and for more examples of .cpf files, see the section titled "Provisioning for Windows Mobile–based Devices" in the Windows Mobile SDK documentation.

> **Note** If you are an enterprise user, you can prevent users from running unapproved applications—even those that are signed by a valid certificate—by removing from the certificate stores all root certificates other than the root certificate for your own code-signing certificates. You could even create your own root certificate, generate your own code-signing certificates, and install just your own root certificate on the device. This stops users from installing applications from other sources.

Summary

This chapter covers a number of topics related to security. The Mobile Configuration and Mobile Authentication Application Blocks from the Microsoft patterns & practices Mobile Client Software Factory support password-based authentication and encryption of sensitive data that meet the security needs of many mobile applications and that are easy to use. This chapter also explains how to use symmetric encryption and how to use public–private key pairs to exchange secrets securely between two individuals.

The chapter then describes how to use SSL to secure communications over HTTP and how to connect successfully to a server that has been secured with your own self-signed server certificate. It also discusses perimeter security, preventing attackers from gaining access to your device, and how the remote management features of Windows Mobile 5.0 and Exchange Server 2003 can enforce some aspects of security policy remotely and initiate a remote wipe of lost or stolen devices. It describes Windows Mobile 5.0 security policy and how you can alter it by using provisioning XML.

The most important advice in this chapter is right at the beginning: Ensure that you establish a security review process as a key component of your software development processes, and carry out frequent reviews throughout a project life cycle to make sure that security vulnerabilities in your software are identified and mitigated.

Chapter 11

Threading

In this chapter:

The topic of writing multithreading code or programming in a free-threaded environment is always a complex one. Herewith it is referred to simply as *threading*, and no assumptions of previous knowledge are made. Threading is the ability for two or more tasks to (appear to) be executing concurrently. Threading can improve the perception of an application's performance.

If there is one chapter in this book that must be read with Microsoft Visual Studio next to you, this is it. We include many code samples, and if you are new to threading, the best way to understand the text is actually to run the code listed and observe the results that the text describes. This chapter is not intended to be read without Visual Studio running because we do not believe threading can be appreciated by using a hands-off approach. Try and make the changes in code as each section instructs, observing the results each time. More often than not, you will be looking at the *output* window in Visual Studio, where the thread of execution will be outlined. Although every sample in this chapter is available for download, you are encouraged to re-create the code as per the listings to gain firsthand experience.

After you've been through this chapter once, you should be able to describe, among other concepts, scheduling, race conditions, thread affinity, deadlocks, critical section synchronization objects, thread pools, and timers, to name but a few.

The next section starts with the reasons why you would want to use threading.

Why Use Threads?

One thing most developers have heard about threading is that it can complicate the code of an application and potentially make it difficult to understand, and that it can potentially lead to issues that are hard to diagnose. So why introduce such a situation by using threads? The answer is throughput and responsiveness.

The last sentence hides one of the most common misconceptions about threading–that it apparently increases performance. Although threading can increase the performance of an application, the performance optimization is not always automatic and primarily occurs on server applications (for example, to service multiple requests) running on hyperthreaded or multiprocessor computers. In this chapter, we focus on devices running Microsoft Windows CE that run on a single processor and specifically on user interface (UI) applications. The concepts described apply equally to desktop applications running on single-processor computers, and because the topic always raises many questions in online forums, our coverage does not assume that you are familiar with threads. Having said that, only the Microsoft .NET Compact Framework application programming interface (API) is examined here, and not its richer counterpart of the full framework.

Every computer user has come across an application that suddenly stops responding. The user tries to interact with the application, but the application appears frozen. As is often said, it "hangs." With correct usage of threads in the program, the issue could have been alleviated.[1] This chapter focuses especially on this topic, starting with the section titled "Mantaining a Responsive User Interface" later in this chapter.

Although on a single processor the actual performance of a task cannot be improved (because the central processing unit can do only one task at a time), you may have an opportunity to introduce parallelism in some circumstances. For example, picture an end user requirement that can be broken down into separate tasks that require different resources. If one task includes waiting for external input, for example, from the user or the network, the CPU will be idle at some points–and a separate thread could use that idle time to perform a different task in parallel. To make this example more concrete, imagine an application in which the user has requested some data from the network. While the bytes from the socket intermittently arrive, the CPU has moments of idleness, and the application can use those idle moments on the main thread to paint the user interface while another thread assembles the bytes to form a complete message, which it would then interpret and eventually pass on to the main thread to place on the already-drawn user interface. At the same time, another thread could have been reading from a database to combine some local data with the network data if the main thread painting the UI also left the CPU with some idle time.

So, to capitalize on CPU idle time and, more important, to ensure that the user interface remains responsive under all circumstances, threads must be used. Before we delve into describing how to use threads correctly through the managed API, first it is important for you to understand some relevant basics of how the operating system works.

---

1 And with incorrect usage of threads, the issue can be amplified!

Understanding Underlying Fundamentals

Today operating systems are expected to be capable of multitasking and multithreading. In the Windows operating system, *multitasking* is the ability to run multiple processes at the same time, each with its own isolated memory area, such as Notepad, Calculator, and Microsoft Office Word, whereas *multithreading* is about each process *appearing* to be performing more than one task at a time, such as searching the file system while the user is still typing.

The .NET Framework introduces an intermediate concept of a lightweight conceptual process, the *application domain (AppDomain)*, that defines isolation, security, and unloading boundaries for managed code. Each managed process has a default *AppDomain*, and in that you create threads. It is very rare in .NET Compact Framework applications that you create an additional *AppDomain*, and regardless, it has no effect on the discussion in this chapter.

Windows CE

Under Windows CE, each process has at least one thread, known as the primary thread or the main thread. Each process may also have additional threads, known as secondary or worker threads. The only limit to the number of threads in a process and indeed in the system is the memory of the device. In simple terms, a thread is a unit of execution that also takes up some memory.[1] Note that a thread is not cheap to construct or to destroy because it constitutes more than just a handle or a simple managed object.

The operating system knows about all the threads on the system and can run only one thread at a time. It runs threads in a round-robin fashion, regardless of what process each thread is running in. Each thread runs for a predefined interval,[2] known as the *thread quantum* or *time slice*. After a thread completes its slice, a *thread context switch* happens: The thread must copy its data out, and the next thread in the queue copies its data in, its stack becomes the active stack, and execution continues. This switch is not cheap, so switching from one thread to the next does come at a cost.

The preceding description of the operating system thread scheduling omits discussion of at least one aspect, thread priority. Each thread has a default priority that can be changed programmatically. The priority of the thread is a factor of the scheduling, and so, plainly put, higher-priority threads get to run before (and even can interrupt) lower-priority ones. If threads of all UI applications on a system did not change their default priority, each one would get an equal overall time slice and run every time its turn was due.

In a .NET Compact Framework application, you can change the priority of a thread by using the *System.Threading.Thread.Priority* property typed as *ThreadPriority* enumeration. However, changing thread priority is rarely justified, and in the overwhelming majority of managed

1 A thread has its own stack, a copy of the CPU registers, and some thread-local storage (TLS).

2 In some versions of the Windows CE operating system, this defaults to 100 milliseconds, whereas in earlier versions it was 25 milliseconds. But because the interval is configurable by the original equipment manufacturer (OEM), the actual figure may vary on your target device.

applications it is absolutely unnecessary to lower or raise the priority of a thread. As a side note, be aware that changing priorities without having a full understanding of the system may lead to issues that are even harder to diagnose. This chapter does not discuss thread priorities any further and always assumes that threads are running at their default normal priority. See the following sidebar titled "Default Threads in a .NET Compact Framework Application" for more details.

Default threads in a .NET Compact Framework application

Every .NET Compact Framework application has more than one thread by default. Native applications start with a single thread, and the application code can create additional ones.

In addition to the main primary thread of the process, managed applications also have another thread that is used to track changes to the active TCP/IP interfaces (simulating the media sense behavior that is present on Windows XP but not Windows CE). An additional thread is used to control various period timers and timeouts that can be scheduled by the system or applications–in version 1.0 of the .NET Compact Framework, this thread is started on application startup, but in version 2.0, it starts only the first time it is needed. In addition, another thread is used to run object *finalizers*. This thread is created when the first finalizable object is collected by the garbage collector (See Chapter 5, "Understanding and Optimizing .NET Compact Framework Performance," for more on garbage collection.) So these three additional threads are out of the developer's control in terms of changing their priority or anything else.

Furthermore, when calling framework methods that begin with *BeginXXX*, under the covers the implementation is using a thread to achieve some asynchronous operation. The thread used is likely coming from the *ThreadPool*, which is examined later in this chapter.

System.Threading

To this point, and in fact throughout most of this book, the examples given assume a single-threaded normal scenario. Your Windows Forms application has a main thread, and all the code you write executes under that main thread. If none of the operations your application performs take a long time, and hence they never block the user interface or you do not want to take advantage of idle CPU time, you probably will not ever *explicitly* need to create a thread. However, if that is not the case, you must become familiar with the *System.Threading* namespace and its types. The code samples of this chapter assume that you have added a *using System.Threading* statement at the top of the code files.[1] All the important Microsoft

1 If the compiler fails to resolve any type in the code sample (for example, *Debug*), you can right-click the type and then click Resolve to resolve the namespace by inserting the namespace at the top of the file for you (for example, *using System.Diagnostics*).

Win32 threading primitives have a counterpart in this namespace, starting with the *Thread* class.

For a table mapping the native synchronization functions to the full .NET threading namespace, please see the article titled "Synchronization Functions" on the Microsoft MSDN Web site at *msdn2.microsoft.com/en-us/library/aa302340.aspx#win32map_synchronizationfunctions*.

The *Thread* class wraps the native thread. This is not guaranteed to remain true going forward, so to future-proof your code do not always assume that there is always a native thread under your managed thread. For this reason, the *Thread* class exposes a *ManagedThreadId* property instead of directly exposing the native thread's handle.[1] A friendlier way to identify managed threads is to give them a name by using the *Name* property. Also note that you can access the current thread executing your code from your code by using the static *Thread.CurrentThread* property.

New in version 2.0

This chapter would be quite different if it were written for version 1.0 of the .NET Compact Framework. Version 2.0 adds many missing members to the *System.Threading* namespace that correspond with the desktop version. These include overloads with timeout parameters for blocking calls such as *WaitHandle.Wait* and new members for the *Thread* class, including *Join*, *Abort*, *IsBackground*, and *Name*. Other new members are the *Monitor.TryEnter* method and some overloads that take generic parameters on the *Interlocked* class. Also, the *ThreadPool* class was fixed and updated. Relevant to threading, the *Control.Invoke* method now accepts any delegate, including passing arguments, and also gains the asynchronous version *BeginInvoke* as well as the ability to check whether they are needed by using *InvokeRequired*.

C# has always supported the *volatile* keyword, and now this is also supported in version 2.0 of the .NET Compact Framework. This has no practical effect because everything in the .NET Compact Framework is treated as volatile, but it does help developers who write cross-platform code to keep their code base the same because previously the keyword would not compile. You can read about the *volatile* keyword in the online documentation for C#, but in a nutshell, it prevents *thread caching* of fields primarily on multiprocessor computers; the optimization is not always desired, and the *volatile* keyword makes sure it does not take place. For more information on this topic, visit the documentation and look up topics such as *memory barriers*. Understanding memory barriers will also help you understand a .NET Compact Framework version 3.5 addition to the *Thread* class: the static method *MemoryBarrier* (which is already part of the full framework version 2.0; see *msdn2.microsoft.com/en-us/library/system.threading.thread.memorybarrier.aspx*).

1 *ManagedThreadId* will be constant if in the future the runtime decides to reuse a single native thread to power more than one managed thread or if the runtime host decides to implement the thread as a fiber (outside the scope of this discussion).

In addition, two new types in the version 2.0 *System.Threading* namespace of the full .NET Framework, *Semaphore* and *EventWaitHandle*, were not implemented for devices. You can download community versions of them from The Moth weblog at *www.danielmoth.com/Blog/2005/01/semaphore.html* and *www.danielmoth.com/Blog/2005/01/eventwaithandle.html*. Note that *EventWaitHandle* is part of the .NET Compact Framework version 3.5.

At this point, by inserting a few lines of code you could use your own existing .NET applications to verify what we just discussed. In an existing or new project, in the *static Main* function in the *Program* class/file, insert the following line above the existing *Application.Run* statement (Microsoft Visual Basic developers, please refer to Chapter 2, "Building a Microsoft Windows Forms GUI," for information about creating a *Main* function):

```
Thread.CurrentThread.Name = "Main UI Thread";
Application.Run(new Form1());
```

In other places of your code, for example, in a button click event handler or in any other method, insert the following two lines of code:

```
Thread t = Thread.CurrentThread;
MessageBox.Show("This thread is " + t.Name +
            ", id=" + t.ManagedThreadId.ToString());
```

Run your application and observe how the same name and ID are returned regardless of which method is executed.

The next example uses the two preceding pieces of code in a more specific scenario. Create a new project, assign the main UI thread a name (as done previously), add an event handler to the left soft key by double-clicking it, and add a method to the form with the code shown earlier. Your form code should look like this:

```
private void DoSomeWork()
{
  // TODO some work

  Thread t = Thread.CurrentThread;
  MessageBox.Show("This thread is " + t.Name +
              ", id=" + t.ManagedThreadId.ToString());
}

private void menuItem1_Click(object sender, EventArgs e)
{
  // UI thread
  this.DoSomeWork();
}
```

> **Tip** When logging information for your application as discussed in Chapter 4, "Catching Errors, Testing, and Debugging," it is a good idea to log the name and ID of the thread as part of the context.

Next, you see how to create a thread and start its execution on the *DoSomeWork* method. Add an event handler to the right soft key, and in the event handler add the code that creates a thread:

```
private void menuItem2_Click(object sender, EventArgs e)
{
  // worker thread
  Thread t = new Thread(new ThreadStart(this.DoSomeWork));
  t.Name = "Worker Thread 1";
  t.Start(); // Thread does not execute until this line.
}
```

Now run the application on your target device. Tap the menu on the left to see the main thread's thread information in a *MessageBox*, and tap the menu on the right to see the information of the worker thread.

Before we dive into a discussion about maintaining a responsive user interface (UI), we must establish a common understanding about what we described earlier as an unresponsive application. Add a *TrackBar* control to the sample application built in this section. Revisit the *DoSomeWork* method and add the following line of code at the top, in place of the comment that was there previously:

```
  Thread.Sleep(5000); //Suspend thread for 5 seconds.
```

> **Note** *Thread.Sleep(X)* results in the thread not entering the queue of available threads for scheduling for at least *X* milliseconds. We use this method liberally in this chapter to simulate long-running tasks and to help demonstrate thread context switching. In real code, *Thread.Sleep* is generally best replaced by options such as a *ManualResetEvent* with a timeout. Note that passing 0 as the argument of *Thread.Sleep* results in an immediate context switch to the next thread. Treat that value as a special case in which the thread gives up its time slice and goes immediately back in the queue, ready to be scheduled again.

Now run the application again and tap the left menu. Notice how no *MessageBox* appears as it did before, and furthermore, if you try to move the slider on the trackbar, you cannot. In fact, if you click the device menu at the upper right or open the software-based input panel (SIP), you may notice that that area of your application is not being painted anymore. This is because the main UI thread of your application is blocked. The application is not responsive. After 5 seconds, the *MessageBox* will appear; dismiss it. Then click the right button; in the

5 seconds it (still) takes for the *MessageBox* to appear, note how you can still interact with the form, for example, by using the *TrackBar*. The following section elaborates on this scenario and gives more examples.

Maintaining a Responsive User Interface

The last section ended with a demonstration of an unresponsive UI. It is interesting to note why an application may become unresponsive.

Message Pump

Every Windows application has what is called a message pump. In reaction to user interaction, Windows sends Windows messages to the message queue of an application. In .NET, the message is handled for the developer and is translated into a friendly .NET event. For example, when the user taps the screen, Windows sends a WM_LBUTTONDOWN message (followed by a WM_LBUTTONUP) to the message pump of your application, and this is translated into *MouseDown*, *MouseUp* events and possibly, depending on the control, into a *Click* event. The main thread of your process is simply waiting for new Windows messages to arrive in the message queue and processes them in order inside a loop. The message pump for your application was created when you called *Application.Run(yourForm)*, and when your form closes, so does the application, as established in Chapter 2.

It may be clear now why the application can become unresponsive: as a result of a Windows message, an event handler was run on the main thread; when your code takes too long to complete its task, the main thread is not processing Windows messages and hence is unresponsive. Some of the Windows messages may be WM_PAINT messages, which also explains why the application is not even repainted. Note that these messages are queued so that when your main thread is freed to return to the loop, it will process all the messages in order.

Long-Running Tasks

In an earlier section, we simulated a long-running activity by using a call to the static method *Thread.Sleep*. Real-world applications contain numerous examples of tasks that should not be done on the main thread if they are time-consuming, such as calling Web services or any other network activity, or interacting with a database, the file system, and generally any form of input/output (I/O). Do not forget that a task that takes a short period of time under your developer's test may take considerably longer under other circumstances. For example, you may test using queries to a database that do not take as long to run as do the queries that a user will use. The user may make a network call when the Domain Name System (DNS) server is absent, for instance, which could result in a lengthy wait. A method that accepts a path to open a file could end up trying to open from a very slow storage card. In addition to scenarios similar to these, your application may be required to perform some genuine heavy calculation that is CPU-bound and, again, that will block the UI if you make the call from the main thread.

For all of the preceding situations, you can use a worker thread to achieve the goal of maintaining a responsive UI. An example will clarify this advice and highlight some of the issues.

Demonstration Example

This fictitious example traverses the file store and lists all files and folders in a *ListBox* control. In a new device project, add a label, add a list box, type **Load** as the text for the left menu/soft key, and type **Cancel** as the text for the right menu item. Then add this code to the form:

```
private ArrayList allFiles = new ArrayList(); // holds the results
private bool stopRequested = false;           // User hit the Cancel button.

private void menuItem2_Click(object sender, EventArgs e)
{
  // cancel
  stopRequested = true;
}

private void menuItem1_Click(object sender, EventArgs e)
{
  // load list
  label1.Text = "";
  listBox1.DataSource = null;
  stopRequested = false;

  this.GetAllFiles(); // will have populated the allFiles ArrayList

  label1.Text = allFiles.Count.ToString();
  listBox1.DataSource = allFiles;
}

private void GetAllFiles()
{
  allFiles.Clear();
  this.PopulateAllFilesFor(@"\");
  Debug.WriteLine("Finished");
}

private void PopulateAllFilesFor(string path)
{
  Debug.WriteLine("Processing new path");
  if (stopRequested)
  {
    return;
  }

  allFiles.Add(path);

  string[] files;
  files = Directory.GetFiles(path);
  allFiles.AddRange(files);
```

```
    Debug.WriteLine(allFiles.Count.ToString());
    label1.Text = allFiles.Count.ToString();

    if (stopRequested)
    {
      return;
    }

    foreach (string  subDirectory in Directory.GetDirectories(path))
    {
      this.PopulateAllFilesFor(subDirectory); //recursion
    }
  }
```

When you run the application and tap the button to read the file store, the application stops responding and hence, tapping the button that requests cancellation of the task has no effect. Also, when you update the label with an intermediate count of files, the label is not updated until the end. This becomes even more visible if you tap the button to load again after loading the files in the list box; notice how the list box and label do not clear even though there is code to do so. The paint message is not being processed.

Note how when the application is running on the target, you can see the *Debug.WriteLine* results in the output window of Visual Studio. This becomes important later.

Nonideal Solutions

If you are happy living with long delays and unresponsive applications but still want to have the application paint its user interface, you can call the form's *Refresh* method, that is, *this.Refresh();*. This does not, for example, make the Cancel button respond to user input, but it does redraw the form. Try it by inserting the call to *Refresh* at the top of the *PopulateAllFilesFor* method. Notice how the label updates while the long task is running and how clicking the Load button for a second run clears the list before repopulating it. However, tapping the Cancel button or trying to close the form still has no effect.

In older single-threaded environments, developers had to resort to a workaround for making the application respond occasionally during its long-running tasks and hence also allow cancellation of the long-running task. They achieved this through a call to *DoEvents*, which still exists in the managed world: *Application.DoEvents*. Recall the discussion about the message pump. *DoEvents* instructs the main thread to process all the messages waiting in the queue and only then to continue executing the code that follows the call to *DoEvents*.

Before we discuss the implications, first let's show it in action. At the top of the *PopulateAllFilesFor* method, instead of the call to *Refresh*, make a call to *Application.DoEvents*, and then run the application. Notice how you can cancel the loading and only partial results are loaded in the list.

DoEvents can be very attractive for simple scenarios, especially when you can avoid using threads, which can complicate code. However, *DoEvents* can be very dangerous. This is evident when you actually digest the earlier statement about what it does: It processes all messages in the queue and then continues to execute the code after the call to *DoEvents*. This can lead to reentrant code. That is, a method that is already running gets to run again concurrently. Dealing with such situations is the same as dealing with threading except that the code is not written with multithreading in mind in the first place; otherwise, the developer would have chosen proper use of threads rather than *DoEvents*.

We could provide many examples of why we think you should not use *DoEvents*, but instead we provide just one: Tun the application again with the *DoEvents* statement as before, and this time tap the Load button twice. Can you rely on those results? Does the label show the correct number of results? One solution to the issue is to redesign the method so that it can cope with reentrancy, and another is to disable the button so that it cannot be clicked more than once. In a larger application with a more complicated UI, it would be harder to analyze all the possibilities of what a *DoEvents* call can affect.

Using a Thread to Solve the Problem

Reset the code to the original, that is, remove the *DoEvents* and *Refresh* calls in the *PopulateAllFilesFor* method.

In the *menuItem1_Click* method, replace the call to *GetAllFiles* with the following:

```
Thread t = new Thread(new ThreadStart(this.GetAllFiles));
t.Name = "Worker: allFiles populator";
t.Start();
```

Run the code, and observe a *NotSupportedException* with the message, "Control.Invoke must be used to interact with controls created on a separate thread." The exception is thrown in the *PopulateAllFilesFor* method on the line that attempts to assign a value to the *label1.Text* property. Although this is very important, we would like to discuss it a bit later, so comment out that line for now.

After you comment out the line that assigns text to the label, run the project again and watch the output window carefully before and after you tap the Load button. Notice how the UI has some items in the list box, the label is blank, and the output window is still showing that processing is taking place. Now that you've introduced a thread, the thread is doing the processing, but the main thread also continues executing its own statements so that it reaches the *ListBox* data-binding statement before the worker thread has had a chance to complete the processing. Run the code a few more times, and note how you can cancel the operation as the output window shows and that the UI is responsive. Those goals were achieved, but new problems were introduced: How can the two threads cooperate? The real answer lies in the

Control.Invoke section, similar to the earlier issue of the *NotSupportedException*. Before we discuss that, though, we explore two alternative solutions.

System.Windows.Forms.Timer

In some scenarios, you can use a *System.Windows.Forms.Timer* instead of or in complement to threading. In the example scenario, rather than figure out the solution to the real problem of having the two threads communicate when the worker thread has the results ready for the main thread to use, you could elect to use a polling technique in which the main thread checks at set intervals if the results are ready. If you add a timer to the form and set it to raise its *Tick* event every second, in the *Tick* event, which is on the main thread of course, you could check a new *boolean* flag if the worker thread has finished its work. If the worker thread has finished, you can stop the timer from ticking and data-bind the *ListBox* control to the *ArrayList* variable. If it hasn't finished, you can check the flag on the next tick. In the worker thread, you would simply set the flag when finished.

One of the issues with using such timers in this way is that the main thread is not notified exactly when the results are ready. This means the worker thread may have completed and the user still has to wait for the main thread to realize it, which can be potentially much later when you use this polling technique. Also, the reverse is not ideal. If the worker thread takes too long to complete the task, the main thread is still checking at frequent intervals for the results when it could be using those CPU cycles for something else.

Another consideration with the use of timers is the impact on battery life. Unnecessarily wasting CPU cycles affects the device's battery life negatively, and this is one of the reasons why event-driven designs are preferred over polling techniques.

Nevertheless, in some scenarios this nonoptimal solution may be applicable.

Thread.Join

The issue at hand can be restated as follows: How can one thread wait for another to exit and only then continue processing its own work? There is a perfect answer to that precise question in the form of the *Thread* instance method: *Join*. Using *Join* works great between worker threads but is definitely not advisable for use by the main thread, as will become obvious in the next paragraph. Nevertheless, this is a good opportunity to explore this method.

In the *menuItem1_Click* method, after the call that starts the thread and before the update of the label, insert the following line of code (read the comment):

```
t.Join(); // whatever thread is running, blocks waiting for it to exit
```

Run the application and tap Load to see the effects of this self-explanatory method call. Note how the main thread does not continue execution and instead waits for the worker thread to exit. At that point, the main thread continues execution, which results in a correct update of the UI with the results. This method works great between worker threads, and you can probably see why it should never be used from the main thread: The UI is once again blocked because the main thread is waiting on the worker thread, unable to process any Windows messages.

Control.Invoke

In this section, we discuss the first rule of threading on the UI and how to use it in the example. Before that, though, we explain the use of *Control.Invoke* with an isolated new example.

Touch UI Elements Only from the Thread That Created Them The rule of Windows, regardless of managed or native code, is that the thread that creates a control (that is, creates its handle) is the only one that can subsequently modify any of the control properties (that is, directly make API calls to its handle), which can also be stated as follows: Windows objects have thread affinity. Every time your code reads or writes to a property of a control or calls a method that does the same, it must be done from the same thread that created the control. In practical terms, this means that only your main thread can "touch" controls, and any worker threads cannot. This begs the question of how you can update the user interface from a worker thread. The answer is by calling the control's *Invoke* (or *BeginInvoke*) method, which, along with *InvokeRequired*, is safe to call from any thread.

Caution With version 1.0 of the .NET Compact Framework, the results of breaking this rule were indeterminate and usually resulted in the application hanging. With version 2.0, a *NotSupportedException* is thrown. This crucial help is applicable only for device projects. Running .NET applications on the desktop can be more forgiving than running them on Windows CE is. Even though you may get away with touching UI elements from a worker thread, you should avoid doing so because it may work in some situations and fail in others. Finally, note that putting a *MessageBox* on the screen is the only UI operation a worker thread is allowed to make.

Here is a short example. On a new device project, place a *TextBox* on the form and create the two event handlers for the soft keys as follows:

```
private void menuItem1_Click(object sender, EventArgs e)
{
  Thread t = new Thread(this.UpdateUI);
  t.Name = "Worker: Assigns form's caption text.";
  t.Start();
}
```

```
private void menuItem2_Click(object sender, EventArgs e)
{
  this.UpdateUI();
}

private void UpdateUI()
{
  this.Text = textBox1.Text;
}
```

Run this application. When you tap the second soft key, the application updates the caption of the form using the text of the text box. When you tap the first soft key, the *NotSupportedException* is thrown. Next, add this method to the form:

```
private void ThreadMethod()
{
   // Do other thread work.
   this.Invoke(new MethodInvoker(UpdateUI));
}
```

The preceding method presumes you have declared in your form this delegate:

```
delegate void MethodInvoker();
```

and that you have changed the thread constructor in *menuItem1_Click* as follows:

```
Thread t = new Thread(this.ThreadMethod);
```

Now running the application works regardless of which soft key you tap.

The *Invoke* method stores in a queue the delegate that was passed to it, and then it sends a custom Windows message to the application message queue. When that message is processed, the processing method notifies the control by calling an internal method. In that method (now on the main thread, of course), the control invokes *all* delegates in its internal queue.

You can pass any delegate to *Invoke*, and if you use the asynchronous version, *BeginInvoke*, execution of the current thread continues to the end of its time slice before the delegate is executed on the main thread.

Sometimes you may prefer an alternative design to extracting a method and pointing a delegate to it. If the method is not called from anywhere else, you can use a new version 2.0 feature of anonymous methods as follows:

```
private void AlternativeThreadMethod()
{
  this.Invoke(new MethodInvoker(
              delegate() { this.Text = textBox1.Text; }
            ));
}
```

Another point to note is that, by design, your methods should almost always know whether they are going to be called on the main thread or on a worker thread. If after analyzing your code you find that your methods do not know if they are being called on the main thread or not, rethink your design—this is often a clue to bad design. Having said that, you can determine programmatically whether *Invoke* is required by checking the property *Control.InvokeRequired*. To see this in action, undo all the changes you have made so far to this short example, and then modify the *UpdateUI* method as follows:

```
private void UpdateUI()
{
  if (this.InvokeRequired)
  {
    // On worker thread-call self again by using Invoke.
    this.Invoke(new MethodInvoker(this.UpdateUI));
    return;
  }
  // Running on main thread, so update directly
  this.Text = textBox1.Text;
}
```

It is important to emphasize the point that you cannot touch UI controls from worker threads. This is true for properties and methods that update the handle of the control as a side effect. Because you do not know what the implementation of control members does internally, follow this rule for all members. For example, in current implementations, accessing the *Tag* property of a control simply stores or retrieves an object and doesn't affect the handle of the control at all. In this case, it is OK to touch the *Tag* member from worker threads.

Using *Control.Invoke* in the Earlier Example Now that you are an expert in updating UI elements, it is useful to revisit the original demonstration example introduced in the section titled "Demonstration Example" earlier in this chapter. The last modification you made was to introduce the *Join* method call.

Recall where the *NotSupportedException* was thrown and that the quick fix was to comment out the line that touched the *label1* control. Now you know how to fix this scenario. Replace the commented line with this line of code:

```
        this.Invoke(
          new EventHandler<LabelEventArgs>(UpdateLabel),
          new object[]{label1, new LabelEventArgs(allFiles.Count)});
```

The preceding code uses the overload of *Invoke* that accepts arguments to be passed to the target method of the delegate. The code statement above assumes you have declared a new *LabelEventArgs* class and a new form method as follows:

```
private class LabelEventArgs : EventArgs
    {
      public LabelEventArgs(int items)
      {
        NumberOfItems = items;
      }
      public int NumberOfItems;
    }

private void UpdateLabel(object sender, LabelEventArgs e)
{
  label1.Text = e.NumberOfItems.ToString();
}
```

Study the code to make sure you understand if this will work. The intention, of course, is to update the label with intermediate results from the worker thread while it is executing. Start the project in debug mode in Visual Studio to see the effect. Was it what you expected? A hung application! The only option now is to stop debugging in Visual Studio and continue reading for an explanation of what went wrong.

What just occurred is called a *deadlock*. The main thread is blocked, waiting for the worker thread to finish (by using the *Join* method call). Meanwhile, the worker thread is waiting for the main thread to process the custom Windows message sent by the call to *Invoke*. One is waiting for the other, and neither can continue. This is the definition of a deadlock, which is one of the pitfalls of multithreading that you must design against. In this specific case, we established earlier that the call to *Join* from the main thread is a huge error. Now, with your knowledge of *Control.Invoke,* you can solve the issue that resulted in introducing the call to *Join*.

The objective is to be notified on the main thread when the worker thread completes its task so that the main thread can make the final update to the UI. Can you see how to achieve this now? Refactor the *menuItem1_Click* method into the following two, eliminating the call to *Join*:

```
private void menuItem1_Click(object sender, EventArgs e)
{
  // Load list.
  label1.Text = "";
  listBox1.DataSource = null;
  stopRequested = false;

  Thread t = new Thread(this.GetAllFiles); // delegate inference
  t.Name = "Worker: allFiles populator";
  t.Start();
}

private void UpdateBox(object sender, EventArgs e)
{
  label1.Text = allFiles.Count.ToString();
  listBox1.DataSource = allFiles;
  Debug.WriteLine("Got results " + listBox1.Items.Count.ToString());
}
```

Then add the following line at the end of the *GetAllFiles* method:

```
  this.Invoke(new EventHandler(this.UpdateBox));
```

Now run the application, and it should work exactly as expected. Once again, observe the output window with the debug messages because they may help clarify the flow. The completed example is available with the downloadable code for this chapter on this book's companion Web site.

BackgroundWorker

Version 2.0 of the full .NET Framework introduces a new component for helping with threading scenarios such as the ones described earlier: the *System.ComponentModel.BackgroundWorker*. Here is an example of its use:

```
BackgroundWorker bw;
private void menuItem1_Click(object sender, EventArgs e)
{
  label2.Text = "will kick it off";

  bw = new BackgroundWorker(this);
  bw.DoWork += new DoWorkEventHandler(bw_DoWork);
  bw.RunWorkerCompleted +=
       new RunWorkerCompletedEventHandler(bw_RunWorkerCompleted);
```

```
    bw.RunWorkerAsync(textBox1.Text);
  }
  void bw_RunWorkerCompleted(object sender, RunWorkerCompletedEventArgs e)
  {
    // can touch UI. Thread communicates to UI.
    // You don't have to Control.Invoke explicitly.
    label2.Text = e.Result.ToString();
  }

  void bw_DoWork(object sender, DoWorkEventArgs e)
  {
    // Do time-consuming work.
    System.Threading.Thread.Sleep(3000);

    // could assign any other object
    e.Result = "finished :) " + e.Argument.ToString();
  }
```

Notice how there is no need to create a thread explicitly, and instead a simple handling of an event results in the worker method running on another thread. Also, passing an argument to the worker method is simple, as is extracting the result on the UI thread without explicitly using *Control.Invoke*. However, the true power of the *System.ComponentModel.BackgroundWorker* component lies in its ability to easily marshal progress from the worker method to the UI and also its ability to cancel the task. In the downloadable code for this chapter on the book's companion Web site, you can find an example that builds on the one in the preceding listing and that further demonstrates progress reporting and cancellation.

Although this class is not available in any version of the .NET Compact Framework, you can find a community version of it along with a great sample of its use on The Moth Web site at *www.danielmoth.com/Blog/2004/12/backgroundworker-sample.html.*

Synchronizing Thread Activities and Access to Data

Earlier we introduced one of the pitfalls of threading: deadlocks. In that example, it was easy to spot the problem, but that is not always the case. Before we look at other deadlock examples, we must introduce another pitfall of threading: race conditions.

Race Conditions

What happens when multiple threads access the same data at the same time? The answer is: indeterminate results. For this reason, you must synchronize access to global data from multiple threads. An example can help convey the message. Consider the following code in a new solution with a form that has a button:

```
long someCounter = 0;

private void button1_Click(object sender, EventArgs e)
{
  someCounter = 0;
  Thread t1 = new Thread(this.ThreadFirst1);
  t1.Name = "Worker Thread 1 ";
  Thread t2 = new Thread(this.ThreadSecond2);
  t2.Name = "Worker Thread 2 ";

  t1.Start();
  t2.Start();

  t1.Join();
  t2.Join();

  MessageBox.Show("Final result = " + someCounter.ToString());
}

private void ThreadFirst1()
{
  for (long j = 0; j < 100000000; j++)
  {
    Debug.WriteLine(Thread.CurrentThread.Name + "before inc");
    someCounter += 1;
  }
  MessageBox.Show(Thread.CurrentThread.Name, "Done");
}

private void ThreadSecond2()
{
  for (long j = 0; j < 100000000; j++)
  {
    Debug.WriteLine(Thread.CurrentThread.Name + "before inc");
    someCounter -= 1;
  }
  MessageBox.Show(Thread.CurrentThread.Name, "Done");
}
```

If you run the preceding code, you would expect to see the final result of *someCounter* be zero (0) because it is incremented and decremented an equal number of times. Indeed, that may be the case when you run the code sometimes, but other times it will not be the case. The variable *someCounter* is declared at the form level and hence is shared between all threads. Therefore, the two threads modify the same variable at the same time, and this can lead to indeterminate results or, in other words, corrupt results.

At this point, you may recall an earlier statement: Threads on a single-processor computer do not really run at the same time; instead, they run in turn as scheduled by the system.

Although that is true, you must consider the statements that access the shared variable: *someCounter += 1* and *someCounter -= 1*. When you look at the disassembly using Ildasm.exe, you can see that the single C# statement actually is five statements:

```
IL_0007:  ldfld      int64 CodeForChapter11cs.frmMoreThreads::someCounter
IL_000c:  ldc.i4.1
IL_000d:  conv.i8
IL_000e:  add
IL_000f:  stfld      int64 CodeForChapter11cs.frmMoreThreads::someCounter
```

The first statement loads the *someCounter* variable on the stack, the second one loads a 4-byte constant (1), the third statement converts the latter to 8 bytes, the fourth statement adds the constant to the variable, and finally the fifth statement stores the result back in the *someCounter* variable. The point here is not to teach intermediate language (IL) statements but simply to demonstrate that a single statement in a high-level language can be multiple lines of code at run time. The scheduler could perform a context switch at any point, and when one thread is switched out, it could be on any of the preceding lines, for example, just before the fifth statement. The other thread then executes its statement, modifying the *someCounter* variable, until at some point the scheduler switches to the first thread. The first thread continues on processing the statement it was on last, which, for example, is to store the value in *someCounter*. The first thread has overridden any changes that the second thread had performed, and hence the data is corrupted. It is worth mentioning here that if a statement represents an indivisible instruction, the problem described does not exist and the statement is said to be *atomic*.

Before we examine a solution, another code example is in order. Add this method to the same form of the preceding example:

```
private void ThreadBoth()
{
  Debug.WriteLine(Thread.CurrentThread.Name + "enters method");
  int localVar = 0;
  localVar += 1;

  if (someCounter == 0)
  {
    Debug.WriteLine(Thread.CurrentThread.Name + "in if block");
    Thread.Sleep(1); // Simulate some longer activity.
    someCounter += localVar;
    Debug.WriteLine(Thread.CurrentThread.Name + "just incremented");
  }
  else
  {
    Debug.WriteLine(Thread.CurrentThread.Name + "in else block");
    someCounter += 3;
  }

  return;
}
```

Modify the two thread constructors in the *button1_Click* method so that both point to *ThreadMethod*. What value do you expect *someCounter* to have when both threads have exited the method? Run the application and try tapping the button a few times. Race conditions are hard to replicate, so you may get the same result all the time, but in theory you could get one of two results: 4 or 2. If you were expecting anything else, you may have been confused by the *localVar* variable: Remember, each thread has its own copy of local variables, so they are never an issue unless you were expecting them to be shared, of course!

In the example just presented, the programmer's intention was for the first thread to initialize the variable to 1 while any subsequent threads increment it by 3, and hence the desired result, 4. To ensure that that happens, code must be added that protects the *someCounter* variable from being concurrently accessed. We examine this in the next section.

Monitor

You can protect a variable from concurrent access by analyzing the code and identifying code regions that must allow only a single thread to enter at a time. These sensitive code regions are known as *critical regions*, and their goal is to treat multiple related operations as atomic. You can use the *System.Threading.Monitor* class to achieve this, as the following code example shows.

```
object someLock = new object();
private void SomeMethod()
{
  // some code

  Monitor.Enter(someLock);
  // critical region, only one thread at a time enters this
  Monitor.Exit(someLock);

  // other code
}
```

The *Monitor.Enter* method accepts an object that is used to guard the region. If in some other part of your application, that is, in another method on another class even, you want to ensure that another region also is not entered while this one is owned by a thread, you would use the same object as the lock.

In the preceding code example, there is a huge flaw. What happens if an exception is thrown inside the critical region? In that case, the *Exit* method would never be called, thus never releasing the lock! To rectify this, the code should look as follows:

```
Monitor.Enter(someLock);
try
{
  // critical region, only one thread at a time enters this
}
finally
{
  Monitor.Exit(someLock);
}
```

This advice is so important that both C# and Visual Basic have keywords that wrap this functionality, and you should use them: *lock* and *SyncLock*, respectively. Revisiting the example of the immediately previous section, protect the region and ensure that the result of *someCounter* is always 4:

```
private object someLock = new object();
private void ThreadBoth()
{
  Debug.WriteLine(Thread.CurrentThread.Name + "enters method");
  int localVar = 0;
  localVar += 1;

  lock (someLock)
  {
    if (someCounter == 0)
    {
      Debug.WriteLine(Thread.CurrentThread.Name + "in if block");
      Thread.Sleep(1); // Simulate some longer activity.
      someCounter += localVar;
      Debug.WriteLine(Thread.CurrentThread.Name + "just incremented");
    }
    else
    {
      Debug.WriteLine(Thread.CurrentThread.Name + "in else block");
      someCounter += 3;
    }
  }
  return;
}
```

When locking or protecting a critical region, choose the lock object with care. Contrary to what you may see in quickly thrown together sample code, never use *this* or *typeOf(SomeClass)* as the lock object because any other thread could also lock on the objects you have chosen, and that could potentially lead to deadlocks. Instead, choose a dedicated object for your lock, one that only the relevant code can access such as *object someLock = new object()*. Finally, be sure to keep the critical regions short because unnecessarily protecting more code than necessary prevents code from being executed by other threads in parallel.

Thread Safe

Like your methods, the framework's methods also contain state. If you call those methods from multiple threads, do you expect them to result in corrupt data or not? The answer depends on which library and which specific method is in question.

A method that can be safely called by multiple threads simultaneously is said to be *thread safe*. Most of the framework is not thread safe. As a rule of thumb, all static methods of the framework are implemented to be thread safe and most instance methods aren't. The documentation states which methods are thread safe. You should follow the same pattern in your own class libraries. Not everything is implemented to be thread safe because obtaining locks is not a cheap operation. So the responsibility for writing thread-safe code with any library is left to the caller of the library. Besides, sometimes the decision to implement thread safety can be made only at a higher level and not in the library.

Chapter 5 describes how to view run-time performance counters. Be sure to explore the threading counters that are relevant to locking to identify potential misuse. Locks should be obtained for as little time as possible, so you must analyze the code carefully to ensure that this is the case.

In addition to the *Monitor* class discussed earlier, take a moment to familiarize yourself with the remaining classes in the *System.Threading* namespace. You may find the *Interlocked* class is more efficient than a *Monitor* is for the scenarios it supports, for example, safely incrementing an Int64: *Interlocked.Increment(ref someLongVar)*.

Collection classes are particularly susceptible to threading issues, so if the design mandates that they be shared among threads, ensure that all access to any members of the collection is protected with the same locking object. Some collections even offer a synchronized wrapper, but that does not perform as well, so manual locking is preferred. As the lock object, you should use the collection's *SyncRoot* property because that is what the private methods of the collection object use to protect access to the private internal state.

Deadlocks Revisited

Now that you understand how to define and obtain locks for critical regions, you can imagine how deadlock situations can occur if you are not careful with your design. The following example demonstrates such a scenario:

```
object someLock = new object();
object someOtherLock = new object();
private void menuItem1_Click(object sender, EventArgs e)
{
```

```
    Thread t1 = new Thread(this.DeadlockOne);
    t1.Name = "Worker Thread 1 ";
    Thread t2 = new Thread(this.DeadlockTwo);
    t2.Name = "Worker Thread 2 ";

    t1.Start();
    t2.Start();
  }

  private void DeadlockOne()
  {
    Debug.WriteLine(Thread.CurrentThread.Name + " enters DeadLockOne");
    lock (someLock)
    {
      Debug.WriteLine(Thread.CurrentThread.Name + " obtained SomeLock");
      // Run some code.
      Thread.Sleep(1); // simulate a context switch
      lock (someOtherLock)
      {
        Debug.WriteLine(Thread.CurrentThread.Name + " obtained SomeOtherLock");
        // Run some more code.
      }
    }
    MessageBox.Show("Thread 1 done");
  }

  private void DeadlockTwo()
  {
    Debug.WriteLine(Thread.CurrentThread.Name + " enters DeadLockTwo");
    lock (someOtherLock)
    {
      Debug.WriteLine(Thread.CurrentThread.Name + " obtained SomeOtherLock");
      // Run some code.
      this.AnotherDemoMethod();
    }
    MessageBox.Show("Thread 2 done");
  }

  private void AnotherDemoMethod()
  {
    Debug.WriteLine(Thread.CurrentThread.Name + " enters AnotherDemoMethod");
    lock (someLock)
    {
      Debug.WriteLine(Thread.CurrentThread.Name + " obtained SomeLock");
      // Run some more code.
    }
  }
```

When you run the preceding code, the two threads will deadlock, each waiting for the other to proceed. Observe the output window as always, and also break into the debugger and notice in the Threads window how the two threads are blocked on the two locks. Finally, notice how in this case there is no visual cue to the situation; your threads are simply not executing any further.

Deadlocks can be prevented only with careful design and by thorough understanding of where your threads can be executing at all times. Also, it should be evident that more communication mechanisms for threads to communicate with one another are needed. This is the subject of the next section.

ManualResetEvent

Most developers learn the principles and APIs described so far in this chapter, write some threaded code, and then at some point encounter a design in which it should be possible for one thread to signal to another that it should stop and block until it is signaled to continue execution. These are situations in which sleeping (using *Sleep*) for a certain interval is not sufficient, joining a thread (using *Join*) when it exits is not applicable because both threads must continue running, and obtaining a lock for a region isn't the exact requirement. Luckily, a mechanism exists and is fundamental to thread communication and cooperation: *System.Threading.ManualResetEvent*.

A *ManualResetEvent* object can be signaled or not signaled. It has a *Wait* method that when called blocks a thread or returns immediately and hence allows the thread to continue. Whether it blocks or not depends on the *boolean* signaled state. The state is toggled by using the *Set* and *Reset* methods. The best way to observe and understand the behavior of this object is to read the following code, type it in Visual Studio pointing two threads to the two methods, and run it while watching the output window.

```
List<long> l = new List<long>(10);
ManualResetEvent mre1 = new ManualResetEvent(false);
ManualResetEvent mre2 = new ManualResetEvent(false);
private void AddFirstAndLast2()
{
  Thread.Sleep(500); // Give the other one a head start; it makes no difference.
  Debug.WriteLine(Thread.CurrentThread.Name + " is running");
  l.Add(1);
  l.Add(2);

  // Tell the other thread to do its job and wait for it to tell you.
  Debug.WriteLine(Thread.CurrentThread.Name + " signals and waits");
  mre2.Set();
  mre1.WaitOne(); // blocks here
  mre1.Reset();
  Debug.WriteLine(Thread.CurrentThread.Name + " is running");

  l.Add(5);
  l.Add(6);

  Debug.WriteLine(Thread.CurrentThread.Name + " signals and waits");
  mre2.Set();
```

```
    mre1.WaitOne(); // could also have been t2.Join() if t2 is available
    mre1.Reset();   // superflous
    Debug.WriteLine(Thread.CurrentThread.Name + " is running and ends.");
  }

  private void AddMiddle2AndMessage()
  {
    // Wait for other thread to do its first set.
    Debug.WriteLine(Thread.CurrentThread.Name + " about to wait");
    mre2.WaitOne(); //blocks here
    mre2.Reset();
    Debug.WriteLine(Thread.CurrentThread.Name + " is running");

    l.Add(3);
    l.Add(4);

    // Tell it you are done and wait again.
    Debug.WriteLine(Thread.CurrentThread.Name + " signals and waits");
    mre1.Set();
    mre2.WaitOne();
    mre2.Reset();
    Debug.WriteLine(Thread.CurrentThread.Name + " is running and breaks in debugger");

    Debugger.Break();
    Debug.WriteLine(Thread.CurrentThread.Name + " ends. You hit F5.");
    mre1.Set();
  }
```

Note that there is also an *AutoResetEvent* class that has just one difference from *ManualResetEvent*: It automatically resets the object, so in the preceding code sample the calls to *Reset* could be omitted if an *AutoResetEvent* class is used. The use of an *AutoResetEvent* is preferable when you know that multiple threads are waiting on the event and you need to ensure that only one executes when the event is signaled.

Another object in the threading namespace is *Mutex*. A mutex is usually introduced first in threading textbooks because, depending on how it is used, it can achieve the goals of most of the other synchronization objects. However, it is more expensive in terms of performance and its primary advantage in Windows is for interprocess communication, which is not available in the .NET Compact Framework because creating named mutexes is not supported. *Mutex* is mentioned here simply to encourage you to visit its documentation.

ThreadPool

In all of the preceding examples, threads were explicitly created. In real-world scenarios, though, most of the time you should use a *ThreadPool* instead. A *ThreadPool* is a pool of threads. It starts out empty, and when your code requests a new thread from the pool, the pool will keep the thread around for the next time your code needs a thread again. The performance gains are impressive because a new thread need not be created most times because threads that are idling in the pool can be reused. Also, threads need not be destroyed immediately, which results in another performance gain. Finally, if an application were to create a large number of tasks, the *ThreadPool* would create a maximum of 25 threads[1] and queue all other work items to be executed when a thread became free. In addition to all the performance gains, it is also much easier to program against the *ThreadPool*, as the following code example exhibits:

```
private void menuItem1_Click(object sender, EventArgs e)
{
  WaitCallback wc = new WaitCallback(RunsOnPoolThread);
  object someState = new object();
  ThreadPool.QueueUserWorkItem(wc, someState);
}

private void RunsOnPoolThread(object state)
{
  // do stuff on thread optionally using state
}
```

As you can see, using a thread from the pool is a single statement. As with the explicit thread creation, you specify a delegate, but this one also accepts some state as an object, which can be useful if you need to pass initialization data to the thread.

Using a thread pool should be the default choice, but it is not the best choice in some scenarios. If your thread does not perform a task and then exit but rather stays alive for a very long period of time, potentially blocking on some synchronization object, a dedicated thread is generally a better choice.

Understanding Threading and Application Shutdown

In Chapter 2, we state that an application terminates when its main form exits. The precise and more correct statement is that an application terminates when all *foreground* threads have exited. If an application does not create any threads, the only foreground thread is the main thread, and it terminates when the main form is closed; hence the original statement is true for such applications. This means you must understand what foreground threads are and how to ensure thatthey are terminated before the main form closes.

Background Threads

.NET threads can be foreground or background threads. By default, every thread explicitly created is a foreground thread and every thread from the *ThreadPool* or otherwise created by

1 In version 2.0, this is configurable through the *SetMaxThreads* method. In version 1.0, it is fixed at 256.

the framework is a background thread. Unless you want a thread to hold up the process when the user has indicated that it should close, you should make all your threads background threads.

The way a thread is made to be background is by setting its *IsBackground* property to *true* before starting it. Our advice is that you make this a good habit for every thread you create: Set to *true* its *IsBackground* property and give it a *Name*. Think of these two property calls as part of the construction process.

An example that enforces this point was already presented earlier in this chapter. Revisit the deadlock example with the two worker threads. When the two threads are deadlocked, try closing the application by using the form's OK button. Notice how Visual Studio debugging does not end. Stop the application process from the integrated development environment (IDE), and then set both threads' properties *IsBackground=true*. Run the application again and observe it closely. We discuss thread termination further later in this chapter.

Another example is shown here:

```
// Start thread that will block.
private void menuItem1_Click(object sender, EventArgs e)
{
  Thread t = new Thread(new ThreadStart(this.KeepTheProcessUp));
  //t.IsBackground = true;
  t.Start();

  MessageBox.Show("Hit the Exit button. Is Visual Studio still debugging?");
}

ManualResetEvent mre = new ManualResetEvent(false);
private void KeepTheProcessUp()
{
  mre.WaitOne();

  MessageBox.Show("Never shown!");
  // Imagine more code here.
}

//Exit
private void menuItem2_Click(object sender, EventArgs e)
{
  this.Close();
  Application.Exit(); // utterly superfluous but just to emphasize the point!
}
```

You can uncomment the *t.IsBackground = true;* line to exhibit the desired behavior.

Unfortunately, the .NET Compact Framework implementation of *IsBackground* does not guarantee that behavior always. One example is networking calls, that is, the managed sockets implementation internally creates worker threads that will not terminate simply by exiting the application. More important, any threads that are blocked on Platform Invocation Services (PInvoke) calls also are not terminated by the runtime when the application exits. The net effect is that you should not rely on a thread not to hold up the process only because of its *IsBackground* property. The property should be set on all threads but only as a backup mechanism and only when there is no deinitilization code the thread must execute.

Also, background threads generally will not keep a process up because the runtime aborts them when the main thread exits. Aborting threads is not a clean way to exit threads, and you should avoid using it. In other words, design your applications in such a way that all threads can exit in a clean way when the application ends. We examine this in the next section.

Thread Termination

A thread can be brutally terminated by using its *Abort* method. This technique is generally frowned upon and is definitely the wrong way to cancel a job. Terminating a thread in such a manner may leave the application in an indeterminate state internally. A better alternative is to use the approach used in one of the earlier examples in this chapter when searching the store. Declare a *boolean* that is visible to both the worker thread and the main thread. Set it from the main thread when it wants to cancel the job, and periodically read it from the worker thread to cleanly exit its task. The termination is not immediate, and this is a good thing because the thread has a chance to shut down and leave any state in a consistent safe state.

The technique just described for canceling a thread is identical to the technique you should use to exit an application. Set to *true* a global static Boolean variable *isClosing* that the application is exiting, and ensure that all your worker threads periodically check the variable and are prepared for a quick, clean exit. An ideal place to set the variable is in the *Form.Closing* event, of course.

If your worker threads are blocked, they will not be able to check the global variable. You must do a few things to prevent your worker threads from being blocked. First, ensure that from the *Closing* event handler you set all synchronization objects to be signaled so that any blocked threads can return at that instance. Wherever in code a thread blocks, on the next line ensure it checks the global *isClosing* variable; this is also true for statements following a *Monitor.Enter* or *lock* statement.

In addition, for all threading, complete one final task. Always use overloads of blocking methods that accept a timeout, to avoid deadlocks, among other things. For example, the *Join* and *Wait* methods shown earlier have overloads that take a maximum number of milliseconds to block for; the return value of the method indicates whether it returned because of success or because of a timeout. Also, as an alternative to the lock statement, investigate the *Monitor.TryEnter* method.

Tip Some of the previous examples demonstrate how the process does not exit because a thread is holding it up even after the main form has closed. In those scenarios, to exit your process we advise that you stop debugging using Visual Studio. If you have run the application on the target and without using Visual Studio, you must manually terminate the process, or another instance of your application will not execute. One way to terminate is to use one of the remote tools, such as the Remote Process Viewer, as mentioned in Chapter 4.

Using .NET Timers

Earlier in this chapter, we demonstrated the use of a *System.Windows.Forms.Timer*, and as stated there, sometimes such a timer can fit a scenario in which implementing true threading would be overkill or would introduce unwanted complexity. It is important to note that Windows Forms timers should be used only for very short tasks because they are not precise and fire on the main thread, thus influencing UI responsiveness.

Another timer available to .NET Compact Framework applications is the *System.Threading.Timer*. This timer is more accurate; it fires on a thread from the *ThreadPool* and is ideal for executing background tasks that do not touch the UI when such tasks should occur after a defined interval. The following code example demonstrates use of a threading timer:

```
System.Threading.Timer tmr;
private void menuItem1_Click(object sender, EventArgs e)
{
  object someState = new object();
  TimerCallback tmrClbck = new TimerCallback(this.AtSetInterval);
  tmr = new System.Threading.Timer(tmrClbck, someState, 5 * 1000, -1);
}

private void AtSetInterval(object state)
{
  // Do something.

  // done with this timer
  tmr.Dispose();
}
```

There are a few interesting points to make about the *Timer*:

- A reference to the timer object must be kept because, like other .NET objects, it is eligible for garbage collection.
- The timer must be disposed of when it has served its purpose.
- The timer has a method called *Change* that has a similar signature to its constructor.

- For the last parameter in the example (which is the *period* parameter) a −1 was passed. Any other numeric value would have resulted in the timer firing repeatedly at that interval. For that to happen, of course, the timer should not be disposed of in the callback.

The last point is worth expanding a bit. If you do specify a *period* parameter, your callback method has to be designed to be reentrant because it is conceivable that two thread pool threads can execute statements in the method concurrently if the first invocation is still executing when the next one fires. It is for this reason that we advise you always to pass −1 as the last value. If you do need the timer to fire again after a set interval and to do so indefinitely, be specific about it in the callback. For example:

```
private void AtSetInterval(object state)
{
  // Do something.
  MessageBox.Show("Test");

  // Restart this timer.
  tmr.Change(5 * 1000, -1);
}
```

This approach guarantees that regardless of what intervals are specified and how long the method takes to execute, only one thread will ever be executing in the method.

Summary

This code-heavy chapter has guided you through understanding why you may use threads and how they work at the operating system level to writing code for marshaling data from worker threads to the main thread and the various synchronization objects available to the .NET Compact Framework developer. The key points to take away are the following:

- Never block the user interface.
- More threads does not equal more performance.
- Avoiding race conditions and deadlocks is possible only through careful design and total knowledge of the system under implementation. Simply testing for these conditions does not necessarily reveal threading issues because such issues are hard to reproduce.
- The *System.Threading* namespace is fairly rich in version 2.0, and you should become very familiar with it before you write any threading code. This chapter only took you on a brief tour.

Chapter 12
Graphics Programming

In this chapter:

Graphics programming skills are not only for games developers. A basic understanding of graphics programming is useful to all developers, whether for creating a good-looking splash screen or for doing your own drawing in a custom control so as to present a user interface (UI) to users that looks more polished and professional than one that is built using only the standard Microsoft Windows Forms controls from the Microsoft Visual Studio 2005 Toolbox.

This chapter shows you how to perform simple graphics programming tasks and demonstrates skills you can use to make your application stand out from the crowd.

Drawing Images, Text, and Shapes

The simplest way of displaying an image is to use the *PictureBox* control, with which most developers are familiar. You can use a *Form* containing a docked *PictureBox* to implement a very simple splash screen (a full-screen image that is displayed to the user while you run code in the background to set up the main form and perform other setup tasks). You can display the splash screen *Form* at application startup by using code such as that shown in Listing 12-1.

Listing 12-1 Logic to Display a Splash Screen During Application Startup

```
using System;
using System.Windows.Forms;

namespace MobileDevelopersHandbook.SimpleGraphic
{
    static class Program
    {
        /// <summary>
        /// The main entry point for the application.
        /// </summary>
        [MTAThread]
        static void Main()
        {
```

```
            // Display splash screen.
            SplashForm spFrm = new SplashForm();
            spFrm.Show();
            spFrm.Refresh();

            // Run setup code and display main form.
            Form1 frm1 = new Form1(spFrm);
            Application.Run(frm1);
        }
    }
}
```

Listing 12-2 shows the code for the splash screen for a smartphone application. Notice that the designer-generated code is not shown in Listing 12-2. To get the sample working, you must drag a *PictureBox* onto the form and dock it to fill the *Form*. Notice that in Listing 12-1 a reference to the *SplashForm* instance is passed to the constructor of *Form1*; *Form1* needs the reference to the *SplashForm* instance because it is responsible for closing the splash screen when its construction work is complete.

Listing 12-2 Splash Screen Using a Docked *PictureBox* in a Form

```
using System;
using System.ComponentModel;
using System.Drawing;
using System.IO;
using System.Windows.Forms;

namespace MobileDevelopersHandbook.SimpleGraphic
{
    public partial class SplashForm : Form
    {
        public SplashForm()
        {
            InitializeComponent();
        }

        private void SplashForm_Load(object sender, EventArgs e)
        {
            // Show full screen.
            this.ControlBox = false;

            // Load graphic into PictureBox.
            string path = GetApplicationDirectory();
            Image img = new Bitmap(Path.Combine(path, "graphic.jpg"));
            pictureBox1.SizeMode = PictureBoxSizeMode.StretchImage;
            pictureBox1.Image = img;
        }
```

```
        private string GetApplicationDirectory()
        {
            return System.IO.Path.GetDirectoryName(
                System.Reflection.Assembly.GetExecutingAssembly()
                .GetModules()[0].FullyQualifiedName);
        }
    }
}
```

In the sample application called SimpleGraphic, which you can find in the downloadable code for this chapter on this book's companion Web site, the splash screen displays the graphic from the cover of this book before displaying the application's main form (see Figure 12-1).

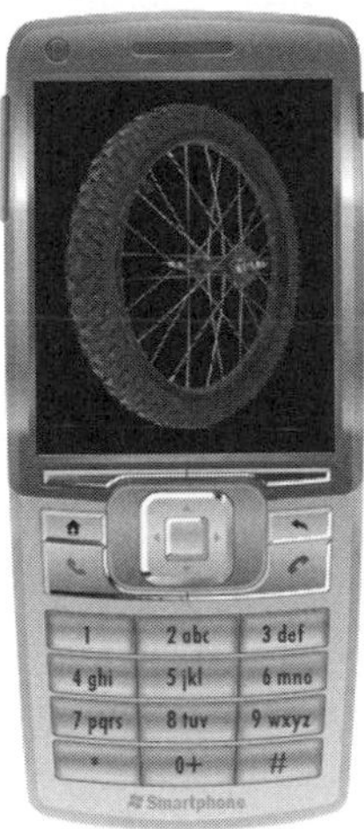

Figure 12-1 Displaying a full-screen image in a *PictureBox*

Understanding Painting Basics

All drawing in Windows Forms applications takes place in response to a *Paint* instruction from the Windows operating system. Windows sends this instruction to a control whenever the operating system determines that the portion of the screen the control occupies is invalid and must be repainted. This occurs in the following situations:

- When the control (or form) first is displayed
- When the form or control is resized (which also occurs when the screen orientation switches between portrait and landscape)
- When a control that was placed in front of another becomes invisible
- When you force a repaint by calling the *Refresh* or *Invalidate* method of the control

Windows sends a *Paint* instruction first to the container control (the *Form* or *Panel*) and then to any child controls inside the container.

Internally, a control handles the *Paint* instruction in its *Paint* method, and it also fires the *Paint* event immediately after executing the *Paint* method. Consequently, you can use one of two ways to do your own drawing:

- Capture the *Paint* event so that any drawing you do augments the built-in drawing of the control
- Override the *OnPaint* method so that your own drawing completely replaces the built-in capabilities

If you are creating a custom control by extending an existing control and it requires custom drawing, you would override the *OnPaint* method.

All drawing takes place through a *System.Drawing.Graphics* object. You can get a *System.Drawing.Graphics* object in a number of ways:

- In the *PaintEventArgs* object that is passed into the *OnPaint* method or the *Paint* event of a control
- By calling the *Control.CreateGraphics* method
- By calling the static (shared in Visual Basic) method *Graphics.FromImage* method, which returns a *Graphics* object from an existing *Image* object, allowing you to draw on the existing *Image*

Important All the *System.Drawing* objects, such as *Graphics*, *Pen*, and *Brush*, are thin managed wrappers around native objects. Always dispose of them properly; otherwise, you may run into memory management problems.

Drawing Images

A *PictureBox* is fine for displaying pictures, but if you want to display graphical content you compose yourself from different components, you'll have to do your own drawing. You can enhance the splash screen example by overriding the *OnPaint* method of a form. The *OnPaint* method takes a parameter of a *PaintEventArgs* object, the *Graphics* property of which exposes the *Graphics* object through which all drawing takes place. The other property of the *PaintEventArgs* object, *ClipRectangle*, gives the area to be drawn.

To draw an image on the form, you can simply use the *DrawImage* method of the *Graphics* object, as follows:

```
using System.Drawing;
…

    protected override void OnPaint(PaintEventArgs e)
    {
```

```
        using (Image backgroundImage =
            new Bitmap(System.Reflection.Assembly.GetExecutingAssembly()
          .GetManifestResourceStream("MobileDevelopersHandbook.Graphic.JPG")))
        {
            // Use the Graphics object from the PaintEventArgs.
            e.Graphics.DrawImage(backgroundImage, 0, 0);
        }
    }
```

Notice that in this example the graphics file called Graphic.jpg is an embedded resource, and hence you must use the rather complicated code shown here to call *Assembly.GetManifestResourceStream*, which returns a *Stream* that you pass to the *Bitmap* constructor. This differs from the example shown in Listing 12-1, where the graphic was included in that project as a content file (meaning the *Build Action* property of the file is set to *Content* so that it is deployed as a separate file alongside your executable).

Tip When you include graphics as an embedded resource, you retrieve them from the executing assembly using code similar to that shown in the preceding code sample. Be careful to get the name right: resource names are case sensitive. In Solution Explorer, the graphic file has the name Graphic.JPG, so when you add it as an embedded resource (by setting the *Build Action* property of the file to *Embedded Resource*), it takes the name MobileDevelopersHandbook.Graphic.JPG, where *MobileDevelopersHandbook* is the default namespace for the project (set in the project properties window). The resource name Graphic.JPG must use exactly the same case as displayed in Solution Explorer. If you have trouble getting the correct name, use the *Assembly.GetManifestResourceNames* method, which returns a string array containing the names of all embedded resources.

Scaling Images

The code you just used does draw the image on the screen, but if you run the application on both the regular smartphone emulator and also the quarter VGA (QVGA) emulator, you get an interesting result, as shown in Figure 12-2. The image we use in this sample is an appropriate size for the higher-resolution 240 × 320 pixel screen on the QVGA device, but on the lower-resolution 176 × 220 pixel display of the regular smartphone, the image doesn't fit the display. (The sample shown in Listing 12-2 does not have this problem because it set the *SizeMode* property of the *PictureBox* to *PictureBoxSizeMode.StretchImage* so that the graphic resizes to fit the dimensions of the *PictureBox*.)

Figure 12-2 Graphic displayed on a QVGA device (left) but that is too big for the regular smartphone display (right)

The answer is to use another form of the *DrawImage* function, one that takes a *Rectangle* parameter for the destination, and another *Rectangle* that selects the source portion of the image to draw (in this example, you draw all of the source image). In fact, if you are working through the examples in this chapter, you will soon add some more shapes and text to the display, so to make space for these additional items, you can use the following code to center the image and reduce it to 50 percent of the width of the display. In this particular example, you can find the width of the display by obtaining the *ClipRectangle* property of the *PaintEventArgs* object that is passed into the *OnPaint* method. The implementation of *OnPaint* now becomes the following:

```
using System.Drawing;
...

    protected override void OnPaint(PaintEventArgs e)
    {
        // Draw the main image.
        using (Image backgroundImage =
            new Bitmap(System.Reflection.Assembly.GetExecutingAssembly()
          .GetManifestResourceStream("MobileDevelopersHandbook.Graphic.JPG")))
        {
            // Fill the background.
            e.Graphics.Clear(Color.Black);

            // Draw the image, but scale it.
            // SourceRect is entire image.
            Rectangle srcRect = new
               Rectangle(0, 0, backgroundImage.Width, backgroundImage.Height);
```

```
            // Set destination rectangle to be 50 percent of the clipping
            // rectangle.
            Rectangle destRect = new Rectangle(
                0, 0, e.ClipRectangle.Width / 2, e.ClipRectangle.Height / 2);
            // Reposition origin to center the image on the screen.
            destRect.Location = new Point(
                (e.ClipRectangle.Width - destRect.Width) / 2,
                (e.ClipRectangle.Height - destRect.Height) / 2);

            // Draw the image.
            e.Graphics.DrawImage(backgroundImage, destRect, srcRect,
                GraphicsUnit.Pixel);
        }
    }
```

Important Do not rely on the *ClipRectangle* property for determining the size of the screen. In this case, it does equal the dimensions of the screen, but you cannot rely on that. In some cases, the *ClipRectangle* might be less than the whole area covered by the control that is being painted because Windows calls the *OnPaint* method only to request painting of whichever area has become invalidated (in need of repainting). For example, if a child control on the *Form* is made invisible, the *OnPaint* method of its container (the *Form*) is called, but the *ClipRectangle* will contain only the dimensions of the region where the child control was located.

Painting the Background

Notice the lines at the beginning of the *OnPaint* method just shown:

```
            // Fill the background.
            e.Graphics.Clear(Color.Black);
```

This is how you color in the background. Without this, the graphic is drawn center screen but is surrounded by white. The *Graphics.Clear* method clears the entire drawing surface and fills it with the specified color.

Painting Shapes and Text

You can now add shapes and/or text to the drawing surface. The *Graphics* object includes the *DrawRectangle*, *DrawEllipse*, *DrawPolygon*, *DrawLines*, and *DrawLine* methods for shapes and the *DrawText* method for text. You can also use the *FillRectangle*, *FillEllipse*, *FillPolygon*, and *FillRegion* methods for filling a shape with a specified color.

All these methods make use of one or more of the following objects:

- ***Pen*** Used for drawing text and for the outlines of shapes. Set the *Width*, *Color*, and/or *DashStyle* properties to affect how items drawn with the *Pen* appear.
- ***SolidBrush*** Defines the background for text or the fill color for a shape. This has only one property: *Color*.
- ***TextureBrush*** Similar to a *SolidBrush*, but fills in the drawn object using an image you select through its *Image* property.

The following example shows how to create a *Pen* and a *SolidBrush* and how to use them to draw a *Rectangle* with some text inside it. It also shows how to use the *Graphics.MeasureString* method, which is useful for measuring the height and width of a string that is to be drawn using a particular font. It is used here so that the size of the rectangle enclosing the text can be determined.

```
using System.Drawing;
...

    protected override void OnPaint(PaintEventArgs e)
    {
        // Draw text positioned inside a rectangle.
        string s = "Mobile Developers Handbook";

        // Set pen and font size.
        int penSize = 4;
        int fontSize = 10;

        using (Pen pen = new Pen(Color.Yellow, penSize))
        {
            using (Font font = new Font("Arial", fontSize, FontStyle.Regular))
            {
                using (SolidBrush brush = new SolidBrush(Color.White))
                {
                    SizeF textSize = e.Graphics.MeasureString(s, font);

                    // Create a rectangle with padding space between string
                    // and box.
                    int rectWidth = Convert.ToInt32((textSize.Width) + 10);
                    int rectHeight = Convert.ToInt32((textSize.Height) + 10);
                    Rectangle r = new Rectangle(
                        (e.ClipRectangle.Width - rectWidth) / 2,
                        e.ClipRectangle.Height - rectHeight - 15,
                        rectWidth,
                        rectHeight);

                    e.Graphics.DrawRectangle(pen, r);
                    e.Graphics.DrawString(s, font, brush,
                        r.Left + 5, r.Top + 5);
                }
            }
        }
    }
```

Tip Although not demonstrated in these code samples (for simplicity), it is good practice to create pen/bitmap/brush objects beforehand when overriding the *OnPaint* event and to reuse the same object instances inside the *OnPaint* event handler because this method could be called a number of times and your application would be slowed down by repeated object construction.

Wrapping Text

The example just shown works for short strings, but if you want to draw a long string, you may be required to wrap it across one or more lines to ensure that it is readable. You can do this by using another override of the *DrawString* method, which takes as its fourth parameter a *RectangleF* instance that defines the area to draw into and as its fifth parameter a *StringFormat* instance. You can horizontally align the text to the left, center, or right by using the *Alignment* property of the *StringFormat* object, and you can set wrapping and clipping behavior by using the *FormatFlags* property. The following code fragment shows how to wrap and center-align a long string. You can see how it appears in Figure 12-3.

```
protected override void OnPaint(PaintEventArgs e)
{
   using (Font font = new Font("Arial", fontSize, FontStyle.Regular))
    {
        using (SolidBrush brush = new SolidBrush(Color.White))
        {
            // Now draw a long string, but use a formatting rectangle and
            // a StringFormat object to wrap and align the text.
            string authors =
               "Authors: Andy Wigley, Daniel Moth, Peter Foot";

            // Define the destination rectangle.
            RectangleF layoutRectangle =
              new RectangleF(15, this.Height - 50, this.Width - 20, 100);

            // Create a StringFormat and set formatting flags.
            StringFormat strFmt = new StringFormat();
            strFmt.Alignment = StringAlignment.Center;
            strFmt.FormatFlags = StringFormatFlags.NoClip;

            // Draw the string.
            e.Graphics.DrawString(authors, font, brush, layoutRectangle,
                strFmt);
        }
    }
}
```

Figure 12-3 Custom drawing used in a splash screen, made up of an image, text, a line, and a shape

Drawing Lines

Drawing lines on a graphics surface is simple. Draw a simple line using the *DrawLine* method, or draw a line that connects many points by using the *DrawLines* method. Use a *Pen* object to determine the color, thickness, and dash style.

```
using System.Drawing;
...

    protected override void OnPaint(PaintEventArgs e)
    {
        // Draw Image (not shown) . . .

        // Draw Text and Rectangle (not shown) . . .

        // Draw a line with e.Graphics.DrawLine.
        // Create pen.
        using (Pen redPen = new Pen(Color.Red, 3))
        {
            int length = e.ClipRectangle.Width - 20;
            int x1 = 10;
            int y1 = 10;
            int x2 = length + 10;
            int y2 = 10;

            // Draw line to screen.
            e.Graphics.DrawLine(redPen, x1, y1, x2, y2);
        }
    }
```

The sample program ShapesLinesText, available in the downloadable code for this chapter on the book's companion Web site, puts these three techniques together to present a more striking splash screen, as shown in Figure 12-3.

Handling Different Resolutions

In the section titled "Scaling Images" earlier in this chapter, you learned how to scale an image to fit the display area. That solution used the *ClipRectangle* property of the *PaintEventArgs* object to determine the size of the area being repainted, and so works well on a standard 176 × 220 pixel smartphone display and also on a 240 × 320 pixel QVGA display.

However, the code shown previously in the section titled "Drawing Images, Text, and Shapes" is not optimized for different resolutions. The pen width of 4 and font size of 10 display well on the standard smartphone (as shown in Figure 12-3), but the text looks a little bit small when displayed on the QVGA device. That is because the QVGA device displays text and graphics using a higher dots per inch (dpi). You must adjust the width and font size on higher-dpi devices. See the sidebar titled "Understanding dpi, VGA, and QVGA" for an explanation of the effect of dots per inch on the display size of graphics items you draw.

Understanding dpi, VGA, and QVGA

It's a common misconception that devices with a high-resolution display always have a larger physical display. They often do, but the physical dimensions of a display area are dependent not only on its resolution (the number of pixels it can display from left to right and from top to bottom) but also on the dots per inch (dpi; the number of pixels it can display per inch).

Older Pocket PC devices had a 240 × 320 pixel display, also known as QVGA. (QVGA stands for quarter Video Graphics Array, where VGA is the de facto graphics standard for computers, which display images and text at a resolution of 640 × 480. Tthe old Pocket PC devices contain a quarter of the total number of pixels contained in a standard VGA display; hence they are called QVGA.) The dpi used on those older devices varied, but a typical figure was 96 dpi, giving physical dimensions of approximately 2.5 inches by 3.3 inches.

Today, handheld devices come in many different screen configurations. Many manufacturers sell Pocket PC devices that have VGA screens, but all manufacturers use a higher dpi on their higher-resolution devices, usually 192 dpi. This results in physical dimensions of—yes—approximately 2.5 inches by 3.3 inches—the same as the older devices. What does change, though, is that the VGA display looks much better. With certain built-in programs such as Microsoft Pocket Internet Explorer and Microsoft Office Excel Mobile, you can zoom out the display to show more information, and the high-dpi resolution means that you can see large amounts of very small text on the screen. However, most standard functionality on a VGA device such as the Today screen, Settings, and so on appears much the same as on a QVGA device, although the graphics are much sharper. The important point to realize is that you do not necessarily see more on a VGA display, but rather you see approximately the same amount of information that simply looks much better.

Of course, how you as a developer use the additional pixels on a VGA or other high-resolution device is up to you. But it is usually a mistake to try to display very much more information. For example, if you display text on a QVGA device using a font size of 8 points at 96 dpi and then display the same text using the same font size on a VGA device at 192 dpi, the text appears much smaller on the VGA device–so small that some users may find it hard to read, despite the higher-quality display.

Graphics developers must be aware of the dpi of the display and modify the size of drawn objects so that they look right to the user. You may be able to take advantage of a higher-resolution display to display more information, but beware of the shrinking effect of a higher-dpi display. You can find the dpi of the current display by using the *Graphics.DpiX* and *DpiY* properties.

If you are not doing any custom drawing, you do not have to worry about different resolution displays. As explained in Chapter 2, "Building a Microsoft Windows Forms GUI," if you set the *AutoScaleMode* property of your *Form* to *Dpi*, it takes care of resizing standard controls to maintain appropriate physical dimensions according to the dpi of the device display.

One point all developers must remember is that if you are providing an icon for your application, you must provide a 32 × 32 pixel icon for use on high-dpi devices as well as the 16 × 16 pixel icon required for lower-dpi devices. You can set the icon for an application in the project properties window; if you then build a .cab file to install your application, as explained in Chapter 6, "Completing the Application: Packaging and Deployment," the icon is displayed in menus on the device, such as in the Programs list on a Pocket PC.

The exact font sizes or pen widths you use on a higher-dpi display are application dependent and so are something you must determine by testing. In the sample application, use the following code to increase the pen width and font size for displays with a resolution greater than 100 dpi:

```
// Set default pen and font size.
int penSize = 4;
int fontSize = 10;

// Find dpi of the current display.
float horResolution = e.Graphics.DpiX;
if (horResolution > 100.0)
{
```

```
        // Increase pen and font size on higher-resolution devices.
        penSize = 5;
        fontSize = 11;
    }

    using (Pen pen = new Pen(Color.Yellow, penSize))
    {
        using (Font font = new Font("Arial", fontSize, FontStyle.Regular))
        {
        ...
```

The effect is quite subtle, as shown in Figure 12-4, but by increasing the font size and pen width, the end result is closer to that on a 96-dpi display, as shown in Figure 12-3.

Figure 12-4 Increasing the pen width and font size on a high-dpi display (right) to counteract the shrinking effect

Rotating Text

One addition to Microsoft .NET Compact Framework version 2.0 that is useful for working with text is support for the *LogFont* class, which defines the characteristics of a font for creating rotated text effects. This class is in the *Microsoft.WindowsCE.Forms* namespace, so you must add a reference to that assembly to use it.

The *LogFont* class is easy to use. Simply create a *LogFont* object, set properties to define the size and angle of the font, and then call the *Font.FromLogFont* method to return the

System.Drawing.Font instance you use for drawing text. The following code shows a method you can use to do this:

```
using System.Drawing;
using Microsoft.WindowsCE.Forms;
...
        private const float POINTS_PER_INCH = 72f;

        private Font CreateLogFont(int angle)
        {
            // Create and define a LogFont structure.
            LogFont fontStruct = new LogFont();

            using (Graphics g = this.CreateGraphics())
            {
                // Scale 10 points for the dpi of the current display.
                // Also make it negative, which means match it against
                // character height of available fonts.
                fontStruct.Height =
                    -1 * (int)(14f * (g.DpiY / POINTS_PER_INCH));
            }

            // Because font width is usually dependent on the height,
            // usual to set width to zero
            fontStruct.Width = 0;

            // Set the font angle.
            // Remember to multiply by 10.
            fontStruct.Escapement = angle * 10;

            // The Escapement member specifies both the
            // escapement and orientation. You should set
            // Escapement and Orientation to the same value.
            fontStruct.Orientation = fontStruct.Escapement;

            // No formatting
            fontStruct.Italic = 0;
            fontStruct.Underline = 0;
            fontStruct.StrikeOut = 0;
            // Weight: 0 = default, 400 = normal, 700 = bold
            fontStruct.Weight = 0;

            fontStruct.CharSet = LogFontCharSet.Default;
            fontStruct.OutPrecision = LogFontPrecision.Default;
            fontStruct.ClipPrecision = LogFontClipPrecision.Default;
            fontStruct.Quality = LogFontQuality.Default;
            fontStruct.PitchAndFamily = LogFontPitchAndFamily.Default;

            fontStruct.FaceName = "Arial";

            // Create the font from the LogFont structure.
            return Font.FromLogFont(fontStruct);
        }
```

Some of the properties of *LogFont* require further explanation, as shown in Table 12-1.

Table 12-1 *LogFont* Properties

Property	Description
Height	Specifies the height of the font in device units (pixels). If this field is 0, the Windows CE font manager returns the default font size for the font family requested in the *PitchOrFamily* or *FaceName* property. Most of the time, however, you will want to use a font of a particular size. The preceding code takes the size of a 10-point font, which is 10 + 2 points for the size of the descent (the distance characters such as *j* descend below the baseline) plus 2 points for the distance between one row of characters and the next (known as the external leading value in the typesetting world). The total size of 14 is then scaled to the screen resolution of the current device by dividing the current vertical resolution (from *Graphics.DpiY*) by 72, which is the standard number of points per inch used in typesetting. The final value is multiplied by -1 to force the font mapper to search for a font with a character height equal to the requested value. If you leave this value positive, the font mapper searches for a font with an equivalent cell height.
Width	Specifies the average character width. Because character width is generally dependent on the font height, you should usually set this to zero so that the Windows CE font manager computes the correct width for the height.
Escapement	Set this to the required angle from the horizontal, but always remember to multiply by 10. For example, the escapement value for 90 degrees is 900.
Orientation	You must always set this to the same value as *Escapement*.
Weight	Set this to a value between 1 (invisible) and 700 (bold). The value 0 represents the default value, which is 400 for normal weight.

After you have your font, you use it in the same way as any other, as shown in the following code fragment:

```
protected override void OnPaint(PaintEventArgs e)
{
    // Draw the image, but scale it.
    … NOT SHOWN (same as before)…

    // Create string to draw.
    string drawString = "Mobile Developers Handbook";
    // Create font and brush.
    SolidBrush drawBrush = new SolidBrush(Color.Yellow);

    // Draw string to screen using the LogFont.
    using (Font ft = CreateLogFont(90))
    {
        e.Graphics.DrawString(drawString,
                              ft,
                              drawBrush,
```

```
                                        5,
                                        this.Height - 20,
                                        new
          StringFormat(StringFormatFlags.NoClip | StringFormatFlags.NoWrap));
        }

        base.OnPaint(e);
    }
```

This code, which is taken from the RotatedText sample in the downloadable code for this chapter on the book's companion Web site, produces output as shown in Figure 12-5.

Figure 12-5 Rotated text drawn using *LogFont*

Reducing Flicker by Using Double Buffering

You may have noticed that even with the relatively simple samples described so far, the screen does not paint all at once. If you use more complex drawing, or you are trying to simulate animation effects by repeatedly repainting an object while moving its position, you will notice a pronounced flickering effect that spoils the results.

The solution to this issue is a technique called *double buffering*, which simply entails creating a background buffer, drawing to the buffer, and painting the result to the screen only when all drawing is complete. One implementation of double buffering is shown in Listing 12-3.

(The designer-generated code is not shown; you will have to hook up the *Form.Resize* event to get this to work.)

Listing 12-3 Drawing Using Double Buffering

```
using System;
using System.ComponentModel;
using System.Drawing;
using System.IO;
using System.Windows.Forms;
using Microsoft.WindowsCE.Forms;

namespace MobileDevelopersHandbook
{
    public partial class SplashForm : Form
    {
        // The background buffer for graphics double buffering
        protected Bitmap backBuffer;

        public SplashForm()
        {
            InitializeComponent();
        }

        private void SplashForm_Load(object sender, EventArgs e)
        {
            // Show full screen.
            this.ControlBox = false;
        }

        protected override void OnPaint(PaintEventArgs e)
        {
            if (backBuffer != null)
            {
                // You need a Graphics object on the buffer.
                using (Graphics gxBuffer = Graphics.FromImage(backBuffer))
                {
                    // Fill the background.
                    gxBuffer.Clear(Color.Black);

                    using (Image backgroundImage =
            new Bitmap(System.Reflection.Assembly.GetExecutingAssembly()
          .GetManifestResourceStream("MobileDevelopersHandbook.Graphic.JPG")))
                    {
                        // Use the Graphics object from the buffer.
                        gxBuffer.DrawImage(backgroundImage, 0, 0);
                    }

                    // Draw text positioned inside a rectangle.
                    string s = "Mobile Developers Handbook";

                    // Set pen and font size.
                    int penSize = 4;
                    int fontSize = 10;

                    using (Pen pen = new Pen(Color.Yellow, penSize))
```

```
                {
                    using (Font font =
                        new Font("Arial", fontSize, FontStyle.Regular))
                    {
                        using (SolidBrush brush =
                            new SolidBrush(Color.White))
                        {
                            SizeF textSize =
                                e.Graphics.MeasureString(s, font);

                            // Create a rectangle with padding space
                            // between string and box.
                            int rcWidth =
                                Convert.ToInt32((textSize.Width) + 10);
                            int rcHeight =
                                Convert.ToInt32((textSize.Height) + 10);
                            Rectangle r = new Rectangle(
                                (e.ClipRectangle.Width - rcWidth) / 2,
                                 e.ClipRectangle.Height - rcHeight - 15,
                                 rcWidth,
                                 rcHeight);

                            gxBuffer.DrawRectangle(pen, r);
                            gxBuffer.DrawString(s, font, brush,
                                 r.Left + 5, r.Top + 5);
                        }
                    }
                }
            }
            // Put the final composed image on screen.
            e.Graphics.DrawImage(backBuffer, 0, 0);
        }
        else
            e.Graphics.Clear(this.BackColor);
    }

    protected override void OnPaintBackground(PaintEventArgs e)
    {
        // Make this a no-op—background is painted in OnPaint.
    }

    private void SplashForm_Resize(object sender, EventArgs e)
    {
        if (backBuffer != null)
        {
            // Dispose of the original one.
            backBuffer.Dispose();
        }

        // Create a new backbuffer of the correct size.
        backBuffer = new Bitmap(this.ClientSize.Width,
            this.ClientSize.Height,
            System.Drawing.Imaging.PixelFormat.Format32bppRgb);
    }
  }
}
```

In Listing 12-3, notice that the background buffer is declared as a private member of the class of type *Bitmap*. The buffer is initialized in the *Form.Resize* event, which is a good place to do it because you can be sure to size the buffer correctly for whichever screen orientation the user selects.

In the *Form.OnPaint* method, the technique is simply to get a *Graphics* object from the back buffer by using *Graphics.FromImage*, draw to that *Graphics* object, and then draw the whole back buffer to the screen when you are finished drawing. The essential statements are as follows:

```
protected override void OnPaint(PaintEventArgs e)
{
    if (backBuffer != null)
    {
        // You need a Graphics object on the buffer.
        using (Graphics gxBuffer = Graphics.FromImage(backBuffer))
        {
            gxBuffer.Clear(Color.Black);
            …
            gxBuffer.DrawImage(backgroundImage, 0, 0);
            …
            gxBuffer.DrawRectangle(…);
            …
            gxBuffer.DrawString(…);
        }
        // Put the final composed image on-screen.
        e.Graphics.DrawImage(backBuffer, 0, 0);
    }
    else
        e.Graphics.Clear(this.BackColor);
}
```

By using this technique, the drawing to the screen appears much smoother, resulting in a much more professional presentation.

Overriding *OnPaintBackground*

If you take care of the drawing of the background in your main *OnPaint* method, you should override the *OnPaintBackground* method of your *Form* to make sure it doesn't also try to paint the background. If you do not override the *OnPaintBackground* method, you may see noticeable flicker, particularly if you have set the form *BackgroundColor* property to a different color from the color you used to paint the background in the *OnPaint* method.

In the sample shown in Listing 12-3, you can see that the background is painted in the *OnPaint* method by using the statement *gxBuffer.Clear(Color.Black)*. The *OnPaintBackground* method is overridden so that it does nothing.

Using Advanced Formatting Techniques

So far in this chapter, we have demonstrated the simpler drawing techniques. This section discusses three techniques that add a little more sparkle to your graphics programming: using a gradient fill to start drawing with one color and change to another color as you move across or down the drawing surface, drawing images with a transparent background, and using alpha blending to draw an image with variable opacity.

Drawing Using Gradient Fill

Gradient fill is a pleasing effect in which you start drawing in one color that gradually changes to a different color. You can paint this transition from top to bottom or from left to right by setting the appropriate flag. There is no direct support for this effect in the *System.Drawing* classes, so you must use Platform Invocation Services (PInvoke) to call the Microsoft Win32 *GradientFill* function. This technique is explained in the .NET Framework Developers Guide in the Microsoft MSDN Library, so we do not repeat the description here. In the downloadable code for this chapter on the book's companion Web site, we include a sample program called GradientFillExample that paints a rectangle using gradient fill and then draws some vertically inclined text over the top of it. This produces the output shown in Figure 12-6.

Figure 12-6 Drawing using *GradientFill*

Drawing Images with a Transparent Background

Bitmaps, JPGs, and the other graphics formats are always rectangular–images have colored backgrounds. In the examples shown in this chapter, an image paints centrally on the screen, but you cannot see the background of the image because it is black, and the background of the graphics surface is also filled with black.

You cannot always rely on this technique, however. What if a user decides to make the background blue? You would have to prepare another graphic with a blue background. Instead, it's far easier to paint images with a transparent background so that the painting of the image is completely independent of the painting of the background. Fortunately, this is quite easy to do in the .NET Compact Framework. You do have to prepare the image using a single background color, and it's a good idea to make this as garish a color as possible—one that is not used in the main part of your image because you do not want to render any parts of the interior of your image transparent as well. We demonstrate this technique in the ImageWithTransparency sample in the downloadable code samples for this chapter on the companion Web site. In the ImageWithTransparency program, we prepared a new version of the central graphic using a fetching pink color (you will have to imagine it on this monochrome image):

To draw an image with transparency, create a *System.Drawing.Imaging.ImageAttributes* instance and call its *SetColorKey* method. In the desktop .NET Framework, you can specify a range of colors, but in the .NET Compact Framework you must specify the same color for the low color and for the high color range. A useful way of getting the background color is by calling the *Bitmap.GetPixel* method on your *Image* object and selecting a pixel you know is on the background, such as that at (0, 0), as demonstrated in the following code sample. Finally, call the override of *Graphics.DrawImage*, which takes an *ImageAttributes* instance as its final parameter, as shown here:

```
protected override void OnPaint(PaintEventArgs e)
{
    using (Image backgroundImage =
        new Bitmap(System.Reflection.Assembly.GetExecutingAssembly()
   .GetManifestResourceStream("MobileDevelopersHandbook.Graphic.JPG")))
    {
        // Fill the background.
        e.Graphics.Clear(Color.Red);

        // The .NET Compact Framework supports transparency but with
        // only one transparency color.
```

```
            // The SetColorKey method must have the same color specified
            // for the low color and high color range.
            System.Drawing.Imaging.ImageAttributes attr =
                new System.Drawing.Imaging.ImageAttributes();

            // Sets the transparency color key based on the upper-left
            // pixel of the image
            attr.SetColorKey(((Bitmap)backgroundImage).GetPixel(0, 0),
                ((Bitmap)backgroundImage).GetPixel(0, 0));

            // Draw the image, but scale it to 50 percent of the clipping
            // rectangle.
            Rectangle destRect =
                new Rectangle(0, 0, e.ClipRectangle.Width / 2,
                                    e.ClipRectangle.Height / 2);
            // Reposition origin to center the image on the screen.
            destRect.Location = new Point(
                (e.ClipRectangle.Width - destRect.Width) / 2,
                (e.ClipRectangle.Height - destRect.Height) / 2);

            // Draw the image using the image attributes.
            e.Graphics.DrawImage(backgroundImage, destRect, 0, 0,
                backgroundImage.Width, backgroundImage.Height,
                GraphicsUnit.Pixel, attr);
        }

        // Other drawing (not shown) . . .
        . . .
    }
```

The ImageWithTransparency sample is a variant of the one used to demonstrate *GradientFill*. Although the drawing of the gradient-filled rectangle and the lettering are not shown in the preceding code sample, the background is no longer black, and the central graphic is drawn using transparency, as shown in Figure 12-7.

Figure 12-7 Graphic drawn using a transparent background

Drawing Using Alpha Blending

You can use the alpha blending technique to draw an image with a degree of opacity so that whatever was previously drawn on the background can be seen through it. As with gradient fill, you must PInvoke to Win32 functions to use this technique. Alpha blending is supported only on Windows Mobile 5.0 and later. This technique was first described in Chris Lorton's Weblog at *blogs.msdn.com/chrislorton/archive/2006/04/07/570649.aspx*. This blog entry also describes a different way to do alpha blending from the one described here.

The sample application in the downloadable code on the companion Web site uses a timer so that the Windows Mobile logo is repainted every 50 microseconds (ms). Each repainting modifies the *BlendFunction.SourceConstantAlpha* property, which controls the degree of opacity of the structure. The degree of opacity starts at 0 (invisible) and ends at 255 (opaque). The *BlendFunction* structure is passed as an argument to the *AlphaBlend* function, which does the actual drawing. The overall effect is that the Windows Mobile logo fades in, as shown in Figure 12-8.

Figure 12-8 Fading in an image by using alpha blending

To use alpha blending, first you must get the PInvoke function declarations right for the *AlphaBlend* function and supporting structures. These are shown in Listing 12-4. See the Windows Mobile 5.0 software development kit (SDK) documentation for precise details of the *AlphaBlend* function.

Listing 12-4 Function Declarations for Alpha Blending

```
using System;
using System.Runtime.InteropServices;

namespace MobileDevelopersHandbook.AlphaBlendExample
{
    // These structures, enumerations, and PInvoke signatures come from
    // wingdi.h in the Windows Mobile 5.0 Pocket PC SDK.

    public struct BlendFunction
    {
        public byte BlendOp;
        public byte BlendFlags;
        public byte SourceConstantAlpha;
        public byte AlphaFormat;
    }

    public enum BlendOperation : byte
    {
        AC_SRC_OVER = 0x00
    }

    public enum BlendFlags : byte
    {
        Zero = 0x00
    }

    public enum SourceConstantAlpha : byte
    {
        Transparent = 0x00,
        Opaque = 0xFF
    }

    public enum AlphaFormat : byte
    {
        AC_SRC_ALPHA = 0x01
    }

    public class PlatformAPIs
    {
        [DllImport("coredll.dll")]
        extern public static Int32 AlphaBlend(IntPtr hdcDest, Int32 xDest,
            Int32 yDest, Int32 cxDest, Int32 cyDest, IntPtr hdcSrc,
            Int32 xSrc, Int32 ySrc, Int32 cxSrc, Int32 cySrc,
            BlendFunction blendFunction);
    }
}
```

The source of the main form that does the drawing is shown in Listing 12-5. The constructor of the *Form* loads the *Image* object from the bitmap file. The sample uses double buffering (described earlier in this chapter), so the *Form.Resize* event handler handles creation of the background buffer. (Note that the designer code is not shown here, and so you will have to wire up this event—and the *Paint* event—for this sample to work.)

The constructor also creates and starts a *Timer* that fires every 50 ms. In the *Timer.Tick* event handler, the code simply increments the *transparencyValue* field by 10 each time (until it reaches the maximum of 255, whereupon it stops the *Timer*), and then calls *this.Refresh* to force a repaint so that the *Paint* event fires.

In the *Paint* event, we create a *Graphics* object for the *Image* containing the logo using *Graphics.FromImage* and set up the *BlendFunction* structure, setting the *SourceConstantAlpha* field to the current value of the *transparencyValue* field. The *AlphaBlend* function requires the *Hdc* of both the image to be drawn and the destination. (*Hdc* stands for "handle to a device context," where a device context [DC] is a mechanism that Windows CE native drawing functions use for controlling access to a drawing destination.) We obtain the *Hdc* information by using *Graphics.GetHdc*. Notice that you must call *ReleaseHdc* when you are finished with the *Hdc* values.

Listing 12-5 Drawing with Alpha Blending

```
using System;
using System.ComponentModel;
using System.Drawing;
using System.Windows.Forms;

namespace MobileDevelopersHandbook.AlphaBlendExample
{
    public partial class Form1 : Form
    {
        protected Bitmap backBuffer;
        protected Image displayImage;
        byte transparencyValue = 0;
        Timer blendTimer;

        public Form1()
        {
            InitializeComponent();

            // Load the image to use with the AlphaBlend API.
            string path =
                System.IO.Path.GetDirectoryName(System.Reflection.Assembly.
                GetExecutingAssembly().GetName().CodeBase);
            displayImage =
                new Bitmap(path + @"\Microsoft_Windows_Mobile_logo.bmp");

            blendTimer = new Timer();
            blendTimer.Interval = 50;
            blendTimer.Tick += new EventHandler(blendTimer_Tick);
            blendTimer.Enabled = true;
        }

        void blendTimer_Tick(object sender, EventArgs e)
```

```
{
    transparencyValue += 10;
    if (transparencyValue == 250)
    {
        transparencyValue = 255; // opaque
        blendTimer.Enabled = false; // Stop the timer.
    }

    // Force a repaint.
    this.Refresh();
}

protected override void OnPaintBackground(PaintEventArgs e)
{
    // Make this a no-op to avoid flicker.
}

private void Form1_Paint(object sender, PaintEventArgs e)
{
    if (backBuffer != null)
    {
        // You need a Graphics object to get a handle to the DC.
        using (Graphics gxBuffer = Graphics.FromImage(backBuffer))
        {
            // Because you made OnPaintBackground a no-op, take care
            // of painting the background here.
            gxBuffer.Clear(this.BackColor);

            // AlphaBlend takes two handles to the DC-one source and
            // one destination.  Here's the source.
            using (Graphics gxSrc = Graphics.FromImage(displayImage))
            {
                IntPtr hdcDst = gxBuffer.GetHdc();
                IntPtr hdcSrc = gxSrc.GetHdc();

                BlendFunction blendFunction = new BlendFunction();
                // AC_SRC_OVER  is the only supported blend operation.
                blendFunction.BlendOp =
                    (byte)BlendOperation.AC_SRC_OVER;
                // Documentation says put 0 here.
                blendFunction.BlendFlags = (byte)BlendFlags.Zero;
                // Constant alpha factor
                blendFunction.SourceConstantAlpha = transparencyValue;
                // Don't look for per-pixel alpha.
                blendFunction.AlphaFormat = (byte)0;

                // Get x co-or based on bitmap width.
                int left = this.Width / 2 - (displayImage.Width / 2);
                int top = 100;   // y co-or
                PlatformAPIs.AlphaBlend(hdcDst, left, top,
                    displayImage.Width, displayImage.Height,
                    hdcSrc, 0, 0,
                    displayImage.Width, displayImage.Height,
                    blendFunction);
```

```
                    gxBuffer.ReleaseHdc(hdcDst); // Reqd cleanup to . . .
                    gxSrc.ReleaseHdc(hdcSrc);    // . . .GetHdc()
                }
            }

            // Put the final composed image on-screen.
            e.Graphics.DrawImage(backBuffer, 0, 0);
        }
        else
            e.Graphics.Clear(this.BackColor);
    }

    private void Form1_Resize(object sender, EventArgs e)
    {
        if (backBuffer != null)
        {
            // Dispose of the original one.
            backBuffer.Dispose();
        }

        // Create a new backbuffer of the correct size.
        backBuffer =
            new Bitmap(this.ClientSize.Width, this.ClientSize.Height,
            System.Drawing.Imaging.PixelFormat.Format32bppRgb);
    }
  }
}
```

Summary

This chapter explains a number of graphics drawing techniques you can use to paint on *Forms* and other controls. It also explains a number of more advanced techniques such as painting using a gradient fill, painting images excluding their background, and combining images using alpha blending.

Note that although the examples in this chapter all painted onto a Windows Form, you can use these techniques also to paint in custom controls. With custom controls, which is the subject of Chapter 15, "Building Custom Controls," you get the added advantage of inheriting the standard docking and anchoring behavior inherent in all controls.

Chapter 13
Direct3D Mobile

By Rob Miles

In this chapter:

Until recently, three-dimensional (3-D) graphics were beyond the capabilities of mobile devices. However, with the launch of Microsoft Windows Mobile 5.0 and because systems contain more powerful processors and even graphics coprocessors, we can now start to contemplate the use of three-dimensional graphics in programs targeted for portable devices. In this chapter, we look at the fundamental concepts behind 3-D graphics and show you how you can start to use the Microsoft Direct3D application programming interface libraries to create graphical applications on mobile devices.

Getting Started with Direct3D

To use Direct3D, you don't actually need a phone handset or mobile device because you can do all the work on the emulators provided by Microsoft Visual Studio .NET 2005 as part of the development environment. However, the emulators do not run at a representative speed when drawing in three dimensions.

Using Direct3D in Your Programs

The Direct3D libraries are not included by default when you create a solution for a device running Windows Mobile 5.0. To use them, you must add them as a reference to a Visual Studio 2005 project. The library you need to add is Windows.Mobile.DirectX.

To make your program simpler, you can also add *using* directives at the top of your program to include the 3-D graphics namespaces:

```
using Microsoft.WindowsMobile.DirectX;
using Microsoft.WindowsMobile.DirectX.Direct3D;
```

The Direct3D Device

All the drawing in the Direct3D program is performed by an instance of the *Device* class. This is an object that represents a graphics display device in a computer system. On a desktop computer, the *Device* maps to a physical adapter connected to a monitor. On a Windows Mobile 5.0–powered system, the *Device* drives the display hardware. You ask a device instance to draw objects for you, and it acts on these requests in the manner appropriate for the actual underlying hardware.

The actual range of options and commands that a given graphics *Device* can understand and act on varies from one platform to another. You can use methods to find out the capabilities of a given device. For the purpose of brevity, we use the set of options known to be offered by devices that run Windows Mobile 5.0.

When a *Device* instance is created, it is given information to describe how it is to use system resources and generate the display. You must set up these presentation parameters prior to the construction of the device. A sequence of statements to construct a device that works on a system running Windows Mobile 5.0 is as follows:

```
public void Init()
{
    PresentParameters presentParams = new PresentParameters();
    presentParams.Windowed = true;
    presentParams.SwapEffect = SwapEffect.Discard;
    device = new Device(
        0,                      // device number 0
        DeviceType.Default,     // default configuration
        this,                   // reference to the parent window
        CreateFlags.None,       // no special creation flags
        presentParams);         // the presentation parameters
}
```

The *Init* method creates a device that we can ask to draw objects for us. You create the device only once when the program starts, and then you use a reference to the device in the method calls that control the drawing process.

Only two items in the *PresentParameters* instance must be set. The 3-D display on a mobile device is always windowed. At present, we do not use any back buffers to draw images prior to display, so we can set the *SwapEffect* to the *Discard* option. A back buffer is an area of memory where a graphics card can assemble the graphics image before copying it to the display memory. The copy process is usually synchronized with the update rate of the monitor attached to the graphics card. However, on the mobile platform we don't have a monitor as such, so we can operate without a back buffer.

The device constructor that we use accepts five parameters:

- The first item is the device number. (This is used for systems with more than one graphics device–number 0 is always the default graphics device.)
- The second is the *DeviceType* selection for this device. Under Windows Mobile 5.0, this is always the default (*DeviceType.Default*) configuration.
- The third item is a reference to the parent form. Because these statements are running inside an instance of a *Form* class, you can simply pass the constructor a reference to this.
- With the fourth item, you can specify any special flags to control the behavior of the device after it is created.
- Finally, you supply the presentation parameters.

Important If any of the device creation parameters are incorrect, the *Device* constructor will throw an exception. You should include code to handle this in your production code.

The Draw Process

Now that you have an instance of a device, you can ask it to draw objects. The best place to do this is in the *OnPaint* method of the parent Windows Form.

```
protected override void OnPaintBackground(PaintEventArgs e)
{
}
protected override void OnPaint(PaintEventArgs e)
{
    Render();
}
```

The *OnPaint* method for the form has been overridden and calls the *Render* method, which uses the *Device* instance to draw. Note that the *OnPaintBackground* method also was overridden and replaced with an empty method. This is to stop the normal form background clear behavior from affecting the drawing. The *Render* method uses the *Device* to draw:

```
private void Render()
{
    device.Clear(ClearFlags.Target, Color.White, 1.0f, 0);
    device.BeginScene();
    device.EndScene();
    device.Present();
}
```

The *Clear* method requests that the device clear the display. The clear operation can target different items through the *ClearFlags* enumeration; the preceding code example requests that the target of the device be cleared. You can supply the color to clear the screen for the operation. The final two parameters are the Z-depth (concerned with the clearing of 3-D images) and the clearing stencil to use (which you can leave at 0 for now). The clearing stencil is a means by which you can get advanced graphical effects by controlling which bits in the pixels are set to 0 when the buffer is cleared. Bits in the display pixels are combined with the stencil using the logical AND operation. Setting all the bits in the stencil to 0 ensures that the values are all cleared to 0.

After the device has been cleared, you begin the scene drawing process by calling *BeginScene*. At the moment, you don't have anything to draw, so you end the process right afterward by calling *EndScene*. Finally, the *Present* method asks the device to present the image for viewing. Listing 13-1 is a complete version of this first graphics program and shows all the components brought together in a form.

Listing 13-1 A Complete Graphics Program

```
public partial class GraphicsForm : Form
{
    /// <summary>
    /// Device we are going to use to render our graphics
    /// </summary>
    private Device device;

    public GraphicsForm()
    {
        InitializeComponent();
    }

    public void Init()
    {
        PresentParameters presentParams = new PresentParameters();
        presentParams.Windowed = true;
        presentParams.SwapEffect = SwapEffect.Discard;
        device = new Device(
            0,                      // device number 0
            DeviceType.Default,     // default configuration
            this,                   // reference to the parent window
            CreateFlags.None,       // no special creation flags
            presentParams);         // the presentation parameters
    }

    protected override void OnPaintBackground(PaintEventArgs e)
    {
    }

    protected override void OnPaint(PaintEventArgs e)
    {
        Render();
    }
```

```
    private void Render()
    {
        device.Clear(ClearFlags.Target, Color.White, 1.0f, 0);
        device.BeginScene();
        device.EndScene();
        device.Present();
    }
}
```

Getting a Direct3D Program Running

You use a different process to start a graphics application from the one you use for a normal Windows application. It is important that you call the *initialize* method before the form is displayed and the application runs. The sequence is as follows:

```
static class Program
{
    /// <summary>
    /// The main entry point for the application
    /// </summary>
    [MTAThread]
    static void Main()
    {
        using (GraphicsForm frm = new GraphicsForm ())
        {
            frm.Init();
            frm.Show();
            Application.Run(frm);
        }
    }
}
```

Although this process looks mostly similar to the way in which Windows applications usually begin running, note that the graphics initialization is called on the instance of the *GraphicsForm* before the *Show* method. If the *GraphicsForm* class is created and run as shown in the preceding code sample, the screen of the target device will turn white. Then, you have to create some objects in three dimensions and have them rendered.

Working in Three Dimensions

Until now, all the code samples in this chapter have simply drawn in two dimensions. The items have been drawn at a given position on the screen that is expressed as two numbers, *X* and *Y*. The *X* value (or X coordinate) specifies how far across the screen the image is to be drawn, and the *Y* value (or Y coordinate) specifies how far down the screen the image is to be drawn. You can move images from left to right by changing the *X* value, and similarly you can move images up or down by changing the *Y* value.

The first thing you must understand is that when you draw in three dimensions, you need a third value (or coordinate) to specify the location in the third dimension. This value is expressed as the *Z* coordinate. Such a position, or point in space, is referred to as a vertex. A vertex is held in Direct3D as three values, for *X*, *Y*, and *Z*. Unlike integer coordinates, these values are floating point, that is, real numbers.

Rendering a Triangle

In 3-D graphics, traditionally the first thing you draw is a triangle, so that is how we shall start. Actually, this is a very sensible tradition because given enough triangles you can draw anything. The triangle is the fundamental building block of every graphical scene.

The position of a triangle can be specified by three vertices. You are going to make your vertices slightly more interesting in that as well as a position in space the vertex structure that you are going to use will also specify the color at that vertex. Direct3D provides several different types of vertex, depending on the needs of the program at the time. The Direct3D class *CustomVertex* holds a number of different vertex structures; among them is one called *PositionColored* that you will use to define the vertices of a triangle. If you create an array of *CustomVertex* structs, you can use this to specify the triangle:

```
CustomVertex.PositionColored[] vertices =
    new CustomVertex.PositionColored[3];
vertices[0].X = 0.0f;
vertices[0].Y = 1.0f;
vertices[0].Z = 0.0f;
vertices[0].Color = Color.Red.ToArgb();

vertices[1].X = 1.0f;
vertices[1].Y = -1.0f;
vertices[1].Z = 0.0f;
vertices[1].Color = Color.Green.ToArgb();

vertices[2].X = -1.0f;
vertices[2].Y = -1.0f;
vertices[2].Z = 0.0f;
vertices[2].Color = Color.Blue.ToArgb();
```

By default, the coordinates have their origin (0,0) in the very middle of the screen and each edge is 1.0 away:

- $X = -1.0$ means the left-hand edge; $X = +1.0$ means the right-hand edge.
- $Y = -1.0$ means the bottom of the screen; $Y = +1.0$ means the top.
- The *Z* value controls how far "into" the screen the triangle is drawn. For the preceding triangle, we have left this value at 0.

You might think that all you need to do now is ask the device to render the array and draw the triangle. However, it is not quite as simple as that. You can view the graphics device as a kind of factory that works on a bunch of scene data and churns out an image based on it. The input to the "factory" must be supplied as a vertex buffer that contains all the items to be drawn.

A program using Direct3D assembles a set of vertices into a vertex buffer and then gives this to the device to render. The program must make a vertex buffer using the triangle data. This is done as follows:

```
// Create a vertex buffer to hold the triangle information.
vertBuffer = new VertexBuffer(
    typeof(CustomVertex.PositionColored), // type of the buffer
    3,                                    // holding 3 vertices
    device,                               // for our device
    Usage.WriteOnly,                      // never going to read it
    CustomVertex.PositionColored.Format,  // source format
    Pool.SystemMemory);                   // mobile 3D requires this

// Set the data in the vertex buffer to your triangles.
vertBuffer.SetData(vertices, 0, LockFlags.None);
```

Don't worry too much about the extra parameters just now. The program now has a vertex buffer containing the data that describes the triangle to be drawn; now you just have to use it in the *Render* method:

```
private void Render()
{
    device.Clear(ClearFlags.Target, Color.White, 1.0f, 0);
    device.BeginScene();

    // Point the device at the vertex buffer.
    device.SetStreamSource(0, vertBuffer, 0);

    // Ask the device to draw the contents of the buffer.
    device.DrawPrimitives(PrimitiveType.TriangleList, 0, 1);

    device.EndScene();
    device.Present();
}
```

A *VertexBuffer* holds information about the vertices that you would like to have drawn by the graphics device. There are many different types of vertices. You select the type of vertex you need depending on what you want to have drawn. In this first example, you are describing the position and color of the points of a triangle, so the *PositionColored* vertex is the one to use.

Later, you will want to use different kinds of vertices, for example, ones that map points in the scene to positions in textures. You create a vertex buffer to hold vertices of a particular type. A draw operation is then directed at a particular vertex buffer and uses the information in the buffer to describe what is to be drawn. You can think of the vertex buffer as being stored inside the graphics adapter (because this is how it would work on a machine with a separate display device). This makes it easy and quick for the device to access the buffer when it is drawing, but it means that changing the content of the vertex buffer from your programs will be slow. Fortunately, as we describe later, you can move objects around the screen without changing the content of the vertex buffer.

The last thing you must do is to tell the Direct3D device that you are setting the colors of the objects. You do this by adding the following line when you have created your device:

```
device.RenderState.Lighting = false;
```

Later, you add lights to the scene. But at this point, you have a complete program that renders a triangle, as shown in Figure 13-1. Note that Direct3D interpolated colors between the points of the triangle.

Figure 13-1 A simple triangle

Understanding Coordinates and Viewing

Right now, you might think that drawing in three dimensions isn't that different from drawing in two. Because the value of *Z* is the same for all the vertices, you are drawing everything in the same plane. In Direct3D, the bigger the value of the *Z* coordinate, the further "into" the screen the vertex is supposed to be.

To explore the way that changes to the positions of the vertices affect the display, you can create an application that you can use to move the triangle.

Moving an Object in Three Dimensions

One way to move an object is to update the values in the vertices and then redraw it.

```
private float step = 0.2f;

private void moveLeft()
{
    vertices[0].X -= step;
    vertices[1].X -= step;
    vertices[2].X -= step;
    updateTriangle();
}

private void moveRight()
{
    vertices[0].X += step;
    vertices[1].X += step;
    vertices[2].X += step;
    updateTriangle();
}
```

The methods *moveLeft* and *moveRight* update the appropriate coordinate element in each of the vertices in the triangle. If these vertices are then reloaded into the vertex and the scene is redrawn, the triangle appears to move in the appropriate direction.

```
private void updateTriangle()
{
    Text = "X:" + vertices[0].X +
           " Y:" + vertices[0].Y +
           " Z:" + vertices[0].Z;
    vertBuffer.SetData(vertices, 0, LockFlags.None);
    Invalidate();
}
```

The methods can be bound to keyboard events so that you can write a program that will move the triangle around the screen.

The program MoveTriangle, which is included in the downloadable code for this chapter on the book's companion Web site, allows you to manipulate the position of a triangle in this way. However, if you run the program, you will notice that it has a problem. Although you can change the position of the triangle by changing the *X* and *Y* values to make it move left or right and up or down, changing *Z* (that is, trying to move toward or away from the triangle) does not have any effect. If you make the value of *Z* more than 1 or less than 0, the triangle disappears completely, which seems very strange. This is because you must give Direct3D more information about the drawing process.

Important We use this form of position manipulation to demonstrate how changes to the coordinate values affect the position of objects in a scene. It is not very efficient to update an existing *VertexBuffer* every time you have to move an object because it entails the following operations: reading out the old vertices, modifying them, and then storing them back in the buffer. On modern 3-D hardware, this buffer is on the Video RAM and accessing it is slow. There is a much more efficient way of transforming positions that involves the use of matrices to describe how to move, scale, or rotate vertex positions. We explore this technique later in the chapter.

From Programmer to Film Director

If you are drawing in two dimensions, life is very easy. You just use *X* and *Y* values to identify the pixel that you want to work with. In three dimensions, however, things are more complex. With the *X*, *Y*, and *Z* coordinate system, you can specify where objects are in the 3-D world, but the coordinates do not specify what the view of objects should be.

Figure 13-2 shows an object on a stage. You can set up a coordinate system to use to tell the computer about every single point (or vertex) in this scene. You could say that the tip of the chess piece is at *X* = 150, *Y* = 200, and *Z* = 10, and that the base is at *X* = 125, *Y* = 150, and *Z* = 9. However, where the object appears in a view of the scene depends on where the viewer is when he or she looks at it and the direction from which the viewer is looking.

Figure 13-2 Object on a stage

The view that you have of a scene is as much a product of where you are looking from and the direction in which you are looking as it is the objects contained in the scene. You must give Direct3D this information so that it can transform the 3-D coordinates into the colored pixels on a screen.

To draw the 3-D scene, you have to position a Direct3D "camera" in the graphics world, point it in the right direction, and hold it the right way up. Fortunately, the designers of the system have found a way to make this easy for the programmer. You start by setting the *View* property of the device:

```
device.Transform.View = Matrix.LookAtLH(
    new Vector3(0.0f, 0.0f, -5.0f), // camera position
    new Vector3(0.0f, 0.0f, 0.0f),  // camera target
    new Vector3(0.0f, 1.0f, 0.0f)   // camera up vector
    );
```

This gives the transformation required to get from "world" coordinate space (that is, the coordinates that express the position of the objects you want to draw) to "screen" coordinates (the position on the screen). The transformation is expressed as a matrix. The static method *LookAtLH* in the *Matrix* class creates this matrix, which is then set as the *Transform.View* property of the device created earlier.

Matrices

It is difficult to get very far in 3-D graphics without dealing with matrices and transformations. Put simply, a transformation matrix is a lump of data that is used to describe mathematically something you would like to do with the position of a vertex. You might want to slide the vertex left or right, scale the vertex so that its values get bigger or smaller, or rotate the vertex to a particular angle.

If you think about it, these are exactly the moves you want to do with the camera. You may want to move the camera in or out (move in on the subject), pan it left or right (slide/translate it), or twist it around (rotate). So a matrix is the ideal form to express camera position and how you are using the camera to view the scene.

You can create a matrix by hand using the appropriate geometry to express how this transformation will be achieved, but DirectX provides a method in the *Matrix* class that does the work for you. This method is called *LookAtLH*. The *LH* stands for "left-handed," which has to do with the way that the *Z* direction travels in relation to the *X* and *Y* coordinates. For now, you can interpret it as meaning that the bigger the *Z* value is, the further into the screen that vertex is.

You must give the method the position of the camera in 3-D space, the direction in which the camera is looking, and the direction that is considered "up." You can express each of these as the value of a vertex.

In the preceding code, the camera is placed at $X = 0$, $Y = 0$, $Z = -5$. Remember that the bigger *Z* is, the further into the screen the vertex is. A value of −5 pulls the camera back "out" of the screen. The more negative that you make Z, the further out of the screen the camera is placed, that is, a *Z* value of −10 moves the camera back even farther, and so everything is drawn smaller because it is farther into the distance.

The camera is pointed at $X = 0$, $Y = 0$, $Z = 0$. This is the origin of the coordinate system and is at the very center of the display. That means that anything placed on the origin will seem to be in the middle of the screen. If you want to change the position in which the camera is pointed, that is, pan the camera, change this value. For example, to pan left make the value of the *X* coordinate smaller.

The vertex $X = 0$, $Y = 1$, $Z = 0$ specifies the up direction. If you are wondering how a vertex can be used to express a direction, think in terms of a line drawn from the origin to the vertex position. A line that goes from one point to another is called a vector. In this case, the vertex is used to describe a vector that points up. This means that from the camera's point of view, *Y* goes up, which means that the camera is presently lined up with the horizon. If you want to tilt the camera, change the position of the vertex. To lay the camera on its side, so that "up" is along the floor, you could use $X = 1$, $Y = 0$, $Z = 0$.

Perspective and Transformations

You now have a camera set up and pointing in an appropriate direction, but you must also tell Direct3D how the scene is to be viewed. Do this by creating another matrix that controls the projection of the scene data. Direct3D provides a static method in the *Matrix* class that you can use to create this matrix. You must give this method some details about the view you want the camera to have:

```
device.Transform.Projection = Matrix.PerspectiveFovLH(
    (float)Math.PI / 4,      // field of view
    1.0f,                    // aspect ratio
    1.0f,                    // near Z plane
    100.0f                   // far Z plane
    );
```

The first parameter is the field of view. This is analogous to selecting a particular lens for the camera you are using to take the picture. The field of view is expressed as an angle given in radians. The preceding value (equivalent to 90 degrees) is very like putting a standard lens on the camera. If you increase the angle value, you can see more of the scene, as you would if you used a wide-angle lens. If you decrease the angle, you see a narrow view, as you would if you used a telephoto lens.

The second parameter is the aspect ratio. This gives the ratio of the width to the height of the display device. It controls how the image rendered by Direct3D is stretched to fit the shape of the screen. This is analogous to filming in widescreen or normal. If the aspect ratio is not set correctly, circles are drawn as ellipses, and squares appear to be rectangular. An aspect ratio value of 1 tells Direct3D that the display is square. You might want to change this to reflect the shape of the device that you are using. You can compute the value by using the height and width properties of the buffer into which the graphics are being drawn:

```
float aspectRatio =
    ((float)device.PresentationParameters.BackBufferWidth) /
    device.PresentationParameters.BackBufferHeight
```

The next two parameters are information to help the Direct3D rendering process. They tell the system which parts of the scene you are interested in having drawn. If you return to the chess piece in Figure 13-2, you can see that the only parts of the scene that need to be drawn are those on the stage, that is, between the front of the stage and the dark backdrop at the back of the stage. The third parameter, the near Z plane, gives the distance from the camera to the "front" of the stage. Anything closer to the camera than this distance will not be drawn. The fourth parameter, the far Z plane, gives the distance from the camera to the "back" of the stage. Anything beyond the back of the stage will not be drawn.

This transformation matrix that is created by the call of *PerspectiveFovLH* also tells Direct3D that you want to use perspective, that is, objects farther away from the camera must be drawn smaller than are objects closer to it.

After Direct3D knows the view transformation and the projection transformation, it can render scenes.

Transformations and Animations

At this point, you know how to position an item in world space and then place a camera to view it. However, the image is static. What you do next is add some animation so that the image appears to move. You can add animation by adding a transformation to the drawing process. This is another matrix that describes how coordinates are to be changed.

The good news is that you don't actually have to create the matrix yourself–as with the view and projection matrices, you can ask Direct3D to do all the hard work:

```
device.Transform.World = Matrix.RotationZ(rotateAngle);
```

This tells Direct3D that when it draws items in the world, it must transform their positions by using the matrix that you have created.

The transformation matrix that we create using the *RotationZ* method in the *Matrix* class specifies a rotation about the *Z*-axis by the angle supplied. The result of this transformation is that when the scene is redrawn, everything is rotated around the *Z*-axis by the angle specified.

However, what you really want is something that moves. You can make an object appear to move by repeatedly drawing the scene using different angles of rotation. This animates the 3-D scene; just drawing objects in slightly different positions makes 2-D items appear to move:

```
float rotateAngle = 0.0f;
float rotateStep = 0.02f;

private void redrawScene ()
{
    device.Transform.World = Matrix.RotationZ(rotateAngle);
    rotateAngle += rotateStep;
    Invalidate();
}
```

You can attach the method *redrawScene* to a timer and call it at regular intervals. Each time it is called, it creates a new transformation matrix and then invalidates the display so that the display is redrawn. Alternatively, you can call *reDrawScene* after each display update. This arrangement, where the scene is repeatedly redrawn at maximum speed, gives the highest possible update rate, but it might not be appropriate for all applications because the speed of the redraw varies on different platforms. We recommend that you use a system in which you use a timer to trigger the redraw; this arrangement allows a program to draw at the same speed on all platforms.

Figure 13-3 shows the triangle rotated. Remember that *Z* is the axis that goes into the screen, and so the triangle spins around its midpoint if you rotate around the *Z*-axis. The project RotateTriangle in the downloadable code for this chapter on the book's companion Web site contains a program that produces this display.

Figure 13-3 A rotated triangle

Important The speed at which the animation takes place depends greatly on the performance of the target hardware. The emulators are not able to use any graphics acceleration that may be present in some devices. If you run the RotateTriangle program in an emulator, you will see the triangle spin very slowly and jerkily.

Adding More Complicated Transformations

The triangle now moves, but it is not really in three dimensions yet. It would be nice to be able to rotate it around several axes at once. Direct3D provides a way to do this:

```
// rotation about Y
float yawAngle = 0.0f;
float yawStep = 0.01f;

// rotation about X
float pitchAngle = 0.0f;
float pitchStep = 0.001f;

// rotation about Z
float rollAngle = 0.0f;
float rollStep = 0.0001f;

private void redrawScene()
{
    device.Transform.World = Matrix.
        RotationYawPitchRoll(yawAngle, pitchAngle, rollAngle);

    yawAngle += yawStep;
    pitchAngle += pitchStep;
    rollAngle += rollStep;

    Invalidate();
}
```

This code is similar to the previous method, but the triangle is now rotated around all three axes at different speeds to give it a much more interesting motion. Unfortunately, this code sample also seems to be faulty in that when you run it the triangle rotates until it is on its edge, and then it vanishes, only to reappear later.

The triangle vanishes because of the way that Direct3D tries to save on the amount of drawing it must do. Essentially, Direct3D decides that when the triangle has its "back" to you, there is no need to draw it. Direct3D can tell when the triangle's back is to the viewer by examining the order in which the vertices are presented for drawing.

Figure 13-4 shows the vertices that make up the triangle. They are created in the order shown. When they are drawn, the points are visited in a clockwise sequence. However, if the back of the triangle is being drawn (that is, if you are drawing the triangle from the point of view of the back of the diagram), the points are visited in a counterclockwise sequence. Direct3D can detect this and decide that, because the rear of the triangle is being drawn, there is no need to draw it on-screen. In other words, this technique allows Direct3D to decide not to draw triangles that are not facing the viewer.

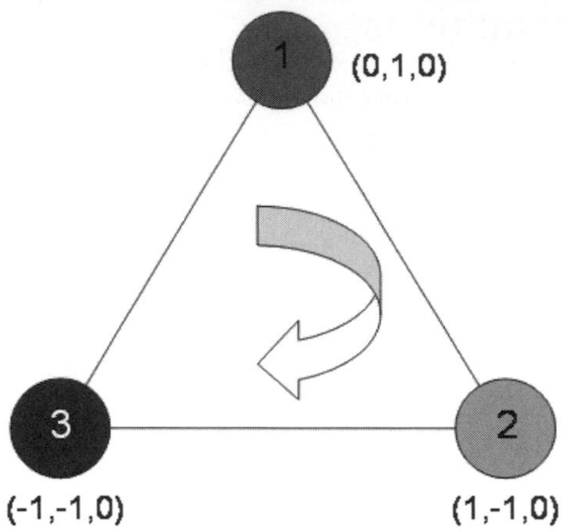

Figure 13-4 The triangle draw order

This process, called *culling*, makes sense when drawing three-dimensional structures that are made up of triangles. Triangles that are facing away from you (that is, those on the far side of the structure) would be on the "back" of the item and so would not be visible anyway.

However, at the moment, because all you are drawing is a single triangle, you do want the back of the triangle to be drawn, so you must turn off culling. You do this by altering the cull mode of the device. By default, Direct3D operates counterclockwise culling. Any triangles that present their vertices to be drawn in this order will not be drawn. However, you can set the cull mode to perform no culling at all. By adding the following line, you tell Direct3D to always draw the triangle, irrespective of the way the triangle is facing.

```
device.RenderState.CullMode = Cull.None;
```

Turning off triangle culling is necessary if you want to see the "backs" of your surfaces. However, you may also find it useful to turn off culling if you draw surfaces that always show their faces toward the camera. In such cases, there is no need to make the renderer decide whether to draw a triangle, so turning off culling can improve drawing speed.

Adding Textures

The current version of the drawing program produces a colored triangle. Each vertex in the scene specifies the location and color of a point that is part of the triangle, and Direct3D interpolates between the colors as it draws the surface. You can also use Direct3D to draw surfaces that contain textures. A texture is a bitmap image that you can add to a scene. When Direct3D draws a triangle with texture, it must have a mapping between a particular vertex and a position in the texture. You supply the mapping by using a different kind of *CustomVertex*, the *PositionTexturedVertex*. Rather than the vertex storing the triangle's color, it instead holds its texel coordinate. A *texel coordinate* is the position in a texture. For example, consider how you add a texture as a background to the scene. The image to be added is a rectangle, which is constructed out of two triangles. Figure 13-5 shows how texels are used to express the position parts of the texture.

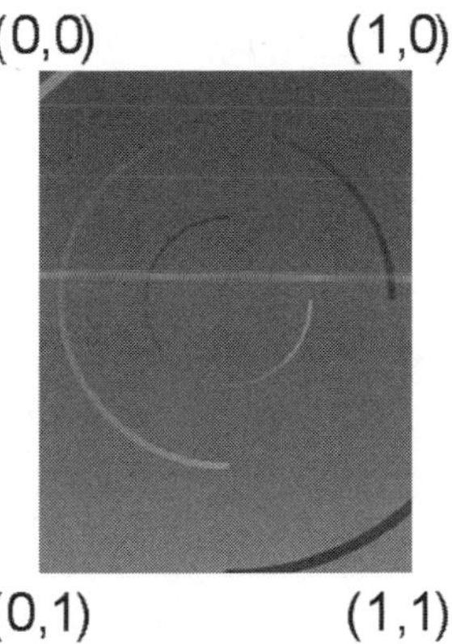

Figure 13-5 Texel coordinates in a texture

The origin of the texel coordinates is 0,0. The texel value can range up to 1.0 in either direction, The diagram shows how the texture is broken into triangles. The code to create the vertices for these triangles is as follows:

```
BackgroundTexture = TextureLoader.FromStream(device, textureStream);

Vertices = new CustomVertex.PositionTextured[6];

Vertices[0] = new CustomVertex.PositionTextured(-sz, -sz, z, 0.0f, 0.0f);
Vertices[1] = new CustomVertex.PositionTextured(-sz, +sz, z, 0.0f, 1.0f);
Vertices[2] = new CustomVertex.PositionTextured(+sz, -sz, z, 1.0f, 0.0f);

Vertices[3] = new CustomVertex.PositionTextured(+sz, -sz, z, 1.0f, 0.0f);
Vertices[4] = new CustomVertex.PositionTextured(-sz, +sz, z, 0.0f, 1.0f);
Vertices[5] = new CustomVertex.PositionTextured(+sz, +sz, z, 1.0f, 1.0f);
```

This code defines two triangles, centered on the origin. The value in *sz* is used to control the size of the triangles, and the value in *z* gives the distance of the triangle into the frame (that is, the higher the *z*, the farther away the background will be). The last two values in the constructor for each vertex are the two values (called *u* and *v*) that define the position on the texture to which each relates. If you examine the code in relation to the image shown in Figure 13-5, you can see that the triangle corners map to the edges of the texture so that the entire texture is drawn. Rendering a texture is similar to drawing ordinary vertices except that the drawing device must be given the texture as well:

```
// Set the data in the vertex buffer to your triangles.
VertBuffer.SetData(Vertices, 0, LockFlags.None);

// Point the device at your vertex buffer.
device.SetStreamSource(0, VertBuffer, 0);

// Assign the texture to the device.
device.SetTexture(0, BackgroundTexture);

// Ask the device to draw the contents of the buffer.
device.DrawPrimitives(PrimitiveType.TriangleList, 0, 2);

// Stop using this texture.
device.SetTexture(0, null);
```

The texture itself is loaded from a bitmap resource:

```
public Texture BackgroundTexture;
...
BackgroundTexture = TextureLoader.FromStream(device, textureStream);
```

The texture type is used to hold textures that you want to use in your program. The *TextureLoader* class provides a static method that can read a texture from a range of sources. In the preceding example, the texture is loaded from a stream. The sample project TextureBackground uses these features to provide a class called *ImageBackground* that you can use in Direct3D programs to provide a textured background for a 3-D scene. The scene can contain other kinds of 3-D objects rendered by different texture types.

A single texture image can be shared among a large number of items in a scene. Different parts of an object, or even textures for different objects, can be stored in a single texture. This can simplify resource management and also removes the need to change drawing textures as a number of items are drawn. By careful manipulation of texel values, you can also use the same texture to draw both the "front" and the "back" of a 3-D object.

Important For performance reasons, it is important that your textures be sized in powers of 2. This has to do with the way that the texture locations are processed as they are rendered. Speaking of performance, remember that drawing with textures is processor intensive.

Creating More Complex Objects

A single triangle is not very interesting, even if you make it spin in three dimensions. However, you can create more complex items by using more triangles. Increase the size of the vertex buffer and add more triangles to describe the scene. Note that you express the fact that some triangles are on the "back" of the 3-D object by specifying the vertices of the rear triangles with the appropriate draw order. To draw a six-sided cube, you need 12 triangles, for a total of 36 vertices:

```
int color = Color.Red.ToArgb();

/// Front face
Vert[0] = new CustomVertex.PositionColored(-0.5f, -0.5f, -0.5f, color);
Vert[1] = new CustomVertex.PositionColored(-0.5f, +0.5f, -0.5f, color);
Vert[2] = new CustomVertex.PositionColored(+0.5f, -0.5f, -0.5f, color);

Vert[3] = new CustomVertex.PositionColored(+0.5f, -0.5f, -0.5f, color);
Vert[4] = new CustomVertex.PositionColored(-0.5f, +0.5f, -0.5f, color);
Vert[5] = new CustomVertex.PositionColored(+0.5f, +0.5f, -0.5f, color);
```

The preceding code shows only how the front face is constructed. The other five faces are created in exactly the same way. The cube will be one unit in size and centered on the origin (which by default is the very center of the screen).

If you are creating complex objects, you should investigate the use of index buffers. As you can see from the preceding code, a particular vertex is used more than once in the triangles. *Vert[2]* and *Vert[3]* both refer to the same position, which is wasteful of memory. When you use an index buffer, you provide a list of vertices and then express your shapes by referring to which particular vertex that you want to use at that position. So rather than using many bytes to express a position, you can simply use a single value that gives the offset into the buffer of the vertex you want to use. This is particularly efficient to use with the cube because there are only eight different vertex positions used. Perhaps the best way to create objects, however, is to use meshes, which we describe in the section titled "Meshes" later in this chapter.

Drawing Multiple Items

You may think that to draw multiple cubes in the 3-D environment requires multiple sets of vertices with position values set to locate the vertices in different places. After all, at the start of this chapter you moved a triangle around by changing the values on the vertices that defined its position. However, this is not actually how you do it.

It might sound strange, but it is easier for you to move the world. By that, we mean that if you want to draw two different-sized cubes in two different positions, you don't create two sets of vertex data but instead apply a transformation to the world, draw the vertex data, apply another transformation, and draw the data again. The key to this is the way that you can use matrices to combine transformations. You can use one matrix to hold the size of a particular block, another matrix to hold the rotation of that block, and a third matrix to hold the 3-D position of that block. If you multiply these three matrices together, you can create a single transformation that tells Direct3D how to put your block where you want it. For example, suppose you want to draw two blocks, side by side, one twice the size of the other, and both rotated by different amounts. You start by creating some matrices:

```
Matrix scale1;
Matrix scale2;

Matrix rot1;
Matrix rot2;

Matrix pos1;
Matrix pos2;
```

These will hold the scale, rotation, and position of the two boxes. You can then create some values for these:

```
scale1 = Matrix.Scaling(2, 2, 2);
scale2 = Matrix.Scaling(0.5f, 0.5f, 0.5f);

rot1 = Matrix.RotationYawPitchRoll(0.5f, 0.5f, 0.5f);
rot2 = Matrix.RotationYawPitchRoll(-0.5f, -0.5f, -0.5f);

pos1 = Matrix.Translation(-0.6f, 0.6f, 0);
pos2 = Matrix.Translation(0.6f, -0.6f, 0);
```

The first block is to be drawn at two times normal size, and the second at half size. The first block is to be rotated forward in each axis, and the second block is to be rotated backward. Finally, the first block will be moved up and to the left, whereas the second will be moved down and to the right. The draw action simply combines these matrices to come up with the final transformation for the draw operation:

```
// Set the data in the vertex buffer to your triangles.
VertBuffer.SetData(Vert, 0, LockFlags.None);

// block 1
device.Transform.World = scale1 * rot1 * pos1;

// Point the device at your vertex buffer.
device.SetStreamSource(0, VertBuffer, 0);

// Ask the device to draw the contents of the buffer.
device.DrawPrimitives(PrimitiveType.TriangleList, 0, 12);
```

```
// block 2
device.Transform.World = scale2 * rot2 * pos2;

// Ask the device to draw the contents of the buffer.
device.DrawPrimitives(PrimitiveType.TriangleList, 0, 12);
```

Figure 13-6 shows the display produced when the two blocks are drawn on the textured background created earlier.

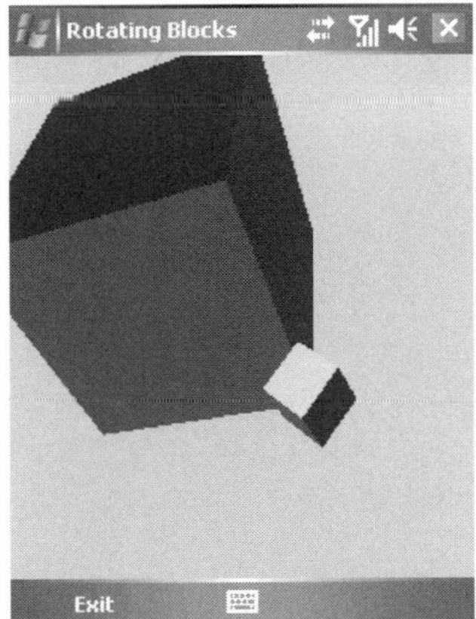

Figure 13-6 Drawing two blocks using transformations

> **Important** Because of the way that matrix multiplication is performed, it is very important that the translation matrix (that is, the one that sets the position of the element in the 3-D world) is multiplied last. If not, the process will generate invalid coordinates. If you want to combine translations, that is, add one position to another, you must do this by adding the transformation matrices together, not by multiplying them.

Remember that you can also modify the camera position and viewing direction by creating appropriate transformation matrices. This makes it easy to make the camera move around objects that are being drawn at their respective positions.

Lighting

You have drawn all the scenes so far with lighting switched off. Direct3D has simply used the colors assigned to the vertices and the bitmap on textures to decide what colors to draw. However, you can use lighting effects in which you can select the type, color, and position of lights in your 3-D scenes.

Adding lighting can significantly increase the amount of work that the processor must do to render a scene. On the PC platform, this is not a problem because the graphics subsystem usually has custom processors to perform image rendering. However, this is not usually the case on a mobile device, so complex graphics that contain large numbers of vertices and lighting can run rather slowly. The only good news in this respect is that the limited number of pixels on a mobile device screen means that there is no point in adding large amounts of detail and also that the processor does not have to generate big pictures.

Vertices and Normals

To actually add lighting to a scene, the Direct3D engine must have some more information about each vertex. For each vertex in a scene, you must supply the normal to that vertex. The *normal* is a perpendicular vector that points away from the face of which the vertex is part.

```
int color = Color.White.ToArgb();

/// Front face
Vertices[0] = new CustomVertex.PositionNormalColored(
    -0.5f, -0.5f, -0.5f, // position
    0.0f, 0.0f, -1.0f,   // normal-looking out of the screen
    color);
Vertices[1] = new CustomVertex.PositionNormalColored(
    -0.5f, +0.5f, -0.5f, // position
    0.0f, 0.0f, -1.0f,   // normal-looking out of the screen
    color);
Vertices[2] = new CustomVertex.PositionNormalColored(
    +0.5f, -0.5f, -0.5f, // position
    0.0f, 0.0f, -1.0f,   // normal-looking out of the screen
    color);
```

The preceding code creates a triangle that is facing the viewer. It uses a new kind of *CustomVertex* called *PostionNormalColored*. This gives the position and color of a vertex, as well as the direction that is perpendicular to the surface of which the vertex is part. The triangle is part of the front face of your cube. Remember that the value of Z (the third dimension) increases as you move "in" to the screen. The camera has been placed at 0.0f, 0.0f, −5.0f, that is, above the screen. This means that the direction perpendicular to a surface lying flat below the camera is looking out of the screen, traveling along the −Z-axis. Note that the actual value of the normal vector does not matter: It could be −1 or −100; the direction is all that Direct3D is interested in. To be able to draw 3-D cubes, you must add this normal information for all the other vertices too.

Lights Setup

If you want to use lights in your scene, you have to change the way that the graphics device is configured. You also must configure and position some lights:

```
PresentParameters presentParams = new PresentParameters();
presentParams.Windowed = true;
presentParams.SwapEffect = SwapEffect.Discard;
presentParams.EnableAutoDepthStencil = true;
presentParams.AutoDepthStencilFormat = DepthFormat.D16;

device = new Device(
    0,                          // device number 0
    DeviceType.Default,         // default configuration
    this,                       // reference to the parent window
    CreateFlags.None,           // no special creation flags
    presentParams);             // the presentation parameters

device.RenderState.Lighting = true;

device.Lights[0].Diffuse = Color.Blue;
device.Lights[0].Type = LightType.Directional;
device.Lights[0].Direction = new Vector3(-.5f, -.5f, -.5f);
device.Lights[0].Update();
device.Lights[0].Enabled = true;

device.Lights[1].Diffuse = Color.Yellow;
device.Lights[1].Type = LightType.Directional;
device.Lights[1].Direction = new Vector3(.5f, .5f, -.5f);
device.Lights[1].Update();
device.Lights[1].Enabled = true;

device.RenderState.Ambient = Color.White;
```

The preceding code sets up a device to use lighting and configures a pair of directional light sources, one yellow and the other blue. Directional light is cast over all parts of a scene from a particular direction and can be used to simulate sunlight or distant light sources. You can also create point light sources. A point source is rather like a candle flame or the filament of a light. It provides a single point from which light will shine on objects around it. For a point source, you specify where it is in the scene and also how the light intensity is attenuated when drawing objects farther away from the point source.

Figure 13-7 shows the two light sources used to illuminate two spinning cubes. Each face is made up of two triangles, one of them colored white. The scene is lit using two lights, one blue and the other white. When the program runs, you can see the effect of the lights on the colors. The background is a texture that is also drawn using lighting. The sample TwoBlocksWith-Lights contains the code for this image on the companion Web site. Note that it does run rather slowly; you can greatly speed it up by removing the background.

Figure 13-7 Drawing two blocks using colored lights

Meshes

You can use collections of vertices to specify the position of the points in your 3-D objects, but Direct3D provides a much better way of doing this called a mesh. Figures or vehicles in computer games almost always are expressed in the form of a mesh. You can use a large number of tools to create meshes. Meshes and the textures that give them their finished appearance are imported as resources. For mobile devices, on the present generation of hardware it is probably not advisable to use complex meshes like those found in computer games. Also, importing meshes can be difficult using Direct3D mobile.

For more information about creating meshes and importing them into Direct3D mobile programs, consult the ManagedDirect3DMobileMeshesTutorial in the Microsoft .NET Compact Framework samples provided by Microsoft. A copy of these samples is supplied in the network resources for this book.

However, meshes are interesting in that some predefined meshes exist that you can use to create 3-D shapes quickly for use in your programs. You can create a box, sphere, cylinder, torus (donut), or polygon with hardly any work.

```
Mesh box = Mesh.Box(device, 1, 1, 1);
```

This code creates a box that is one unit in size in each direction. *Box* is a static method in the *Mesh* class, and it accepts the Direct3D device and the dimensions (width, height, and depth) and creates a mesh that describes a box that size. If you want to create a sphere, the code is similar:

```
Mesh sphere = Mesh.Sphere(device, 1, 18, 18);
```

The first parameter after the device is the radius; the last two are the number of slices and stacks in the sphere. These specify how "lumpy" the sphere will be. You know that everything you draw is actually made up of triangles. This means that you cannot draw curved surfaces; all you can do is make the triangles so small that the resulting shape closely approximates a curved surface. The slices and stacks values control how many triangles you have in the vertical and horizontal directions, respectively. The higher these values, the better the resulting object will look–but of course it will occupy more memory and take longer to draw.

The predefined meshes are useful for creating simple shapes very easily, but unfortunately it is not possible to add textures to meshes created in this way. Instead, the way they appear is controlled by the material selected when they are drawn.

Lighting and Materials with Meshes

Now you can consider how meshes will appear when they are drawn. With Direct3D, you can create *Materials* that specify the color and reflective behavior of surfaces on an object.

```
boxMaterial = new Material();
boxMaterial.Ambient = Color.Red;
```

This code creates a new material that has an ambient color of red and diffuse color of white. The following subsections describe what these terms mean.

Ambient Light

When you light a scene, you can specify the color of the ambient light for that scene:

```
device.RenderState.Ambient = Color.Gray;
```

Ambient light does not come from anywhere specific; you can think of it as all around. In essence, it is the color objects are when no light falls on them. The ambient light used to render a scene combines with the ambient color of material to set the color of the unlit items.

For example, if you set the ambient light color to blue and the material ambient color to blue, any object that uses that material is rendered blue. However, if you set the ambient color of the material to yellow, objects that use that material are rendered black because yellow objects appear black in blue ambient light. If you set the ambient material color to white, objects appear in the color you have set for the objects. This is directly analogous to shining a white light on a colored item. Conversely, anything with a material ambient color set to white is rendered in the color of the ambient light. This is directly analogous to shining a colored light on a white item.

In the examples, we set the ambient light color to gray to make it appear that objects that have no light on them are in shadow.

Diffuse Light

You can also set the diffuse color of a material as follows:

```
boxMaterial.Diffuse = Color.Red;
```

The diffuse color of a material is the color that is combined with the color produced by lights shining on the material. For example, if you shine a white light on a material that has the *Diffuse* property set to *Red*, the points on which the light shines will appear red. If you shine a green light on the same material, the illuminated points will appear black because green objects appear black in red light.

> **Tip** You can use the diffuse and ambient settings to color objects in ways that are not possible in real life and that may not look very good. For a realistic appearance, set the diffuse color to *Gray* and set the diffuse and ambient colors for given objects to the same values.

To draw a mesh using a particular material, you must select the material during the draw operation.

```
device.Material = boxMaterial;
box.DrawSubset(0);
```

You can use the same material for a number of items.

Figure 13-8 shows a sphere and a block being drawn. They are being drawn with red and blue material and the ambient light color set to *Gray*. The sample program BlockAndSphereWithMaterial, which you can find on this book's companion Web site, contains the code for this image.

For more information about the use of lights, including point lights, a good place to start is the ManagedDirect3DMobileLightingSample provided by Microsoft in the .NET Compact Framework Samples.

Figure 13-8 Drawing a block and a sphere using materials

Direct3D on Mobile Devices

Now you know the basics of drawing in three dimensions. Now consider the interaction between the Direct3D system and a device running Windows Mobile.

Direct3D and Events

When a graphics program is running, a number of events, such as a change in the size of the display, an application being minimized, or another application acquiring the graphics adapter, can happen to which the program must respond. Direct3D provides events as a way of allowing a program to detect and respond to such events. It turns out that on the mobile platform the number of significant events is actually quite small.

Device Reset

If a graphics device is reset, the program must restore the state of some Direct3D objects, including textures, meshes, surfaces, *vertexBuffers*, *indexBuffers*, and lights. Your program can detect when this event occurs by binding to the *DeviceReset* event when initializing your graphics device:

```
device.DeviceReset += new EventHandler(DeviceReset);
DeviceReset(device, EventArgs.Empty);
```

The first line in the preceding code binds to the reset event; the second line makes a call to the *DeviceReset* method, which contains all the required setup code.

Managing Orientation Change

Many mobile devices can operate in landscape and portrait modes, and the user of the device can change orientation as the device is running. When the orientation changes, your application should scale the view of the scene accordingly. You have already seen how to handle the *DeviceReset* event. This event is also generated when the orientation of the screen changes. Handling a change in orientation effectively means adjusting the field of view so that the aspect ratio of the objects drawn is retained—so that circles remain circles and squares remain squares. You can adjust the field of view by using the aspect ratio of the screen to calculate the field of view as follows:

```
float aspectRatio =
    ((float)device.PresentationParameters.BackBufferWidth) /
    device.PresentationParameters.BackBufferHeight;

device.Transform.Projection = Matrix.PerspectiveFovLH(
    (float)Math.PI / 4,     // field of view
    aspectRatio,            // aspect ratio
    1.0f,                   // near Z plane
    100.0f                  // far Z plane
    );
```

The back buffer properties give you the width and height of the display area available. The computed aspect ratio is then used to modify the camera projection. If this is performed during a device reset, the graphics will be drawn correctly. Of course, your program must make sure that all the required objects are still visible because important objects may be unintentionally cropped when the dimensions of the screen change. You can address this by moving the camera farther out from the scene or by adjusting the field of view.

Important Not all implementations of Direct3D on mobile devices are able to manage the orientation changes without some screen corruption. If this feature is important to your application, you should test it on a real device prior to deployment. If your application works only in one orientation, you should test for the correct aspect ratio and display an error if an incorrect orientation is requested.

Direct3D Drawing Performance

The graphics performance on mobile devices is not as good as it is on desktop computers. Therefore, it is important that you monitor the performance of your application very carefully. Graphical performance is expressed in terms of the number of frames per second (fps) that a program can display. On high-performance desktop computers, this value can be more than

100 fps. However, on a mobile device, the limitations of the display hardware mean that frame rates of more than 20 fps will not be drawn correctly.

One way to monitor performance is to add an fps counter to your program. The counter displays the number of frames per second that your application is generating. A number of counters are available. The sample program called ManagedDirect3DMobileLightingSample on the companion Web site contains one such example.

You can always improve fps speed by removing textures, reducing the lighting effects, and turning off triangle culling, if appropriate. Remember to size all textures in powers of 2, and if you are converting an existing application from computer to mobile device, resize all the textures to save on resources. The development philosophy is to start simple and add complexity, carefully monitoring performance on the lowest specified device that you want to target.

Handling Platform Diversity

If you are writing a program that contains moving graphics, perhaps a game, you will want the program to run at the same speed on all platforms. One way to achieve this is to use a timer to trigger the redraw action. If the timer fires at a rate of 20 events per second, say, your game will update at this speed.

You can modify the frame rate without affecting the speed at which the game plays by measuring the time between display updates and then moving the items in the 3-D environment by a proportionate amount. Unfortunately, Windows Mobile 5.0 does not provide a high-resolution timer for use in these calculations, but the *Environment.TickCount* property, which gives the number of milliseconds that have elapsed since the system was started, can be used for this.

Battery Life

Programs that produce 3-D graphics displays make heavy demands on the underlying processor. If the hardware supports 3-D graphical acceleration, this hardware is also used when 3-D displays are produced. This means that battery consumption increases accordingly. You should remember that running at maximum update rate may produce the best possible display but may also result in very poor battery life. It might therefore be a good idea to cap the frame rate, perhaps by pausing execution after a frame has been drawn, on very high performance systems.

If you want to take your Direct3D graphics skills further, you can investigate the range of examples and tutorials on the Microsoft MSDN Mobile Direct3D Programming Web site at *msdn2.microsoft.com/en-us/library/aa452478.aspx*. Although not all the techniques described are available on mobile devices, you may also find a Microsoft DirectX 9 reference useful.

Summary

This chapter discusses how 3-D graphics can be implemented on a Windows Mobile 5.0–powered device using Direct3D. We walk you through creating a display device and using this to draw simple two-dimensional shapes with textures on them. Then we move into three dimensions and discuss rendering shapes in three dimensions. We also discuss matrices and how these can be used to specify the position, orientation, and size of items drawn in three dimensions. Finally, you perform some animation and lighting and look at issues that affect the use of 3-D graphics on the mobile platform.

Chapter 14

Interoperating with the Platform

In this chapter:

Throughout this book, we have made references to using functionality outside the Base Class Library (BCL) available in the Microsoft .NET Compact Framework. You can create your own business logic purely in managed code, but rarely will you write an entire application that does not need to go beyond this and call into some native code. Although version 2.0 of the Compact Framework has a much richer class library than version 1.0 does, there are still cases when you'll need to use other functionality, including device-specific application programming interfaces (APIs). This may take the form of system APIs that are part of Microsoft Windows CE, or a third-party software development kit (SDK), or perhaps your own legacy native code. This chapter investigates in detail the techniques available to cross the managed to native code boundary. First, we look at the simplest scenario of calling static native functions and then look at the way the runtime marshals .NET types and structures. We also investigate more advanced techniques that allow native code to call back into your managed code. We put this all together by using a worked class example that is a .NET Compact Framework 2.0 implementation of a subset of the *System.Media* namespace, which will be part of the .NET Compact Framework version 3.5. In the second half of this chapter, we look at Component Object Model (COM) interoperability, including using COM objects from your managed code and exposing your managed code as a native COM interface. Platform interop is a vital part of application development–you can find a need to step outside the Compact Framework class library on almost any application project.

Understanding Platform Invocation Services

The .NET Framework includes a set of functionality known as Platform Invocation Services, or PInvoke for short. With PInvoke, you can call native methods, written in C or C++, from managed code, which is necessary to make use of any functionality outside the .NET class libraries. Internally, the base class libraries use Platform Invoke to interoperate with the host operating system. Although the .NET Compact Framework provides a rich programming model, oftentimes you must go beyond this and use additional functionality such as from your existing legacy native code or functionality that is part of the Windows CE operating system. Luckily, the Compact Framework has a powerful platform invocation subsystem that you can use to call into external code. The functionality required is located in the *System.Runtime.InteropServices* namespace.

This first section of the chapter looks at calling static native methods, which are methods written in C and compiled into machine code in a dynamic-link library (DLL). For example, you may have legacy code written in this way that you would like to reuse in a managed code project. The examples in this chapter are based on features already present in the underlying operating system that are not available directly through the Compact Framework class libraries.

When you define a native method that you want to invoke, the syntax is similar to that of defining your own method in managed code, with only a few key differences. You can find numerous examples of PInvoke declarations online in an MSDN article at *msdn2.microsoft.com/en-us/library/aa446550.aspx* and at *www.pinvoke.net*. The following code sample shows a simple API call that plays a sound based on a member of the MB enumeration.

```
using System.Runtime.InteropServices;

[DllImport("coredll.dll")]
internal static extern void MessageBeep(MB type);

internal enum MB
{
  ICONHAND = 0x00000010,
  ICONQUESTION  = 0x00000020,
  ICONEXCLAMATION = 0x00000030,
  ICONASTERISK = 0x00000040,
}
```

The *extern* keyword tells the runtime that the method body is defined elsewhere. Because of this, you do not define a body for the method but instead follow the definition by a semicolon as the end of the statement. Above the method declaration, you add an attribute of type *System.Runtime.InteropServices.DllImportAttribute*. This tells the runtime in which library to look for the method and optionally what name or index the method is exported to, if different from the method name as you have defined it. The properties of the *DllImportAttribute* are shown in Table 14-1.

Table 14-1 *DllImportAttribute* Properties

Property	Description
CallingConvention	Currently unused in the Compact Framework because only *CallingConvention.WinApi* is supported.
CharSet	Can be set to either *Auto* or *Unicode*; however, on Windows CE, *Auto* uses *Unicode* because Windows CE is an all-Unicode operating system.
EntryPoint	Defines the name (or ordinal number prefixed with a number sign, for example, "#24") of the exported native method. With *EntryPoint*, you can use a friendly name for your PInvoke method if the native method is exposed by ordinal only or has a C++ mangled name.
PreserveSig	Used with COM interop (which is discussed later in the chapter).
SetLastError	Toggles whether to store the last error code following a call to the method so that the error code can be retrieved by using *Marshal.GetLastWin32Error()*. This is activated by default when using Microsoft Visual Basic but is disabled by default with C#.

Methods can be exposed by a DLL either by name or by ordinal. If the library is written in C, the name of the method is also the name of the export. In C++, the name is altered, known as "mangling," so that it retains information about the method signature. This allows tools to determine the method signature by "unmangling" the name. You can use a tool such as Depends.exe or Dumpbin.exe to list exported functions in a DLL. These run on your development computer, although they can be used with device-specific DLLs. The sample project called NativeDll, which you can find in the downloadable code samples for this chapter on the book's companion Web site, contains an example of both types of method, and Figure 14-1 shows the exported methods as they appear in Depends.exe.

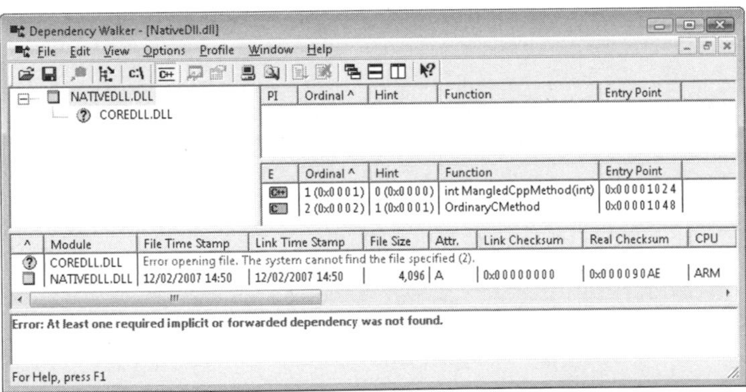

Figure 14-1 Exported native methods as they appear in Depends.exe

You can see that with the Depends.exe tool you can switch between mangled and unmangled names; for example, the C++ export shows as *?MangledCppMethod@@YAHH@Z* and *int MangledCppMethod(int)*, respectively. To call a method with a mangled name you add the

EntryPoint property to the *DllImportAttribute* applied to the managed method declaration and specify the exact mangled name, for example:

```
[DllImport("NativeDll.dll", EntryPoint="?MangledCppMethod@@YAHH@Z")]
private static extern int MangledCppMethod(int arg);
```

In the case of a method exported with no name, you can call it as long as you know the ordinal, which you can determine from Depends.exe. In this case, the *EntryPoint* is the ordinal prefixed with the number sign, for example:

```
[DllImport("NativeDll.dll", EntryPoint="#1")]
private static extern int MangledCppMethod(int arg);
```

Beyond defining the actual function name, you must understand how to declare the arguments a method will accept and how these types are marshaled between native and managed code. Because the .NET type system is different from the types available in C and C++, you must take care to define the types used correctly. Understanding marshaling will allow us to investigate more complex PInvoke declarations.

Marshaling

A set of rules define how the various managed types in the base class library are marshaled to native code. They are illustrated in Table 14-2. The default behavior can be overridden using the *MarshalAs* attribute, which is new in version 2.0 of the Compact Framework and which removes a lot of manual conversion that was necessary to PInvoke in version 1.0 of the .NET Compact Framework.

Table 14-2 .NET Types and Default Marshaling Behavior

.NET Type	Size (Bytes)	C++ Type
System.Boolean	2	short
System.Byte	1	uchar
System.SByte	1	char
System.Int16	2	short
System.UInt16	2	ushort
System.Int32	4	LONG
System.UInt32	4	DWORD, UINT, ULONG
System.Int64	8	LONGLONG
System.UInt64	8	ULONGLONG
System.IntPtr	4	HANDLE, HWND, PBYTE, etc.
System.UIntPtr	4	—
System.Single	4	Float

Table 14-2 .NET Types and Default Marshaling Behavior

.NET Type	Size (Bytes)	C++ Type
System.Double	8	—
System.Guid	16	GUID
System.String	4 (Pointer)	LPWSTR
System.Array	—	LPVOID for PInvoke methods, SAFEARRAY for COM Interop
System.Enum		Enumeration types are marshaled based on their base type. Unless you specify otherwise, all Enums are created with the *Int32* type.

As long as your native methods export only these types with their default behavior, you don't have to worry–the .NET runtime will do the marshaling for you. If you must force a specific marshalling behavior, you can apply the *MarshalAsAttribute*. For example, when calling the native method *CloseHandle*, which is used with various native APIs, you must specify that the return value is actually a 4-byte native *BOOL* type.

```
[DllImport("coredll.dll", SetLastError = true)]
[return: MarshalAs(UnmanagedType.Bool)]
internal static extern bool CloseHandle(IntPtr hObject);
```

CloseHandle closes a native system handle that is attached to some resource, such as a named event, mutex, or database table. The runtime then knows that the value returned is an unmanaged *BOOL* type and that it should be converted to a managed *System.Boolean* (*bool* keyword in C#) automatically.

MarshalAsAttribute

With the *MarshalAs* attribute, you can override the default marshalling behavior of parameters or fields. It uses the *UnmanagedType* enumeration, which contains various special behaviors that can be applied. Table 14-3 contains the most important of these.

Table 14-3 *UnmanagedType* Members

AsAny	The default behavior; determines the appropriate marshalling at run time based on the object type.
Bool	Marshals a *Boolean* value as a 4-byte *BOOL* type. Zero is false, and nonzero is true.
BStr, AnsiBStr	Generally used with COM Interop, the *BStr* is a length-prefixed string. You are unlikely to use the *Ansi* variety because Windows CE is Unicode only and all APIs should be designed similarly.
ByValArray	Marshals a managed array as a single block with each item directly following the last in memory. You must specify *SizeConst* parameter for the size of the array.

Table 14-3 *UnmanagedType* Members

ByValTStr	Used for marshalling a string as an inline character array rather than as a string pointer. Again, you must specify the *SizeConst* parameter because this affects the size of the overall structure.
FunctionPtr	Used with delegates; passes the delegate to native code as a function pointer that native code can call back into.
IDispatch, Interface, IUnknown	Marshals an object as a COM interface. Interface uses the interface type from the object type *IDispatch,* and *IUnknown* uses the generic COM interface types.
LPArray	Marshals an array as a pointer to the first item in the array. The array contents are arranged flat in memory, and you must specify the *SizeConst* if used for marshalling from native to managed code.
LPStr, LPTStr, LPWStr	Marshals a string as a pointer to the character array. Because only Unicode is supported on the Windows CE platform, *LPTStr* behaves the same as *LPWStr*. *LPStr* is unlikely to be required; marshals as American National Standards Institute (ANSI) chars.
LPStruct	Used only with the *Guid* type to pass it with an extra layer of indirection.
VariantBool	Used to pass a *Boolean* value as a 2-byte COM type; 0 is false, –1 is true.

Native Structures

When you consider defining a native structure in managed code, you have the choice of creating it as a class or as a struct. Fundamentally, the difference is that a struct is marshaled by value on the stack and a class is placed in the heap and is marshaled by reference. Often, you will come across native methods that receive a pointer to a structure; these are to be marshaled by reference, so either of the following is valid:

```
internal class SomeInteropClass
{
}
private static extern int SomeInteropMethod(SomeInteropClass data);
```

```
internal struct SomeInteropStruct
{
}
private static extern int SomeInteropMethod(ref SomeInteropStruct data);
```

Where your choice becomes important is when a structure has another structure as a member. In native code, the internal structure is placed inline and therefore must be defined as a struct for the marshaler to treat it the same way as the native version. For example, the following code sample shows the *SYSTEMTIME* type defined as a *struct* and appearing inline in a *TIME_ZONE_INFORMATION* structure. We have also applied the *StructLayoutAttribute* to tell the runtime to lay out the structure sequentially in the order we have defined it; this avoids the runtime optimizing the layout automatically. This is important because the structure must match the native definition exactly.

```
[StructLayout(LayoutKind.Sequential)]
internal struct TIME_ZONE_INFORMATION
{
  int Bias;
  [MarshalAs(UnmanagedType.ByValTStr, SizeConst=32)]
  string StandardName;
  SYSTEMTIME StandardDate;
  int StandardBias;
  [MarshalAs(UnmanagedType.ByValTStr, SizeConst=32)]
  string DaylightName;
  SYSTEMTIME DaylightDate;
  int DaylightBias;
}

[StructLayout(LayoutKind.Sequential)]
internal struct SYSTEMTIME
{
  ushort wYear;
  ushort wMonth;
  ushort wDayOfWeek;
  ushort wDay;
  ushort wHour;
  ushort wMinute;
  ushort wSecond;
  ushort wMilliseconds;
}
```

Many native structures include a member (usually at the beginning) that specifies the length of the structure. This member is used for versioning because newer versions may be extended and hence have a greater size. The runtime can return the size of any structure using the *Marshal.SizeOf* method. It is important that your structure be defined exactly because if you call an API method with an invalid size specified, it will most likely fail. If you define the structure too small, the native method will write data into unallocated memory beyond your structure that will result in a native exception; if the structure is too big, the data will not match up with the correct fields in the structure. See "The Log Files" in Chapter 4 for details of the interop log that can help to diagnose marshaling problems.

NativeMethods

It is not good practice to mix PInvoke declarations in your managed classes. Instead, the .NET Framework Design Guidelines suggest that PInvoke declarations should be placed in a static internal class called *NativeMethods*. You should also never expose raw PInvoke methods publicly for other assemblies to call directly. In almost all cases, you must validate arguments before calling the native method. If you run the Run Code Analysis feature in Microsoft Visual Studio, Platform Invoke declarations that are not in a *NativeMethods* class are flagged as a warning. On the desktop, there are stricter security checks around calls to unmanaged functions as a result of the Code Access Security (CAS) implemented in the full .NET Framework. On the Compact Framework, CAS is not supported, so calling native methods is much simpler. It's usually good practice to put any structures used only internally when dealing with these PInvokes in the *NativeMethods* class too.

Media Example

To illustrate a number of the techniques described so far, we work through the definition of a reusable class that demonstrates wrapping native API functionality in a managed class. In this case, we take an often-requested piece of functionality, that of sound playback, and create a wrapper class. We modeled the class on the *SoundPlayer* component, which can be found in the desktop .NET Framework but is absent from version 2.0 of the Compact Framework. This class will be available in the .NET Compact Framework version 3.5. The full code sample appears as Listing 14-1. You can see that we have placed all PInvoke-related code in a *NativeMethods* class. The result is very simple but provides a class that matches the behavior of the desktop equivalent, which should make it very easy to port any code consuming it to .NET Compact Framework 3.5 later on because only the namespace needs to be changed from *Chapter14.Media* to *System.Media*.

Listing 14-1 Sample Media Classes

```
using System.Runtime.InteropServices;

namespace Chapter14.Media
{
    public sealed class SoundPlayer : Component
    {
        //path to the file
        private string soundLocation = "";

        public SoundPlayer() { }

        public SoundPlayer(string soundLocation)
        {
            //Set the path.
            this.soundLocation = soundLocation;
        }

        public string SoundLocation
```

```
    {
        get
        {
            return soundLocation;
        }
        set
        {
            if (File.Exists(value))
            {
                soundLocation = value;
            }
            OnSoundLocationChanged(EventArgs.Empty);
        }
    }

    public event EventHandler SoundLocationChanged;

    private void OnSoundLocationChanged(EventArgs e)
    {
        if (this.SoundLocationChanged != null)
        {
            this.SoundLocationChanged(this, e);
        }
    }

    public void Play()
    {
        //Play async.
        NativeMethods.PlaySound(soundLocation, IntPtr.Zero,
           NativeMethods.SND.FILENAME | NativeMethods.SND.ASYNC);
    }

    public void PlaySync()
    {
        //Play sync.
        NativeMethods.PlaySound(soundLocation, IntPtr.Zero,
           NativeMethods.SND.FILENAME | NativeMethods.SND.SYNC);
    }

    public void PlayLooping()
    {
        //Play looping.
        NativeMethods.PlaySound(soundLocation, IntPtr.Zero,
           NativeMethods.SND.FILENAME | NativeMethods.SND.ASYNC |
           NativeMethods.SND.LOOP);
    }

    public void Stop()
    {
        NativeMethods.PlaySound(null, IntPtr.Zero,
           NativeMethods.SND.NODEFAULT);
    }
}
```

```
public static class SystemSounds
{
    public static SystemSound Beep
    {
        get
        {
            return new SystemSound(0);
        }
    }

    public static SystemSound Asterisk
    {
        get
        {
            return new SystemSound(NativeMethods.MB.ICONASTERISK);
        }
    }

    public static SystemSound Exclamation
    {
        get
        {
            return new SystemSound(NativeMethods.MB.ICONEXCLAMATION);
        }
    }

    public static SystemSound Question
    {
        get
        {
            return new SystemSound(NativeMethods.MB.ICONQUESTION);
        }
    }

    public static SystemSound Hand
    {
        get
        {
            return new SystemSound(NativeMethods.MB.ICONHAND);
        }
    }
}

public sealed class SystemSound
{
    //type of sound
    private NativeMethods.MB soundType;

    internal SystemSound(NativeMethods.MB soundType)
    {
        //Set type.
        this.soundType = soundType;
    }
```

```
        public void Play()
        {
            //play
            NativeMethods.MessageBeep(soundType);
        }

    }

    internal static class NativeMethods
    {
        [DllImport("coredll")]
        internal static extern void MessageBeep(MB type);

        internal enum MB
        {
            ICONHAND = 0x00000010,
            ICONQUESTION  = 0x00000020,
            ICONEXCLAMATION = 0x00000030,
            ICONASTERISK = 0x00000040,
        }

        [DllImport("coredll", EntryPoint = "PlaySoundW")]
        [return:MarshalAs(UnmanagedType.Bool)]
        internal static extern bool PlaySound(string lpszName,
             IntPtr hModule, SND dwFlags);

        [Flags()]
        internal enum SND
        {
            //ALIAS = 0x00010000,
            FILENAME = 0x00020000,
            //RESOURCE = 0x00040004,
            SYNC = 0x00000000,
            ASYNC = 0x00000001,
            NODEFAULT = 0x00000002,
            //MEMORY = 0x00000004,
            LOOP = 0x00000008,
            NOSTOP = 0x00000010,
            NOWAIT = 0x00002000
        }
    }
}
```

Callbacks into Managed Code

In some situations, you may want to communicate in the opposite direction. For example, you may start a long-running process in a native library and need to communicate back to your managed application when it has completed. You may also have a native component that must notify your managed application of some event at any time. There isn't the equivalent of Platform Invoke for native code to simply call methods in your managed code. Instead, you require some form of callback mechanism.

There are three ways in which native code can call back to managed code to inform of an event or pass some data. The first is to use Windows messages, which are an integral part of any Windows application. The .NET Compact Framework supplies a *MessageWindow* class that you can use to process incoming Windows messages. The second technique is to use a system event handle and the *WaitForSingleObject* API method on a background thread. This method will block until the handle is signaled. The downside of using this approach is that you must use it in conjunction with another technique to pass any data. The third method, which is new to version 2.0 of the Compact Framework, is the ability to pass a managed delegate to a native API function. The delegate is marshaled as a function pointer and allows the native application to call directly into a managed method. As long as you are careful that the types used in the method signature are suitably matched on both the native and managed sides, this method is quite flexible.

MessageWindow

MessageWindow is a special type specific to the .NET Compact Framework, and to use it you must add a reference to the *Microsoft.WindowsCE.Forms* assembly. *MessageWindow* was introduced to allow a managed application to process incoming Windows messages because usually these would be handled by overriding the form's *WndProc* method. For performance reasons, the Compact Framework does not expose the *WndProc* as the full framework does.

Windows messages are inherent to the architecture of the user interface services in the Windows operating system. The operating system manages sending Windows messages backward and forward between all the windows on the system, and each window will interpret these in order to provide their specific function. Natively, every control is a window, not just a form. The windows form a hierarchy in which the desktop, which contains each top-level window, is at the top followed by contained controls. *MessageWindow* is exposed to native code as a hidden window that is a child of your main application form. It exposes the window handle that you can pass to native code and contains an overridable *WndProc* method. In this method, you can check the received message and act on it accordingly.

All Windows messages are processed in the user interface thread, which means that you should not perform long-running operations from in your *WndProc* implementation because it stops the user interface from updating. In managed code, an individual message is described by the *Message* structure in the *Microsoft.WindowsCE.Forms* namespace. Along with the handle of the destination window, this structure contains two members, *LParam* and *WParam*. Each member is an *IntPtr* type that can contain supporting data. A special message, *WM_COPYDATA*, is used to copy a block of memory from one process to another. With this message, the *LParam* is a pointer to a *COPYDATASTRUCT* structure, and this and the raw data it points to are copied to the context of the receiving application. This makes it a very easy to implement method of interprocess communication.

To illustrate the *MessageWindow* approach, we extend the *ConnectionManager* sample introduced in Chapter 9, "Getting Connected." We created a basic wrapper around the Connection Manager APIs but did not pass an optional window handle that would receive events upon changes in the connection state. If a window handle and a message ID are specified in the *CONNMGR_CONNECTIONINFO* structure, the message will be delivered to the window identified by the handle. In this case, the *WParam* is used to pass the new connection status, but you must cast it to the correct type so that it is interpreted as a member of the *ConnectionStatus* enumeration. To support raising a managed event, you must define a delegate to define the method that will handle the event, and you must define an internal method to raise the event that can be called from the separate message *Window* class. The *ConnectionStatusChangedEventArgs* class gives you the ability to return the *ConnectionStatus* to the event handler.

```
public delegate void ConnectionStatusChangedEventHandler(
   ConnectionStatusChangedEventArgs e);

public class ConnectionStatusChangedEventArgs : EventArgs
{
   private ConnectionStatus connectionStatus;

   public ConnectionStatusChangedEventArgs(ConnectionStatus status)
   {
      this.connectionStatus = status;
   }

   public ConnectionStatus ConnectionStatus
   {
      get
      {
         return connectionStatus;
      }
   }
}
```

In the *ConnectionManager* class, we added the *ConnectionStatusChangedEvent* and an internal method used to raise the event.

```
//raises the connectionstatuschanged event
internal void OnConnectionStatusChanged(ConnectionStatusChangedEventArgs e)
{
   if (ConnectionStatusChanged != null)
   {
      ConnectionStatusChanged(e);
   }
}

//event fired when Connection Manager sends a status changed message
public event ConnectionStatusChangedEventHandler ConnectionStatusChanged;
```

A message ID is simply an integer; however, many are reserved for generic events and settings or those of the various built-in native *Window* types. To pass a unique message ID to Connection Manager, call the native *RegisterWindowMessage* API method, which takes a string and returns a message ID that is safe to use. The PInvoke definition is added to the *NativeMethods* class, as you'll see in the following code.

```
[DllImport("coredll", SetLastError = true)]
internal static extern int RegisterWindowMessage(string lpString);
```

If different processes call *RegisterWindowMessage* using the same string, the same message ID is returned. This makes *RegisterWindowMessage* a useful tool for when you use the *MessageWindow* for interprocess communication.

To use the *MessageWindow*, you must create a new class that inherits from *MessageWindow*—you cannot simply instantiate a *MessageWindow* object directly because you must override the window procedure (*WndProc*) to add your own behavior. In this example, the custom class is called *ConnectionManagerMessageWindow*. To register just a single message ID for the lifetime of the application, you call *RegisterWindowMessage* statically from the *ConnectionManagerMessageWindow* class. This class is internal and contains a simple constructor that takes a reference to the parent *ConnectionManager* object. After performing your own custom actions in the *WndProc* method, you should call the base *WndProc* implementation in *MessageWindow* to ensure the system processes standard window messages correctly.

```
internal class ConnectionManagerMessageWindow : MessageWindow
{
   internal static int WM_ConnectionManager =
       NativeMethods.RegisterWindowMessage("ConnectionManagerEvent");
   private ConnectionManager connectionManager;

   internal ConnectionManagerMessageWindow(ConnectionManager parent)
   {
       this.connectionManager = parent;
   }

   protected override void WndProc(ref Message m)
   {
       if (m.Msg == WM_ConnectionManager)
       {
          //This is a Connection Manager message.

          //convert the status
          ConnectionStatus status =
               (ConnectionStatus)m.WParam.ToInt32();
         //Raise the event on the parent ConnectionManager class.
         this.connectionManager.OnConnectionStatusChanged(
               new ConnectionStatusEventArgs(status));
         }

         //Pass control to base WndProc implementation.
         base.WndProc(ref m);
   }
}
```

The constructor for the *ConnectionManager* class has been modified to create a new instance of *ConnectionManagerMessageWindow*. It writes the window handle of the message window, the *HWnd* property, to the *CONNMGR_CONNECTIONINFO* structure.

```
public class ConnectionManager
{
    private IntPtr handle;
    private NativeMethods.CONNMGR_CONNECTIONINFO connectionInfo;
    private ConnectionManagerMessageWindow messageWindow;

    public ConnectionManager()
    {
        messageWindow = new ConnectionManagerMessageWindow(this);

        connectionInfo = new NativeMethods.CONNMGR_CONNECTIONINFO();
        connectionInfo.cbSize = Marshal.SizeOf(connectionInfo);
        connectionInfo.dwFlags = NativeMethods.CONNMGR_FLAG.NO_ERROR_MSGS;
        connectionInfo.dwParams = NativeMethods.CONNMGR_PARAM.GUIDDESTNET;
        connectionInfo.dwPriority =
              ConnectionPriority.HighPriorityBackground;

        // Window handle
        connectionInfo.hWnd = messageWindow.Hwnd;
        // Unique message ID
        connectionInfo.uMsg =
              ConnectionManagerMessageWindow.WM_ConnectionManager;
    }
```

After the *EstablishConnection* method is called, the Connection Manager will begin sending messages to the message window with the connection status. Even after the connection is established, the Connection Manager will send messages if the connection is canceled by the user or otherwise broken.

Named Events

The Windows operating system supports a synchronization entity know as an event handle, which is effectively a unique numerical handle you can perform operations on by using system API methods. This is completely different from the .NET event system that you are probably already familiar with. Windows allows applications to register event handles using a unique name, and you can write code to then wait until the handle is signaled. When different applications attempt to create an event handle using the same name, the same handle is returned. This makes named events a very useful interprocess communication method.

Although the Compact Framework has some underlying support for system events in the *System.Threading* namespace, it doesn't have the *EventWaitHandle* included in the full .NET Framework, which supports creating or opening existing named events. *EventWaitHandle* inherits from the abstract *WaitHandle* class, which defines methods such as *WaitOne* that must be implemented. This is used to halt execution in the current thread until the handle is signaled. Once again, you must resort to some Platform Invoke to take advantage of this functionality.

The following code sample re-creates the desktop *EventWaitHandle* class and should prove to be a handy piece of reusable code. As well as the functionality to work with a single handle, the following code also includes a static *WaitAny* method that accepts an array of handles and waits until any single handle is signaled. First, you must create an internal *NativeMethods* class to hold the API method declarations.

```
internal static class NativeMethods
{
   internal enum EVENT
   {
       PULSE = 1,
       RESET = 2,
       SET = 3,
   }

   [DllImport("coredll", SetLastError = true)]
   [return:MarshalAs(UnmanagedType.Bool)]
   internal static extern bool EventModify(IntPtr hEvent, EVENT ef);

   [DllImport("coredll", SetLastError = true)]
   internal static extern IntPtr CreateEvent(IntPtr lpEventAttributes,
   bool bManualReset, bool bInitialState, string lpName);

   [DllImport("coredll", SetLastError=true)]
   [return:MarshalAs(UnmanagedType.Bool)]
   internal static extern bool CloseHandle(IntPtr hObject);

   [DllImport("coredll", SetLastError = true)]
   internal static extern int WaitForSingleObject(IntPtr hHandle,
       int dwMilliseconds);

   [DllImport("coredll", SetLastError = true)]
   internal static extern int WaitForMultipleObjects(int nCount,
       IntPtr[] lpHandles, bool fWaitAll, int dwMilliseconds);
}
```

CreateEvent is used to create a new event handle or open an existing handle. Although the name is optional, calling the method with the same name is the only way to create a shared handle across different processes. You can set the event from one process by using *EventModify* and wait for the signal in another process by using *WaitForSingleObject*. To wait on a handle, you call *WaitForSingleObject* on a worker thread, which will block until the handle is signaled or until a specified timeout elapses. The *EventWaitHandle* class inherits from the abstract *WaitHandle* class and provides a constructor to create a handle and implementations for the *WaitOne* and *Close* methods. The *Set* method is added to wrap *EventModify* to signal the event.

```
public class EventWaitHandle : WaitHandle
{
    public const int WaitTimeout = 0x102;

    public EventWaitHandle(bool initialState, EventResetMode mode,
        string name)
    {
        this.Handle = NativeMethods.CreateEvent(IntPtr.Zero,
            mode == EventResetMode.ManualReset, initialState, name);
    }

    public bool Set()
    {
        return NativeMethods.EventModify(this.Handle,
            NativeMethods.EVENT.SET);
    }

    public bool Reset()
    {
        return NativeMethods.EventModify(this.Handle,
            NativeMethods.EVENT.RESET);
    }

    public static int WaitAny(WaitHandle[] waitHandles)
    {
        return WaitAny(waitHandles, Timeout.Infinite, false);
    }

    public static int WaitAny(WaitHandle[] waitHandles,
        int millisecondsTimeout, bool exitContext)
    {
        IntPtr[] handles = new IntPtr[waitHandles.Length];
        for (int i = 0; i < handles.Length; i++)
        {
            handles[i] = waitHandles[i].Handle;
        }

        return NativeMethods.WaitForMultipleObjects(handles.Length,
            handles, false, millisecondsTimeout);
    }


    public override bool WaitOne()
    {
        return WaitOne(Timeout.Infinite, false);
    }

    public override bool WaitOne(int millisecondsTimeout, bool exitContext)
    {
        return NativeMethods.WaitForSingleObject(this.Handle,
            millisecondsTimeout) == 0;
    }
```

```
    public override void Close()
    {
        if (this.Handle != WaitHandle.InvalidHandle)
        {
            NativeMethods.CloseHandle(this.Handle);
            this.Handle = WaitHandle.InvalidHandle;
        }
    }
}

public enum EventResetMode
{
    AutoReset = 0,
    ManualReset = 1,
}
```

This class now has the ability to create an event handle and wait for it to be signaled or to signal it if you want to alert another process or thread. To demonstrate this in action, we created a sample project using this class. We use a Windows CE API that tells the system to signal a named event when a system change occurs. These are defined in the notify.h header in the SDK, and the supported events are described as the *NOTIFICATION_EVENT_** constants that we defined in the *NotificationEvent* enumeration.

```
public enum NotificationEvent
{
    None              = 0,
    TimeChange        = 1,
    SyncEnd           = 2,
    OnACPower         = 3,
    OffACPower        = 4,
    NetConnect        = 5,
    NetDisconnect     = 6,
    DeviceChange      = 7,
    IrDiscovered      = 8,
    RS232Detected     = 9,
    RestoreEnd        = 10,
    Wakeup            = 11,
    TZChange          = 12,
    MachineNameChange = 13,
}
```

The API call to set up this registration is *CeRunAppAtEvent*. As the name may suggest, this function is used for launching an application on these events, but it can also be used to signal a named event by using a specific format for the application name. To differentiate the event name from an executable file, the name of the event must be prefixed with the following:

```
"\\\\.\\Notifications\\NamedEvents\\"
```

To unregister this named event you must call the same function using the *None* event type. In the sample, we created a *Notify* class to wrap this and expose the *RegisterNamedEvent* and *UnregisterNamedEvent* methods.

```
internal static class NativeMethods
{
   internal const string EventPrefix =
       "\\\\.\\Notifications\\NamedEvents\\";

   [DllImport("coredll")]
   internal static extern bool CeRunAppAtEvent(string pwszAppName,
       NotificationEvent lWhichEvent);
}

public static class Notify
{
   public static void RegisterNamedEvent(NotificationEvent whichEvent,
       string eventName)
   {
       NativeMethods.CeRunAppAtEvent(NativeMethods.EventPrefix +
           eventName, whichEvent);
   }

   public static void UnregisterNamedEvent(string eventName)
   {
       NativeMethods.CeRunAppAtEvent(NativeMethods.EventPrefix +
           eventName, NotificationEvent.None);
   }
}
```

In the sample, we create two named events and register them to be signaled on the *NetConnect* and *NetDisconnect* methods, respectively. In the application, we run a background thread that uses the static *EventWaitHandle.WaitAny* method to wait on both handles. When one is signaled, the thread unblocks and invokes a method in the user interface (UI) thread. This will change the color of the form based on the connection state.

Note Although this example illustrates the technique of using named events, if you are developing with Windows Mobile 5.0 or later, you can use the managed *Microsoft.WindowsMobile.Status* functionality to make your application react to changes in network state.

To avoid the background thread blocking inevitably, you can create an additional *EventWaitHandle* that you can signal from the UI thread. Therefore, if the user closes the application, the background thread will be safely ended.

```
private void EventThread()
{
    //event to kill the worker thread
    hQuit = new Chapter14.Threading.EventWaitHandle(false,
        EventResetMode.AutoReset, null);
    //Set up the named events.
    EventWaitHandle hConnected = new EventWaitHandle(false,
        EventResetMode.AutoReset, "PowerConnected");
    EventWaitHandle hDisconnected = new EventWaitHandle(false,
        EventResetMode.AutoReset, "PowerDisconnected");

    while (true)
    {
        int eventIndex = EventWaitHandle.WaitAny(new WaitHandle[] {
            hQuit, hConnected, hDisconnected });

        switch (eventIndex)
        {
            case 0:
                hConnected.Close();
                hDisconnected.Close();
                hQuit.Close();
                return;
            case 1:
                //You are on a background thread, so invoke.
                Invoke(new EventHandler(Connected));
                break;
            case 2:
                Invoke(new EventHandler(Disconnected));
                break;
        }
    }
}
```

Function Pointers

A form of native to managed interop that was introduced in version 2.0 of the .NET Compact Framework is the ability to marshal managed delegates as function pointers. A delegate is a definition for a method that handles a particular managed event. In native code, it's possible to define a method that takes a pointer to a native function and uses this to call back to provide status or multiple callbacks. It is used in the Windows CE APIs to support enumeration of system resources such as windows, fonts, locales, and so forth. The following example uses this technique to retrieve all of the top-level windows on the device and display them in the managed application.

First, we look at the definition of the native API and the associated callback function in the SDK documentation. The *lParam* argument is provided so that you can pass your own identifier, which will be sent back when your callback is called. This might be useful if there is a case when your callback may be called from more than one original call of the *EnumWindows* API.

```
BOOL EnumWindows(
  WNDENUMPROC lpEnumFunc,
  LPARAM lParam
);

BOOL CALLBACK EnumWindowsProc(
  HWND hwnd,
  LPARAM lParam
);
```

This method is fairly simple and is therefore easy to define in managed code. The default behavior for a delegate passed to a native method is for it to be marshaled as a function pointer. As in previous examples, we place the platform invoke declarations in a *NativeMethods* class.

```
private static class NativeMethods
{
   [DllImport("coredll")]
   [return: MarshalAs(UnmanagedType.Bool)]
   internal static extern bool EnumWindows(EnumWindowsDelegate lpEnumFunc,
       int lParam);

   [DllImport("coredll")]
   internal static extern int GetWindowText(IntPtr hWnd,
       System.Text.StringBuilder lpString, int nMaxCount);
}
```

One thing we discovered while building the sample application is that the delegate used in this process must return an *Int32* type. *Boolean* is not supported even if accompanied by the *MarshalAsAttribute*. Therefore, we declare the delegate and the handling method as follows.

```
private delegate int EnumWindowsDelegate(IntPtr hwnd, int lParam);

// This method will be called by the native EnumWindows API.
private int EnumWindowsProc(IntPtr hwnd, int lParam)
{
   // Add to list on UI thread.
   NativeMethods.GetWindowText(hwnd, sb, sb.Capacity);
   this.Invoke(new AddToListDelegate(AddToList),
       new object[] { hwnd, sb.ToString() });

   //BOOL true
   return -1;
}
```

In the handling method, we call another Windows CE API, *GetWindowText*, to retrieve the text for the specific window handle. Then we pass the handle and the text to another method called *AddToList*, which is invoked on the UI thread as it updates the list box. This is necessary because the delegate will be called back by the system on a different thread from which we cannot directly update UI elements. (See Chapter 11, "Threading," for more information about updating the UI thread.) The delegate is se tup and the native API is called from a button press in the sample application:

```
private void button1_Click(object sender, EventArgs e)
{
   listBox1.Items.Clear();
   NativeMethods.EnumWindows(new EnumWindowsDelegate(EnumWindowsProc), 0);
}
```

The system will keep calling the function until all the windows have been enumerated or the function returns *false*. In this case, we always return –1, which is the integer equivalent of the *BOOL true* value. Because this returns all top-level window handles and not just the visible ones, it returns a lot more results than the usual Settings, Memory, Running Programs list does. It gives an interesting insight into what else is running on the system, so you can interrogate the handles even more in your implementation to look at the flags or locations of the specific windows. This example uses a feature straight out of the platform SDK, but you may encounter a similar approach in third-party SDKs or in your own native libraries.

Understanding COM Interop

Component Object Model (COM) is a native object-oriented programming model that has been supported on Windows CE since the earliest versions. COM components are exposed by interfaces and are reference counted so that when the last reference is deleted, the object can safely release any resources it uses. COM components are referenced by a pointer. In memory, this points to a VTable that is a list of function pointers to each method in the interface. All COM interfaces are derived from *IUknown*, which includes methods for increasing (*AddRef*) and decreasing (*Release*) the reference count and querying for another interface type (*QueryInterface*). A component can support multiple interfaces, and each interface is identified by a unique *Guid*. The *IDispatch* interface is derived from *IUnknown* and adds support for late binding. COM components supporting automation use interfaces derived from the *IDispatch* interface.

Although the .NET Framework included COM interop support from its creation, the Compact Framework gained a subset of COM interop support in version 2.0. With COM interop support, you can call COM components from your managed code after providing a type library or manually defining the supported COM interfaces in your code. The Compact Framework does not allow you to register your managed components as COM types such that they can be activated from native code by using their class identifier (CLSID). This means, for example, that you can't write shell extensions or ActiveX controls in managed code.

One feature that is supported in .NET Compact Framework is the ability to expose your class to a COM interface such that it can call back in to your code. This is used as a notification mechanism by several system APIs. The following code sample creates a wrapper around the messaging system and supports a callback that will be executed when a new e-mail message is received on the device. The Windows CE Messaging API (CEMAPI) is a complex set of COM interfaces, and we leave it as an exercise for you to extend the sample as required.

Like PInvoke, COM Interop incurs a performance hit. This is because when you create your COM component, the runtime has to create an interop object based on your interface definition that maintains a pointer to the COM object. On each method call, the runtime has to use the interface definition to marshal the data through to the COM interface and process the return value, throwing an exception on failure. Because there is a fixed cost associated with each method call, it is better to implement the COM object to use fewer methods but pass more data in each method call. Obviously this is an option only if you write the particular COM component yourself.

Importing COM Libraries

If you have the .dll file or the type-library (.tlb) file available on your development computer, you can have Visual Studio automatically create a wrapper library for you that generates the required interface definitions. You can use a similar method when adding a reference to a .NET DLL: in the Add Reference dialog box, select Browse, and then locate the .dll or .tlb file. Visual Studio will create a new .dll file for you that is a managed interop library for the COM library you selected.

Manually Defining Interfaces

Because there isn't a type library for CEMAPI, you must manually create the interface definitions. This may seem like a daunting task, but you will use the native header files from the SDK and work through copying the interface definitions. There are a number of syntax changes between the C++ COM header and the C# definition, and you must make sure you replace native types with their managed equivalents. The main interface into CEMAPI is *IMAPISession*.

To show that an interface belongs to a COM component, you must add the *ComImportAttribute* to the interface. You must also add a *GuidAttribute* that contains the interface identifier. CEMAPI headers are slightly nonstandard, so the full globally unique identifier (GUID) is not documented for each interface; however, GUIDs are all of the form *xxxxxxxx*-0000-0000-C000-000000000046, where the first 8 digits are documented in *mapiguid.h*. In practice, this looks like the following declaration for *IMAPISession*.

```
[ComImport, Guid("00020300-0000-0000-C000-000000000046"),
    InterfaceType(ComInterfaceType.InterfaceIsIUnknown)]
internal interface IMAPISession
```

Interface Types

The third and final attribute required is the *InterfaceTypeAttribute*, which specifies whether the interface you are declaring is derived from *IUnknown* or *IDispatch*. The interface type affects the layout of the VTable because *IDispatch* contains other methods before those you are declaring. *IUnknown* contains only methods to maintain the object's reference count and to retrieve alternative interfaces for the object. Every other method must be called explicitly from its position on the VTable. On the other hand, *IDispatch* also has methods for querying the methods on the interface and invoking them by ID. You can use this method to call code to use the object without explicitly knowing the supported methods and VTable definition, which is known as late binding and is fundamental to ActiveX and scripting of objects.

Three members are defined in the *ComInterfaceType* enumeration:

- ***InterfaceIsDual*** The default value that specifies that the defined interface follows the standard *IDispatch* method in the VTable. Calling code can call methods either through early binding to the VTable or through late binding by calling the *IDispatch* methods (*GetIDsOfNames* and *Invoke*).
- ***InterfaceIsIDispatch*** Indicates that only the *IDispatch* methods are exposed and that all the methods you have defined must be called through late binding.
- ***InterfaceIsIUnknown*** Specifies that the interface you have declared follows the *IUnknown* methods in the VTable. These can be called only by early binding.

All the CEMAPI interfaces are derived from *IUnknown*, so that you must add the *InterfaceTypeAttribute* to the definition.

COM Error Handling

COM methods normally return an *HRESULT*, which is a 4-byte integer that contains 0 on success or an error code. There is a standard range of error codes for COM errors, and there may be additional codes specific to a component. When you define a COM method in your code, you set the return type to *void* by default because the runtime checks the return value and will throw an exception specific to the error code returned. If the error doesn't match a framework exception, a generic *COMException* containing the error code is thrown.

You can override this behavior by adding the *PreserveSigAttribute* to a method and setting the return type, for example, to *Int32*. In this way, you can get the return value and act on it without necessarily throwing an exception. This is necessary in some cases when methods don't return an *HRESULT* but some other value. If you want to throw a relevant exception manually based on an *HRESULT* value, you can use the *Marshal.ThrowExceptionForHR* method.

Specific Device Issues

In the CEMAPI sample, some methods are not implemented, and therefore you must not call them; each unimplemented method is marked with a comment. The reason some methods are not implemented is that the interface matches the *IMAPISession* interface used on the desktop version of Windows. Even though these methods are unused, they must be declared so that the following methods are in the correct location in the VTable. Because these methods are not implemented, the function pointer at the unused method's position in the VTable is null. Also, notice that when comparing the *IMAPISession* interface in managed code with the original in *cemapi.h,* we declared some output parameters as *IntPtr* types even though they should return a specific interface type, such as the *GetMsgStoresTable* method.

```
void GetMsgStoresTable(int ulFlags, out IntPtr lppTable);

//This is how the method _should_ be defined.
//void GetMsgStoresTable(int ulFlags, out IMAPITable lppTable);

//This is the native definition.
//MAPIMETHOD(GetMsgStoresTable)
//        (THIS_  ULONG                      ulFlags,
//                LPMAPITABLE FAR *          lppTable) IPURE;
```

Typically, returning a specific interface is supported, but CEMAPI doesn't follow the golden rules of COM and fails to implement the key method from the *IUnknown* interface–*QueryInterface*. Usually, *QueryInterface* should at the very least support a request with the GUID for *IUnknown* or the specific interface's own identifier and return a copy of itself. It should fail only if the requested interface identifier passed in is not supported. This is a problem because the COM interop support in .NET Compact Framework performs a *QueryInterface* on the pointer as soon as it gets it, and this operation will fail with all the CEMAPI interfaces. The only time you have declared a COM interface type as a parameter is to the *Advise* method because you know that the .NET Compact Framework runtime will correctly implement *IUnknown* on the *IMAPIAdviseSink* interface you are exposing.

To work around this issue–which should not be a problem with well-written COM components–you can use a third-party class to perform some manipulation on the pointer before casting it to the correct interface type. This problem is known to occur with a number of operating system interfaces that are part of the CEMAPI, Object Exchange (OBEX), and Imaging APIs. The workaround is implemented in the Mobile In The Hand library, of which a free Community Edition exists containing this functionality (*www.inthehand.com/WindowsMobile.aspx*). We look at the library again in Chapter 17, "Developing with Windows Mobil," because it contains some useful Windows Mobile–specific functionality.

You are now ready to look at the completed interface declaration in Listing 14-2, which is accompanied by some additional required declarations.

Listing 14-2 Managed Definition of COM Interfaces for CEMAPI

```
using System;
using System.Runtime.InteropServices;

namespace COMInterop
{
    internal static class NativeMethods
    {
        [DllImport("cemapi.dll")]
        internal static extern int MAPIInitialize(IntPtr lpMapiInit);

        [DllImport("cemapi.dll")]
        internal static extern int MAPIUninitialize();

        [DllImport("cemapi.dll")]
        internal static extern int MAPILogonEx(int ulUIParam,
              string lpszProfileName, string lpszPassword, int flFlags,
              out IntPtr lppSession);

        [DllImport("cemapi.dll")]
        internal static extern int MailDisplayMessage(byte[] lpEntryID,
              int cbEntryID);
    }

    [ComImport, Guid("00020300-0000-0000-C000-000000000046"),
    InterfaceType(ComInterfaceType.InterfaceIsIUnknown)]
    internal interface IMAPISession
    {
        void GetLastError();//Not supported

        void GetMsgStoresTable(int ulFlags, out IntPtr lppTable);

        void OpenMsgStore(int ulUIParam, int cbEntryID, byte[] lpEntryID,
              int lpInterface, int ulFlags, out IntPtr lppMDB);

        void OpenAddressBook();//Not supported
        void OpenProfileSection();//Not supported
        void GetStatusTable();//Not supported

        void OpenEntry(int cbEntryID, byte[] lpEntryID, int lpInterface,
              int ulFlags, out int lpulObjType, out IntPtr lppUnk);

        void CompareEntryIDs(Int32 cbEntryID1, byte[] lpEntryID1,
               Int32 cbEntryID2, byte[] lpEntryID2, int ulFlags,
               out int lpulResult);

        void Advise(int cbEntryID, byte[] lpEntryID, fnev ulEventMask,
               IMAPIAdviseSink lpAdviseSink, out int FlpulConnection);

        void Unadvise(int ulConnection);

        void MessageOptions();//Not supported
        void QueryDefaultMessageOpt();//Not supported
        void EnumAdrTypes();//Not supported
        void QueryIdentity();//Not supported
```

```
        void Logoff(int ulUIParam, int ulFlags, int ulReserved);

        void SetDefaultStore();//Not supported
        void AdminServices();//Not supported
        void ShowForm();//Not supported
        void PrepareForm();//Not supported

    }

    [ComImport, Guid("00020302-0000-0000-C000-000000000046"),
    InterfaceType(ComInterfaceType.InterfaceIsIUnknown)]
    internal interface IMAPIAdviseSink
    {
        void OnNotify(uint cNotif, ref NOTIFICATION lpNotifications);
    }

    [Flags()]
    internal enum fnev
    {
     ObjectCopied = 0x00000040,
        ObjectCreated = 0x00000004,
        ObjectDeleted = 0x00000008,
        ObjectModified = 0x00000010,
        ObjectMoved = 0x00000020,
    }
```

Structures with Unions

The *NOTIFICATION* type is an example of a union where a structure can contain different nested structures at the same position, depending on the event type. To support this, you can add the *StructLayoutAttribute* to the structure and specify that fields will be laid out explicitly. Then you can add the *FieldOffsetAttribute* to each field to define its position in the structure; in this way, multiple nested structures can appear at the same field offset. You must be careful when reading from the structure that you use the correct type so you do not misinterpret the data. We commented out the original union from the definition, and because we are only supporting new mail notifications in this sample, we have defined only the *NEWMAIL_NOTIFICATION* nested structure.

```
[StructLayout(LayoutKind.Explicit)]
internal struct NOTIFICATION
{
   /* notification type, i.e. fnevSomething */
   [FieldOffset(0)]
   public fnev   ulEventType;

   //This is how the union member was originally defined.
   //union
   //{
        //ERROR_NOTIFICATION          err;
        [FieldOffset(8)]
```

```
        public NEWMAIL_NOTIFICATION   newmail;
        //OBJECT_NOTIFICATION         obj;
        //TABLE_NOTIFICATION          tab;
        //EXTENDED_NOTIFICATION       ext;
        //STATUS_OBJECT_NOTIFICATION  statobj;
    //} info;
}

internal struct NEWMAIL_NOTIFICATION
{
    public int cbEntryID;
    public IntPtr lpEntryID;  /* identifies the new message */
    public int cbParentID;
    public IntPtr lpParentID; /* identifies the folder it lives in */
    public uint ulFlags;      /* 0 or MAPI_UNICODE */
    [MarshalAs(UnmanagedType.LPTStr)]
    public string lpszMessageClass; /* message class */
    public uint ulMessageFlags; /* copy of PR_MESSAGE_FLAGS */
}
```

To add support for the other event types, you must repeat with the other structure types and also mark them with a field offset of 8. Then you must hook up some code on the application form to initialize Messaging API (MAPI) and hook up the *IMAPIAdviseSink* interface. For simplicity, make the main form expose this interface.

```
Using InTheHand.Runtime.InteropServices

internal partial class Form1 : Form, IMAPIAdviseSink
    {
        //MAPI session
        IMAPISession session;
        //an ID used by the advise method
        int connection;
```

Store the connection ID that the session assigns to each caller of the *Advise* method. You must pass this to *Unadvise* when you close down the application. All of the initialization is placed in the *Load* event hander for the form.

```
private void Form1_Load(object sender, EventArgs e)
{
    int hresult = NativeMethods.MAPIInitialize(IntPtr.Zero);
    IntPtr psession;
    hresult = NativeMethods.MAPILogonEx(0, null, null, 0, out psession);
    //fix for improper COM implementation
    session = (IMAPISession)Marshal2.GetTypedObjectForIUnknown(psession,
        typeof(IMAPISession));

    session.Advise(0, null, fnev.ObjectCreated, this, out connection);
}
```

The *OnNotify* method is very simple and uses *MailDisplayMessage*, a Windows Mobile 5.0 native API, to display the affected message. If you want to get properties from the specific message, you can define additional interfaces and structures, but this is beyond the scope of this example.

```
public void OnNotify(uint cNotif, ref NOTIFICATION lpNotifications)
{
   switch (lpNotifications.ulEventType)
   {
       case fnev.ObjectCreated:
             byte[] entryid =
                    new byte[lpNotifications.newmail.cbEntryID];
             Marshal.Copy(lpNotifications.newmail.lpEntryID, entryid, 0,
                    entryid.Length);
            //Play a notification sound.
            Chapter14.Media.SystemSounds.Asterisk.Play();
            NativeMethods.MailDisplayMessage(entryid, entryid.Length);
            break;
   }
}
```

ActiveX Controls

As already mentioned, the Compact Framework has only a subset of the full COM interop functionality present in the full .NET Framework. The Compact Framework does not directly support hosting ActiveX controls; however, the underlying COM support makes it possible by defining additional classes. For more information about adding ActiveX control hosting and the required sample code to do it, see the Microsoft MSDN Web site at *msdn2.microsoft.com/en-us/library/aa446515.aspx*.

Summary

In this chapter, we investigated the various methods available to interoperate with native code, including functionality that is part of the underlying platform or in third-party SDKs or your own legacy C++ code. Version 2.0 of the Compact Framework has greatly improved interop functionality and supports both Platform Invoke for static C++ functions and COM interop for COM interfaces. After you can apply the basic techniques of defining your Platform Invoke declarations and know how to marshal the various types available in managed code, you can access a wide array of functionality without losing all your existing native code assets.

Chapter 15

Building Custom Controls

In this chapter:

The Microsoft .NET Compact Framework version 2.0 includes a powerful set of Windows controls. Although these controls are a subset of what is available to a desktop developer, controls for dealing with a wide variety of data types and interaction scenarios are available. In this chapter, we investigate how you can go beyond the built-in controls. First, we examine extending the functionality of existing controls, and then we look at creating new custom controls from scratch. We create the necessary design-time support so that your controls can be easily used in the Microsoft Visual Studio Form Designer.

Extending Existing Controls

The simplest scenario you will encounter when requiring a specific control is one in which you want to alter the behavior of an existing control or add some functionality to it. All the standard controls are wrappers around native common controls that are present in Microsoft Windows CE. These standard controls, as you can imagine, are a subset of those included in desktop versions of the Windows operating system, which is one of the reasons why the .NET Compact Framework controls are more limited than their desktop counterparts. All standard controls are derived from the *Control* class in the *System.Windows.Forms* namespace.

The *Control* class has a *Handle* property that is the native window handle (HWND) for the native control that is wrapped. There are two ways to interact with an existing control: you can intercept managed events from the control and override the behavior, or you can use native interop on the control using the value of the *Handle* property to set a native style that is not implemented in the managed control.

Overriding Events

Sometimes you will require text input in a particular format, for example, you must allow only numerals to be entered. You don't have to build your own control from scratch to achieve this. In this section, we implement a text control designed to accept only numerals. By inheriting from the *TextBox* control, you can override the way the control responds to key presses and ignore those you don't want to accept. You must override the *OnKeyPress* and *OnKeyDown* methods and check the key code received. Depending on the type of keyboard the device has, key codes can be either the *Keys.D0* to *D9* values or *Keys.NumPad0* to *Numpad9*. You must also let the *Keys.Back* through so that the user can delete a character from the text box. You check the value in the *OnKeyDown* method and set a flag if you want to block the character. If this flag is set when *OnKeyPress* is called, you mark the keyboard event by setting the *Handled* property to *true* to ensure that it is not passed to the native control. The *NumericTextBox* is defined in Listing 15-1.

Listing 15-1 *NumericTextBox* Control

```
using System;
using System.Windows.Forms;

namespace Chapter15.Windows.Forms
{
    public class NumericTextBox : TextBox
    {
        private bool blockedKey = false;

        protected override void OnKeyPress(KeyPressEventArgs e)
        {
            if (blockedKey)
            {
                e.Handled = true;
            }
        }
        protected override void OnKeyDown(KeyEventArgs e)
        {
            blockedKey = false;
            if (e.Shift == true || e.Alt == true)
            {
                blockedKey = true;
                return;
            }
            if (e.KeyCode < Keys.D0 || e.KeyCode > Keys.D9)
            {
                if (e.KeyCode < Keys.NumPad0 || e.KeyCode > Keys.NumPad9)
                {
                    if (e.KeyCode != Keys.Back)
                    {
                        blockedKey = true;
                    }
                }
            }
        }

    }
}
```

Because the standard forms controls in the Compact Framework are built around the native Windows controls, it is not possible to change the drawing behavior of the controls. If you must change the appearance of a standard control, you need to build your own custom control with custom drawing code.

Creating Custom Controls

When you must create a new control from scratch, you have two different classes from which you can inherit. The first is *Control*, which is the base class from which all controls are derived, including the standard framework controls. The other is *UserControl*, which is a special class, new to .NET Compact Framework 2.0, that is designed especially to support user-designed and user-created controls. It is important to understand the functional differences between the two classes before you start to create a custom control.

UserControl is derived from the *ContainerControl* class, which in turn inherits from *ScrollableControl*. These two classes add support for hosting child controls, managing their layout, and supporting scrolling. The scrolling support can be very useful because you can define the control's area and lay out controls, but if the user control is resized, it will automatically have scroll bars applied to it if necessary. *UserControl* adds support for a design canvas for the control that you can use to lay out elements of the control visually, just like designing a form. It also adds properties for common functionality such as setting the border appearance for the control.

UserControl

To help you understand the *UserControl*, you will build a sample control that uses the designer functionality available for the *UserControl*. The control is designed specifically for entering a 4-digit personal identification number (PIN) and is composed of a *NumericTextBox*, which was created earlier in this chapter, and a keypad made up of several *Button* controls.

You can do the majority of the work to create the control in the designer. Just as when you design a form, you have access to the properties and events of each control from the designer window. You can add buttons to make up a keypad that includes buttons for the characters 1 to 9, along with a zero button and a backspace button. To simplify the code, you can hook the *Click* event of each of the numbered buttons to a single event handler method. This looks at the sending control and places its caption in the text box.

```
private void btn_Click(object sender, EventArgs e)
{
   Button b = (Button)sender;
   if (!IsEntered)
   {
      txtPin.Text += b.Text;
   }
}
```

The backspace button has a separate event handler that removes the last character from the text box. Figure 15-1 shows the *PinUserControl* in the Visual Studio designer.

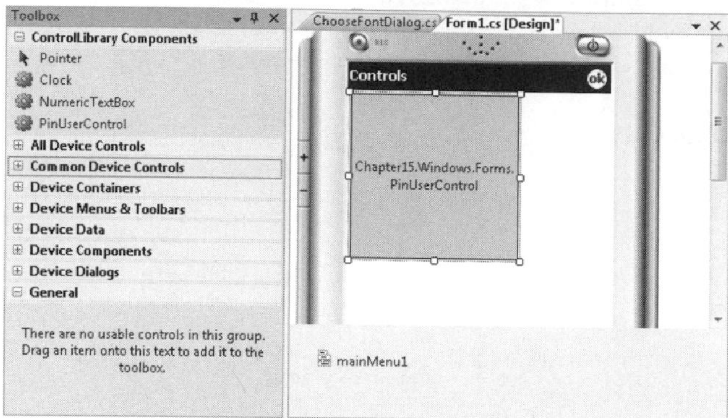

Figure 15-1 *PinUserControl* in the Visual Studio designer

Exposing Properties

You now have a functioning control that you can add to a project and build and deploy; however, although you have added functionality to the control, you haven't exposed any public properties. This means the form you put the control onhas no idea what PIN (if any) was entered. Because all classes derived from *Control* have a *Text* property, you can override this property so that it instead returns the text from the numeric text box, which is a child of the control. You must provide read-only access to the *Text* property so that the calling application can retrieve the PIN. It would also be useful to expose a property to indicate whether the entered PIN is the required 4 digits long. These two properties are defined as follows:

```
public override string Text
{
   get
   {
      return txtPin.Text;
   }
}

public bool IsEntered
{
   get
   {
      return (txtPin.Text.Length == 4);
   }
}
```

Exposing Events

As described, the custom control has no specific events of its own, and neither are the events of any of the child controls accessible to the hosting form. An important event to include in this control is one to signal when the user has changed the entered text. You can add the *PinChanged* event that is triggered whenever the *TextChanged* event occurs in the numeric text box. The event and a helper method to raise the event are included in the following code sample. The helper method simply checks whether there is a method registered to handle the event–you must raise an event only when there is at least one handler set to react to it.

```
public event EventHandler PinChanged;

protected virtual void OnPinChanged(object sender, EventArgs e)
{
   if (this.PinChanged != null)
   {
      PinChanged(sender, e);
   }
}
```

The following handler method for the *TextChanged* event of the text box calls the *OnPinChanged* method.

```
private void txtPin_TextChanged(object sender, EventArgs e)
{
   OnPinChanged(sender, EventArgs.Empty);
}
```

Control

Although deriving a class from the *Control* class doesn't give you the same designer experience, it does give you a very similar array of inherited functionality. If you are building a control that must draw its own content and doesn't simply wrap existing controls, building from the *Control* base class can make sense because you won't be able to see the effect of your painting code anyway.

To understand a custom-drawn control, you can create a clock control to display an analog clock face. This can help demonstrate how you can redraw your control without just reacting to external events. The control hosts a *Timer* component to update once every second and redraw the correct hand positions. But first, before you create the control, we must introduce the concept of double buffering.

Double Buffering

Drawing individual items to the screen in the *OnPaint* method of the control can introduce flickering. You can mitigate screen flicker by using a technique called double buffering, which is covered in Chapter 12, "Graphics Programming." In this case, because the *Timer* specifies when the redrawing is required, you perform all the drawing operations in the *Tick* handler of the timer control. A helper method, *GetHandPoint* is included to use the *System.Math* functionality to determine the positions of each of the clock hands.

```
protected override void OnPaint(PaintEventArgs pe)
{
   // Draw the previously created buffer.
   pe.Graphics.DrawImage(doubleBuffer, 0, 0);

   // Calling the base class OnPaint
   base.OnPaint(pe);
}

private void timerClock_Tick(object sender, EventArgs e)
{
   // Update the hands.
   DateTime d = DateTime.Now;
   double angle = d.Second * (Math.PI / 30);
   second = GetHandPoint(center, angle, minuteHand);
   angle = d.Minute * (Math.PI / 30);
   minute = GetHandPoint(center, angle, minuteHand);
   angle = d.Hour * (Math.PI / 6);
   hour = GetHandPoint(center, angle, hourHand);

   Graphics g = Graphics.FromImage(doubleBuffer);
   g.Clear(this.BackColor);

   g.FillEllipse(new SolidBrush(faceColor), 0, 0,
     shortestSide, shortestSide);
   g.DrawEllipse(grayPen, 0, 0, shortestSide, shortestSide);

   //Draw quarter marks.
   g.DrawLine(grayPen, center.X, 2, center.X, hourMarks);
   g.DrawLine(grayPen, 2, center.Y, hourMarks, center.Y);
   g.DrawLine(grayPen, shortestSide - hourMarks, center.Y,
     shortestSide - 2, center.Y);
   g.DrawLine(grayPen, center.X, shortestSide - hourMarks,
     center.X, shortestSide - 2);

   //Draw hands.
   g.DrawLine(blackPen, center.X, center.Y, hour.X, hour.Y);

   g.DrawLine(blackPen, center.X, center.Y, minute.X, minute.Y);
   g.DrawLine(grayPen, center.X, center.Y, second.X, second.Y);

   g.FillEllipse(new SolidBrush(Color.Black),
     center.X - 2, center.Y - 2, 4, 4);
```

```
    g.Dispose();

    Refresh();
}

private static Point GetHandPoint(Point center, double angle,
    int handlength)
{
    Point p;

    if (angle > 270)
    {
      angle = angle - 270;
      int height = Convert.ToInt32(Math.Sin(angle) * handlength);
      int width = Convert.ToInt32(Math.Cos(angle) * handlength);
      p = new Point(center.X + width, center.Y + height);
    }
    else if (angle > 180)
    {
      angle = angle - 180;
      int width = Convert.ToInt32(Math.Sin(angle) * handlength);
      int height = Convert.ToInt32(Math.Cos(angle) * handlength);
      p = new Point(center.X - width, center.Y + height);
    }
    else if (angle > 90)
    {
      angle = angle - 90;
      int height = Convert.ToInt32(Math.Sin(angle) * handlength);
      int width = Convert.ToInt32(Math.Cos(angle) * handlength);
      p = new Point(center.X + width, center.Y + height);
    }
    else
    {
      int width = Convert.ToInt32(Math.Sin(angle) * handlength);
      int height = Convert.ToInt32(Math.Cos(angle) * handlength);
       p = new Point(center.X + width, center.Y - height);
    }

    return p;
}
```

Screen Resizing

Many devices have the ability to change their screen size on the fly, either by using software or by hardware manipulation such as rotating a screen panel. Devices can also come in a wide variety of screen resolutions, so when you build reusable controls you must be aware of how they might appear on different devices. In the *Clock* control, you handle the *Resize* event so that if the control's dimensions change at run time you can recalculate the size of the clock face and hands so that the clock is displayed correctly in the available screen space.

```
protected override void OnResize(EventArgs e)
{
    if(Width > Height)
    {
      shortestSide = this.Height;
    }
    else
    {
      shortestSide = this.Width;
    }

    center = new Point(shortestSide / 2, shortestSide / 2);

    //Dispose of old buffer.
    if (doubleBuffer != null)
    {
      doubleBuffer.Dispose();
    }

    doubleBuffer = new Bitmap(shortestSide, shortestSide);
    minuteHand = (shortestSide / 2) - 4;
    hourHand = (shortestSide / 4);
    hourMarks = (shortestSide / 8);

    base.OnResize(e);
}
```

Programming the Design-Time Experience

Visual Studio applies the most basic design-time experience to a custom control with no additional work. If your library contains any Platform Invocation Services (PInvoke) code, Visual Studio works on the assumption that your control may not be compatible with the host Windows operating system, and it simply draws a sizable box with the name of the control as a placeholder. The control is visible in the Toolbox only in other projects in the same solution.

To customize the design-time experience, you must add a number of attributes to describe the designer behavior. When you create controls for smart device projects, these attributes are not applied to the code directly but rather are applied by using a special Extensible Markup Language (XML) format in an .xmta file. If you are familiar with creating controls for the full .NET Framework, you will be accustomed to applying attributes directly to your control code.

During the build process, the .xmta file is used to create a design-time .dll file that contains this metadata. The name of this .dll file is the name of your assembly, followed by the platform type you are targeting (PocketPC, Smartphone, or WindowsCE), and finally the .asmmeta.dll extension. This .dll file contains no actual code, just stubs with the required design-time attributes. After you build this library, the designer will use it only on the specific platform for which it was built. You will write the example control library to target the PocketPC platform.

This means that if you were to try to use the control library from a Smartphone project, the .asmmeta file would be ignored and the default behavior would be applied. We look at the process of custom-building .asmmeta files in the section titled "Custom Metadata Assemblies" later in this chapter.

Attributes

To add attributes to the custom control, you must add a new type of file to the project. Select Add New Item from the Project menu, and then select Design-Time Attribute File for device projects. This adds an .xmta file to the project, and in this file you can add the XML to describe the attributes to apply to the custom control. You can have a single .xmta file in a project and define several different controls in it, or you can create a separate .xmta file for each control—the choice is entirely yours.

Visual Studio includes Microsoft IntelliSense support to show valid items as you type, and the document starts with the required *Classes* element. In this, you add a *Class* item for each custom control, specifying the full namespace and class name in the *Name* attribute. You can then add subitems to this element for each *Property* and *Event* you want to describe. The majority of the attributes are direct equivalents of the desktop attributes you would apply directly in the code; these are used to add descriptions and default values and to define in which groups the events and properties appear in the project properties window in the designer. In the following sections, we look into a few device-specific attributes.

DesktopCompatible

If your library contains any PInvoke code, the designer doesn't trust that a custom component is safe to instantiate on the desktop. In such a scenario, the designer uses a generic designer that allows you only to site the control on the form, as illustrated in Figure 15-2.

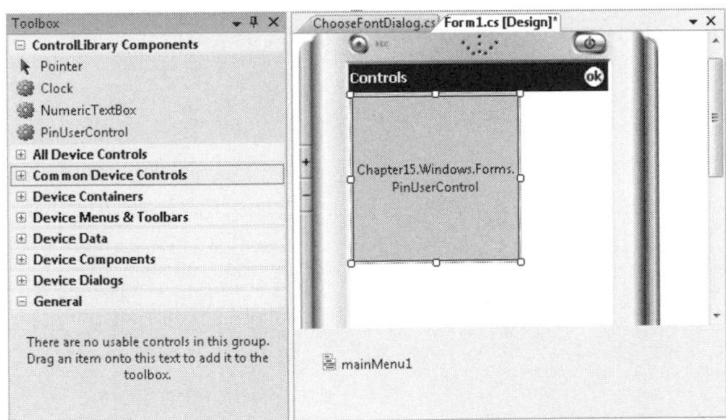

Figure 15-2 *PinUserControl* in a consuming application, when not marked as *DesktopCompatible*

If your control code is completely desktop compatible and doesn't contain any device-specific functionality, you can easily inform the designer by adding the *DesktopCompatible* attribute with a value of *true* to your class definition in the .xmta file. With this set and the project recompiled, the designer will use your custom drawing logic and the control will appear in the designer as it will be drawn on a real device. Figure 15-3 shows the result of adding the *DesktopCompatible* attribute to the *PinUserControl*.

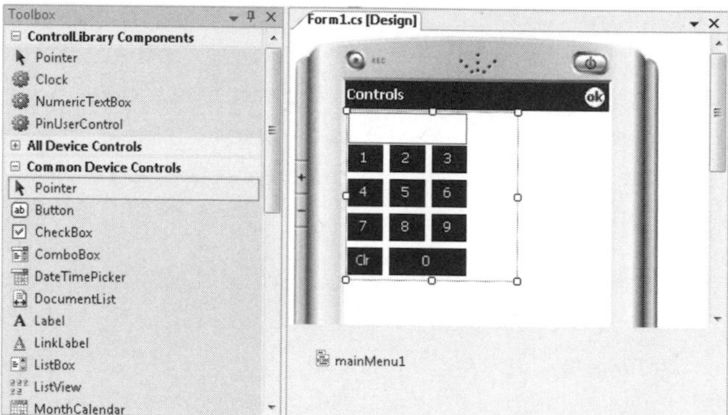

Figure 15-3 *PinUserControl* in a consuming application, when marked as *DesktopCompatible*

Custom Property

When you add a new property to a control, the designer shows it as long as the designer can support the datatype. However, the new property will not have as rich functionality as the standard control properties. The standard designer behavior for new properties is to add them to the *Misc* section of the properties table, and they will have no description. This is shown in Figure 15-4.

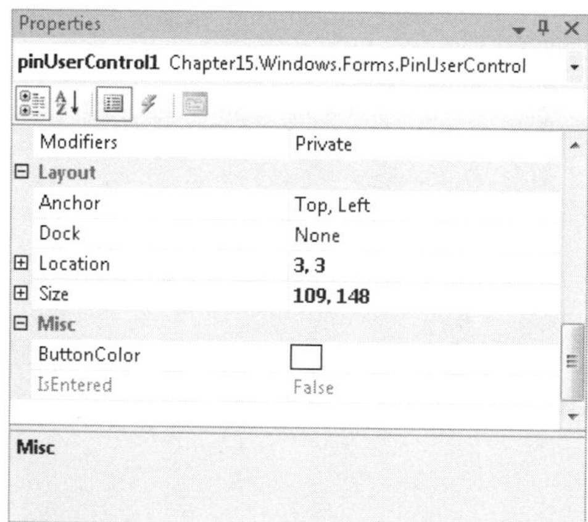

Figure 15-4 Default appearance of the *ButtonColor* property

You can add an attribute for the category that is specified as a string value. Use the existing category names before creating different ones. For example, a control's *BackColor* property appears in the *Appearance* category; the *PinUserControl* introduces a *ButtonColor* property for the keypad buttons, so we assign this to the *Appearance* category also.

When you write the code to create the control, you set certain default values for properties. By specifying the default value for the *ButtonColor* property, you can tell the designer not to generate code when the default value is chosen and to correctly highlight the property in bold type when it has been changed to an alternative value. When you set a default value, you must specify both the data type and the value in string form. Unless the data type is defined in Mscorlib, you must specify the full type name, including the assembly name, version, culture, and public key token. This is illustrated in the following code sample, which shows the attributes applied to the *ButtonColor* property. The result of applying this customization is shown in Figure 15-5. Applying these attributes to the control's properties and events can greatly improve the design-time experience.

```
<Property Name="ButtonColor">
   <Category>Appearance</Category>
      <DefaultValue>
         <Type>System.Drawing.Color, System.Drawing, Version=2.0.0.0, Culture=neutral,
PublicKeyToken=b03f5f7f11d50a3a</Type>
         <Value>ActiveCaption</Value>
   </DefaultValue>
   <Description>Sets a color for the keypad button faces.</Description>
</Property>
```

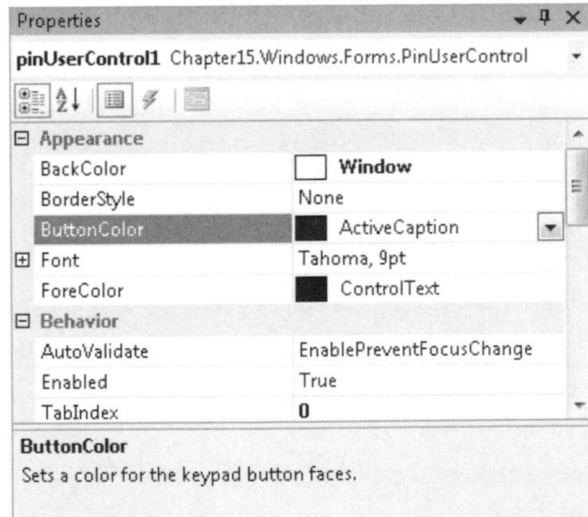

Figure 15-5 Results of applying design-time attributes to the *ButtonColor* property

DefaultEvent

By adding a *DefaultEvent* attribute to the control you can specify which event is selected when the user double-clicks the control on the design surface. For example, on the *Button* control this would be the *Click* event. For the *PinUserControl*, this is set to the *PinChanged* event because you are not exposing individual button presses occurring in the control. The event is specified by name:

```
<DefaultEvent>PinChanged</DefaultEvent>
```

EditorBrowsable

Sometimes you'll want to hide functionality from the designer, such as when a property is relevant only at run time. When the designer inspects your control to build the properties list, it includes properties that are read-only, which appear dimmed and unavailable. In the *PinUserControl*, the *IsEntered* property can be queried at run time to determine whether the full PIN code has been entered. At design time, this has no meaning, and therefore this property can be hidden by setting the *EditorBrowsable* attribute to *false*.

```
<Property Name="IsEntered">
   <EditorBrowsable>false</EditorBrowsable>
</Property>
```

Custom Property Types

The designer implements standard design-time behavior for standard .NET types such as strings, integers, colors, and so forth. If your control uses a custom type in one or more of its properties, you must provide additional details to the designer to describe how the type should be handled. For example, the *Clock* class implements the *ColorScheme* property, which is of type *ColorScheme*. This type consists of a number of *Color* properties used to define the clock appearance. Visual Studio does not know how to display this property, so the property remains unavailable in the properties window.

For types that are themselves a collection of standard framework types, you can apply the *TypeConverter* attribute with the *ExpandableObjectConverter* type. This adds the property as an expandable tree showing the properties in the type. You can add descriptions and default values by adding entries for your custom type, in this case, the *ColorScheme* type, in the .xmta file. The code for the *Clock* and *ColorScheme* types is shown in Listing 15-2.

Listing 15-2 Clock Control Attributes

```
<?xml version="1.0" encoding="utf-16"?>
<Classes>
  <Class Name="Chapter15.Windows.Forms.Clock">
    <DesktopCompatible>true</DesktopCompatible>

    <Property Name="ColorScheme">
      <Category>Appearance</Category>
```

```
      <Description>The color scheme used to render the clock.</Description>
      <TypeConverter>System.ComponentModel.ExpandableObjectConverter,
System, Version=2.0.0.0, Culture=neutral,
PublicKeyToken=b77a5c561934e089</TypeConverter>
    </Property>

  </Class>

  <Class Name="Chapter15.Windows.Forms.ColorScheme">
    <TypeConverter>
      System.ComponentModel.ExpandableObjectConverter, System,
      Version=2.0.0.0, Culture=neutral,
      PublicKeyToken=b77a5c561934e089
    </TypeConverter>
    <DesktopCompatible>true</DesktopCompatible>

    <Property Name="BorderColor">
      <Description>Color used for the clock border</Description>
      <DefaultValue>
        <Type>System.Drawing.Color, System.Drawing, Version=2.0.0.0,
Culture=neutral, PublicKeyToken=b03f5f7f11d50a3a</Type>
        <Value>Gray</Value>
      </DefaultValue>
      <NotifyParentProperty>true</NotifyParentProperty>
    </Property>
    <Property Name="FaceColor">
      <Description>Color used for the clock face</Description>
      <DefaultValue>
        <Type>System.Drawing.Color, System.Drawing, Version=2.0.0.0,
Culture=neutral, PublicKeyToken=b03f5f7f11d50a3a</Type>
        <Value>LightBlue</Value>
      </DefaultValue>
      <NotifyParentProperty>true</NotifyParentProperty>
    </Property>
    <Property Name="HandColor">
      <Description>Color used for the hour and minute hands</Description>
      <DefaultValue>
        <Type>System.Drawing.Color, System.Drawing, Version=2.0.0.0,
Culture=neutral, PublicKeyToken=b03f5f7f11d50a3a</Type>
        <Value>Black</Value>
      </DefaultValue>
      <NotifyParentProperty>true</NotifyParentProperty>
    </Property>
  </Class>
</Classes>
```

The properties window now shows the *ColorScheme* property as an expandable type (see Figure 15-6), and, as expected, changes in the properties of the *ColorScheme* object are reflected in the control in the designer.

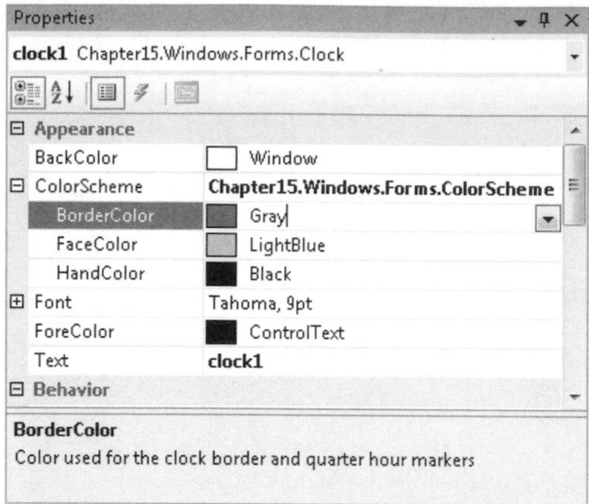

Figure 15-6 Expandable property in the designer

Class Diagrams

In the previous examples, you have worked directly with the .xmta file to specify attributes for the controls. You can also modify these same attributes through the Class Diagram Designer in Visual Studio. When an item is selected in the diagram, the properties window will contain an entry called Custom Attributes, as shown in Figure 15-7.

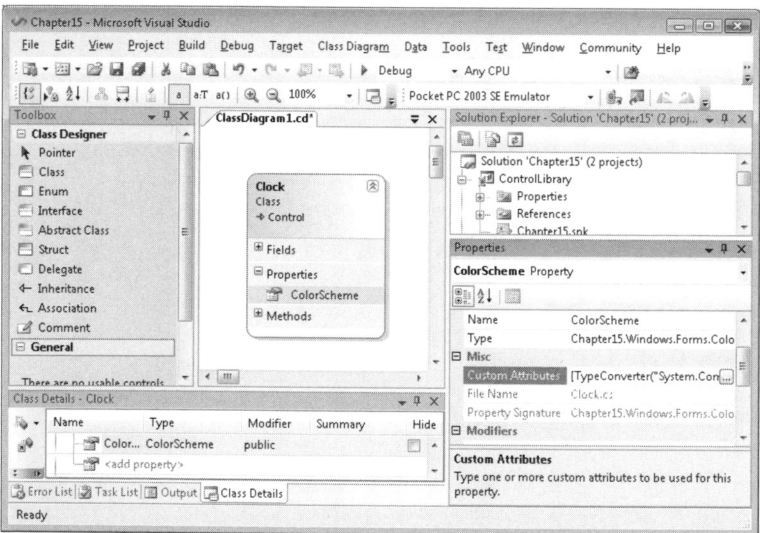

Figure 15-7 Custom Attributes in the class diagram

This property has an ellipsis (...) button that allows you to open the Custom Attributes list in a dialog box for easier editing. Attributes entered here are in their .NET syntax rather than how you would define them in an .xmta file. Figure 15-8 shows the attributes applied to the *Clock.ColorScheme* property.

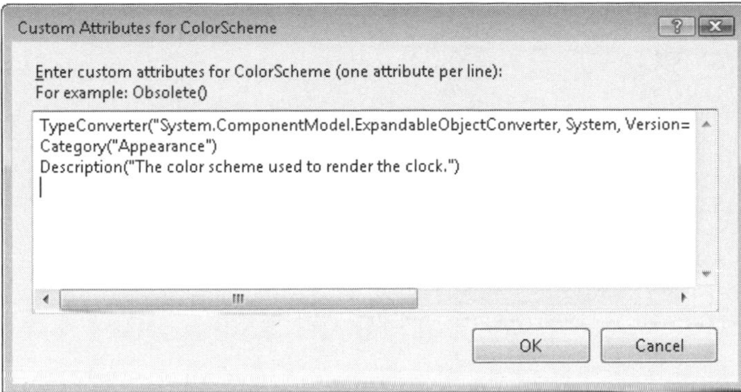

Figure 15-8 Custom Attributes dialog box showing attributes applied to the *ColorScheme* property

Listing 15-3 shows the complete .xmta file for the *ControlLibrary* project. It shows how to hide properties derived from the parent class, how to override default values, and how to add descriptions and designer behavior to newly defined properties.

Listing 15-3 Attribute File Listing

```
<?xml version="1.0" encoding="utf-16"?>
<Classes xmlns="...">
  <Class Name="Chapter15.Windows.Forms.Clock">
    <DesktopCompatible>true</DesktopCompatible>

    <Property Name="Width">
      <DefaultValue>
        <Type>System.Int32</Type>
        <Value>128</Value>
      </DefaultValue>
    </Property>
    <Property Name="Height">
      <DefaultValue>
        <Type>System.Int32</Type>
        <Value>128</Value>
      </DefaultValue>
    </Property>

    <Property Name="ColorScheme">
      <Category>Appearance</Category>
      <Description>The color scheme used to render the clock.</Description>
      <TypeConverter>System.ComponentModel.ExpandableObjectConverter,
System, Version=2.0.0.0, Culture=neutral,
PublicKeyToken=b77a5c561934e089</TypeConverter>
    </Property>

  </Class>

  <Class Name="Chapter15.Windows.Forms.ColorScheme">
    <TypeConverter>
      System.ComponentModel.ExpandableObjectConverter, System,
      Version=2.0.0.0, Culture=neutral,
      PublicKeyToken=b77a5c561934e089
```

```
    </TypeConverter>
    <DesktopCompatible>true</DesktopCompatible>

    <Property Name="BorderColor">
      <Description>Color used for the clock border</Description>
      <DefaultValue>
        <Type>System.Drawing.Color, System.Drawing, Version=2.0.0.0,
Culture=neutral, PublicKeyToken=b03f5f7f11d50a3a</Type>
        <Value>Gray</Value>
      </DefaultValue>
      <NotifyParentProperty>true</NotifyParentProperty>
    </Property>
    <Property Name="FaceColor">
      <Description>Color used for the clock face</Description>
      <DefaultValue>
        <Type>System.Drawing.Color, System.Drawing, Version=2.0.0.0,
Culture=neutral, PublicKeyToken=b03f5f7f11d50a3a</Type>
        <Value>LightBlue</Value>
      </DefaultValue>
      <NotifyParentProperty>true</NotifyParentProperty>
    </Property>
    <Property Name="HandColor">
      <Description>Color used for the hour and minute hands</Description>
      <DefaultValue>
        <Type>System.Drawing.Color, System.Drawing, Version=2.0.0.0,
Culture=neutral, PublicKeyToken=b03f5f7f11d50a3a</Type>
        <Value>Black</Value>
      </DefaultValue>
      <NotifyParentProperty>true</NotifyParentProperty>
    </Property>
  </Class>
  <Class Name="Chapter15.Windows.Forms.NumericTextBox">
    <DesktopCompatible>true</DesktopCompatible>
  </Class>
  <Class Name="Chapter15.Windows.Forms.PinUserControl">
    <DesktopCompatible>true</DesktopCompatible>
    <DesignTimeVisible>true</DesignTimeVisible>

    <!-- Hide some properties from parent class -->

    <Property Name="AutoScroll">
      <Browsable>false</Browsable>
      <Supported>false</Supported>
    </Property>
    <Property Name="AutoScrollMargin">
      <Browsable>false</Browsable>
      <Supported>false</Supported>
    </Property>
    <Property Name="ContextMenu">
      <Browsable>false</Browsable>
      <Supported>false</Supported>
    </Property>

    <!-- set some default values for existing properties -->
```

```
    <Property Name="BackColor">
      <DefaultValue>
        <Type>System.Drawing.Color, System.Drawing, Version=2.0.0.0,
Culture=neutral, PublicKeyToken=b03f5f7f11d50a3a</Type>
        <Value>Window</Value>
      </DefaultValue>
    </Property>
    <Property Name="Width">
      <DefaultValue>
          <Type>System.Int32</Type>
          <Value>109</Value>
      </DefaultValue>
    </Property>
    <Property Name="Height">
      <DefaultValue>
        <Type>System.Int32</Type>
        <Value>149</Value>
      </DefaultValue>
    </Property>

    <!-- Describe some new properties -->

    <Property Name="IsEntered">
      <Browsable>false</Browsable>
      <DesignerSerializationVisibility>Never
   </DesignerSerializationVisibility>
    </Property>

    <DefaultEvent>PinChanged</DefaultEvent>
    <Event Name="PinChanged">
      <Category>Action</Category>
      <Description>Occurs when the pin entered by the user changes.
   </Description>
    </Event>

    <Property Name="ButtonColor">
      <Category>Appearance</Category>
      <DefaultValue>
        <Type>System.Drawing.Color, System.Drawing, Version=2.0.0.0,
Culture=neutral, PublicKeyToken=b03f5f7f11d50a3a</Type>
        <Value>ActiveCaption</Value>
      </DefaultValue>
      <Description>Sets a color for the keypad button faces.</Description>
    </Property>
  </Class>
</Classes>
```

Custom Metadata Assemblies

When you are building a control library, Visual Studio doesn't include built-in support to create multiple .asmmeta files. If you want to support multiple platforms, you have two options: To provide exactly the same functionality on different platforms, you can copy the existing .asmmeta file and rename it to the required platform name; to provide different functionality on different platforms, you must do a little extra work.

For example, you may implement different functionality on different platforms in a control library that contains a number of controls, one or more of which are unsuitable for Smartphones because they rely on components not available on Smartphones, such as the *Button* control. In this case, you can hide the control from the designer to avoid run-time errors if the control is used.

You can manually create .asmmeta.dll files by using the Genasm.exe tool, which is part of Visual Studio. This is a command-line tool that takes the compiled .dll assembly and the .xmta metadata file and outputs the .asmmeta.dll file. Use of this tool is not well documented, and it is outside the scope of this book to explain it. Instead, we look at creating additional platform versions from the same code using Visual Studio.

First, create a new project in the solution, for example, use the project name *ControlLibrary.Smartphone* and target the Windows Mobile 5.0 Smartphone platform. Remove the existing AssemblyInfo.cs and UserControl.cs that are created for you. From the Project menu, select Add Existing Item, select the All Files (*.*) filter, and then browse to the existing control library project folder. Select all of the source files in this folder except the .xmta files, and then select Add As Link. This second project now uses all of the same source files as the first control library project. Repeat this process to add the AssemblyInfo.cs file—this ensures the library has the same name and version. Finally, add a new design-time attribute file for the project, and paste in the contents of the .xmta file you created for Pocket PC. Now you can amend this to change the behavior for Smartphone. Then create a new .xmta file that specifies designer behavior for the controls when used with the Smartphone platform. Listing 15-4 shows the Smartphone version of the attributes file.

Listing 15-4 Smartphone .xmta File

```
<?xml version="1.0" encoding="utf-16"?>
<Classes xmlns="http://schemas.microsoft.com/VisualStudio/2004/03/SmartDevices/
XMTA.xsd">

  <Class Name="Chapter15.Windows.Forms.Clock">
    <DesktopCompatible>true</DesktopCompatible>

    <Property Name="Width">
      <DefaultValue>
        <Type>System.Int32</Type>
        <Value>96</Value>
      </DefaultValue>
    </Property>
    <Property Name="Height">
      <DefaultValue>
        <Type>System.Int32</Type>
        <Value>96</Value>
      </DefaultValue>
    </Property>

        <Property Name="ColorScheme">
```

```
      <Category>Appearance</Category>
      <Description>The color scheme used to render the clock.</Description>
      <TypeConverter>System.ComponentModel.ExpandableObjectConverter,
System, Version=2.0.0.0, Culture=neutral,
PublicKeyToken=b77a5c561934e089</TypeConverter>
    </Property>

  </Class>

  <Class Name="Chapter15.Windows.Forms.ColorScheme">
    <TypeConverter>
      System.ComponentModel.ExpandableObjectConverter, System,
      Version=2.0.0.0, Culture=neutral,
      PublicKeyToken=b77a5c561934e089
    </TypeConverter>
    <DesktopCompatible>true</DesktopCompatible>

    <Property Name="BorderColor">
      <Description>Color used for the clock border</Description>
      <DefaultValue>
        <Type>System.Drawing.Color, System.Drawing, Version=2.0.0.0,
Culture=neutral, PublicKeyToken=b03f5f7f11d50a3a</Type>
        <Value>Gray</Value>
      </DefaultValue>
      <NotifyParentProperty>true</NotifyParentProperty>
    </Property>
    <Property Name="FaceColor">
      <Description>Color used for the clock face</Description>
      <DefaultValue>
        <Type>System.Drawing.Color, System.Drawing, Version=2.0.0.0,
Culture=neutral, PublicKeyToken=b03f5f7f11d50a3a</Type>
        <Value>LightBlue</Value>
      </DefaultValue>
      <NotifyParentProperty>true</NotifyParentProperty>
    </Property>
    <Property Name="HandColor">
      <Description>Color used for the hour and minute hands</Description>
      <DefaultValue>
        <Type>System.Drawing.Color, System.Drawing, Version=2.0.0.0,
Culture=neutral, PublicKeyToken=b03f5f7f11d50a3a</Type>
        <Value>Black</Value>
      </DefaultValue>
      <NotifyParentProperty>true</NotifyParentProperty>
    </Property>
  </Class>

  <Class Name="Chapter15.Windows.Forms.NumericTextBox">
    <DesktopCompatible>true</DesktopCompatible>
  </Class>

  <Class Name="Chapter15.Windows.Forms.PinUserControl">
    <DesignTimeVisible>false</DesignTimeVisible>
    <Supported>false</Supported>
  </Class>

</Classes>
```

For Smartphone clients, the preceding code sets the *PinUserControl* as unsupported and invisible at design time. This makes no difference to the compiled ControlLibrary.dll, but the ControlLibrary.Smartphone.asmmeta.dll will stop this control from being added to the Toolbox. The preceding code also changes the default size of the *Clock* component because Smartphone devices generally have smaller screen sizes. The ControlLibrary.Smartphone.asmmeta.dll file is copied to the same folder as ControlLibrary.dll for testing. In a separate project built for Smartphone, you can see the results after adding the library to the Toolbox, as shown in Figure 15-9.

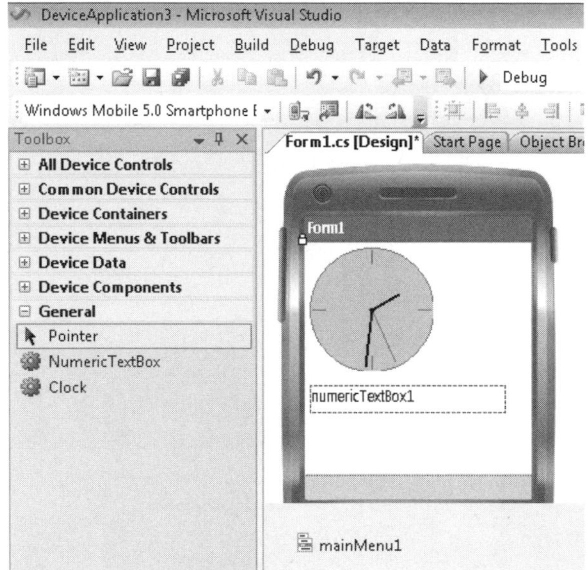

Figure 15-9 Visual Studio Toolbox showing controls from the *ControlLibrary* project in a Smartphone project

Migrating Old Controls

Controls created for Visual Studio 2003 used a completely different architecture for design-time support and are not supported in Visual Studio 2005 and later. A full description of the steps necessary to rewrite a legacy control is beyond the scope of this book; however, a good article on this topic is available on the Microsoft MSDN Web site at *msdn2.microsoft.com/en-us/library/aa446500.aspx*.

Adding to Visual Studio 2005 Toolbox

When you create a control library and reference it in the same solution, you gain instant access to the designer support for your controls without deploying any code, as shown in Figure 15-10.

Figure 15-10 Visual Studio Toolbox showing controls from the *ControlLibrary* project

After you have created a library of reusable controls, you will likely want to reuse them in other projects. In this section, we look at how to deploy your compiled assemblies to get the same designer support in other device projects.

To redistribute your control library as an installable package, you must copy your compiled .dll file into a location where Visual Studio can locate it so that it is shown in the Add Reference dialog box. The exact path will vary depending on the language settings on the computer and preferences set when installing Visual Studio. You can retrieve the required path by querying the registry for the default value at:

```
HKEY_LOCAL_MACHINE\SOFTWARE\Microsoft\.NETCompactFramework\v2.0.0.0\
PocketPC\AssemblyFoldersEx
```

In this folder is a subfolder called DesignerMetadata, which is where you should place the .asmmeta.dll file generated for your library. With these two files copied, you are able to add a reference to this library from other device projects as if it were just a code library. Next, you must customize the Toolbox.

To keep the Toolbox easy to browse, add these custom controls to a new tab: Right-click the Toolbox, select Add Tab, and in the caption box type a description such as **Sample Custom Controls**. This new tab is empty, so you can right-click in it, and select Choose Items. You are presented with a list of .NET components currently available to the Toolbox. Click the Browse button to locate your control library. After you have selected the ControlLibrary.dll, when you return to the Choose Items dialog box, you'll see that all available controls in the library are selected, as illustrated in Figure 15-11.

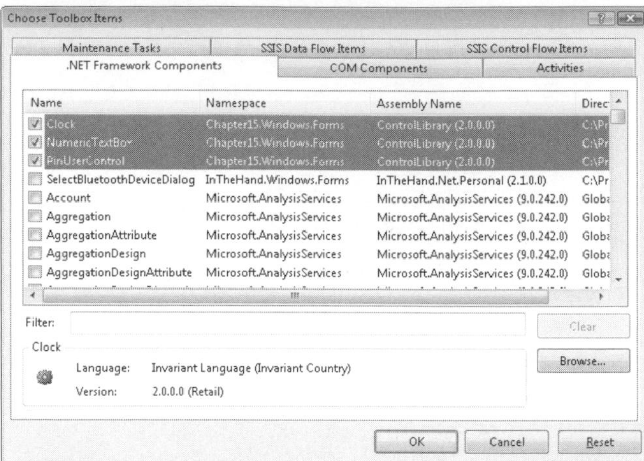

Figure 15-11 Choose Toolbox Items dialog box populated with new custom controls

Click OK to return to the Visual Studio designer. The Toolbox tab is populated with the custom controls. If you drag one to your form, a reference to the ControlLibrary.dll is automatically added to your project. Figure 15-12 shows the completed Toolbox in use in a new device project.

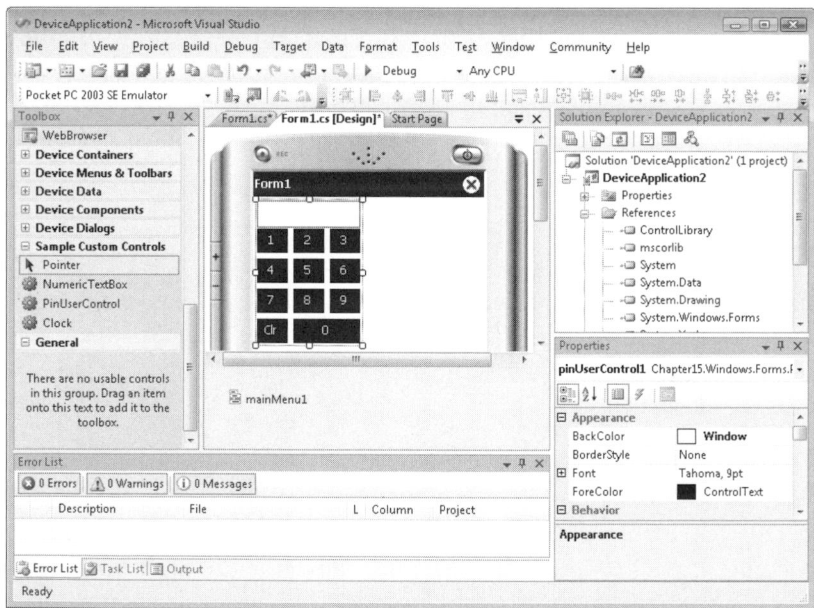

Figure 15-12 Smart device project showing custom Toolbox items and control designer support

It is possible to automate these steps and automatically populate the Toolbox if you are building a redistributable control library, but doing so is outside the scope of this book and requires knowledge of the Visual Studio software development kit (SDK).

Summary

This chapter examines the creation of several custom control types and follows the development of the control code with the necessary designer support to provide a rich experience in the Visual Studio Form Designer. Initially, we looked at the different possible starting points when creating a control—whether to inherit from an existing control, start with a basic *Control* type, or use the powerful *UserControl*, which is new in .NET Compact Framework 2.0. We investigated how building design-time behavior for smart device controls differs from using the full .NET Framework. We added the necessary designer attributes to support both simple and complex property types and provide descriptions and default values. Finally, we looked at the steps necessary to customize the Toolbox in Visual Studio so that your controls are easily accessible.

Chapter 16

Internationalization

In this chapter:

For many years there has been the promise of a "global marketplace," and today that is definitely a reality. In this online and connected world, the chances of your software application being used in different countries are very high and very real. The question is: How do you make your software cope with the challenges of respecting local culture-specific information and rendering a user interface (UI) in various languages? There is a two-part answer:

1. Don't hard-code decisions that work only in your specific country, for example, using the colon (:) or dot (.) as the time separator between hours and minutes; physically isolate such decisions (this process is known as globalization).
2. Translate the country-specific elements to satisfy various world markets, for example, French in Canada or English in South Africa (this process is known as localization).

Both the Microsoft Windows operating system and the Microsoft .NET Framework support globalization and localization. In fact, globalizing and localizing an application under the .NET Compact Framework on Windows CE–powered devices is almost identical to doing it under the full .NET Framework on desktop platforms. If you are familiar with the desktop model, you can skim through this chapter. Similarly, if you are not familiar with the desktop model, after reading this chapter you can get more in-depth information by using other materials that describe the desktop model because most of the principles apply equally to devices.

Understanding the Challenges of Globalization

Before we look at the steps needed to ready software for the global marketplace, we must explain some of the challenges.

Imagine an application that displays the time or maybe parses a string to obtain a time that it will then use somehow. The code for those two scenarios might look like this:

```
private void button1_Click(object sender, EventArgs e)
{
  this.DisplayThis(DateTime.Now);
}
private void DisplayThis(DateTime dt)
{
  string timeSeparator = ":";
  label1.Text = dt.Hour + timeSeparator + dt.Minute;
}

private void menuItem1_Click(object sender, EventArgs e)
{
  this.ParseThat("13/1/06 23.31.54");
}
private void ParseThat(string someTime)
{
  // someTime comes in as "13/1/06 23.31.54"
  DateTime dt = DateTime.Parse(someTime);
  MessageBox.Show(dt.ToString());
}
```

The problem with the preceding code is that it makes assumptions about the date and time formats. In the first method, it assumes that the time separator is the colon (:). Having a colon in a time display will look wrong to an Italian user who is accustomed to the dot (.) time separator. The second method will work on a device that is set up for Italian because the string that comes in representing the date and time is formatted as per the Italian rules. However, if the device is running under an English culture, the result will be a *FormatException* when the *DateTime.Parse* method is called.

A different example follows:

```
private void menuItem2_Click(object sender, EventArgs e)
{
  string s = this.ExtractDecimalPoints(12.34);
  label1.Text = s;
}
private string ExtractDecimalPoints(double valueFromNetwork)
{
  // valueFromNetwork comes in as 12.34, but on French culture
  // becomes 12,34.
  string temp = valueFromNetwork.ToString();
  int decimalPoint = temp.IndexOf('.');
  return temp.Substring(decimalPoint + 1);
}
```

If you are looking at that code and thinking that it returns *34*, you are right in some cases and wrong in others. For example, in most French-speaking countries (but not Switzerland!), the decimal separator is a comma (,), and that means the preceding code would incorrectly return *12,34*.

Try to spot what is wrong with this third example:

```
private void button2_Click(object sender, EventArgs e)
{
  label1.Text = this.FirstDayOfWeekToString();
}
private string FirstDayOfWeekToString()
{
  return DayOfWeek.Monday.ToString();
}
```

Most Europeans would agree that Monday is the first day of the week; however, in the United States, Sunday is considered the first day of the week. Furthermore, regardless of which day you determine to be the first day of the week, calling *ToString* on the enumeration will always produce an English string, which clearly is not desired if the device is set up for a non-English language.

In all three examples, the code would either fail at run time or produce incorrect results. In some cases, it should be rewritten to be aware of the settings that the user has chosen, and in others it should be rewritten to behave consistently regardless of the device settings. For example, storing and retrieving a value from a database may have to happen in a consistent format regardless of how the value is rendered on the screen. Of course, globalization is not limited to dates and numbers; it extends to calendars, currencies, string comparisons, and more. You must write code that is aware of all these cases.

Globalization even affects how you address folders in the file system. You should never hard-code paths to files or folders under *\My Documents* or *\Program Files* because these standard folders have local language names on devices running localized versions of Windows CE or Windows Mobile. To find the correct folder name for these standard folders, use the *Sstem.Environment.GetFolderPath* method, which takes as a parameter a *System.Environment.SpecialFolder* enumerated value to indicate the folder that you want. For example, use the following code to get the correct path to the folder, which in English is *\My Documents*:

```
string  myDocsPath =
    System.Environment.GetFolderPath(Environment.SpecialFolder.Personal);
```

Next, we revisit the important concept of a *culture* and then see how to take advantage of culture in your .NET applications.

Culture

The words *country* and *language* are not fine-grained concepts because some countries use more than one official language (for example, Belgium) and some languages are used in more than one country (for example, French in Canada and French in France). It is for this reason that in computing, International Organization for Standardization (ISO) standards describe unique combinations of languages and regions; for example, fr-FR specifies French in France whereas fr-CA denotes French in Canada. In addition, Windows defines a locale culture identifier (LCID) for each unique locale. The following table shows a few examples:

ISO Name	English Name	Windows LCID
fr-FR	French (France)	1036
fr-CA	French (Canada)	3084
en-CA	English (Canada)	4105
en-GB	English (United Kingdom)	2057
el-GR	Greek (Greece)	1032

At any one time, Windows is running under a particular locale. The end user can change the locale through the Regional Settings panel, as shown in Figure 16-1.

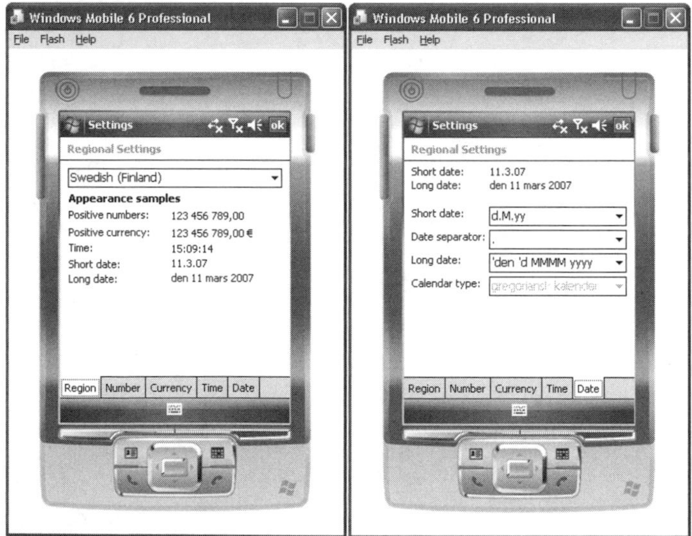

Figure 16-1 Regional Settings in the Windows Mobile 6 Professional emulator

.NET applications typically must be restarted for changes to a locale to take effect because they don't automatically respond to a setting change. This is not a big issue because Windows Mobile–powered devices must typically be soft-reset for a locale change to take effect. In any case, when an application is started, it uses the current locale for any locale-specific decisions.

From managed code, the entry point to obtaining and using locale information is the *CultureInfo* class from the *System.Globalization* namespace.

CultureInfo

To obtain the current culture settings, use code as follows:

```
CultureInfo ci = CultureInfo.CurrentCulture;
this.Text = ci.Name;
```

Note In addition to *CurrentCulture*, *CultureInfo* also has another property: *CurrentUICulture*. For device projects targeting Windows Mobile, the two properties return the same results, so do not let that confuse you. Note that custom Windows CE–based devices with Multilingual User Interface (MUI) support may potentially return different values. See *msdn2.microsoft.com/en-us/library/ms904030.aspx* for more information about MUI support in Windows CE.

All threads in a smart device application are set to use the *CultureInfo* representing the device settings. On the full framework, you can change the culture on a per-thread basis, but this is not possible on the .NET Compact Framework, so the properties are not available on the *Thread* class. However, you can still explicitly create a *CultureInfo* object and use it accordingly. For example, drag a combo box and some label/text box pairs onto a form, as shown in Figure 16-2.

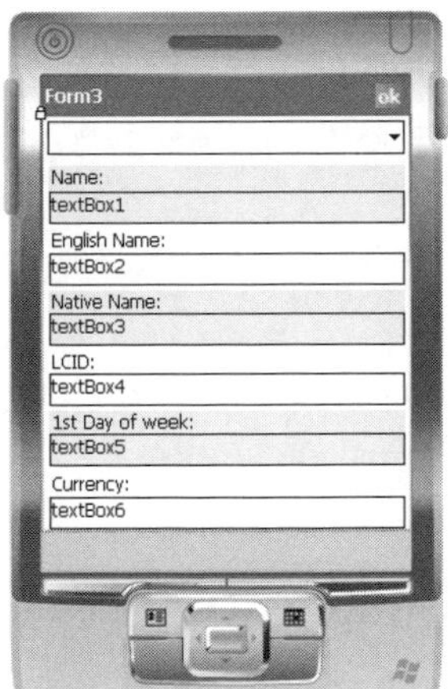

Figure 16-2 Playing with *CultureInfo* objects

Then add the following code to the form code-behind:

```
private void Form3_Load(object sender, EventArgs e)
{
  comboBox1.Items.Add(new CultureInfo("fr-FR"));
  comboBox1.Items.Add(new CultureInfo("fr-CA"));
  comboBox1.Items.Add(new CultureInfo("en-GB"));
  comboBox1.Items.Add(new CultureInfo("en-CA"));
  comboBox1.Items.Add(new CultureInfo("el-GR"));
  comboBox1.Items.Add(new CultureInfo("de-DE"));
  comboBox1.Items.Add(new CultureInfo("es-ES"));
  comboBox1.Items.Add(new CultureInfo("de-AT"));
  comboBox1.Items.Add(new CultureInfo("ru-RU"));

  // PlatformNotSupportedException for Japanese
  // comboBox1.Items.Add(new CultureInfo("ja-JP"));

  comboBox1.SelectedIndexChanged +=
         new EventHandler(comboBox1_SelectedIndexChanged);
}

void comboBox1_SelectedIndexChanged(object sender, EventArgs e)
{
  this.Render((CultureInfo)comboBox1.SelectedItem);
}

private void Render(CultureInfo ci)
{
  textBox1.Text = ci.Name;
  textBox2.Text = ci.EnglishName;
  textBox3.Text = ci.NativeName;
  textBox4.Text = ci.LCID.ToString();
  // Note the use of ToString on enumeration. Bad practice used for demo only.
  textBox5.Text = ci.DateTimeFormat.FirstDayOfWeek.ToString();
  textBox6.Text = ci.NumberFormat.CurrencySymbol;
}
```

Run the project and change the selection in the combo box to observe different data for each locale. Figure 16-3 shows a few results.

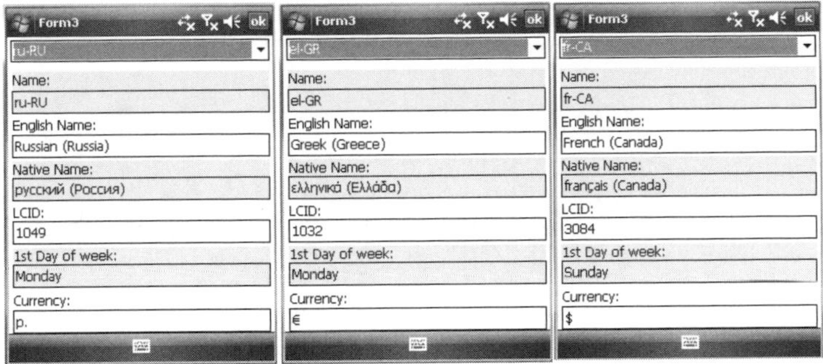

Figure 16-3 *CultureInfo* data for Russian, Greek, and French (Canada)

Notice that if you try to create a Japanese *CultureInfo* object and then try to run in the emulator, a *PlatformNotSupportedException* is thrown. That is because you can create *CultureInfo* objects only for locales that are supported by your device/target. It is not possible to use a locale that is not supported on the device or to create a custom culture. Also not possible is support for right-to-left (RTL) languages such as Hebrew and Arabic. The issue with the latter is that the .NET Compact Framework controls do not expose the *RightToLeft* property.[1]

Caution You are advised not to try to display your application resources (including dates, numbers, and other localizable entities) in a language different from the one currently selected on the device. Although you can program your application to do that, it is generally more trouble than it is worth; simply advise your user to change the language of the device in the Regional Settings dialog box and then restart the application.

Revisiting the Challenges

You can use the *CultureInfo* object to solve the challenges of device application globalization mentioned earlier in this chapter. Compare and contrast the following code with the code given earlier. The methods that required changes are shown in bold type:

```
private void DisplayThis(DateTime dt)
{
  CultureInfo ci = CultureInfo.CurrentCulture;
  string timeSeparator = ci.DateTimeFormat.TimeSeparator;
  label1.Text = dt.Hour + timeSeparator + dt.Minute;
}
```

In the preceding code, notice how we use the current *CultureInfo* to determine what the separator should be. Whenever you find yourself hard-coding cultural decisions like this, look at the *CultureInfo* object, which contains a host of information.

1 For a discussion of RTL and some possible unsupported workarounds for the simplest of applications, please see Daniel Moth's blog *www.danielmoth.com/Blog/2005/03/progress-on-rtl.html*

Here we revisit two other methods:

```
private void ParseThat(string someTime)
{
  // someTime comes in as "13/1/06 23.31.54"
  CultureInfo ci = new CultureInfo("it-IT");
  DateTime dt = DateTime.Parse(someTime, ci);
  MessageBox.Show(dt.ToString());
}

private string ExtractDecimalPoints(double valueFromNetwork)
{
  // valueFromNetwork comes in as 12.34 but in French becomes 12,34.
  string temp = valueFromNetwork.ToString(new CultureInfo("en-US"));
  int decimalPoint = temp.IndexOf('.');
  return temp.Substring(decimalPoint + 1);
}
```

In both of the examples, observe how we use different overloads of the framework methods to force the formatting of our choice rather than using the default. In one case, the *Parse* method and in the other the *ToString* method is passed in a *CultureInfo* object that we explicitly create. Whenever you call framework methods such as these that have an overload that accepts an *IFormatProvider* object, you should consider carefully whether the default or invariant[1] culture is what you require. If not, you should pass in an *IFormatProvider* object that conforms to your business logic.

It is worth clarifying here that formatting data as discussed in this section is important in two specific areas: how you *display* it and how you *store* it. Typically, you display the data formatted to match the end user's expectations and to match the current device settings. However, typically you store data in a format that is independent of how you render it, for example, always storing string representations of doubles with a dot (.) rather than in a locale-specific way. Between the storage and the UI layer, the formatting translation takes place. In particular, when storing dates, an additional element to consider is the time zone. Storing date and time information using one time zone and reading it in another can result in incorrect data. If you have such a scenario, you should use Coordinated Universal Time (UTC) for internal representation and storage. Please see the methods of the *DateTime* type, for example, *ToUniversalTime*, *SpecifyKind*, and others, described in the online documentation on the Microsoft MSDN Web site at *msdn2.microsoft.com/en-us/library/system.datetime.aspx*.

1 The Invariant culture is a culture-independent *CultureInfo* object accessible via *CultureInfo.InvariantCulture*. It is associated with the English language but not with any specific region.

Finally, let's re-examine the last challenge.

```
private string FirstDayOfWeekToString()
{
   DayOfWeek dow =
     CultureInfo.CurrentCulture.DateTimeFormat.FirstDayOfWeek;
    switch (dow)
    {
      case DayOfWeek.Monday:
        return "Monday";
      case DayOfWeek.Sunday:
        return "Sunday";
      default:
        return "Monday"; //arbitrary decision
     }
 }
```

The *FirstDayOfWeekToString* method has been completely rewritten to read the value from the current *CultureInfo* rather than make assumptions. It has also been changed not to call *ToString* on the enumeration. However, it still uses hard-coded English text, and we revisit this example later in this chapter. We haven't yet described anything that demonstrates how to work with translated text. That is the subject of the next section.

Using Language Translation (or Localization)

Although formatting data is very important and is in fact the area where most bugs surface in the process of internationalizing an application, the most visible part of the internationalization process is displaying strings in the chosen language. .NET Compact Framework developers achieve language translation in the same way that desktop developers do:

1. Create all localizable strings and images in resource files (text or Extensible Markup Language [XML] files that are compiled into binary resources files that are then embedded in fallback or satellite assemblies). A good example of localizable strings is error messages that your application may display to the user.
2. Rather than hard-coding anything, read from the embedded resources using a *ResourceManager* class.
3. Translate the resources, and take advantage of the .NET satellite assembly infrastructure to get the correct set loaded in memory at run time. In other words, the *ResourceManager* automatically picks the correct set of resources to load.

Creating Resource Files

Developers add .resx files to their projects (see Figure 16-4) and enter name/value pairs using a designer (see Figure 16-5).

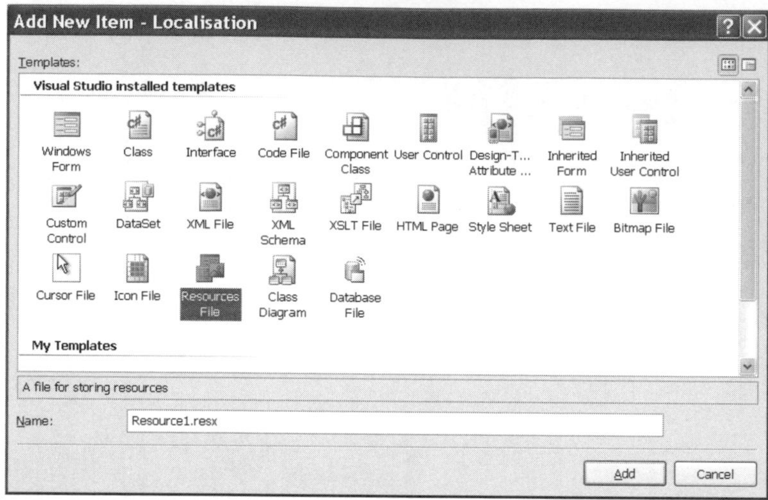

Figure 16-4 Adding a .resx file to a project

The *value* is the actual string to be translated, and the *name* is the key that is used in code to retrieve the value. The first set of resources to be created is typically the *fallback* resources. That is, these are the resources that are used by default when a resource for a chosen language does not exist.

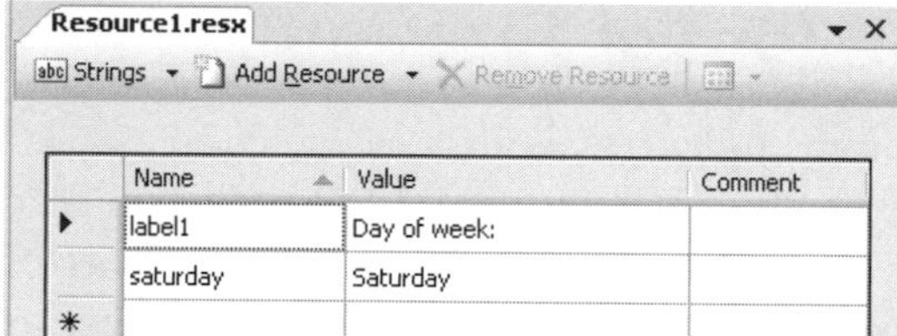

Figure 16-5 Entering name/value pairs for the localizable resources

In Microsoft Visual Studio 2005, the project already has a global .resx file included (and you can add ones if you wish) that you can access in the project properties window (in Microsoft Visual Basic, it is located in My Project) on the Resources tab. Select a .resx file in Solution Explorer, and then look at the file properties. Observe how its *Build Action* is set to *Embedded Resource*, as shown in Figure 16-6.

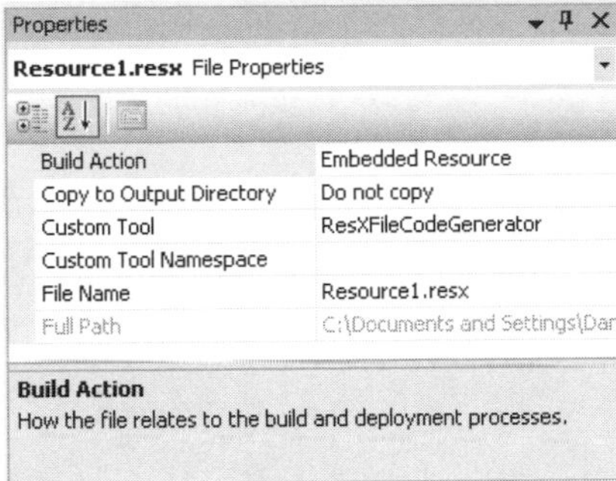

Figure 16-6 .resx files are built as embedded resources

Earlier, we hard-coded the strings *Sunday* and *Monday*. Instead, you could create a name for each one and enter it together with the value in a .resx file. For that particular example, note that there is a better solution because the translation exists in the framework. Change the code as follows:

```
private string FirstDayOfWeekToStringCorrect()
{
  DateTimeFormatInfo dtfi = CultureInfo.CurrentCulture.DateTimeFormat;
  DayOfWeek dow = dtfi.FirstDayOfWeek;
  return dtfi.DayNames[(int)dow]; //DayNames returns localized strings
}
```

Next we describe how to access the .resx values from code.

Reading from Resources

After all your strings are in one or more .resx files and out of the code, you must be able to access them somehow. This is achieved by using a *ResourceManager*. Before Visual Studio 2005, you had to create the *ResourceManager* manually and point it to the appropriate resource in its constructor. Subsequently, you would call its methods (that is, *GetString*, *GetObject*) that accepted a name as a string parameter and returned the localized result. This process is error prone because it is string-based and a single typo in the creation or retrieval causes a run-time exception. With Visual Studio 2005, you get an easier programming model and compile-time checking.

Behind every .resx file that you add, and indeed behind the default .resx file in the project properties window (My Project, in Visual Basic), there is an auto-generated class that wraps the creation of the *ResourceManager* and that exposes strongly typed properties for resources that were added to the .resx file by the designer. For example, consider the following code, which uses hard-coded strings:

```
label1.Text = "Day of week:";
textBox1.Text = "Saturday";
```

Next, add to the project the .resx file shown earlier in Figure 16-5. Then you need to change the code to use the resource file. In Visual Studio 2005, you can do this as follows:

```
label1.Text = Resource1.label1;
textBox1.Text = Resource1.saturday;
```

Note Because you don't know at design time how long the translation for a piece of text will be, it is best to place Label controls in their own horizontal space on the Form and size them large enough so that they can accommodate the longest local language translation you expect to need.

In the preceding code, *Resource1* is a class that is generated by Visual Studio, and the static properties it exposes also are generated for every name/value pair you add in the designer. It is good to look at the auto-generated code to understand how the process works under the covers. To examine the code, in Solution Explorer expand the .resx file node to reveal the code-behind file (in Visual Basic, select Show All Files first); see Figure 16-7.

Figure 16-7 .resx files have an auto-generated class that helps access the resources at run time

The benefit of keeping the strings in one place is that if you need to change them later (because of branding or a change in UI guidelines), it is easier. Also, having all text in one place makes it easier to spot inconsistencies in terminology. However, the biggest benefit is that .NET supports swapping one set of resources for another in a different language, with no changes to the code. We discuss how later, in the section "Locale-Specific Resources and Satellite Assemblies."

Form's *Localizable* Property

If you select a form in Solution Explorer and examine the properties, you'll find two properties: *Localizable* and *Language*. You may also notice that each form has an associated .resx file (in Visual Basic, show all files in Solution Explorer to observe the .resx file). If you change the *Localizable* property to *true* and then select a *Language* from the combo box, you'll notice that an additional .resx file is created. For example, setting the language to French creates a *Form1.fr.resx* file, as shown in Figure 16-8.

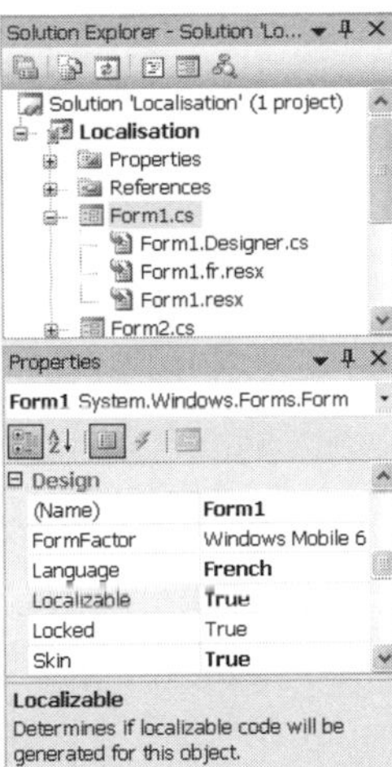

Figure 16-8 Setting separate localizable resources for a form

The point here is that each form has its own .resx file. When you use *Localizable* for the form, a .resx file is automatically created for each language you choose. Each .resx file persists not only the text but also the other properties of the controls such as location and size. Note that you cannot have a different set of controls per locale, and that is why you can add controls only when the *Language* property is set to *Default*. If you want to have a slightly different set of controls for each culture, you can add all controls to the form and toggle their *Visible* property as appropriate per culture. Always remember to switch back the *Language* to *Default* before building or closing the project.

The benefit of the *Localizable* property is that each form is self-contained and you can design different layouts for each locale you want to support. The disadvantage is that if you do not require different layouts for each language, you pay a very small performance penalty at load time, especially for larger forms. Different needs dictate different decisions, but, especially in a resource-constrained environment such as on a mobile device, it may be better to explicitly use your own .resx files and leave the form's *Localizable* property set to *False*.

As stated in Chapter 5, "Understanding and Optimizing .NET Compact Framework Performance," always measure the performance impact in your specific scenario before making such decisions. If you decide not to use the *Localizable* property, it means that you do not enter any text into the properties of controls and instead set them in the form's constructor (or in the form's *Load* event method handler) by reading from the resource class, as discussed in the preceding section. The tradeoff is between a potential performance penalty and additional code that you have to write yourself. Writing the code gives you the option to choose to store form resources in a single file rather than have an individual .resx file for each form. If you store form resources in a single file, you can use the same resource key/value pair across multiple forms, which translators may appreciate.

Locale-Specific Resources and Satellite Assemblies

At this stage, you have an application that has separated the localizable resources from the code. The next step is to truly take advantage of that separation.

Each .resx file in your project that contains resources you'd like to localize requires a corresponding culture-specific or culture-neutral .resx file. Culture-neutral resources are ones that apply to a language regardless of location, for example, French. Culture-specific resources are those that apply to a specific language–location combination, for example, French (Canada). For example, if you have a .resx file in your project called Resources1.resx, you must add a resource file with the same file name but culture-specific extension for each supported culture. So, for French, you could add a .resx file named Resources1.fr.resx to contain culture-neutral resources for French, and you could further add a Resources1.fr-FR.resx file with resources that apply only to French in France. The runtime will try to find the most specific resources to use. For every culture-specific entry that is missing, it will fall back to the culture-neutral resources and for anything missing there, it will fall back to the language-neutral resources that are embedded in the executable assembly (for example, Resources1.resx). Note that .resx files that have a language's two-letter code in their name do not have a separate generated class associated with them, of course.

Build the project after adding the language .resx files, and browse to your build directory, that is, browse to your project's location, and then go to bin/Debug/. In addition to what you normally find there, you will see an additional directory named fr. For every supported language in your project (for which you added a set of .resx files) there will be a directory named after the two-letter language code. Open the fr folder, and you will find the *AppName*.Resources.dll, where *AppName* is the name of the project. These culture-neutral and culture-specific assemblies are called satellite assemblies. The language XML .resx files in a project are compiled into binary satellite assemblies (Figure 16-9).

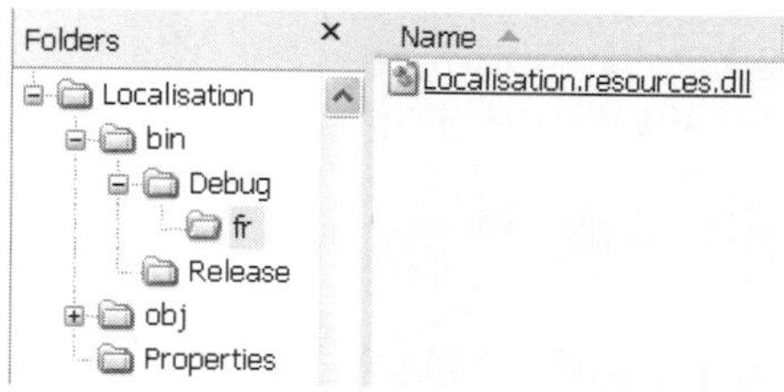

Figure 16-9 Satellite assemblies

When you deploy your solution to the user's device, you must re-create this directory hierarchy: Under the folder where your executable is deployed, copy the language folders that contain the resources assembly for that language. That means that even after your application is deployed, you can still make an additional deployment step at a later stage without touching the original executable, and you can simply add language translation by adding a directory containing a new satellite resource assembly.

Actually Translating the Text

Usually, you may require a third party to translate the text from one language to another. If the translator has Visual Studio, that person can load the .resx files and translate the text by preserving the same *key* and replacing the *value* with the localized text. Chances are that the translator will not have Visual Studio. Instead, there are many third-party products that specialize in resource localization, for example, Alchemy Catalyst and other free ones such as Lutz Roeder's Resourcer for .NET.

These tools can read the .resx format so that you need to send to your translators only the English .resx file, and they will send you back a localized .resx file (for example, someName.es.resx for Spanish) that you can add to your Visual Studio project and build the Resources.dll. This is where using the *Localizable* property of the form mentioned earlier can be beneficial. Some of these tools can display the UI layout when they open the FormX.resx file. This means that the translator can see the text in the context of a user interface. Note that this is not possible with Visual Studio .NET 2003 and .NET Compact Framework version 1.0 projects because the RESX format for device projects is different, so the tools cannot read that format and re-create the UI (although they can still read the .resx file in a textual list format). In Visual Studio 2005 and .NET Compact Framework version 2.0, the RESX format used for device projects and for desktop projects is identical, so that issue has gone away.

Caution In the software development kit (SDK), you can use the tool named Winres to translate form .resx files as per the earlier description about the *Localizable* property. Beware that it is not aware of device-specific .resx files, and although the file format is the same now, there are still properties that are missing from device controls such as *RightToLeft*. With Winres, you can assign such properties and you will find out only with run-time exceptions. We suggest that you do not use Winres.

Should your translator not be willing or able to use the .resx files, the translator can still translate your content by using text files. You can easily convert the .resx file to a text file and send that to the translator. The text file for the .resx file in Figure 16-5 would contain the following two lines of text:

```
label1=Day of week:
saturday=Saturday
```

The translator opens the file that contains a series of key/value pairs separated by equal signs (=) and replaces the text on the right with the localized text. The translator then sends back to you the text file, which you convert back to the .resx format and rename accordingly (for example, *someName*.de.resx for German). The question you probably have at this stage is how to convert the .resx file to text and vice versa. You can use the SDK tool Resgen from the command line. (In previous versions where the .resx file format is different, you have to use Cfresgen.) An example of what the command-line syntax looks like follows:

```
resgen Resource1.resx Resource1.txt
```

Summary

Writing software for the global marketplace is an ever more important requirement for large enterprises operating in multiple countries, and for independent software vendors. In this chapter, we saw how code should be written in a locale-independent way and how to isolate and then translate the locale-specific resources. You can test localized applications even without having foreign devices because you can download localized images of the emulators from MSDN.

This chapter has given you a brief introduction to this topic. For more information, please consult the online documentation on the MSDN Web site at *msdn2.microsoft.com/en-us/library/f45fce5x.aspx*.

Chapter 17

Developing with Windows Mobile

In this chapter:

The Microsoft Windows Mobile operating system contains a number of application programming interfaces (APIs) that are exclusive to Windows Mobile–powered devices. Some we have already discussed in previous chapters, for example, Connection Manager in Chapter 9, "Get Connected." Windows Mobile 5.0 and later feature a set of managed APIs that can easily be used in both Microsoft .NET Compact Framework version 1.0 and version 2.0 projects. In this chapter, we investigate these managed APIs along with some of the native functionality that you can also use in application development, such as the Global Positioning System (GPS) API.

Pocket Outlook

The Windows Mobile managed APIs include functionality for a number of different areas, but by far the most complex and widely used is the *Microsoft.WindowsMobile.PocketOutlook* library, an easy-to-use managed class library around two separate native APIs: the Microsoft Office Pocket Outlook Object Model (POOM), which is responsible for Calendar, Contacts, and Tasks on the device, and Windows CE Mail API (CEMAPI), which handles all e-mail and Short Message Service (SMS) functionality on the device. In Windows Mobile 5.0, this set of functionality was renamed Outlook Mobile; however, the programming interface retains the Pocket Outlook name. All activities using the Pocket Outlook functionality are based on the central *OutlookSession* class. Therefore, you should create an instance somewhere central to your application, for example, as a member of the main application form. The following sample application uses this approach: The session is initialized in the *Form_Load* method.

```
using Microsoft.WindowsMobile.PocketOutlook;

namespace Chapter17
{
        public class OutlookForm : System.Windows.Forms.Form
        {
                private OutlookSession session;
...
```

Personal Information Management

The Pocket Outlook Object Model, the native API on which this managed class library is built, is designed as a subset of the Outlook Object Model present in the desktop Microsoft Office Outlook application. With the Pocket Outlook Object Model, you can access the Calendar, Contacts, and Tasks data held on the device; these are referred to as Personal Information Management (PIM) items.

Because of the limitations of the applications on the device, the Pocket Outlook Object Model is notably missing a number of features that an experienced Outlook developer is familiar with. For example, each type of data has only a single folder, whereas Outlook supports a rich nested folder structure. There is no e-mail support in the Pocket Outlook Object Model; e-mail is accessed by using a separate API, which we discuss later in this chapter in the section titled "Messaging." All of the PIM data held on the device can be synchronized with Outlook on the user's desktop computer or a Microsoft Exchange Server, depending on the synchronization settings applied.

PimItem

All individual PIM items are derived from the *PimItem* base class. This class defines standard functionality supported by all item types such as the ability to display the item to the user with the *ShowDialog()* method and the ability to copy and delete items. Each *PimItem* is uniquely identified by its *ItemId* property. Internally, the *ItemId* contains a numerical ID assigned by the database engine on the device. These IDs do not persist across a backup and restore and are not synchronized with desktop Outlook.

All of the properties in the *PimItem*-derived classes have accompanying events that fire if the property value is changed. For example, the *Body* property, which contains the plain text notes for the item, has an accompanying *BodyChanged* event. These events reflect only changes made in your own code–if the user modifies items in the standard PIM applications or in a third-party application, the data in your application will not automatically update. All items contain a *Categories* property, which is a string value containing the names of categories to which the item is assigned. Internally, Pocket Outlook maintains a master categories list that is not exposed through the managed class library.

Appointments

Windows Mobile supports both one-time and recurring appointments. You can create a new *Appointment* either by using the *AppointmentCollection.AddNew()* method or the *Appointment* constructor. If you use the *Appointment* constructor, you must call *AppointmentCollection.Add()* to add your new item to the calendar on the device; otherwise, when you call *Update()* to save the item, an exception will be thrown. Strongly typed collection classes are implemented for each of the item types, and these support a number of standard .NET interfaces and with them you can easily data-bind controls to the PIM data. For example, the sample application that accompanies this chapter displays all the Appointment data in a *DataGrid* control using just the following code:

```
private void OutlookForm_Load(object sender, System.EventArgs e)
{
        //Create new Outlook application instance.
        session = new OutlookSession();
        dataGrid1.DataSource = session.Appointments.Items;
}
```

You can data-bind to controls just as you would with other collections or data sources. The *Appointment* class offers a range of unique properties for setting the start and end times for the event. Appointments can be marked as all-day events by setting the *AllDayEvent* property to *true*. This ignores the time component of the *Start* and *End* properties, and it also affects the way the items are displayed in the Calendar application. All-day events are always listed at the top of the day view and do not scroll out of view. Appointment behavior is also affected by the *BusyStatus* property, which you can use to set the status to Free, Busy, Tentative, and Out Of Office. Each status has a color key when the items are displayed in the Calendar application. Figure 17-1 shows a few different types of appointment.

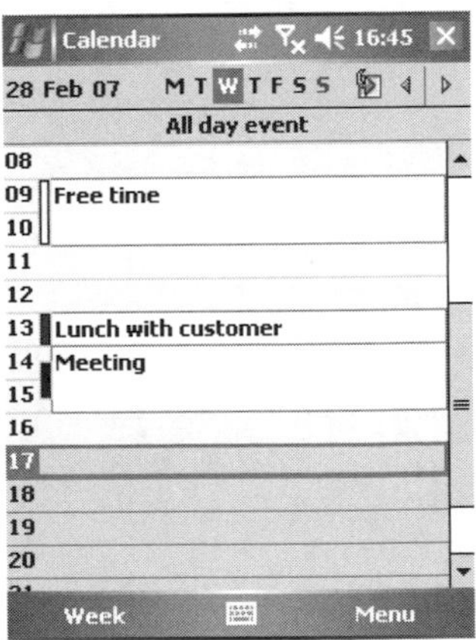

Figure 17-1 Calendar application showing different appointment types

Tasks

The Task item is used to store the user's to-do list. Tasks have properties for setting due date, completion status, and priority. Other than the task-specific properties, working with tasks is the same as working with the other item types. The *DateCompleted* and *Complete* properties are linked–because *DateCompleted* is read-only, the value is set to the current time whenever the *Complete* property is set to *true*. Because tasks are synchronized with the user's Outlook task list, they can be very useful for recording outstanding work from a mobile application. The following code example shows how to create a *Task* item.

```
private void SaveTask(string customerid, int jobNumber, string description)
{
   Task t = new Task();
   t.Subject = jobNumber.ToString() + ": " + description;
   t.StartDate = DateTime.Now;
   //Set due date to 7 days.
   t.DueDate = DateTime.Today.AddDays(7);
   //Add custom properties.
   t.Properties.Add("CustomerId", typeof(string));
   t.Properties.Add("JobNumber", typeof(int));
   t.Properties["CustomerID"] = customerid;
   t.Properties["JobNumber"] = jobNumber;
   //Assign category.
   t.Categories = "Maintenance";

   t.Update();
}
```

Reminders

A reminder can be set for appointment and task items. The time of appointment reminders can be overridden using the *ReminderMinutesBeforeStart* property. For task items, you set the *ReminderTime* property using the exact *DateTime* value. You can also set the way in which the reminder behaves by using a number of Boolean properties:

- *ReminderDialog*
- *ReminderLED*
- *ReminderRepeat*
- *ReminderSound*
- *ReminderVibrate*

If the *ReminderSound* property is set to *true*, you can override the default reminder sound by passing the full path of a .wav audio file to the *ReminderSoundFile* property. The following example shows how to create an *Appointment* and set a reminder.

```
private void AppointmentWithReminder(DateTime start, TimeSpan duration,
        string subject)
{
    Appointment a = new Appointment();
    a.Start = start;
    a.Duration = duration;
    a.Subject = subject;
    a.BusyStatus = BusyStatus.Busy;
    a.Categories = "Samples";

    //Remind user one hour before start.
    a.ReminderMinutesBeforeStart = 60;
    a.ReminderDialog = true;
    a.ReminderLed = true;
    a.ReminderSound = true;
    a.ReminderRepeat = true;
    a.ReminderSoundFile = "\\Windows\\Alarm3.wav";

    a.Update();
}
```

Recurrence Patterns

Appointment and *Task* items can be created with a recurrence pattern. You must take some care in setting up recurrence patterns because the *Recurrence* class has a number of properties, but their use depends on the recurrence type set. Therefore, the *RecurrenceType* property is always the first property you should set when creating a *RecurrencePattern*. Table 17-1 shows the possible values for *RecurrenceType* and the other *Recurrence* properties that must be used with it.

Table 17-1 *RecurrenceType* and *Recurrence* Properties

***RecurrenceType* Value**	***Recurrence* Properties**	**Property Type**
NoRecurrence		
Daily	*Interval*	*Int32* (Days)
Weekly	*DaysOfWeekMask*	*DaysOfWeek*
	Interval	*Int32* (Weeks)
Monthly	*DayOfMonth*	*Int32*
	Interval	*Int32* (Months)
MonthByNumber	*DaysOfWeekMask*	*DaysOfWeek*
	Instance	*WeekOfMonth*
	Interval	*Int32* (Months)
Yearly	*DayOfMonth*	*Int32*
	MonthOfYear	*Month*
YearByNumber	*DaysOfWeekMask*	*DaysOfWeek*
	Instance	*WeekOfMonth*
	MonthOfYear	*Month*

The difference between the *Monthly* and *MonthByNumber* recurrence types (and the *Yearly* and *YearByNumber* types) is that *Monthly* occurs on a specific date every *n* months, and *MonthByNumber* occurs on a specific occurrence of a weekday every *n* months. A typical example of a *MonthByNumber* recurrence is "the second Thursday of every month." Some of these enumerations look similar to .NET types, but they have different values and behaviors. For example, because *DaysOfWeek* is a Flags enumeration, and multiple items can be combined by using the OR operator, the values are not the same as *System.DayOfWeek*. Therefore, to convert between the two requires some additional code that includes a *switch* statement:

```
private DaysOfWeek DayOfWeekToDaysOfWeek(DayOfWeek dow)
{
        switch (dow)
        {
                case DayOfWeek.Monday:
                        return DaysOfWeek.Monday;
                case DayOfWeek.Tuesday:
                        return DaysOfWeek.Tuesday;
                case DayOfWeek.Wednesday:
                        return DaysOfWeek.Wednesday;
                case DayOfWeek.Thursday:
                        return DaysOfWeek.Thursday;
                case DayOfWeek.Friday:
                        return DaysOfWeek.Friday;
                case DayOfWeek.Saturday:
                        return DaysOfWeek.Saturday;
                case DayOfWeek.Sunday:
                        return DaysOfWeek.Sunday;
        }

        return 0;
}
```

The next enumeration of note is *Month*. This contains values for each of the 12 months, each of which has numerical values 1 through 12. This means that you can cast a numerical month value to the enumeration and vice versa. This is useful because the *DateTime* type exposes the month numerically, so you can convert this easily to set up a recurrence:

```
ar.MonthOfYear = (Month)dtStart.Month;
```

The *WeekOfMonth* enumeration is used with the *MonthByNumber* and *YearByNumber* recurrence types. You can determine the week value from any specific date by using the following code:

```
private WeekOfMonth GetWeekOfMonth(DateTime dt)
{
       int week = (dt.Day / 7) + 1;
       return (WeekOfMonth)week;
}
```

You can set up a simple recurrence pattern using a few lines of code:

```
private void RecurringAppointment(DateTime start, int occurrences)
{
   Appointment a = session.Appointments.Items.AddNew();
   a.Start = start;
   a.Duration = new TimeSpan(1,0,0);
   a.Subject = "Recurrence";

   AppointmentRecurrence ar = a.RecurrencePattern;
   ar.RecurrenceType = RecurrenceType.Daily;
   ar.Interval = 1;
   ar.Occurrences = occurrences;

   a.Update();
}
```

Contacts

Contact is another class derived from *PimItem*, and it contains properties to describe the various contact methods for that item, including telephone numbers, e-mail addresses, and postal addresses. Each communication type includes multiple properties so that a contact can contain both a *HomeTelephoneNumber* and a *BusinessTelephoneNumber*, for example. As with the other PIM, the *ContactCollection* supports data binding.

The display string used for a contact can be retrieved from the contact's *FileAs* property, which is automatically generated based on the *FirstName* and *LastName* properties you provide, although you can manually change the *FileAs* property if required. When you create a new contact, all fields are optional; however, you should at least set the *FileAs* or the name properties. The following code shows how to add a new *Contact* item.

```
Contact c = session.Contacts.Items.AddNew();
c.FirstName = "Michael";
c.LastName = "Allen";
c.Email1Address = "michael@contoso.com";
c.MobileTelephoneNumber = "555-0132";
c.CompanyName = "Contoso Pharmaceuticals";
c.Update();
```

ChooseContactDialog Unique to contacts is the functionality to display the list of contacts to the user so that the user can choose a specific contact, such as is common when creating an e-mail message. The *Microsoft.WindowsMobile.Forms* namespace includes a component specifically designed to address this–the *ChooseContactDialog*. This can be used to select a specific contact, select a specific property of a contact, or select a combination of both. When selecting contacts, you can also apply a restrict filter using the same syntax as used with the *ContactCollection.Restrict()* method. With the *RequiredProperties* property, you can specify which properties must be present on the items to be shown. For example, the user can choose not to show contact items that have no e-mail address. Some special entries in the *ContactProperty* enumeration act as wildcards; for example, *ContactProperty.AllEmail* is equivalent to combining the *Email1Address*, *Email2Address*, and *Email3Address* properties. If the selected contact has more than one matching property, a second screen is shown to the user so that the user can choose the specific property to use. The prompt on this screen is defined with the *ChoosePropertyText* property. The following code example shows the *ChooseContactDialog* being used to select a specific e-mail address:

```
ChooseContactDialog ccd = new ChooseContactDialog();
ccd.ChoosePropertyText = "Select an email address:";
ccd.ChooseContactOnly = false;
ccd.Owner = this;
ccd.Title = "Choose an email recipient";
ccd.RequiredProperties = new ContactProperty[] {
ContactProperty.AllEmail };

if (ccd.ShowDialog() == DialogResult.OK)
{
       txtEmailAddr.Text = ccd.SelectedPropertyValue;
}
```

In Windows Mobile 6, some additional properties are available, such as *EnableGlobalAddressListLookup*. This is a Boolean property that when set to *true* allows the user to browse the Global Address List (GAL) as well as the user's local contacts. Another useful addition is the *NoUIOnSingleOrNoMatch* property. When set to *true*, the dialog box is not shown to the user if there is no possible choice or only one possible option. The *ChooseContactDialog* dialog box has a look and feel just like the standard Contacts application, as illustrated in Figure 17-2.

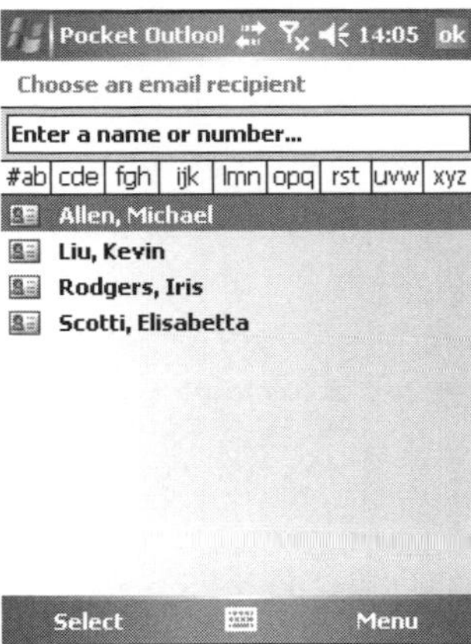

Figure 17-2 The *ChooseContactDialog* in action

Custom Properties

The standard properties available on the PIM items are sufficient for most uses but are, as expected, a subset of those available in Outlook. You can add your own custom properties to items; however, these are not synchronized and are not displayed in the standard Outlook Mobile dialog boxes for viewing and editing items. Each type of *PimItem* has a specific set of strongly typed properties, and it also has the *Properties* collection, which is of the type *PimPropertySet*. This collection allows you to access property values from their property identifiers using the *AppointmentProperty*, *ContactProperty*, and *TaskProperty* enumerations. It also supports retrieving properties by using their name, and it is this mechanism that is used to retrieve custom properties. A custom property must first be added to the collection by using the *Add* method. It is not necessary to specify the type of the property, in which case a string type will be used, but an additional override of the *Add* method accepts a .NET type:

```
c.Properties.Add("LastInvoice", typeof(int));
c.Properties["LastInvoice"] = 3124;
```

Although *Add* takes a *Type*, custom properties can be of only a few specific types—anything else results in an *ArgumentException* being thrown. The supported property types are the following:

- *Bool*
- *Byte[]*
- *DateTime*
- *Double*
- *Int16*
- *Int32*
- *UInt16*

- *UInt32*
- *String* (default)

After you have added a custom property to a particular item, that property is available to the whole collection of that item type. So, for example, you need to add the *LastInvoice* property only once to a contact, and then you can directly set that property on any other contact. It is your responsibility to ensure that whatever value you assign to the property matches the type used when creating the custom property; otherwise, an *ArgumentException* will be thrown.

Messaging

The messaging system on Windows Mobile encompasses the e-mail and SMS functionality. The managed class libraries give you the ability to send both e-mail and SMS messages and perform some basic automation of the messaging application.

E-Mail

The *EmailMessage* class represents a single e-mail message and contains properties to set the recipients, message contents, and file attachments. The managed APIs do not include functionality to read messages already on the device, which would require Platform Invocation Services (PInvoke) around the CEMAPI functionality or use of a third-party library such as Mobile In The Hand (*www.inthehand.com/WindowsMobile.aspx*).

To send an e-mail message programmatically, first you must create a new instance of *EmailMessage*. The *To* property contains a *RecipientCollection* that represents one or more recipients for the message. The *EmailMessage* class also contains collections of carbon copy (CC) and blind carbon copy (BCC) recipients. A *Recipient* object is created using either just an e-mail address or a display name and an e-mail address.

The message contains string properties to set the subject line and the message body. You can set some additional properties on the message, including the *Importance* (*High*, *Low*, or *Normal*) and *Sensitivity* (*Private*, *Confidential*, *Personal*, and *Normal*). The message also contains an *Attachments* property. This is an *AttachmentCollection* that can be used to attach files to the message. An *Attachment* contains a single property that is the full path to the file. The file must exist at this location or an *ArgumentException* will be thrown. The following code sample shows a complete example of creating an e-mail message, populating the recipients, creating the message contents, and adding a file attachment:

```
private void SendGenericEmail()
{
      EmailMessage m = new EmailMessage();

      Recipient r = new Recipient("Elisabetta Scotti",
                  "elisabetta@fourthcoffee.com");
      m.To.Add(r);

      m.Subject = "Important customer update";
```

```
m.BodyText = "This is an automatically generated email";
m.Importance = Importance.High;

Attachment a = new Attachment(openFileDialog1.FileName);
m.Attachments.Add(a);

m.Send(session.EmailAccounts[0]);
}
```

Sending and Receiving The default behavior for the messaging application is for messages to be placed in the Outbox until the e-mail account is explicitly synchronized by the user. This gives the user complete control over when to establish a network connection for exchanging this data. You can programmatically force a send and receive operation on the user's behalf by using the *MessagingApplication.Synchronize* method. There are a couple of overloads for this method, the default of which takes no arguments and performs a send and receive on the currently active e-mail account. The two other overloads take either an *EmailAccount* argument or a string that contains the name of the account. The synchronization occurs asynchronously, and there is no way to determine whether the operation was successful or when it completed. The sample application has a Sync button that calls the following code:

```
private void btnSync_Click(object sender, EventArgs e)
{
        // send/receive default account
        MessagingApplication.Synchronize(session.EmailAccounts[0]);
}
```

Composing a New Message Rather than build a message in your own code, you may prefer to present the user with the standard new message dialog box. With the *MessagingApplication.DisplayComposeForm* method, you can do this. This method is very flexible because it features numerous overloads so that you can prepopulate the form before showing it to the user and specify which e-mail account to use. The sample application includes a Compose button that calls this method, passing in the recipient address, subject and body, and a file attachment:

```
private void btnCompose_Click(object sender, EventArgs e)
{
        string[] attachments = new string[] { };

        if (File.Exists(openFileDialog1.FileName))
        {
                attachments = new string[] { openFileDialog1.FileName };
        }
        MessagingApplication.DisplayComposeForm(
                session.EmailAccounts[0].Name, txtEmailAddr.Text,
                "Populated Compose Form", txtBody.Text, attachments);
}
```

The resulting screen is shown in Figure 17-3.

Figure 17-3 Compose E-Mail dialog box

SMS

The *SmsMessage* type is similar to its e-mail equivalent, and both are derived from the base *Message* class. Because SMS is a simpler messaging system, it has fewer properties than e-mail does. The other big difference is that SMS messages are always sent immediately (subject to cellular network coverage) rather than being placed in the Outbox until a connection is made. An individual SMS message is 160 characters long; however, you can work around this limitation by splitting a long message across multiple SMS messages. The messages are then reassembled on the receiving device. Because each 160-character message is billed as a separate message, and because many mobile phones don't have user interfaces suited to reading long text content, you should keep SMS messages concise.

You can send an SMS message to multiple recipients by passing several *Recipient* objects to the *To* collection; however, these are sent internally as separate messages and therefore each copy is billed as a separate message. You can optionally request a delivery report for the message that will be received in the SMS Inbox when the recipient device acknowledges receipt of the message. Because SMS is a store-and-forward mechanism, a message can take some time to get to its destination based on network traffic levels and the recipient's cellular coverage. The operations to send a single SMS message are shown in the following code example:

```
private void SendGenericSms()
{
        SmsMessage s = new SmsMessage();

        Recipient r = new Recipient("Andrey Gladkikh", "555-0171");
        s.To.Add(r);

        s.Body = "This is an automatically generated SMS";
        s.RequestDeliveryReport = true;

        s.Send();
}
```

Chapter 9 discusses the SMS interception functionality in the *Microsoft.WindowsMobile.PocketOutlook.MessageInterception* namespace. You can use SMS send functionality described in this chapter to work in conjunction with a *MessageInterceptor* on another device, for example, for peer-to-peer data transfer. Simply ensure that the message you send matches the rule you specified in the *MessageInterceptor* instance.

State and Notifications

Windows Mobile 5.0 introduces a centralized API for querying device settings and raising events when these settings change. This is known as the State and Notifications Broker and is available to both native code and managed code projects through the *Microsoft.WindowsMobile.Status* namespace. The settings are held in the system registry, and thanks to new functionality in Windows CE 5.0 the system is capable of providing events when certain registry values change. The *SystemState* class is the central point for the State and Notifications Broker. It features static properties you can use to quickly access all of the available system properties. For example, you can retrieve the cellular phone signal strength by using a single line of code:

```
int signal = SystemState.PhoneSignalStrength;
```

The *SystemProperty* enumeration contains all the properties available from the API. These include properties related to the network connectivity, hardware configuration, and phone hardware on the device. Windows Mobile 6 extends this list of properties to include WiFi, Bluetooth, and more detailed cellular phone properties. The ability to retrieve system property values is only one part of the API; you can also write code so that you can be notified when any of these properties change. This is very powerful because in previous versions of the platform you must work with a number of different low-level native APIs to get change information in the power management and telephony subsystems. To start monitoring a particular property you must create an instance of *SystemState*. Each instance can monitor only a single property.

In the example code for this section, we look at two ways of monitoring a property. The first is to use the *SystemState* class to monitor the property for the lifetime of your application, and the second is to set up an application launcher registration so that your application is launched when a property changes.

The standard constructor for *SystemState* takes a *SystemProperty* member to define which property to monitor. In the example, you monitor the battery level by using *PowerBatteryStrength*. In the *Form_Load* method, you create the *SystemState* instance and add a handler for the *Changed* event:

```
private void Form1_Load(object sender, EventArgs e)
{
        batteryState = new SystemState(SystemProperty.PowerBatteryStrength);
        batteryState.Changed += new ChangeEventHandler(batteryState_Changed);
        UpdateBatteryStrength(SystemState.PowerBatteryStrength);
}
```

UpdateBatteryStrength is a helper method you can create to update a progress bar and colored panel on the form to reflect the current battery level. You call it here to set the initial values; it will be called again whenever the *Changed* event is raised.

Different property values have different data types. The *PowerBatteryStrength* uses the *BatteryLevel* enumeration, so *UpdateBatteryStrength* checks the value and sets an appropriate value for the progress bar to show a rudimentary battery meter:

```
void UpdateBatteryStrength(BatteryLevel newLevel)
{
        switch (newLevel)
        {
                case BatteryLevel.VeryHigh:
                        pnlPower.BackColor = Color.Green;
                        pbBattery.Value = 100;
                        break;
                case BatteryLevel.High:
                        pnlPower.BackColor = Color.LimeGreen;
                        pbBattery.Value = 75;
                        break;
                case BatteryLevel.Medium:
                        pnlPower.BackColor = Color.Yellow;
                        pbBattery.Value = 50;
                        break;
                case BatteryLevel.Low:
                        pnlPower.BackColor = Color.Orange;
                        pbBattery.Value = 25;
                        break;
                case BatteryLevel.VeryLow:
                        pnlPower.BackColor = Color.Red;
                        pbBattery.Value = 0;
                        break;
        }
}
```

After you have created this helper function, writing the code required in the *Changed* event handler is fairly simple. The only complication is that the *ChangeEventArgs* passed to the event handler contains a *NewValue* property that is the raw value as retrieved from the registry. Because the registry supports only a small number of data types, the registry values will not be what you would expect from the *SystemState* static properties. For example, Boolean properties are stored as *DWORD* values (4-byte integers) in the registry, with nonzero representing *true*. If you do not want the complication of converting the value to the correct type, you can ignore *ChangeEventArgs* and retrieve the value from the appropriate *SystemState* property. The *BatteryLevel* value is stored as a *DWORD* with the numerical value of the enumeration member. In this case, you can cast the value to the *BatteryLevel* type:

```
void batteryState_Changed(object sender, ChangeEventArgs args)
{
UpdateBatteryStrength((BatteryLevel)args.NewValue);
}
```

When this code is implemented, you can see the progress bar and the panel color changes when the device battery transitions between the various *BatteryLevel* steps. As mentioned previously, you can register your application to be started when a particular property changes. You do this by using the members of the *IApplicationLauncher* interface, which is also exposed by the *MessageInterceptor* class described in Chapter 9. You can use an application launch ID to uniquely identify your registration and details of the property, and your application .exe file is stored in the registry so that it can be started if the property changes.

An attempt to use the same application launch ID as one that is already registered results in an exception, so you should always check with the *IsApplicationLauncherEnabled* method before registering. A specific overload of the *SystemState* constructor takes an existing application launch ID. The sample code checks for an existing registration; if present, you can use the existing ID, and if not, you set up a new *SystemState* for the required property, and then call *EnableApplicationLauncher*. The code to set up your registration will always follow this pattern:

```
if(SystemState.IsApplicationLauncherEnabled("Chapter17.Cradle"))
{
        cradleState = new SystemState("Chapter17.Cradle");
}
else
{
        cradleState = new SystemState(SystemProperty.CradlePresent);
        cradleState.EnableApplicationLauncher("Chapter17.Cradle");
}

cradleState.Changed+=new ChangeEventHandler(cradleState_Changed);
```

The only limitation with this notification mechanism is that your application will be launched every time the property changes, and not just when it changes to a specific value. For example, you may want your application to start only when the device is placed in the cradle, not when it is removed from the cradle. The only workaround here is to check the value in your code and close the application if the current value isn't the required state. If you are going to do this, you should check the state as early as possible in your application code so that you can close the application quickly with as little disruption to the user as possible. The earliest opportunity would be to place the code in your *Main* method:

```
static class Program
{
        /// <summary>
        /// The main entry point for the application.
        /// </summary>
        [MTAThread]
        static void Main()
        {
                if (SystemState.CradlePresent)
                {
                        Application.Run(new Form1());
                }
        }
}
```

As you have seen, the State and Notifications Broker is a very powerful set of functionality. It can make your life much easier by placing system properties in a single location where properties can be queried and notifications set up using relatively little code.

Pictures

The *Microsoft.WindowsMobile.Forms* namespace contains two components for working with pictures: *SelectPictureDialog* provides an alternative to the traditional *OpenFileDialog* by displaying images using thumbnails. This makes it much easier to work with image files because you can see what you are choosing rather than just picking by the file name alone. Figure 17-4 shows the standard appearance of the *SelectPictureDialog*.

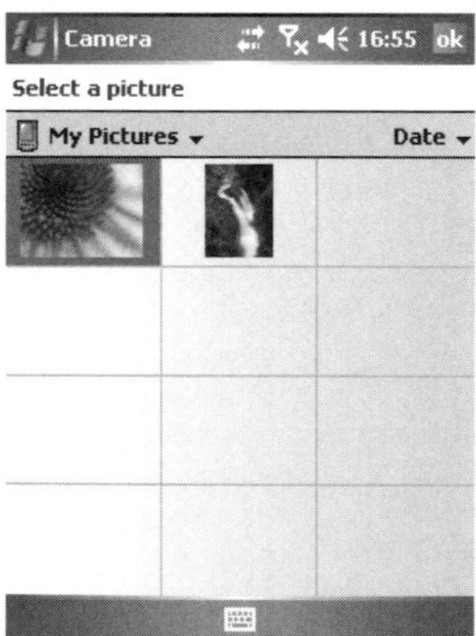

Figure 17-4 The *SelectPictureDialog*

Using the default settings, you can open the dialog box by using just a couple of lines of code. If the device has a built-in camera, the first item in the list on the picker will be a link to the camera application. You can customize this behavior by disabling access to the camera by setting *CameraAccess* to *false*. You can also add your own title to the dialog box by using the *Title* property. You can toggle whether distributed rights management (DRM) content is displayed to the user. One of the properties of this dialog box, *LockDirectory*, is documented as being able to block the user from browsing outside the *InitialDirectory* you specify; in actual fact, this property is not implemented, and the user will still be able to browse outside the initial directory. The following example shows how to set up and display the *SelectPictureDialog*:

```
private void mnuChoose_Click(object sender, EventArgs e)
{
        SelectPictureDialog spd = new SelectPictureDialog();
        spd.Owner = this;
        spd.Title = "Select a picture";
        spd.CameraAccess = false;
        spd.LockDirectory = true;

        if (spd.ShowDialog() == DialogResult.OK)
        {
                pbImage.Image = new Bitmap(spd.FileName);
        }
}
```

Camera

As well as providing a method to select a picture already on the device, you can programmatically invoke the camera to add picture-taking functionality to your application. The *CameraCaptureDialog* provides a simple interface over the platform's camera support. The API is consistent across all Windows Mobile–powered devices, even though each manufacturer is responsible for implementing the camera functionality and user interface. For this reason, the actual camera dialog box can vary between different devices. Figure 17-5 shows an example of the *CameraCaptureDialog* in use.

Figure 17-5 The *CameraCaptureDialog*

The dialog box can be set to still image or video mode, and you can specify a preferred resolution for the output, although device capabilities can vary. The following code example shows how to invoke the camera dialog box:

```
private void mnuCapture_Click(object sender, EventArgs e)
{
        CameraCaptureDialog ccd = new CameraCaptureDialog();
        ccd.Mode = CameraCaptureMode.Still;
        ccd.StillQuality = CameraCaptureStillQuality.High;
        ccd.Title = "Say Cheese";

        if (ccd.ShowDialog() == DialogResult.OK)
        {
                pbImage.Image = new Bitmap(ccd.FileName);
        }
}
```

GPS

All consumer GPS receivers output data over a serial port in a text format devised by the National Marine Electronics Association (NMEA). Prior to Windows Mobile 5.0, you needed to establish a connection to the attached device by a serial port, or a virtual serial port for devices connected by Bluetooth, to receive incoming NMEA data, and then parse it yourself. Windows Mobile introduces a centralized GPS service that the user can configure through the Settings menu on the device. Because only the system is connected directly to the GPS device, with this approach multiple applications can access the same GPS data at once through a virtual COM port or a set of API methods.

Unfortunately, the managed APIs for Windows Mobile don't include support for the new GPS API, but sample code is shipped with the Windows Mobile software development kit (SDK). The sample code for this chapter on the book's companion Web site contains a modified version optimized for version 2.0 of the Compact Framework. The code can be simplified by using the *EventWaitHandle* class created in Chapter 14, "Interoperating with the Platform," and by taking advantage of improved platform interop support for complex structures in .NET Compact Framework 2.0. The definition of the *GPS_POSITION* structure is simplified to the following:

```
[StructLayout(LayoutKind.Sequential)]
internal struct GPS_POSITION
{
        private const int GPS_MAX_SATELLITES = 12;

        public int dwVersion;
        public int dwSize;
        public GPS_VALID dwValidFields;
```

```
        public GPS_DATA_FLAGS dwFlags;
        public SYSTEMTIME stUTCTime;
        public double dblLatitude;
        public double dblLongitude;
        public float flSpeed;
        public float flHeading;
        public double dblMagneticVariation;
        public float flAltitudeWRTSeaLevel;
        public float flAltitudeWRTEllipsoid;
        public FixQuality FixQuality;
        public FixType FixType;
        public FixSelection SelectionType;
        public float flPositionDilutionOfPrecision;
        public float flHorizontalDilutionOfPrecision;
        public float flVerticalDilutionOfPrecision;
        public int dwSatelliteCount;
        [MarshalAs(UnmanagedType.ByValArray, SizeConst = GPS_MAX_SATELLITES)]
        public int[] rgdwSatellitesUsedPRNs;
        public int dwSatellitesInView;
        [MarshalAs(UnmanagedType.ByValArray, SizeConst = GPS_MAX_SATELLITES)]
        public int[] rgdwSatellitesInViewPRNs;
        [MarshalAs(UnmanagedType.ByValArray, SizeConst = GPS_MAX_SATELLITES)]
        public int[] rgdwSatellitesInViewElevation;
        [MarshalAs(UnmanagedType.ByValArray, SizeConst = GPS_MAX_SATELLITES)]
        public int[] rgdwSatellitesInViewAzimuth;
        [MarshalAs(UnmanagedType.ByValArray, SizeConst = GPS_MAX_SATELLITES)]
        public int[] rgdwSatellitesInViewSignalToNoiseRatio;
}
```

This is now passed by reference to the *GPSGetPosition* method, which is defined as follows:

```
[DllImport("gpsapi.dll")]
Private static extern int GPSGetPosition(IntPtr hGPSDevice,
ref GPS_POSITION pGPSPosition, int dwMaximumAge, int dwFlags);
```

The *GetPosition* method that calls this method and returns the *GpsPosition* object is defined as follows:

```
public GpsPosition GetPosition(TimeSpan maxAge)
{
        if (Opened)
        {
                GPS_POSITION position = new GPS_POSITION();
                position.dwVersion = 1;
                position.dwSize = Marshal.SizeOf(typeof(GPS_POSITION));

                // Call native method passing in your native struct.
                int result = GPSGetPosition(gpsHandle, ref position, 500000, 0);
                if (result == 0)
                {
```

```
                    // Native call succeeded; create managed wrapper class.
                    GpsPosition gp = new GpsPosition(position);

                    if (maxAge != TimeSpan.Zero)
                    {
                        // Check to see if the data is recent enough.
                        if (!gp.TimeValid || DateTime.Now - maxAge > gp.Time)
                        {
                            return null;
                        }
                    }

                    return gp;
                }
            }
        return null;
}
```

Externally, the *Gps* class is kept consistent so that you can use it in the same way as the original sample version. Because the events raised by this object initiate from a background worker thread, you must not update any user interface elements directly from an event handler. Instead, you must use *Invoke* to call a method on the user interface thread. In the following example, when the *LocationChanged* event occurs, the *OnLocationChanged* method is called on the user interface thread and the current location is displayed on a *StatusBar* control.

```
private void Form1_Load(object sender, EventArgs e)
{
        gps.DeviceStateChanged += new
            DeviceStateChangedEventHandler(gps_DeviceStateChanged);
        gps.LocationChanged += new
            LocationChangedEventHandler(gps_LocationChanged);
        gps.Open();
}

void gps_LocationChanged(object sender, LocationChangedEventArgs args)
{
        //Invoke your handler on the UI thread.
        this.Invoke(new LocationChangedEventHandler(OnLocationChanged),
            new object[] { sender, args });
}

void OnLocationChanged(object sender, LocationChangedEventArgs args)
{
        statusBar1.Text = "Lat/Lon: " + args.Position.Latitude.ToString("f5") +
            ", " + args.Position.Longitude.ToString("f5");
}
```

Configuration

Windows Mobile supports an Extensible Markup Language (XML) configuration subsystem that you can use in a variety of ways, from operator-provisioned over the air (OTA) settings to deployment packages to calling configuration APIs to register settings programmatically. The platform consists of a range of configuration service providers, each responsible for a particular group of settings. It is beyond the scope of this book to describe each of the providers, and the reader should consult the Windows Mobile SDK documentation online for a full reference (*msdn2.microsoft.com/en-us/library/ms889540.aspx*).

Configuring the Device Programmatically

The *Microsoft.WindowsMobile.Configuration* assembly provides two methods for testing and processing configuration documents. The Configuration sample application contains code to load an XML file containing the basic settings for a General Packet Radio System (GPRS) network connection and to process it on the device. The document is loaded into an *XmlDocument* instance and passed to the *ProcessConfigXml* method.

```
private void btnGPRS_Click(object sender, EventArgs e)
{
       System.Xml.XmlDocument d = new System.Xml.XmlDocument();
       d.Load(Assembly.GetExecutingAssembly().GetManifestResourceStream(
              "Chapter17.GprsSettings.xml"));
       System.Xml.XmlDocument d2 = ConfigurationManager.ProcessConfiguration(
              d, true);
       MessageBox.Show(d2.OuterXml);
}
```

Deploying Configuration Settings

When deploying applications to Windows Mobile–powered devices, you can also build installer packages from XML provisioning documents. These compiled files have the .cpf file type and are started in a way similar to how .cab files are started, as described in Chapter 6, "Completing the Application: Packaging and Deployment." You cannot build a .cpf file in Microsoft Visual Studio. Instead you must resort to the MakeCab.exe command-line utility, which is installed with Visual Studio 2005 and later in the SmartDevices\SDK\SDKTools folder beneath your Visual Studio installation. The setup XML file you create must be named _setup.xml. You create a .cpf file by passing MakeCab.exe the XML file you have created and specifying the output file name:

```
makecab.exe _setup.xml MySettings.cpf
```

More detail on the MakeCab.exe tool can be found in an article titled "Creating a .cpf file" on the Microsoft MSDN Web site at *58*.

Telephony

The *Telephony* namespace contains functionality for programmatically establishing a voice call. This is discussed in Chapter 9 in the section titled "Voice Calls."

Earlier Versions of Windows Mobile

On devices running versions of Windows Mobile earlier than version 5.0, these managed class libraries are not available. To include some of the functionality, you can PInvoke the native APIs or use a third-party wrapper. Mobile In The Hand (*www.inthehand.com/WindowsMobile.aspx*) provides a subset of the Windows Mobile 5.0 managed APIs that works on devices running Windows Mobile 2003 and later. This library can make it easier to write a single set of code across a wider range of devices. A free community edition that provides the basic functionality from the *Configuration*, *PocketOutlook*, *Status*, and *Telephony* namespaces is available.

Summary

In this chapter, we investigated the functionality available when specifically targeting Windows Mobile–powered devices. Although the underlying Windows CE operating system is modular and can vary greatly between different device types, the Windows Mobile platform provides a tightly defined set of APIs that you know will be present across the range of Windows Mobile–powered devices. Windows Mobile 5.0 introduces some powerful managed class libraries to simplify development on the platform.

Part III
New Developments

In this part:

Chapter 18

Introducing .NET Compact Framework Version 3.5 and Visual Studio Code Name "Orcas"

In this chapter:

Microsoft .NET Compact Framework version 2.0–with which the bulk of this book is concerned–was released as part of the Microsoft Visual Studio 2005 product at the end of 2005. At the time of this writing, Microsoft is gearing up to release the next version of these products. The code name for the next version of Visual Studio is "Orcas," and included in "Orcas" will be .NET Compact Framework version 3.5, the follow-up to version 2.0. There never was and never will be a version 3.0 of the .NET Compact Framework because Microsoft keeps version numbering in sync with the full .NET Framework, which also reaches version 3.5 in Visual Studio "Orcas." (.NET Framework version 3.0 was released in late 2006 around the same time the Windows Vista operating system was released, and it included the first releases–for the full .NET Framework only–of the Microsoft Windows Communication Foundation [WCF], Windows Presentation Foundation [WPF], Windows Workflow Foundation [WF], and Windows CardSpace.)

In this chapter, we introduce the new features of .NET Compact Framework 3.5 and describe the new tools for mobile application developers included in Visual Studio "Orcas."

Important The new features described in this chapter are based on the beta 1 release of Visual Studio "Orcas." We can make no guarantee that the features described will be present in the final released product or will operate as described, and we can't guarantee that the code samples included in this chapter will compile and run using the final released product. However, we will ensure that updated information is available on this book's companion Web site.

Introducing .NET Compact Framework 3.5

The new version of the .NET Compact Framework runtime is supported on exactly the same platforms as v2.0: Pocket PC 2003 and later, smartphones running Microsoft Windows Mobile 2005 and later, and embedded hardware running Windows CE 4.2 and later. As with earlier versions of the .NET Compact Framework, you can install version 3.5 to run alongside earlier versions of the runtime.

.NET Compact Framework 3.5 includes many additions that make it more compatible with corresponding functionality in the full .NET Framework. Some exciting new features, including the following, address particular challenges mobile application developers face:

- Compact Windows Communication Foundation (Compact WCF) allows mobile applications to interact with WCF services. Compact WCF supports Hypertext Transfer Protocol (HTTP) as a message transport, but the most innovative feature is support for e-mail as a transport so that you can use a Microsoft Exchange Server as a store-and-forward transport for messaging over unreliable networks. See the section titled "Programming Compact WCF" later in this chapter for more information.
- The *System.IO.Compression* namespace, which includes the *DeflateStream* and *GZipStream* classes, allows easy compression of data using royalty-free compression algorithms. You can also use these classes with HTTP requests, such as when calling Web services, to reduce costs associated with transferring data over public networks such as with data calls over phone networks using General Packet Radio Service (GPRS) or Code-Division Multiple Access (CDMA). See the section titled "Programming *System.IO.Compression*" later in this chapter for more information.
- Compact Language Integrated Query (LINQ) supports a subset of LINQ Standard Query Operators that you can use to query in-memory objects, *DataSet* objects, and Extensible Markup Language (XML). You cannot, however, make direct queries to data in Microsoft SQL Server 2005 or SQL Server 2005 Compact Edition. See the section titled "Programming Language Integrated Query" later in this chapter for more information.
- The *System.Media* namespace is supported, including support for *SoundPlayer* using *WaveOut*, which allows multiple sounds to play at once, and support for *SystemSound* and *SystemSounds*.
- Client certificates are supported to authenticate Web Service calls and calls with *System.Net.HttpWebRequest*. To use client certificates for authentication, you install the certificate on the device, create a *System.Security.Cryptography.Certificates.X509Certificate* specifying the name of the installed certificate, and then add the certificate object to the *ClientCertificates* property of the *WebRequest* or your Web service proxy using code such as *myWebRequest.ClientCertificates.Add(mycertificate);*.

- The new *SystemSettings.WinCEPlatform* property in the *Microsoft.WindowsCE.Forms* namespace helps you easily distinguish Smartphone, Pocket PC, and embedded solutions and makes it easier for developers to build software to run on all these platforms. The property returns an enumeration that has values *WinCEGeneric*, *PocketPC*, or *Smartphone* according to the platform the application is currently running on.
- Numerous application programming interface (API) additions implement features that are available in the full .NET Framework 2.0 and that are now included in version 3.5 to make the full and compact frameworks more compatible. These include not only the *System.IO.Compression* and *System.Media* namespaces mentioned earlier, but also the following:
    - *System.Threading.EventWaitHandle*.
    - *System.Diagnostics.Stopwatch*.
    - Support for the *Resize* method of the *Array* class, plus the addition of some new *Sort* method overloads.
    - *System.Runtime.CompilerServices.CompilerGeneratedAttribute*.
    - *System.Runtime.Serialization.SerializationException*.
    - *System.Text.StringBuilder*, which gets a new overload for the *AppendFormat* method and also both overloads of the *AppendLine* method.
    - *System.Threading.Thread.MemoryBarrier* method.
    - Support for *String.Contains*.
    - Addition of a public *Dispose* method to many classes, including *GraphicsStream*, *FileStream*, *MemoryStream*, *StreamReader*, *StreamWriter*, *StringReader*, *StringWriter*, *TextReader*, and *TextWriter*.
    - *System.IO.InvalidDataException* and a new enum *System.Net.DecompressionMethods* that is the type of the new property *AutomaticDecompression* on the *HttpWebRequest* class, which support the addition of the *System.IO.Compression* namespace already mentioned earlier (see the section titled "Programming *System.IO.Compression*" later in this chapter).
    - Support for two classes in the *System.ComponentModel* namespace: *AsyncCompletedEventArgs* and *AsyncCompletedEventHandler*.
    - Support for *System.Diagnostics.TraceListener* so that you can implement your own class that inherits from *TraceListener* to implement run-time logging by calls to *Trace.** methods. You can direct the output to the destination of your choice by using the custom *TraceListener*. There is also support for *TextWriterTraceListener*, which redirects trace and debug output to a *TextWriter* or to a *Stream* such as *FileStream*.

- Four overloads for each of the methods *Write*, *WriteIf*, *WriteLine*, and *WriteLineIf* in the *System.Diagnostics.Trace* class (in version 2.0, the *Trace* class supports only the *Assert* method for output of tracing diagnostics). It also gets the *Fail*, *Flush*, and *Close* methods.

- Debugging enhancements, including the following:
  - Support for nested func-evals. (A *func-eval* is a function evaluator or property evaluator that Visual Studio uses when you evaluate functions and get properties when stopped at a breakpoint; a func-eval is also used by visualizers, such as the DataSet visualizer.)
  - Stack trace enhancements.
  - Provision for log files to be read at run time. See Chapter 4, "Catching Errors, Testing, and Debugging," for details about how to turn on logging. In .NET Compact Framework 2.0, log files are locked at run time so that you can read the file only when the program stops execution, but this restriction is removed in version 3.5.
  - Enhanced logging for interop functionality with native code.
  - Improved logging of finalizer activities to enhance product supportability.
- Support for strong-name keys that are greater than 1,024 bytes in length.
- Support for performing runtime version redirection for all applications on the device by placing an app.config file in the Windows folder. In .NET Compact Framework 2.0, you can create a .config file called {*myapplication*}.exe.config and place it in the application folder. You can use this technique to cause an application that was compiled against an earlier version of the runtime to run instead using a later version that you have installed on the device. If you do not use this technique, and the version that your application was compiled against is still installed on the device, the default behavior is for the application to run using the same version it was compiled against.

  In version 3.5, you can create a .config file called device.config and place it in the Windows folder to perform run-time redirection for every application on the device. For example, to redirect all applications to run using the version 3.5 runtime, place a device.config file containing the following in the Windows folder (replace **v3.5.*xxxx*** with the correct version number when version 3.5 is finally released):

```
<configuration>
  <startup>
    <supportedRuntime version="v3.5.xxxx"/>
  </startup>
</configuration>
```

Introducing Visual Studio Code Name "Orcas"

In addition to the new items included in the .NET Compact Framework runtime and libraries, Visual Studio "Orcas" introduces new tools designed to help the mobile application developer. Note that although these tools are included in Visual Studio Code Name "Orcas" beta 1, in future releases some or all of the tools for mobile device application development may be distributed as a separate download.

- In Visual Studio Team Developer Edition and Visual Studio Team Suite, you can generate and run unit tests from within the Visual Studio Integrated Development Environment (IDE).
- The Remote Performance Monitor (first released with .NET Compact Framework 2.0 Service Pack 1 [SP1]) is included in "Orcas" and installs run-time components on the device automatically, in comparison with the manual installation process required by earlier versions, as explained in Chapter 5, "Understanding and Optimizing .NET Compact Framework Performance."
- The Remote Performance Monitor in version 2.0 includes menu options to activate and disable network, loader, and native interop logging. In version 3.5, these options are moved into a separate tool, the Device Logging Configuration tool.
- The Remote Performance Monitor gains a new feature that you can use to take several snapshots of the common language runtime (CLR) heap and then analyze object allocation trends using those snapshots. (This feature was actually first introduced in the tools update shipped as part of Compact Framework 2.0 SP2.) This feature can be very helpful in diagnosing the cause of memory leaks. In managed code, a memory leak occurs when you believe you have removed references to objects, but the objects cannot be collected by the garbage collector because there is still a well-concealed reference to them somewhere in your object tree. The heap snapshot feature of the Remote Performance Monitor helps you track down the cause of problems such as this. For more information, see Steven Pratschner's Weblog at *blogs.msdn.com/stevenpr/archive/2007/03/08/finding-managed-memory-leaks-using-the-net-cf-remote-performance-monitor.aspx.*
- The CLR Heap Profiler tool from the full .NET Framework software development kit (SDK) is ported to operate with the .NET Compact Framework. With this useful tool, you can analyze object allocations over time, identify where objects are being created in your code, and identify memory allocation by object type.

- The Device Security Manager PowerToy for Windows Mobile 5.0 mentioned in Chapter 10, "Security Programming for Mobile Applications," is included in "Orcas" on the Tools menu as the Device Security Manager.
- Device Emulator 3.0 includes a number of new features, including the ability to automate/script interaction with the emulators through a Component Object Model (COM) API. It also includes the enhancements introduced in version 2.0 of the Device Emulator, such as the ability to simulate low-battery scenarios.
- The New Project Wizard has been redesigned for mobile applications. In the New Project dialog box, a single option called Smart Device Project for mobile device projects is available. When you select that option, the New Project Wizard for mobile applications starts, as shown in Figure 18-1.

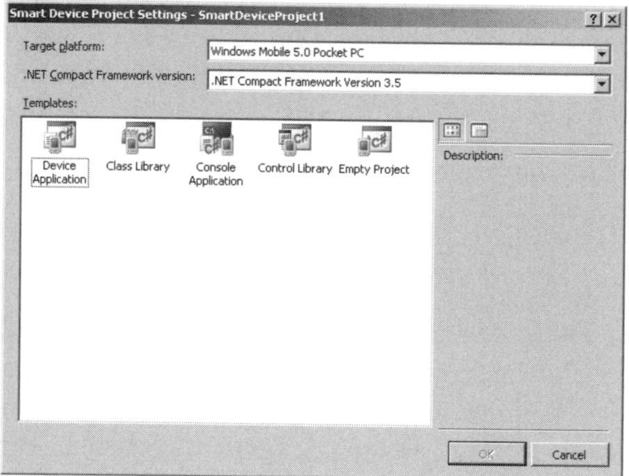

Figure 18-1 New Project Wizard for mobile applications

Note Late in 2007, another exciting new technology will come out: the Microsoft Synchronization Services for ADO.NET, which is a new, easy-to-use programming model for synchronizing data between a client database, such as SQL Server 2005 Compact Edition on a mobile device, and another database on a server, such as SQL Server 2005. We do not discuss Synchronization Services for ADO.NET in this chapter because the tool support for using it with mobile device applications didn't make it into the "Orcas" release but instead will be released separately later. Synchronization Services for ADO.NET has the potential to replace Remote Data Access (covered in Chapter 7, "Exchanging Data with Backend Servers") because it is easier to configure and use. For more information, download "Microsoft Synchronization Services for ADO.NET Books Online Community Technology Preview" from the Microsoft Download Center Web site at *go.microsoft.com/fwlink/?LinkId=80742*.

Developing Applications with .NET Compact Framework 3.5

In this section, we take a more in-depth look at some of the more exciting additions to the Compact Framework introduced in version 3.5.

Programming Compact WCF

The Windows Communication Foundation (WCF) for desktop computers and servers was released in .NET Framework 3.0 late in 2006. WCF (formerly known as Indigo) is the new unified messaging framework that provides developers with a single, consistent, easy-to-use programming model for building messaging in distributed applications. It provides a framework for working with the different messaging techniques in use to date, such as Web Services, Microsoft Message Queuing (MSMQ), and .NET Remoting. Instead of the different and varied APIs each of these techniques requires, programmers must learn only a single API. Also, the framework is easily extensible to support new message transports. It unifies both messaging style and Remote Procedure Call (RPC) style and can use both binary protocols and Simple Object Access Protocol (SOAP)–based XML protocols at the message transport level.

.NET Compact Framework 3.5 includes a subset of WCF called Compact WCF. Compact WCF allows applications on mobile devices to interoperate with WCF services on desktop computers and servers. There is no support for hosting WCF services on a device, so your device application is always a client requesting the services of a service running on a desktop computer or server. Compact WCF offers two different predefined bindings (a *binding* is a defined set of characteristics, such as the protocol used to transfer the message, the kind of security and transactional support available, and the message formatting and encoding supported), the first of which, *BasicHttpBinding*, is essentially equivalent to calling a Web service in version 2.0 because it supports traditional client/server interaction over HTTP, where the client sends a request to the service and waits for the response.

The second predefined binding, which at the time of this writing has not been formally named, but which we call the *WindowsMobileMailBinding*, is truly innovative in respect to messaging to devices. It uses e-mail as the message transport and offers a duplex messaging channel that allows for unsolicited asynchronous bidirectional messaging. For example, a client application running on a device used by a van driver who travels around picking up packages from customers may register with a service running on a backend server that notifies client applications whenever a new pickup request is received on the server. The service sends out pickup requests to clients in an unsolicited fashion whenever one is ready. The client need not poll the server every few minutes to ask whether any updates are available, which is the programming model you must use with Web Services today.

WCF is a layered protocol stack, so the way messages are formatted is independent of the way the messages are transported. One other significant characteristic of WCF is that it has extensibility points that you can use to create custom components and plug them into the overall WCF architecture. The .NET Compact Framework team took advantage of these extensibility points to create the unique e-mail WCF message transport, which is particularly well suited to the specific connectivity problems mobile devices encounter.

Using E-Mail as a WCF Transport, and the Story of the Lunch Launcher

In his blog (at *blogs.msdn.com/romanbat*), Roman Batoukov of the .NET Compact Framework team at Microsoft tells the story of how e-mail came to be supported as a transport in Compact WCF. Prior to the release of .NET Compact Framework 1.0, the development team often spent time imagining what kinds of applications mobile developers would build. Roman explains:

> *"One of the really simple ideas that came up then and remained unimplemented was the 'Lunch Launcher.' Many folks on the team prefer local restaurants to Microsoft cafeterias. Getting several people to go out to the same place often requires lots of coordination over the phone or e-mail, especially when people are away from their offices, in different buildings. Usually someone wants Indian food, someone had Indian three days in a row and wants to go for Mexican, and someone else has strong cravings for a slice of bad pizza. . . .*
>
> *"As most people on the team have some sort of Windows Mobile device connected to WiFi or a mobile carrier network, we thought it would be nice to have an application that allows one person to send a lunch invite with a list of a few good local restaurants to other people and let them vote where to go to. When the poll is finished, its results (the place of choice) are communicated back to everyone and everyone hopefully is heading to the same place. Sounds trivial, doesn't it?"*

The Lunch Launcher was never built (until now!) because a number of difficulties with the network addressability of devices that are hard to overcome had to be addressed. Mobile devices that connect to the Internet through a mobile operators network have dynamically assigned TCP/IP addresses that change frequently. Also, devices connect through numerous firewalls and Network Address Translation (NAT) devices that make it very difficult to establish the true publicly addressable TCP/IP address of a device, and almost impossible to initiate a TCP/IP connection from a backend server or another device to connect to a device on a mobile phone operators network.

Consider another example: A worker who uses a device to connect to the Internet over WiFi while working in one building goes outside, whereupon the device switches to connect through the mobile operators network over GPRS or CDMA. The worker then enters a different building and connects to WiFi again, but in a different subnet and with an IP address different from the one used in the first building. In that short walk from one building to another, the device maintained connectivity to the Internet but had three different IP addresses.

Applications such as the Lunch Launcher require that an application running on one device be able to send a message out to other devices. Unless all your devices connect to your local network using virtual private networks (VPNs) or are permanently connected to the same WiFi network (such as in a warehouse application) and you use a static IP addressing scheme, you cannot reliably connect to another device. Until now, the problem of addressing devices connected to mobile phone networks has been solved either by the use of expensive middleware or by a polling scheme, in which the application on the device calls in to the server every few minutes to check whether there are any messages waiting for it.

However, since the release of Exchange Server 2003 SP2 and the Messaging and Security Feature Update to Windows Mobile 5.0 (which came out shortly after the initial release of Windows Mobile 5.0 and is otherwise known as Adoption Kit Update 2 [AKU2]), Microsoft has had a reliable way of addressing mobile devices anywhere on the public networks, and that is through push e-mail. Push e-mail works because the device connects to Exchange Server through a Microsoft Internet Information Server (IIS) server, and it makes a series of long-lived HTTP requests (a long-lived request is a request that has a very long timeout associated with it) to the Exchange Server. If Exchange Server receives a message for the e-mail address associated with the device, it sends it straight on to the device as the HTTP response. If the HTTP request times out, then, no problem, the device just issues a new long-lived request. If the device is offline, Exchange Server acts as a store-and-forward transfer and saves the e-mail message until the device comes back online.

As you can see, this kind of behavior is ideal for use as a message transport for applications such as the Lunch Launcher, providing device addressability (through the e-mail address) and store-and-forward behavior for handling devices that are connected to transient and unreliable networks.

Supported Connectivity for Compact WCF

As mentioned previously, WCF is a layered architecture in which individual layers act independently of one another. The messaging layer is concerned with the correct formatting of messages, while the transport layer is concerned with the transfer of messages from one point to another. At the messaging level, WCF is based on a number of Web Services WS-* standards and protocols, which are standards defined by industry bodies to achieve interoperability between Web Services implementations from different vendors. The Compact WCF messaging layer supports the following specifications:

- **WS-Addressing** This specification defines a standard format for the message header and defines information such as the destination address and return address for any response.

- **WS-Security** This specification defines how a message is encrypted and how digital signatures are transferred for authenticating the sender and recipient. Note that these security measures are independent of the message transport used, so they work if the message is routed from one message transport node onto another, whereas transport layer security such as Secure HTTP (HTTPS) operates only between one computer and another.
- **WS-ReliableMessaging** This specification is concerned with ensuring guaranteed delivery of a message even over transient and unreliable networks.

A WCF service provides an endpoint to which clients send requests. An endpoint consists of three pieces of information:

- **The address of the service** The format of the address varies according to the transport protocol used. So, for a service that you access over HTTP, the address is of the form *http://myserver/LunchService/LunchService.svc*, whereas for the new store-and-forward e-mail transport, it is something like *myLunchService@microsoft.com/LunchService*.
- **The binding supported by the service** The binding for a service describes how a client can connect to the service and the format of the data expected by the service. It specifies the transport protocol, the encoding format of messages, and the security and transactional requirements of the service.
- **The contract implemented by the service** This is an interface stored in a .NET assembly that has been annotated with the *[ServiceContract]* attribute. It defines the methods on the service the client can call, in other words, what operations the service supports.

This chapter can give you only the briefest of introductions to Windows Communication Foundation. To find out more, see the documentation provided on the Microsoft MSDN Web site at *msdn2.microsoft.com/en-us/netframework/aa663324.aspx*. For your first steps in programming WCF, we recommend the book *Microsoft Windows Communication Foundation Step By Step*, written by John Sharp and published by Microsoft Press (2007).

Programming WCF Using the *BasicHTTPBinding*

The first of the two bindings provided out of the box with Compact WCF is the *BasicHTTPBinding*. This is easy to understand because it is essentially identical to making a call to a Web service. Your application sends an HTTP request to the WCF service using a SOAP-encoded message and waits for the HTTP response. In contrast with the store-and-forward e-mail transport, no unsolicited messaging is possible, so the WCF service can send messages only in a response to a request from the client. The connectivity options are essentially the same as those for a Web service, as shown in Figure 18-2.

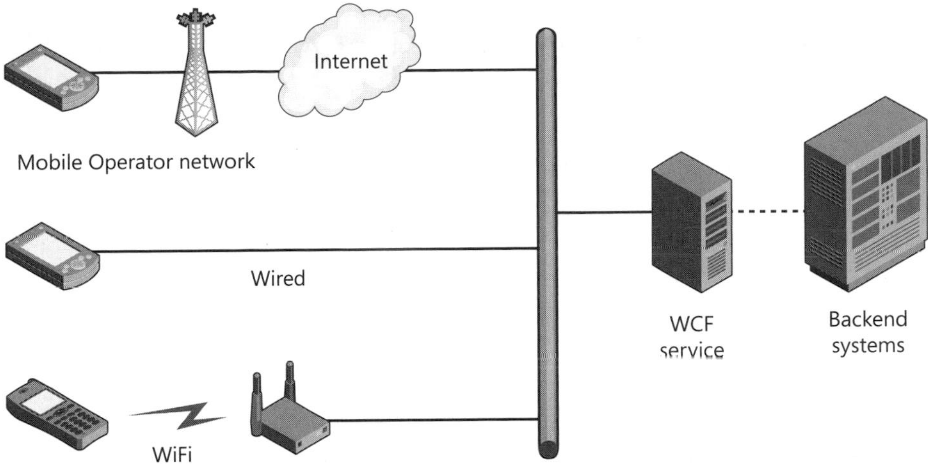

Figure 18-2 Connectivity options for WCF using the *BasicHTTPBinding*

Creating a WCF Service for Compact WCF Clients The standard way to create a WCF service is to define a class annotated with the *[DataContract]* attribute that describes the serializable class that you use to encapsulate the data for transfer, and an interface annotated with the *[ServiceContract]* attribute that describes the operations exposed by the service. Then, to write the implementation of the service, you create a class that implements the service contract interface, such as the following example:

```
using System.Runtime.Serialization;
using System.ServiceModel;

...
    // WCF Service class that implements the IMobileDataService service
    // contract interface
    public class MobileDataImpl : IMobileDataService
    {
        public MobileWCFObject GetMessage()
        {
            MobileWCFObject dataContract =
                new MobileWCFObject(1, "Hello, World");
            return dataContract;
        }
    }
...
```

This kind of simple implementation will not work with Compact WCF clients because the standard serializer associated with the WCF *DataContract* attribute has too large a footprint for implementation in the Compact WCF. As a result, we have to implement a custom serializer that extends *XmlObjectSerializer* for use in serializing and deserializing Compact WCF messages.

For example, Listing 18-1 shows an example of a class called *MobileWCFObject* that we use as our message payload and a custom serializer class that we use to serialize and deserialize it. You need to add a reference to *System.ServiceModel* and *System.Xml.Serialization* to your project.

Listing 18-1 Definition of a Class for Transfer over WCF with Its Serializer

```
using System;
using System.ServiceModel;
using System.ServiceModel.Description;
using System.ServiceModel.Channels;
using System.Xml;
using System.Xml.Serialization;
using System.Runtime.Serialization;

namespace NetCFDevelopersReference.WCFSample.Common
{
    [System.SerializableAttribute()]
    [System.Xml.Serialization.XmlTypeAttribute(
        Namespace = "http://Microsoft.ServiceModel.Samples")]
    public class MobileWCFObject
    {
        [System.Xml.Serialization.XmlElementAttribute(Order = 0)]
        public string message;

        [System.Xml.Serialization.XmlElementAttribute(Order = 1)]
        public int i;
    }

    public sealed class XmlSerializerWrapper : XmlObjectSerializer
    {
        XmlSerializer serializer;
        string defaultNS;
        Type objectType;

        public XmlSerializerWrapper(Type type)
            : this(type, null, null)
        { }

        public XmlSerializerWrapper(Type type, string name, string ns)
        {
            this.objectType = type;
            if (!String.IsNullOrEmpty(ns))
            {
                this.defaultNS = ns;
                this.serializer = new XmlSerializer(type, ns);
            }
            else
            {
                this.defaultNS = "";
                this.serializer = new XmlSerializer(type);
            }
        }
```

```
        public override bool IsStartObject(XmlDictionaryReader reader)
        { throw new NotImplementedException(); }

        public override object
        ReadObject(XmlDictionaryReader reader, bool verifyObjectName)
        { throw new NotImplementedException(); }

        public override void WriteEndObject(XmlDictionaryWriter writer)
        { throw new NotImplementedException(); }

        public override void
        WriteObjectContent(XmlDictionaryWriter writer, object graph)
        { throw new NotImplementedException(); }

        public override void
        WriteStartObject(XmlDictionaryWriter writer, object graph)
        { throw new NotImplementedException(); }

        public override void
        WriteObject(XmlDictionaryWriter writer, object graph)
        {
            this.serializer.Serialize(writer, graph);
        }

        public override object ReadObject(XmlDictionaryReader reader)
        {
            string readersNS;

            readersNS =
      (String.IsNullOrEmpty(reader.NamespaceURI)) ? "" : reader.NamespaceURI;
            if (String.Compare(this.defaultNS, readersNS) != 0)
            {
                this.serializer =
                    new XmlSerializer(this.objectType, readersNS);
                this.defaultNS = readersNS;
            }

            return (this.serializer.Deserialize(reader));
        }
    }

    ...
}
```

You need to use the classes shown in Listing 18-1 on both the client and the server.

One thing that distinguishes WCF from Web Services is that—with the appropriate coding—you can host WCF services in any process, not just in IIS. For example, you can create a Windows Service or a simple Windows Forms application, add a reference to the project containing the common code from Listing 18-1, and write code to programmatically build a channel, listen on a specific port, and respond to requests, such as that shown in Listing 18-2.

Listing 18-2 WCF Service for Compact WCF Clients

```
using System.ServiceModel;
using System.ServiceModel.Description;
using System.ServiceModel.Channels;
using System.Xml;
using System.Xml.Serialization;
using System.Runtime.Serialization;
using NetCFDevelopersReference.WCFSample.Common;

namespace NetCFDevelopersReference.WCFSample
{
    public class CompactWCFServer
    {
        public void ReceiveCompactWCFMessage()
        {
            // Build the channel using the BasicHTTPBinding.
            BasicHttpBinding binding = new BasicHttpBinding();
            BindingParameterCollection parameters =
                new BindingParameterCollection();

            IChannelListener<IReplyChannel> listener =
                binding.BuildChannelListener<IReplyChannel>(
                new Uri("http://LocalHost:8000/MobileService"), parameters);

            // Start listening for incoming requests.
            listener.Open();

            // Create the XMLSerializer wrapper for the object we will
            // receive.
            XmlSerializerWrapper wrapper =
                new XmlSerializerWrapper(typeof(MobileWCFObject));

            // Accept request and open response channel.
            IReplyChannel channel = listener.AcceptChannel();
            channel.Open(TimeSpan.MaxValue);

            // Receive the message and process it.
            RequestContext r = channel.ReceiveRequest(TimeSpan.MaxValue);

            MobileWCFObject transferObj =
                r.RequestMessage.GetBody<MobileWCFObject>(wrapper);

            // Do something with it. Here, we modify its contents
            // and send it back.
            transferObj.message = transferObj.message + "World";
            transferObj.i = transferObj.i + 1;

            // Build the response message.
            Message m = Message.CreateMessage(
                MessageVersion.Soap11, "urn:test", transferObj, wrapper);
            // Send response.
            r.Reply(m, TimeSpan.MaxValue);
        }
    }
}
```

Programming the WCF Client On the device side, the first thing to realize is that in Compact WCF, unlike in WCF for the full .NET Framework, there is no support for configuration files to define to which address to make the request or the binding to use. Coupled with the requirement for custom serialization already discussed, the result requires rather more code than you may be accustomed to when programming WCF clients in the full .NET Framework.

You must create your device project and add a reference to the project containing the class library shown earlier in Listing 18-1. Then write code to define the channel, make the request, and wait for the response, as shown in Listing 18-3.

Listing 18-3 Compact WCF Client

```
using System.ServiceModel;
using System.ServiceModel.Description;
using System.ServiceModel.Channels;
using System.Xml;
using System.Xml.Serialization;
using System.Runtime.Serialization;
using NetCFDevelopersReference.WCFSample.Common;

namespace NetCFDevelopersReference.WCFSample
{
    public class CompactWCFClient
    {
        public void SendCompactWCFMessage()
        {
            // Build the message to send.
            MobileWCFObject wcfMsg = new MobileWCFObject ();
            wcfMsg.message = "hello";
            wcfMsg.i = 5;

            XmlSerializerWrapper wrapper =
                new XmlSerializerWrapper(typeof(MobileWCFObject));

            Message m =
    Message.CreateMessage(MessageVersion.Soap11, "urn:test", wcfMsg, wrapper);

            // Create the channel. In this example, we use the built-in
            // text encoder and http transport to construct a channel factory.
            BasicHttpBinding binding = new BasicHttpBinding();
            BindingParameterCollection parameters =
                new BindingParameterCollection();

            IChannelFactory<IRequestChannel> channelFactory =
                binding.BuildChannelFactory<IRequestChannel>(parameters);

            channelFactory.Open();

            // Open the channel.
            IRequestChannel outChannel = channelFactory.CreateChannel(
                new EndpointAddress(
                        new Uri("http://MyServer:8000/MobileService")));
```

```
            outChannel.Open(TimeSpan.MaxValue);

            // Send the message and wait for the reply.
            Message reply = outChannel.Request(m, TimeSpan.MaxValue);

            // Do something with the response.
            MobileWCFObject to1 = reply.GetBody<MobileWCFObject>(new
                XmlSerializerWrapper(typeof(MobileWCFObject)));

            MessageBox.Show(to1.message + " " + to1.i.ToString());

            // Tidy up.
            m.Close();
            reply.Close();
            outChannel.Close();
            channelFactory.Close();
        }
    }
}
```

Generating a Proxy Class Using Compact Svcutil In the full .NET Framework, you can use the command-line utility called Svcutil to query the metadata for a service and generate a proxy class that you can add to your project to call the service. Using a tool-generated proxy in this way avoids the need for programmatic access to the service such as that shown in the preceding section. When you use the Add Service Reference feature in a full .NET Framework project, underneath the wrappers Visual Studio just runs Svcutil and automatically adds the proxy to your project–a process you will recognize as being very similar to the Add Web Reference feature for Web Services that you may be more familiar with using.

A version of Svcutil for Compact WCF will generate proxies suitable for .NET Compact Framework 3.5, although in the initial release this will work only for services you call using the *BasicHttpBinding*. So you will still have to call the *WindowsMobileMailBinding* programmatically. When you use the tool-generated proxy, you do not have to use the code shown in the preceding section. Instead, you simply instantiate an instance of the proxy class and then call methods on it to make the WCF call, just as you do with Web Services proxies. At the time of this writing, the compact Svcutil tool will not be included in the initial release of Visual Studio Code Name "Orcas" but instead will be released shortly afterward as a separate download.

Programming WCF Using the E-Mail Transport

The e-mail message transport requires Exchange Server 2007–not for the device to Exchange Server connection, which uses the push e-mail capability (also called AirSync) that has been available for Windows Mobile for some time now, but for the server-side application for Exchange Server communications. The WCF libraries Microsoft has created for the e-mail message transport communicate with Exchange Server using Exchange Web Services, which are not supported on earlier versions of Exchange Server. It is to be hoped that a custom e-mail channel implementation for Exchange Server 2003 will be available from the developer community at some point. The connectivity options are shown in Figure 18-3.

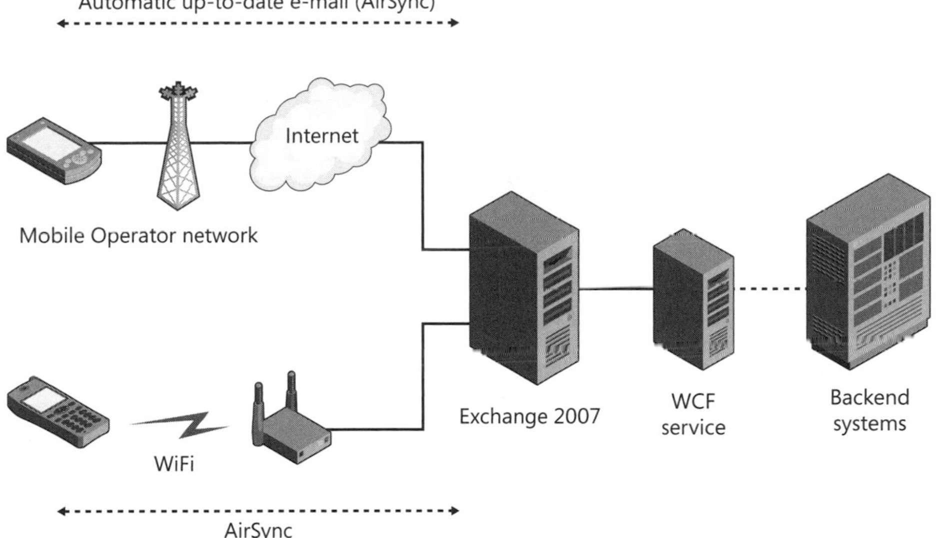

Figure 18-3 Connectivity options for WCF using the *ExchangeBinding*

Programming WCF for the E-Mail Transport The e-mail transport is not tied to the request–response pattern required by the HTTP transport. As a consequence, you can think of it as one-way messaging, although of course you could open separate channels for both send and receive on both a backend server and on a client device to enable two-way communication. Listing 18-4 shows how to send an unsolicited message from a program on a backend server to a program on a mobile device. This example is somewhat simpler than is the *BasicHTTPBinding* example shown previously.

The logic for a Windows console application, which is the sender, is shown in Listing 18-4. Note that you still need the *XmlCustomSerializer* custom serializer class shown previously in Listing 18-1. It sends a message containing a string—the name of a fictional employee—to the remote application.

Listing 18-4 Sending a Message Using the E-Mail Transport

```
using System;
using System.Collections.Generic;
using System.Text;
using System.Net;
using System.ServiceModel;
using System.ServiceModel.Channels;
using Microsoft.ServiceModel.Channels.Mail;
using Microsoft.ServiceModel.Channels.Mail.ExchangeWebService;
```

```
namespace NetCFDevelopersGuide.EmployeeUpdate
{
    class Program
    {
        private static Uri ExchangeServer =
            new Uri("http://mail.contoso.com.107.72.20");
        private static string UserEmail = "test@contoso.com";
        private static string Password = "P@ssw0rd";

        private static string DestinationEmail = "test1@contoso.com";
        private static string OutputChannelName = "EmployeeViewer";

        static void Main(string[] args)
        {
            ExchangeWebServiceMailBinding mailBinding;
            IChannelFactory<IOutputChannel> factory;
            IOutputChannel outputChannel;
            CFMessagingSerializer serializer;
            Message message;

            // NetworkCredential can be null here if you want to use
            // Windows Integrated Security.
            mailBinding = new ExchangeWebServiceMailBinding(
                Program.ExchangeServer,
                new NetworkCredential(Program.UserEmail, Program.Password));

            factory = mailBinding.BuildChannelFactory<IOutputChannel>(
                new BindingParameterCollection());
            factory.Open();

            outputChannel = factory.CreateChannel(
                                new EndpointAddress(MailUriHelper.Create(
                                        Program.OutputChannelName,
                                        Program.DestinationEmail)));
            outputChannel.Open();

            serializer = new XmlSerializerWrapper(typeof(string));
            message = Message.CreateMessage(MessageVersion.Default,
                          "AddEmployee", "Jeff Smith", serializer);

            Console.Write("Sending the update... ");
            outputChannel.Send(message);
            Console.WriteLine("done.");

            outputChannel.Close();
            factory.Close();
            mailBinding.Close();
        }
    }
}
```

The client application is a Windows Forms application running on a device. This opens a listener channel on a background thread and waits for messages. When it receives a message containing the name of the new employee, it adds it to the list of names shown in the *ListBox* on the form. The code is shown in Listing 18-5. As with the other examples, this too requires the *XmlSerializerWrapper* custom serializer class.

Listing 18-5 Device Application That Receives Messages Using the E-Mail Transport

```
using System;
using System.Collections.Generic;
using System.ComponentModel;
using System.Threading;
using System.Drawing;
using System.Text;
using System.Windows.Forms;
using System.ServiceModel;
using System.ServiceModel.Channels;
using Microsoft.ServiceModel.Channels.Mail;
using Microsoft.ServiceModel.Channels.Mail.WindowsMobile;

namespace NetCFDevelopersReference.EmployeeViewer
{
    public partial class MainForm : Form
    {
        public static string InputChannelName = "EmployeeViewer";

        private delegate void AddEmployeeDelegate(string employeeName);

        private WindowsMobileMailBinding mailBinding;
        private IChannelListener<IInputChannel> listener;
        private IInputChannel inputChannel;

        private Thread listenerThread;
        private bool isClosed;

        private XmlSerializerWrapper serializer;

        public MainForm()
        {
            InitializeComponent();
        }

        private void menuItemClose_Click(object sender, EventArgs e)
        {
            this.Close();
        }

        private void MainForm_Load(object sender, EventArgs e)
        {
            this.isClosed = false;
```

```
        this.listenerThread =
            new Thread(new ThreadStart(this.ListenerThread));
        this.listenerThread.Start();
    }

    private void MainForm_Closed(object sender, EventArgs e)
    {
        this.isClosed = true;

        if (this.inputChannel != null)
        {
            // Closing the channel will unblock the
            // inputChannel.Receive() call on the listener thread.
            this.inputChannel.Close();
        }

        this.listenerThread.Join();
    }

    private void ListenerThread()
    {
        BindingParameterCollection parameters;
        Message message;
        string employeeName;

        this.mailBinding = new WindowsMobileMailBinding();
        parameters = new BindingParameterCollection();

        this.listener =
            this.mailBinding.BuildChannelListener<IInputChannel>(
                 MailUriHelper.CreateUri(InputChannelName, ""),
                  parameters);
        this.listener.Open();

        this.inputChannel = this.listener.AcceptChannel();
        this.inputChannel.Open();

        this.serializer = new XmlSerializerWrapper(typeof(string));

        while (!this.isClosed)
        {
            message = this.inputChannel.Receive();

            // The Receive() method will return null if the input channel
            // has been closed (for example, from a different thread).
            if (message != null)
            {
                employeeName = message.GetBody<string>(this.serializer);
                this.BeginInvoke(
                    new AddEmployeeDelegate(this.AddEmployee),
                    new object[] { employeeName });
            }
        }
```

```
            this.inputChannel.Close();
            this.listener.Close();
            this.mailBinding.Close();
        }

        private void AddEmployee(string employeeName)
        {
            this.listBox.Items.Add(employeeName);
            MessageBox.Show(employeeName +
                " has been added to the list of employees");
        }
    }
}
```

Programming Language Integrated Query

.NET Framework 3.5 uses new versions of the Microsoft Visual C# and Visual Basic compilers, which introduce new syntax into the languages to support querying operations in your programming code. This is called Language Integrated Query (LINQ). With LINQ, you can write declarative code to query data sources regardless of their origin. In the full framework, the current plans are for LINQ to operate on in-memory object collections, XML, *DataSets*, SQL Server, and Entities. The Compact Framework does not support LINQ to SQL Server (including SQL Server CE) or Entities. The query syntax is somewhat similar to SQL, so it will be familiar to developers who have written database code.

This section is not intended to be a comprehensive reference for LINQ. Instead, we highlight the LINQ functionality that will be available in .NET Compact Framework 3.5. You can read more about LINQ on the LINQ Project Web site at *msdn2.microsoft.com/en-us/netframework/aa904594.aspx*.

You can find an explanation of the programming constructs on which LINQ is based on the LINQ Resources page of the Moth Web site at *www.danielmoth.com/Blog/2007/02/linq-resources.html*.

Query Syntax

A simple expression will be familiar to anyone who has used structured query language (SQL):

```
var contacts =
    from c in customers
    where c.State == "WA"
    select new { c.Name, c.Phone };
```

This simple query uses a number of innovations introduced with C# 3.0 and Visual Basic 9, which we look at in the following sections. The *customers* object can be any collection that implements *IEnumerable*, and *c* represents a single item in the collection, which you can see in this particular example has at least the *Name*, *Phone*, and *State* properties. As with an SQL statement, you can use one or more *where* clauses to restrict the results. Here we compare the *State* string property to "*WA*". The *select* keyword defines a projection for the query and results in a collection of items with just the *Name* and *Phone* properties. These results are actually strongly typed but use the new support for anonymous types introduced with the C# (and Visual Basic) language enhancements; this is why we are not naming a particular return object type but instead use the *var* keyword for the type of the contacts variable (see the section titled "Type Inference" later in this chapter for more information about the *var* keyword).

Lambda Expressions

C# version 2.0 introduced the concept of anonymous delegates, which you can use to define the contents of a delegate method in the code you write to hook up the delegate. Behind the scenes, it creates the delegate type and method for you, but the type isn't exposed to your code; hence it is anonymous. To support LINQ, this is taken one step further, and the concept of lambda expressions is introduced. Take the following longhand example:

```
delegate bool NumberCrunchDelegate(int i);
public void SomeMethod()
{
   NumberCrunchDelegate ncd = new NumberCrunchDelegate(NumberCrunch);
   // other code here
   CallTheDelegate(ncd);
}
private bool NumberCrunch(int i)
{
   return i > 2;
}
private void CallTheDelegate(NumberCrunchDelegate f)
{
   bool result = f(5);
   Console.WriteLine(result.ToString());
}
```

The *NumberCrunch* method receives an integer and returns *true* if it is greater than 2. The *NumberCrunchDelegate* provides a delegate for this method signature. *SomeMethod* creates a new instance of this delegate using the *NumberCrunch* method, and *CallTheDelegate* calls the method from the passed delegate. This can be rewritten using anonymous methods in C# 2.0:

```
delegate bool NumberCrunchDelegate(int i);
private void SomeMethod()
{
   NumberCrunchDelegate sd = delegate(int i){return i > 2;} ;
```

```
    // other code here
    CallTheDelegate(sd);
}
private void CallTheDelegate(NumberCrunchDelegate f)
{
    bool result = f(5);
    Console.WriteLine(result.ToString());
}
```

Here the *NumberCrunch* method is no longer used and the method body is defined when the instance of *NumberCrunchDelegate* is created using the *delegate* keyword. With lambda expressions, this can be made even more concise by using the new => operator. The following two expressions are equivalent:

```
delegate(int i){return i > 2;}
(int i) => { return i > 2;}
```

Furthermore, lambda expressions support inference, which means that in the preceding code you do not have to state that *i* is an integer. Also, if the body of the lambda expression is a single *return* statement (as in the preceding example), you do not have to enclose it in braces, and you do not need to use the *return* keyword:

```
i => i > 2
```

Although LINQ supports the new query syntax, all operations have an equivalent lambda expression that can be used behind the scenes to build your code. For example, the following two statements are equivalent:

```
var contacts =
    from c in customers
    where c.State == "WA"
    select new { c.Name, c.Phone };

var contacts =
    customers
    .Where(c => c.State == "WA")
    .Select(c => new { c.Name, c.Phone });
```

Extension Methods

You can replace all of the standard methods used in querying, such as *Select*, with your own custom implementations. This is supported by another new language feature called extension methods. With extension methods, you can create a new static method that appears as an instance member of a particular type. This is achieved by adding the *this* keyword to the first argument passed to the method. For example, the following extension method applies to the *String* type:

```
public static bool IsAllUpper(this string s)
{
    ...
}
```

The method is supported in Microsoft IntelliSense in Visual Studio, as shown in Figure 18-4.

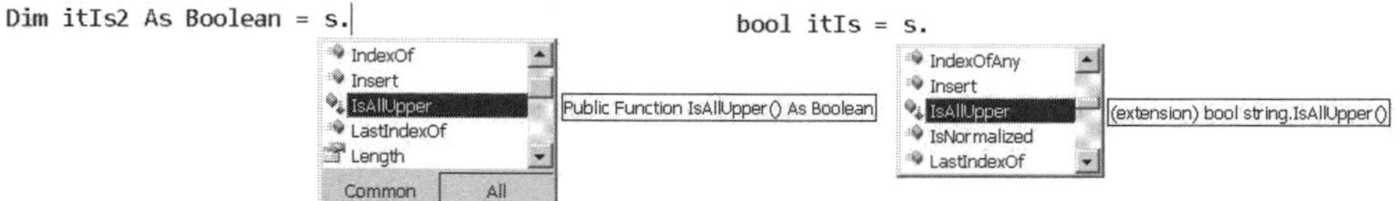

Figure 18-4 IntelliSense for the *IsAllUppercase* extension method

Extension methods are not limited to use in LINQ code; however, they are a key part of the way that LINQ works.

Type Inference

The compiler can infer the type of local variables through the *var* keyword. The *var* keyword is used to create a local variable that is strongly typed (not the same as a variable of type *object*). For example, the following code example creates items of *int*, *string*, and *double* types, respectively:

```
var i = 7;
var s = "Hello";
var d = 3.4;
```

The *var* keyword can be used only for local variables that are immediately followed by an assignment in the same statement. They cannot be used as a return type for methods or for members of a class or structure, or for parameters of methods. Because the compiler knows the strong type of these *var* variables, it shows the correct IntelliSense help as you code and generates an error if you try to pass the variable to a method that accepts a different argument type.

Anonymous Types

With anonymous types, you can define a type at the time you create an object. This is useful when performing a projection operation when you want to return a specific subset of properties that you won't use as a type elsewhere in your code. An example of creating an anonymous type to store personal information can be written as follows:

```
var x = new {
    Name = "Stephanie",
    Email = "stephanie@adventure-works.com"
};
```

X is an object of an anonymous type that exposes the *Name* and *Email* string properties. If you pass in just the values of properties on another object and don't define the property names, the property names will be inferred from the other object. For example, the following code example creates another anonymous typed object with *Name* and *Phone* properties:

```
var y = new {
   x.Name,
   Phone = "+1 555-0123"
}
```

LINQ to Objects

You can query any collection of objects that exposes the *IEnumerable<T>* interface by using LINQ. To demonstrate, following is a simple query on the built-in *FontFamilies* collection:

```
InstalledFontCollection ifc = new InstalledFontCollection();

var results = from p in ifc.Families
              select p;

foreach (var o in results)
{
   Debug.WriteLine(o.ToString());
}
```

LINQ to XML

Probably one of the most powerful uses of LINQ is for querying and generating XML. With LINQ to XML, you can use the simple declarative syntax to work with complex XML content easily. A new set of XML classes is provided to implement LINQ support: *XDocument*, *XElement*, and *XAttribute*.

These new classes provide a simpler programming model for creating and manipulating XML than is possible in previous versions of .NET. For example, the following code is what you would write to create a simple XML output:

```
XmlDocument doc = new XmlDocument();
XmlElement books = doc.CreateElement("Books");
XmlElement book  = doc.CreateElement("Book");
XmlElement title = doc.CreateElement("Title");
XmlElement price = doc.CreateElement("Price");

doc.AppendChild(books);
books.AppendChild(book);
book.AppendChild(title);
book.AppendChild(price);

title.AppendChild(
doc.CreateTextNode("Microsoft Mobile Development Handbook"));
price.AppendChild(doc.CreateTextNode("99.95"));

doc.Save("MyBooks.xml");
```

This creates the following XML output:

```
<Books>
  <Book>
    <Title>Microsoft Mobile Development Handbook</Title>
    <Price>99.95</Price>
  </Book>
</Books>
```

The same XML can be generated using the following code in .NET Compact Framework 3.5:

```
XDocument doc =
new XDocument(
  new XElement("Books",
    new XElement("Book",
      new XElement("Title", "Microsoft Mobile Development Handbook"),
      new XElement("Price", "99.95")
    )
  )
)

doc.Save("MyBooks.xml");
```

Not only is the code far more concise, it's also easier to read because its structure follows that of the XML output.

The following example works on an XML version of the Northwind sample database. First, the contents are loaded into an *XDocument* container, a query is run, and then the results are written out as a new *XDocument*. The query performs a join on the orders and customers on the *CustomerID* field. Next, a *where* clause is issued to select only records for which the order shipping country is the same as the customer's country. A projection is run to output just the required fields from the resulting table. Finally, this transformed data is saved to disk and opened in Microsoft Internet Explorer Mobile for viewing.

```
public static void ProcessNorthwind()
{
string path = System.IO.Path.GetDirectoryName(
Assembly.GetExecutingAssembly().GetName().CodeBase);

XDocument doc = XDocument.Load(System.IO.Path.Combine(path,
"northwind.xml"));

var customers = doc.Root.Elements("Customers");
var orders = doc.Root.Elements("Orders");

XDocument transformed = new XDocument(
new XElement("OrdersWithCustomers",
   from o in orders

         join c in customers
         on (String)o.Element("CustomerID")
         equals (String)c.Element("CustomerID")

         let country = (string)c.Element("Country")
         let shipCountry = (string)o.Element("ShipCountry")

         where   (country != null) &&
                 (shipCountry != null) &&
                 (country == shipCountry)

         select new XElement("OrderWithCustomerInfo",
         new XAttribute("ID", (String)o.Element("OrderID")),
               new XAttribute("Company", (String)c.Element("CompanyName")),
               new XAttribute("City", (String)c.Element("City")),
               new XAttribute("Country", country),
               new XAttribute("Date", (String)o.Element("OrderDate"))
         )));


// Write the transformed XML.
   transformed.Save("customersOrders.xml");

// Open the created XML document.
System.Diagnostics.Process.Start(@"file://\customersOrders.xml", null);
}
```

This generates output XML in the following format:

```
<OrdersWithCustomers>
   <OrderWithCustomerInfo ID="10643" Company="Alfreds Futterkiste"
       City="Berlin" Country="Germany" Date="1997-08-25T00:00:00-07:00"/>
</ OrdersWithCustomers>
```

LINQ to *DataSet*

Because the *DataSet* exposes an enumerable collection of rows, it's not surprising that you can also use LINQ with the contents of a *DataSet*. To support this, the *DataTable* class has a new method called *AsEnumerable()* that returns a collection suitable for use in a LINQ query. The row objects returned have a *Field* accessor so that you can refer to individual field values in your query. For example, to select a list of users' first names from a table where their last name is Smith, you can use the following:

```
var query = from dataRow in usersDataTable.AsEnumerable()
            where r.Field<string>("LastName") == "Smith"
            select r.Field<string>("FirstName");
```

You can use any of the LINQ syntax we have already discussed when targeting a *DataSet* with your query.

LINQ to *DataSet* is something that you should use with care from a smart device project. Because a *DataSet* is an in-memory copy of data, it is not a particularly efficient method of working with a local data source. Instead, in most cases you would be wise not to use LINQ to *DataSet* but instead to use the traditional ADO.NET classes to execute your query directly against a SQL Server CE database using a *SqlCeResultSet* object to step through the data directly.

Programming *System.IO.Compression*

As mobile developers, we are used to working in a constrained environment. We are also used to the high cost of transferring data over a phone network and the difficulty in doing large data transfers over slow, unreliable networks. It follows, then, that we are interested in compression. The full .NET Framework included the *System.IO.Compression* namespace in version 2.0 to support compression using industry-standard gzip or deflate algorithms, and this support is extended to devices in .NET Compact Framework 3.5.

The *GZipStream* and *DeflateStream* classes in *System.IO.Compression* support compression of any generic stream, such as *FileStream*, *MemoryStream*, *TextWriter*, *XmlWriter*, *NetworkStream*, and so on. As a simple example, consider the following methods you can use to compress and decompress a file:

```
using System.IO;
using System.IO.Compression;
...
private void Compress(string infile, string outfile)
{
    using (FileStream inStream = File.OpenRead(infile))
    {
        using (FileStream outStream = File.OpenWrite(outfile))
        {
            using (GZipStream compressedStream =
                new GZipStream(outStream, CompressionMode.Compress))
            {
                byte[] data = new byte[inStream.Length];
                inStream.Read(data, 0, data.Length);
                compressedStream.Write(data, 0, data.Length);
            }
        }
    }
}

private void Decompress(string infile, string outfile)
{
    using (FileStream inStream = File.OpenRead(infile))
    {
        using (FileStream outStream = File.OpenWrite(outfile))
        {
            using (GZipStream decompressedStream =
                new GZipStream(inStream, CompressionMode.Decompress))
            {
                int data;
                while ((data = decompressedStream.ReadByte()) != -1)
                    outStream.WriteByte((byte)data);
            }
        }
    }
}
```

This support for compression in the Base Class Libraries can also be used for automatic decompression of data you read over HTTP using *System.Net.WebRequest* or when calling a Web service.

When making requests for Web content using *System.Net.WebRequest*, just set *WebRequest.AutomaticDecompression* to *DecompressionMethods.GZip* or *DecompressionMethods.Deflate* (or you can *OR* them together to accept both), and *WebRequest* inserts the appropriate *Accept-Encoding=gzip* and/or *Accept-Encoding=deflate* headers into your outgoing HTTP request. If the Web server is configured to do so, it will send compressed content in the response. Back on the client, the *HttpWebResponse* object will automatically decompress the response it receives. For example:

```
using System.Net;
using System.IO.Compression;
...
Uri address = new Uri ("http://mywebresource/dest.htm");
HttpWebRequest request = WebRequest.Create(address) as HttpWebRequest;
request.AutomaticDecompression =
    DecompressionMethods.GZip | DecompressionMethods.Deflate;

using (HttpWebResponse response = request.GetResponse() as HttpWebResponse)
{
    // HttpWebResponse automatically decompresses response stream.
    Stream stream = response.GetResponseStream();
    StreamReader reader = new StreamReader (stream);
    string line = reader.ReadLine();
    MessageBox.Show (line);
}
```

You can get the same behavior with calls to Web services by setting the *EnableDecompression* property to *true* on your Web Services proxy class.

```
MyApp.MyService webServiceProxy = new MyApp.MyService();
webServiceProxy.EnableDecompression = true;
```

In Chapter 7, we discussed how to receive compressed data from a Web service in .NET Compact Framework 2.0 using SOAP extensions. The method described there is still valid in version 3.5 and is still a good way of compressing the outgoing request from the client to the server, which setting the *EnableDecompression* property doesn't do. For receiving compressed content in the response, the built-in support in version 3.5 just described makes this task much simpler.

To find out how to enable IIS to compress HTTP responses automatically for those clients that support compressed content, see the article titled "Enabling HTTP Compression" on the Microsoft TechNet Web site at *technet2.microsoft.com/WindowsServer/en/library/ae342c42-fbc4-4ab7-b9ac-20a89f0fa4ad1033.mspx?mfr=true.*

Unit Testing in Visual Studio Code Name "Orcas" Team System

The different editions of Visual Studio that are part of the Team System family integrate tools to help with the full software development life cycle, from design through development, testing, build, and bug tracking and resolution. The editions of Team System that are targeted at software developers are Visual Studio Team Developer Edition and Visual Studio Team Suite. With these editions, you can create and run unit tests. In Visual Studio 2005, unit testing is available only for applications built on the full .NET Framework, but in "Orcas" these capabilities extend to applications built on the .NET Compact Framework.

If you are unfamiliar with unit testing, refer to Chapter 4. The idea is that as you develop your application code, in parallel if not before, you also develop a suite of unit tests to test your code. You run the tests continuously during the development cycle, and obviously, you should not ship your product if any tests fail. The test suite also provides an essential tool for regression testing–as your application changes over time and new features are added, you can verify that your changes have not broken any existing functionality by rerunning the unit tests.

If done properly, your test code should consist of a large number of tests and should rival the actual product for lines of code. There is even a particular approach to software development called Test-Driven Development (TDD), in which you identify the feature you are about to implement in your solution, but before you write the code for that feature, you write the test or tests that will verify its correct implementation. Only when the test code is complete do you go on to make the changes to your application code. This technique is favored by many groups at Microsoft, including the patterns and practices group, who wrote the Mobile Client Software Factory mentioned frequently throughout this book.

Writing Unit Tests in Visual Studio Code Name "Orcas"

To get the best out of unit testing, it's advisable to architect your applications to place as much logic as possible in class libraries, and not in Windows Forms. The Visual Studio Team System tools for unit testing work best when the test target is a class library. The tools do not offer any features for user interface (UI) testing, such as the ability to script tests that enter text in text boxes or click buttons.

There are plenty of good reasons for building applications with a thin UI layer and as much logic as possible in class libraries, quite apart from unit testing. One reason is that if you have a thin UI layer, you can easily replace it with a different UI should you choose to move your application to a different device with a different form factor or screen size.

To understand how it works, consider the trivial example of a calculator application that you can use to add, subtract, multiply, and divide integers. The logic of this class is contained in a class called *CalculatorLogic*. Ideally, you'll be doing Test-Driven Development, so your first iteration of this class will contain just the empty method stubs, and you will create unit tests before you write the logic. But for brevity in this example, we have supplied the class logic (see Listing 18-6). In Listing 18-6, you can see that the developer made two mistakes in the logic, one in the *Subtract* method, which is obvious, and a subtler one in the *Divide* method—but this is by design for the purposes of this illustration. These mistakes are what you intend to uncover through writing unit tests.

Listing 18-6 Class Containing Erroneous Logic for a Calculator

```
namespace MobileDevelopersHandbook.UnitTestingExample
{
    public class CalculatorLogic
    {
        public int Add(int p1, int p2)
        {
            return p1 + p2;
        }

        public int Subtract(int p1, int p2)
        {
            return p1 + p2;
        }

        public int Multiply(int p1, int p2)
        {
            return p1 * p2;
        }

        public float Divide(int p1, int p2)
        {
            return p1 / p2;
        }
    }
}
```

There are a number of ways to write unit tests, but the easiest way for a class such as this is simply to right-click the class and click Create Unit Tests on the shortcut menu, as shown in Figure 18-5.

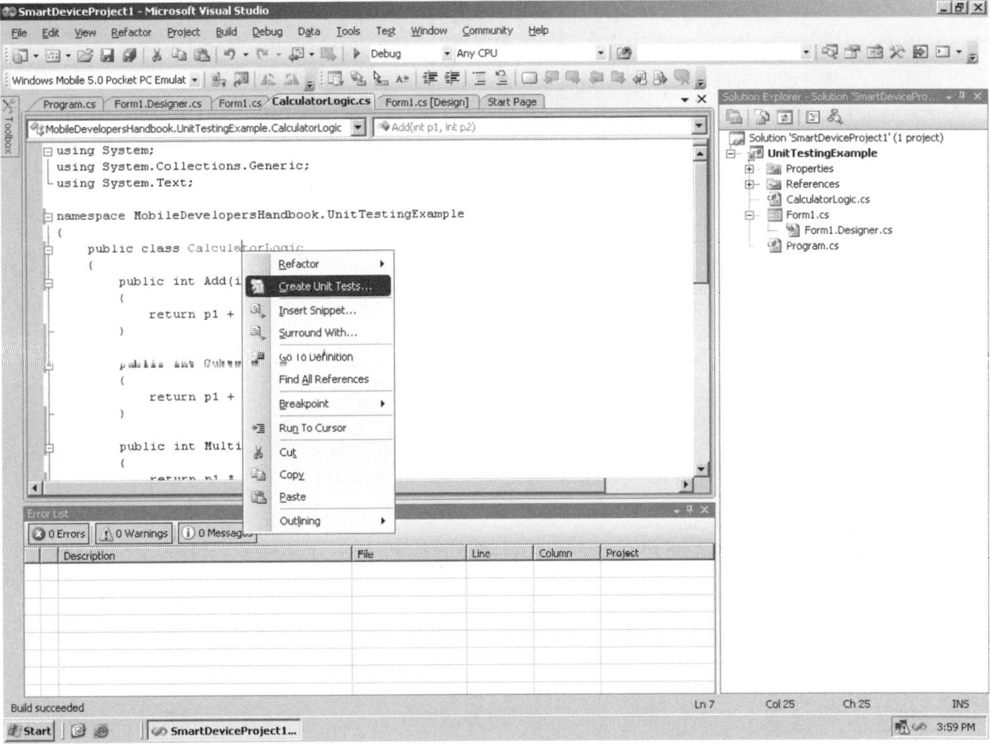

Figure 18-5 Creating unit tests for a class from in the Code Editor

Next, Visual Studio asks for which classes in your project it should generate tests, as shown in Figure 18-6. Remember to select Create A New Smart Device *C#/VB* Test Project in the drop-down menu at the bottom of this dialog box.

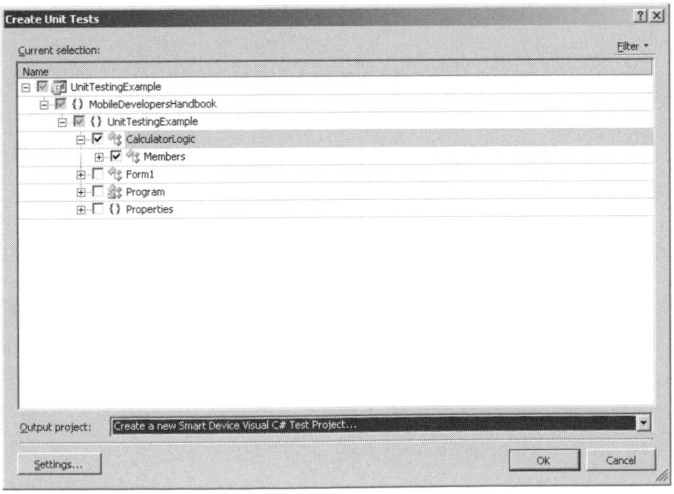

Figure 18-6 Selecting the classes to test

After this, Visual Studio creates a new Test project and adds it to your solution. It also generates a class that contains stubs for tests for each public method, as well as some methods that are called at the start and end of each test run. You can add setup and cleardown code to the start and end of each test run. The stub for a test looks like the following:

```
/// <summary>
///A test for Multiply (int, int)
///</summary>
[TestMethod()]
public void MultiplyTest()
{
    CalculatorLogic target = new CalculatorLogic();

    int p1 = 0; // TODO: Initialize to an appropriate value

    int p2 = 0; // TODO: Initialize to an appropriate value

    int expected = 0;
    int actual;

    actual = target.Multiply(p1, p2);

    Assert.AreEqual(expected, actual,
"MobileDevelopersHandbook.UnitTestingExample.CalculatorLogic.Multiply " +
            " did not return the expected value.");
    Assert.Inconclusive(
        "Verify the correctness of this test method.");
}
```

As you can see, Visual Studio generates the outline for a simple test. You must edit it to perform the testing you need. You can report whether the test succeeded or failed by calling one of the *Assert* class methods, such as *Assert.AreEqual*, as used in the preceding sample. When your test is complete, you should remove the call to *Assert.Inconclusive* from the last line–Visual Studio inserts that line to alert you to tests that you have not written yet because the *Inconclusive* status will be reported when you come to run a test that still includes this line. Needless to say, you can create additional tests–just decorate them with the *[TestMethod]* attribute to ensure that they are run.

Running Unit Tests

After your tests are complete, you need to run them. There are two ways of doing this: through the Test View window or by using the Test Manager. Neither is visible by default, so make one or both of them visible by clicking the Windows option on the Test menu.

By default, the Test View window opens as a tab in Solution Explorer, as shown in Figure 18-7. In the Test View window, you can select one or more tests and then run them by clicking the arrow at the top of the window.

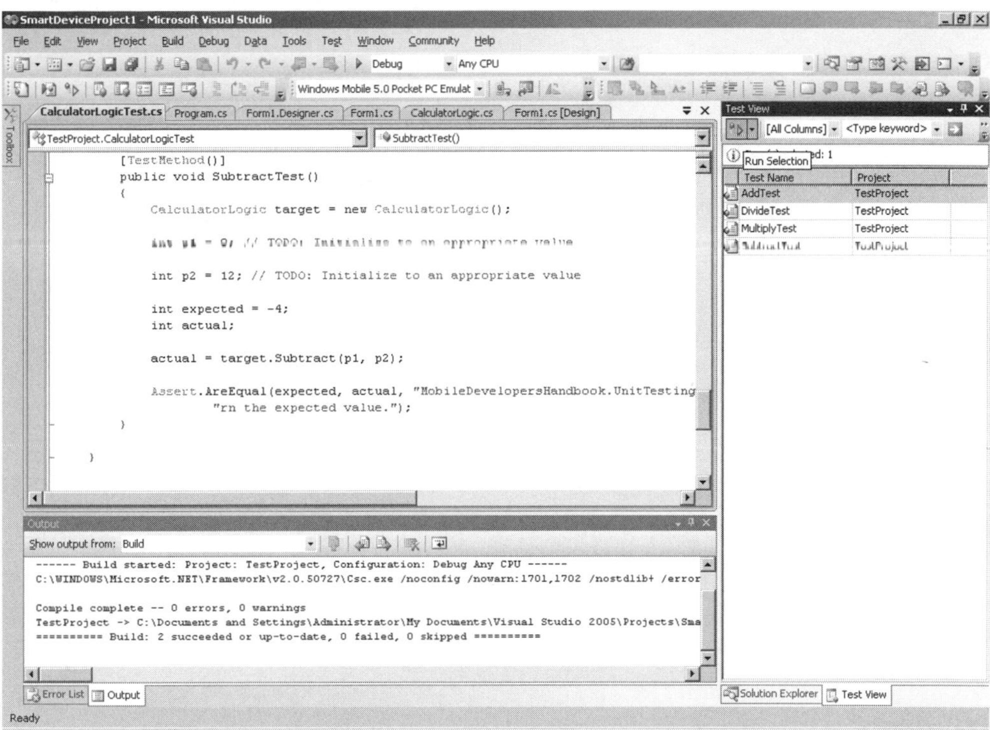

Figure 18-7 Running tests from the Test View window

After you click the arrow, Visual Studio deploys the tests to your target device or emulator and runs them. No UI is displayed on the device, but instead the results are displayed in the Test Results window, as shown in Figure 18-8.

Each time you run the tests, the results are stored in a folder called TestResults in your project, and if your solution is under source control, they are stored in your Source Code Controller along with your application code. The test suite and results become part of your overall solution.

As your project progresses, your test suite grows and provides an invaluable tool to ensure that your solution receives proper testing. Another feature of the Team System testing tools is that you can also view test coverage to identify parts of your code that your unit tests are not running. Unit tests are also really valuable for identifying unanticipated failures when you make changes in one part of your application that inadvertently cause breakage elsewhere.

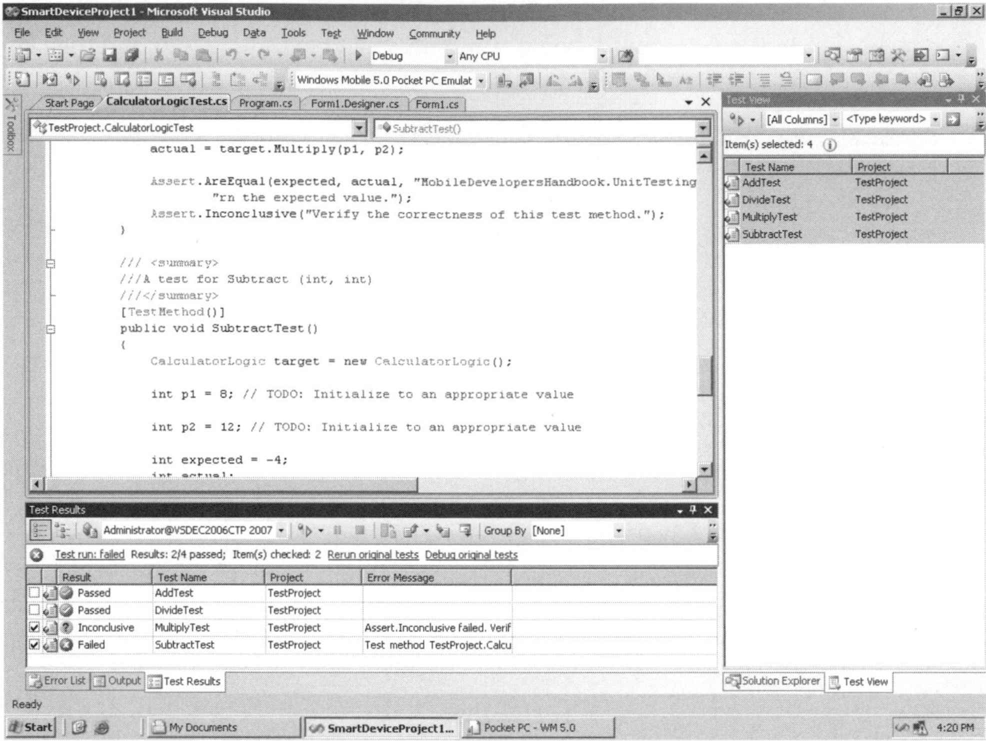

Figure 18-8 Viewing test results

Summary

In this chapter, we discuss the new features for device application developers included in Visual Studio Code Name "Orcas" and in the new runtime .NET Compact Framework version 3.5. The information presented is based on the beta 1 release of Visual Studio "Orcas," so we can make no guarantee that the features described will be present or will operate in the final released product as described.

.NET Compact Framework 3.5 builds on the feature set of version 2.0 by adding much-requested features from the full .NET Framework 2.0, such as compression and the ability to play sound files. Subsets of exciting technologies available in the full .NET Framework 3.5, such as LINQ and Windows Communication Foundation (WCF), will now also be available in the new version of the Compact Framework. Compact WCF introduces an innovative message transport built on e-mail that provides a solution for the particular problems we experience with addressability of mobile devices connected to public networks.

In addition, the .NET Compact Framework team and the Visual Studio for Devices team have delivered new and improved tools that help with mobile application development, testing, and logging and monitoring applications at run time.

Index

B

C

D

E

F

G

H

M

N

O

Q

R

S

T

Additional Resources for C# Developers

Published and Forthcoming Titles from Microsoft Press

Microsoft® Visual C#® 2005 Express Edition: Build a Program Now!

Patrice Pelland • ISBN 0-7356-2229-9

In this lively, eye-opening, and hands-on book, all you need is a computer and the desire to learn how to program with Visual C# 2005 Express Edition. Featuring a full working edition of the software, this fun and highly visual guide walks you through a complete programming project—a desktop weather-reporting application—from start to finish. You'll get an unintimidating introduction to the Microsoft Visual Studio® development environment and learn how to put the lightweight, easy-to-use tools in Visual C# Express to work right away—creating, compiling, testing, and delivering your first, ready-to-use program. You'll get expert tips, coaching, and visual examples at each step of the way, along with pointers to additional learning resources.

Microsoft Visual C# 2005 *Step by Step*

John Sharp • ISBN 0-7356-2129-2

Visual C#, a feature of Visual Studio 2005, is a modern programming language designed to deliver a productive environment for creating business frameworks and reusable object-oriented components. Now you can teach yourself essential techniques with Visual C#—and start building components and Microsoft Windows®–based applications—one step at a time. With *Step by Step*, you work at your own pace through hands-on, learn-by-doing exercises. Whether you're a beginning programmer or new to this particular language, you'll learn how, when, and why to use specific features of Visual C# 2005. Each chapter puts you to work, building your knowledge of core capabilities and guiding you as you create your first C#-based applications for Windows, data management, and the Web.

Programming Microsoft Visual C# 2005 Framework Reference

Francesco Balena • ISBN 0-7356-2182-9

Complementing *Programming Microsoft Visual C# 2005 Core Reference*, this book covers a wide range of additional topics and information critical to Visual C# developers, including Windows Forms, working with Microsoft ADO.NET 2.0 and Microsoft ASP.NET 2.0, Web services, security, remoting, and much more. Packed with sample code and real-world examples, this book will help developers move from understanding to mastery.

Programming Microsoft Visual C# 2005 *Core Reference*

Donis Marshall • ISBN 0-7356-2181-0

Get the in-depth reference and pragmatic, real-world insights you need to exploit the enhanced language features and core capabilities in Visual C# 2005. Programming expert Donis Marshall deftly builds your proficiency with classes, structs, and other fundamentals, and advances your expertise with more advanced topics such as debugging, threading, and memory management. Combining incisive reference with hands-on coding examples and best practices, this *Core Reference* focuses on mastering the C# skills you need to build innovative solutions for smart clients and the Web.

CLR via C#, Second Edition

Jeffrey Richter • ISBN 0-7356-2163-2

In this new edition of Jeffrey Richter's popular book, you get focused, pragmatic guidance on how to exploit the common language runtime (CLR) functionality in Microsoft .NET Framework 2.0 for applications of all types—from Web Forms, Windows Forms, and Web services to solutions for Microsoft SQL Server™, Microsoft code names "Avalon" and "Indigo," consoles, Microsoft Windows NT® Service, and more. Targeted to advanced developers and software designers, this book takes you under the covers of .NET for an in-depth understanding of its structure, functions, and operational components, demonstrating the most practical ways to apply this knowledge to your own development efforts. You'll master fundamental design tenets for .NET and get hands-on insights for creating high-performance applications more easily and efficiently. The book features extensive code examples in Visual C# 2005.

Programming Microsoft Windows Forms
Charles Petzold • ISBN 0-7356-2153-5

CLR via C++
Jeffrey Richter with Stanley B. Lippman
ISBN 0-7356-2248-5

Programming Microsoft Web Forms
Douglas J. Reilly • ISBN 0-7356-2179-9

Debugging, Tuning, and Testing Microsoft .NET 2.0 Applications
John Robbins • ISBN 0-7356-2202-7

For more information about Microsoft Press® books and other learning products, visit: **www.microsoft.com/books** *and* **www.microsoft.com/learning**

Andy Wigley

Andy Wigley has been building mobile computing solutions for many years and has been awarded Most Valuable Professional (MVP) status by Microsoft every year since 2003 for his work assisting the Microsoft .NET Compact Framework developer community. He leads the mobile development and consulting company, Andy Wigley Computing Ltd (*www.wigleycomputing.co.uk*). He has enjoyed a long working relationship with Content Master, delivering consultancy and creating books, Microsoft MSDN articles, and other training materials mainly aimed at those early adopters working at the "bleeding edge" of the newest Microsoft development technologies. Andy is a regular speaker at major Microsoft conferences such as MEDC and TechEd, and he is the co-author of Microsoft Press books on the .NET Compact Framework version 1.0 and on developing ASP.NET Web sites for mobile devices.

Outside computing, Andy is a climber/mountaineer, both on the crags of Wales where he lives, and also in the Alps and the Himalaya. He also performs regularly in the pubs of North Wales in a three-piece rock band.

Daniel Moth

Daniel Moth works in the United Kingdom for Microsoft in the Development and Platform group. Daniel gets to "play" with the latest and greatest Microsoft software, and then explains and demonstrates it in his blog, articles, webcasts, screencasts, online chats, and in person at developer events. Before joining Microsoft, he worked for a large consultancy, and before that in an R&D department. In addition to significant industry experience, he holds a BSc in Computing for Business, an MSc with distinction in Object-Oriented Software Technology, and Microsoft certifications, and he has been working with the Microsoft .NET Framework since the first public beta in 2000. Daniel gained the Most Valuable Professional (MVP) award in .NET Compact Framework development for his community contributions in 2004 and 2005, and you can find his active blog at *www.danielmoth.com/Blog*.

In his spare time, he loves to travel the world-be it on city breaks, lazing on the beach, or scuba diving the oceans.

Peter Foot

Peter Foot is the founder of In The Hand Ltd, a company providing development and consulting services for mobile devices. In The Hand also produces software components for the Microsoft .NET Compact Framework to assist other developers, from hobbyists to small and medium enterprises. Prior to working with Pocket PCs, Peter led a test team for a major

U.K. mobile Internet portal and the United Kingdom's first consumer General Packet Radio Service (GPRS) service. Peter holds a BSc in Computer Science.

Peter has been awarded Most Valuable Professional (MVP) by Microsoft each year since 2003 for his community contributions. Peter established the 32feet.NET shared-source community project bringing Bluetooth and IrDA technologies into easy reach of .NET developers. Peter has also been an active contributor to other shared-source initiatives for mobile and embedded developers. Peter is an active blogger at www.peterfoot.net where he posts on a range of mobile development issues and has had developer articles published on the Microsoft MSDN Web site.

Away from the keyboard, Peter enjoys traveling to new places with his digital camera. He also enjoys listening to a wide variety of music.